Women's Lives: A Topical Approach

Claire A. Etaugh

Bradley University

Judith S. Bridges

University of Connecticut at Hartford, Emeritus

PEARSON

Boston • New York • San Francisco
Mexico City • Montreal • Toronto • London • Madrid • Munich • Paris
Hong Kong • Singapore • Tokyo • Cape Town • Sydney

Psychology Editor-in-Chief: Susan Hartman
Series Editorial Assistant: Therese Felser
Marketing Manager: Karen Natale
Production Editor: Patrick Cash-Peterson
Editorial Production Service: Stratford Publishing Services, Inc.
Manufacturing Buyer: JoAnne Sweeney
Electronic Composition: Stratford Publishing Services, Inc.
Cover Designer: Kristina Mose-Lisbon

For related titles and support materials, visit our online catalog at www.ablongman.com.

Between the time website information is gathered and then published, it is not unusual for some sites to have closed. Also, the transcription of URLs can result in typographical errors. The publisher would appreciate notification where these errors occur so that they may be corrected in subsequent editions.

Library of Congress Cataloging-in-Publication Data

Etaugh, Claire.
   Women's lives : a topical approach / Claire A. Etaugh, Judith S. Bridges.
      p. cm.
   Includes bibliographical references and index.
   ISBN 0-205-43920-9 (alk. paper)
      1. Women—Psychology.   2. Women—North America—Social Conditions.
   I. Bridges, Judith S. II. Title.

HQ1206.E883 2006
305.4—dc22   2005053917

Printed in the United States of America

10 9 8 7 6 5 4 3   09 08 07

DEDICATION

To my new granddaughter Isabel, a treasured addition to my circle of women.

—*C.E.*

To my husband, Barry, my life partner and best friend,
who is always there for me and to my children, Rachel and Jason,
and their spouses, Gray and Nora, who reflect the promise
of a more gender-equal tomorrow.

—*J.S.B.*

TABLE OF CONTENTS

v

PREFACE

Over the last three decades the burgeoning interest in the psychology of women has been reflected in a rapidly expanding body of research and a growing number of college-level courses in the psychology of women or gender. *Women's Lives: A Topical Approach* draws on this rich literature to present a broad range of experiences and issues of relevance to girls and women. Because it does not presuppose any background in psychology, this book can be used as the sole or primary text in introductory-level psychology of women courses and, with other books, in psychology of gender or interdisciplinary women's studies courses. Additionally, its presentation of both current and classical research and theory make it a suitable choice, along with supplementary materials, for more advanced courses focused on the psychology of women or gender.

Every chapter reflects substantial changes in this field during the past few years. We have made several changes based on the extremely helpful comments from reviewers and the many students and faculty who have used the two lifespan editions of this book. This new topical version includes the following highlights.

- Over 2,000 twenty-first-century references emphasize the latest research and theories.
- *Explore Other Cultures*, a boxed feature in each chapter, provides students with an understanding of the role of cultural, social, and economic factors in shaping women's lives around the world.
- The unique lifespan approach of two previous editions is embedded within topical chapters on sexuality, reproduction and childbearing, education and achievement, employment, physical health, mental health, and violence against girls and women.
- Coverage of the lives of women in the middle and later years is far more extensive than in any other textbook in the field.
- An expanded list of Websites at the end of each chapter provides students with resources for additional study and research.
- Expanded coverage of many topics reflects scientific and social developments of the new millenium. These topics include women and leadership, salary negotiation issues, men and feminism, intersexuality, the "New View" of women's sexual problems, social support and mental health, civil unions and gay marriage, recent trends in dating, human trafficking, cybersex, and alternatives to hormone replacement therapy.
- Expanded use of vignettes and quotes from women help students personally connect with the material.

Special Continuing Features Related to Content and Organization

Lifespan Approach Embedded within Topical Chapters.   Almost all textbooks in this field use a topical approach and also include two or three chronological chapters. Typically, there is a chapter or two on childhood and adolescence, and one on women in the middle and later years. Almost all coverage of midlife and older women is contained in that one chapter. The result is that many of the issues and experiences relating to women in midlife and beyond are barely touched on or simply are not covered at all. These older women remain relatively invisible.

Our approach is different. We have taken the unique lifespan approach of our two earlier chronologically focused texts and have embedded this approach within almost all chapters, including topical chapters on sexuality, reproduction and childbearing, education and achievement, employment, physical health, mental health, and violence against girls and women. Midlife and older women are discussed in all chapters except the one on infancy, childhood, and adolescence.

Integration of Women's Diversity throughout the Text.   The text provides extensive coverage of women of color and lesbian and bisexual women. Although there is less information available, we also include material on poor women and women with disabilities whenever possible. We chose to integrate women's diversity throughout each chapter rather than in separate chapters on subgroups of women. An integrated approach demonstrates similarities and differences in life stage experiences of diverse groups of women without creating the impression that certain groups of women are treated separately because they deviate from the norm.

Thorough Examination of Balancing Family and Work.   It is clear that at this point in our history, the balancing of family and work is a major issue facing North American families. We devote an entire chapter to this timely topic in order to thoroughly explore the theories, challenges, benefits, and solutions associated with this great challenge of the twenty-first century.

Pedagogical Features

Introductory Outline.   Each chapter begins with an outline of the material, thus providing an organizational framework for reading the material.

Opening Vignettes.   In order to grab students' attention and connect the material to real life, each chapter begins with one or two actual or hypothetical experiences illustrating one or more issues discussed in the chapter.

What Do You Think? Questions.   The text includes critical-thinking questions in every chapter. The end-of-the-chapter What Do You Think? questions foster skills in synthesis and evaluation by asking the student to apply course material or personal experiences to provocative issues from the chapter.

Get Involved Exercises.   As a means of providing firsthand involvement in the material, each chapter contains a number of student activities. Some require collecting data on a small number of respondents and others focus solely on the student. Furthermore, each exercise is accompanied by critical-thinking What Does It Mean? questions that focus on explanations and implications of the activity's findings.

The active learning involved in these activities serves several purposes. First, it reinforces the material learned in the text. Second, those exercises that involve surveys of other people or analyses of societal artifacts introduce students to the research process, which, in turn, can stimulate interest in research, increase familiarity with a variety of assessment techniques, and provoke critical evaluation of research techniques. Third, the Get Involved activities demonstrate the relevance of the course material to students' experiences or to the experiences of important people in their lives.

Explore Other Cultures. In order to provide students with a deeper appreciation of women in a global context, each chapter contains between one and five boxed features highlighting the role of cultural, social, and economic factors in shaping women's lives around the world.

Learn about the Research. To stimulate student interest in and appreciation of research as a source of knowledge about girls and women, each chapter has one or two boxed sections that focus on research. These Learn about the Research sections either highlight an interesting current study or present an overview of recent findings in an intriguing research area. We expose students to a variety of research techniques (content analysis, interviews, questionnaires) without requiring that they have any background in psychological research methods. Furthermore, to highlight the importance of diversity in research samples, our selections include studies of underrepresented populations.

Following the research presentation are What Does It Mean? questions. These provoke more critical thinking by asking the student to consider a variety of issues related to the research, such as explanations and implications of the findings.

Key Terms. Bolded terms and italicized definitions within the text help students preview, understand, and review important concepts.

Summary. The point-by-point end-of-the-chapter summary helps the student synthesize the material.

If You Want to Know More. Recommended readings related to each chapter facilitate more extensive examination of the material.

Websites. An expanded list of Websites at the end of each chapter provides students with additional resources.

Writing Style

In order to engage the student and construct a nonhierarchical relationship between ourselves and the student, we use a nonpedantic first-person writing style. To reinforce this relationship in some of the opening vignettes and within the text, we also present our own experiences or those of our friends and families.

Ancillary Materials

Instructor's Manual and Test Bank.   The Instructor's Manual and the Test Bank contain a variety of activities to stimulate active learning. The Instructor's Manual includes critical thinking discussion topics and offers exercises that the instructor can use instead of, or supplementary to, the Get Involved activities incorporated within the text. In addition, the manual includes film and video listings as well as additional Internet Websites. Finally, it contains multiple-choice and essay questions for each chapter.

Acknowledgments

We owe a great deal to the many reviewers whose expert suggestions and insights were invaluable in the development of this book. Our sincere thanks to all of you: Jill Johnson, Carl Sandburg College; Barbara A. Rienzo, University of Florida; Harriet Amster, University of Texas at Arlington; Judith LeMaster, Scripps College; Susan K. Johnson, University of North Carolina—Charlotte; Maria Lavooy, University of Central Florida; Leslee Koritzke, Los Angeles Trade Tech College; Jo-Ellen Asbury, Bethany College; Laura Madson, New Mexico State University; Sandra Harris, Troy State University; Kristen Kling, St. Cloud State University; Wendy Bartkus, Pennsylvania State University—Schuylkill Campus.

It has been a pleasure to work with the publishing professionals at Allyn & Bacon. In particular, we acknowledge the invaluable support and assistance of Susan Hartman, our editor, for this book. We also are deeply indebted to Pat Campbell and Holly Conarro, who flawlessly and cheerfully carried out the mind-boggling tasks of locating and keeping track of over 1,000 new references, securing permissions, revising author and subject indexes, proofreading, and carrying out numerous other tasks essential to the production of this book.

Thanks also to the students in our Psychology of Women courses who provided excellent editorial suggestions on earlier versions of the manuscript and for whom, ultimately, this book is written.

Finally, the book could not have been completed without the loving support of our families. Judith thanks her mother, Ruth, mother-in-law, Hilde, children, Rachel and Jason, and their spouses, Gray and Nora, for providing support and inspiration throughout this project. Also, her deepest appreciation goes to her husband Barry for his unwavering patience, understanding, and encouragement. Claire's heartfelt thanks go to the women and men who have enriched her life and have been an endless source of encouragement and support throughout this project: her late mother, Martha, her father, Lou, siblings, Paula, Bonnie, and Howard, children, Andi and Adam, and their spouses, Jeff and Jen, grandchildren, Anthony and Isabel, and "extended family" of friends, Peggy, Pat, Pat, Barbara, Michael, and Bill.

1

Introduction to the Psychology of Women

History and Research

In 1965 when I (Judith) was applying to graduate schools, the chair of one psychology department informed me that my college grades met the criterion for male, but not female, admission into the program. That department (and others) had two sets of standards and, obviously, fewer women than men were admitted. When I look back at that time it is amazing to me to realize that I quietly accepted this pronouncement. I was disappointed but not outraged. I rejoiced at my acceptance by a comparable department but never thought to protest discriminatory admission policies (which were not unique to that department). A generation ago I did not identify this issue or any other gender inequality in institutional, legal, or interpersonal practices as a problem. However, over the last several decades my awareness and concern about these issues dramatically changed. Claire and I are deeply committed to gender equality in all areas of life and hope that this text will help illuminate both the progress women have made and the challenges that remain in the attainment of this important goal.

In this chapter we set the groundwork for the study of the psychology of women. We present major definitions, explore relevant history, examine research issues, and discuss the themes of the book. We begin with a look at the difference between sex and gender.

Definitions: Sex and Gender

Psychologists do not agree completely on the definitions of the words *sex* and *gender*. *Sex* is used to refer either to whether a person is female or male, or to sexual behavior. This ambiguity of definition sometimes can cause confusion. For example, Claire offered a course several years ago entitled "The Psychology of Sex Differences." The course dealt with behavioral similarities and differences of females and males. After the first day of class, some students approached her with a puzzled look on their faces. The course title had led them to believe that the subject matter of the course was human sexuality.

The words *sex* and *gender* have often been used interchangeably to describe the differences in the behaviors of women and men. One example is the term *sex roles*, which is sometimes used to refer to culturally prescribed sets of behaviors for men and women. *Sex Roles* is even the name of a highly respected journal. Yet many psychologists believe that the term *gender roles* is more appropriate to describe the concept of culturally assigned roles.

To avoid confusion, we use the term **sex** to refer to *the classification of individuals as female or male based on their genetic makeup, anatomy, and reproductive functions.* Even these definitions may be too simple: Recent research on intersexed individuals has led to the suggestion that there are more than two sexes (Fausto-Sterling, 2000; Pryzgoda & Chrisler, 2000). See Chapter 3 for further discussion of that issue. We will use **gender** to refer to *the meanings that societies and individuals give to female and male categories* (Becker & Eagly, 2004).

Women and Men: Similar or Different?

Scholars who study sex and gender issues usually take one of two approaches. Either they emphasize the similarities between women and men or they focus on the differences between them.

Similarities Approach

Those who adhere to the similarities viewpoint seek to show that *men and women are basically alike in their intellectual and social behaviors. Any differences that do occur are produced by socialization, not biology* (Bohan, 2002; Eagly, Wood, & Johannesen-Schmidt, 2004; Yoder & Kahn, 2003). This approach, also called the **beta bias,** has its origins in the work of early twentieth-century women psychologists. As we shall see later in the chapter, a number of these psychologists carried out research that challenged the prevailing belief that women were different from (and inferior to) men. Most feminist theory and research dealing with gender differences has retained this similarities approach (Bohan, 2002).

Differences Approach

The differences viewpoint, also known as the **alpha bias,** *emphasizes the differences between women and men.* Historically, these differences have been thought to arise from *essential qualities within the individual that are rooted in biology* (Bohan, 2002; Wood & Eagly, 2002; Yoder & Kahn, 2003). This concept is known as **essentialism.**

The differences perspective has ancient origins in both Western and Eastern philosophies, which associate men with reason and civilization and women with emotion and nature (Hare-Mustin & Marecek, 1990). As we have seen, early psychologists often equated women's differences from men with inferiority and "otherness." Men set the standard while women were seen as deviations from that standard (Strickland, 2000). For example, Sigmund Freud stated that because women do not have a penis, they suffer from penis envy. Using the same logic, one could argue just as persuasively that men experience uterus envy because they cannot bear children. (Karen Horney [1926/1974], a psychoanalyst who challenged many of Freud's views, made this very proposal.)

Contemporary feminists regard female-male differences as arising from a culture's expectations of how individuals should behave. In other words, any behavioral differences between the genders are not inborn but are socially constructed (Bohan, 2002; Marecek et al., 2004; Wood & Eagly, 2002). As we shall see at the end of the chapter, the social construction of gender is one of the three major themes of this book.

Some feminists have added still another twist to the differences approach. They embrace cultural feminism, a view that celebrates those positive qualities historically associated with women, such as a sense of human connection and concern for other people (Bohan, 2002; Jordan et al., 2003; Miller & Stiver, 1997). The theories of Nancy Chodorow (1990) and Carol Gilligan (1982, 1993) illustrate the cultural feminist approach. According to Chodorow, early childhood experiences forever set females and males down different paths in their development of identity, personality, and emotional needs. Girls develop an early attachment to their mother, whom they perceive as similar to themselves. This leads girls to develop relational skills and a desire for close emotional connections. Boys, on the other hand, reject their emotional attachment to their mother, who is perceived as dissimilar. Boys instead identify with male figures who are often more distant. In the process, they become more invested in separation and independence and develop a more abstract and impersonal style (Basow & Rubin, 1999). Gilligan (1982, 1993) also sees women's identity as based on connections and relationships to others. She believes that women reason and make moral judgments in a "different voice," a voice concerned with caring and responsibility. Men, on the other hand, are more concerned with abstract rights and justice. These different patterns of reasoning are equally valid and sophisticated, according to Gilligan. We shall discuss moral reasoning in females and males in greater detail in Chapter 5.

Regardless of one's approach to gender comparisons, the study of gender and the psychology of women is rooted in a feminist perspective. Therefore, let's now examine the meaning of feminism.

Feminism

"Feminism . . . means you promote that men and women should have equal rights—economic, political, and with health care" (Meghann McCluskey, college sophomore, quoted in Dube, 2004, p. B5). "Feminists are . . . bra-burning, hairy-legged, man-hating lesbians. They constantly look for sexism and find it everywhere . . . " (Dube, 2004, p. B5, describing how another of her college students views feminism). Do either of these definitions reflect your own view of feminism? Although the term *feminism* is frequently used by the media, in opinion polls, and in casual conversation, people obviously differ in their conceptions of its meaning. There is even diversity among feminists. Although united in their belief that women are disadvantaged relative to men (Worell, 1996), feminists differ in their beliefs about the sources of this inequality and the ways to enhance women's status. Let's examine five different types of feminism embraced by feminist scholars.

Liberal feminism is *the belief that women and men should have the same political, legal, economic, and educational rights and opportunities* (Henley et al., 1998; Ens & Sinacore, 2001). Liberal feminists advocate reform; their goals are to change attitudes and laws that are unfair to women and to equalize educational, employment, and political opportunities. For example, they seek the creation of an educational environment that encourages women's growth in all academic fields, removal of barriers to full participation and advancement in the workplace, and more political leadership positions for women. Liberal feminists stress the similarities between females and males and contend that gender differences are a function of unequal opportunities.

In contrast, **cultural feminism** reflects *the belief that women and men are different and that more respect should be given to women's special qualities, such as nurturance, concern about others, and cooperativeness* (Ens & Sinacore, 2001; Henley et al., 1998). Cultural feminists are concerned about destructive outcomes related to masculine traits, such as aggressiveness and lack of emotional expressiveness, and want to empower women by elevating the value attached to their interpersonal orientation.

Another type of feminism, **socialist feminism,** reflects *the attitude that gender inequality is rooted in economic inequality* (Ens & Sinacore, 2001; Henley et al., 1998). Socialist feminists believe that oppression based on gender, ethnicity, and social class interact with one another and cannot be eliminated until the capitalistic structure of North American society is changed.

Radical feminism, on the other hand, is *the belief that gender inequality is based on male oppression of women* (Ens & Sinacore, 2001; Henley et al., 1998; Johnson, 1997). Radical feminists contend that **patriarchy,** *male control over and dominance of women*, has existed throughout history and must be eliminated to achieve gender equality. In other words, different from socialist feminists, radical feminists see men, rather than capitalism, as the source of women's oppression. Consequently, they are concerned not only about inequality in societal institutions, such as the workplace, but also about power differential in the family and other types of intimate relationships.

Many women of color have argued that the feminist movement is concerned primarily about issues that confront White women. Consequently, they embrace **women of color feminism** (also known as womanism), which is *the belief that both* **racism,** *bias against people because of their ethnicity, and* **classism,** *bias based on social class, must be recognized as being as important as* **sexism,** *gender-based bias* (Boisnier, 2003; Ens & Sinacore, 2001; Henley et al., 1998).

Clearly, there is no reason why a feminist perspective has to be limited to one viewpoint. Many individuals combine two or more into their personal definition of feminism. Now, perform the exercise in Get Involved 1.1 to more closely examine each of these types of feminism.

GET INVOLVED **1.1**
How Do People View Feminism?

Answer the following questions and then ask several female and male acquaintances to do the same. Save your own answers but do not refer back to them after completing this chapter.

First, indicate which of the following categories best characterizes your identity as a feminist:

1. consider myself a feminist and am currently involved in the Women's Movement
2. consider myself a feminist but am not involved in the Women's Movement
3. do not consider myself a feminist but agree with at least some of the objectives of feminism

4. do not consider myself a feminist and disagree with the objectives of feminism

Second, on a scale from 1 (strongly disagree) to 6 (strongly agree), indicate the extent to which you disagree or agree with each of the following statements.

1. Women should be considered as seriously as men as candidates for the presidency of the United States.
2. Although women can be good leaders, men make better leaders.
3. A woman should have the same job opportunities as a man.
4. Men should respect women more than they currently do.

5. Many women in the workforce are taking jobs away from men who need the jobs more.
6. Doctors need to take women's health concerns more seriously.
7. Women have been treated unfairly on the basis of their gender throughout most of human history.
8. Women are already given equal opportunities with men in all important sectors of their lives.
9. Women in the United States are treated as second-class citizens.
10. Women can best overcome discrimination by doing the best they can at their jobs, not by wasting time with political activity.

What Does It Mean?

Before computing your scores for the 10 items, reverse the points for statements 2, 5, 8, and 10. That is, for a rating of 1 (strongly disagree), give 6 points, for a rating of 2, give 5 points, and so on. Then sum the points for the 10 items. Higher scores reflect greater agreement with feminist beliefs.

1. Are there differences in the feminist labels and/or feminist attitude scores between your female and male respondents?
2. For each respondent, including yourself, compare the feminist attitude score to the selected feminist category. Did you find that individuals who gave themselves a

feminist label (i.e., placed themselves in category 1 or 2) generally agreed with the feminist statements and obtained a score of 40 or higher? Similarly, did the individuals who did not label themselves as feminists (e.g., category 3 or 4) tend to disagree with the feminist statements and receive a score below 40? If there was no correspondence between the feminist identity label and the feminist beliefs, give possible reasons.

3. Do you think that individuals who vary in ethnicity and social class might hold different attitudes about feminism? If yes, explain.

Source: Reprinted with permission from Plenum Publishing Corp. from Morgan (1996).

History of Women in Psychology

The first women in psychology faced a number of obstacles, especially in establishing their credentials, since many universities in the late 1800s and early 1900s did not welcome women who sought advanced degrees (Hogan & Sexton, 1991; Milar, 2000). Judith's experience described at the beginning of this chapter indicates that overt sexist policies toward women in psychology continued well into the twentieth century. Nevertheless, several women overcame the odds to become pioneers in the field (Kimmel & Crawford, 2001; "Once Behind," 1999). Margaret Floy Washburn was the first woman to receive a Ph.D. in psychology in America in 1894. It took another 40 years before doctorates in psychology were awarded to Black women—Inez Beverly Prosser and Ruth Winifred Howard ("February is Black History Month," 2004).

Women and the American Psychological Association

One year after the founding of the American Psychological Association (APA) in 1892, 2 of the 14 new members admitted were women: Mary Whiton Calkins and Christine Ladd-Franklin. Calkins went on to become the first woman president of the APA in 1905. Margaret Floy Washburn was elected the second woman president in 1921. It would be 51 years before the APA had another female leader. From the 1930s through the 1960s, women constituted about one-third of APA membership, but they did not attain high-level offices, editorships, or important committee positions at the same rate as their male colleagues (Hogan & Sexton, 1991).

Since the early 1970s, the number of women in APA leadership roles has increased notably and 10 women have become president (Carpenter, 2000; American Psychological Association, 2003). In 2002, women represented 50 percent of the APA members, 38 percent of the council of representatives, and 30 percent of the board of directors, although only one-fourth of APA fellows, the most prestigious membership category. One-third of the reviewers and 41 percent of the associate editors of APA journals (but only 26 percent of the editors) are women

Ten women have been elected president of the American Psychological Association: Mary Whiton Calkins (shown here), *Margaret Floy Washburn, Anne Anastasi, Leona Tyler, Florence Denmark, Janet Spence, Bonnie Strickland, Dorothy Cantor, Norine Johnson, and Diane Halpern.*

(American Psychological Association, 2003). Of the 96 psychologists who received the APA's annual Award for Distinguished Scientific Contributions from 1956 to 1987, only 5 were women. Between 1990 and 2000, however, 8 of the 33 winners were women ("Awards," 1998; Kite et al., 2001).

Women's Contributions

Women have been relatively invisible in psychology; their contributions to the field have often been overlooked or ignored (Scarborough, 2005). Coverage of gender-related topics has also been limited. However, the situation is improving. Florence Denmark (1994) examined undergraduate psychology textbooks in 1982 and 1993 for the inclusion of women's contributions and of gender-related topics. The more recent books showed progress in both areas. Claire and her students (Etaugh et al., 1995) similarly found that coverage of gender-related topics in introductory psychology textbooks increased by nearly 40 percent between the early 1970s and the early 1990s.

Even when the works of women psychologists are cited, they may still be overlooked. There are two related reasons for this apparent invisibility of many women psychologists. First, the long-standing practice in psychology books and journal articles is to refer to authors by their last name and first initials only. (Ironically, even if this practice were to change, some women authors still might choose to use their initials in order to avoid possible gender-biased devaluation of their scholarly work [Walsh-Bowers, 1999].) Second, in the absence of gender-identifying information, people tend to assume that the important contributions included in psychology books and articles have been carried out by men. When Claire learned about the Ladd-Franklin theory of color vision in introductory psychology, she assumed that two men named Ladd and Franklin had developed the theory. Only later did she discover that it was the work of Christine Ladd-Franklin. Similarly, most people assume that it was *Harry* Harlow who established the importance of touch in the development of attachment. How many individuals know that his wife, psychologist Margaret Kuenne Harlow, was his research partner and a codeveloper of their groundbreaking theory? In order to make the contributions of women psychologists more visible in this book, we frequently use first names when identifying important researchers and theorists.

History of the Psychology of Women

> *Ignorance about women pervades academic disciplines in higher education, where the requirements for the degree seldom include thoughtful inquiry into the status of women as part of the human condition.* (Carolyn Sherif, cited in Denmark, Rabinowitz, & Sechzer, 2000, p. 1)

How has the psychology of women developed as a field since Carolyn Sherif wrote that sentence about 25 years ago? Let us turn to a brief history of the feminist approach to the study of gender.

The Early Years

Rachel Hare-Mustin and Jeanne Marecek (1990) call the early years of psychology "womanless" psychology. Not only were there few women psychologists, but also women's experiences were not deemed important enough to study. Concepts in psychology were based on the male experience. For example, as we shall see in Chapter 3, Sigmund Freud formulated his views of the Oedipus complex and penis envy from a male perspective but applied them to both genders. The same is true of Erik Erikson's notion of the development of identity during adolescence, as we shall see in Chapter 6.

In addition, early psychologists viewed women as different from and inferior to men (Shields & Eyssell, 2001). For example, male psychologists reported that women's brains were smaller than men's to explain their premise that women are less rational and less intelligent than men (Angier & Chang, 2005; Hines, 2004b; see Gould, 1981, for a historical review). This theory seemed to be discredited by the discovery that *relative* brain size—the weight of the brain relative to the weight of the body—is actually greater in women than in men. But stereotypes are not that easily erased. Scientists began comparing various segments of the brain in the two genders in an attempt to find the cause of women's purported inferior intelligence. No differences were found (Caplan & Caplan, 1999). Yet the search continued. In 1982, the prestigious journal *Science* published a study claiming that the corpus callosum (the connection between the two hemispheres of the brain) is larger in women than in men. The researchers stated that this difference might account for women's supposedly inferior spatial skills. (See Chapter 6 for a detailed discussion of this topic.) The study had many flaws, including the fact that only nine males' brains and five females' brains had been examined. Ruth Bleier, a neuroanatomist, and her colleagues did a study that corrected the flaws and used a much larger number of brains. They found no gender differences. Yet *Science* refused to publish their findings on the grounds that they were too "political" (Caplan & Caplan, 1999; Spanier, 1997).

The first generation of women psychologists carried out research that challenged assumptions of female inferiority (Milar, 2000). Helen Thompson Woolley found little difference in the intellectual abilities of women and men. Leta Stetter Hollingworth tackled the prevailing notion that women's menstrual cycles were debilitating, rendering women unfit to hold positions of responsibility. She demonstrated that intellectual and sensory-motor skills did not systematically vary across the menstrual cycle (Bohan, 2002).

The Recent Years

A number of events in the 1960s signaled the beginning of the modern feminist movement in the United States, including the publication of Betty Friedan's (1963) book *The Feminine Mystique,* the passage of the Equal Pay Act (see Chapters 9 and 14), and the formation of the National Organization for Women (NOW). In each case, the spotlight turned on glaring economic, social, and political inequities between women and men.

During these years, the psychology of women emerged as a separate field of study. In 1969, the Association for Women in Psychology was founded, followed in 1973 by the APA Society of the Psychology of Women. Several textbooks on the psychology of women were written, journals such as *Psychology of Women Quarterly* and *Sex Roles* were established, and college courses on the topic began to appear. Feminist theorists and researchers demonstrated the sexist bias of much psychology theory, research, and practice. They set about expanding knowledge about women and correcting erroneous misinformation from the past (Bohan, 2002; Kimmel & Crawford, 2001). Today, women make up nearly half of the psychologists in the workforce. This percentage is very likely to increase because two-thirds of doctoral degrees in psychology now are awarded to women (Bailey, 2004).

Studying the Psychology of Women

With a basic understanding of the history of the psychology of women, we now turn to an examination of issues involved in performing psychological research. As you probably learned in introductory psychology, our understanding of human behavior stems from research conducted by psychologists and other scientists who use the scientific method to answer research questions. Although you might have learned that this method is value-free, that it is not shaped by researchers' personal values, feminist scholars (Rabinowitz & Martin, 2001) argue that values can influence every step of the research process. Let's turn now to a brief discussion of these steps to see how researchers' own ideas about human behavior can influence our understanding of the psychology of women.

Bias in Psychological Research

Selecting the Research Topic.   The first step in any scientific investigation is selecting the topic that will be examined. Just as your personal preferences lead you to choose one term paper topic over another, scientists' personal interests influence the topics they decide to investigate. Throughout the history of psychology, most psychologists have been male; thus, for many years topics related to girls and women were rarely investigated (Kimmel & Crawford, 2001). Since 1970, however, the increasing number of female psychologists and the growth of the psychology of women as a discipline have been accompanied by steadily increasing research attention to topics of importance to women. This progression of interest has been documented by Judith Worell (1996), who notes a dramatic increase in publications on issues of importance to women between 1974 and 1993. For instance, she reports that, while no studies on female achievement were published in 1974, 161 were published in 1993, and published investigations of rape increased from 35 to 306 during the same period.

Another influence on topic selection is the researcher's assumptions about gender characteristics. For example, a psychologist who believes leadership is primarily a male trait is not likely to investigate the leadership styles of women. To give another example, aggressive behavior typically is associated with males. Consequently, very little is known about aggressive behavior in girls and women (Cummings and Leschied, 2002).

Bias in topic selection is even more evident when we focus on women of color. Not only is there a limited number of psychologists of color (Feldman, 1998) but researchers, influenced by the biased assumption that people of color are deviant, deficient, and helpless, have also examined ethnic minority women in relation to only a narrow range of topics (Kimmel & Crawford, 2001; Tucker & Herman, 2002). For example, women of color are more likely to be included in examinations of poverty and teen pregnancy than in investigations of other topics (Reid, 1999). The tendency to treat women of color as helpless deviates substantiates a negative image of ethnic minority females and denies their full personhood as women with a wide breadth of concerns and experiences.

Formulating the Hypothesis. Once the topic is selected, the researcher generally formulates a hypothesis (a prediction) based on a particular theoretical perspective. Consequently, the researcher's orientation toward one theory or another has a major influence on the direction of the research. To better understand this effect, we look at the link between two theories of rape and related research hypotheses. One theory proposes that rape has evolved through natural selection, which leads to the hypothesis that rape is present in nonhuman animals (e.g., Thornhill & Palmer, 2000). A very different theory contends that rape stems from a power imbalance between women and men. One hypothesis stemming from this theory is that regions of the country with more gender inequality of power should have higher rates of rape than regions with less power imbalance (e.g., Whaley, 2001). As we see in the next section, these different hypotheses lead to very different kinds of research on rape.

Theoretical perspectives about ethnicity can similarly influence the hypotheses and direction of research. As Pamela Trotman Reid and Elizabeth Kelly (1994) noted, many studies on women of color are designed to "illuminate deficits and deviance from White norms" (p. 483). Rather than examining strengths of women of color, this deviance perspective leads to research that focuses on ethnic minority women as powerless victims.

Designing the Study. Because the methods used to gather data stem from the underlying predictions, hypotheses based on disparate theories lead to different procedures. This, in turn, affects the type of knowledge we gain about the topic under investigation. Returning to our rape example, the hypothesis that rape is not unique to humans has led to investigations of forced copulation in nonhuman species (Thornhill & Palmer, 2000), research which would not be appropriate to the investigation of a power hypothesis. The prediction that rape is linked to the degree of gender inequality in society has led to studies of the relationship between a city's rape rate and its occupational and educational gender inequality (e.g., Whaley, 1999). Each of these procedures provides very different kinds of information about rape that can lay the foundation for different attitudes about

Psychologist Pamela Trotman Reid notes that many studies of women of color are designed to show deviance from White norms.

this form of violence (see Chapter 11). Examining specific aspects of research design will show us the ways bias can also affect the choice of procedures.

Selecting Research Participants.   One of the consistent problems in psychological research has been the use of samples that do not adequately represent the general population. A **sample** refers to *the individuals who are investigated in order to reach* *conclusions about the entire group of interest to the researcher* (i.e., the **population**). For example, a researcher might be interested in understanding the emotional experiences of first-time mothers in the first months following childbirth. It would be impossible, however, to assess the experiences of all new mothers *(population)*. Instead, the investigator might seek 100 volunteers from among mothers who gave birth in any one of three hospitals in a specific geographical area *(sample)*.

Unfortunately, research participants are not always representative of the larger population. Throughout most of the history of psychology, psychologists have focused primarily on White, middle-class, heterosexual, able-bodied males (Kimmel & Crawford, 2001; Unger, 2001). This procedure can lead to unfortunate and incorrect generalizations about excluded groups. It would be inappropriate, for example, to draw conclusions about women's leadership styles by examining male managers. Furthermore, focusing on selected groups can lead to the disregard of excluded groups.

Have there been changes in the gender bias of research samples? The answer is somewhat complex. Since the 1970s there has been a progressive decline in the reliance on male-only samples (Gannon et al., 1992). One study (Ader & Johnson, 1994) found that, although a minority of 1990 journals published studies using single-gender samples, twice as many of these studies used female-only samples than used male-only samples. Perhaps this is because of a growing interest in women's issues, at least some of which are relevant exclusively or primarily to females (e.g., personal reactions to menopause, techniques for coping with rape).

Another related issue is whether and how researchers specify the gender composition of their samples. A continuing problem is that a sizable minority of authors do not report this information. For example, between 30 percent and 40 percent of studies published in 1990 in a large variety of major psychology journals failed to mention the gender makeup of their participants (Ader & Johnson, 1994; Zalk, 1991). Therefore, the reader does not know whether the findings are applicable to both genders. Interestingly, the failure to report gender in the title of the article or to provide a rationale for sampling only one gender was more common in studies with male-only participants than in studies with female-only participants. Furthermore, discussions based on male participants were more likely to be written in general terms, whereas those based on only female participants were likely to be restricted to conclusions about females. According to Deborah Ader and Suzanne Johnson (1994, pp. 217–218), these practices suggest "there remains a significant tendency to consider male participants 'normative,' and results obtained from them generally applicable, whereas female participants are somehow 'different.'" That is, it appears that males are considered to be the standard against which all behavior is measured.

Although there has been improvement in the gender balance of participants in psychological research, samples have been limited in other ways. One problem is the relative invisibility of people of color (Russo & Vaz, 2001; Williams et al., 2002). In fact, several top psychology journals have shown a steady *decline* in the examination of Black participants, and in the late 1980s, only 0.3 percent to 5 percent of the studies in these journals investigated Blacks' experiences (Graham, 1997).

Even psychologists critical of the male bias in traditional psychology have erred by using primarily White samples (Hall, 2003; Reid & Kelly, 1994). For example, between 1989 to 1991, only about 10 percent of the articles published in journals that focus on women and gender roles examined the ethnicity of the participants (Reid & Kelly, 1994). A positive development is that these journals now require a description of the ethnicity of the sample even if it is restricted to typically studied White participants. However, it should be noted that specifying the ethnic composition of the sample does not imply that the researcher actually examined the relationship between the participant's ethnicity and the behavior under investigation.

Samples have been restricted, additionally, in their socioeconomic status: Most participants have been middle class and poor women are nearly invisible (Lott, 2002; Saris & Johnston-Robledo, 2000). As a result, problems that have a much greater impact on poor women than on middle-class women are rarely studied. For example, very little is known about the sexual harassment of low-income women by their landlords, even though this is unfortunately a common occurrence (Reed et al., 2005). In addition, most studies of employed women have focused on those in professional and managerial jobs. Unfortunately, we know relatively little about women in blue-collar jobs (Nelson et al., 2002). More-over, when researchers do study poor and working-class individuals, they tend to focus on people of color (Reid, 1999), perpetuating a biased assumption about ethnicity and social class as well as limiting our understanding of both poor White women and middle-class women of color.

It should also be noted that many of the middle-class individuals who serve as research participants are college students. As reported by David Sears (1997), in 1985 nearly three-quarters of the studies published in major social psychology journals were based on American undergraduates. Because this group is restricted in age, education, and life experiences compared to the general population, there are numerous findings based on these samples that cannot be generalized to other types of people.

Other groups, such as lesbian, gay, and bisexual individuals and people with disabilities, have rarely been studied in psychological research, and proportionally less research has focused on older women than on younger women or girls (Olkin & Pledger, 2003; Walsh & LeRoy, 2004). What can explain researchers' narrow focus on White, middle-class, heterosexual, able-bodied, younger individuals? One possibility is that psychologists are more interested in understanding the experiences of people like themselves, and the majority of investigators fit the characteristics of the typical participants. Another possibility is that psychologists might use these individuals in their research because it is easier to recruit them. These are the people most likely to be located within the situational contexts—such as academic or professional environments—inhabited by researchers. Also, due to cross-group mistrust and/or misunderstanding, it is sometimes more difficult for nonminority investigators to recruit minority individuals (Russo & Vaz, 2001). Whatever the causes, the exclusion of certain groups of people from psychological examination not only devalues their experiences but can also lead to inaccurate conclusions about them based on faulty generalizations. To get firsthand knowledge about the extent of biased samples in recent psychological research, complete the exercise in Get Involved 1.2.

GET INVOLVED **1.2**

Are Samples in Psychological Research Biased?

In this exercise you are to evaluate samples used in recent psychological studies and to compare descriptions of samples published in journals oriented toward women or gender to mainstream psychological journals. At your campus library select one recent issue of *Psychology of Women Quarterly* or *Sex Roles*. Also, select a recent issue of one of the following: *Journal of Personality and Social Psychology, Journal of Experimental Social Psychology, Developmental Psychology, Child Development*, or *Journal of Consulting and Clinical Psychology*. For each article in these issues, read the brief section that describes the participants. This is found in the Method section of the article and is usually labeled Participants, Sample, or Subjects. As you read these sections, make note of the following information:

1. a. Is the gender of the participants specified?
    b. If yes, does the sample include females only, males only, or both females and males?
2. a. Is the ethnicity of the participants specified?

    b. If yes, does the sample include predominantly or exclusively Whites, predominantly or exclusively individuals of another single ethnic group, or a balanced mixture of individuals from two or more ethnic groups?

3. a. Is the social class of the participants specified?
    b. If yes, is the sample predominantly or exclusively middle class, predominantly or exclusively working class or poor, or a mixture of social classes?
4. a. Are any other characteristics of the participants (e.g., sexual orientation, presence of a disability, etc.) given?
    b. If yes, specify.

After recording the information for each article from one journal, add up the number of articles that specified the gender of the sample, the number that specified ethnicity, and so on. Similarly, sum the articles that included both genders, those that included more than one ethnic group, and so forth. Follow the same procedure for the other journal.

What Does It Mean?

1. Which participant characteristic was described most frequently? Explain why.
2. Which participant characteristic was represented in the most balanced way? Explain why.
3. Which participant characteristic was specified least often? Explain why.

4. Did the two journals differ in their descriptions of their samples? If yes, explain any observed differences.
5. What are the implications of your findings?

Source: Reprinted with permission from Plenum Publishing Corp. from Morgan (1996).

Women with disabilities rarely are included in psychological research.

Selecting the Measures. Another step in the design of a study is the selection of procedures to measure the behaviors or characteristics under investigation. These procedures can determine the results that we find. For example, in their comparison of female and male aggression, Mary Harris and Kelly Knight-Bohnhoff (1996) obtained different findings depending on how they measured aggressive behavior. When participants were asked to indicate their physical aggression, males reported more aggression than females; however, when asked about their verbal aggression, there was no gender difference. As you can see, relying on only one of these measures would have distorted the conclusion.

Analyzing and Interpreting the Findings. Once the data have been collected, the researcher performs statistical analyses to discover whether the findings support the hypotheses. Although there are numerous types of statistical tests, they all provide information about the **statistical significance** of the results, which means that *the findings are not due to chance alone.* For example, in a study of college students' perceptions of rape, Judith asked respondents to rate the degree to which a specific rape was due to the victim's failure to control the situation, from 0 (not at all) to 10 (to a great extent) (Bridges, 1991). The findings showed that females had an average rating of 2.75 and males had a rating of 4.59. These numbers have no meaning in themselves. However, a statistical analysis applied to these data indicated that the difference of 1.84 between the male and female averages was not due to chance alone; males, more than females, believed the victim failed to adequately control the situation.

Once statistical tests have been applied to the data, the researcher must interpret the findings. Statistical analyses inform us only about the likelihood that the data could have been produced by chance alone. Now, the researchers must discuss explanations and implications of the findings. One type of bias occurring at this stage is interpreting the findings in a way that suggests a female weakness or inferiority. For example, studies have shown that females use more tentative speech than males do (see Chapter 11). They are more likely than men to say, "I *sort of* think she would be a good governor" or "She *seems* to be a strong candidate." Some researchers (e.g., Lakoff, 1990) have suggested this is an indication of females' lack of confidence—an interpretation pointing to a female deficit. Another equally plausible and more positive interpretation is that females use more tentative speech as a means of encouraging other people to express their opinions (e.g., Wood, 1994).

A second problem related to interpretation of findings is generalizing results based on one group to other groups. As discussed earlier in this chapter, psychologists frequently examine narrowly defined samples, such as White male college students, and sometimes they generalize their findings to other people, including females, people of color, and non-middle-class individuals. Linda Gannon and her associates (Gannon et al., 1992) examined evidence of generalization from one gender to the other found in several major psychology journals published from 1970 to 1990. Although there has been improvement since the 1970s, when inappropriate gender generalizations occurred in 19 percent to 76 percent of the articles, these researchers found that even in 1990 percentages ranged from 13 percent to 41 percent.

A third bias in the interpretation of data has been the assumption that the presence of gender differences implies biological causes (Hyde & Mezulis, 2001). For example, Camilla Benbow and Julian Stanley (1980) found that more males than females are mathematically gifted. Although these investigators did not examine biological factors, they interpreted their findings to suggest that the difference was based on biological factors rather than on differing life experiences.

Communicating the Findings
Publishing.　　The primary way that psychologists communicate their research findings to others is by publishing their studies, usually in psychological journals. Unfortunately, there is a publication bias. Editors and reviewers who make decisions about which studies are worthy of publication tend to favor those that report statistical significance over those that do not. This publication bias can affect the body of our knowledge about gender. Studies that show a statistically significant gender difference are more likely to be published than those that do

not and can lead to exaggerated conclusions about the differences between females and males (Hyde & Mezulis, 2001).

Another type of publication bias exists as well. Victoria Brescoll and Marianne LaFrance (2004) found that politically conservative newspapers were more likely than liberal newspapers to use biological explanations for gender differences. Moreover, readers tended to believe whatever bias was represented in these news stories. Let the reader beware!

Gender-Biased Language.   The language that researchers use in their research papers is another possible source of gender bias in the communication of findings. Gender-biased language, such as the use of the male pronoun to refer to both genders, can lead to serious misinterpretation. As is discussed in Chapter 2, the male pronoun tends to be interpreted as males only, not as males and females (Crawford, 2001). Fortunately, although this practice was prevalent in 1970, the *Publication Manual of the American Psychological Association* (American Psychological Association, 2001) now specifies that gender-biased language must be avoided. As of 1990 only a small minority of studies employed the inappropriate use of the male pronoun (Gannon et al., 1992).

Another, more subtle type of biased language is the use of nonparallel terms when writing about comparable female and male behaviors, thus implying an essential difference between the genders. For example, much of the research on gender and employment refers to women who work outside the home as "employed mothers" but refers to men who work outside the home as simply "employed" (Gilbert, 1994). This distinction carries the implicit assumption that the primary role for women is motherhood whereas the primary role for men is the provider role.

Conclusion.   Although it is unlikely that most researchers attempt to influence the research process in order to support their preconceived ideas about a topic, the biases they bring to the research endeavor can affect their choice of topic, hypotheses, research design, interpretation of findings, and communication about the study. Given that researchers have very human personal interests, values, and theoretical perspectives, they do not fit the image of the objective scientist (Caplan & Caplan, 1999).

Despite these inherent biases, we do not want to give the impression that psychological research is unduly value-laden or that it provides no useful information about the psychology of women. Most researchers make a concerted attempt to be as unbiased as possible, and research from psychology and other social scientific disciplines has provided a rich body of knowledge about females' experiences. However, we must read this research critically, with an understanding of its possible limitations—especially its failure to focus on the diversity of girls and women. For a look at doing gender research around the world, see Explore Other Cultures 1.1.

EXPLORE OTHER CULTURES 1.1
Doing Cross-Cultural Research on Gender

Cross-cultural research has made important contributions to our understanding of gender development (Best & Thomas, 2004). Nevertheless, there are methodological pitfalls that need to be avoided in order to draw meaningful conclusions from such research. Judith Gibbons (2000) gives an example of how similar findings may have different meanings depending upon the culture being studied. She and her colleagues studied adolescents' drawings of the ideal woman. In a variety of cultures, many adolescents drew the ideal woman as working in an office. However, when the drawings were then presented to peers in the same culture for interpretation, adolescents gave responses that were both similar across cultures, but also culturally specific. For instance,

in all countries studied, women working in offices were described as hardworking. However, Guatemalan adolescents also viewed them as working for the betterment of their families, Filipino teenagers described them as adventurous and sexy, and U.S. teens saw them as bored with the routine of office work.

Another formidable methodological challenge in cross-cultural research is the issue of sampling. In studying gender issues, samples often are drawn in a certain setting, such as colleges and universities, as a way to ensure equivalent samples. But college or university students do not reflect the population similarly in different countries because the proportion of the population attending university differs widely internationally.

Feminist Research Methods

Traditional psychological research emphasizes objectivity, control, and quantitative measures as a means of understanding human behavior, and some feminist psychologists advocate adherence to this general methodology. Others, however, contend that more accurate representations of women's lives are achieved with subjective procedures, such as women's qualitative accounts of their experiences (Jarviluoma et al., 2003; Naples, 2003). For example, a subjective investigation of women's friendships might ask participants to describe, in their own words, the most important friendships they have had. In contrast, an objective measure might ask them to complete a questionnaire written by the researcher in which they indicate how often they have experienced a variety of feelings and interactions in their most important friendships. Whereas the subjective approach attempts to capture each participant's unique perspective, the objective approach compares participants' responses to a standard situation. For a more detailed examination of principles of feminist research, look at Learn About the Research 1.1.

Drawing Conclusions from Multiple Studies

Researchers use one of two procedures to draw conclusions about gender differences on the basis of large numbers of published studies. This section examines these two techniques.

LEARN ABOUT THE RESEARCH 1.1

Principles of Feminist Research

Although feminists have a variety of opinions about the most effective methods for studying girls and women, they agree that such research should increase our understanding of females and help change the world for them (Kimmel & Crawford, 2001; Rabinowitz & Martin, 2001). Thus, feminists, like all researchers, bring a set of values to the research process, values that can direct the nature and interpretation of the research. An important assumption of the feminist approach to knowledge is that research cannot be value-free (Weatherall, 1999). Accordingly, Claire and her colleague, Judith Worell, (Worell & Etaugh, 1994) have articulated a set of principles that are based on the values of feminist research. These are summarized as follows:

1. Challenging the traditional scientific method.
   a. Correcting bias in the research process.
   b. Expanding samples beyond White middle-class participants.
   c. Acknowledging the legitimacy of both quantitative and qualitative methods.
2. Focusing on the experiences of women.
   a. Examining diverse categories of women.
   b. Investigating topics relevant to women's lives.
   c. Attending to women's strengths as well as their concerns.
3. Considering gender imbalances in power.
   a. Recognizing that women's subordinate status is a sign of power imbalance, not deficiency.
   b. Attempting to empower women.
4. Recognizing gender as an important category for investigation.
   a. Understanding that a person's gender can influence expectations about and responses to that person.
5. Recognizing the importance of language.
   a. Changing language to be inclusive of women.
   b. Understanding that language can both influence thought and be influenced by thought.
6. Promoting social change.
   a. Creating a science that benefits women.
   b. Guiding action that will lead to justice for women.

What Does It Mean?

1. Assume you are a feminist researcher interested in examining how women handle their paid employment and family obligations. Using the feminist principles outlined above, describe the characteristics of the sample you might wish to study, and the research methods you would use in collecting your data.
2. A hypothetical study of the educational expectations of White, Mexican American, and Vietnamese American eighth-grade girls found that the White girls expect to complete more years of schooling than the other groups. The researcher concluded that Latina and Asian American girls have lower educational expectations than White girls. Critique this conclusion, using feminist research principles.

Source: Based on Worell & Etaugh (1994).

Narrative Approach. The traditional way of examining psychological gender differences has been to sift through dozens or even hundreds of studies on a particular topic and to form an impression of the general trends in their results. The first major attempt to synthesize the research on gender differences in this narrative fashion was carried out by Eleanor Maccoby and Carol Nagy Jacklin in 1974. In this massive undertaking, they tallied the results of over 1,600 published and unpublished studies appearing in the 10 years prior to 1974. Gender differences were declared to exist when a large number of studies on a given topic found differences in the same direction. Although the contribution of this pioneering work is enormous, a major drawback is its use of a simple "voting" or "box-score" method, which gave each study the same weight regardless of sample size or magnitude of the reported difference (Eagly et al., 1995). In addition, the possibility of subtle biases is always present in any narrative review.

Meta-Analysis. A more sophisticated and objective technique of summarizing data has been developed in recent years. **Meta-analysis** is *a statistical method of integrating the results of several studies on the same topic.* It provides a measure of the magnitude, or size, of a given gender difference rather than simply counting the number of studies finding a difference (Hyde & Mezulis, 2001; Kimball, 2001).

Gender researchers using meta-analysis first locate all studies on the topic of interest. Then they do a statistical analysis of each study that measures the size of the difference between the average of the men's scores and the average of the women's scores. This difference is divided by the standard deviation of the two sets of scores. The standard deviation measures the variability or range of the scores. For example, scores ranging from 1 to 100 have high variability, while scores ranging from 50 to 53 show low variability. Dividing the difference between men's and women's scores by the standard deviation produces a *d* statistic. Finally, the researchers calculate the average of the *d* statistics from all the studies they located. The resulting *d* is called the **effect size.** *It indicates not only whether females or males score higher but also how large the difference is.* This is one of the major advantages of meta-analysis over the traditional narrative method of summarizing research (Eagly et al., 1995; Hyde & Mezulis, 2001).

The value of *d* is large when the difference between means is large and the variability within each group is small. It is small when the difference between means is small and the variability within each group is large (Halpern, 2000). Generally a *d* of 0.20 is considered small, 0.50 is moderate, and 0.80 is large. However, these guidelines still do not settle the debate of whether a particular difference is *meaningful* or important (Deaux, 1999). In cancer research, for example, even a very small effect size can have powerful consequences. Suppose a treatment was discovered that completely cured a small number of women with a highly lethal form of cancer. Although the effect size might be quite small, this discovery would be hailed as a major medical breakthrough. As we discuss later in the book, the effect sizes for some psychological gender differences are greater than those found in most psychological research (Halpern, 2000) while others are close to zero.

Now that we have explored the historical and methodological framework for understanding the psychology of women, we focus on the major themes that characterize this book.

Themes in the Text

Science is not value-free. As we have seen, the evolving belief about the importance of women has had a powerful impact on topics and methods of psychological research. Similarly, this text is not value-neutral. It is firmly rooted in a feminist belief system, which contends (1) that the diversity of women's experiences should be recognized and celebrated; (2) that men hold more power than women; and (3) that gender is shaped by social, cultural, and societal influences. These beliefs are shared by many feminist psychologists and are reflected throughout this book.

Theme 1: Diversity of Women's Experiences

As we saw in the discussion of research biases, minimal attention given to females throughout most of the history of psychology not only devalues women's experiences but also often leads to incorrectly generalizing men's experiences to include women. Similarly, a psychology of women restricted to White, middle-class, heterosexual, able-bodied, young females minimizes the importance of women of color, poor and working-class women, lesbian and bisexual women, women with disabilities, and older women, and it can lead to the false conclusion that the experiences of the majority are applicable to all.

Consequently, this text examines the heterogeneity of females' experiences. We discuss both similarities and differences in the attitudes, emotions, relationships, goals, and behaviors of girls and women who have a diversity of backgrounds. For example, we explore interpersonal relationships of heterosexual and lesbian women (Chapter 8), health concerns of White women and women of color (Chapters 6 and 12), problems on campus and in the workplace faced by women with disabilities (Chapters 8 and 9), and health, employment, and interpersonal issues of older women (Chapters 8, 10, and 12). However, because most of the research to date on the psychology of women has been based on restricted samples, it is important to note that our presentation includes a disproportionate amount of information about middle-class, heterosexual, able-bodied White women and girls.

When referring to cultural variations among people we use the term *ethnicity* or *ethnic group* rather than *race*. **Race** is *a biological concept that refers to physical characteristics of people* (Feldman, 1998). However, experts disagree about what constitutes a single race (Feldman, 1998) and there is considerable genetic variation among people designated as a single race. **Ethnicity**, on the other hand, refers to *variations in cultural background, nationality, religion, and/or language* (Feldman, 1998), a term more closely associated with the variations in attitudes, behaviors, and roles that we discuss in this book.

Unfortunately, there are no universally acceptable labels that identify a person's ethnicity. Some terms are based on geographical origin as in *African American* and *Euro-American* whereas others are based on color, such as *Black* and *White*. Furthermore, each major ethnic category encompasses a diversity of ethnic sub-types. For example, Americans with Asian ancestry, regardless of their specific origin (e.g., Japan, China, Korea, Vietnam) are generally grouped into a single category of Asian Americans. Similarly, Whites from countries as diverse as Ireland, Germany, and Russia are combined into one ethnic group. With the hope that our usage does not inadvertently offend anyone, ethnic group labels used in this book are Asian American, Black, Latina/o, Native American, and White, recognizing that each of these broad ethnic categories actually encompasses a diversity of cultures.

Theme 2: Gender Differences in Power

> *In no known societies do women dominate men. . . . Men, on average, enjoy more power than women, on average, and this appears to have been true throughout human history.* (Pratto & Walker, 2004, p. 242)

Two interlocking ideas characterize our power theme. One is that the experiences of women in virtually all cultures are shaped by both **organizational power**, *the ability to use valuable resources to influence others*, and **interpersonal power**, *the ability to influence one's partner within a specific relationship*. The greater organizational power of males compared to that of females is evident in our discussion of numerous topics, including gender differences in salary (Chapter 10), the underrepresentation of women in high-status occupations (Chapter 10), and sexual harassment (Chapter 14). Additionally, gender differences in interpersonal power are clearly reflected in our discussions of interpersonal violence (Chapter 14), rape (Chapter 14), and the allocation of household responsibilities (Chapter 11).

Both of these power differentials reflect an undesirable imbalance in a form of power, which Janice Yoder and Arnold Kahn (1992) call **power-over**, *a person's or group's control of another person or group*. This type of power is distinguished from **power-to**, *the individual's control over her/his own behavior and goals* (Yoder & Kahn, 1992). Whereas the former is a negative type of power that restricts opportunities and choices of members of the less powerful group, the latter allows for personal growth for all. Thus, feminist psychologists want to eliminate the former and increase the latter.

A second component of our theme of power differences is that many women experience more than one type of power imbalance. In addition to a gender difference in power, women can experience power inequities as a function of their ethnicity, social class, sexual preference, age, and physical ability (Jenkins, 2000). Furthermore, the effects of these imbalances are cumulative. For example, women of color experience greater discrimination in the workplace than do White women (Chapter 10). As bell hooks (1990) stated, "By calling attention to interlocking systems of domination—sex, race, and class—Black women and many other groups of women acknowledge the diversity and complexity of female experience, of our relationship to power and domination" (p. 187).

One consequence of gender differences in power is that women and women's issues receive less emphasis and visibility than men and men's issues. In this chapter, for example, we saw that women's contributions to psychology have often been overlooked. We examine other instances of this problem in our discussion of specific topics, such as the underrepresentation of females in the media (Chapter 2) and the exclusion of women from major studies of medical and health issues (Chapter 12).

Theme 3: Social Construction of Gender

As indicated at the beginning of this chapter, social scientists differentiate between sex, the biological aspects of femaleness and maleness, and gender, the nonbiological components. Our third theme, the **social construction of gender,** points out that *the traits, behaviors, and roles that we associate with females and males are not inherent in one's sex; they are shaped by numerous interpersonal, cultural, and societal forces.* Even if some aspects of being a female or a male are biologically based, we live in a society that emphasizes gender, and our development as women and men as well as our conceptions of what it means to be a female or a male are significantly influenced by cultural and societal values. We do not exist in a sterile laboratory; instead, we are continually affected by an interlocking set of expectations, pressures, and rewards that guide our development as women and men.

Furthermore, our experience and conceptions of femaleness and maleness cannot be viewed as separate from our ethnicity and social class (hooks, 1990) or from our sexual orientation and physical ability/disability. Each of these identities is also socially constructed. Lesbian women, for example, are affected not only by societal expectations about what women are like, but also by people's beliefs about and attitudes toward lesbianism.

The social construction of gender is discussed in relation to several topics in the text. For example, we examine theories that explain how children develop their ideas about gender (Chapter 3); we explore the processes of instilling a child with expectations about what it means to be a girl or boy (Chapter 4); and we examine social influences on gender in our discussion of gender differences in self-esteem (Chapter 5), friendship (Chapter 8) and the division of household labor (Chapter 11).

S U M M A R Y

Definitions: Sex and Gender

- Sex refers to classification of females and males based on biological factors. Gender refers to social expectations of roles and behaviors for females and males.

Women and Men: Similar or Different?

- The similarities approach (beta bias) argues that women and men are basically alike in

their behaviors and that any differences are a product of socialization.
- The differences approach (alpha bias) emphasizes that women and men are different and that these differences are biologically based.

Feminism

- Liberal, cultural, socialist, radical, and women of color feminism all posit that women are disadvantaged relative to men. They differ in their assumptions about the sources of this inequality.

History of Women in Psychology

- For many years, women attained few leadership positions and awards in the American Psychological Association, but gains have been made in recent years.
- Women's contributions to psychology have often been overlooked or ignored, but that situation is improving.

History of the Psychology of Women

- In the early years of psychology, women were viewed as inferior to men and their experiences were rarely studied.
- Early women psychologists carried out research that challenged the assumptions of female inferiority.
- In the 1970s, the psychology of women emerged as a separate field of study.

Studying the Psychology of Women

- Psychological research is not value-free. Throughout most of its history, psychology did not pay much attention to the experiences of girls and women in either the topics investigated or the participants studied.
- Since 1970 there has been an increase in research focus on females; however, most of this research has been focused on White, middle-class, heterosexual, able-bodied women.
- Generalizing results based on one type of participant to other types of people can lead to inaccurate conclusions.
- The researcher's theoretical perspective influences the hypothesis examined in the research, which, in turn, affects the type of information learned from the research.
- The measures used to study the research topic can influence the findings of the research.
- Due to a publication bias, published studies are more likely to present gender differences than gender similarities.
- Very few studies use blatantly biased gender language, but a more subtle bias can be detected in the use of nonparallel terms for comparable female and male behaviors.
- Some feminists advocate the use of traditional objective, quantitative research methods.
- Others favor the use of subjective, qualitative procedures.
- There are several principles that characterize most feminist research.
- The narrative approach and meta-analysis are two methods of integrating results of several studies on the same topic.
- Meta-analysis is a statistical method that provides a measure of the magnitude of a given difference, known as the effect size.

Themes in the Text

- Three themes are prominent in this text.
- First, psychology must examine the experiences of diverse groups of women.
- Second, the greater organizational and interpersonal power of men compared to women negatively shapes and limits their experiences. Women of color, poor and working-class women, lesbian women, and women with disabilities experience additional power inequities, with cumulative effects.
- Third, gender is socially constructed; it is shaped by social, cultural, and societal values.

KEY TERMS

sex	essentialism	radical feminism
gender	liberal feminism	patriarchy
beta bias	cultural feminism	women of color feminism
alpha bias	socialist feminism	racism

classism	meta-analysis	interpersonal power
sexism	effect size	power-over
sample	race	power-to
population	ethnicity	social construction of gender
statistical significance	organizational power	

WHAT DO YOU THINK?

1. Do you prefer the similarities approach or the differences approach to the study of gender issues? Why?

2. Which definition of feminism or combination of definitions best reflects your own view of feminism? Why?

3. Do you think it would be desirable for women and/or men if more people identified themselves as feminists? Explain your answer.

4. We noted a few experiences of women that are influenced by a gender imbalance in power, and we will cover other examples throughout the text. However, can you now identify any behaviors or concerns of women that you think are influenced by a power imbalance?

IF YOU WANT TO LEARN MORE

Caplan, P. J., & Caplan, J. B. (1999). *Thinking critically about research on sex and gender* (2d ed.). New York: HarperCollins.

Collins, L. H., Dunlap, M. R., & Chrisler, J. C. (Eds.). (2002). *Charting a new course for feminist psychology.* Westport, CT: Praeger.

Estrich, S. (2000). *Women and power.* New York: Riverhead Books.

Fenstermaker, S., & West, C. (2002). *Doing gender, doing difference: Social inequality, power, and resistance.* New York: Routledge.

Jarviluoma, H., Moisala, P., & Vilkko, A. (2003). *Gender and qualitative methods.* Thousand Oaks, CA: Sage.

Johnson, A. G. (1997). *The gender knot: Unraveling our patriarchal legacy.* Philadelphia: Temple University Press.

Jordan, J. V., Walker, M., & Hartling, L. M. (Eds.). (2004). *The complexity of connection: Writings from the Stone Center's Jean Baker Miller Training Institute.* New York: Guilford.

Meezan, W., & Martin, J. I. (Eds.). (2004). *Research methods with gay, lesbian, bisexual, and transgender populations.* Binghamton, NY: Harrington Park Press.

Naples, N. A. (2003). *Feminism and method: Ethnography, discourse analysis and activist research.* New York: Routledge.

O'Connell, A. N., & Russo, N. J. (Eds.). (1990). *Women in psychology: A bio-bibliographic sourcebook.* New York: Greenwood.

Pilcher, J., & Whelehan, I. (2004). *50 key concepts in gender studies.* London: Sage.

Rothenberg, P. S. (2003). *Race, class, and gender in the United States* (6th ed.). New York: Freeman.

Wyche, K. F., & Crosby, F. J. (Eds.). (1996). *Women's ethnicities: Journeys through psychology.* Boulder, CO: Westview.

WEBSITES

Feminism

Feminist Utopia
http://www.amazoncastle.com/feminism/feminism.htm

Women of Color Web
http://www.hsph.harvard.edu/grhf/woc

CHAPTER 2

Cultural Representation of Gender

Stereotypes of Females and Males
The Content of Gender Stereotypes
The Perceiver's Ethnicity and Gender Stereotypes
The Target's Characteristics and Gender Stereotypes
Stereotypes of Girls and Boys
Bases for Gender Stereotypes
Stereotypes Based on Identity Labels

Sexism
Ambivalent Sexism
Changes in Sexist Attitudes over Time
Modern Sexism
Experiences with Sexism

Representation of Gender in the Media
Pattern 1: Underrepresentation of Females
Pattern 2: Underrepresentation of Specific Groups of Females
Pattern 3: Portrayal of Gender-Based Social Roles
Pattern 4: Depiction of Female Communion and Male Agency
Pattern 5: Emphasis on Female Attractiveness and Sexuality
Significance of Gender-Role Media Images

Representation of Gender in the English Language
Language Practices Based on the Assumption That Male Is Normative
Negative Terms for Females
Significance of the Differential Treatment of Females and Males in Language

In September 1970, on the day I (Judith) enthusiastically (but somewhat nervously) began my academic career, there was a meeting of the faculty at my small campus. As is generally the custom, the campus director took this opportunity to introduce me and another new professor to the rest of the faculty and staff. His introduction of my male colleague in the physics department was both unsurprising and appropriate; he identified him as "Dr. Lantry Brooks" and then provided his academic credentials. Although my educational background was also given, the director introduced me, quite awkwardly, as "Dr., Mrs. Judith Bridges."

What images of women's and men's roles does this dual title suggest? Is there a power difference implied by the different forms of address used for my male colleague and me?

Leap ahead to 1996. At that time, a colleague of mine went through a lengthy decision-making process about the surname she would use after her forthcoming marriage. She knew her fiancé was not going to change his name, and she considered taking his name, retaining her birth name, or hyphenating their names. She decided to hyphenate.

Does this colleague's decision have any effect on people's impressions of her? When students read her name in the course schedule, when she applies for grants, when she is introduced to new acquaintances, does her hyphenated name suggest a different image than her alternative choices would have? Why do we associate different characteristics with different surname choices; that is, what social experiences help shape these images?

These issues and similar ones are explored in this chapter as we examine stereotypes of females and males, the nature of sexism, and the representations of gender in the media and in language.

Stereotypes of Females and Males

Before we begin, think about your conception of the *typical* adult woman and the *typical* adult man. Then indicate your ideas in Get Involved 2.1.

The Content of Gender Stereotypes

The characteristics shown in Get Involved 2.1 reflect **gender stereotypes,** that is, *widely shared beliefs about the attributes of females and males.* As this sample of traits indicates, *personality characteristics associated with women, such as sympathy and warmth, reflect a concern about other people.* Social scientists call this cluster of attributes **communion.** *The group of traits associated with men, including achievement orientation and ambitiousness,* on the other hand, *reflects a concern about accomplishing tasks* and is called **agency.**

Consistent with the tendency to associate communal traits with females and agentic traits with males is people's tendency to expect different roles for women and men (Prentice & Carranza, 2002). For example, although most women are employed (U.S. Census Bureau, 2003c), many individuals continue to expect that women will be the primary caregivers of both children and elderly parents and that men will be the primary providers (e.g., Novack & Novack, 1996).

Interestingly, some of these stereotypes have remained relatively unchanged since the 1970s, especially those involving experiencing and expressing emotion and caring as more typical of women and those involving assertiveness, independence, and activity as more typical of men (Kite, 2001; Nesbitt & Penn, 2000; Pierce et al., 2003). However, the typical woman is no longer considered to be less logical, direct, ambitious, or objective than the typical man or to have greater difficulty in making decisions or separating ideas from feelings. These traits represent a cluster of agentic characteristics having to do with competence and the capacity to be effective (Nesbitt & Penn, 2000).

You might have noted that the attributes comprising the male stereotype are more highly regarded in North American society and are more consistent with a powerful image than those comprising the female cluster. In Western culture, with its strong emphasis on the value of hard work and achievement, we tend to associate agentic qualities, such as ambition and independence, with power and prestige and to evaluate these traits more positively than communal attributes, such as gentleness and emotionality. On the other hand, highly competent and agentic women often are disliked, especially by men (Eagly & Karau, 2002; Masser & Abrams, 2004). Thus, gender stereotypes are the first indication of the power imbalance discussed in Chapter 1.

GET INVOLVED **2.1**

How Do You View Typical Females and Males?

Indicate which of the following characteristics reflect your conception of a *typical* adult woman and a *typical* adult man. Write W next to each characteristic you associate with women and M next to each characteristic you associate with men. If you think a particular trait is representative of both women and men, write W and M next to that trait.

_____ achievement oriented	_____ emotional
_____ active	_____ gentle
_____ adventurous	_____ independent
_____ affectionate	_____ kind
_____ aggressive	_____ people oriented
_____ ambitious	_____ pleasant
_____ boastful	_____ rational
_____ charming	_____ softhearted
_____ daring	_____ sympathetic
_____ dominant	_____ warm

What Does It Mean?

Did your conceptions of a typical woman and a typical man match those reported by samples of university students from the United States and 28 other countries? These students described the typical woman with traits including affectionate, charming, emotional, gentle, kind, people oriented, softhearted, sympathetic, and warm; they described the typical man with characteristics such as achievement oriented, active, adventurous, ambitious, boastful, daring, independent, rational, and showing initiative.

1. If your impressions of the typical woman and the typical man did not agree with the descriptions reported by these samples of college students, give possible reasons.

2. What was the ethnic identity of the typical woman and man that you considered when performing this activity? If you thought about a White woman and man, do you think your conceptions would have varied had you been asked to specifically consider Blacks, Latinas/os, Asian Americans, or Native Americans? If yes, what are those differences and what can explain them?

3. Similarly, did you think of a middle-class woman and man? Would your impressions have varied had you thought about working-class or poor females and males? Explain any possible differences in gender stereotypes based on social class.

Source: Based on De Lisi & Soundranayagam (1990) and Williams & Best (1990).

Gender stereotypes are relevant to another theme introduced in Chapter 1, the social construction of gender. Regardless of their accuracy, gender-related beliefs serve as lenses that guide our expectations and interpretations of other people. They can elicit stereotypic behaviors from others. For example, a high school teacher who believes that females are more nurturant than males might ask female students to volunteer in a day-care center run by the school. This would provide females but not males the opportunity to develop their caregiving traits. Thus, the teacher's stereotype about the communal characteristics of girls and women might actually contribute to the construction of female-related traits in her female students.

The importance of gender stereotypes in the social construction of gender is also evident in the choices individuals make about their own behavior. For example, based on gender-related beliefs, more adolescent females than males might be likely to seek out babysitting experiences and, thus, more strongly develop traits such as nurturance and compassion.

The traits we have examined thus far are those that North Americans see as *representative* of most women and men. However, an examination of the characteristics people view as *ideal* for each gender indicates some discrepancy between people's stereotypes about most women and men and their conceptions of what women and men should be like. Sue Street and her colleagues (Street, Kromrey et al., 1995; Street, Kimmel et al., 1995) studied college students' and faculty's conceptions about the *ideal* woman and the *ideal* man as well as beliefs about *most* women and *most* men. Their findings showed that both students and faculty perceived most women as communal and most men as agentic. However, they viewed the ideal woman as very high in both female-related and male-related traits; that is, they believed she should be caring, sensitive, gentle, and compassionate as well as logical, intelligent, achievement oriented, and assertive. Additionally, although these respondents saw the ideal man as highest in agentic traits, they believed he should be relatively high in compassion as well. Thus, both students and faculty believe ideal persons of both genders should have both types of characteristics.

The Perceiver's Ethnicity and Gender Stereotypes

When you performed Get Involved 2.1, did your selection of traits for females and males match those found in previous research? Alternatively, did you find that you were either less restrictive than the samples investigated in these studies or that you used different stereotypes? Possibly you indicated that some of these characteristics were reflective of both females and males or that some were more representative of the gender not usually associated with the stereotype. Although there is considerable consistency among people in their gender stereotypes, all individuals do not think alike.

In fact, there is evidence that people from different ethnic backgrounds vary in the degree to which they believe the ideal characteristics for females are different from the ideal traits for males, with Blacks less stereotypic in their views than

Latinas/os or Whites (Kane, 2000; Leaper, 2002). For example, Allen Harris (1994) asked 500 female and 500 male shopping-mall patrons from each of these three ethnic groups to rate the desirability of personality traits for either a woman or a man in their culture. The Blacks were less likely than the Whites or Latinas/os to associate specific characteristics with each gender; instead they considered a larger variety of traits as desirable for both females and males. For example, Blacks rated assertiveness, independence, and self-reliance as equally desirable for Black women and men, whereas the other two ethnic groups evaluated these traits as more desirable for men than women in their cultural groups. Also, Blacks viewed eagerness to soothe hurt feelings as equally desirable for individuals of both genders, but Whites and Latinas/os perceived it as more desirable for women than men. The results of this and other studies indicate that among these three ethnic groups, Blacks are the least likely to adhere to rigid gender stereotypes for women and men.

The Target's Characteristics and Gender Stereotypes

We have seen that people with diverse ethnic backgrounds differ somewhat in their perception of stereotypes of women and men. Now let's examine how these stereotypes vary as a function of the characteristics of the person who is the object, or target, of the stereotype. These characteristics include a woman's age, ethnicity, social class, sexual orientation, and ability/disability.

Age.   One of the challenges facing older people in North America is the presence of stereotypes (mostly negative) that many people hold about the elderly (Grunbaum et al., 2004; Kite et al., 2002). Even young children express stereotyped views about older adults, some positive (kind, friendly, wise) and others negative (unhealthy, inactive, unattractive, feeble) (Montepare & Zebrowitz, 2002). Such stereotypes are part of a concept known as **ageism.** This term refers to *bias against people on the basis of their age* (Nelson, 2002). Ageism can be targeted toward any age group ("Children don't respect their elders"; "teenagers are rebellious"). But ageism is usually directed at people in later life. Ageism resembles sexism and racism in that all are forms of prejudice that limit people who are the object of that prejudice. Unlike sexism and racism, however, everyone will confront ageism if they live long enough (Cuddy & Fiske, 2002).

Ageism seems to be more strongly directed toward women than men. For centuries, unflattering terms have been used to describe middle-aged and older women: crone, hag, wicked old witch, old maid, dreaded mother-in-law (Have you ever heard any jokes about fathers-in-law?) (Markson, 2001; Sherman, 2001). Another example of negative attitudes toward older women is the double standard of aging that we will examine later in the chapter.

Still another example is the relative invisibility of elderly women in the media. When Betty Friedan (1993) examined close to 400 illustrations in the magazines *Ladies Home Journal, Vanity Fair,* and *Vogue,* she located fewer than 10 women who appeared to be 60 or older. Few elderly characters appear on television shows and only a small fraction of these are women (Pasupathi & Löckenhoff, 2002). The few older women who do appear are portrayed less favorably than older men. They are often depicted as comic or eccentric figures, asexual, marginal, passive, unsuccessful, or downright villainous (Palmore, 2001; Sherman, 2001; Wilkinson & Ferraro, 2002; Zebrowitz & Montepare, 2000). Whereas prime-time male characters age 65 and older are depicted as active, middle-aged mature adults, women of that age are more likely to be designated as elderly (Signorielli & Bacue, 1999).

Psychologists seem to share society's negative views of older women. In one study, for example, 1,200 psychotherapists were asked to rate characteristics of individuals who were described as either old or young and either White or Black (Turner & Turner, 1991). Older women of both races were viewed as less assertive, less willing to take risks, and less competitive than younger women.

Negative attitudes toward the elderly are far from universal, however. For a look at some of the factors that influence views of older individuals, turn to Learn about the Research 2.1.

Although aging women have traditionally been viewed less positively than aging men, there is some indication that attitudes toward older women may be improving. One positive sign is what psychologist Margaret Matlin (2001) calls the "Wise and Wonderful Movement." Since the early 1990s, there has been an explosion of books on women who discover themselves in middle or old age. The books present a positive picture of the challenges and opportunities for women in their later years. Two of these books, by Betty Friedan (1993) and Ruth Jacobs (1997), are listed as recommended readings at the end of this chapter.

Ethnicity. Studies find both commonalities and differences in stereotypes of individuals who vary in ethnicity. In one investigation, Yolanda Niemann and her colleagues (Niemann et al., 1994) asked a multiethnic sample of college students to list adjectives that came to mind when they thought of individuals in each of eight different ethnic/gender groups: White, Black, Mexican American, and Asian American females and males. Examination of the most frequently mentioned traits showed that all women, regardless of their ethnicity, were seen as pleasant. However, other traits varied as a function of ethnic identification. For example, whereas Black women were viewed as speaking loudly, Asian American women were seen as speaking softly. Further, only Mexican Americans were characterized as family oriented and only Blacks were described as antagonistic.

Unfortunately, in this study and others (e.g., Weitz and Gordon, 1993), college students attributed a greater number of negative traits to Black women than to other women. Black women were viewed as antagonistic, unmannerly, loud, and argumentative, that is, traits connoting a threatening stereotype. Weitz and Gordon suggest two possible explanations for this image. First, it might reflect the cultural stereotype of Black women as domineering matriarchs. Second, because non-Blacks have not been exposed to a clear image of Black women, they might associate Black women with the more common threatening stereotype associated with Black men. Regardless of the explanation, this negative stereotype indicates

LEARN ABOUT THE RESEARCH 2.1

Who Is Ageist?

Many factors are related to attitudes toward the elderly. Two of these are age and ethnicity. Older adults have more positive attitudes toward aging and the elderly than do younger adults (Chasteen, 1998; Harris et al., 1988). In a 1993 *New Woman* magazine survey of over 6,000 of its readers, younger women were more fearful of growing old than older women. Among women in their twenties, 54 percent expressed such a fear compared with only 23 percent of those over 60. Women over age 50 expressed positive views of older women. Half reported that the best part of aging is feeling a firm sense of self. Older women were more satisfied with their lives than younger women. In response to the question "How do you feel about life as a whole?" 26 percent of women over 50 were "delighted, pleased" and

37 percent were "mostly satisfied," as compared with only 17 percent and 28 percent, respectively, of women under 30 (Perlmutter et al., 1994). Among younger adults, those with positive, supportive relationships with their grandparents have less negative stereotypes and more positive feelings about older adults (Mitchell & Stricker, 1998).

Views toward older adults also vary among ethnic groups. Whites generally show less favorable attitudes than do ethnic minority groups. In research by Mary Harris and her colleagues (Harris et al., 1988), for example, Whites were less likely to enjoy spending time with the elderly than were Latinos and Native Americans. Other studies (e.g., Boduroglu et al., 2002) show that views of the elderly are more positive in China than in the United States.

What Does It Mean?

1. Why do you think young women are more afraid of growing old than are older women?
2. Why do you think members of ethnic minority groups hold more positive views of the elderly than Whites do?
3. What are some factors, other than age and ethnicity, that might be related to attitudes toward the elderly?

that some Americans perceive Black women through a racist lens, a problem experienced by other ethnic minority women as well.

Social Class.   Studies have found that lower-class individuals are typically characterized as dishonest, dependent, lazy, stupid, uneducated, promiscuous, drug using, and violent (Bullock et al., 2001; Cozzarelli et al., 2001). One study (Lott & Saxon, 2002) found that a working-class woman was judged as more crude and irresponsible than a middle-class woman, even when she was running for PTO president in her child's school.

Sexual Orientation.   Some heterosexual people believe that in lesbian relationships one partner consistently assumes the masculine role in sexual relations as well as in other behaviors and dress, the so-called butch role, while the other part-ner assumes the femme, or traditional feminine role. Contrary to popular assump-tions, sexual and other behaviors of lesbians seldom reflect butch-femme gender roles. Many gays and lesbians claim that the labels "masculine" and "feminine" represent efforts of the heterosexual community to pigeonhole them in traditional ways (Rathus et al., 2005).

Women with Disabilities. Although there has been little research on this topic, there is some evidence that people attribute more negative characteristics to women with disabilities than to able-bodied women. Such *biases against people because of their disability* is known as **ableism.** Women with disabilities, unlike able-bodied women, are not assumed to be wives and mothers. Rather than expecting these women to function as nurturers, stereotypical images of women with disabilities emphasize their dependence on others (Olkin & Pledger, 2003).

In summary, we can see that gender stereotypes are not applied uniformly to all women. A woman's age, ethnicity, social class, sexual orientation, and ability/ disability influence stereotypes of her.

Stereotypes of Girls and Boys

We have seen that people have different expectations of the traits and behaviors of adult females and males. Now let's examine adults' gender-stereotypic expecta-tions of children.

As early as the first few days of life, newborn girls and boys are perceived dif-ferently, at least by their parents. Studies performed two decades apart showed that parents rated newborn daughters as finer featured, less strong, and more delicate than newborn sons, despite medical evidence of no physical differences between them (Karraker et al., 1995; Rubin et al., 1974). Thus it is apparent that adults hold gender stereotypes of the physical characteristics of children immediately after the child's birth.

Adults' stereotypes of children are not restricted to early infancy. In one study (Martin, 1995) Canadian college students were asked to rate the typical characteristics of 4- to 7-year-old girls and boys. The evidence for gender stereo-types was quite clear. Out of 25 traits, these young adults rated 24 as being more typical for one gender than the other. Additionally, the traits seen as typical for girls versus boys reflected the communion-agency stereotypes evident in gender stereotypes of adults. For example, these students rated girls, compared to boys, as more gentle, sympathetic, and helpful around the house and they rated boys as more self-reliant, dominant, and competitive than girls.

Bases for Gender Stereotypes

Our exploration of the origins of gender stereotypes focuses on two related issues: (1) the reasons why people stereotype on the basis of gender, and (2) the reasons why these stereotypes center on communal traits for females and agentic attributes for males. In other words, we will consider explanations for both the *process* and the *content* of gender stereotyping.

Social Categorization.   The process of gender stereotyping makes sense if we consider how individuals attempt to understand their complex social environments. Because we are bombarded daily with diverse types of people, behaviors, situations, and so on, we simplify our social perceptions by *sorting individuals into categories,* a process called **social categorization.** It would be hard for us to understand and remember the multitude of people we encounter if we were to treat each as completely different from all others. Instead, we sort people into groups and focus on the characteristics they share with other members of that category. As an example, in a hospital we might categorize the individuals we encounter as doctors, nurses, patients, and visitors. Then the differential set of characteristics we associate with physicians versus nurses serves as a behavior guide when we interact with them, enabling us to ask questions appropriate to each of their skills and knowledge.

Although we make use of a variety of cues for the sorting process, social categorization is frequently based on easily identified characteristics, such as ethnicity, age, and gender (Baker, 2001). This makes sense because these attributes are usually the first that we observe and provide an easy basis on which to sort people. Thus, the process of gender stereotyping begins with the categorization of individuals as females or males with the implicit assumption that the members of each gender share certain attributes. Then, when we meet a new individual, we attribute these characteristics to this person.

Although the social categorization and stereotyping processes help simplify our understanding of and interactions with people, they can lead us astray: Neither all females nor all males are alike. Fortunately, we are most likely to rely on stereotypes when we have little differentiating information about the person (e.g., Swim et al., 1989). Once more details about a person are available, we use that information in addition to the person's gender to form our impression and guide our interactions. For example, when evaluating an individual's level of ambition, we might make use of the person's gender if no other information were available. However, this information would be much less important if we knew the individual was a CEO in a major corporation.

Social Role Theory.   Given that people naturally divide others into gender categories and attribute to all members of a category similar characteristics, we turn now to the question of why people associate communion with females and agency with males. One possibility is that these stereotypes stem from our observations of the types of behaviors individuals typically perform in their social roles. According to **social role theory** (Eagly et al., 2004), *stereotypes of women and men stem from the association of women with the domestic role and men with the employee role.* This theory contends that because we have observed primarily women in the domestic role, we assume women have the nurturing traits characteristic of that role. Similarly, because more men than women have traditionally been seen in the employment role, we perceive men as having the agentic traits displayed in the workplace.

Support for this theory of gender stereotypes comes from numerous studies that show an influence of a person's social role on the application of gender-related traits to her/him. For example, there is evidence that social roles can override gender when assigning communal or agentic characteristics to others. Specifically, when participants are asked to describe a woman and a man who are homemakers, they view them as equally communal. Similarly, when asked to describe a full-time female and male employee, they perceive both as agentic. In addition, women and men who are employed are viewed as more agentic than those who are not (Mueller & Yoder, 1997; Riggs, 1997), mothers are seen as more communal than nonmothers (Bridges et al., 2000; Etaugh & Poertner, 1992), and married women are perceived as more communal than unmarried women (Etaugh & Nekolny, 1990; Etaugh & Poertner, 1991). Clearly, when people are aware of an individual's social role, their stereotypes of the person are influenced by that role information.

The influence of social roles on gender stereotypes is evident even when people are asked to describe women and men in both the past and the future. When both college and noncollege adults were asked to rate the average woman and the average man in 1950, 1975, 2025, and 2050, they viewed females as becoming dramatically more masculine over time and males as becoming somewhat more feminine (Diekman & Eagly, 1997). What accounts for these perceptions? In support of social role theory, the researchers found that the decreasing degree of gender stereotyping was related to the belief that the occupational and domestic roles of women and men during this time period have become and will continue to become increasingly similar.

Keep in mind, however, the evidence presented earlier in this chapter—that stereotypes have remained relatively constant, at least since the 1970s. What can explain the discrepancy between the increased participation of women in the labor force and the consistency of gender stereotypes over time? Although a greater number of women are now employed than was the case in the past, the proportion of women in the paid workforce continues to be lower than the corresponding proportion of men. Also, regardless of their employment role, women still have the primary caregiving responsibility in their families and are more likely than men to be employed in caregiving occupations, such as nursing and early childhood education. Although social roles are gradually changing, women remain the primary nurturers and men the primary providers. Consequently, it is not surprising that our stereotypes of females and males have been resistant to change.

Stereotypes Based on Identity Labels

Recall the experience Judith described at the beginning of the chapter when she was introduced as "Dr., Mrs. Bridges." The fact that the campus director introduced her this way but did not present her male colleague as "Dr. Lantry Brooks who happens to be married," implies he believed that a woman's identity, more than a man's, is shaped by her marital role. Although his use of a dual title was highly unusual, his belief about a woman's identity is consistent with the long-standing cultural norm that a woman is defined in terms of her relationship to a man (e.g., Lakoff, 1990). Given that a woman's title of address can signify her marital role and that her marital status has been viewed as an important aspect of her identity, we might expect different stereotypes of women who use different titles for themselves. Consider the woman who chooses not to use the conventional "Miss" versus "Mrs." labels that inform about her marital status but instead identifies herself with the neutral "Ms." Kenneth Dion and his colleagues (Dion & Cota, 1991; Dion & Schuller, 1990) found that women who prefer the modern title Ms. are perceived as more achievement oriented, socially assertive, and competent, but less warm and likable than traditionally titled women. Thus, the Ms. title is a powerful cue eliciting a stereotype consistent with the male gender-related traits of agency and inconsistent with the female communal traits. More recent research indicates that the meaning of the title Ms. may be changing. Carol Lawton and her colleagues (Lawton et al., 2003) found that Ms. was often defined as a title for unmarried women, especially by younger adults. Older unmarried women were more likely to prefer Ms. as their own title than were younger unmarried women, while married women overwhelmingly preferred the use of Mrs.

Given that our impressions of a woman are influenced by her preferred title, a related question is whether these stereotypes vary according to another identity label, a woman's choice of surname after marriage. Similar to the preference for Ms. as a title of address, a woman's choice of a surname other than her husband's, such as her birth name or a hyphenated name, is a nontraditional practice that separates the woman's personal identity from her identity as a wife. Thus, it is not surprising that studies by Claire, Judith, and their students (Etaugh et al., 1999; Etaugh & Conrad, 2004; Etaugh & Roe, 2002) showed that college women and men view married women who use a nontraditional surname as more agentic and less communal than women who follow the patriarchal practice of taking their husband's name after marriage.

Why do a woman's preferred title and surname influence the characteristics attributed to her? One possibility is that individuals have observed more women with nontraditional forms of address (i.e., title and/or surname) in the workplace than in the domestic role and, thus, attribute her with more agentic traits. For example, there is evidence that married women who use nonconventional surnames are highly educated and have prestigious occupations (Guzman, 2002; Johnson & Scheuble, 1995). Thus, consistent with social role theory (Eagly et al., 2004), stereotypes of women who prefer nontraditional forms of address might be due to the belief that they are in nontraditional roles.

Sexism

The definition of sexism as bias against people because of their gender can be directed at either females or males. However, women have a power disadvantage relative to men and are, therefore, more likely to be targets of sexism (Goodwin & Fiske, 2001).

Therefore, our discussion focuses on the more specific definition of sexism as *stereotypes and/or discriminatory behaviors that serve to restrict women's roles and maintain male dominance.* For example, stereotypes, such as "women are dependent and passive," "women should be the primary caregivers," and "women are not competent to be police officers or university presidents," serve to shape women's role choices. *Violating these gender stereotypes can result in social and economic reprisals*—a phenomenon referred to as the **backlash effect** (Rudman & Fairchild, 2004). For example, a highly qualified female job applicant may be viewed as socially deficient, leading to hiring discrimination, and ultimately the maintenance of male dominance in the culture at large.

Consider the real-life case of Ann Hopkins, a high-achieving professional at Price Waterhouse, one of the country's most prestigious accounting firms. In 1982 Ms. Hopkins was one of 88 candidates for partner and the only female candidate. At that time she had more billable hours than any other contenders. Additionally, she had brought in $25 million worth of business and was highly esteemed by her clients. However, Ann Hopkins was turned down for the partnership. She was criticized for her "macho" style and was advised to "walk more femininely, talk more femininely, dress more femininely, wear makeup, have her hair styled, and wear jewelry" (Fiske et al., 1991, p. 1050).

Ms. Hopkins filed a lawsuit, asserting that her promotion had been denied on the basis of her gender. Although she won this suit, her employer appealed the decision all the way up to the Supreme Court. The Court decided in Ann Hopkins's favor and in 1990, a federal district court judge concluded that gender-based stereotyping had played a role in the firm's refusal to promote Ms. Hopkins to partner. After this decision, Ann Hopkins did become a partner and was awarded financial compensation for her lost earnings (Hopkins, 1996).

Ambivalent Sexism

Generally, we consider sexism to comprise *negative* stereotypes about women, such as the beliefs that women are fragile, submissive, and less competent than men. And, of course, we can see how stereotypes such as these are detrimental to women. Interestingly, however, Peter Glick and Susan Fiske (2001; Fiske, 2002) have proposed that sexism can be **ambivalent,** encompassing both **hostile sexism,** or negative stereotypes of women, as well as **benevolent sexism,** or positive characterizations such as "women are pure" and "women should be protected."

Although hostile sexist beliefs are overtly demeaning, benevolent sexist views are usually accompanied by genuine affection and the holder of these attitudes might be unaware of their implicit sexist bias. For example, a husband who shields his wife from the family's financial difficulties because he believes she would be unable to cope might be unaware of the biased assumptions implicit in his desire to protect her. According to Glick and Fiske (2001), hostile and benevolent sexism both imply that women are weak and best suited for traditional gender roles. Both serve to justify and maintain patriarchal social structures. In other words, ambivalent sexism includes both positive and negative beliefs about women, but both serve to maintain the power imbalance between women and men. In support of this view, research shows that individuals who endorse benevolent sexism also endorse the concept of "paternalistic chivalry," that is, being courteous and considerate to women but at the same time favoring traditional courtship behaviors for women (Viki et al., 2003). Some aspects of benevolent sexism may appeal to some women. For example, beliefs that women are less physically strong or more emotionally sensitive allow women to not engage in distasteful activities ranging from taking out the garbage to fighting in wars (Goodwin & Fiske, 2001). For a look at ambivalent sexism around the world, see Explore Other Cultures 2.1.

Changes in Sexist Attitudes over Time

Since 1970 the United States has experienced a significant decrease in overt sexism. For example, in 1970, 48 percent of a sample of college students expressed the belief that married women with children should stay home (Twenge, 1997a); however, only 21 percent expressed agreement with this belief in 2002 ("This Year's Freshmen," 2003). Further, a meta-analysis of 71 undergraduate samples from 1970 to 1995 (Twenge, 1997a) showed a steadily decreasing adherence to overt sexism by both females and males. Unfortunately, little is known about the sexist beliefs of noncollege adults, such as working- or middle-class women and men or adults on welfare.

EXPLORE OTHER CULTURES 2.1

Benevolent Sexism Is a Global Phenomenon

Peter Glick, Susan Fiske, and their colleagues (2000) measured ambivalent sexism in over 15,000 participants in 19 countries in Africa, Asia, Europe, the Americas, and Australia. While both hostile and benevolent sexism were prevalent in all cultures, these attitudes were strongest in Africa and Latin America and weakest in Northern Europe and Australia. Without exception, men showed more hostile sexism than women. In contrast, women in about half the countries endorsed benevolent sexism as much as or even more than men did (Figure 2.1). What accounts for these cross-cultural differences? The key factor appears to be the degree to which gender inequality exists in the various nations. Gender inequality is measured by such things as women's (relative to men's) participation in a country's economy and political system, their life expectancy, educational level, and standard of living. In countries with the greatest gender inequality (i.e., in Africa and Latin America), both men's and women's sexism scores were highest. Furthermore, the more hostile sexism the men showed, the more likely women were to embrace benevolent sexism, even to the point of endorsing it more strongly than men. How can this be explained? According to Glick and Fiske (2001), the greater the threat of hostile sexism from a society's men, the stronger the incentive for women to adopt benevolent sexism's protective nature.

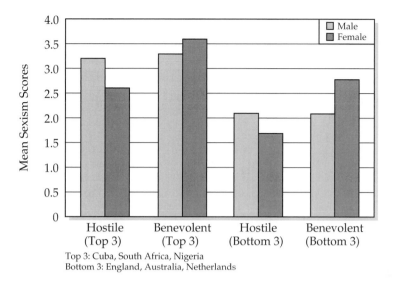

Top 3: Cuba, South Africa, Nigeria
Bottom 3: England, Australia, Netherlands

FIGURE 2.1　Hostile and Benevolent Sexism across Countries: The Top Three versus the Bottom Three

Modern Sexism

It is likely that the reduction in sexism is due, in part, to legislative actions (e.g., 1960s legislation prohibiting education and workplace discrimination on the basis of sex) and other social changes (e.g., the significant influx of married women into the workplace in the last few decades). However, some of the decline in overt sexism might actually reflect the decreased social acceptability of blatantly sexist views, rather than a real weakening of beliefs that serve to maintain traditional roles and power differences. Several theorists have suggested that a more subtle type of sexism has emerged in North America. This ideology, called **modern sexism** (Swim & Campbell, 2000), is based on the coexistence of conflicting attitudes. According to this perspective, some people hold egalitarian values but, at the same time, harbor negative feelings toward women. The resulting ideology is *characterized by the belief that gender discrimination is no longer a problem in society and is manifested by harmful treatment of women in ways that appear to be socially acceptable*. For example, a modern sexist might argue that policies that foster gender equality, such as affirmative action, should not be implemented. Thus, it is possible for a person to espouse sexist beliefs such as these but not appear to be prejudiced against women.

Do you know anyone who endorses modern sexism? See Get Involved 2.2 for examples of modern sexist beliefs.

Experiences with Sexism

Have you ever experienced unfair treatment by teachers, employers, strangers, romantic partners, and others because of your gender? Have you ever been the

GET INVOLVED **2.2**

Who Holds Modern Sexist Beliefs?

On a scale from 1 (strongly disagree) to 7 (strongly agree), indicate the extent to which you disagree or agree with each of the following statements. Also, ask several female and male acquaintances who vary in age to respond to these statements.

1. It is rare to see women treated in a sexist manner on television.
2. Society has reached the point where women and men have equal opportunities for achievement.
3. Over the past few years, the government and news media have been showing more concern about the treatment of women than is warranted by women's actual experiences.
4. Discrimination against women is no longer a problem in the United States.
5. Women's requests in terms of equality between the sexes are simply exaggerated.
6. Universities are wrong to admit women in costly programs such as medicine, when in fact, a large number will leave their jobs after a few years to raise their children.
7. Due to social pressures, firms frequently have to hire underqualified women.

What Does It Mean?

Sum the ratings you gave to these seven statements. Do the same for each of your respondents. Note that each statement reflects a sexist belief; therefore, the higher the score, the greater the sexism.

1. Are there differences between the views of your female and male respondents? Explain your finding.
2. Are there differences between the views of respondents who vary in age? Explain your finding.
3. Do you think it is possible that a person could endorse one or more of these beliefs but not be supportive of traditional roles and male dominance? Why or why not?

Source: Based on Swim, Aikin, Hall, & Hunter (1995) and Tougas, Brown, Beaton, & Joly (1995).

target of inappropriate or unwanted sexual advances or sexist name calling? Have you ever been forced to listen to sexist jokes? Elizabeth Klonoff and Hope Landrine (1995) asked 631 culturally diverse college and noncollege women how often incidents like these had happened to them. All except 6 women (99 percent) reported experiencing sexist discrimination at least once in their lives. Among the most commonly experienced events, reported by more than 80 percent of the women, were being forced to listen to sexist jokes, being sexually harassed, and experiencing a lack of respect. Although less common, 40 percent of the women reported some type of employment discrimination and 19 percent indicated they had taken legal or institutional action to pursue discrimination on the basis of gender.

The perception of sexism is dependent, in part, on a woman's interpretation. To one woman a joke that sexually degrades women is sexist, but to another woman that joke is simply funny. Not only do women vary in their interpretation of sexist incidents, but they also differ from one another in their willingness to acknowledge their own experience with discrimination. In a study of college students, Kobrynowicz and Branscombe (1997) found that women who have a strong desire for social approval are less likely to acknowledge they had experienced discrimination than are those willing to risk disapproval. According to these researchers, claiming sexism might be perceived as socially undesirable for women who are greatly concerned about the amount of approval they receive from others.

Another factor that can explain variations in the interpretation of a specific behavior as discriminatory is the perpetrator's gender. When people decide whether a behavior is sexist, they take into account the gender of the person who performed the action. For example, in one study (Baron et al., 1991), researchers asked college students to read vignettes in which a woman or a man responded to a woman in accordance with traditional roles and stereotypes (e.g., discouraged a female applicant who applied for a job as a tractor-trailer driver; counseled a female student to change from premed to nursing). The results showed that the same behaviors were more likely to be perceived as sexist if they were performed by a male than by a female perpetrator. Possibly, people consider it unlikely that women will discriminate against other women; thus, they fail to label women's gender-stereotypic comments and behaviors as sexist.

Representation of Gender in the Media

We have seen that North American adults have different conceptions of females and males. We turn now to the depiction of these stereotypes in the media. On a daily basis we are bombarded with differential images of females and males on television, in the movies, in books, and in magazines. Are these images consistent with gender stereotyping? Try the exercise in Get Involved 2.3 to examine television portrayals of gender.

Numerous investigations of the depiction of females and males in both electronic and print media have revealed several consistent patterns: the underrepresentation of females, the underrepresentation of specific groups of females, the portrayal of gender-based social roles, the depiction of female communion and male agency, and the emphasis on female attractiveness and sexuality. Our first task is to examine these patterns. Then we consider the effects of media images on gender stereotypes and attitudes.

Pattern 1: Underrepresentation of Females

As we have previously seen, women are perceived as less powerful than men; men's roles are viewed as more important. This imbalance of power and value is reflected in the media's underrepresentation of females. Although the percentage

GET INVOLVED **2.3**

How Are Females and Males Portrayed on Prime-Time Television?

Watch five different prime-time shows and record the following information: (1) the number of major female and male characters; (2) the ethnicity of these characters; (3) the employment status and occupation, if employed, of each major female and male character; (4) the marital and parental status of these characters; (5) the approximate age of each of these characters (e.g., 20s, 30s); and (6) whether or not each character's physical appearance was mentioned or otherwise appeared to be an important characteristic of that person. After recording this information, examine commonalities and differences in the depiction of females and males and in the portrayal of different age groups. Also, if these shows featured women and/or men of color, compare portrayals of characters of varying ethnicities.

What Does It Mean?

1. Are your findings consistent with those presented in this chapter? If not, what do you think might explain any differences you observed?
2. Do your findings indicate that members of each gender are depicted similarly, regardless of their ethnicity or age? If you found differences related to ethnicity or age, explain them.
3. Do you think that media images of gender, as described in this chapter and as shown by your analysis, help shape our construction of gender? Explain your answer.

---

of female characters in television shows increased from 28 percent in the 1970s to 39 percent in the 1990s (Signorielli & Bacue, 1999), it is clear that the proportion of females continues to be low. Similarly, the percentage of female characters in TV commercials (Bartsch et al., 2000; Ganahl et al., 2003; Signorielli, 1997), music videos (Signorielli, 1997), and movies (Lauzen, 2003; Signorielli, 1997) ranges from approximately 20 percent to 45 percent. This underrepresentation is also mirrored in children's television programs (Calvert, 1999), video games (Dietz, 1998), and even in computer clipart images (Milburn et al., 2001).

This situation has improved in recent years in certain types of children's reading material. For example, picture books of the 1990s featured males and females equally in titles, as central characters, and in pictures (Gooden & Gooden, 2001; Lane & Etaugh, 2001).

Pattern 2: Underrepresentation of Specific Groups of Females

Ethnicity.   The invisibility of females is most evident when considering females in less powerful social categories. Women and girls of color, especially Latinas, Asian Americans, and Native Americans are featured very infrequently in children's and adult's television shows, commercials (Calvert, 1999; Coltrane & Messineo, 2000; Van Evra, 2004), and movies (Lauzen, 2003). Latina characters are especially likely to be shown in low-status occupations such as maids (Navarro, 2002). On prime-time television shows, Black women and men, compared to Whites, were found to be more provocative and less professional in dress, were shown as more passive, and were judged as the laziest and least respected ethnic group (Mastro & Greenberg, 2000). Ethnic minority women are also underrepresented in advertisements in a wide variety of periodicals (Jackson & Ervin, 1991; Taylor et al., 1995) and are nearly invisible in fiction stories in large-circulation women's magazines (Peirce, 1997). Even college-level textbooks pay little attention to women of color. For example, a study of 11 developmental psychology texts reported that ethnic minority women were mentioned only four times (Conti & Kimmel, 1993), and an analysis of 20 leading marriage and family texts found that only 2 percent of the material dealt with people of color, and this coverage completely excluded Native Americans (Shaw-Taylor & Benokraitis, 1995). Similarly, a study of sociology textbooks noted that Latina women were nearly invisible (Marquez, 1994).

Age. Another seriously underrepresented group is older women. In television shows (Fouts & Burggraf, 1999; Signorielli & Bacue, 1999), television commercials

The media often depict Latina characters in low-status occupations, as in the movie Maid in Manhattan.

(Ganahl et al., 2003), and movies (Hornblow, 2002; Lauzen, 2003), female characters are younger than male characters, with most women under age 35. In
fact, women over 50 are portrayed in only 12 percent of the roles in popular
movies and, among the top actors aged 50 or older, only 20 percent are women
(Haskell & Harmetz, 1998). Older women of color are rarely seen (Robinson et al.,
2004).

Those older women who do appear in the media are praised for their youthful appearance and for hiding the signs of aging. Editors of women's magazines
admit that signs of age are removed from photographs through computer imag-
ing, making 60-year-old women look 45. *Lear's,* a magazine for midlife women,
rarely shows photographs of gray-haired women (Chrisler & Ghiz, 1993). In the
words of Susan Bordo,

> *I'm 56. The magazines tell me that at this age, a woman can still be beautiful. But they don't
> mean me. They mean Cher, Goldie, Faye, Candace. Women whose jowls have disappeared as
> they've aged, whose eyes have become less droopy, lips grown plumper, foreheads smoother
> with the passing years. 'Aging beautifully' used to mean wearing one's years with style, con-
> fidence, and vitality. Today, it means not appearing to age at all.* (2004, p. 246)

In our youth-oriented society, the prospect of getting older is generally not
relished by either sex. For women, however, *the stigma of aging is much greater than
it is for men.* Susan Sontag (1979) has labeled this phenomenon the **double standard of aging**. The same gray hair and wrinkles that enhance the perceived status and attractiveness of an older man diminish the attractiveness and desirability
of an older woman. Some researchers account for this by noting that a woman's
most socially valued qualities—her ability to provide sex and bear children—are
associated with the physical beauty and fertility of youth. As she ages, she is seen
as less attractive because her years of social usefulness as childbearer are behind
her. Men, however, are seen as possessing qualities—competence, autonomy, and
power—which are not associated with youth but rather increase with age
(Halliwell & Dittmar, 2003).

Older women in popular films are portrayed as more unfriendly, unintelligent,
unattractive, and wicked (Bazzini et al., 1997). Attractive actresses such as Meryl
Streep, Jessica Lange, and Diane Keaton are labeled "geezer babes"—and thus too
old for romantic parts—while male actors many years their senior are paired with
young ingenues (Genzlinger, 2004; Haskell, 1998; Hornblow, 2002). Along the
same lines, an analysis of Academy Award nominations for Best Actress and
Best Actor from 1927–28 to 1990 found that women over the age of 39 accounted
for only 27 percent of all winners for Best Actress, while men in the same age
category won 67 percent of Best Actor awards (Markson & Taylor, 1993). Holly-
wood's long-standing tendency to add years to actresses and subtract them from
actors has led to some interesting—and biologically impossible—movie relationships. For example, 29-year-old Angelina Jolie played the mother of 28-year-old
Colin Farrell in the 2004 film *Alexander* (Beumont, 2005). Before going further, try
Get Involved 2.4.

Older men are often portrayed as powerful and distinguished, while older women are perceived as losing their attractiveness.

GET INVOLVED **2.4**

Media Ads and the Double Standard of Aging

Look through newspapers and magazines for advertisements that include middle-aged adults. Then answer the following questions:

1. Are there differences in the appearance of the women and the men?

2. Do females and males advertise different products?

3. In ads with two or more people, what is the role of the principal male or female in relationship to others?

What Does It Mean?

1. Do the ads show evidence of a double standard of aging?

2. What can advertisers do to minimize differences in the portrayal of middle-aged females and males?

3. How do media images of midlife adults help shape our perceptions of middle-aged women and men?

Source: Berk, Wholeben, & Bouchey (1998).

Sexual Orientation.   Lesbians and gay men have been another underrepresented group in the media. As recently as 15 years ago, there were few visible gay characters, and they were usually portrayed as psychopaths, suicidal, unattractive, or isolated (D'Erasmo, 2004; Weinraub & Rutenberg, 2003; Stanley, 2004; Wloszezyna, 2003). But as gays and lesbians have become more accepted in recent years, gay characters are increasingly featured in mainstream television shows, films, and theater. Television shows such as *Will and Grace* (a straight woman and a gay man are best friends), *Queer Eye for the Straight Guy* (gay experts in fashion, food, and interior design do a makeover on "aesthetically challenged" straight men), and *Queer as Folk* (a portrayal of gay men's lives) are mainstream hits. The year 2004 saw the debut of *It's All Relative,* featuring a woman raised by two liberal gay men who is engaged to the son of Irish-Catholic conservatives, and *The L-Word,* the first lesbian-focused series. In 2005, a long-time character on *The Simpsons* came out of the closet and Homer Simpson conducted dozens of same-sex weddings to boost tourism in his town (Waxman, 2005). Also in that year, MTV started the first cable television channel directed at gay and lesbian viewers (Carter & Elliott, 2004). The trend-setting *New York Times* began publishing same-sex wedding and commitment ceremony announcements in 2002. And a 2003 issue of the popular magazine *Brides* had a feature on what to wear to a same-sex wedding (Toussaint, 2003).

Angelina Jolie (left), age 29, plays the mother of 28-year-old Colin Farrell (right) in the film Alexander.

Pattern 3: Portrayal of Gender-Based Social Roles

Females and males are portrayed differently in the media not only in terms of their numbers but also in relation to their social roles. Over the last few decades there has been an increase in the percentage of prime-time TV shows that feature female characters who are employed, with 60 percent of female characters depicted as working in the 1990s (Signorielli & Bacue, 1999). Furthermore, their range of jobs has broadened; in the 1990s only one quarter were shown in traditional female jobs, such as secretary or nurse (Signorielli & Bacue, 1999). But although women lawyers, doctors, and police officers appear on television, many of these depictions are unrealistic. For example, not all women in these professions are young and beautiful (Van Evra, 2004)!

On the other hand, consistent with the stereotypical association of men in the worker role and women in the family role, popular television shows (National Partnership for Women & Families, 1998; Signorielli & Bacue, 1999), commercials (Das, 2000; Signorielli, 1997), and movies (Signorielli, 1997) still show more men than women with jobs, and, more women than men in families. In the movies, women are more likely than men to hold powerless occupations, such as retail clerk, and they rarely are shown in leadership roles (Lauzen, 2003). Also, although most married men in TV shows are employed, there are few married working women in these shows (Signorielli, 1997). Thus, despite the presence of several positive employed-female role models on television and the fact that the majority of American married women are employed (U.S. Census Bureau, 2003c), there is little depiction of women who successfully combine a career and marriage. Television seems to be saying that successful women professionals cannot have rewarding home lives, if indeed they have any at all (Garfinkel, 2002).

Similarly, the Sunday comics feature more women than men at home and fewer women than men in career activities (Brabant & Mooney, 1997; LaRossa et al., 2001). Children's picture books also reflect this role difference by depicting women as homemakers and nurturers (Lane & Etaugh, 2001; Lehr, 2001). In addition, when females are portrayed as working, children's readers (Purcell & Stewart, 1990) and cartoons (Spicher & Hudak, 1997) show them in a smaller variety of occupations, and teen magazines for girls portray both genders in gender-stereotypical occupations (e.g., men as physicians and women as nurses) (Peirce, 1993). Furthermore, the majority of feature articles in the leading teen magazine for girls, *Seventeen*, focus on traditional topics, such as appearance and relationships (Schlenker et al., 1998). Only 40 percent address more feminist themes, such as self- and career development. The world of work is dominated by powerful men, and fashion modeling is presented as the pinnacle of "women's work" (Massoni, 2004). Moreover, stereotyped depictions of women in both general interest and fashion magazine advertisements have decreased only slightly over the past 50 years (Lindner, 2004).

Despite the increasing participation of women in sports, female athletes continue to be underrepresented in the media (Zill et al., 2004). Moreover, those who participate in traditional feminine sports such as tennis, golf, or gymnastics get more coverage than women who compete in more masculine team sports such as basketball or softball (Fink & Kensicki, 2002; Tuggle et al., 2002). In the 2000 Olympics, women who competed in sports involving power or hard physical contact—discus throw, javelin throw, shot put, weightlifting, martial arts—received almost no television coverage (Tuggle et al., 2002).

Pattern 4: Depiction of Female Communion and Male Agency

Consistent with the depiction of females and males in different social roles, the communion stereotype for females and the agency stereotype for males are both evident in the media. Despite the growing body of movies and TV shows featuring women fighting and committing mayhem—*Survivor, Fear Factor, Buffy the Vampire Slayer, Kill Bill, Charlie's Angels,* and others (Lee, 2003; Leland, 2003)—boys and men are depicted as more assertive, aggressive, and powerful than females in a range of media. These include adult films (Hedley, 1994), MTV music videos (Sommers-Flanagan et al., 1993), children's cartoons (Browne, 1998; Spicher & Hudak, 1997), Disney films (Levant, 1997), and children's literature (Etaugh et al., 2003; Louie, 2001). The lack of agency on the part of females is reflected in both teen (Peirce, 1993) and women's (Peirce, 1997) magazine fiction, where the female main character generally has to depend on other people to help her solve her problems. Furthermore, consistent with their greater power, males are presented as narrators in approximately 70 to 90 percent of commercials that use voice-overs (e.g., Bartsch et al., 2000; Craig, 1992), thus projecting an image of authority and expertise.

The media also feature females as communal, as oriented toward other people. For example, even when a woman is depicted as an action hero—such as Xena the Warrior princess—she is liked best when she embodies traditionally valued feminine traits such as nurturance, compassion, and using the mind over the sword (Calvert et al., 2001). In both television and movies, women are more likely than men to focus on their romantic relationships (Signorielli, 1997). Most mothers in children's literature are nurturers. Many are homemakers, while others are in traditional female nurturing occupations such as teaching, nursing, or social work (Lehr, 2001).

Pattern 5: Emphasis on Female Attractiveness and Sexuality

The media define females, more than males, by their looks and sexuality. For example, commercials show more women than men as physically attractive (Lin, 1998), and commercials, television shows, and movies portray women as more likely than men to receive comments about their appearance (Lauzen & Dozier, 2002; Signorielli, 1997). In the pursuit of physical perfection, women routinely risk their health to undergo extensive plastic surgery on TV reality shows such as *Extreme Makeover* and *The Swan* (Orenstein, 2004; Pozner, 2004).

Music videos emphasize women's sexuality rather than their musical talent (Lin, 1998; Van Evra, 2004). In the words of one researcher (Arnett, 2002, p. 256), ". . . a typical music video . . . features one or more men performing while beautiful, scantily clad young women dance and writhe lasciviously." Sports announcers and writers frequently refer to a female athlete's attractiveness, emotionality, femininity, and heterosexuality, thus conveying to the audience that her stereotypical gender role is more salient than her athletic role (Billings et al., 2002; Fink & Kensicki, 2004; Knight & Giuliano, 2001). Furthermore, in the photographs of the media guide put out by the National Collegiate Athletic Association (NCAA), women athletes are less likely than men athletes to be portrayed as active participants in sport and are more likely to be shown in passive and feminine poses (Buysse & Embser-Herbert, 2004).

This emphasis on females' appearance is apparent in print as well as electronic media. In 1996, 78 percent of the covers of the most popular magazines for women presented text about bodily appearance, such as messages about diet or exercise. However, none of the covers of frequently read men's magazines contained comparable messages (Malkin et al., 1999). Websites of teen magazines such as *CosmoGIRL!*, *Teen People*, *Seventeen*, and *Teen* emphasize that beauty is essential for success and can only be achieved by using products to perfect one's body (Labre & Walsh-Childers, 2003). Similarly, popular women's magazines prey on women's insecurities to get them to buy the advertisers' wares (Blyth, 2004). Kate Peirce (1997) contends that magazines targeted at working women focus as much on appearance as beauty and fashion magazines do. She notes that in one 1995 issue of *New Woman*, 12 pages of makeup ads preceded the table of contents. Moreover, the depiction of women is more sexualized than that of men. For example, female fashion ads are more likely than male ads to feature models in sexy attire (Plous & Neptune, 1997). Even popular children's fairy tales, such as Cinderella, Snow White, and Sleeping Beauty, highlight youthful feminine beauty, which often is associated with being White, virtuous, and economically privileged (Baker-Sperry & Grauerholz, 2003).

Not only is a woman's attractiveness portrayed as highly important but that attractiveness is also depicted as overly thin. For example, most *Playboy* centerfolds are underweight, and approximately one-third are so thin that they meet the World Health Organization's standard for anorexia nervosa, a severe eating disorder (see Chapter 13) (Spitzer et al., 1999). Gregory Fouts and Kimberley Burggraf (1999, 2000) examined the body weight of characters in Canadian situation comedies and found that the number of below-average-weight female characters was greater than that found in the general population. Additionally, they observed that comments from male characters were contingent on a female character's weight. The thinner the female, the more positive comments she received, and the heavier the woman, the more derogatory remarks she got. On the show *America's Next Top Models*, dangerously underweight young women reaped praise for their looks, while normal-weight contestants at 5 feet 8 inches and 130 lbs were mocked as "plus-sized" (Pozner, 2004). Overweight women not only are underrepresented on television and considered less attractive, but they are also less likely to interact with romantic partners (Greenberg et al., 2003).

Thus, the media still portray appearance and sexuality as two highly valued aspects of a woman's identity. More specifically, they present the message that it is White beauty that is valued (Baker, 2005; Pacheco & Hurtado, 2001). Black actresses and models who are depicted as physically desirable are likely to be light-skinned and to possess White facial features (Perkins, 1996), thus informing the Black viewer that not just beauty but White beauty is important.

The media's portrayal of women's appearance does have some recent bright spots. In 2004, for example, Dove launched "The Dove Campaign for Real Beauty," a global effort intended to act as a catalyst for widening the definition and discussion of beauty. The campaign targeted the United States and Great Britain and featured billboard images of six women of various ages, sizes, types, and shapes (Hoggard, 2005). Each photograph showed a woman whose appearance challenges traditional stereotypes of beauty, and asked viewers to judge her looks by casting votes and joining a discussion of beauty issues at the campaign's Website. For example, "Oversized? Outstanding?" were the choices next to Tabatha Roman, 34, a plus-size woman, and "Wrinkled? Wonderful?" appear next to the photo of Irene Sinclair, 96.

Significance of Gender-Role Media Images

As this discussion indicates, despite the nearly equal numbers of North American females and males, the media portray a world more heavily populated by males than by females, a world in which males are more likely than females to have jobs and be active and assertive and where beauty and romantic relationships are central to females' identity. Research shows that media not only reflect and transmit existing stereotypes but also have a socializing effect (Bryant & Zillman, 2002; Reichert & Lambiase, 2003; Van Evra, 2004). For example, exposure to music videos leads to and is associated with stronger endorsement of traditional gender roles and greater acceptance of dating violence (Ward et al., 2005; Ward, 2002). Thus, the media can play an important role in shaping our construction of gender and in providing us with expectations of what females and males are like—their personality traits, social roles, and value to society. In addition, the very limited depiction of non-White or older females can reinforce perceptions of the powerlessness of these groups and communicate that their experiences are not important (Van Evra, 2004).

Consider other types of media that might portray females and males stereotypically. See, for example, Learn about the Research 2.2 to find out about stereotypes in greeting cards.

Representation of Gender in the English Language

The last section demonstrated how communication via the mass media, such as television and magazines, portrays different images of females and males. This section examines language itself: the different ways females and males are

wrinkled?
wonderful?

Will society ever accept
old can be beautiful?

Irene Sinclair, age 96, in a Dove commercial challenging traditional stereotypes of beauty.

LEARN ABOUT THE RESEARCH 2.2

Are Babies Portrayed Stereotypically in Birth Congratulations Cards?

We have seen that girls and boys are portrayed stereotypically in virtually all media. To explore how infant girls and boys are portrayed, Judith and her students examined the visual images and verbal messages present in 61 birth congratulations cards for girls and 61 cards for boys.

Not surprisingly, pink was the most common color used on the cards for girls and blue on the cards for boys. Boys were more likely to be shown performing physical activities, such as walking or building, whereas girls were pictured passively sitting or lying down. Similarly, more of the cards for boys featured toys, such as sports equipment and vehicles, that require considerable action, whereas girls were pictured with baby toys, such as rattles and mobiles, that required less physical involvement. Larger animals, including bears and dogs, were more common on the cards for boys and smaller, less aggressive birds and rabbits were shown on the cards for girls.

Although there were few gender-specific verbal messages in the cards, there were several interesting differences. Girls, more than boys, were described as "little" and "sweet," while the happiness of parents or the child was included more often in the verbal message to boys than in the message to girls.

What Does It Mean?

Answer these questions before reading the remaining part of the research description.

1. The pictures on the cards for girls and boys differed in terms of the types of activities the children were doing, and the types of toys and animals presented. How do these differential images fit in with gender stereotypes of females and males as discussed in this chapter?
2. Do any of the study's findings suggest that one gender is more culturally valued than the other? Explain your answer.
3. If you were buying a birth congratulations card for a friend or relative, would you look for a gender-stereotypic or a nonstereotypic card? Why?

One conclusion of this study was that birth congratulations cards do portray newborns in gender-stereotypic ways. In keeping with the stereotypical conception that males are more active than females, the types of activities, toys, and animals shown on the cards portrayed boys as more active than girls. Similarly, the tendency to characterize girls more than boys as "little" and "sweet" is consistent with the stereotypic conception of more passive and less powerful females. It is possible that the more frequent reference to happiness on the cards for boys might reflect a greater societal value placed on males than on females and/or it might be indicative of a stronger preference for a son than for a daughter.

Source: Bridges (1993).

depicted in the English language and how this differential portrayal can shape our conceptions of gender. *Language that unnecessarily differentiates between females and males or excludes and trivializes members of either sex* is called **sexist language.** Let's examine different types of sexist language.

Language Practices Based on the Assumption That Male Is Normative

Numerous language practices reflect the assumption that **male is normative;** that is, that *male behaviors, roles, and experiences are the standards (i.e., norms) for society.* Integral to this perspective are the assumptions that males are more important than females and that female behaviors, roles, and experiences are deviant, that is, different from the norm (Wood, 1994). One indication of this assumption is that adults tend to think of males as persons, as standard or normative individuals in society. For example, Mykol Hamilton (1991) found that college students were more apt to describe typical persons as males than as females and to refer to a male as a *person* but a female as a *woman.* Try Get Involved 2.5 and see if your findings match those reported by Hamilton. Even animals, flowers, and inanimate objects tend to be conceived as male when their sex is unspecified (Lambdin et al., 2003).

Now let's examine some of the language practices that reflect this belief of male as normative.

GET INVOLVED 2.5

Are Both Women and Men Persons?

Ask two acquaintances of each gender to help you with this activity. Tell them you are studying people's choices about grammatical structure; that is, you are examining students' selections of specific words in a sentence. Therefore, you would like them to fill in the blank in each of the following:

1. Debra Cook won the raffle at the charity fund-raising event. The event organiz-

ers will send the prize to this _____ in two weeks.

        person   **woman**

2. Dave Sherman moved to a new town and went to the Town Hall to register to vote. The registrar of voters gave this _____ the application form.

        person   **man**

What Does It Mean?

Examine the selections made by your respondents.

1. Did they select different terms depending on the gender of the person?
2. Were there any differences between the answers of the females and males?

3. Did these answers correspond to the findings of Hamilton, as discussed in this chapter?
4. What interpretation can you offer for your findings?

Source: Based on Hamilton (1991).

Masculine Generic Language.   Consider the following situation.

> *At the first session of a training program called "Reducing Man's Addictions" the program's director informed participants that they would be divided into small groups for discussion of the material and that each group should appoint a chairman to facilitate its discussion. Also, the director indicated that at the end of the training program each participant would have sufficient knowledge so that he could work at a drug rehabilitation center.*

Describe your image of this event. Does the program deal with addiction problems of both women and men or men only? Will the chairs of the groups be men or women? What is the gender of the participants? Are these gender images clear?

Now substitute *woman*'s for *man*'s, *chairwoman* for *chairman*, and *she* for *he*. Ask yourself the same questions.

Regardless of your own interpretations of these two verbal descriptions, note that the latter was written using gender-specific (i.e., female) terms whereas the former was written in **masculine generic language,** which is *language that uses male terms but purports to be inclusive of females and males*. Both male pronouns, such as *he* and *his*, as well as male nouns, such as *chairman, freshman, businessman, man-hours, and forefathers*, are used not only in reference to males but also as inclusive of both genders (reflecting the assumption that male is standard).

Are these masculine generic terms actually interpreted as gender neutral; that is, are they as likely to elicit images of females as males? An abundance of research suggests they are not. Far from communicating gender-neutral images, these terms tend to be exclusionary, connoting just what they directly indicate, that is, men and boys (Conkright et al., 2000; Crawford, 2001; Klein & Larson, 2004). For example, in one study (Switzer, 1990) first- and seventh-grade children listened to the following story:

> Pretend that [teacher's name] told you that a new student is coming to be a part of your class. Tomorrow will be _____ first day. Describe how you think _____ will feel on the first day. (p. 74)

Students heard the story with one of the following pronouns inserted in the blanks: *he, he or she*, or *they*. The results clearly showed that *he* is not assumed to mean both females and males. Its exculsionary interpretation was demonstrated by the finding that 93 percent of the children who heard the *he* story, wrote that the student was a boy. On the other hand, when the pronouns were the inclusive *he or she* or *they*, the girls were more apt to write about a girl than a boy and the boys were more likely to write about a boy than a girl.

Given that male pronouns are evidently not gender neutral, it is not surprising that the use of male nouns as gender neutral similarly connotes male images. In one study (McConnell & Fazio, 1996) college students rated a *chairman* as more masculine than either a *chair* or a *chairperson*, suggesting that the former leads to more male-related mental imagery than the other two. Therefore, it is not surprising that the newer, gender-neutral terms, chair and chairperson, are more likely used in reference to women whereas the traditional term, chairman, is more often used to indicate a man (Romaine, 1999).

Spotlighting.   **Spotlighting** refers to *the practice of emphasizing an individual's gender*, as in *"Female* professor receives prestigious grant" or, as in a recent headline about a spy who for decades had handed British atomic secrets to Russia, "Grandma led two lives" (Knightley, 1999). Consistent with the male as normative perspective, this practice of highlighting a woman's gender serves to reinforce the notion that males are the standard (Basow, 2001). That is, although spotlighting does give recognition to specific females, at the same time, it conveys the message that these females are exceptions.

One investigation of gendered spotlighting involved the examination of televised broadcasts of the 1989 women's and men's National Collegiate Athletic Association final four basketball tournaments (Messner et al., 1993). The researchers observed spotlighting an average of 26 times per game during the women's tournament with commentary, such as ". . . is a legend in *women's* basketball" or "this NCAA *women's* semifinal is brought to you by . . . " (p. 125). However, there was no evidence of spotlighting during the men's games.

Diminutive Suffixes for Female Terms.   The English language sometimes differentiates genders by using a root word to designate a male and an added suffix to specify a female. This language feature, like others discussed in this section, is based on the assumption of the male as the standard. A suffix is needed to indicate the nonnormative exception, the female. Examples of this include *actor/actress*, *poet/poetess*, and *author/authoress*. In fact, according to Suzanne Romaine (1999), the only English words where the female term is the root word with a male suffix added are *widower* and *bridegroom*. Why do these words have female roots? Perhaps the term, *widower*, reflects the fact that women generally outlive men and *bridegroom* might be based on the traditional expectation that women's roles are linked to marriage and the family.

Romaine (1999) contends that this practice of marking the female with a suffix added to the male root is one way the English language signifies that a woman is a "lesser man" (p. 140). Similarly, Casey Miller and Kate Swift state, "the significance of a word like authoress is not that it identifies a female but that it indicates deviation from what is consciously or unconsciously considered the standard" (1991, p. 171).

Negative Terms for Females

Another language practice that reflects the differential treatment of females and males is the greater number of negative terms depicting women than men.

Parallel Terms.   There are numerous pairs of words in the English language in which the objective meaning of the female and male term are comparable, but the female word has a negative connotation. Consider, for example, *bachelor* and *spinster* or *old maid*. All three refer to unmarried persons, but the female terms connote an undesirable state reflecting rejection and old age. Another example is *master* versus *mistress*. Originally these referred to a man and woman in charge of a

Tide twists Vols' title plans

Disappearing act won't help Vols' status

TUSCALOOSA, Ala.

If you're a Tennessee men's basketball fan, you can rest easy today.

You no longer have to fret about those whispers concerning the possibility of one or more Vols jumping to the NBA early.

Let's just put it this way: junior Tony Harris and sophomore Vincent Yarbrough should be thankful there was only one NBA scout in the building to witness the second half of UT's 80-75 loss to Alabama on Saturday.

"Both of those Tennessee guys have a tremendous future," Seattle SuperSonics regional scout Yvan K. Kelly said diplomatically.

Note: The key word is "future."

As for the present, that's another story. Harris was 1 for 9 against Alabama and scored four points.

GARY LUNDY

"It's going to be a big transition for Tony to play the point in the pros, and size (under 6 feet) is going to be more of a problem in the pros than in college," Kelly said.

Hot second half helps Alabama ambush No. 7 UT

By Mike Strange
News-Sentinel sportswriter

TUSCALOOSA, Ala. — Among the several costly turnovers Tennessee fumbled away in the closing minutes Saturday, the biggest was this: the chance to control its own destiny.

The SEC men's basketball championship the Vols covet hasn't fallen completely out of reach, but now it also will be decided in places such as Gainesville and Lexington.

"We just put the ball in somebody else's hands," sai' UT's Vincent Yarbrough, assessing the damage after No. 7-ranked Tennessee was upset by Alabama 80-75.

UT arrived at Coleman Coliseum in the driver's seat of a tight SEC race. However, the Vols got unseated by a young Alabama team that rose to the occasion, cheered on by a crowd of 9,053.

The Crimson Tide (13-13, 6-8 SEC) overturned a 10-point Tennessee lead early in the second half and held the cold-shooting, fumble-fingered Vols at bay down the stretch.

The intensity Tennessee showed in its victory over Kentucky three days earlier was nowhere to be found.

"We came in thinking because we're Tennessee, they'd lay down for us," senior C.J. Black said, searching for an explanation.

"You look at our defense against Kentucky," UT coach Jerry Green said, "and our offense and how much enthusiasm and energy we've got to expend.

Lady Vols seek a repeat defense against LSU

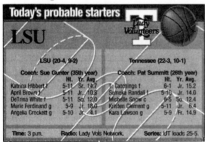

Today's probable starters

LSU (20-4, 9-2)				Tennessee (22-3, 10-1)			
Coach: Sue Gunter (35th year)				Coach: Pat Summitt (26th year)			
	Ht.	Yr.	Avg.		Ht.	Yr.	Avg.
Katrina Hibbert f	5-11	Sr.	14.7	Tamika Catchings f	6-1	Jr.	15.2
April Brown f	5-11	Jr.	10.8	Semeka Randall f	5-10	Jr.	14.0
DeTrina White f	5-11	So.	12.0	Michelle Snow c	6-5	So.	12.4
Marie Ferdinand g	5-9	Jr.	18.0	Kristen Clement g	5-11	Jr.	6.4
Angelia Crockett g	5-10	Jr.	4.1	Kara Lawson g	5-9	Fr.	14.9
Time: 3 p.m.		Radio: Lady Vols Network		Series: UT leads 25-5.			

By Dan Fleser
News-Sentinel sportswriter

A visit from LSU today recalls the finest hour for Tennessee's defense.

The 3 o'clock tip-off at Thompson-Boling Arena is the second regular-season meeting for these SEC rivals. The first game, Jan. 6 in Baton Rouge, La., probably was second to none for the Lady Vols.

"That could've been our best game of the year," UT coach Pat Summitt said of the 86-50 victory.

One of the biggest reasons for the one-sided result was Tennessee's defenders helping limit the Tigers to 36.8 percent shooting

from the floor. They also played a part in 25 LSU turnovers.

Striving for a repeat performance would be a noble quest, but probably not realistic. Summitt conceded to the one-of-those-nights nature of the first encounter.

"We were on a roll," she said. "They couldn't get on track. It snowballs."

Nonetheless, taking a stab at better defensive consistency would be a useful objective. Before the first LSU-Tennessee game, the defense was viewed as good but not great. Thirteen games later, the same perspective applies.

The Lady Vols are more apt to have their moments on defense.

Obviously they've had their share, as evidenced by their record (22-3, 10-1 SEC) and their national ranking (2nd). A nine-game winning streak adds to their stature.

"I believe we can get a (defensive) stop against any team in the country at any time," freshman guard Kara Lawson said.

She offered this assessment after UT's defenders held Mississippi State scoreless during the final 2:35 of last Thursday's 79-75 comeback victory. This work was a crucial accompaniment to the Lady Vols' 11-point finishing kick across the same time span.

The defensive stand was a

Please see **LADY VOLS**, page C7

Highlighting the female gender but not the male gender reinforces the assumption that males are the standard and females are the exception.

household, a usage that still pertains to *master. Mistress,* however, has developed a sexual connotation with negative overtones (Romaine, 1999).

Childlike Terms. Have you ever heard the term *girl* in reference to an adult woman? Perhaps you have noted a male manager say something like the following to one of his associates: "I'll have my *girl* phone your *girl* to schedule a lunch meeting for us." Given that neither of the secretaries to whom he is referring is likely to be "a female child" a dictionary definition of girl, the term *girl* is not appropriate. However, it is more common for people to refer to ☺ adult women as *girls* than to adult men as *boys* (Basow, 2001). For example, in the investigation (Messner et al., 1993) of televised commentary of women's and men's sports discussed above, the researchers found that, although the female athletes were not younger than their male counterparts, the broadcasters referred to female basketball and tennis players as *girls* but never called the male athletes *boys*.

Other childlike terms that are applied more to women than to men include *baby*, *babe*, and *sweetie*. Although these terms might be perceived as signs of affection in an intimate relationship, their use by nonintimates reflects the childlike quality of many terms used to identify women.

Is the use of these terms detrimental to women? Research suggests that it might be. For example, when female and male respondents in a study were asked about their impressions of adult women, they described women who were referred to as *girls* as being less responsible than women who were labeled *women* (Kitto, 1989). Such a negative depiction could clearly apply to other childlike terms.

Animal and Food Terms.   Researchers of the gender biases of language (e.g., Wood, 1994) point to the heavy use of animal names and food products in reference to women as another example of the negative depiction of females. Examples of these include the animal labels *fox*, *chick*, *bitch*, and *cow*, and the food-related terms *honey*, *cookie*, *dish*, and *feast for the eyes*.

Sexualization of Women.   As discussed earlier in this chapter, the media treat a woman's sexuality as an important aspect of her identity. American English also places a strong emphasis on a woman's sexuality. In one study (Grossman & Tucker, 1997), college students were asked to list all of the slang words they could think of for either a woman or a man. Although there was no difference in the number of terms associated with each gender, approximately 50 percent of the terms used for females were sexual (e.g., *slut*) whereas less than 25 percent of those used for males were. Furthermore, there are far more negative sexual terms for women than for men (Crawford, 2001).

In Grossman and Tucker's study of slang, the terms used for women were more negative than those used for men. For example, among the most frequently listed terms were *bitch* and *slut* for women but *guy* and *dude* for men.

Significance of the Differential Treatment of Females and Males in Language

We have examined several indications that English depicts males as the societal standard and that many language conventions portray females in negative terms. Do these practices matter? According to Janet Swim and her colleagues (Swim et al., 2004; Swim et al., 2003), they certainly do. Sexist language reinforces and perpetuates gender stereotypes and status differences between women and men. Whether or not the speaker or writer intends harm, sexist language can have a negative effect on how girls and women perceive themselves.

The words of Jessica, a 25-year-old college senior, make this point vividly.

Using animal and food terms to refer to women is obviously degrading, and hazardous to a woman's self-esteem. If a woman hears herself being called a cow or bitch enough, she will believe that she is one. I didn't think it could happen if you were a strong person; I mean, I know I'm not a bitch, right? Wrong. After five years of hearing it from a significant other, I actually found myself calling myself these names aloud! It's powerful.

SUMMARY

Stereotypes of Females and Males

- Based on the tendency to sort others into gender categories, we assume that certain characteristics, behaviors, and roles are more representative of females and others of males. These are called gender stereotypes.
- Stereotypes vary according to the ethnicity of the person holding the stereotype and the ethnicity and social class of the target person.
- Stereotypes of women with disabilities differ from stereotypes of able-bodied women.
- According to social role theory, because we associate females with the domestic role and males with the employment role, our female stereotype tends to center on communion and our male stereotype on agency.
- Women who choose to be called "Ms." or who use a nontraditional name after marriage are perceived as more agentic and less communal than women who prefer conventional titles of address.

Sexism

- Several different forms of sexism have been proposed by scholars. Ambivalent sexism includes both hostile and benevolent attitudes. Modern sexism is a subtle form of sexism, based on egalitarian values combined with underlying negative feelings toward women.
- Large numbers of women have experienced either minor or major sexist incidents.

Representation of Gender in the Media

- Females are underrepresented in the media.
- Certain groups of women are particularly underrepresented, including ethnic minority women, older women, and lesbians.
- The stigma of aging is greater for women than men. This double standard is based on society's emphasis on youthful physical beauty for women.
- Although the media do depict women in occupational roles, TV features few women who combine family and work roles.
- Similarly, the Sunday comics, children's books, and teen magazines present messages consistent with the importance of the domestic role for women and the provider role for men.
- Many forms of media portray males as more agentic than females and show females as being relationship oriented.
- Media images emphasize the importance to females of physical attractiveness and sexuality.
- The media both reinforce and contribute to our stereotypes of gender.

Representation of Gender in the English Language

- Numerous English language practices, including the use of the masculine generic, spotlighting, and diminutive suffixes for female terms, are based on the assumption that the male is normative.

- Other practices that deprecate women include the use of parallel terms, childlike terms, animal and food terms, sexual terms, and negative slang.

- The differential treatment of females and males in language both reflects and helps shape our gender images.

KEY TERMS

gender stereotypes	social role theory	double standard of aging
communion	backlash effect	sexist language
agency	ambivalent sexism	male is normative
ageism	hostile sexism	masculine generic language
ableism	benevolent sexism	spotlighting
social categorization	modern sexism	

WHAT DO YOU THINK?

1. We have seen that women who use the title Ms. or who do not take their husband's surname after marriage are perceived as more agentic and less communal than women who use Miss or Mrs. or who take their husband's name. One explanation for this is provided by social role theory. Can you think of any other possible explanations?

2. Consider the work by Glick and Fiske on ambivalent sexism.

    a. Do you agree that positive stereotypes of women can serve to maintain patriarchal roles and relationships? Why or why not?

    b. Do you believe that benevolent and hostile sexism are equally detrimental to women? Why or why not?

3. We have examined numerous sources of societal representations of gender, such as greeting cards, children's books, and television commercials. What other types of media might reflect gender stereotypes?

4. Which of the various language features that treat females and males differently do you think has the most detrimental effect on girls and women? Why?

5. Provide evidence, from the chapter or from your own experience, that language influences our perceptions of gender.

IF YOU WANT TO LEARN MORE

Black, P. (2004). *The beauty industry: Gender, culture, pleasure.* New York: Routledge.

Cortese, A. J. (2004). *Provocateur: Images of women and minorities in advertising.* (2d ed). Lanham, MD: Rowman & Littlefield.

Douglas, S. J. (1995). *Where the girls are: Growing up female with the mass media.* New York: Times Books.

Friedan, B. (1993). *The fountain of age.* New York: Simon & Schuster.

Halmlund, C. (2002). *Impossible bodies: Femininity and masculinity at the movies.* New York: Routledge.

Jacobs, R. H. (1997). *Be an outrageous older woman.* New York: HarperCollins.

Kilbourne, J., & Pipher, M. (2000). *Can't buy my love: How advertising changes the way we think and feel.* New York: Touchstone Books.

Lehr, S. (Ed.). (2001). *Beauty, brains, and brawn: The construction of gender in children's literature.* Portsmouth, NH: Heinemann.

MacDonald, M. (1998). *Representing women: Myths of femininity in the popular media*. New York: Edward Arnold.

Tannen, D. (1990). *Gendered discourse*. New York: Oxford University Press.

Wilson, C. C., Gutierrez, F., & Chao, L. (2004). *Racism, sexism, and the media*. (3rd ed.). Thousand Oaks, CA: Sage.

WEBSITES

The Media

Media Watch
http://www.mediawatch.com

Representation of Gender in Language

Gender Neutral Language
http://dir.yahoo.com/society_and_culture/gender/gender_neutral_language/

Gender Self-Concept: Developmental Processes and Individual Differences

In 1965, shortly after starting graduate school, Judith participated in a discussion about graduate student issues with her eight male classmates. During this conversation, much to her surprise and dismay, one of the men offered his impression of her lack of femininity. When asked for clarification, he said without hesitation, "Judith is too highly achievement oriented to be feminine."

Now consider the lighthearted mockery of gender-expected behaviors shown by Judith's daughter and son-in-law during their wedding ceremony. On the one hand, the setting was traditional with the bride in a long white gown, the groom in a formal tuxedo, and an entourage of bridesmaids and ushers. On the other hand, inconsistent with traditional expectations, at the end of a beautiful and serious service celebrating the bride and groom's love for each other, the officiate concluded with "Now you may kiss the groom!"

The comment by Judith's classmate suggests that, in his mind, people cannot combine female-stereotypic and male-stereotypic characteristics. Do you see problems with this type of thinking?

Do you know people who, like Judith's daughter and son-in-law, believe our behaviors should not be dictated by our gender? Do you know others who see value in separate roles for women and men? In this chapter we focus on issues like these as we examine the integration of gender into one's personal identity. After a brief look at the components of gender self-concept, we look at prenatal sex development and its influence on these gender concepts. Then we explore theoretical perspectives of gender learning and conclude with an examination of variations among people in their gender self-concepts.

Gender Self-Concept

One component of gender self-concept is **gender identity:** *one's self-definition as a female or male*. This identity generally develops between the ages of 2 and 3. Most individuals establish a gender identity in accordance with their external reproductive organs. **Transgendered individuals,** however, do not. They have a *gender identity inconsistent with their reproductive organs*. They firmly believe they were born with the body of the wrong sex and really feel that they are the other sex (Wylie, 2004).

Despite the usual consistency between anatomy and gender identity, there are variations in the degree to which people incorporate gender stereotypes into their own personalities and attitudes. As we saw in Chapter 2, there are numerous commonly held expectations about the appropriate traits and roles for females and males. However, these gender stereotypes reflect *beliefs* about individuals; they do not tell us what anyone is *actually* like. Although these stereotypes are descriptive of some people, they are not representative of all. Instead, individuals differ from one another in their adherence to cultural stereotypes about gender. That is, they differ in the extent to which their traits, behaviors, interests, and roles conform to those expected for their gender. Moreover, they differ in their **gender attitudes**, their *beliefs about the appropriate traits, interests, behaviors, and roles of females and males.*

Are various domains of an individual's gender self-concept associated with one another? Although most people's gender identity is consistent with their anatomy, that does not imply a connection between gender identity and gender-related attributes. A person can feel that she is a female but have male-related traits, such as ambition and independence or engage in roles generally associated with men, such as construction worker or engineer. Furthermore, a person's gender-related attributes are not linked to her or his **sexual orientation**. *Preference for a same- or other-gender sexual partner* does not reflect the individual's gender-related traits, behaviors, interests, or roles (Zucker, 2001).

Prenatal Development

Our journey toward understanding the development of a personal sense of gender begins with an examination of **prenatal sex differentiation**, that is, *the biological processes that influence the making of our physical sex.* As we shall see, prenatal sex differentiation consists of a highly complex set of processes. The first step, the joining of the sex chromosomes in the fertilized egg, is followed by several other prenatal events that collectively contribute to the determination of sex (see Table 3.1). Furthermore, not only is the biological process highly complex, but also the meaning of biological sex is multidimensional; it is defined by our chromosomes, hormones, reproductive organs, and brain organization (Hines, 2004b; Tobach, 2001).

Stages of Prenatal Sex Differentiation

The stages of prenatal sex differentiation begin with the sex chromosomes, followed by the development of the gonads and hormones, internal reproductive organs, and external genitalia and differentiations of the brain. Let us examine each of these steps in greater detail.

TABLE 3.1   Stages of Prenatal Sex Differentiation of Females and Males

Stages	Females	Males
1. Chromosomes	XX	XY
2. Gonads and hormones	ovaries (estrogens)	testes (androgens)
3. Internal reproductive organs	uterus, fallopian tubes, and upper vagina	vas deferens, seminal vesicles, and prostate
4. External genitalia	clitoris, labia, and vaginal opening	penis and scrotum
5. Brain	female differentiation of the hypothalamus	male differentiation of the hypothalamus

Chromosomes. Sex differentiation begins with the combining of the sex chromosomes at conception. Normally individuals inherit 23 pairs of chromosomes from their parents. Twenty-two of these pairs contain genes that determine the general nature of the human species and the individual's specific characteristics (e.g., eye color), and one pair consists of the sex chromosomes, containing the genetic material that begins the process of sex differentiation. Genetic females have two X chromosomes, one received from each parent, and genetic males have one X chromosome received from their mother and one Y from their father.

Gonadal Development. Until the sixth week of development there are no anatomical differences between XX and XY embryos. In fact, all embryos contain the same undifferentiated tissue that will later develop along sexual lines (Biason-Lauber et al., 2004). However, at that point in time, the Y chromosome in XY embryos directs the previously undifferentiated gonadal tissue to develop into testes, the male sex glands. In XX embryos gonadal development begins at approximately the twelfth week after conception; the previously undifferentiated gonadal tissue develops into ovaries, the female sex glands. Recent evidence suggests that the X chromosome might direct this development (Tobach, 2001).

Once the gonads develop, the remaining process of sex differentiation is regulated by the sex hormones. Most research has examined XY development and we know that prenatal male differentiation requires the presence of the *male sex hormones*, collectively known as **androgens.** Until recently, it was believed that no gonadal hormones were necessary for female development; differentiation of female sex organs would proceed in the absence of androgens (Hughes, 2004). Now there is evidence that the *female sex hormones*, collectively known as **estrogens,** play a more active role in female development than previously believed (Tobach, 2001).

Development of Internal Reproductive Organs. The female and male internal reproductive organs develop from the same previously undifferentiated tissue. Both XX and XY fetuses contain two sets of tissues. One of these, the **mullerian ducts,** are *the foundation for female structures*, and the other, the **wolffian ducts,** serve as *the basis for male internal reproductive structures*. In XX individuals, the mullerian ducts differentiate into the uterus, fallopian tubes, and upper vagina and the wolffian tissue degenerates. In XY development, two substances produced by the testes govern the process of developing male internal reproductive structures. **Testosterone,** an androgen, is necessary for the transformation of the wolffian ducts into the male organs, including the vas deferens, seminal vesicles, and prostate; and the **mullerian inhibiting substance** is necessary for the degeneration of the mullerian ducts (Hughes, 2004).

External Genitalia. Similar to the development of the internal reproductive structures, the external structures develop from previously undifferentiated tissue present in both XX and XY individuals. In XX fetuses, estrogen differentiates this tissue as the clitoris, labia, and vaginal opening. In XY development, testosterone transforms the tissue into the penis and the scrotum (Tobach, 2001).

Brain Differentiation.   Sex differences in the brain are less observable and, predictably, more controversial than sex differences in reproductive organs. However, experimentation on lower animals and case histories of humans whose prenatal exposure to androgens was abnormal for their genetic sex shows there is a critical period of time during which exposure to sex hormones can affect the hypothalamus and, thereby, influence the threshold for subsequent behaviors. For example, in both animals and humans, this early exposure to androgens organizes the hypothalamus so that it becomes insensitive to estrogen (Rathus et al., 2005). The result is the elimination of the normal hormonal cyclical pattern associated with the menstrual cycle. We explore behavioral and sexual effects in humans in the next section as we examine the outcomes of certain variations in prenatal sex differentiation.

Intersexuality

The pattern of sex differentiation just described is the typical one that characterizes the prenatal development of most individuals. However, several variations can occur, and examination of these can help us understand the role of the chromosomes and hormones on gender identity and gender-related attributes.

Intersexuality, *the intermingling of female and male sexual characteristics,* occurs about once in every 2,000 births. In some cases the baby has ambiguous genitalia that look like an enlarged clitoris or a mini-penis. In other cases, the external genitalia are at odds with the baby's gonads (Hines, 2004b). In Western cultures, which recognize only two genders, the typical course of action has been early genital surgery, coupled with gender reassignment (Navarro, 2004). (See Explore Other Cultures 3.1 for a different view.) But genital surgery can lead to loss of fertility, reduced sexual functioning, urinary difficulties and psychological problems, without providing the individual with any further sense of gender identity (Lerner, 2003; Minto et al., 2003). The Intersex Society of North America (ISNA), along with an increasing number of researchers, recommend that any surgery be postponed until adolescence, when the individual can make an informed choice (Fausto-Sterling, 2000; Gorman & Cole, 2004; Navarro, 2004; Pinholster, 2005). Let us take a closer look at some of the varieties of intersexuality.

Turner Syndrome.   **Turner syndrome** is *a condition in which the individual has a single X chromosome rather than a pair of sex chromosomes.* The missing chromosome could have been an X or a Y but is defective or lost. Because two chromosomes are necessary for the development of the gonads, the individual has neither ovaries nor testes. Externally, the genitalia are female and the individual is reared as a girl. Estrogen therapy at puberty enables girls with Turner syndrome to develop female secondary sex characteristics, such as breasts and pubic hair (Hines, 2004b; Sybert & McCauley, 2004).

Congenital Adrenal Hyperplasia (CAH).   **Congenital adrenal hyperplasia** is *an inherited disorder in which the adrenal glands of a genetic female malfunction and*

Multiple Genders

All societies recognize female and male genders and roles, although there is considerable cross-cultural variability in how these roles are expressed. The United States and virtually all Western nations formally recognize only two genders, and any variations from these are considered abnormal. Recent efforts to be more flexible in recognizing additional gender categories (e.g., Fausto-Sterling, 2000) are highly controversial. A number of non-Western cultures, however, recognize third and fourth genders. These are women and men who do not fit typical gender identities and roles. Often, these individuals are considered spiritually enlightened by having an alternative gender, and they may be respected and accepted (Kimmel, 2002; Whelehan, 2001). The Hijras of India are hermaphrodites or castrated men who are viewed as a third gender embodying the spirits of both females and males. Frequently called upon to bless new babies, they dress as females, live in hijra communities, and some maintain a monogamous relationship with a man (Mahalingam, 2003). In Indonesia, transvestites known as "waria"—a combination of the words for woman and man—have been welcomed for centuries as entertainers and beauticians (Perlez, 2003). Many Native North American societies recognized so-called "two-spirit" individuals (Balsam et al., 2004). Biological female two-spirits typically were found west of the Rockies among the Apache, Cheyenne, Mohave, Navajo, and Tlingit. The "manly-hearted woman," for example, wore men's clothes, led war parties, and was completely accepted in that role. As native societies assimilated European beliefs, however, third- and fourth-gender roles often disappeared, changed, or came to be viewed negatively (Balsam et al., 2004; Roscoe, 1998).

---

produce an androgen-like hormone (Berenbaum et al., 2004). Because this hormone is not produced until after the internal reproductive organs develop, these individuals have a uterus. However, the disorder causes either a partial or complete masculinization of the external genitals with the formation of an enlarged clitoris or a penis. Usually CAH is diagnosed at birth and the baby is reared as a girl, receiving some degree of surgical feminization of the genitals. Additionally, because this condition does not cease at birth, the individual generally receives hormonal therapy to prevent continued masculinization of her body.

Androgen-Insensitivity Syndrome. The **androgen-insensitivity syndrome** is *an inherited disorder in which the body of a genetic male cannot utilize androgen* (Hines, 2004b). Analogous to CAH in which prenatal exposure to androgen masculinizes the external genitals of a genetic female, this inability of body tissue to respond to androgen feminizes the external genitals of a genetic male. Usually, the feminization of the external genitalia is complete and there is no suspicion that the baby is a genetic male (see photo on p. 70). Similarly, the inability of the body to respond to androgen prevents the wolffian ducts from differentiating into the internal male reproductive structures. However, because of the presence of the mullerian inhibiting substance, the mullerian ducts do not develop into the internal female organs. Consequently, the individual has no internal reproductive organs.

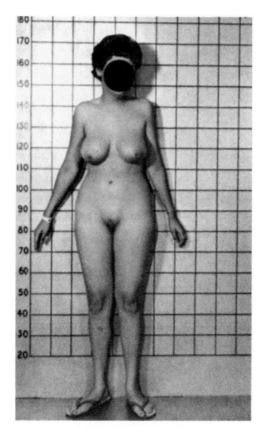

This genetic male has androgen-insensitivity syndrome.

Source: From J. Money, & A. A. Ehrhardt, *Man & woman, boy & girl: The differentiation and dimorphism of gender identity from conception to maturity* (Baltimore: Johns Hopkins, 1972), p. 116, Figure 6.4.

5 Alpha-Reductase Deficiency.   The **5 alpha-reductase deficiency** is *an inherited condition in a genetic male which prevents the prenatal differentiation of the external genital tissue into a penis* (Zucker, 2001). In other ways, prenatal development follows a male blueprint; testes and male internal reproductive organs develop. At birth these genetic males appear to be girls and are labeled as such. However, the surge of testosterone at puberty causes a belated masculinization of the external genitals and the development of male secondary sex characteristics, such as a deepening voice and facial hair. Thus, these genetic males, generally raised as girls, now develop the body of a male. In the Dominican Republic, where certain communities have a high frequency of the disorder, it is known as *guevdoces*, or "eggs (i.e., testicles) at twelve" (Lippa, 2005).

Case Studies.   The relative influence of prenatal and postnatal experiences on gender-related development has been the focus of considerable controversy. Case histories of intersexuals have examined the role of prenatal hormones on the development of nonsexual gender-related attributes, gender identity, and sexual orientation and have produced inconsistent findings. Several researchers contend that prenatal biological factors are highly influential, whereas others conclude that experiences after birth play the most significant role in shaping individuals' gender-related attributes.

First, let's examine the effects of prenatal hormones on gender-related interests and activities. On the one hand, higher levels of testosterone in pregnant women are related to more masculine-typed toy choices and activities in their daughters at age 3.5 years (Hines et al., 2002). In addition, girls with CAH, who were exposed to an androgen-like substance prenatally, show stronger than average preferences for boys' toys and activities and for boys as playmates (see review by Hines, 2004b; Pasterski et al., 2005). However, evidence about aggressive behavior is mixed (Hines, 2004a). Most of the affected women are heterosexual, and their sexual and gender identity is almost always female (Berenbaum & Bailey, 2003; Speiser & White, 2003).

Investigations on the effects of prenatal estrogen suggest that it might not be necessary for the development of female gender-related interests or role expectations. For example, girls with Turner syndrome, who lack prenatal estrogen, are similar to matched controls in their preferences for female playmates and female-style clothing, satisfaction with the female gender role, and interest in marriage and motherhood. Similarly, androgen-insensitive (XY) individuals raised as females tend to have female-related interests, although they also lack prenatal estrogen. Such individuals are generally romantically and sexually attracted to males. On tests of verbal and spatial skills, they also perform more like females than males (Lippa, 2005; Sybert & McCauley, 2004).

Turning to the development of gender identity, research similarly provides inconsistent findings. Some investigators have pointed to the importance of the gender of rearing, that is, experiences after birth, on gender identity (Zucker et al., 1996). Others, such as Milton Diamond (1997), contend that prenatal experiences predispose individuals toward a female or male identity. He notes, for example, that prenatal processes influence some intersexuals to switch from the gender of rearing to an identity with the other gender. One recent study examined genetic males who had normal male hormones, but were born without a penis, underwent early sex-reassignment surgery and were raised as girls. Nearly half still developed male gender identity by adolescence (Reiner & Gearhart, 2004).

There is some evidence that cultural values also play a role in the development of gender identity. Consider, for example, studies of individuals who have experienced the female-to-male body change caused by 5 alpha-reductase deficiency. In the Dominican Republic, 16 of 18 who were raised as girls elected to reverse their gender identity at puberty and become males (Imperato-McGinley and colleagues, cited in Deaux & Stewart, 2001). Another study in New Guinea found that some changed and some did not, but that those who did switch from a female to a male identity did so as a result of social pressure stemming from their inability to fulfill their female role (Herdt & Davidson, 1988). Although there might be a variety of explanations for these cultural differences, the researchers suggest that cultural expectations have some influence in shaping gender identity, at least for individuals with conflicting body signals.

Last, in examining influences on sexual orientation, case studies of intersexual individuals have led some researchers to contend that sexual orientation has its origins in prenatal development. Melissa Hines (2004a), for example, points to an increased lesbian or bisexual orientation among women with CAH and suggests that prenatal exposure to androgen may serve as one influence on sexual orientation. However, based on their review of research on the topic, Amy Banks and Nanette Gartrell (1995) conclude that atypical prenatal hormone exposure is not related to increased same-gender sexual orientation.

What can we conclude about this controversial issue? Unfortunately, it is difficult to evaluate the relative contribution of biological and postnatal factors because case studies do not allow for adequate control (Zucker, 2001). For example, CAH girls have somewhat masculinized genitalia. Consequently, it is difficult to separate effects of their atypical exposure to prenatal hormones from the psychological and interpersonal reactions they might experience after birth. Both CAH girls and their parents are aware of their masculinization and this knowledge might serve as a powerful influence on the girls' gender-related self-concept and on their parents' treatment of them (Hines, 2004a). At this time, the most accurate conclusion to be drawn appears to be that gender is both a biological and social phenomenon. The challenge for researchers is to examine how biological processes interact with social influences from the earliest years onward (Ruble, in Dingfelder, 2004).

Theories of Gender Typing

Now we turn to an exploration of the major theories that attempt to explain *the acquisition of the traits, behaviors, and roles that are generally associated with one's gender*, a process known as **gender typing.** Although these theories propose different processes involved in the learning of gender, only one (psychoanalytic theory) contends that the development of gender-related attributes is rooted in biological sex differences. The other perspectives share the assumption that gender traits, behaviors, and roles are socially constructed, that they develop from children's interactions with others and are not inherent in our biology. Furthermore, even psychoanalytic theory emphasizes the perceived significance of anatomical differences, rather than the effect of hormonal or other biological sex differences on gender development. For a summary of the major theories of gender typing, see Table 3.2.

Psychoanalytic Theory

We begin our theoretical exploration with an examination of psychoanalytic theory, a complex theory of personality and psychotherapeutic treatment developed by the Viennese physician Sigmund Freud. **Psychoanalytic theory** proposes that *gender typing stems from children's awareness of anatomical differences between females and males combined with their strong inborn sexual urges*. According to this theory, children have sexual urges that shift from one bodily region to another as they

TABLE 3.2   Theories of Gender Typing

Theory	Major Theorist	Sources of Learning	Motive	Sequence of Events
Psychoanalytic Theory	Sigmund Freud	Parents; emotional bond with same-sex parent is critical	Internal: reduce fear and anxiety; no reinforcement necessary	(Same-sex) parental attachment → identification (modeling) → gender identity
Social Learning Theory	Walter Mischel	Parents, larger social system provide models; child is relatively passive	External: reinforcements Internal: Expected reinforcements. "I want rewards. I am rewarded for doing girl things. Therefore, I want to be a girl."	(Same-sex) parental attachment (due to rewards) → modeling (identification) → gender identity
Social Cognitive Theory	Albert Bandura	Parents, larger social system provide models; child is more active than in social learning theory in evaluating social standards; cognition plays a greater role	Similar to social learning theory	Similar to social learning theory
Cognitive-Developmental Theory	Lawrence Kohlberg	Parents and larger social system interacting with child's cognitive system	Internal: desire for competence. "I am a girl. Therefore, I want to do girls things. Therefore, doing girl things is rewarding."	Gender identity → modeling (same-sex parent) → (same-sex) parental attachment
Gender-Schema Theory	Sandra Bem	Parents and larger social system interacting with child's cognitive system. Society dictates that gender is an important schema, so child organizes information around this schema.	Similar to cognitive-developmental theory	Because child learns that gender is an important schema, child develops gender identity. Sequence then proceeds as in cognitive-developmental theory.

develop. During each psychosexual stage of development a different body part produces pleasure and children's attempts to obtain this pleasure can have major effects on their personality development.

During the third, so-called phallic, stage (between the ages of 3 and 6 years) two experiences occur that have dramatic consequences for gender-related development. The first is the child's discovery of the anatomical differences between females and males and the second is the child's love for the parent of the other gender.

The child's sexual attraction for the other-gender parent, known as the **Oedipus complex**, runs a different course in the development of boys than it does in girls and leads to very different outcomes. For the little boy, the sexual attraction for his mother is accompanied by a belief that his father is a rival for his mother's affections and that his father, similarly, perceives him as a competitor. The boy's growing awareness of the anatomical differences between males and females serves to resolve his Oedipus complex. He assumes that females have been castrated, and that he, too, will be castrated by his powerful rival, his father. The boy's *fear of castration by his father*, called **castration anxiety**, is strong enough to induce him to give up his Oedipal feelings for his mother. When he does so, he forms *a close emotional bond* with his father, an attachment called **identification**. Through this identification process the boy adopts his father's masculine behaviors and traits and incorporates his father's values into his superego (the moral component of personality), thus developing a strong sense of morality.

The phallic stage of development follows a different sequence of events for the little girl. Her discovery of the anatomical distinction between females and males does not resolve the Oedipus complex as in boys but rather sets it in motion. Sometimes referred to as the Electra complex, the girl develops **penis envy**, *a desire to possess the male genitals*, and blames the mother for her castrated state. Her desire for a penis is replaced by a desire for a child and she turns to her father to fulfill that wish. Because the girl lacks the fear of castration (having already been castrated), the chief motive for resolving the Oedipus complex is absent. Thus, she does not completely resolve her Oedipal feelings. However, with the realization that she will never possess her father, the girl gradually gives up her Oedipal feelings, identifies with her mother, and begins the acquisition of her mother's feminine traits and behaviors. Although she, too, begins superego development, this development is weak because it is not driven by the powerful motivator of castration anxiety.

Freud believed that the girl's continuing wish for a penis into adulthood contributes to the woman's sense of inferiority and her sharing of the "contempt felt by men for a sex which is the lesser in so important a respect" (Freud, 1925/1989, p. 192).

Evaluation.   First, as is fairly obvious, Freud's theory is highly male-biased. His use of the male term *phallic* to label the third stage of psychosexual development, his strong emphasis on the superiority of the male organ, and his assumption that females are doomed to feelings of inferiority because they lack a penis are a few of the numerous indications of Freud's promale bias. For these reasons, psychoanalytic theory is not widely embraced by feminist scholars (Basow, 2001). Second, psychoanalytic theory cannot be subjected to empirical examination. Important psychoanalytic concepts, such as penis envy and castration anxiety, are conceptualized as unconscious; thus, they are not translatable into clearly defined scientific measures. Third, Freud has been criticized for his emphasis on the anatomical foundations of gender development to the virtual exclusion of societal influences. From Freud's perspective, gender is constructed from the presence or absence of a penis and not the societal value attached to males. Subsequent psychoanalytic thinkers have placed greater emphasis on the psychological and sociocultural aspects of gender development (Bell, 2004; Bornstein & Masling, 2002; Callan, 2001). Others, including Karen Horney, Nancy Chodorow, Jessica Benjamin, and Ellen Kaschak, have proposed psychoanalytic views that minimize the masculine orientation of Freud's theory (Bell, 2004; Casey, 2002; Shields & Eyssell, 2001).

Social Learning Theory

Whereas psychoanalytic theory envisions the growing child as pushed around by her/his inborn desires, **social learning theory**, originally proposed by Walter Mischel (1966), views *gender development as influenced by the social environment.* Based on learning theory principles, this perspective proposes that *children acquire behaviors associated with their gender because those behaviors are more likely to be imitated and to be associated with positive reinforcement.*

Observational Learning. One mechanism through which gender-related behaviors are acquired is **observational learning** (also called imitation or modeling); that is, *the acquisition of behaviors via the observation of role models.* Children are continually exposed to both real-life and media models who engage in gender-stereotypic behaviors. Because they are more likely to emulate similar models than to emulate dissimilar models, they are more likely to observe and imitate same-gender individuals rather than other-gender individuals (Bussey & Bandura, 2004). Through observation of these models children learn which behaviors are considered appropriate for someone of their gender. For example, 5-year-old Jenny sees her mother bake cookies and then uses her play kitchen to pretend she is baking. And, because the nurses in her pediatrician's office are females, Jenny believes that only women can be nurses. Jenny also learns that it is important for women to be pretty because she sees televised female role models who are frequently concerned about their appearance.

Reinforcement and Punishment. Social learning theory maintains that even though children sometimes engage in cross-gender observational learning in addition to same-gender imitation, they are likely to perform primarily gender-appropriate behaviors. The mechanisms that explain this phenomenon are reinforcement and punishment. If people expect a positive reinforcement (reward) for performing the behavior, it is likely they will engage in that behavior. On the other hand, if they anticipate a negative consequence (punishment), they are not likely to perform that act. Thus, girls and boys learn, both through observing the consequences to models and as a result of the outcomes received for their own behaviors, that girls are more likely to be rewarded for certain actions and boys for others. For example, a girl playing "dress-up" might be praised for her beauty as she parades around wearing her mother's old dress and high heels. If her brother wears the same outfit, however, his parents might tell him to take off the clothes.

Cognition.   A modification of social learning theory, known as **social cognitive theory**, states that *observational learning and rewards and punishments following behavior cannot alone account for gender typing; thought processes (cognitions) also play a role.* As children develop, they not only receive rewards and punishments from others but also begin to internalize standards about appropriate gender-related behavior (Bandura, 2002; Bussey & Bandura, 2004). Consequently, children initially engage in gender-appropriate behaviors because of the anticipation of rewards from others. However, as they gain experience and maturity, they develop internal standards about gender-related behavior, which motivates them to engage in gender-appropriate activities in order to gain self-satisfaction and avoid self-censure. For example, Pablo might refuse to play with his sister's dolls because playing with them would violate his personal standard of appropriate behavior for boys.

Evaluation.   Unlike psychoanalytic theory, the concepts of the social learning perspective are clear and observable. Therefore, numerous studies have examined the theory's assumptions. These studies have provided support for some aspects of the theory and are inconclusive about others.

One assumption of social learning theory is that girls and boys receive encouragement and reinforcement for different behaviors. In support of this perspective, several studies show that parents do treat their daughters and sons differently, at least in regard to some behaviors. For example, mothers encourage their preschool daughters more than their sons to talk about interactions with other people, thus fostering a greater interpersonal interest and concern (Flannagan et al., 1995). In addition, parents buy their daughters and sons different types of toys, encourage different play activities, and assign them different chores (see Chapter 4).

According to social learning theory, the other process in gender typing is observational learning. Although children do imitate same-gender role models, observational learning is not restricted to the behaviors of individuals of the same gender as the child (Martin et al., 2002). Other characteristics, such as a model's power, can influence the selection of role models. Thus, while children no doubt learn from the behaviors of important adults in their lives, including parents and teachers, this learning is not restricted to adults of the same gender as the child.

According to social learning theory, children acquire gender roles by imitating same-gender models and receiving reinforcement for doing so.

Cognitive Developmental Theory

Cognitive developmental theory, originally formulated by Lawrence Kohlberg (1966), contends that *children are neither pushed by their biological desires nor pulled by external rewards and punishments. Instead, children are active learners, attempting to make sense of the social environment.* They actively search for patterns and rules that govern the functioning of females and males and then follow these in an attempt to best adapt to social demands.

By approximately 3 years of age, children can correctly label their own gender. However, they do not yet know that gender is unchangeable, that neither time nor behavioral and appearance modifications can alter one's gender. For example, Kohlberg (1966) reported that most 4-year-olds believe that a girl could become a boy if she wanted to if she engaged in boy-related activities, or if she wore a boy's clothes. As an example of this thinking, he reported the following conversation between two preschool children (p. 95):

JOHNNY: I'm going to be a airplane builder when I grow up.

JIMMY: When I grow up, I'll be a Mommy.

JOHNNY: No, you can't be a Mommy. You have to be a Daddy.

JIMMY: No, I'm going to be a Mommy.

JOHNNY: No, you're not a girl, you can't be a Mommy.

JIMMY: Yes, I can.

It appears that Johnny, but not Jimmy, has developed the concept of **gender constancy,** *the belief that gender is permanent regardless of changes in age, behavior, or appearance,* a belief that generally develops between the ages of 4 and 7 years.

According to Kohlberg (1966), the absence of gender constancy in young children is not a function of their lack of knowledge of genital differences. Even children who have this awareness at an early age do not conclude that gender cannot be altered. Instead the absence of gender constancy is due to the young child's reliance on obvious physical characteristics, such as clothing or hair length, as informative, even if they are not. Kohlberg notes that this type of thinking parallels children's beliefs about the changeability of other entities. Preschool children do not recognize that changes in any object's visible characteristics do not necessarily alter its quality. For example, Kohlberg (1966) writes that most 4-year-olds believe a cat would become a dog if its whiskers were cut off.

Gender constancy is an important concept in cognitive developmental theory. The theory contends that gender typing cannot take place until children understand that their gender is unchangeable. Once they acquire that understanding, they begin to behave in gender-appropriate ways. Engaging in gender-consistent activities enables children to effectively master the environment and to competently adapt to the social world. To learn which behaviors are performed by females and which are performed by males, children actively observe parents and other role models. In this process they seek out information and use rewards and punishments as a source of information about which behaviors are gender-appropriate and which are not. Then they engage in the gender-appropriate behaviors because behaving in a gender-consistent manner is, in itself, rewarding.

You might think this sounds similar to the social learning theory assumption that children learn about gender from external rewards and punishments and from observation of others. However, Kohlberg (1966) notes that the cognitive developmental view of children's use of the social environment is very different from the social learning perspective. According to social learning theory, rewards for gender-appropriate behavior lead to the development of gender-appropriate behaviors and attitudes. Cognitive developmental theory, on the other hand, argues that rewards for gender-consistent behavior merely inform the child what is gender-appropriate and that children engage in these behaviors because acting in a gender-consistent manner is, in itself, rewarding. Let's look at an example to help clarify the distinction. Six-year-old Caitlin has been praised for helping her mother cook dinner. According to social learning theory, she then wants to cook again because she anticipates positive reinforcement from others (and possibly from herself) for cooking. The attainment of gender constancy would not be necessary because her desire to cook stems from her expectation of positive reinforcement, not because cooking is defined as a female activity. According to cognitive developmental theory, on the other hand, the praise received by Caitlin serves as information that cooking dinner is a female activity. If she has attained gender constancy, she now wants to cook because behaving in a gender-consistent manner is, in itself, rewarding.

Evaluation.   The concepts of cognitive developmental theory, like those of social learning theory, are clearly defined and easily measured and have generated considerable research. One important assumption of this perspective is that gender typing is dependent on an awareness of the unchangeability of gender. Examination of this assumption has provided mixed results (Maccoby, 2000; Martin, 2000; Martin et al., 2002). Some, but not all, studies have shown that children who have achieved gender constancy are more likely than their peers to select gender-appropriate activities and to have knowledge of gender stereotypes (Evans et al., 2003).

A second assumption of cognitive developmental theory is that children tend to value same-gender activities once they attain gender constancy. On this point the theory receives considerable support; numerous studies show that children value their own gender more highly than they value the other gender (e.g., Powlishta, 2001).

A major criticism of cognitive developmental theory is that it does not specify why children use gender as a classifying concept. Kohlberg (1966) asserts that children want to adhere to social rules so as to best master the social environment, but his theory does not explain why these rules are structured around gender. As Bem (1983, p. 601) stated, "The theory fails to explicate why sex will have primacy over other potential categories of the self such as race, religion, or even eye color."

Gender Schema Theory

Gender schema theory, proposed by Sandra Bem (1983), incorporates elements of cognitive developmental and social learning theories. Like the former, it proposes that *children develop an interrelated set of ideas or schema about gender that guides their social perceptions and actions.* However, unlike cognitive developmental theory, gender schema theory postulates that the use of gender as an organizing principle is not inevitable; it does not naturally stem from the minds of children. Similar to social learning theory, it assumes that *gender schema development stems from learning the gender norms and practices of society.*

The theory proposes that children formulate conceptions of the traits and roles associated with females and males on the basis of societal expectations. Then they use this information to regulate their own behavior, and their self-esteem becomes contingent on their adherence to these gender schemas (Bem, 1981).

A significant difference between gender schema and cognitive developmental theories lies in the basis for gender schema development. Whereas Kohlberg (1966) assumes the development of cognitive conceptualizations about gender is a natural process, Bem (1981) contends that the use of gender as a way of processing social information occurs because societal norms and practices emphasize its importance. Thus, children do not organize the social environment on the basis of physical attributes, such as eye color or hair color, because society does not give these characteristics the same significance it applies to gender. Bem argues that children cannot avoid noticing that different toys, activities, jobs, and chores are deemed acceptable for girls and boys by their parents, peers, and teachers. As one illustration, Bem (1983) points out that elementary school teachers do not line up children separately by race because they do not want to emphasize race as a distinguishing characteristic. They might, however, group children by sex, thus increasing its perceived importance as a distinguishing characteristic.

Bem (1983) claims that individuals vary in the degree to which they use gender schemas to understand and evaluate others and to guide their own behavior. According to Bem, people who have strong gender schemas consider a narrower range of activities as acceptable for individuals of each gender, including themselves. For example, boys have more powerful gender schemas than girls (Gelman et al., 2004). This finding is consistent with research showing that boys are more likely than girls to maintain gender boundaries (see Leaper, 2000, for a review).

Even within a given sex, some individuals have stronger, less flexible gender schemas than do others. Bem suggests that variations among people might be influenced by individual differences in exposure to gender as an organizing characteristic. Consequently, she proposes several strategies parents can use for minimizing the development of gender schemas and, consequently, for reducing the development of gender-stereotypic attitudes and behavior. Can you think of parental practices that might be effective? Read Get Involved 3.1 and answer the questions to learn about Bem's proposal.

GET INVOLVED **3.1**
Parental Strategies for Minimizing Gender Schemas in Children

Bem (1983) suggests that the following parental practices might help reduce gender schema development in children:

1. Elimination of gender stereotyping from parental behavior. For example, parents could share household duties instead of dividing them along gender lines.
2. Elimination of gender stereotyping from the choices parents present their children. That is, they could offer toys, activities, and clothing associated with both females and males.
3. Definition of femaleness and maleness along anatomical and reproductive lines only. That is, parents could reduce children's tendency to organize the social

world according to gender by teaching their children that one's sex is relevant only for reproduction. Bem offers the following anecdote about her four-year-old son Jeremy and his nursery school classmate as an illustration of the limiting outcomes of a cultural definition of gender and the greater flexibility of a biological definition:

One day Jeremy decided to wear barrettes to school. Several times that day, another little boy told Jeremy that he, Jeremy, must be a girl because "only girls wear barrettes." After trying to explain to this child that "wearing barrettes doesn't matter" and that "being a boy means having a penis and testicles,"

Jeremy finally pulled down his pants as a way of making his point more convincingly. The other child was not impressed. He simply said, *"Everybody has a penis; only girls wear barrettes." (p. 612)*

What Does It Mean?

1. Do you agree that each of the practices proposed by Bem could help reduce gender schema development? Why or why not?
2. Which of these, if any, do you think you would use, or are using, in raising your own children? Explain your answer.
3. According to gender schema theory, minimizing the use of gender schemas for perceiving the social world should reduce the development of gender stereotypes. Are there other practices that might help reduce gender stereotyping?
4. What advantages and/or disadvantages might result if all children were raised to restrict their definition of gender to reproductive characteristics only?

Evaluation. Kohlberg's cognitive developmental theory (1966) does not explain why children structure their social perceptions around gender. One strength of gender schema theory, on the other hand, is that it illustrates how societal messages can influence the formation of gender schemas.

In addition, there is considerable research support for the theory (Casey, 2002; Martin & Dinella, 2001). For example, one of its assumptions is that gender schemas help individuals organize their memories, thus facilitating the recollection of gender-consistent information. Consistent with this view, research shows that individuals remember material consistent with their own gender better than they remember material consistent with the other gender (Ganske & Hebl, 2001; Martin et al., 2002; Susskind, 2003). For example, Isabelle Cherney and Brigette Ryalls (1999) asked adults to recall items that were located in a room where they were waiting for an experiment to begin. Females were better able to remember female-related items, such as a makeup kit, a cookbook, and a purse, whereas males were better at recalling male-related objects, including aftershave, a sports video, and a necktie.

Gender-Related Traits

We have explored a variety of theories that explain gender typing. Now let's examine variations in individuals' conformity to stereotyped expectations about their gender. As mentioned previously, people differ in the degree to which their own traits, behaviors, interests, and roles are consistent with gender stereotypes.

The most commonly measured variation has been in the gender-related traits individuals ascribe to themselves, that is, in their personal identification with female-related and male-related characteristics. Historically, these two sets of traits were viewed as bipolar, that is, as opposite extremes of a single continuum. In the opening vignette in Chapter 1, we saw that Judith's classmate believed she could not be both feminine and achievement oriented. This belief reflects the bipolar view that a person cannot have characteristics stereotypically associated with both females and males.

In the 1970s, there was a change in this characterization of female-related and male-related traits. At that time psychologists began to conceptualize the two dimensions as independent, rather than opposite, of one another. Unlike a bipolar dimension, such as tall-short, in which it is impossible to be described by both traits, the new perspective posited that individuals can exhibit any combination of female-stereotypic and male-stereotypic characteristics. That is, a high degree of one does not imply a low degree of the other.

In 1974 Sandra Bem proposed that femininity and masculinity should be assessed independently and developed the Bem Sex Role Inventory (BSRI) to accomplish that goal. The BSRI includes one set of traits viewed as more desirable for females than for males and another set of items seen as more desirable for males than for females. At approximately the same time, Janet Spence, Robert Helmreich, and Joy Stapp (1974) published the Personal Attributes Questionnaire (PAQ) which also has two separate dimensions to measure gender-related personality characteristics. On the PAQ these two scales comprise personality characteristics seen as desirable for both females and males but viewed as more representative of one gender than the other. On both instruments the female-related scale comprises communal traits and the male-related scale reflects agentic traits (see Chapter 2); however, when used as measures of gender-related trait identification, they have typically been labeled either "femininity" and "masculinity" or "expressiveness" and "instrumentality."

The scoring of the BSRI and the PAQ reflects the goal of each to evaluate femininity/expressiveness and masculinity/instrumentality as independent dimensions. Thus, respondents receive a score on each dimension and the combination of the two indicates which of four categories best describes their gender-related traits. These categories are (1) **femininity,** *a high score on the femininity/expressiveness scale and a low score on the scale for masculinity/instrumentality*; (2) **masculinity,** *a high score on the masculinity/instrumentality scale and a low score on the femininity/expressiveness scale*; (3) **androgyny** (derived from the ancient Greek words for male—*andro*—and female—*gyn*), *high scores on both scales*; and (4) **undifferentiation,** *low scores on both scales*. Any individual, regardless of gender, can be characterized by any of these categories.

Although most investigations of gender-related traits have focused on White college students, a few have examined college and/or noncollege women with diverse ethnic backgrounds. These have shown that Black college women report greater masculinity than White (De Leon, 1995; Harris, 1993) or Puerto Rican (De Leon, 1995) women. To assess your own gender-related traits, try Get Involved 3.2.

GET INVOLVED 3.2
What Are Your Gender-Related Traits?

The following is a partial set of characteristics from the Personal Attributes Questionnaire. For each item, choose the letter that best describes where you fall on the scale. Choose **A** if you feel the characteristic on the left strongly describes you and choose **E** if the trait on the right is strongly descriptive of you. Choose **C** if you are in the middle, and so on. Also, ask a friend to rate you on these characteristics.

1. Not at all independent	**A.B.C.D.E**	Very independent
2. Not at all emotional	**A.B.C.D.E**	Very emotional
3. Very rough	**A.B.C.D.E**	Very gentle
4. Not at all competitive	**A.B.C.D.E**	Very competitive
5. Not at all helpful to others	**A.B.C.D.E**	Very helpful to others
6. Not at all kind	**A.B.C.D.E**	Very kind
7. Not at all self-confident	**A.B.C.D.E**	Very self-confident
8. Gives up very easily	**A.B.C.D.E**	Never gives up easily
9. Not at all understanding of others	**A.B.C.D.E**	Very understanding of others
10. Goes to pieces under pressure	**A.B.C.D.E**	Stands up well under pressure

What Does It Mean?

To score yourself, give 0 points to a response of **A**, 1 point to **B**, and so on. Then add up your points for items 2, 3, 5, 6, and 9; this comprises your femininity/expressiveness score. Similarly, sum your points for items 1, 4, 7, 8, and 10; this comprises your masculinity/instrumentality score. Use the same procedure to score your friend's ratings of you.

1. Are your two scores similar to each other or is one much higher than the other? Does your pattern of scores reflect the gender-related trait category you think best describes you? Why or why not?
2. Is your pattern of scores similar to the pattern based on your friend's ratings?

If not, describe the differences. Also, explain why your friend views your gender-related traits differently than the way you perceive them.
3. Although the Personal Attributes Questionnaire is widely used today, it was based on 1970s' perceptions of traits more typical of either females or males. Are there any characteristics presented here that no longer seem to be more representative of one gender than the other? Which ones? What evidence do you have for the gender similarity on those traits?

Source: From *Masculinity and Femininity: Their Psychological Dimensions, Correlates and Antecedents* by Janet T. Spence and Robert L. Helmreich, Copyright (c) 1978. By permission of the University of Texas Press.

Changes in Gender-Related Traits over Time

> *College women and high school girls' . . . assertiveness . . . increased from 1931 to 1945, decreased from 1946 to 1967 and increased from 1968 to 1993 . . . . Why did women's assertiveness scores switch twice over the century?* (Twenge, 2001, pp. 133, 141)

In the 1970s studies showed that more female than male college students scored high on femininity whereas more males than females scored high on masculinity and approximately one-third of both genders were androgynous (e.g., Spence & Helmreich, 1978). To determine whether there has been any change over time, Jean Twenge (1997b) performed a meta-analysis of femininity and masculinity scores based on samples from over 50 different college campuses since the 1970s. Interestingly, the most notable change found by Twenge was the dramatic increase in masculinity scores of women. Also, there was a significant increase in androgyny among women and a weaker increase among men. Other research (Harper & Schoeman, 2003; Spence & Buckner, 2000; Twenge, 2001) has found that women and men no longer differ on a number of items long considered to be masculine. These include being active, independent, self-reliant, ambitious, assertive, acting as a leader, and defending one's beliefs. When compared to their own mothers, today's college women show more masculine-typed and less feminine-typed behaviors (Guastello & Guastello, 2003).

Jean Twenge, Janet Spence, and Camille Buckner suggest that these changes in gender-related traits may be accounted for by societal changes that have occurred in recent years. Girls have been encouraged to become more assertive, to stand up for their rights, to be independent rather than helpless, and to have high occupational aspirations. They have been given more opportunities to develop their agentic skills, especially in the educational, vocational, and sports arenas.

Similarly women were expected to be self-sufficient during the Great Depression and World War II, in the early-to-middle years of the twentieth century, whereas passive domesticity was encouraged in the 1950s and early 1960s. These shifts in women's status and roles closely parallel the changes in women's assertiveness over the course of the century (Twenge, 2001).

Thus, today's young women are more likely than their counterparts in the seventies to have witnessed or experienced roles that involve male-stereotypic characteristics. This could have contributed to the development of their greater masculinity and, in turn, their greater androgyny. Thus, consistent with the view that gender is socially constructed, changes in women's personal sense of gender seem to be related to their social experiences.

Gender-Related Traits and Psychological Adjustment

Once psychologists started to conceptualize gender-related traits as being more complex than a single dimension of femininity-masculinity, they began to examine the psychological well-being of individuals who varied in their pattern of gender-stereotypic traits. For example, Bem hypothesized that because androgynous individuals are comfortable engaging in both feminine and masculine behaviors, they can adapt more adequately to various situational demands and should report greater well-being than nonandrogynous individuals (Bem, 1975). Research shows, however, that it is high masculinity, and not the specific combination of high masculinity and high femininity, that is strongly related to well-being and self-esteem (Helgeson, 1994; Saunders & Kashubeck, 2002; Ward, 2000). Predictably, it is the positive aspects of masculinity (e.g., independence, ambition), not its negative components (e.g., aggressiveness, selfishness), that are linked with psychological health (Woodhill & Samuels, 2003).

What can explain the positive relationship between masculinity and psychological adjustment? As we saw in Chapter 2, male-related traits are more highly valued in North America than female-related traits. Therefore, people with male-stereotypic traits feel better about their ability to function effectively. Derek Grimmell and Gary Stern (1992) found support for this explanation in college students' BSRI self-ratings, their BSRI ratings of the ideal person, and their psychological well-being. These investigators found that students' masculinity score was related to their psychological adjustment. Moreover, respondents' adjustment was predicted by the difference between their self-reported masculinity and their ratings of masculinity for the ideal person. The higher their own masculinity in relation to their perception of ideal masculinity, the higher their own self-esteem and the lower their anxiety and depression. Thus, it appears that the degree to which we feel we possess highly valued masculine traits is a good predictor of our psychological adjustment.

However, before we conclude that androgyny is not related to psychological well-being, let's consider a different conceptualization of androgyny. See Learn about the Research 3.1 for a newer approach to androgyny measurement and its psychological benefits.

Evaluation of the Concept of Androgyny

When the psychological measurement of androgyny was introduced in the 1970s, it was received enthusiastically by feminist scholars. It replaced the notion that psychological health required that females be feminine and males be masculine. By embodying socially desirable traits for both females and males, androgyny seemed to imply the absence of gender stereotyping. Furthermore, by incorporating both feminine and masculine behaviors it appeared to broaden the scope of behaviors that can be used to handle different situations and, thus, lead to more flexible and adaptive behaviors.

Although androgyny continues to be viewed by feminist scholars as more positive than restrictions to either femininity or masculinity, several feminist criticisms have been leveled against this concept. One is that the notion of androgyny, similar to the bipolar differentiation of femininity-masculinity, is based on the division of gender into female-stereotypic and male-stereotypic characteristics (Bem, 1993; Hoffman & Youngblade, 2001). Rather than making traits *gender-neutral*, androgyny

LEARN ABOUT THE RESEARCH 3.1
A Real-Life Approach To Androgyny

Examination of gender-related traits indicates that masculinity, and not the coexistence of masculinity and femininity, best predicts psychological adjustment. Recently, however, Jayne Stake argued that the psychological benefits of androgyny should not be dismissed on the basis of measuring individuals' ratings of their gender-related traits. Instead, she suggested we consider androgyny as the integration of communal and agentic behaviors given in response to expectations demanded by specific life situations. That is, measurement of these behaviors must be grounded in situational contexts.

Stake focused on work-related expectations because job settings tend to require a wide range of behaviors from the worker. Her specific interest was in individuals' responses to demands on the job that required both communal and agentic behaviors. She wanted to discover whether people who use both types of behaviors when they respond to these situations experience any benefits compared to those who rely on one type or neither type. Accordingly, in individual interviews, 194 undergraduate students were asked to describe a work situation in which they were expected to behave with both "sensitivity and caring" (e.g., "Be sensitive to the needs of others," "Show others you care about them") and "mas-

tery and independence" (e.g., "Always show that you can handle things on your own—without the help of others," "Show you have technical know-how"). Then they were asked to describe the behaviors they used to cope with these dual expectations. Similarly, they were asked to consider the overall expectations in their job and to describe what they usually did to respond to these expectations. These coping strategies in both the specific situation as well as in the job setting overall were coded into one of the four categories generally used to classify gender-related traits. In addition, students indicated to what extent their well-being was affected by work situations that expected both types of behaviors.

The results showed that androgynous coping behaviors used in response to dual expectations in specific job situations and dual expectations in the job overall were related to the highest level of well-being. Individuals who used both communal and agentic behaviors experienced more rewards and fewer negative outcomes than those using other types of strategies. Thus, it is possible that examining gender-related attributes as behavioral responses to specific situations rather than as general personality traits might be a fruitful approach to understanding the beneficial effects of various gender-related orientations.

What Does It Mean?

1. Stake examined expectations for communal and agentic behaviors in the workplace. Can you think of other situations that might make simultaneous demands?

2. Identify a job experience you had where both types of demands were made. Describe how you handled it and how you felt in this situation. Was your experience consistent with the results reported here?

Source: Stake (1997).

involves the combination of *gender-specific* orientations. A second concern is that androgyny might be erecting unrealistic goals for individuals—the requirement that people be competent in both the communal and agentic domains. Third, according to Bem (1993), the concept of androgyny does not deal with masculinity and femininity in their unequal cultural context. It neither acknowledges nor attempts to eliminate the greater cultural value placed on male activities. Last, Bem is concerned that androgyny will not lead to the elimination of gender inequality, a goal that requires *societal* rather than *personal* change. That is, the mere existence of individuals with both feminine and masculine traits does not alter the patriarchal power structure in society.

Gender Attitudes

Let's turn now to an examination of variations in gender attitudes. People differ in the degree to which they believe that gender should dictate females' and males' roles. Some individuals hold a **traditional gender attitude**, *the belief that females should engage in communal behaviors and roles and males should engage in agentic behaviors and roles.* They might believe, for example, that women should be the primary rearers of children whereas men should be the primary financial providers or that women are better suited than men to nursing whereas men are better suited than women to corporate management. Others adhere to a **nontraditional or egalitarian gender attitude**, *the belief that behaviors and roles should not be gender-specific.* To get more familiar with the meaning of gender attitudes, take the test in Get Involved 3.3.

The Sex-Role Egalitarianism Scale (King & King, 1990), which is shown in part in Get Involved 3.3, illustrates the multidimensional nature of gender attitudes. This scale comprises beliefs about appropriate roles within five life domains: marital, parental, employment, social-interpersonal-heterosexual, and educational. There is considerable evidence that gender attitudes are not uniform across these dimensions. Instead, North American college students tend to have more nontraditional beliefs about women's employment roles than they do about women's combined family and work roles (Anderson & Johnson, 2003; Holland & Andre, 1992; Powell & Yanico, 1991). For example, Holland and Andre found that approximately 84 percent of a college student sample disagreed with the statement that it is more important for a wife to help her husband with his career than for her to have a career of her own. However, only 42 percent believed a woman should accept an employment opportunity if it meant her husband would have to find another job and her family would have to move. For a look at gender role attitudes in other countries, read Explore Other Cultures 3.2 (see p. 92).

Individual Differences in Gender-Related Attitudes

As we have seen, gender attitudes can vary from traditional to egalitarian. Now let's examine demographic and personality characteristics that are related to differences in gender attitudes.

GET INVOLVED **3.3**

What Are Your Gender Attitudes?

On a scale from 1 (strongly agree) to 7 (strongly disagree), indicate the degree to which you agree or disagree with each of the following statements:

1. The husband should be the head of the family.
2. Keeping track of a child's out-of-school activities should be mostly the mother's responsibility.
3. Home economics courses should be as acceptable for male students as for female students.
4. A person should generally be more polite to a woman than to a man.
5. It is more appropriate for a mother rather than a father to change their baby's diaper.
6. It is wrong for a man to enter a traditionally female career.
7. Things work out best in a marriage if a husband leaves his hands off domestic tasks.
8. Women can handle pressures from their jobs as well as men can.
9. Choice of college is not as important for women as for men.

What Does It Mean?

Before computing your score, reverse the points for statements 3 and 8. That is, if you answered "1" (strongly agree) to these two questions, give yourself 7 points, if you answered "2," give yourself 6 points, and so on. Then sum the points for the 9 items. Note that higher scores reflect more nontraditional or egalitarian gender attitudes.

1. These statements come from the Sex-Role Egalitarianism Scale, developed in the 1980s. Are there any questions that you think are no longer adequate measures of egalitarian gender beliefs? If yes, give your reasons.
2. Look at your answers to Get Involved 3.2. Is there any consistency in the extent to which you describe yourself as communal and/or agentic and your beliefs about appropriate gender-related behaviors and roles? For example, if you received high scores on both communion and agency, reflecting an androgynous identity, did your answers to the questions in this activity indicate egalitarian beliefs? Can you explain why a person's gender-related traits might not be associated with her or his gender attitudes?
3. If most North Americans were to endorse egalitarian gender beliefs, what positive outcomes might be experienced by women and girls? By men and boys? Would there be any negative consequences for either gender? Explain.

Source: Reproduced by permission of Sigma Assessment Systems, Inc., P.O. Box 610984, Port Huron, MI 48061-0984. Tel: (800) 265-1285.

Gender. Not surprisingly, one characteristic is gender. Dozens of studies have shown that, among Whites, males have more traditional beliefs about the appropriate roles for women than females (e.g., Anderson & Johnson, 2003; Brewster & Padavic, 2002; Burt & Scott, 2002; Eagly et al., 2004; Frieze et al. 2003; Riggio & Desrochers, 2005; Robinson et al., 2004). Similarly, Black men (Kane, 2000) and

Asian men (Anderson & Johnson, 2003) hold more traditional gender role attitudes than their female counterparts.

Ethnicity.   Another demographic characteristic that is related to gender attitudes is ethnicity. As we saw in Chapter 2, Black women are less likely than White or Latina women to adhere to gender stereotypes. Thus, we might think their attitudes about gender-related behaviors and roles would be uniformly more egalitarian.

Interestingly, research comparing Black and White views about gender roles shows a complex pattern. On the one hand, Black women seem to hold more traditional views about the domestic domain. They have more stereotypical views about children's domestic roles (Dugger, 1988) and women's responsibilities for housework and child care (Binion, 1990). According to Dugger (p. 439) this traditional view might reflect a defensive reaction against the "labeling of Black women as 'matriarchs' . . . who rob their sons and men in general of their manhood." On the other hand, there is some evidence that Black women hold more egalitarian views about women's employment and political roles than White women do (Harris & Firestone, 1998). Also, Black college women, compared to White college women, perceive less conflict in the combination of the provider and domestic roles (e.g., Bridges & Etaugh, 1996), a difference possibly due to Black women's longer history of combining work and family roles.

What about gender attitudes of Latinas? Traditionally, Latina/o families have been characterized as patriarchal with a dominant, powerful husband/father and a submissive, self-sacrificing wife/mother. Thus, it is not surprising that Latina women have been found to hold more traditional views about women's employment and political roles than either Black or White women (Harris & Firestone, 1998). However, there is evidence that the views held by Latina women are becoming less traditional, over time. The Latina/o family has been undergoing many changes related to gender (Castaneda, 1996). They have been experiencing an increasingly greater flexibility in the division of household responsibilities and a more egalitarian approach to family decision making (Gonzalez & Espin, 1996). For example, Donna Castaneda (1996) notes that second-and third-generation Latinas/os are less likely than first-generation women and men to believe that the husband should be the sole provider and decision maker within the family and that females should do all of the housework and obey the husband's/father's demands. Thus, the degree of acculturation of Latina women and Latino men seems to be strongly related to their gender attitudes.

Research on Native Americans has focused on their actual gender-related behaviors and roles rather than on their attitudes and has shown great variations over time and across tribal groups. According to scholars such as Theresa LaFromboise and her associates (LaFromboise et al., 1999), women's behaviors and roles in traditional Native American life included caregiving, spiritual continuation of their people, and transmission of cultural knowledge. Many Native American societies were characterized by complementary but equally powerful roles for some women and men while other groups institutionalized alternative female roles. For example, within several Plains tribes, women's roles included masculine ones, such as the "warrior woman" and the "manly-hearted woman" (aggressive and independent) in addition to the traditional role of the submissive, hard-working wife. Other tribes, such as the Navajo and Iroquois, were matrilineal; women owned the material goods and passed these on to their daughters and sisters and played important economic, political, and spiritual roles.

In traditional Navajo and Iroquois culture, women played important economic, political, and spiritual roles.

Interestingly, LaFromboise and her colleagues (1999) contend that colonization by Europeans and the continuing acculturation process by which Native Americans have become more involved in the dominant White culture have contributed in several Native American societies to a breakdown in complementary female-male roles and to an increase in male dominance and the subjugation of women. However, in many tribes women continue to experience considerable political power because of their traditional roles of caretakers for the community and transmitters of the culture. In order to learn more directly about the gender attitudes of women of different ethnicities, perform the interviews described in Get Involved 3.4.

In addition to the differences in gender attitudes across ethnic groups in the United States, cross-national differences exist as well. For a closer look, see Explore Other Cultures 3.2.

Other Factors. There is some evidence that gender attitudes are related to religious factors. Among college students, Jews tend to have less traditional gender beliefs than Protestants (Lottes & Kuriloff, 1992; Willetts-Bloom & Nock, 1994), and Catholics fall somewhere in between (Harville & Rienzi, 2000). Moreover, the more strongly individuals embrace religion in their lives, the more traditional their

GET INVOLVED **3.4**
Ethnic Variations in Gender Attitudes

Interview two college women of approximately the same age (i.e., both traditional-age students or both older adults), from each of two different ethnic groups. Ask the following questions:

1. Do you think there should be different roles for women and men in the family? In dating relationships? In the workplace? If your respondent answered "yes" to any of these, ask her to be specific.
2. What is your career goal?
3. How important is your future/current career to your personal identity?
4. Do you want to get married and have children? If yes, do you think you will have any difficulty balancing your family and work roles?
5. Who do you think should be the primary provider in your family?
6. How do you think you and your spouse/partner will divide up the household responsibilities, including child care?

What Does It Mean?

1. Although your sample is very small, did you observe any ethnic differences? Did these differences match those discussed in the text? If yes, show the connections. If no, explain why your results might differ from those reported in past research.
2. You interviewed college women. Do you think your findings might have been different had your respondents been college graduates? Working-class or poor women without a college education? Explain your answers.

EXPLORE OTHER CULTURES **3.2**
Gender Attitudes in Global Context

Deborah Best and her colleagues (Best, 2001; Best & Thomas, 2004) have conducted studies of the gender attitudes of university students in 14 different countries. Their research indicates that gender attitudes range from traditional to more egalitarian both across and within cultures. For example, the most egalitarian attitudes were found in northern European countries (the Netherlands, Germany, Finland, England). The United States was in the middle of the distribution, and the most traditional attitudes were found in Africa and in Asian countries (Nigeria, Pakistan, India, Japan, Malaysia). Other studies have found that Muslim nations in the Middle East and North Africa are the least likely of all nations to endorse gender equality (Norris & Inglehart, 2004). In general, Best and colleagues found that women held more egalitarian views than men. Within a given country, however, the gender attitudes of women and men corresponded highly. Now go back to Chapter 2, and compare these results with those of Glick and Fiske on hostile and benevolent sexism across cultures.

gender attitudes are (Brewster & Padavic, 2002; Frieze et al., 2003; Harville & Rienzi, 2000; Robinson et al., 2004).

Other demographic characteristics related to gender attitudes are social class, academic achievement, age, and political ideology. Among both Blacks and Whites, higher social class and educational level tend to be associated with more nontraditional views about gender (Brewster & Padavic, 2002). Furthermore, students' levels of traditionalism decline during the college years (Bryant, 2003; Etaugh & Spiller, 1989). Similarly, a high GPA is related to nontraditional gender attitudes (Ahrens & O'Brien, 1996; Bryant, 2003). Young adults and those with politically liberal views hold less traditional attitudes than older adults, and those who are politically conservative (Apparala et al., 2003).

In addition, gender attitudes are related to a personality characteristic known as authoritarianism, which is characterized by intolerance of ambiguity and is strongly related to prejudice toward members of perceived outgroups such as Blacks, Jews, gays, and disabled people. As you might guess, both women and men who are high in authoritarianism endorse traditional societal roles for women and men (Duncan et al., 2003). Traditional attitudes about gender are also associated with the belief that gender differences are caused by biological or religious (divine) causes as opposed to differences in socialization or opportunities (Neff & Terry-Schmitt, 2002).

Perceived Value of Female versus Male Gender-Related Attributes

Derek Grimmell and Gary Stern (1992) found that college students value masculinity more strongly than femininity. This is consistent with our previous discussion of the greater power held by males in North American society. Is it,

---

GET INVOLVED **3.5**

Would You Rather Be a Female or a Male?

Have you ever considered what life would be like if you were the other gender? Think about what is has been like to be a female or male. Then think about any advantages and/or disadvantages that would occur if you were the other gender. For each of the following three categories, list any advantages and/or disadvantages of being the other gender: (1) *social roles*, that is,

opportunities that are not equally available to the two genders and/or behaviors that are considered more appropriate for one gender than the other; (2) *physical appearance expectations*; and (3) *physical differences*, for example, reproductive, size, or strength differences. Also, ask another-gender friend to perform the same exercise. Discuss your answers with your friend.

What Does It Mean?

1. Did you imagine more advantages and/or disadvantages in one category than the others? If yes, how can you explain the pattern of perceived advantages and disadvantages?
2. Are the responses of your other-gender friend complementary to your own responses? In other words, are your friend's perceptions of the advantages of being your gender consistent with your perceptions of the disadvantages of being your friend's gender? Why or why not?

3. Examine the number of advantages relative to disadvantages that you associated with being the other gender and consider the relative importance of each. Do the same for your friend's responses. Do you and/or your friend attach greater value to one gender or the other? If yes, how can you explain this?
4. If you or your friend perceive a relative advantage of one gender over the other, discuss some societal changes that would have to occur to reduce this discrepancy?

Source: Cann & Vann (1995).

---

therefore, more advantageous to be a male than to be a female? Alternatively, are gender-related advantages and disadvantages equally distributed between the genders or, perhaps, balanced in favor of females? To examine this question, try the exercises in Get Involved 3.5.

When Arnie Cann and Elizabeth Vann (1995) asked college students to list as many advantages and disadvantages as they could associate with being the other gender, they found that, overall, both women and men associated more advantages with being male. Specifically, these students considered differences in physical appearance requirements and actual physical differences as more disadvantageous to females than to males. For example, they believed that more females than males must be concerned about their appearance and that biological differences, such as pregnancy and menstruation, are disadvantageous to females. Interestingly, these students did not perceive males to have more social-role advantages than females. Although females were seen to be limited by workplace discrimination and the expectation to be subordinate in their relationships, males were viewed as hurt by the social pressure on them to be successful and to play a leadership role. Thus, these students seemed to be aware that the gender imbalance in power puts women at a disadvantage and that the social construction of the agentic, achievement-oriented male role establishes potentially difficult expectations for men.

Given the evidence that males are seen as having more advantages than females, it is not surprising that people evaluate males more negatively than they do females who violate gender expectations (Ruble & Martin, 1998). Scholars have proposed two possible explanations for this difference. The **social status hypothesis** contends that *because the male gender role is more highly valued than the female role is, a male is seen as lowering his social status by engaging in female-stereotypic behaviors, whereas a female performing male-stereotypic behaviors is perceived as raising her status* (e.g., McCreary, 1994). Consequently, males who engage in cross-gender behaviors are viewed more negatively than are females who deviate from gender expectations. As stated by Bem (1993), our society so thoroughly devalues whatever thoughts, feelings, and behaviors are culturally defined as feminine that crossing the gender boundary has a more negative cultural meaning for men than it has for women—which means, in turn, that male gender-boundary-crossers are much more culturally stigmatized than female gender-boundary-crossers (pp. 149–150).

The social status hypothesis receives some support from the finding that people believe that occupations with higher prestige require skills associated with masculine characteristics and that these jobs should pay more than those requiring feminine characteristics (Kite, 2001).

The other explanation of the more negative evaluation of male gender-role violation is the **sexual orientation hypothesis** (e.g., McCreary, 1994). This perspective argues that *cross-gender behavior in boys but not girls is considered a sign of actual or potential same-sex sexual orientation.* Several investigations have provided support for this perspective. For example when Donald McCreary (1994) asked college students to evaluate either a child or an adult who had cross-gender traits and interests, he found they considered it more likely that the feminine male was or would become a gay man than that the masculine female was or would become a lesbian.

S U M M A R Y

Gender Self-Concept

■ Gender self-concept includes gender identity and gender attitudes.

Prenatal Development

■ Prenatal sex differentiation is a multistage process. The joining of the sex chromosomes at conception is followed by the differentiation of the gonads, the development of the internal and external reproductive organs, and the organization of the hypothalamus.

■ After the gonads develop, the presence or absence of androgens influences the development of the reproductive organs and the brain.

■ Estrogens appear to play a role in female development.

■ Some individuals experience variations in their prenatal development known as intersexuality.

- Turner syndrome is a chromosomal disorder in which the individual has a single X chromosome. These individuals are raised as girls and have female gender expectations although they have no sex glands and no prenatal estrogen.
- Genetic females with CAH are usually reared as girls, although they have a partial or complete masculinization of their external genitals.
- Genetic males with the androgen-insensitivity syndrome have feminized external genitals and are reared as girls.
- Genetic males with a 5 alpha-reductase deficiency experience a female-to-male body transformation at puberty.
- Case studies of intersexuals provide mixed evidence regarding the influence of prenatal biological factors on nonsexual gender-related attributes, gender identity, and sexual orientation. Some researchers claim that gender-related development is dependent on prenatal factors and others point to the importance of the gender of rearing.

Theories of Gender Typing

- Psychoanalytic theory proposes that gender typing stems from the child's identification with the same-gender parent, a process that occurs when the child resolves the Oedipus complex.
- For the boy the resolution stems from fear of castration by the father. For the girl it stems from the realization that she will never possess her father.
- Because the girl's desire for a penis continues, she experiences inferiority feelings throughout her life.
- Social learning theory proposes that children acquire gender behaviors via imitation of same-gender models and positive reinforcement of their own gender-consistent behaviors. Social cognitive theory stresses the added role of cognition.
- Cognitive developmental theory contends that once children attain gender constancy, they are motivated to behave in gender-appropriate ways. Thus, they actively seek out the rules that characterize female behavior and male behavior. They then engage in gender-consistent behaviors because it enables them to competently adjust to the social environment.
- Gender schema theory proposes that children develop an interrelated set of ideas about gender. They learn the societal norms and practices that signify the importance of gender. They then organize the social world on the basis of gender and guide their own actions accordingly.

Gender-Related Traits

- On the basis of their gender-related traits, individuals can be categorized as feminine, masculine, androgynous, or undifferentiated.
- Research has shown an increase in masculinity and androgyny in women over time.
- Masculinity is related to psychological adjustment.
- Androgyny was once considered to be highly desirable, but recently feminist scholars have criticized it.

Gender Attitudes

- Gender attitudes are multidimensional.
- College students have less-traditional beliefs about the value of the employment role for women but more-traditional views about the combination of women's employment and family roles.
- Among Whites, women are generally more nontraditional in their beliefs than men are.
- Among women, Blacks hold more traditional views about domestic responsibilities than Whites, but they have more nontraditional views about the combination of women's employment and family roles.
- The roles of Latina/o women and men have become more egalitarian over time, but Latinas have more traditional views than Black and White women.
- The gender-related behaviors and roles of Native American women vary greatly across tribes and in several societies increased acculturation has been accompanied by greater male dominance.

- Traditional gender attitudes are linked to being older, more religious, less educated, of lower social class, politically conservative, and authoritarian.

- College women and men associate more advantages with being male than with being female.
- Males, compared to females, are more negatively evaluated for engaging in cross-gender behavior.

KEY TERMS

gender identity
transgendered individuals
gender attitudes
sexual orientation
prenatal sex differentiation
androgens
estrogens
mullerian ducts
wolffian ducts
testosterone
mullerian inhibiting
    substance
intersexuality
Turner syndrome

congenital adrenal
    hyperplasia
androgen-insensitivity
    syndrome
5 alpha-reductase deficiency
gender typing
psychoanalytic theory
Oedipus complex
castration anxiety
identification
penis envy
social learning theory
observational learning
social cognitive theory

cognitive developmental
    theory
gender constancy
gender schema theory
femininity
masculinity
androgyny
undifferentiation
traditional gender attitude
nontraditional or egalitarian
    gender attitude
social status hypothesis
sexual orientation hypothesis

WHAT DO YOU THINK?

1. If you gave birth to an intersexual child, would you decide on surgerical restructuring of the child's reproductive system and genitalia early in life, or would you wait until closer to puberty when your child could participate in the decision? Give reasons for your answer.

2. Evidence indicates that boys, more than girls, select role models who are powerful. Explain this finding.

3. As discussed in Chapter 2, it is possible that the media not only reflect gender stereotypes but also help shape them. Now that you are familiar with theories of gender typing, use one of these theories to explain how the media might contribute to an individual's acquisition of gender stereotypes.

4. Which gender-typing theory or theories best explain(s) the development of gender-related traits, behaviors, and roles? Explain.

To help you develop your reasons, critically think about the evaluations presented in the text. Indicate why you believe that some of the evaluative comments seem to be more credible than others. Additionally, if you have had any contact with young children, try to provide anecdotal support for some of the theoretical concepts.

5. Discuss the advantages and disadvantages to girls/women and boys/men of gender-related trait identifications consistent with stereotypes, that is, femininity in females and masculinity in males. Can you think of the advantages and disadvantages of an androgynous identity?

6. There is some evidence that individuals who internalize their religious beliefs and attempt to live by them hold more traditional gender attitudes than individuals who do not. Consider possible explanations for this finding.

IF YOU WANT TO LEARN MORE

Anselmi, D. L., & Law, A. L. (1998). *Questions of gender: Perspectives and paradoxes*. Boston: McGraw Hill.

Bem, S. L. (1993). *The lenses of gender: Transforming the debate on sexual inequality*. New Haven, CT: Yale University Press.

Colapinto, J. (2000). *As nature made him: The boy who was raised as a girl*. New York: HarperCollins.

Fausto-Sterling, A. (2000). *Sexing the body: Gender politics and the construction of sexuality*. New York: Basic Books.

Hines, M. (2004). *Brain gender*. New York: Oxford University Press.

Preves, S. (2003). *Intersex and identity: The contested self*. Rutgers, NJ: Rutgers University Press.

WEBSITES

Gender Identity

Border Crossings
http://www.uiowa.edu/~commstud/resources/bordercrossings/

Myth, Stereotype, and Cross-Gender Identity in the DSM-IV

http://www.gicofcolo.org/gd/writings/awptext.html

Women's Studies Links

http://dir.yahoo.com/health/diseases_and_conditions/intersexuality

CHAPTER

4 Infancy, Childhood, and Adolescence

I was 6 when I realized there were different expectations for boys and girls. My brother and I used to play dress up at home all the time. It was an Easter Sunday and I wanted to wear the tie and my brother wanted to wear the dress. My father got really mad and my mom told us that since we were going to church I had to wear the dress and my brother had to wear the suit. I had a fit about the hose itching and my father told me to get used to it because girls were supposed to dress like girls and boys like boys. (Traci, 23-year-old college senior)

My mom wanted me to wear pink and my brother blue. At Christmas all of the granddaughters were given make-up and Barbie dolls whereas the boys were given GI Joe or hunting gear. My mother raised me to know how to cook, clean, budget, and do all of the work to take care of children and a household. However, my brother has never even washed a dish. (Jamie, 20-year-old college junior)

Both my parents encouraged me to do well in school, but while my brother was signed up for karate lessons at the YMCA I was signed up for things like jazz dance. When I joined girls' football in high school, my mother cringed every time I left the house in a jersey or came back with a bloody lip. She kept telling me she would "never understand." I was teased constantly, mostly by boys. They told me I would never be good enough at football, but I kept my head high and ignored them. (Erika, 20-year-old college junior)

An old nursery rhyme declares that little girls are made of "sugar and spice and everything nice," while little boys are made of "frogs and snails and puppy dogs' tails."

Are girls and boys really as different as the nursery rhyme suggests? Is there even a kernel of truth in these age-old stereotypes? And if so, what factors might be responsible? The childhood recollections of Traci, Jamie, and Erika indicate the important contributions made by family members. In this chapter, we focus on the development of girls in infancy, childhood, and adolescence and examine both similarities and differences between girls and boys during these years. We also explore factors that influence gender development, including the roles played by parents, schools, peers, and the media. We then look at the physical transformations of adolescence, examining puberty and individual differences in rates of physical maturation. Finally, we turn to psychosocial development in adolescence, exploring identity, self-esteem, gender, intensification, and body image.

Children's Knowledge and Beliefs about Gender

Early childhood is a time when much of the social construction of gender takes place. Let's examine some of these processes more closely. For a summary of the major milestones of gender stereotyping and gender-role adoption, see Table 4.1.

TABLE 4.1   Milestones of Gender Typing

Age	Gender Stereotyping and Gender-Role Adoption	Gender Identity
1–5 years	• "Gender-appropriate" toy preferences emerge. • Gender stereotyping of activities, occupations, and behaviors appear. • Gender segregation in peer interaction emerges and strengthens. • Girls' preference for play in pairs, boys' for play in larger groups, appears.	• Gender constancy develops in a three-stage sequence: gender labeling, gender stability, and gender consistency.
6–11 years	• Gender segregation reaches a peak. • Gender-stereotyped knowledge expands, especially for personality traits and achievement areas. • Gender stereotyping peaks between ages 5–7, then becomes more flexible.	• "Masculine" gender identity strengthens among boys; girls' gender identity becomes more androgynous.
12–20 years	• Gender-role conformity increases in early adolescence and then declines. • Gender segregation becomes less pronounced.	• Gender identity becomes more traditional in early adolescence ("gender intensification"), after which highly stereotypic self-perceptions decline.

Note: These milestones represent overall age trends. Individual differences exist in the precise age at which each milestone is attained and in the extent of gender typing.
Source: Adapted from Berk (2003).

Distinguishing between Females and Males

From birth, infants are surrounded by abundant cues signifying gender. They are given gender labels and are outfitted in color-coded clothing, diapers, and blankets (Eisenberg et al., 1996). It is not surprising that children learn to differentiate between females and males at an early age. Six-month-old infants can tell the difference between pictures of adult females and males (Walsh et al., 1991), and 10-month-olds are able to distinguish between their faces (Leinbach & Fagot, 1993; Younger & Fearing, 1999). By the age of 18 months, children can match the face and voice of men and women (Poulin-Dubois et al., 1998). Between the ages of 2 and 2½ years, they can accurately label pictures of girls and boys (Etaugh & Duits, 1990; Etaugh et al., 1989). Young children who learn to identify females and males early show more gender-typical preferences for toys and peers than children of the same age who do not make this distinction (Martin, 1999).

Gender Identity and Self-Perceptions

As we saw in Chapter 3, children develop gender identity between 2 and 3 years of age. By that time they can accurately label their own gender and place a picture of themselves with other same-gender children (Campbell et al., 2002; Ruble & Martin, 1998). As children grow aware of their membership in a particular gender category, they begin to view their own gender more favorably than the other gender (Powlishta, 1997; Ruble & Martin, 1998). In one study of children in second through tenth grade, for example, girls believed that girls were nicer, harder workers, and less selfish than boys. Boys, on the other hand, felt that *they* were nicer, harder workers, and less selfish than girls (Etaugh et al., 1984).

Gender Stereotypes

In Chapter 2, we discussed how gender stereotypes are formed. This process begins early in life. Rudimentary knowledge about gender-typical objects and activities develops during the second year. Children as young as 24 months know that certain objects (e.g., ribbon, dress, purse) are associated with females and that others (e.g., gun, truck, screwdriver) are associated with males (Levy et al., 1998; Poulin-Dubois et al., 1997). By age 3, they display knowledge of gender stereotypes for toys, clothing, occupations, and activities (Campbell et al., 2004; Fagot et al., 1992; Weinraub et al., 1984). For example, children of this age generally agree that boys play with cars and trucks and help their fathers, whereas girls play with dolls and help their mothers (Etaugh & Rathus, 1995). Gender-stereotyped knowledge of activities and occupations increases rapidly between ages 3 and 5 and is mastered by age 7 (Martin & Little, 1990; Serbin et al., 1993; Signorella et al., 1993). For a closer look at how occupational stereotypes develop throughout childhood, read Learn about the Research 4.1.

In addition, preschoolers demonstrate a rudimentary awareness of gender stereotypes for personality traits. Traits such as "cries a lot," "gets feelings hurt easily," "needs help," "likes to give hugs and kisses," and "can't fix things" are applied to girls, while "hits people," "likes to win at playing games," "is not afraid of scary things," and "fixes things" are seen as characteristics of boys (Bauer et al., 1998; Ruble & Martin, 1998). In general, knowledge of gender-typical personality traits emerges later than other stereotype information (Eisenberg, et al., 1996) and increases throughout elementary school (Best & Williams, 1993).

The gender stereotypes learned in the toddler and preschool years become quite rigid between 5 and 7 years of age. They then become more flexible until early adolescence (Liben & Bigler, 2002; Martin et al., 2002; Martin & Ruble, 2004). For example, Thomas Alfieri and his colleagues (Alfieri et al., 1996) presented 12 trait-related terms, half of them feminine and half masculine, to children ranging in age from 9 to 16 years. The children were asked whether the items described males, females, or both. Gender-trait flexibility, indicated by choosing the "both" option, peaked at ages 11 and 12 and declined thereafter.

LEARN ABOUT THE RESEARCH 4.1
Gender Stereotypes about Occupations

The stereotype that certain occupations are more appropriate for one gender than the other emerges early in childhood (Helwig, 1998; Phillips & Imhoff, 1997). Even children as young as 2 and 3 years of age make a distinction between "women's jobs" and "men's jobs" (Etaugh & Rathus, 1995). Girls generally are less rigid in their occupational stereotypes than boys (Helwig, 1998; Jessell & Beymer, 1992). In addition, girls are more likely to have nonstereotyped career aspirations for themselves (Belansky et al., 1993; Kresevich, 1993). In one study (Etaugh & Liss, 1992), kindergarten through eighth-grade children were asked about their occupational aspirations. Through the third grade, most girls chose traditional feminine occupations, such as nurse and teacher. About 25 percent listed traditionally male occupations, such as doctor and pilot. Older girls, however, were more likely than younger ones to choose a traditionally masculine career and were less likely to pick a feminine one. Boys, on the other hand, aspired to masculine careers at all ages and *never* chose a feminine occupation. The results for females may be related to the finding that, by fourth grade, children view stereotypical feminine occupations less favorably than masculine occupations (Bukatko & Shedd, 1999). In studies done in the early 1970s, boys aspired to a wider variety of occupations than did girls. However, more recent studies report that girls are now selecting more varied occupations than boys (Helwig, 1998; Phipps, 1995; Trice et al., 1995).

What Does It Mean?

1. Why are girls more flexible in their career aspirations than boys?
2. Why are male-dominated careers more attractive to both girls and boys than female-dominated careers are?
3. What are some ways that gender stereotypes about occupations can be reduced?

Boys showed less flexibility than girls, particularly regarding masculine traits. Similarly, research by Elaine Blakemore (2003) and by Lisa Serbin and her colleagues (Serbin et al., 1993) has found that 11-year-olds know more about stereotypes than younger children but are also more aware of gender-role exceptions, such as girls using tools and sports equipment, and boys engaging in domestic chores. While these older children retain the broad stereotypes, their increasing cognitive maturity allows them to recognize the arbitrary aspects of gender categories, and they are more willing to accept and even try behaviors that are typical of the other gender (Etaugh & Rathus, 1995; Katz & Walsh, 1991). How do gender stereotypes develop in other cultures? Read Explore Other Cultures 4.1.

How Do Children Develop Gender Stereotypes in Other Cultures?

Deborah Best and John Williams (described in Best & Thomas, 2004) developed a Sex Stereotype Measure to assess children's knowledge of gender stereotypes. When they gave it to 5-, 8-, and 11-year-olds in 25 countries, they found that stereotype learning in all countries accelerated during the early school years and was completed during adolescence. Girls and boys learned the stereotypes at the same rate. There was a tendency for male-typed traits to be learned somewhat earlier than female-typed traits. However, female-typed traits were learned earlier than male traits in Latin/Catholic cultures (Brazil, Chile, Portugal, Venezuela) where, according to Best and Williams, the female stereotype is more positive than the male stereotype. In predominantly Muslim countries, children learned the stereotypes at an earlier age than in non-Muslim countries, perhaps reflecting the greater divide between female and male roles in Muslim cultures.

Gender-Related Activities and Interests

We have seen that children acquire gender stereotypes at an early age. Are these stereotypes reflected in the interests children develop and the play activities they choose? Let's now examine this question.

Physical Performance and Sports

In the preschool and elementary school years, girls and boys are fairly similar in their motor skills. Boys are slightly stronger, and they can typically run faster, throw a ball farther, and jump higher (Mondschein et al., 2000). Their activity levels also tend to be greater, at least in some settings (Danner et al., 1991). Girls are better at tasks requiring overall flexibility, precise movement, and coordination of their arms and legs. This gives them an edge in activities such as jumping jacks, balancing on one foot, and gymnastics (Etaugh & Rathus, 1995).

Gender differences in motor skills favoring boys become increasingly pronounced from childhood through adolescence (Small & Schultz, 1990; Thomas & French, 1985). What might account for this change? Thomas and French suggest that childhood gender differences in motor skills (with the exception of throwing) are more likely a result of environmental factors than biological ones. They note that boys receive more opportunities, encouragement, and support for participating in sports. It is not surprising that by middle childhood, boys in most cultures spend more time than girls in vigorous, competitive, athletic activities (Larson & Verma, 1999).

During puberty, hormonal changes increase muscle mass for boys and fat for girls, giving boys an advantage in strength, size, and power. But hormones are only

Girls are better than boys at tasks requiring flexibility and precise movement.

part of the story. Social pressures on girls to act more feminine and less "tomboyish" intensify during adolescence, contributing to girls' declining interest and participation in athletic activities (McHale et al., 2004; Ruble & Martin, 1998; Vilhjalmsson & Kristjansdottir, 2003). This trend is troubling, given that involvement in sports is associated with a number of positive traits in girls and women, including higher self-esteem, enhanced sense of competence and control, reduced stress and depression, delayed sexual activity, lessened likelihood of substance abuse and better academic performance (Giuliano et al., 2000; Kulig et al., 2003; Pate et al., 2000; Pedersen & Seidman, 2004; Richman & Shaffer, 2000). The good news is that the participation of girls and young women in sports has increased dramatically since the passage in 1972 of Title IX of the Education Amendments Act. This federal legislation bars discrimination in all educational programs, including athletics. The number of girls and women in high school and college athletic programs is 5 to 10 times greater now than before Title IX (Meadows, 2002; National Coalition, 2002). For example, 1 in 3 high school girls now participate in sports, compared to 1 in 27 in 1972 (Pennington, 2004). Currently, 42 percent of college athletes are women, with the percentage being highest in larger institutions (Suggs, 2004). The bad news is that schools still spend disproportionately more

Participation of girls and women in sports has increased dramatically since Title IX, but men's sports are better funded.

money on scholarships, recruiting, and operating expenses for men's sports and on the salaries of coaches (mostly White males) of men's teams (Jacobson, 2001; Longman, 2002; Navarro, 2001; Suggs, 2003). Moreover, since the passage of Title IX, the percentage of college women's teams coached by female head coaches has dropped from 90 percent to 44 percent (Acosta & Carpenter, 2002). Only 8 percent of Division I college programs have women as athletic directors (Suggs, 2005). Furthermore, Black women have made fewer gains than White women, both as players and coaches (Rhoden, 2002; Suggs, 2005).

Toys and Play

Gender differences in children's play activities and interests are more evident than they are in other areas such as personality qualities or attitudes (McHale et al., 1999). Girls and boys begin to differ in their preference for certain toys and play activities early in life. By the time they are 12 to 18 months old, girls prefer to play with dolls, domestic equipment, and soft toys, while boys choose vehicles, sports equipment, and tools (Serbin et al., 2001; Campbell et al., 2000). By 3 years of age, gender-typical toy choices are well established (Eisenberg et al., 1996), and these differences persist throughout childhood (e.g., McHale, Kim et al., 2004; McHale, Shanahan et al., 2004). However, girls are more likely than boys to display neutral or cross-gender toy choices and activities (Campbell & Stevenson, 2002; Green et al., 2004; McHale, Kim et al., 2004; Wood et al., 2002). For example, girls are more likely to request transportation toys and sports equipment as gifts than boys are to ask for dolls (Etaugh & Liss, 1992).

Why are girls more likely to depart from the stereotype? In most cultures, masculine activities have greater prestige than feminine ones. Thus, according to the social status hypothesis (see Chapter 3) a girl who plays with "boys'" toys will be viewed more positively, whereas a boy who plays with "girls'" toys will be seen as lowering his status. Moreover, children generally find boys' toys more interesting and appealing than girls' toys (Rosenblum, 1991). You can do lots more things with Legos than with a tea set!

Because of their preferences, girls and boys experience very different play environments (Edwards et al., 2001). During the preschool and elementary school years, boys spend more time than girls in vigorous physical outdoor activities such as playing with large vehicles, climbing, exploratory play, sports, and **rough-and-tumble play,** which consists of *playful chasing, tumbling, hitting and wrestling, often accompanied by laughter and screaming* (Hofferth & Sandberg, 2001; Lindsey & Mize, 2001; Maccoby, 2002; Pellegrini et al., 2002). Boys are more likely to engage in competitive activities, to play in large groups of five or more children, and to take more physical risks in their play (Benenson et al., 2001; Ginsburg et al., 2002). In conflict situations with other children, they are more likely to use powerful, controlling strategies (Sims et al., 1998). Girls' play preferences, on the other hand, include dolls, domestic play, reading, and arts and crafts. They also engage in more symbolic (i.e., "pretend") play than boys (Edwards et al., 2001; McHale et al., 2001). Girls' play is more sedentary, more cooperative, more socially competent, and more supervised and structured by adults. Also, girls are more likely than boys to play with a small group of children or just one other child (deGuzman et al., 2004; Fabes et al., 2003; Holmes-Lonergan, 2003; Maccoby, 2002). To take a closer look at play patterns of girls and boys, try Get Involved 4.1.

Gender Segregation

By 3 years of age, children prefer playing with children of the same gender, with girls showing this preference somewhat earlier than boys (Campbell et al., 2004;

Boys spend more time in vigorous physical outdoor activities; girls' play is quieter, more symbolic, and more socially competent.

GET INVOLVED **4.1**

Play Patterns of Girls and Boys

Observe preschool-aged children in a day-care center or preschool during a free-play session. Keep a record of the following behaviors:

1. The toys that girls choose and those that boys choose.

2. The activities girls engage in and those that boys engage in.
3. How often (a) girls play with other girls; (b) boys play with other boys; (c) girls and boys play with each other.

What Does It Mean?

1. Did boys and girls show different patterns of toy choice and activity preference? If so, describe these patterns. How do you account for the differences you observed (if any)?
2. Which toys in general were most in demand? Were these "girl" toys, "boy" toys, or gender-neutral toys?

3. Did boys prefer to play with same-gender peers more than girls did, was it the other way around, or were there no differences? How do you account for the differences you observed (if any)?

Hay et al., 2004; Martin & Fabes, 2001). Gender segregation increases during childhood and is especially strong in the elementary school years (Maccoby, 1998, 2002). Even when children choose seats in the lunchroom or get into line, they frequently arrange themselves in same-gender groups. Peer pressure can be a powerful motivator, as illustrated in Barrie Thorne's (1993) observation of second graders seating themselves in the lunchroom. One table was filling with both boys and girls, when a high-status second-grade boy walked by. He commented loudly, "Too many girls" and headed for a seat at another table. The boys at the first table picked up their trays and moved, leaving no boys at the first table which had now been declared taboo. Children who cross the "gender boundary" are unpopular with their peers, although there are certain conditions under which contact with the other gender is permissible. Often these overtures involve playful teasing, pushing, and grabbing (Pellegrini, 2001), as seen in Table 4.2.

Why do children play primarily with children of their own gender? According to Eleanor Maccoby (1998), there are two reasons why girls may avoid boys. One is that they don't like the rough, aggressive, dominant play style of boys. A second is that boys are unresponsive to their polite suggestions. Analogously, boys may avoid girls because girls are not responsive to their rough play (Eisenberg et al., 1996). An alternative view is that rather than actively trying to avoid children of the other gender, children simply prefer the company of their own gender (Sippola et al., 1997). This, in turn, may be because they share a preference for gender-typed toys and activities (Etaugh & Liss, 1992; Hay et al., 2004).

TABLE 4.2   Knowing the Rules: Under What Circumstances Is It Permissible to Have Contact with the Other Gender in Grade School?

Rule:	The contact is accidental.
Example:	You're not looking where you are going, and you bump into someone.
Rule:	The contact is incidental.
Example:	You go to get some lemonade and wait while two children of the other gender get some. (There should be no conversation.)
Rule:	The contact is in the guise of some clear and necessary purpose.
Example:	You may say "pass the lemonade" to persons of the other gender at the next table. No interest in them is expressed.
Rule:	An adult compels you to have contact.
Example:	"Go get that map from X and Y and bring it to me."
Rule:	You are accompanied by someone of your own gender.
Example:	Two girls may talk to two boys though physical closeness with your own partner must be maintained and intimacy with the others is disallowed.
Rule:	The interaction or contact is accompanied by disavowal.
Example:	You say someone is ugly or hurl some other insult or (more commonly for boys) push or throw something at them as you pass by.

Source: From Sroufe et al. (1993). Reproduced with permission of the Society for Research in Child Development, Inc.

Influences on Gender Development

Socialization refers to *the process by which each generation passes along to children the knowledge, beliefs, and skills which constitute the culture of the social group.* Since societies prescribe somewhat different social roles for adult females and males, girls and boys are typically socialized differently in order to prepare them for the adult roles they will play (Lott & Maluso, 2001; Pomerantz et al., 2004). This is a restatement of the third theme of our book; namely, that much of gender is socially constructed. A variety of sources help shape the behaviors and interests of boys and girls. These include parents, teachers, peers, and the media. In Chapter 3, we briefly mentioned the role of these influences when we discussed theories of gender typing. In this section, we examine these factors in greater detail.

Parents

When I was 4 or 5, my father asked me what I wanted to be when I grew up.

ME: *I'll be a carpenter and make furniture.*
HIM: *Oh, no, Holly, girls can't be carpenters. Only boys can.*
ME: *Okay, then I'll be a fisherman.*
HIM: *No, girls can't be fishermen either. They aren't strong enough.*

(Holly, 45-year-old middle-school teacher)

Children's gender-typed views about themselves and others are closely linked to the gender self-concepts and attitudes of their parents (Tenenbaum & Leaper, 2002). How do parents transmit their views on gender to their children? One of the most obvious ways in which parents influence gender development is by providing their sons and daughters with distinctive clothing, room furnishings, and toys. Infant girls are likely to be dressed in a ruffled pink outfit (sometimes with a bow attached to wisps of hair), whereas baby boys typically wear blue (Pomerleau et al., 1990; Shakin et al., 1985). The bedrooms of infant and toddler girls contain dolls and are decorated in pastel colors, frills, and flowery patterns. Baby boys' rooms feature animal themes, sturdy furniture, blue bedding, and a variety of sports equipment, vehicles, and military toys (Pomerleau et al., 1990). Clearly, infants are too young to express their preference in these matters.

Could it be that infant girls and boys give off subtle cues that influence their parents' gender-typed behavior? Research suggests that this is not the case. For example, in some studies, adults are asked to play with an unfamiliar infant who has a girl's name and is dressed in girls' clothing. Other adults play with an infant who wears boys' clothes and has a boy's name. (In fact, it is actually the same baby, who is dressed and named according to whether it is introduced as one gender or another.) Adults who believe the child is a boy are more likely to offer "him" a football or hammer and to encourage physical activity. Those who think the baby is a girl are more apt to offer a doll (Etaugh & Rathus, 1995; Stern & Karraker, 1989).

Parents and other adults are less likely to purchase cross-gender toys than to purchase gender-typical toys for children, even when children request the cross-gender toy (Etaugh & Liss, 1992). Boys are even less likely than girls to receive such toys (Fisher-Thompson et al., 1995). Parents, especially fathers, also tend to offer gender-typical toys to children during free play and are more supportive when children engage in gender-typical activities than in cross-gender activities (Ruble & Martin, 1998). Both mothers and fathers play more roughly with little boys than with little girls, and fathers in particular roughhouse with their young sons (Lindsey & Mize, 2001; Maccoby, 1998). Given that fathers treat children in more gender-typical ways than mothers do, it is not surprising that children's gender-typical activity preferences are more closely linked to their father's gender-related attitudes than to their mother's (McHale et al., 1999).

One way in which parents foster gender stereotypes in their children is through conversation. Susan Gelman and her colleagues (Gelman et al., 2004) videotaped mothers and their daughters or sons (ages 2, 4, or 6) discussing a picture book that focused on gender. Although mothers rarely expressed gender stereotypes directly, they emphasized gender concepts indirectly. For example, they provided gender labels (e.g., "That's a policeman"), contrasted males and females (e.g., "Is that a girl job or a boy job?"), and gave approval to their children's stereotyped statements (e.g., "Ballet dancers are girls!").

Parents also shape their children's environment by assigning chores based on gender (Cunningham, 2001; Dodson & Dickert, 2004). In many cultures around the world, girls are more likely to be given domestic and child-care tasks

Isabel or Isaac? Adults are more likely to offer a doll to "Isabel" and a football to "Isaac." (In fact, both babies are Claire's granddaughter, Isabel.)

centered around the home, whereas boys typically are assigned outside chores such as yard work and taking out trash (Eisenberg et al., 1996; Larson & Verma, 1999). For a closer look at the relationship between toy giving, chore assignments, and children's gender-related development, read Learn about the Research 4.2.

Parents treat daughters and sons differently in other ways than encouraging activities or assigning chores. For example, mothers talk more and use warmer, more supportive speech with daughters than with sons (Gleason & Ely, 2002). Earlier, we saw that mothers also talk more about emotions with their daughters. Parents also emphasize prosocial behaviors and politeness more with their daughters than their sons (Eisenberg & Fabes, 1998) and act more warmly toward their daughters (Zhou et al., 2002). In addition, parents control their daughters more than their sons, while granting their sons greater autonomy and greater opportunities to take risks (Leaper, 2002; Morrongiello & Hogg, 2004; Smetana & Daddis, 2002). For example, parents are more likely to make decisions for girls and to give them help even if it is not requested. Boys, on the other hand, are encouraged to make their own decisions and to solve problems on their own (Pomerantz & Ruble, 1998). Moreover, mothers expect more risky behaviors from sons than from daugh-

---

LEARN ABOUT THE RESEARCH **4.2**

Learning Gender-Related Roles at Home and at Play

Are the toys children request and receive and the chores adults assign them related to gender differences in play activities and occupational goals? To study this question, Claire Etaugh and Marsha Liss (1992) gave questionnaires to 245 5- to 13-year-olds before and after Christmas, asking which gifts they requested and which ones they received.

The children also were asked to name their friends, play activities, assigned chores, and occupational aspirations. Children generally requested and received gender-typical toys. They were less likely to receive requested cross-gender toys (such as a girl asking for a baseball glove). Children who wanted and received gender-typical toys were also more likely to be assigned gender-typical chores (such as yard work and taking out the garbage for boys, and kitchen work and dusting for girls), to engage in gender-typical play activities and to have same-gender friends. Girls preferred masculine toys and jobs more than boys preferred feminine ones. As they got older, both girls and boys increasingly preferred masculine toys, and girls increasingly chose masculine occupations.

What Does It Mean?

1. Why do you think parents and other adults are more likely to give children a requested gender-typical toy than a requested cross-gender toy? What message does this send? Did you ever ask for a gender-atypical toy? Did you get it?

2. Why do girls prefer masculine toys and jobs more than boys like feminine ones? Explain.
3. How might the assignment of gender-typical chores help influence the formation of gender roles?

In many cultures girls are more likely than boys to be assigned domestic chores in the home.

ters and consequently intervene less frequently to stop boys' injury-risk behavior in play settings (Morrongiello & Hogg, 2004; Morrongiello & Dawber, 2004).

Parents serve as role models for their children's development of gender concepts. Take the case of maternal employment. More mothers work outside the home today than ever before. Also, although to a lesser degree, more fathers are participating in child care and household chores (see Chapter 11). Not surprisingly, researchers have found that maternal employment is associated with less stereotyped gender-related concepts and preferences in boys and girls from the preschool years through adolescence (Etaugh, 1993). Children also show less stereotyping in their activity preferences if their fathers are highly involved in sharing child care and housework and if their mothers frequently engage in traditional "masculine" household tasks such as washing the car and doing yard work (Serbin et al., 1993; Etaugh & O'Brien, 2003; Murray & Steil, 2000).

Children growing up in single-parent homes tend to be less traditional in their gender stereotypes and activities than those from two-parent homes (Leaper, 2000). One reason for this is that a single parent engages in activities normally carried out by both parents, such as housework, child care, home repairs, and going to work. In addition, the absent parent is most often the father, who usually encourages children's adherence to gender norms more strongly than the mother does (Etaugh & Rathus, 1995; Katz, 1987).

Parents in both North America and Europe react negatively to children who do not adhere to traditional gender roles. As we saw in Chapter 2, this is especially true for boys (Iervolino et al., 2005). In one study (Sandnabba & Ahlberg, 1999), for example, Finnish parents expected cross-gender boys to be less well adjusted psychologically and more likely to become gay than cross-gender girls.

Young children whose parents strongly encourage gender-typical play learn gender labels at an earlier age than other children (Fagot & Leinbach, 1993). Moreover, preschool boys choose more stereotyped toys when they believe that their fathers think cross-gender play is "bad" (Raag & Rackliff, 1998). More than one male college student has confided to Claire that as a child he longed to play with his sister's Barbie dolls but would do so only when no one else was home.

Siblings

The role of siblings in gender role socialization has received less attention than that of parents and peers. Yet siblings are the most frequent out-of-school companions for children and young adolescents (Updegraff et al., 2000). Not surprisingly, siblings make significant contributions to each other's development (G. Brody, 2004). Consistent with social-learning predictions about the importance of role models (see Chapter 3), older siblings appear to play a role in the gender socialization of their younger siblings (McHale et al., 2001). For example, a large-scale longitudinal study in England (Rust et al., 2000) found that both girls with older sisters and boys with older brothers were more gender-typed than only children of their gender. These only children, in turn, were more gender-typed than children with other-gender older siblings.

School

Schools convey powerful messages to children about gender typing. For one thing, the school social structure is biased. Women hold most of the low-paying elementary school teaching positions, while males occupy more than half of the higher-paying high school teaching jobs. Additionally, men are more often in the leadership positions of principal and superintendent (Ruble & Martin, 1998). A clear signal is sent that men hold more power than women, one of the themes of this book.

In the classroom, girls are often treated unequally by their teachers. That was the conclusion of the American Association of University Women (AAUW, 1992) in a report reviewing over 1,000 publications about girls and education. Both the AAUW report and a more recent meta-analysis of empirical studies (Jones & Dindia, 2004) showed that teachers pay far less attention to girls than to boys. This finding is strikingly documented by Myra and David Sadker (1994) in their book *Failing at Fairness*. The Sadkers found that teachers call on boys more often and give them more time to answer questions. Boys are more likely to be praised, corrected, helped, and criticized constructively, all of which promote student learning. Girls are more likely to receive a bland and ambiguous "okay" response. Black girls are the least likely to be given clear feedback. Teachers are more likely to accept calling out from boys, while girls are reprimanded for the same behavior. Boys are rewarded for being smart, while girls are rewarded for being neat, pretty, and compliant. In addition, teachers are likely to give girls the answer when they ask for help but tend to help boys use strategies to figure out the answer themselves (DeZolt & Hull, 2001). Unfortunately, teachers are generally unaware that they are treating boys and girls differently. Later in the chapter, we will see how such unequal treatment may contribute to the declining self-esteem of adolescent girls.

As we saw in Chapter 2, girls are also shortchanged in school textbooks, which often ignore or stereotype females (AAUW, 1992; DeZolt & Henning-Stout, 1999). Worksheets and other teaching materials may also reflect such biases. A few years ago, for example, a friend of Claire's was very upset when her 5-year-old brought home a particular worksheet from school. At top of the page were the pictures of a woman and a man. At the bottom were various objects, such as a lawnmower, pots and pans, a hammer, and a vacuum cleaner. The instructions were to draw a line from the woman to the objects that belong with her, and a line from the man to the objects that go with him. In their home, Claire's friend did the yard work and her husband vacuumed and cooked. Their child drew the lines accordingly and received an F on the worksheet!

Peers

Children exert strong pressures on each other to engage in gender-appropriate behavior. As early as the preschool years, they modify their activity and toy preferences to conform to the patterns their peers reward. The mere presence of other children inhibits gender-inappropriate play (Eisenberg et al., 1996; Lott & Maluso, 2001). Children who show gender-typical behavior are accepted by their peers (Yunger et al., 2004), while those who dare to violate gender norms are teased, ridiculed, rejected, or ignored (Etaugh & Liss, 1992).

Boys who routinely engage in traditionally feminine activities are viewed more negatively than girls who display masculine activities (Fagot et al., 2000; Rubin et al., 1998). Even the label given to boys who show cross-gender behavior—"sissy"—has negative overtones, whereas the term used for girls who display cross-gender behavior—"tomboy"—does not.

Media

We saw in Chapter 2 that females are underrepresented in the media and that females and males are portrayed in stereotyped ways. What is the impact of these media messages on children's gender-related learning? Most of the research has focused on television. Children's television viewing averages 2–5 hours a day for preschoolers and peaks at about 4 hours a day at age 11 (Fabes & Martin, 2003), but there are large individual differences in viewing. Children who are heavy viewers have greater knowledge of gender stereotypes (Huston & Wright, 1998; Lott & Maluso, 2001; Signorella et al., 1993). In these correlational studies, it is difficult to know the direction of influence. Television may cause children to develop stronger stereotypes. On the other hand, children with stronger stereotypes may choose to watch more television because it shows images that are consistent with their beliefs (Ruble & Martin, 1998). A third alternative is that both factors are involved.

Stronger evidence of the impact of television comes from experiments that examined whether television can undo or counter the stereotypic messages. These studies found that exposure to characters who engage in nontraditional behaviors and roles (nurturing boys and girl auto mechanics, for example) reduced children's gender stereotypes about activities, domestic roles, and occupations (Comstock, 1991; Huston & Wright, 1998).

For a closer and more personal look at influences on gender role development, try the exercise in Get Involved 4.2.

Puberty

> *I think what is happening to me is so wonderful, and not only what can be seen on my body, but all that is taking place inside [. . .] Each time I have a period (and that has only been three times) I have the feeling that in spite of all the pain, discomfort, and mess, I have a sweet secret, and that is why, although it is nothing but a nuisance to me in a way, I always long for the time that I shall feel that secret within me again.*
> (Frank, 1995, pp. 158–159)

One of the most moving accounts of a young woman's entry into adolescence was written by Anne Frank, a Jewish girl who lived in Nazi-occupied Holland in

---

GET INVOLVED 4.2
Influences on Gender Development

Describe your own gender socialization. Focus on specific things that were said, done, or modeled by (a) your parents and other family members; (b) your teachers; (c) your peers; (d) television, books, and other media. Then ask two female friends and two male friends to do the same.

What Does It Mean?

Include your own responses when answering the following questions.

1. Did the females and the males you interviewed describe different kinds of socialization experiences? If so, what were they?
2. Identify aspects of your own socialization and that of your friends that are consistent with the material presented in the chapter.
3. When did you realize there were social expectations for your gender?
4. What happened in situations when you crossed gender lines?
5. How have your socialization experiences affected your current choices in activities friends, major, career, etc.?

Source: Based on Gilbert and Scher (1999).

World War II. Anne kept a diary during the two years she and her family hid from the Germans in an attic. Anne wrote about her sudden physical growth, commenting on the shoes that no longer fit her and the undershirts that became "so small that they don't even cover my stomach" (Frank, 1995, p. 101). She also grew concerned about her appearance and asked her sister "if she thought I was very ugly" (p. 55). A few months before she and her family were discovered and sent to die in a concentration camp, Anne wrote the above entry about the "wonders that are happening to [my] body."

In this section we will explore the physical transformations of adolescence. First we describe the events of puberty. We then discuss gender differences in these events. Finally, we examine individual differences in rates of physical maturation.

Events of Puberty

Puberty is the *period of life during which sexual organs mature and the ability to reproduce emerges.* Increasing levels of sex hormones stimulate development of primary and secondary sex characteristics. **Primary sex characteristics**—in girls, the ovaries, fallopian tubes, uterus, and vagina—*are structures that make reproduction possible.* **Secondary sex characteristics** are *visible signs of sexual maturity that are not directly involved in reproduction,* such as breast development and the appearance of pubic and underarm hair (Rathus et al., 2005). Table 4.3 summarizes these changes.

Most White girls begin to show signs of puberty by the age of 10, and Black girls do so about a year earlier (Belkin, 2000; Biro et al., 2003; O'Sullivan et al., 2001). Other studies confirm that feelings of sexual attraction, one of the behavioral hallmarks of puberty, also first appear between the ages of 9 and 10 (Marano, 1997). However, recent research shows that many girls start puberty far earlier than previously thought. For example, Marcia Herman-Giddens and her colleagues (Herman-Giddens et al., 1997; Herman-Giddens et al., 2004) found that by the age of 8, more than 10 percent of White girls and about one-third of Black girls have some breast development, pubic hair, or both.

Menarche

Menarche, *the first menstrual period,* is a dramatic and meaningful event in women's lives. Many women have vivid memories of their first menstrual period and, even years later, can describe details of the experience (Chrisler & Johnston-Robledo, 2000). (If you, the reader, are female, can you?)

The average age of menarche in the United States is about 12.1 years for Black girls and 12.6 years for White girls, although it is quite normal for a girl to begin to menstruate any time between 9 and 16 (Anderson et al., 2003; Herman-Giddens et al., 2004). *Over the past 150 years, the onset of puberty and the attainment of adult height and weight have occurred at progressively earlier ages in the United States and western Europe* (Graber & Brooks-Gunn, 2002). This **secular trend** is most likely a result of better nutrition and medical care. The onset of puberty seems to be triggered when individuals reach a certain body weight. Improved nutrition, health,

TABLE 4.3   Stages of Pubertal Development in Females

Beginning sometime between ages 8 and 11

Pituitary hormones stimulate ovaries to increase production of estrogen.
Internal reproductive organs begin to grow.
Pubic hair begins to appear.
Breast development begins.

Beginning sometime between ages 9 and 15

First the areola (the darker area around the nipple) and then the
breasts increase in size and become more rounded.
Pubic hair becomes darker and coarser.
Growth in height continues.
Body fat continues to round body contours.
A normal vaginal discharge becomes noticeable.
Sweat and oil glands increase in activity, and acne may appear.
Internal and external reproductive organs and genitals grow, which makes
the vagina longer and the labia more pronounced.

Beginning sometime between ages 10 and 16

Areola and nipples grow, often forming a second mound sticking out
from the rounded breast mound.
Pubic hair begins to grow in a triangular shape and to cover the center of the mons.
Underarm hair appears.
Menarche occurs.
Internal reproductive organs continue to develop.
Ovaries may begin to release mature eggs capable of being fertilized.
Growth in height slows.

Beginning sometime between ages 12 and 19

Breasts near adult size and shape.
Pubic hair fully covers the mons and spreads to the top of the thighs.
The voice may deepen slightly (but not as much as in males).
Menstrual cycles gradually become more regular.
Some further changes in body shape may occur into the early 20s.

Note: This table is a general guideline. Changes may appear sooner or later than shown, and not
always in the indicated sequence.
Source: Rathus et al. (2005), p. 440. Reprinted with permission from Allyn & Bacon.

and living conditions have led to the achievement of that weight at a younger age
(Frisch, 2002). The rise in obesity among American children may play a role as
well, since girls with a high percentage of body fat in early childhood show more
advanced pubertal development at age 9 (Davison et al., 2003).

Environmental stress is also linked to an earlier onset of puberty (Ellis,
2004). Research has found that girls from divorced families or families high in

parental conflict begin to menstruate earlier than girls whose parents are married or have lower levels of conflict (Ellis & Garber, 2000; Graber & Brooks-Gunn, 2002). One explanation for these findings is that stress may lead to overeating, which increases body weight, which then triggers the onset of puberty. Alternatively, early-maturing mothers may tend to have early-maturing daughters because of genetic factors. Early maturers become sexually active, marry, and give birth at younger ages than others. But early marriages are more likely to end in divorce. So, girls who parents divorce may reach puberty early not because of parental conflict and divorce, but simply because their own mothers matured early (Mustanski et al., 2004).

In North America, girls have mixed feelings about starting to menstruate, with Black and Latina girls reporting more negative attitudes than White girls (Chrisler & Johnston-Robledo, 2000). On the one hand, menstruation is an eagerly awaited sign of growing up. According to one adolescent girl, "It's a great feeling knowing that one day when you want to have a baby, that you can do it. To me that's just amazing" (Commonwealth Fund, 1997, p. 39). Still, girls also believe that menstruation is embarrassing, frightening, or disgusting (Chrisler & Johnston-Robledo, 2000; Roberts et al., 2002). Young adolescent girls also worry about having an "accident" and about someone knowing they have their menstrual period. "When you're in middle school and you're getting your period, you don't want to tell anyone. I was ashamed when I got my period," (Commonwealth Fund, 1997, p. 39).

Feminine hygiene advertisements reflect and reinforce these concerns by focusing on the discomfort and messiness of menstrual periods and the potential embarrassment of "showing" (Merskin, 1999). Women are taught to conceal the fact that they are menstruating. Even within the family household, menstruation often is not openly discussed. One of Claire's students shared the following experience: "When I started my period, I didn't tell a soul. I wrote down 'pads' on my parents' grocery list and they showed up in the bathroom closet. That was the extent of the 'birds and bees' talk in my family." Cultural pressure to hide menstrual cycles, and marketing pitches for products that keep a woman clean and deodorized during her menstrual cycles send a clear message to women that their bodies are unacceptable in their natural state. It is not surprising that women who place a great deal of emphasis on their appearance and body image have more negative attitudes and emotions, including disgust and shame, toward their menstrual cycles (Roberts, 2004).

A negative attitude toward menstruation before menarche is associated with greater menstrual discomfort (Yeung, Tang, & Lee, 2005). For example, girls whose mothers lead them to believe that menstruation will be uncomfortable or unpleasant later report more severe menstrual symptoms. Moreover, girls who begin to menstruate earlier than their peers, or who are otherwise unprepared and uninformed about pubertal changes find menarche especially distressing (American Psychological Association, 2002). When 14- and 15-year-old girls were asked what advice they would give to younger girls about menarche, they recommended emphasizing the normalcy of menstruation, providing practical information on handling menstrual periods, and discussing what menarche actually feels like (American Psychological Association, 2002).

Gender Differences in Puberty

Besides the obvious differences in secondary sex characteristics, girls and boys differ in other ways as they move through puberty. For one thing, girls begin and finish puberty about two years before boys, on average (Fechner, 2003). The **adolescent growth spurt,** *a rapid increase in height and weight*, also starts earlier in girls, at about age 9, while boys start their spurt at about age 11. The period of peak growth occurs at age 12 for girls and 14 for boys, on average, and then tapers off for two years or so. Boys grow more than girls during their spurt, adding an average of 12 inches to their height, while girls grow slightly over 11 inches. Boys also gain more weight than girls do during their growth spurt (Susman & Rogol, 2004).

Body shape changes in puberty as well. Girls gain twice as much fatty tissue as boys, largely in the breasts, hips, and buttocks, while boys gain almost twice as much muscle tissue as girls (Fechner, 2003). These changes produce the more rounded shape of women as compared to men.

As the growth spurt begins to slow down, adolescents reach sexual maturity. In girls, the most obvious sign is menarche. We shall discuss other aspects of menstruation in Chapter 7.

Early and Late Maturation in Girls

I remember when I got my first period. It was the summer between fourth and fifth grades—I guess I was 10 . . . By sixth and seventh grades, I had this intense desire to hang out with older kids, usually older boys. I tried pot for the first time when I was 12. I could usually convince people I was 15 when I was in seventh grade and I started hanging out with other girls who looked older . . . Sometimes we would go off with older boys. Often we were drinking or smoking pot . . . Overall, I was pretty unhappy during the teen years; at times, I guess, depressed. I had a hard time fitting in at school even though I got good grades. I was always looking for a group where I belonged. It wasn't until college that I really found my niche. (Graber & Brooks-Gunn, 2002, p. 35)

The timing of the events of puberty vary considerably from one girl to another (Susman et al., 2003), as shown in Table 4.3. Early-maturing girls may feel awkward and self-conscious because they begin the physical changes of puberty earlier than their peers. Boys may tease them about their height and developing breasts, which some early-maturing girls try to hide by wearing heavy sweaters and loose clothing (Summers-Effler, 2004). In addition, because they look older than they actually are, others may place sexual and other expectations on them that are difficult to meet. No wonder that early maturers tend to have lower self-esteem, higher levels of depression and anxiety, and a poorer body image than girls who mature later (Ellis, 2004; Susman & Rogol, 2004; Weichold et al., 2003).

The timing of puberty varies considerably from one girl to another.

Early-maturing girls tend to associate with older peers. This may explain why they begin sexual activity at an earlier age and are more likely to engage in risky behavior such as smoking, drinking, substance abuse, and delinquent behavior (Ellis, 2004; Haynie, 2003; Weichold et al., 2003). But not all early maturing girls suffer negative consequences. Instead, early maturation seems to accentuate behavioral problems in girls who had already shown adjustment difficulties earlier in childhood (Weichold et al., 2003).

Once early-maturing girls reach high school, they come into their own socially. They are envied by other girls because of their grown-up looks. They may also serve as advisors to their later maturing girlfriends on such increasingly important topics as makeup, dating, and sex. They are likely to cope better than their peers with the challenges of adolescence, perhaps because of skills developed in dealing with problems of early maturation (Etaugh & Rathus, 1995). By the end of high school, early-maturing girls seem to be as well adjusted as other girls (Brody, 1999b). By age 30, they appear to be more self-possessed and self-directed than their later-maturing peers. Perhaps learning to cope with the stresses of puberty at an early age prepares early-maturing girls to deal effectively with later stressful events (Weichold et al., 2003).

Late-maturing girls may have relatively low social status during the middle school and junior high school years. They look and are treated like "little girls" and are often excluded from boy-girl social activities. Late-maturing girls often are dissatisfied with their appearance and lack of popularity. By tenth grade, however, they are noticeably showing the physical signs of puberty. They often wind up more popular and more satisfied with their appearance than early-maturing girls (Simmons & Blyth, 1987). One reason for this may be that late maturers are more likely to develop the culturally valued slender body shape than early maturers, who tend to be somewhat heavier.

Psychosocial Development in Adolescence

How much do I like the kind of person I am? Well, I like some things about me, but I don't like others. I'm glad that I'm popular since it's really important to me to have friends. But in school I don't do as well as the really smart kids. That's OK, because if you're too smart you'll lose your friends. So being smart is just not that important. But what's really important to me is how I look. If I like the way I look, then I really like the kind of person I am. I've also changed. It started when I went to junior high school. I got really depressed. There was this one day when I hated the way I looked, and I didn't get invited to this really important party, and then I got an awful report card, so for a couple of days I thought it would be best to just end it all. I was letting my parents down, I wasn't good-looking anymore, and I wasn't that popular and things were never going to get better. I talked to Sheryl, my best friend, and that helped some. (adapted from Harter, 1990, pp. 364–365)

This self-description from a 15-year-old girl illustrates some of the psychological characteristics of adolescent females. Notice how important physical appearance is to her self-esteem. Note also that she discloses her private thoughts to her best friend. Can you recall what was important to you at age 15?

Adolescence is a time of learning more about oneself and others. Two key issues are developing a sense of who you are and how you feel about yourself. Adherence to traditional gender roles often becomes stronger and girls begin to focus a great deal on their appearance. In this section we explore four aspects of psychosocial development in the adolescent girl: identity formation, self-esteem, gender intensification, and body image.

Identity

One of the most important tasks of adolescence is to develop a sense of **identity,** that is, *deciding who we are and what we want to make of our lives.* According to Erik Erikson (1968, 1980), adolescent identity formation involves commitment to a vocation and a philosophy of life. In order to do so, adolescents must **individuate,** that is, *see themselves as separate and unique.* Carol Gilligan (1982), Sally Archer (1992), Ruthellen Josselson (1994), and others maintain that this model describes the traditional identity development of males better than that of females. They believe that achieving identity for both female and male adolescents requires an interplay between separateness (meeting one's own needs) and connectedness (satisfying the needs of those one cares for) (Jaffe, 1998).

Research supports the view that adolescent females and males take similar paths in their quest for identity. Elements of career choice, personal competence, and interpersonal relationships are central to the identity of both genders (Archer,

1992; Giesbrecht, 1998; Murray, 1998). For one thing, adolescent girls' educational and career aspirations have increased in recent years and now parallel those of boys (Denmark, 1999). In addition, an increasing number of teenagers (83 percent of females and 72 percent of males) say that having a good marriage and family life is extremely important to them as a life goal (Popenoe & Whitehead, 1999). However, whereas most adolescent girls see interconnections between their career goals and family goals, most adolescent boys perceive no connection between the two. For example, young women place greater emphasis than young men do on flexible working hours that facilitate the coordination of employment and childrearing (see Chapter 11). Still, it appears that nowadays, individual differences in identity development may be more important than gender differences (Archer, 1993; Marcia, 1993).

Unfortunately, little research has been conducted on the identity formation of ethnic minority adolescent girls. The few studies that have been done find that one key factor in this process is the family unit, often an extended kinship network, which is a highly valued part of life among Asian Americans, Blacks, Latinas/os, and Native Americans. Identity with the family and community seems to provide strength and resources for adolescent girls of color as they strive to integrate their ethnicity and their femaleness within a larger society that devalues both (de las Fuentes & Vasquez, 1999; Vasquez & de las Fuentes, 1999).

Self-Esteem

> *The two really blonde girls in our class dressed better than the rest of the girls, and I always felt like I couldn't compete with them. This feeling carried on throughout high school. Even though I felt like I was smarter than the boys, I didn't feel better because I didn't look nice enough to impress them. Basically, I grew up not really caring for boys and thinking that they were stupid, but that it was important to impress them by looking nice. I was so confused. I felt superior, but not. And I felt anxious around both males and females, but probably more anxious around males.* (Jamie, 25-year-old college senior)

Self-esteem is *the sense of worth or value that people attach to themselves.* High self-esteem has long been associated with healthy psychological adjustment and happiness (American Psychological Association, 2002; Baumeister et al., 2003; Donnellan et al., 2005). Beginning in early adolescence, self-esteem diminishes for both genders, with girls showing lower self-esteem than boys (Eccles et al., 1998; Frost & McKelvie, 2004; Hoffmann et al., 2004; Major et al., 1999; Quatman & Watson, 2001; Thomas & Daubman, 2001). According to a recent meta-analysis of over 97,000 respondents by Kristen Kling and her colleagues (Kling et al., 1999), this gender gap becomes greatest in late adolescence, with a small to moderate effect size of 0.33 (see Chapter 1). For example, in one survey of 2,400 girls and 600 boys in grades four through ten, 60 percent of girls and 69 percent of boys 8 and 9 years old reported feeling confident and happy with themselves. By the ages of 16 and 17, however, the percentage who reported these positive feelings dropped to only 29 percent for girls compared with 46 percent for boys. Many more Black adolescent girls, 58 percent, remained confident and positive than did White girls or Latinas (AAUW, 1992). Two recent meta-analyses revealed a similar increasing gap between the self-esteem of Black and White females during late adolescence and young adulthood (Gray-Little & Hafdahl, 2000; Twenge & Crocker, 2002). Other studies have found that, compared to White adolescent girls, Black girls have more confidence in their physical attractiveness, sports ability, femininity, popularity, and social relations (Eccles et al., 2002; Michael & Eccles, 2003).

What causes girls' self-esteem to decline in adolescence and why do Black girls remain more self-confident than others? For one thing, perceived physical appearance is closely linked to self-esteem (Fingeret & Gleaves, 2004; Klomsten et al., 2004). Girls are more dissatisfied with their appearance than boys, a difference that increases during adolescence (Harter, 1998; Klomsten et al., 2004). But Black girls, as we shall see, are less concerned about body shape and size than White girls, and physical appearance is less important to their sense of self-worth (Erkut et al., 1999; Schwartz & Abell, 1999). Upon entering adolescence, for example, the self-esteem of obese Latina and White girls drops more than that of nonobese girls, but obese Black girls do not show this decline (Strauss, 2000).

In addition, we saw earlier in this chapter that schools shortchange girls in ways that undermine girls' perceptions of their competence and importance (AAUW, 1992; Sadker & Sadker, 1994). Black girls, however, seem less dependent on school achievement for their self-esteem. Their view of themselves is more influenced by their community, family, and sense of ethnic identity (American Psychological Association, 2002; Tolman & Brown, 2001; Vasquez & de las Fuentes, 1999). Some researchers believe that Black females are socialized early in life by their mothers and other female relatives to be strong, independent women who can cope with a society in which racism, sexism, and classism can be barriers to the development of a positive identity (Vasquez & de las Fuentes, 1999; Way, 1995). In one study of African American female college students, for example, over 75 percent mentioned a sense of strength as a key component of their sense of identity (Shorter-Gooden & Washington, 1996).

Several theorists, notably Carol Gilligan (1993, 2002) and scholars at the Stone Center (e.g., Jordan, 1997) maintain that as girls make the transition to adolescence, they become aware of growing up in a patriarchal society which devalues women and which views the desirable stereotype of the "good woman" as being nice, pleasing to others, and unassertive. This places girls in conflict with their view of themselves as self-sufficient, independent, and outspoken. Many girls respond to this conflict by losing confidence in themselves and by suppressing their thoughts, opinions, and feelings, that is, by "losing their voice."

However, research by Susan Harter and her colleagues (Harter, 1998, 1999) found that adolescent boys and girls did not differ with respect to the loss of voice. About a third of young people of both genders said they disguised their true feelings and thoughts in dealing with certain categories of individuals, but a large majority of these females and males did not report doing so. Harter and her colleagues found that *gender role identity*, not gender itself, predicted the level of voice, a finding since confirmed by other researchers (e.g., Smolak & Munster-tieger, 2002). Masculine and androgynous adolescents of both genders reported higher levels of voice and higher self-esteem than those with a feminine orientation. Although the feminine girls in Harter's study reported loss of voice in public contexts, such as school and group social situations, this did not occur with parents or close friends. Support, approval, and acceptance from parents and teachers appear critical to the development of high esteem and to the expression of one's thoughts and feelings (Harter, 1998).

Gender Intensification

> *All through grade school, I had been very active in sports. Basketball was my favorite and I was really good at it. Basketball gave me self-esteem. When I was 13, I set my life's goal—to one day coach the Boston Celtics. I will never forget the reactions I got when I told people this. Everyone—my friends, my parents' friends, other adults—all said the same thing: A girl could never coach a professional men's team. Until then, it hadn't occurred to me that gender mattered. I just thought you needed talent and desire, which I had. I was totally heartbroken. Then I began to question whether women were as good as men in basketball. If not, why was I playing? I didn't ever again want people to tell me I couldn't do something because I was a girl. So I quit basketball and became a cheerleader. I didn't really want to, but I felt people wouldn't like me unless I became a "complete and total girl."* (Liz, 21-year-old college senior)

Gender differences in value orientation become pronounced at the onset of adolescence. For example, a study by Kimberly Badger and her colleagues (Badger et al., 1998) of geographically diverse American adolescents found that as early as sixth grade, girls were more likely than boys to place a high value on (1) compromising; (2) being kind and forgiving; (3) expressing feelings; (4) wanting to know what people are like inside; (5) enjoying people; (6) getting along with others; and (7) having friends, cooperating, and helping. Early adolescence is also marked by an increase in rigidity of gender-role stereotypes, although girls continue to remain more flexible than their male peers (Basow & Rubin, 1999). This *increasing divergence in gender-related behaviors and attitudes of girls and boys that emerges in early adolescence* is known as **gender intensification** (Galambos, 2004). At this age, perceiving yourself to be a typical member of your same-sex peer group is important to a sense of psychological well-being (Carver et al., 2003; Yunger et al., 2004).

Several factors contribute to the development of gender intensification. For one thing, the physical changes of puberty accentuate gender differences in appearance. Peers, parents, and other adults, especially those with traditional views of gender, apply increasing pressure on girls to display "feminine" behaviors (Crouter et al., 1995; Raffaelli & Ontai, 2004), as illustrated poignantly by Liz's experience. This magnification of traditional gender expectations is stronger for girls than for boys, probably because girls have been given more latitude than boys have to display cross-gender behaviors in middle childhood (Crockett, 1991). In addition, when adolescents begin to date and enter romantic relationships, they may increase their gender-stereotypical behavior in order to enhance their appeal to the other gender. For example, girls become intensely interested in appearing physically attractive to boys and spend long hours focusing on their clothes, hairstyles, complexions, and weight (Maccoby, 1998). Furthermore, cognitive changes make adolescents more aware of gender expectations and more concerned about what others think of them (Crockett, 1991). The resulting adherence to a traditional construction of gender seems at least partly responsible for the gender differences in self-esteem, friendship patterns, dating behaviors, and cognitive skills that we discuss in this chapter and in Chapters 5 and 8.

Gender intensification starts to decrease by middle to late adolescence. Gender-related occupational stereotypes (see earlier in this chapter) become more flexible, and sexist attitudes (see Chapter 2) become less pronounced. Also, the understanding that gender-related traits, behaviors, and roles are culturally created and modifiable increases (Crockett, 1991).

Body Image

> *I was always heavier than other females my age, but was very healthy and athletic as a child and into high school. I played basketball, soccer, tennis and softball. My weight was never an issue for me until I reached adolescence. I suddenly became very conscious of my weight. Boys in my class would make comments. It took me several years before I could become comfortable with my weight and grow to like my body.* (Becky, 22-year-old senior)

The weight gain associated with puberty occurs within a cultural context that emphasizes a female beauty ideal of extreme thinness (Cash & Pruzinsky, 2002; Stice, 2003). According to some feminist theorists (Fingeret & Gleaves, 2004; Murnen et al., 2003; Slater & Tiggemann, 2002), girls and women in Western culture internalize society's view of the body as a sexualized object to be looked at and evaluated, a process termed *self-objectification*. As girls internalize the "thin ideal" body image of Western society, which is unattainable for most women, they become intensely dissatisfied with their weight and shape (Calogero et al., 2005; Forbes, Doroszewicz, et al., 2004; Muehlenkamp et al., 2005). Ironically, preschool girls are more positive about their appearance than boys are about theirs (Marsh et al., 2002). However, by adolescence, girls are much more concerned with body weight and appearance than are males of the same age. They have a less positive body image, are less satisfied with their weight, and are more likely to be dieting (Field et al., 2003; Grunbaum, 2004; Rozin et al., 2003; Safir et al., 2005; Yates et al., 2004). American adolescent girls and women often view themselves as too heavy even at average weight levels, and many of them have a negative view of their overall appearance (Brody, 2002; Markey et al., 2004;

Many adolescent girls are dissatisfied with their weight and shape.

Sarwer et al., 2005). Similarly, a recent body image survey conducted by a British teen magazine found that only 8 percent of the teenage girls responding were happy with their body. Even though 58 percent said they were of normal weight, two-thirds of the entire sample thought they needed to lose weight. A quarter of the respondents admitted that they already suffered from an eating disorder (Barton, 2005).

The importance of body image to adolescent females is indicated by the close association between teenage girls' body image and their self-esteem. The more negative their body image is, the lower their self-esteem. For adolescent boys, however, the relationship is minimal or nonexistent (Kelly et al., 2004; McHale, Corneal et al., 2001; Siegel, 2002; Tiggemann, 2001). Being heavier is associated with having a poorer self-image and greater body image dissatisfaction with one's body in girls as young as age 5 and 6 (Davison & Birch, 2002; Stice, 2002), and continuing into adolescence (Jones, 2004).

Gender differences in body image have grown since the middle of the twentieth century according to a meta-analysis of 222 studies by Alan Feingold and Ronald Mazzella (1998). Their analysis showed a dramatic increase in the number of women with a poor body image, particularly during the adolescent years. Men's body image, however, has remained relatively stable over time (Cash et al., 2004). Along these same lines, Joan Jacobs Brumberg (1997), after reviewing 150 years of girls' diaries, concluded that the focus of adolescent girls has shifted from developing their talents, interests, character, and contributions to society to worrying about their weight, shape, and appearance. According to one therapist who works with teenage girls, (Netburn, 2002, pp. ST1, ST7), "'Who am I?' has been replaced by 'What image should I project?' and part of that image involves for many girls engaging in unhealthy behaviors: dieting, tanning, smoking to keep your weight down." We will discuss the unhealthy weight control behaviors known as eating disorders in Chapter 13.

A major factor contributing to the increase in poor body image is the increasing emphasis in Western culture on thinness as the ideal female body shape

(Bordo, 2004; Rubin et al., 2004). Studies of *Playboy* centerfolds, Miss America contestants, and fashion models over the last few decades have found that the average size and shape of the idealized woman has become thinner and more boyish (Rubinstein & Caballero, 2000; Spitzer et al., 1999; Voracek & Fisher, 2002). For example, the average fashion model in 1985 was a size 8, while today she is a size 0 or 2 (Betts, 2002). Magazines designed for an audience of women or girls are far more likely than magazines aimed at men or boys to focus on becoming slim, trim, and beautiful through diet, exercise, and cosmetic surgery (Malkin et al., 1999). Furthermore, as mentioned in Chapter 2, thin central women characters are overrepresented in television situation comedies and receive more positive comments from male characters the thinner they are (Fouts & Burggraf, 1999). So powerful is the cultural emphasis on slenderness in adolescent girls and young women that simply viewing photographs or media images of physically attractive women with idealized physiques is associated with diminished self-evaluations of attractiveness, less body-image satisfaction, lower self-esteem, increased anger, anxiety, depressed mood, eating disorder symptoms, and approval of surgical body-alteration (Groesz et al., 2002; Harrison, 2003; Van Evra, 2004; Vaughan & Fouts, 2003). This is especially true for White women (Schooler et al., 2004; Van Evra, 2004). In addition, adolescent girls who read beauty and fashion magazines and articles about dieting are more likely to use unhealthy dieting methods (Thomsen et al., 2002; Utter et al., 2003). In one study (Commonwealth Fund, 1997), adolescent girls generally agreed that there is considerable pressure to be thin, especially from the media:

> *There's such pressure. I look at movie stars and I'm like, "Oh, my God. She's so pretty. She's so thin. I want to look like that." I'm not a small person. I am never going to be like a size 2. I should be happy with what I am and just accept that. But inside I'm freaking out because I can't eat.* (p. 67)

Pressure from parents and peers to be thin and to look good may be as influential as the media in undermining girls' body images (Davison & Birch, 2002; Field et al., 2001; Murray & Corson, 2004; Stice & Whitenton, 2002). Overweight teenagers are more likely than normal-weight children to be physically bullied by their peers or excluded from social activities (Janssen et al., 2004). Furthermore, girls whose peers tease them about their weight and pressure them to lose weight have poorer body esteem and engage in more disordered eating behaviors (Littleton & Ollendick, 2003). Even simply having conversations with peers about appearance lowers body satisfaction in girls (Jones, 2004). Mothers are three times as likely to identify weight as a problem in girls than in boys. In some cases, parents will talk in their daughter's presence about her need to lose weight (Goode, 2003b). Teasing—especially by girls' fathers and brothers—is also emerging as a powerful influence on those who feel bad about their bodies (Eisenberg et al., 2003; Thompson, in Berger, 2000). Marla Eisenberg and her colleagues (2003) found that adolescents who were teased by family members or peers about their weight were more likely than other teenagers to be depressed and to think about or attempt suicide.

In their search for the "perfect look," more teenage girls are choosing to undergo cosmetic surgery (Springen, 2004). Moreover, the procedures requested are changing from a generation ago. While nose reshaping still is the most popular surgery, girls are increasingly choosing breast augmentation, liposuction, and tummy tucks (Duenwald, 2004; Smolak & Striegel-Moore, 2001). Preteen girls, or "tweens" as they are now called, get manicures, pedicures, and facials (Tyre & Pierce, 2003). It's not unusual to see girls age 12 or younger trying to look like Britney Spears or Christina Aguilera, with pierced bellybuttons, skimpy tube tops, strappy high-heeled shoes and revealing shorts. Marketers call it K.G.O.Y., or Kids Getting Older Younger (Trebay, 2003).

Females of color and those who are less affluent are more satisfied with their bodies and are less concerned about weight loss and dieting than are White females and those of higher socioeconomic status (Kelly et al., 2004; Padgett & Biro, 2003; Breitkopf & Berenson, 2004; Jones & Shorter-Gooden, 2003; Mack et al., 2004; Shulman & Horne, 2003; Wardle et al., 2004). Standards of beauty and attractiveness in Black and Latina cultures appear to place less emphasis on thinness than in White culture (Gil-Kashiwabara, 2002; Omari & Mitchell, 2003; Sherry et al., 2004). However, even though females of color may be more satisfied with their bodies than their White counterparts, they still have concerns about weight and are more likely than males of color to be dieting (Cash & Pruzinsky, 2002; Grunbaum, 2004; Mulholland & Mintz, 2001). Moreover, cosmetic surgery is gaining in popularity among Black women, with the most popular procedures being tummy tucks, breast reduction, and liposuction compared to nose reshaping, liposuction, and breast augmentation in White women (Samuels, 2004). Both body dissatisfaction and eating disorders have been reported among Asian, Black, Latina, and Native American girls and women, and among the urban poor as well as the suburban middle class (Franzoi & Chang, 2002; LaFromboise et al., 1994; Pastore et al., 1996; Robinson et al., 1996). The more that American ethnic minority women and non-Western women have adopted the values of mainstream U.S. society, the more likely they are to suffer from eating problems (Reijonen et al., 2003; Stark-Wroblewski et al., 2005). Try Get Involved 4.3 for a closer look at the body images of Black and White women.

Lesbians are less preoccupied with weight and dieting and have higher levels of body self-esteem than heterosexual women, but they have still more weight concerns than heterosexual men (Morrison et al., 2004; Lakkis et al., 1999; Rothblum, 2002; Share & Mintz, 2002). Why are lesbians less concerned about their body image? According to Judith Daniluk (1998), lesbians are branded by society as sexually unappealing because of their sexual orientation, no matter how slender and beautiful they might be. This decoupling of physical attractiveness and sexual appeal may help protect lesbians from developing a negative body image. Another explanation (Heffernan, 1999) is that lesbians may be less likely than heterosexual women to base romantic relationships on physical appearance (see Chapter 8).

GET INVOLVED 4.3

Perceptions of Actual and Desirable Physique

For this exercise, survey four young adult females, two Black and two White. Show each woman the following nine figure drawings and ask her the following questions.

1. Using the numbers under the figures, which represents your perception of *your current body*?

2. Which represents your perception of *your ideal body*?

3. Which is the body you feel *men find the most attractive*?

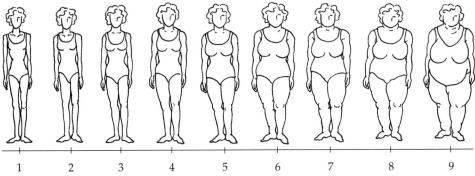

What Does It Mean?

1. How did the women's perceptions of their current body compare with their perception of their ideal body?

2. How did women's perceptions of their current body compare with what they feel men find most attractive?

3. Were there any differences in the perceptions of Black and White women?

SUMMARY

Children's Knowledge and Beliefs about Gender

- Children are able to distinguish females and males as early as 6 months of age.
- By age 2 or 3 years, they can label their own gender and they show some awareness of gender-typical objects, activities, and occupations.
- Awareness of gender stereotypes for personality traits emerges later in the preschool years.
- Stereotypes become more flexible after age 7.

Gender-Related Activities and Interests

- Preschool girls and boys are similar in their motor skills.
- Differences favoring boys become more pronounced in adolescence as a result of both enviornmental and biological factors.
- Participation in sports is associated with positive traits in females. Their participation has soared since the passage of Title IX.
- By age 3, gender differences in toy choices and activities are well established.

- Gender segregation, the preference for same-gender children, emerges by age 3 and increases during childhood.

Influences on Gender Development

- Both parents, but fathers more than mothers, encourage gender-typical toys, play activities, and chore assignments for their children.
- Parents talk more to their daughters, give them less autonomy, and encourage their prosocial behaviors.
- Maternal employment is associated with less stereotyped gender-related concepts and preferences in sons and daughters.
- Older siblings influence the gender development of younger siblings.
- Boys receive more attention from teachers than girls do. They are more likely to be called on, praised, and criticized constructively
- Girls are also shortchanged in school textbooks.
- Children exert strong pressures on each other to engage in gender-typical behavior.
- Boys are viewed more negatively than girls when they engage in cross-gender activity.
- Children who are heavy TV viewers are more aware of gender stereotypes.

- Exposure to characters who show nontraditional behaviors reduces children's gender stereotypes.

Puberty

- During puberty, sexual organs mature and secondary sex characteristics appear.
- Menarche is a major event of puberty.
- Girls who mature early tend to adjust less easily than late-maturing girls.

Psychosocial Development in Adolescence

- Adolescent girls and boys show similar patterns of identity development, focusing both on occupational choices and interpersonal relationships.
- Girls begin to show lower self-esteem than boys in early adolescence, and the gender gap widens during adolescence. Explanations include girls' dissatisfaction with their physical appearance, shortchanging of girls in school, and girls' "losing their voice."
- Early adolescents show an increasing divergence in gender-related behaviors and attitudes, known as gender intensification.
- Adolescent girls, compared to boys, have a more negative body image and are more likely to diet. Cultural pressures for slimness are partly responsible.

KEY TERMS

rough-and-tumble play	secondary sex characteristics	identity
socialization	menarche	individuate
puberty	secular trend	self-esteem
primary sex characteristics	adolescent growth spurt	gender intensification

WHAT DO YOU THINK?

1. Should parents attempt to raise their children in gender-neutral ways? If so, why? What would be the advantages? What would be the disadvantages? Incorporate material from Chapters 2 and 3 into your answers.

2. Why do you think teachers pay more attention to boys than to girls? What can be done to ensure more equal treatment of girls in the classroom?

3. In your opinion, why are boys who engage in feminine activities viewed more

negatively than girls who engage in masculine activities?

4. Lois Gould (1990), in her fictional *X: A Fabulous Child's Story*, wrote about Baby X, whose gender was concealed from everyone except its parents. This created considerable consternation among relatives and family friends. Why do you think that was?

5. The earlier onset of puberty in the United States and Western Europe has not been accompanied by earlier gains in social and emotional development that would help children successfully manage their sexuality. What are the implications for individual adolescents and for society?

6. Using what you know about gender-role identity, explain why masculine and androgynous adolescents have higher self-esteem than feminine adolescents.

7. What actions can parents and teachers take to help enhance the self-esteem of adolescent girls?

8. How does the social construction of gender influence women's body images versus men's body images?

IF YOU WANT TO LEARN MORE

American Association of University Women. (1992). *How schools shortchange girls: The AAUW report*. Washington, DC: AAUW Educational Foundation.

Bettis, P. J., & Adams, N. G. (2005). *Geographies of girlhood: Identities in-between*. Mahwah, NJ: Erlbaum.

Bordo, S. (2004). *Unbearable weight: Feminism, western culture and the body*. Los Angeles: University of California Press.

Brown, L. M. (1998). *Raising their voices: The politics of girls' anger*. Cambridge, MA: Harvard University Press.

Brumberg, J. J. (1997). *The body project: An intimate history of American girls*. New York: Random House.

Cash, T. F., & Pruzinsky, T. (Eds.). (2002). *Body image: A handbook of theory, research and practice*. New York: Guilford.

Haag, P. (1999). *Voices of a generation: Teenage girls on sex, schools, and self*. Washington, DC: American Association of University Women.

Harris, A. (Ed.). (2004). *All about the girl: Culture, power, and identity*. New York: Routledge.

Johnson, N. G., Roberts, M. C., & Worell, J. (Eds.). (1999). *Beyond appearance: A new look at adolescent girls*. Washington, DC: American Psychological Association.

Kimmel, M. S. (2000). *The gendered society*. New York: Oxford Press.

Maccoby, E. E. (1998). *The two sexes: Growing up apart, coming together*. Cambridge, MA: Harvard University Press.

Roan, S. L. (2001). *Our daughters' health: Practical and invaluable advice for raising confident girls ages 6–16*. New York: Hyperion.

Sadker, M., & Sadker, D. (1994). *Failing at fairness: How America's schools cheat girls*. New York: Scribner.

Yelland, N. (Ed.). (1998). *Gender in early childhood*. New York: Routledge.

Zager, K., & Rubenstein, A. (2002). *The inside story on teen girls*. Washington, DC: American Psychological Association.

Zimmerman, T. S. (2002). *Integrating gender and culture in parenting*. New York: Haworth.

WEBSITES

Sports

Empowering Women in Sports
http://www.feminist.org/sports

http://www.girlpower.gov/
http://www.girlsinc.org/
http://www.nedic.ca/

Gender Comparisons: Social Behavior, Personality, Communication, and Cognition

Gender-Related Social Behaviors and Personality Traits
Aggression
Prosocial Behavior
Influenceability
Emotionality
Moral Reasoning

Communication Style
Verbal Communication
Nonverbal Communication

Gender Comparison of Cognitive Abilities
Verbal Ability
Visual-Spatial Ability
Mathematics Ability

In high school, I once struggled with some concepts in my advanced algebra class. My teacher did not help me much. He kept telling me not to worry about it; that I would not be using algebra in my future. I excelled in that class, and kept taking math courses, which surprised him. (Nathalie, 22-year-old college senior)

Gender-Related Social Behaviors and Personality Traits

In Chapter 2, we examined numerous gender stereotypes. How accurately do these stereotypes reflect actual differences in the social behaviors, personality characteristics, communication style, and cognitive abilities of females and males? In this chapter, we review all four of these areas. As we shall see, some stereotypes have at least a grain (or more) of truth to them, whereas others are not supported by the evidence. Two cautionary notes: First, even when gender differences are found, they are typically small. Second, there is considerable overlap in the characteristics of females and males (Barnett & Rivers, 2004; Halpern, 2004a). For example, girls are generally more nurturant toward younger children than boys are, but some boys show greater nurturance than some girls.

Aggression

She talks about you.
You talk about her.
She glares at you.
You stare at her.
Is it a rumor, or is it the truth?
She lies to you, you lie right back.
You need a friend, but for sure not her.
She takes your guy.
You want him back.
Too much stress, too much pressure.
But I guess this is life.
(Kelsey, 12 years old)

Few gender differences in aggression are noted in the infancy and toddler years, although by age 2, boys show higher levels of toy grabbing and other negative behavior (Campbell et al., 2002). By the time children begin to interact with each other during the preschool period, however, the differences become striking (Hay et al., 2004; NICHD, 2004). Boys are more physically aggressive than girls and this difference increases into adulthood (Archer, 2004; Bongers et al., 2004; Frieze, 2005; Pepler et al., 2004; Rutter, 2003). The differences hold across socioeconomic groups and across cultures (Archer, 2004; Hines, 2004a). Girls, however, are more likely than boys to use **relational aggression,** which involves *harming others through nonphysical hurtful manipulation of their peer relationships.* For example, girls might exclude a peer from their play group, or spread malicious rumors and gossip about her, as illustrated in Kelsey's poem in the beginning of this section and in the 2004 movie *Mean Girls* (Harmon, 2004). Girls are also more likely than boys to be victims of relational aggression (Cummings & Leschied, 2002; French et al., 2002). This gender difference in how children display aggression is so striking that even preschool children are aware of it (Giles & Heyman, 2005).

Interestingly, although aggression is typically associated with rejection by peers, girls who use relational aggression tend to be both popular and powerful within their peer group (Cillessen & Mayeux, 2004; Rose et al., 2004). What might account for this unexpected finding? According to Suzanna Rose and her colleagues (Rose et al., 2004), strategic use of relational aggression may serve to maintain social dominance as well as to display superiority.

Both biological and environmental influences may contribute to gender differences in aggression (Brendgen et al., 2005). On the biological side, it has been noted that the gender difference emerges early and appears across most cultures. In addition, the sex hormone testosterone appears to play a role, at least in animal aggression. Research on the relationship between aggressive behavior and testosterone in humans, however, has produced mixed results (Frieze, 2005; Ramirez, 2003). A meta-analysis by Angela Book and her colleagues (Book et al., 2001) yielded a weak, positive correlation between testosterone and aggressive behavior in humans. However this correlation is difficult to interpret, since the causal direction can go either way. That is, increasing testosterone levels can lead to aggression, but it is also the case that acting aggressively (such as winning a wrestling match) leads to a rise in testosterone levels (Frieze, 2005). Jacquelyn White and Robin Kowalski (1994) suggest that studies showing a connection between aggression and testosterone may be unduly emphasized because they are consistent with the stereotype of the aggressive male and the submissive female.

Environmental factors are probably even more important than biological ones in producing gender differences in aggression. For one thing, parents, teachers, and peers are less tolerant of aggressive acting-out behaviors in girls (White, 2001; Zahn-Waxler & Polanichka, 2004). Consequently, girls expect more guilt, more peer and parental disapproval, and fewer material gains for aggression than boys do (Eisenberg et al., 1996). In addition, parents' encouragement of boys' physical play and the use of gender-typical toys such as guns may serve to promote aggression. Furthermore, the rougher, dominance-oriented play of boys' groups may contribute to the maintenance of higher aggression levels in boys (Coie & Dodge, 1998).

Prosocial Behavior

Prosocial behavior is *voluntary behavior intended to benefit someone else.* It includes helping, comforting others, sharing, and cooperating (Eisenberg & Morris, 2004). The stereotype is that females are more nurturant, supportive, and helpful than males. Are they?

Girls are more likely than boys to use relational aggression.

Most studies of children have found no gender differences in prosocial behavior, but when differences are found they favor girls (Eisenberg & Fabes, 1998). For example, toddler girls under the age of 2 years are more likely than boys to comfort someone in distress (Kiang et al., 2004). Girls also help others more than boys

Preschool girls are more likely than preschool boys to comfort someone in distress.

do (Caprara et al., 2001; Eisenberg & Fabes, 1998), but studies have found that the opposite is true for adults. This is partly because studies with adults frequently involve male-oriented situations, such as rescuing strangers, sometimes in potentially dangerous situations (for example, helping to change a tire or picking up a hitchhiker). Women, on the other hand, are more likely to offer psychological assistance and help to friends and family members (Eisenberg & Fabes, 1998; Eisenberg & Morris, 2004; Hamilton, 2001). Unfortunately, this aspect of helpfulness has largely been overlooked by researchers.

Gender differences in helping styles are consistent with stereotyped expectations for males and females. How do the differences arise? In many societies, girls are expected to be more nurturant, kind, and emotionally supportive than boys, and they are rewarded for these behaviors. Boys, meanwhile, are more often rewarded for helping behaviors that involve rescuing, risk taking, and chivalry (Eagly, 1998; Eisenberg & Morris, 2004).

Influenceability

Females tend to be stereotyped as more easily influenced and more conforming than males. Is there any evidence to support this view? Again, the answer depends on several factors, such as the type of measure used and even the gender of the researcher. The two major types of tasks used to measure the ability to influence are persuasion studies and group pressure conformity studies. In **persuasion studies,** *participants indicate their position on a controversial topic. A different position supported by arguments is presented by another individual and the participant's position is again measured.* **Group pressure conformity studies** are similar, except that a *group of people, not just one individual, supports a position discrepant with the participant's.*

Alice Eagly and Linda Carli (1981) performed a meta-analysis on both kinds of studies and found that women were more easily influenced than men. The gender difference was greater for the conformity studies, but all differences were small. Females were influenced more when masculine topics, such as technology or sports, were used. The gender difference was also greater when the researchers were male.

Several factors may account for these findings. For one thing, females are socialized to yield to social influence, while males are trained to do the influencing. Remember also that from an early age, females show more cooperation and less conflict in group settings. Accepting the views of others can be viewed as a mechanism for maintaining social harmony and avoiding conflict. In addition, consistent with our theme that females have less power than males, women are accorded a lower status than men in most societies. Individuals of lower status generally learn to conform to the wishes of higher-status individuals (Eagly et al., 2000).

Emotionality

Females are thought to be more emotional than males: more fearful, anxious, easily upset, and emotionally expressive. Males are viewed as more likely to express anger and pride and to hide or deny their emotions (Dittman, 2003; Plant et al., 2000; Plant et al., 2004). Is there any truth to these stereotypes?

Preschool girls express less anger and more fearfulness than boys. They are also better at labeling emotions and understanding complex emotions such as pride (Bosacki & Moore, 2004). In elementary school, boys start to hide negative emotions such as sadness, while girls begin to hide negative emotions, such as disappointment, that might hurt others' feelings. By adolescence, girls report more sadness, shame, and guilt, whereas boys deny experiencing these feelings. Girls also report experiencing emotions more intensely than boys (Eisenberg et al., 1996; Polce-Lynch et al., 1998). Note that these findings do not answer the question of whether females are actually more emotional than males or whether they simply are more likely to report their feelings.

Another aspect of emotionality is **empathy,** which involves *feeling the same emotion that someone else is feeling.* The stereotype is that women are more empathic than men. Are they in reality? The answer depends on how you measure empathy. When individuals are asked to report how they feel in certain situations (for example, "Does seeing people cry upset you?"), females show more empathy than males (Eisenberg & Morris, 2004; Karniol et al., 1998). However, when individuals' behaviors are observed unobtrusively or when their physiological reactions are measured, no gender differences in empathy are found (Eisenberg et al., 1996). These findings suggest that when people know what is being measured and can control their reactions, they may act in the socially acceptable gender-typical manner.

Socialization seems to be an important factor in the development of differences in emotionality (or in the willingness to report emotions). Parents report being more accepting of fear in girls and anger in boys. Mothers focus more on emotions, particularly sad emotions, when talking to their daughters (Fivush et al., 2000; Gleason & Ely, 2002). In addition, parents put more pressure on sons to control their emotions, while encouraging their daughters to be emotionally expressive (DeAngelis, 2001). Parents emphasize closer emotional relationships with daughters than with sons. As early as preschool, mothers and daughters already are closer emotionally than mothers and sons (Benenson et al., 1998).

A series of studies by Penelope Davis (1999) on adults' memories of childhood events provides an interesting illustration of the apparent social construction of gender differences in emotionality. She found that, in general, females and males did not differ either in the number of memories recalled or in how quickly they recalled them. However, females consistently recalled more childhood memories of events associated with emotion and were faster in accessing these memories. Furthermore, this difference was observed across a wide range of emotions experienced by both the individuals and others.

Moral Reasoning

Are there gender differences in moral reasoning? The question has been hotly debated ever since Lawrence Kohlberg (1985) proposed that males show higher levels of moral reasoning than females. In his research, Kohlberg asked individuals to respond to moral dilemmas. In one dilemma, a druggist refuses to lower the price of an expensive drug that could save the life of a dying woman. Her husband, who cannot afford the drug, then steals it. Was he right or wrong in doing so, and why? Kohlberg reported that males' answers emphasized abstract justice and "law and order," which he believed to be more advanced than the emphasis on caring and concern for others expressed by females. As we saw in Chapter 1, Carol Gilligan (1982, 1993) argued that females' moral reasoning is just as advanced as that of males, but that females speak "in a different voice" that emphasizes personal connections rather than abstract legalities.

Research, however, generally fails to support Kohlberg's and Gilligan's view that there are gender differences in the underlying basis of moral reasoning (Eakin, 2002). For example, a meta-analysis of 113 studies by Sara Jaffee and Janet Hyde (2000) found only slight differences in the care orientation favoring females and in the justice orientation favoring males. In addition, an extensive review by Lawrence Walker (1991) revealed that females score as high as males on Kohlberg's measure of moral reasoning. And, among college students in the United States, women are more concerned with moral issues than are men (Skoe et al., 2002).

Moral reasoning appears to be more dependent on the context of the situation than on the gender of the individual. For example, both women and men are more likely to use a care-based approach when interacting with a friend than with a stranger, or when interacting with a member of their in group as opposed to someone outside their group (Ryan et al., 2004).

Communication Style

> *In short, feminine talk is a lot of polite talk about silly things; whereas masculine talk is a little blunt talk about important things.* (D. Spender, 1979, quoted in Popp et al., 2003)

People believe that men have demanding voices, swear, are straight to the point, forceful, and boastful. Women, on the other hand, are thought to talk a lot, speak politely and emotionally, enunciate clearly, use good grammar, talk about trivia, and gossip (Popp et al., 2003). According to a bestselling book, women and men are so different in their communication styles that it is as if *Men Are from Mars, Women Are from Venus* (Gray, 1992). What does research tell us about differences between the communication styles of females and males?

Verbal Communication

Evidence supports a number of gender differences, and one of these is, indeed, a difference in talkativeness. Interestingly, however, the talking behavior of females and males is the opposite of the stereotype. In many situations studied by researchers, including online discussion groups, males talk more than females, speak more frequently, and for longer periods of time. Furthermore, this gender difference is apparent as early as the preschool years and continues throughout adulthood (Carli & Bukatko, 2000; Gleason & Ely, 2002; Kramarae, 2001).

Given the gender difference in talkativeness, we might expect that males also interrupt others more than females do. Research indicates that gender differences in the number of interruptions depend on the situations and also that women and men have different goals when they interrupt others (Gleason & Ely, 2002). One purpose of an interruption is *to show interest and affirm what the other is saying*—an **affiliative interruption**—for example, by saying "uh-huh." A second reason for interrupting is *to usurp the floor and control the conversation*—an **intrusive interruption.** This might be accomplished by taking over the conversation even though the previous speaker shows no signs of relinquishing the floor. It might not surprise you to learn that females are more likely to engage in affiliative interruption and males, in intrusive interruption (Athenstaedt et al., 2004; Eckert & McConnell-Ginet, 2003; Leman et al., 2005). These differences are consistent with both the social construction of females as other-directed and caring and the gender inequality in power. Affiliative interruptions are one way to express an interest in other people, and females might have learned through their socialization that this was one means of showing concern about and reinforcing others. On the other hand, both intrusive interruptions and talkativeness are associated with the desire to maintain dominance and with the power to do so. More powerful individuals are seen as having the right to dominate the conversation and to usurp the floor. This connection between power and communication behavior is illustrated in a study by Elizabeth Cashdan (1998), who observed female and male college students in group discussions and asked them to rate their housemates on characteristics of power. Her findings showed that the more powerful students were the ones who talked the most.

Gender differences have also been found in conversational style. Consistent with communal and agentic stereotypes, studies show that females use more emotional, polite, soothing and supportive speech while males use more direct, goal-oriented, and abrupt speech (Kramarae, 2001; Leaper, 2004; Leaper & Smith, 2004; Mulac et al., 2001). For example, women are more likely than men to refer to emotions, and use intensive adverbs ("She is *really* friendly"), whereas men tend to use directives ("Think about this") and judgmental adjectives ("Working can be a drag") more than women do. Women also are more apt to use personal pronouns (Brownlow et al., 2003; Pennebaker et al., 2003).

Another gender difference in conversational style is that females use speech that is sometimes referred to as more tentative. Such speech may contain uncertainty verbs (e.g., "It *seems* that the class will be interesting"), hedges (e.g., "*I kind of feel* you should not be too upset about this"), tag questions ("It's hot in here, *don't you think*?"), and disclaimers of expertise ("*I may be wrong, but . . .*") (Carli & Bukatko, 2000; Goldshmidt & Weller, 2000; Mulac, 1998).

One explanation for this gender difference in speech is that females have lower self-esteem than males and, consequently, speak more tentatively (Lakoff, 1990). Another interpretation is that women's tentativeness results not from their uncertainty but from their lower status (Weatherall, 2002). Less powerful individuals are more likely to use more tentative speech, regardless of their own confidence in what they are saying, and, as we have noted throughout this text, women have less power than men. In support of this explanation, research suggests that females use more tentative language in their conversations with men but not in their interactions with other women (Carli & Bukatko, 2000).

Still another perspective on this gender difference in conversational style is that the language features used by women do not reflect tentativeness at all but instead are due to women's communal orientation—their desire to leave open the lines of communication and encourage the participation of others (Weatherall, 2002). Research has found that tag questions in fact serve a variety of functions depending on the situation. For example, in one study (Cameron, in LaFrance, 2001a), both women and men in powerful roles used tag questions to generate talk from other participants. However, women and men in less powerful roles used them to seek reassurance for their opinions. This finding indicates that gender differences in verbal communication depend in part on the situation. For example, conversational style is generally more gender-stereotyped in same-sex groups than in mixed-sex groups (Athenstaedt et al., 2004; Leaper, 2004). In the latter groups, women and men tend to adjust their behaviors to each other. Whatever the explanation for women's greater use of so-called tentative speech, such speech makes people seem less credible, powerful, or persuasive (Brownlow et al.,

2003). Can you think of how this perception might be problematic for women in leadership positions?

Another aspect of conversational style is the way people respond to a friend's troubles. Shari Michaud and Rebecca Warner (1997) found that women were more likely than men to offer sympathy in response to a friend's problems, whereas men were more likely to change the subject. In addition, women were more likely than men to appreciate receiving advice or sympathy, whereas men were more likely to resent it. On the other hand, recent research by Erina MacGeorge and her colleagues (MacGeorge et al., 2004) found only slight differences in the way women and men responded. Both sexes preferred to listen, sympathize, and give thoughtful advice. Men were only slightly more likely to give advice, and women were slightly more likely to provide support. Similarly, both women and men appreciated advice that was relevant to their problems and was given in a respectful, kind manner. MacGeorge and her colleagues concluded that women and men do not come from two different communication cultures but are instead from the same "planet." Do Get Involved 5.1 to see whether your findings support the view of Tannen or MacGeorge.

Like Erina MacGeorge, Anthony Mulac (1998) argues that gender differences in communication style are subtle, and that it is difficult to identify the gender of speakers simply from their words. Mulac and his colleagues performed several studies in which college students were asked to determine the gender of a communicator after reading a written communication, such as a transcription of a speech from a public speaking class or an essay describing landscape photos. In none of these situations were respondents able to guess accurately the gender of the communicator. Mulac concluded that, "spoken and written language used in everyday communication by women and men, as well as girls and boys, displays a high degree of similarity" (p. 131).

Similar to conversational style, the actual content of females' and males' conversations, at least with their same-gender friends, is characterized by both gender similarities and differences. In an attempt to learn what young adult women and men talk about with their friends, Ruth Anne Clark (1998) asked college students to list all the topics discussed in a recent conversation with a same-gender close friend and to indicate the dominant topic. Not surprisingly, given the importance of romantic relationships to young adults, both females and males talked about the other gender. However, women's conversations more than men's were dominated by interpersonal issues. Whereas 64 percent of the women reported that other people (both male and female) were the dominant topic of their conversations, this was true for only 40 percent of the men. Furthermore, 36 percent of the men said that sports and other leisure activities were their primary focus. Another difference in content was the type of discussion about other people, with women more likely than men to discuss the nature of their relationships or problems in these relationships. Despite these gender differences, it is important to keep in mind that this study was done with college students and tells us little about the topics of interest to older women and men or to girls and boys.

GET INVOLVED **5.1**

"Troubles Talk": Effects of Gender on Communication Styles

Give the following two-part survey to two female and two male traditional-aged college students.

PART I. Imagine your friend is upset because of having one of the PROBLEMS listed below. For each problem, indicate how likely you would be to make each of the listed RESPONSES.

PROBLEM A: Your friend says "I'm upset because I may be breaking up with my dating partner." What do you do?

| Offer sympathy | very unlikely | 1 | 2 | 3 | 4 | 5 | very likely |
| Change the subject | very unlikely | 1 | 2 | 3 | 4 | 5 | very likely |

PROBLEM B: Your friend says "I'm upset because I may fail a course." What do you do?

| Offer sympathy | very unlikely | 1 | 2 | 3 | 4 | 5 | very likely |
| Change the subject | very unlikely | 1 | 2 | 3 | 4 | 5 | very likely |

PART II: Now imagine that *you* have each of the problems cited above. Indicate how you FEEL when your friend makes the indicated RESPONSES.

PROBLEM A: You tell your friend "I'm upset because I may be breaking up with my dating partner." Your friend offers SYMPATHY. How much do you feel the following?

| Grateful | not at all | 1 | 2 | 3 | 4 | a lot |
| Resentful | not at all | 1 | 2 | 3 | 4 | a lot |

PROBLEM B: You tell your friend "I'm upset because I may fail a course." Your friend gives ADVICE on solving the problem. How much do you feel the following?

| Grateful | not at all | 1 | 2 | 3 | 4 | a lot |
| Resentful | not at all | 1 | 2 | 3 | 4 | a lot |

Source: Adapted from Michaud & Warner (1997).

What Does It Mean?

For Part I, compare the scores of your female and male respondents on the "sympathy" scale of the two problems. Do the same for the "change the subject" scale. For Part II, compare the female and male respondents in terms of how grateful or resentful they are for receiving sympathy (Problem A), and how grateful or resentful they are for receiving advice (Problem B).

1. Did you find the same results as Michaud and Warner (1997) for Parts I and II of the survey? If not, give reasons.
2. As described in the chapter, Deborah Tannen theorizes that women and men come from two different cultures of communication, whereas Erina MacGeorge disagrees. Do your findings support the view of Tannen or MacGeorge? Explain.

3. Your data, like those of Michaud and Warner (1997), were collected from traditional-aged college students. Do you think that middle-aged women and men would respond differently? (You would, of course, have to make the problems age-appropriate by, for example, substituting "spouse" for "dating partner," and "get a poor job performance evaluation" instead of "fail a course.") Explain your answer.

Nonverbal Communication

Consistent with the communal stereotype, people believe that females are more likely than males to engage in nonverbal behaviors that demonstrate interpersonal interest and warmth. Are these beliefs accurate? Considerable evidence shows that they are. For one thing, girls and women are more likely than boys and men to engage in mutual eye contact with another individual for longer periods of time, particularly if that individual is female (Goldshmidt & Weller, 2000; Hall et al., 2000). This gender difference in gazing behavior is not present at birth but appears as early as 13 weeks of age and continues through adulthood (Leeb & Rejskind, 2004). Females also smile, lean forward more, and approach others more closely (Hall et al., 2000; Hall et al., 2001; LaFrance et al., 2003). Girls and women also are more sensitive to the meanings of nonverbal messages portrayed by others and more accurately interpret their emotions (Brody & Hall, 2000). In addition, research on interpersonal sensitivity indicates that females are better than males at initially getting to know the personality traits, emotional states, and behavioral tendencies of other people. They are also more accurate at recalling the appearance of social targets (Horgan et al., 2004).

One explanation for these gender differences is the differential socialization of females and males, with females receiving greater societal encouragement for being socially concerned (McClure, 2000). Smiling and gazing communicate interest and involvement in another person. In addition, women's ability to accurately decipher other people's emotional states might stem from their greater interest in others and their more extensive experience with emotional communication.

A different explanation of females' superior sensitivity skills lies in their subordinate status within society. In order to adapt best socially—to know how to respond appropriately and to structure their own action—less powerful individuals must be good interpreters of the nonverbal cues of more powerful people (LaFrance, 2001a). They must be able to anticipate the reactions of those with power. In other words, the ability to decipher the nonverbal behavior of others might serve as a protective mechanism that guides the interpersonal relationships of all lower-status individuals, including women.

Touch is another form of nonverbal communication. Nancy Henley (1995) proposed a framework for understanding gender differences in tactile communication. She contended that there is an unwritten societal rule that high-status individuals can touch low-status individuals, but those of low status cannot touch those of high status. For example, it is more likely that the president of a corporation will pat a janitor on the back than the reverse. Based on this assumption, Henley asserted that because males in North America have a greater degree of power than females, there is more male-to-female touching than the reverse. Despite the logic of this perspective, research on gender differences in touching has provided mixed findings, with no overall gender differences in touching (Hall, 1996).

Of course, tactile communication can vary widely—from hugs that show affection, to inappropriate sexual touching that is harassing, to formal handshakes that communicate respect. Given the complexity of the types of touch and the nature of relationships in which touching can take place, it is not surprising that researchers have failed to observe any overall gender differences in touching (Hall, 1996). One investigation, however, suggests an interesting relationship among gender, status, and touching. Judith Hall (1996) trained college students to unobtrusively observe and record touching behavior that occurred among professionals attending either a psychology or a philosophy convention. Her results indicated no overall tendency for one gender to touch the other gender more nor for more touching to be initiated by higher-status professionals (based on factors such as the prestige of their university or the academic rank of the individual) than by lower-status professionals. However, when the toucher and recipient were of similar status, males were more likely to touch females than vice versa. Hall suggested that when individuals are similar in professional status, gender serves as a status cue that can dictate rules about touching. Obviously, gender and status differences in touching are more complex than were originally believed. Additional variables, such as age and type of relationship, also can affect who touches whom (Hall & Veccia, 1992).

Gender Comparison of Cognitive Abilities

Research into questions about sex differences and similarities in intelligence is fraught with political minefields and emotional rhetoric from all ends of the political spectrum. But research is the only way we can distinguish between those stereotypes that have some basis in fact and those that don't. (Diane Halpern, president-elect of the American Psychological Association, cited in Kersting, 2003a)

Although females and males do not differ in general intelligence, they do vary in certain cognitive skills. Some differences emerge in childhood while others do not appear until adolescence (Halpern, 2004a; Hines, 2004a). No doubt some of these differences have a bearing on the career choices made by females and males. Remember our cautionary notes from the beginning of this chapter. Gender differences, where they exist, are generally small. Females and males are much more alike in cognitive abilities than they are different. Even when there is a small *average* difference favoring one gender on a test of a particular cognitive skill, many individuals of the other gender will score well above the average. Also, recall from Chapter 1 that the presence of a gender difference does not tell us anything about the *causes* of the difference. Finally, keep in mind that cognitive skills, like the social behaviors and personality traits we discussed earlier in this chapter, develop within a social context. As we shall see throughout this section of the chapter, attitudes and expectations about the cognitive performance of females and males play an important role in socially constructing that performance.

Verbal Ability

Verbal abilities include a variety of language skills such as vocabulary, reading comprehension, writing, spelling, grammar, and word fluency. Females show superior performance on most verbal tasks, although the differences are small (Halpern, 2001, 2004a; Hyde & Kling, 2001). Gender differences in verbal ability appear earlier than other cognitive gender differences. Girls are more vocal than boys during infancy, talk at an earlier age, produce longer utterances, have larger vocabularies, and are more fluent (Halpern, 2001; Karass et al., 2002; Leaper & Smith, 2004; Tamis-LeMonda et al., 2004). They also are less likely to have developmental delays involving language (Sices et al., 2004).

Girls continue to show an edge in verbal skills throughout the grade school years (Feingold, 1993; Halpern, 2001; Leventhal & Brooks-Gunn, 2004). They achieve higher scores on tests of reading comprehension and are less likely to display reading problems such as reading disability (dyslexia) and reading below grade level (Rutter et al., 2004; U.S. Department of Education, 2004). In adolescence, girls continue to outperform boys in reading, writing, and speech production (Halpern, 2004a; Programme for International Student Assessment, 2004; U.S. Department of Education, 2004).

Some researchers have suggested that gender differences in verbal skills and other cognitive abilities are becoming smaller (Feingold, 1988; Hyde & Linn, 1988). More recent reviews, however, have concluded that these differences are not diminishing and have remained relatively stable for decades (Nowell & Hedges, 1998; Voyer et al., 1995).

What might account for the greater verbal ability of girls? In Chapter 4, we saw that parents vocalize more to their infant daughters than to their infant sons. This may lead to increased vocalization by female infants which may in turn encourage parents to talk even more to their young daughters. Girls' early advantage with language may lead them to rely more on verbal approaches in their interactions with others, further enhancing their verbal ability (Halpern, 2000).

Parental expectations also may play a role in girls' superior verbal skills. Studies in Finland, Japan, Taiwan, and the United States find that as early as first grade, children and their mothers generally believe that girls are better than boys at reading (Lummis & Stevenson, 1990; Räty et al., 2002). In addition, girls whose mothers think that girls are better readers receive higher scores on reading comprehension and vocabulary than girls whose mothers think girls and boys read equally well.

Visual-Spatial Ability

Visual-spatial ability refers to skill in visualizing objects or shapes and in mentally rotating and manipulating them. Visual-spatial skills are used extensively in engineering, architecture, and navigation, and in everyday activities such as doing jigsaw puzzles or reading maps.

Types of Visual-Spatial Ability. Gender differences in visual-spatial ability are larger and more consistent than in other cognitive skills, with males outperforming females (Halpern, 2004a; Voyer et al., 2000). The pattern of differences, however, depends on the spatial ability being measured. For example, females do better than males on remembering the location of various objects (Cherney & Ryalls, 1999). Three separate facets of visual-spatial ability have been identified by Marcia Linn and Anne Petersen (1985). Tasks used to measure these three components are shown in Figure 5.1.

a. **Mental Rotation**
Choose the responses that show the standard in a different orientation.

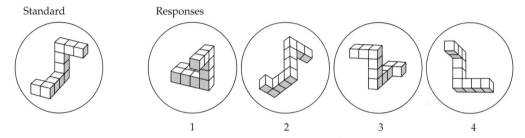

b. **Spatial Perception**
Pick the tilted bottle that has a horizontal water line.

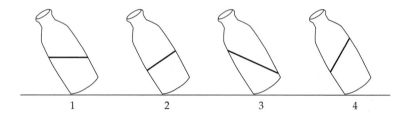

c. **Spatial Visualization**
Find the figure embedded in the complex shape below.

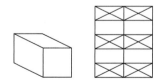

FIGURE 5.1 Types of spatial tasks. Large sex differences favoring males appear on mental rotation, and males also do better than females on spatial perception. In contrast, sex differences on spatial visualization are weak or nonexistent.

Source: M. C. Linn and A. C. Peterson, "Emergence and Characterization of Sex Differences in Spacial Ability: A Meta-Analysis," *Child Development 56*, 1985. © The Society for Research in Child Development, Inc. Reprinted by permission.

Mental rotation involves *the ability to rapidly manipulate two- or three-dimensional figures* (See Figure 5.1a). Meta-analyses (see Chapter 1) show that the largest gender difference in spatial skills occurs on tests of this ability, with an overall *d* value of 0.60 (Voyer et al., 1995). Boys begin to outperform girls as early as age 4 (Levine et al., 1999), consistently do so by age 9, and the gender difference increases into adolescence and adulthood (Ruble & Martin, 1998; Voyer et al., 1995).

Tests of **spatial perception** involve the *ability to locate the vertical or the horizontal while ignoring distracting information*. For example, individuals may be asked to identify a horizontal water line in a tilted bottle (see Figure 5.1b). Gender differences on spatial perception tests like this are smaller than those found on mental rotation tasks (overall *d* = 0.40) (Voyer et al., 1995; Ruble & Martin, 1998). Boys begin to perform better than girls by age 9 and this difference gets larger during the adolescent and adult years.

Tasks measuring **spatial visualization** include *finding simple shapes hidden within larger, complex shapes* (see Figure 5.1c). Gender differences favoring males are much smaller or absent on these tasks (overall *d* = 0.20) (Voyer et al., 1995).

The size of gender differences on spatial visualization and spatial perception tasks has been decreasing over time (Feingold, 1993; Voyer et al., 1995). Differences on mental rotation tests, however, have remained stable or even increased (Ruble & Martin, 1998; Voyer et al., 1995).

Explanations of Gender Differences.   Several biological and environmental theories have been proposed to account for gender differences in visual-spatial abilities. Biological theories focus on genes, hormones, or the organization of the brain. According to one theory, visual-spatial ability is influenced by sex-linked recessive genes on the X chromosome. Research does not support this view, however (Halpern, 2000).

Another biological theory is that sex hormone levels affect visual-spatial skills in either of two ways (Halpern, 2000; Hines, 2004b). One possibility is that hormones circulating in the bloodstream might directly affect visual-spatial performance (Hampson & Moffat, 2004). Studies have shown that women with higher testosterone levels achieve better spatial scores than women with lower testosterone levels, whereas the reverse is true in men (Moffat & Hampson, 1996). Keeping in mind that women's testosterone levels, on average, are lower than those of men, these findings suggest that the optimal level of testosterone for certain spatial skills is in the low male range (Hampson & Moffat, 2004). Other research, however, finds that actively circulating sex hormones do not affect spatial performance in adolescent girls and boys (Liben et al., 2002).

Another possibility is that prenatal sex hormones might irreversibly organize the brain to enhance certain spatial functions. Evidence for this view comes from studies of girls with congenital adrenal hyperplasia (CAH) (see Chapter 3) which exposes them to high levels of prenatal androgens. At birth, the hormone imbalance is corrected and they are raised as girls. Some studies find that CAH girls display better visual-spatial skills than unaffected girls, but others do not (Berenbaum,

2000; Liben et al., 2002). Some psychologists (e.g., Hines, 2004a), however, point out that parents' awareness of the possible masculinizing effects of androgens may influence their treatment of and expectations for their daughters.

Some theorists have attributed gender differences in visual-spatial skills to differences in the lateralization of female and male brains. **Lateralization** refers to the *specialization of the cerebral hemispheres of the brain to perform different cognitive functions*. For most of us, the left hemisphere is involved in language and mathematical computation, whereas the right hemisphere is more involved in processing visual and spatial information (Halpern, 2000). Some evidence suggests that male brains may be more completely lateralized or specialized than female brains (Halpern, 2000), but it is not clear that lateralization leads to better performance in visual-spatial or other cognitive skills (Caplan & Caplan, 1999).

Numerous environmental theories have been proposed to explain gender differences in visual-spatial skills. Most of these focus on the impact of cultural gender stereotypes, observational learning, and encouragement of gender-typed activities and interests in shaping the experiences and attitudes of females and males. Participation in spatial activities fosters the development of spatial abilities in both girls and boys (Bjorklund & Brown, 1998; Caldera et al., 1999; Halpern, 2000), yet females engage in fewer spatial activities than males. Why is this? For one thing, gender-stereotyped "boys'" toys, such as blocks, Erector sets, Legos, and model planes and cars, provide more practice with visual-spatial skills than gender-stereotyped "girls'" toys. Boys also are encouraged more than girls to participate in sports, which often involves moving balls and other objects through space (Etaugh & Rathus, 1995). Action video games, which are especially popular with boys, also appear to exercise and develop spatial skills (Huston & Wright, 1998). If experience enhances the development of visual-spatial skills, appropriate training ought to improve these skills. Research indicates that it does, for both females and males (Lawton & Morrin, 1999; Halpern, 2000). Some training procedures have reduced or eliminated gender differences (Casey, cited in Monastersky, 2005; Newcombe, 2002; Vasta et al., 1996; Voyer et al., 2000).

The stereotyping of visual-spatial activities as masculine also influences performance. Studies have found that females and males with more masculine self-concepts perform better on visual-spatial tasks than those with less masculine self-concepts (Halpern, 2000). For example, college men and women who describe themselves as having few stereotypical feminine traits or many stereotypical masculine traits get better scores on visual-spatial tests than students who show the reverse pattern (Signorella & Frieze, 1989). Simply changing the instructions on spatial tests also has a marked effect on the performance of females and males. In one study (Sharps et al., 1993), college students were given one of two sets of instructions before performing a mental rotation task. One set of instructions emphasized that the test measured spatial abilities and that these abilities are involved in mechanical skills, navigation, map reading, and work with tools. The other instructions made no mention of spatial ability or masculine-typed activities. The "spatial" instructions lowered the performance of women, but not men. Under the "nonspatial" instructions, women improved and performed as well as men.

Mathematics Ability

In the most comprehensive review to date of gender differences in mathematics performance, Janet Hyde and her colleagues (Hyde et al., 1990) did a meta-analysis of 100 studies involving more than 3 million individuals. They found a small difference in computation skills favoring girls up to age 15. Girls and boys did equally well at understanding mathematical concepts at all ages. In tests of problem solving, boys began to do better than girls starting at age 15. In studies that sampled from the general population, overall gender differences were smallest, with females showing a slight edge over males. However, in highly select samples (for instance, college students or mathematically precocious youth), differences in mathematics performance were larger and favored males.

Gender differences in mathematics performance have decreased over time (e.g., Feingold, 1993). One striking example is the change in the number of mathematically gifted girls and boys who score 700 on the math section of the SAT exam at age 13. Twenty-five years ago, there were 13 boys for every girl at that high level, achieved by only 1 out of every 10,000 students. Now, the ratio is only 2.8 to 1 (Monasterky, 2005). In addition, gender differences in mathematics performance no longer exist among U.S. elementary school students, although they still are present in high school (Mullis et al., 2004; U.S. Department of Education, 2004). In one large-scale study of college-bound juniors and seniors, boys outperformed girls on standardized tests of mathematics, as well as on tests of physics, chemistry, computer science, and biology (Stumpf & Stanley, 1998). An international study of high school seniors (Bronner, 1998), yielded the same pattern of results for math and sciences in 18 out of 21 countries. Gender differences in science performance are typically greatest in physics, and smallest (or nonexistent) in the life sciences (Martin et al., 2004). The magnitude of the gender difference in mathematics and science is not the same in all cultures, however, as shown in Explore Other Cultures 5.1.

When we shift from scores on standardized tests to grades in mathematics classrooms, a different picture emerges. Girls receive higher grades than boys, a pattern found in a number of countries including the United States and Canada (Kimball, 1998). This female advantage in grades is found even in samples of mathematically precocious youth, where the male advantage on standardized tests is greatest (Benbow & Arjmond, 1990). When female and male college students in the same mathematics courses are compared, females earn the same or higher grades than males who have received higher scores on the mathematics portion of the SAT (Wainer & Steinberg, 1992). (This finding applies to other academic subjects as well. In other words, women receive higher grades in college than their SAT scores would predict [Leonard & Jiang, 1999]. Thus, of the women and men who would receive the *same grades* in college, fewer of the women are admitted because of their lower SAT scores.) Let us now examine more closely some of the factors associated with women's math performance.

EXPLORE OTHER CULTURES **5.1**

Gender Differences in Mathematics Achievement Around the World

Cross-cultural studies have generally found that males outperform females in mathematics and science and have higher mathematics self-efficacy (Halpern, 2004a; Penner, 2003; Martin et al., 2004; Programme for International Student Assessment, 2004). Of particular interest, however, is the finding that the size of the gender difference varies with the status of women in the countries studied (Riegle-Crumb, 2000, cited in Penner, 2003). One key factor appears to be the role of women in the workforce. According to Riegle-Crumb, female students are aware of the opportunities available to them, which then influences the amount of effort they invest in their education. The greater the percentage of women in a nation's labor force and the more opportunities they have to enter high-status occupations, the more positive are girls' attitudes toward math, and the smaller is the gender gap in mathematics test scores (Baker, & Jones, 1993). Even though much has been written about the gender gap in math in the United States, the gap is larger in East Asian countries such as Japan and Taiwan, with their greater emphasis on traditional gender roles (Evans et al., 2002). One particularly interesting finding is that East Asian girls, although they lag behind boys in their own countries, still score higher in math than boys of many other nations, including the United States (Evan et al., 2002). In Iceland, girls contradict the gender stereotype completely, habitually outperforming Icelandic boys on all parts of their national math exams (Angier & Chang, 2005). These results suggest the powerful role of culture in the social construction of math performance.

Factors Associated with Math Performance.   The single best predictor of scores on mathematics achievement tests is the number of mathematics courses an individual has taken. But starting in adolescence, girls are less likely than boys to take advanced mathematics courses, even when they show superior mathability (Catsambis, 1999; AAUW, 1998a). A synthesis of 1,000 studies by the AAUW (1998a) reports both good news and bad news. The good news is that since 1992, high school girls' enrollment in math and science courses has increased. Moreover, they are reducing the gender gap in scores on standardized tests of computer science (Stumpf & Stanley, 1998). The bad news is that girls are still less likely than boys to take advanced mathematics, chemistry, and physics before they graduate. Girls also take fewer computer science and computer design courses (AAUW, 1998a; Adelman, 1999; Clewell & Campbell, 2002).

In college, many women avoid choosing math and science courses and careers even when they are gifted in mathematics (Ashcraft, 2002; Halpern, 2000). This is troubling, since mathematics is a critical factor in career development, paving the way to high-status and high-salary careers in the sciences, medicine, engineering, and business (Ayalon, 2003). Why, then, do many girls begin to avoid math and science in high school and college?

One important clue is found in the attitudes and feelings that girls and boys develop toward mathematics. Nancy Betz and Gail Hackett (1997) have developed the concept of **mathematics self-efficacy** to refer to *a person's beliefs concerning her or his ability to successfully perform mathematical tasks*. Numerous studies around the world show that males have greater mathematics self-efficacy than females (Crombie et al., 2005; Kurman, 2004; Nosek, Banaji & Greenwald, 2002; Programme for International Student Assessment, 2004). Compared to males, females are more anxious about math and have less confidence in their ability to learn it, despite their equal or superior performance on tests and in the classroom. This self-perception emerges as early as elementary school, when girls begin to view math and science as part of the male domain (Ashcraft, 2002; Clewell & Campbell, 2002), and it continues into adolescence (Beyer, Riesselman et al., 2002; Beyer, Rynes et al., 2002; Fredricks & Eccles, 2002; Lips, 2004; Vermeer et al., 2000; Wigfield & Eccles, 2002). The more that girls endorse this stereotype, and the lower their self-confidence in math, the less effort they exert in their math classes (Greene et al., 1999), the poorer their math performance (Crombie et al., 2005; Pietsch, Walker, & Chapman, 2003), and the less interest they have in continuing math studies (Crombie et al., 2005; Schmader et al., 2004). Adolescent girls are also less likely than adolescent boys to view mathematics as useful and important for their future careers (Eccles et al., 1999). These negative attitudes have been found in Black, Latina, and White girls (Catsambis, 1999). Keep in mind, however, that many girls and women have positive views about math. For a more detailed look at factors that are associated with womens' perspectives on math, see Learn About the Research 5.1.

Girls receive higher grades than boys in math courses, but lower scores on standardized math tests such as the SAT. Why the discrepancy?

LEARN ABOUT THE RESEARCH 5.1
Factors Linked to Womens' Perspectives on Math

Women's experiences with math and their attitudes toward it differ greatly. Debra Oswald and Richard Harvey (2003) set out to identify college women's differing perspectives and experiences regarding math. They used a technique called the Q-method, which is considered a useful tool for feminist research (Kitzinger, 1999). In the first phase of the Q-method, women are interviewed about their thoughts, experiences, and attitudes regarding a topic, in this case, math. Researchers then select a large number of statements, called Q-sort items, and ask a new group of women to sort the items on scale ranging from *strongly disagree* to *strongly agree*. Finally, participants with shared viewpoints are grouped together. Oswald and Harvey identified three groups of college women who differed in their experiences, attitudes, and awareness of stereotypes about math. Over half the women, labeled the Successfully Encouraged group, had high self-perceived math ability, found math to be personally relevant, and had positive attitudes toward it. They had been encouraged by parents and teachers and were relatively unaware of negative stereotypes. About 20 percent of women were in the Math-

ematically Aversive group. They did not like math, had negative perceptions of their ability, and were somewhat aware of negative stereotypes about women and math. Although not directly discouraged in math, neither were they encouraged to pursue it. Nearly 20 percent of women belong to the Stereotypically Discouraged group, consisting of women who were very aware of negative gender stereotypes regarding math, lacked parental and teacher support, and had negative experiences in math. These women were fairly neutral in their attitudes toward math and in their own math abilities.

This study clearly shows that a number of variables, including self-perceived ability, experience with math, encouragement (or discouragement), and degree of awareness of stereotypes, are key factors linked to women's perspectives about mathematics. The authors were encouraged that their largest group consisted of Successfully Encouraged women. They saw this as a possible indicator that women may become better represented in math-related fields in the future.

What Does It Mean?

1. The Stereotypically Discouraged group was keenly aware of gender stereotypes about math. Do you think these women might be experiencing *stereotype threat*? (See p. 154.) Explain your answer.
2. Do you think the results of this study would have been different if the partici-

pants had been a group of noncollege women? Explain your answer.
3. Into which of the three groups would you place yourself? Explain your answer.

Explanations of Gender Differences.   Several theories have been proposed to account for gender differences in math performance and attitudes. One viewpoint is that genetic, hormonal, and/or structural brain differences underlie gender differences in mathematic ability (Lubinski & Benbow, 1992; Geary, cited in

Monastersky, 2005). Critics have argued that research fails to support this inter-pretation (Halpern, 2000; Kimball, 1995), and the biological approach remains controversial.

Most researchers who study gender differences assert that whatever biolog-ical factors might exist are dwarfed by social forces that steer girls and young women away from mathematics (Monastersky, 2005). For starters, parents and peers give less encouragement and support to girls than to boys for studying math (Clewell and Campbell, 2002). As early as first grade, parents in the United States, Japan, China, Finland, and Great Britain believe that boys are better than girls in mathematics (Furnham et al., 2002; Lummis & Stevenson, 1990; Räty et al., 2002). These beliefs and expectations influence parents' perceptions and behaviors toward their children and also the children's own perceptions and behaviors (Tiedemann, 2000). For example, a series of studies by Jacquelynne Eccles and her colleagues (e.g., Eccles et al., 2000) found that parents with stronger stereotypes about the abilities of girls and boys in math, English, and sports had different expectations of their own daughters' and sons' abilities in these areas. These expectations, in turn, were linked to their children's performance and self-perceptions of competence regardless of their actual ability levels.

How are parents' expectations transmitted to their children? Among other things, parents provide different experiences for their daughters and sons. For example, they are more likely to buy their sons science-related toys (Bleeker, 2003; Fisher-Thompson, 1991) and to enroll them in summer computer camps (D'Amico et al., 1995). (See Learn about the Research 5.2 for a discussion of gender, computers, and video games.) In addition, when parents take their young children to interactive science exhibits at museums, they are more likely to explain the science to their sons than to their daughters (Crowley et al., 2001). Similarly, fathers are more likely to use scientific concepts and vocabulary when explaining a physics task to a son than to a daughter (Tenenbaum & Leaper, 2003).

Children receive the same message in the math and science classroom, as illustrated in Nathalie's comments at the start of the chapter. High school math and science teachers believe boys to be more interested, more confident, and higher achievers in these school subjects than girls (Plucker, 1996). Teachers not only expect boys to do better, but they also overrate male students' capacity to do math (Halpern, 2000; Li, 1999). Since expectations often guide behavior, it is not sur-prising to find that math teachers spend more time instructing, interacting with, and giving feedback to boys than to girls (AAUW, 1992; Jovanovic & Dreves, 1997). Even the president of Harvard University, Lawrence Summers, recently asserted that women may be innately inferior to men in mathematics (Angier & Chang, 2005). These remarks highlight the prejudices women scientists face at every stage of their careers (Kantrowitz, 2005). And who knows how many young women are discouraged by such remarks from pursuing such careers in the first place?

These prejudices provide another explanation for the poorer math perfor-mance of females, namely, the concept of **stereotype threat.** According to this view, developed by Claude Steele and his colleagues, *members of stereotyped groups (for example, women and ethnic minorities) feel threatened in those test situations in which*

LEARN ABOUT THE RESEARCH 5.2
Gender, Computers, and Video Games

Girls and boys both like to play video games, but boys spend more time playing them (DeBell & Chapman, 2004; Subrahmanyam et al., 2001; Wartella, Caplovitz, & Lee, 2004). Over 80 percent of video-game players are male (Hafner, 2004). Why is this? One major reason is the content of video games, many of which have violent themes (Haninger & Thompson, 2004). The few females who appear in the games are often portrayed as "Barbies in sexy combat gear" (Vogt, 1997, p. 6). They are more likely than male characters to be shown partially nude or engaging in sexual behaviors (Beasley & Standley, 2002; Haninger & Thompson, 2004). Feminist critics, such as bell hooks, challenge the notion that video-game portrayals of hypersexualized women as heartless killers represent an advance for women (Marriott, 2003). In fact, presenting women in this negative manner may decrease the attractiveness of many video games for girls and thus their time commitment. Girls and women prefer video games that are less violent, less focused on action and sports themes, more reality based, and that emphasize intellectual challenge, such as classic board games, quiz games, and puzzle games (Hafner, 2004 Wartella et al., 2004). Unfortunately, very little software is designed to appeal to girls or to children of both sexes, although that situation began to change in the mid-1990s (Cassell & Jenkins, 1998; Elrich, 1997). Since 1995, the number of games designed for girls has increased sharply, but girls' games are as stereotyped as those designed for boys, featuring Barbies, makeovers, jewelry, and cooking (Hafner, 1998; Rabasca, 2000; Van Evra, 2004). In 1999, Mattel released the Barbie PC, a pink Barbie-themed computer for girls. But to the dismay of several critics, the Barbie PC comes with just a little more than half of the educational software found on Mattel's companion computer for boys (blue, of course), the Hot Wheels PC. Omitted were programs dealing with logic, human anatomy, and spatial visualization (Headlam, 2000).

The gender gap in video game usage has important implications for girls' experience with computers. Video games often provide a child's introduction to the computer (Subrahmanyam et al., 2001). By the time children enter school, and well into adulthood, males have more positive attitudes toward computers than girls and have greater confidence in their computer skills (AAUW, 2000; Jackson et al., 2001; Van Evra, 2004). Boys are more likely than girls to attend summer computer camps and enrichment programs and to enroll in computer programming courses in high school and college (AAUW, 1998a; Levesque, 2003; Morahan-Martin & Schumacher, 1998; Newman, Cooper, & Ruble, 1995). Although overall computer and Internet use rates for girls and boys are now about the same (DeBell & Chapman, 2004), an AAUW (2000) report reached the troubling conclusion that a new gender gap in technology has developed. Boys are using computers to program, create Web pages, and solve problems, whereas girls' computer use tends to focus on verbal activities such as word processing, sending e-mail, or visiting chat rooms rather than on activities that help them understand technology (DeBell & Chapman, 2004; Stabiner, 2003; Wartella et al., 2004).

How can girls' attitudes toward computing be improved? Video games and educational software should be less gender-biased instead of being constructed around male themes of violence and adventure (Sheldon, 2004). Girls perform better on educational software when less masculine-typed themes are used (Littleton, Light et al., 1993). The AAUW (2000) report also suggests the following:

- Teachers should use computers throughout the curriculum, including areas in which girls excel.

Girls, more than boys, prefer video games that are less violent, less focused on sports, and emphasize intellectual challenge.

- Efforts should be made to combat girls' popular stereotype that computer work is antisocial.

- Computer clubs and summer computer classes for girls should be encouraged.

What Does It Mean?

1. Why are most video games and educational software dominated by themes of violence and adventure?
2. What do you think accounts for gender differences in computer-related attitudes?

3. What can be done to minimize or eliminate these differences?
4. Why are positive attitudes toward computers important in today's society?

---

their performance might confirm to themselves or others the negative stereotypes held about the group's ability to perform. This anxiety can impair performance (Cadinu et al., 2005; Jaffe, 2004; Kersting, 2003b; Steele et al., 2002; Quinn & Spencer, 2001). Picture, for example, two college-bound straight-A high school students, one a girl and one a boy, taking the math portion of the SAT or ACT exam. While both experience frustration and difficulty with some of the problems, she has the additional performance-impairing stress of knowing that her performance may confirm the stereotype of female inferiority in math (Quinn & Spencer, 2001). Stereotype threat theory further predicts that performance suffers only when stereotype threat is activated, but not when it is reduced or removed.

To test this prediction, Claude Steele and his colleagues (Spencer et al., 1999) gave mathematically skilled students two math tests. Before the tests, students were told that in the past, men had done better than women on one test but not the other. On the test in which men supposedly outperformed women (thus activating stereotype threat), the women did worse than the men. But on the test in which women and men supposedly performed at the same level (thus eliminating the threat), women performed as well as men. Similar results have been found in many academic settings, using various manipulations to either activate or minimize stereotype threat (Davies et al., 2005; Ford et al., 2004; Johns et al., 2005; Keller & Dauenheimer, 2003). The good news is that the pressures associated with negative stereotypes can be overcome by teaching students ways to reduce stereotype threat. For example, Catherine Good and her colleagues (Good et al., 2003) assigned college students to mentor seventh graders in a low-income ethnically diverse school district. Some children were told that intelligence developed over time, and that they could overcome challenges and achieve academic success. Others were given unrelated information about drug use. Girls given the positive message about their academic skills scored higher on a standardized math test than girls given the unrelated message. Similarly, minority and low-income students given the positive academic message did better on a standardized reading test than those in the unrelated message group.

Gender Equity in Science and Math Education.   In the past decade, increasing emphasis has been given to establishing gender equity in the fields of science, mathematics, and engineering education. The National Science Foundation and the AAUW Educational Foundation alone have spent almost $90 million to fund over 400 projects aimed at increasing the participation of girls and women in these fields. The publication *Under the Microscope* (AAUW, 2004) provides an outstanding summary of these efforts. About two-thirds of the funded projects involve extracurricular activities such as field trips and museums; a large number include mentoring activities; and others provide workshops for teachers. Most projects, however, have occurred outside the regular school curriculum, rather than focusing on changing the formal school curriculum and the classroom environment.

What are some things teachers can do to make the math and science classroom more "girl friendly"? Females respond more positively to math and science instruction if it is taught in a cooperative manner, using an applied perspective and a hands-on approach rather than in the traditional competitive manner using a theoretical perspective and a book-learning approach. When the former practices are used, both girls and boys are more likely to continue taking courses in math and science and to consider future careers in these fields (Eccles et al., 1998; Eccles & Roeser, 1999).

SUMMARY

Gender-Related Social Behaviors and Personality Traits

- Girls and boys are more alike than different in their social behaviors and personality traits. Gender differences, when found, are generally small.
- Boys are more physically aggressive than girls, whereas girls are more likely to use relational aggression.
- Girls and boys are similar in prosocial behavior, but the few observed differences favor girls.
- Females are somewhat more easily influenced than males in certain situations.
- Girls are more likely than boys to express their emotions and report feeling empathy. Whether this reflects actual differences in emotionality or in the willingness to report feelings remains an open question.
- Research does not support Kohlberg's and Gilligan's claim of gender differences in the underlying basis of moral reasoning. Both females and males show caring and justice concerns in resolving moral conflicts.

Communication Style

- Gender differences in verbal communication include males' greater talkativeness and intrusive interruptions, and females' greater affiliative interruptions and their use of speech characterized as tentative. When responding to friends' troubles, women are more likely than men to give support and less likely to give advice.
- Both college women and men like to talk to their friends about the other gender. However, women's conversations focus on interpersonal issues more than do men's.

- Females smile and gaze at their conversational partner more than males do. They are also better able to interpret nonverbal messages. These differences might reflect the communal socialization of females. Another possibility is that women's ability to understand others is an adaptive mechanism that stems from their lower societal status.
- Explanations for these gender differences focus on females' interpersonal orientation and the gender imbalance in power.

Gender Comparison of Cognitive Abilities

- Females and males do not differ in general intelligence but show some differences in certain cognitive skills.
- Girls have a slight advantage in verbal skills beginning in infancy. Girls outperform boys in reading, writing, and speech production and are less likely to have reading problems.
- On visual-spatial tests, gender differences favoring boys are greatest in mental rotation, less in spatial perception, and smaller or absent in spatial visualization.
- Girls are better than boys in mathematics computation skills and get better grades in mathematics courses. Boys are better at problem solving starting in midadolescence and perform better on standardized mathematics tests.
- Biological explanations for gender differences in cognitive skills focus on genetics, hormones, and brain structure or organization.
- Environmental explanations include differential socialization of girls and boys by parents and teachers, gender typing of activities as feminine or masculine, gender differences in attitudes toward various cognitive skills, and stereotype threat.

KEY TERMS

relational aggression
prosocial behavior
persuasion studies

group pressure conformity
studies
empathy

affiliative interruption
intrusive interruption
mental rotation

spatial perception   lateralization   stereotype threat
spatial visualization   mathematics self-efficacy

WHAT DO YOU THINK?

1. Why do you think girls are more likely than boys to engage in relational aggression?

2. Adolescent girls report feeling more sadness, shame, and guilt than adolescent boys do. Do you think that females are actually more emotional than males or are simply more likely to report their feelings? Explain your answer.

3. Explanations for gender differences in verbal communication style focus on females' interpersonal orientation and the gender imbalance in power. Which of these explanations do you favor? Explain your answer.

4. What can parents do to maximize girls' potential for learning and liking math?

IF YOU WANT TO LEARN MORE

Canary, D. J., & Dindia, K. (Eds.). (1998). *Sex differences and similarities in communication*. Mahwah, NJ: Erlbaum.

Cooper, J., & Weaver, K. D. (2003). *Gender and computers: Understanding the digital divide*. Mahwah, NJ: Erlbaum.

Halpern, D. F. (2000). *Sex differences in cognitive abilities*. (3rd ed). Mahwah, NJ: Erlbaum.

Howes, E. V. (2002). *Connecting girls and science: Constructivism, feminism, and science education reform*. New York: Teachers College Press.

Margolis, J., & Fisher, A. (2002). *Unlocking the clubhouse: Women in computing*. Cambridge, MA: MIT Press.

Putallaz, M., & Bierman, K. L. (Eds.). (2004). *Aggression, anti-social behavior, and violence among girls*. New York: Guilford.

Shields, S. A. (2002). *Speaking from the heart: Gender and the social meaning of emotion*. Cambridge: Cambridge University Press.

Simmons, R. (2002). *Odd girl out: The hidden culture of aggression in girls*. San Diego, CA: Harcourt.

Underwood, M. K. (2003). *Social aggression among girls*. New York: Guilford.

Van Evra, J. (2004). *Television and child development*. (3rd ed). Mahwah, NJ: Erlbaum.

Xie, Y., & Shauman, K. A. (2003). *Women in science: Career processes and outcomes*. Cambridge, MA: Harvard University Press.

WEBSITES

Association for Women in Mathematics

http://www.awm-math.org/

Girl Tech: Getting Girls Interested in Computers

http://math.rice.edu/~lanius/club/girls.html

Women in Engineering: Programs and Advocates Network

http://wepan.cecs.ucf.edu

CHAPTER

6 Sexuality

I don't want to be forced to take care of a child that I'm not ready for or get an S.T.D . . . As for sex, it'll happen someday, but just not today. (17-year-old female high school senior; in Villarosa, 2003, p. D6)

We didn't have the choice of time when the kids were young. Now we have time during the day. We seldom make love at nighttime. Now we can choose. It might be 10 A.M. or 2 P.M.—whenever we're feeling turned on. (65-year-old woman; in Doress-Worters & Siegal, 1994, p. 85)

Did these opening vignettes surprise you? Both of them run counter to the popular stereotypes of the hormonally driven, sexually active teenager, on the one hand, and the sexually disinterested older woman, on the other. In this chapter, we explore the fascinating diversity of women's sexuality throughout the lifespan, including sexual attitudes, behaviors, problems, and orientations.

Sexuality

We start with a discussion of women's sexual anatomy and sexual response. Then we look at sexual attitudes, behaviors, and problems.

Sexual Anatomy and Sexual Response

External Female Sexual Anatomy. The *external female sexual organs*, collectively called the **vulva,** are shown in Figure 6.1. Women can get a clear view of their own vulva by squatting and looking into a hand mirror. The **mons pubis** (also *mons veneris*, mountain of Venus) is *a pad of fatty tissue covering the pubic bone.* During

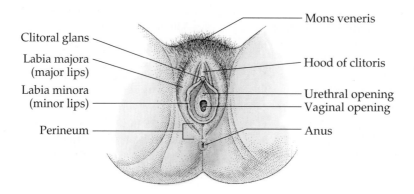

Clitoral glans

Labia majora
(major lips)

Labia minora
(minor lips)

Perineum

Mons veneris

Hood of clitoris

Urethral opening
Vaginal opening

Anus

FIGURE 6.1   Female External Sex Organs

Source: Rathus et al., 2005, p. 69, Fig. 3.5. Reprinted with permission from Allyn & Bacon.

puberty, it becomes covered with coarse hair. The hair continues between the legs and around the anus, the opening of the large intestine. The *fatty hair-covered area between the legs forms flaps called* the **labia majora** (outer lips). They surround *soft hairless flaps of skin*, the **labia minora** (inner lips). Between the inner lips and the anus lies the perineum (Rathus et al., 2005). Spreading the inner lips apart reveals that they join at the upper end to form a fold of skin, or *hood* over the **clitoris.** *This highly sensitive organ, whose only known function is sexual pleasure, consists of erectile tissue that swells during sexual stimulation* (somewhat like the penis). Although smaller than the penis, the clitoris has more than twice as many nerve fibers (Schulman, 2003). Right below the clitoris is the urethral opening, through which urine passes. Below that is the larger vaginal opening. The **vagina** is *the canal leading to the uterus.* The menstrual blood passes through it and it is the birth canal during childbirth (Rathus et al., 2005).

The Sexual Response Cycle.   William Masters and Virginia Johnson (1966) first described the **sexual response cycle,** *the physiological responses of women and men to sexual stimulation from any source* (sexual intercourse, masturbation, etc.). They pointed out that women and men respond similarly during the four phases of the cycle. Here we discuss women's responses.

In the *excitement phase*, a major response is **vasocongestion,** *the swelling of genital tissues with blood.* Vasocongestion produces vaginal lubrication within 30 seconds after stimulation. The clitoris and labia swell with blood. The inner two-thirds of the vagina expand, the uterus elevates, the breasts enlarge, the nipples become erect, and the skin becomes flushed. Heart rate, breathing rate, and muscle tension increase.

During the *plateau phase*, the clitoris, now extremely sensitive, shortens and withdraws under the clitoral hood. *The low third of the vagina becomes engorged with blood, forming* the **orgasmic platform.** Heart rate, blood pressure, and breathing rate continue to rise.

In the *orgasmic phase*, the orgasmic platform, uterus, and anal sphincters contract strongly between 3 and 15 times, at intervals of less than a second. These contractions constitute the orgasm.

During the *resolution* phase, the *body returns to its pre-arousal state* within 15 to 30 minutes. Blood is released from engorged areas, the clitoris, vagina, uterus, and labia return to normal size, and muscle tension dissipates. Heart rate and breathing rate return to pre-arousal levels.

Multiple Orgasms. Alfred Kinsey and his colleagues (Kinsey et al., 1953) reported that 14 percent of the women they interviewed experienced multiple orgasms. However, Masters and Johnson (1966) reported that most women are capable of multiple orgasms. In a more recent survey of over 700 nurses, 48 percent reported reaching multiple orgasms (Darling et al., 1991). Unlike women, few, if any, men are physiologically capable of multiple orgasms. This is one of the major gender differences in sexual response, the other being that men but not women ejaculate during orgasm. While having multiple orgasms can be a good thing, some women now feel that they are sexually inadequate if they don't. One orgasm can be quite satisfying, as can sex that does not culminate in orgasm.

One or Two Kinds of Orgasm? Freud (1938) proposed that there were two types of female orgasm: clitoral and vaginal. Clitoral orgasms were achieved through clitoral stimulation during masturbation. This form of orgasm, practiced by young girls, was considered immature and sexually inadequate in adult women. Women were expected to shift to vaginal orgasms, brought on by sexual intercourse. Masters and Johnson (1966), however, demonstrated that there is only one kind of orgasm, physiologically, whether it is brought on by clitoral or vaginal stimulation. Furthermore, the clitoris is indirectly stimulated even in vaginal intercourse. While orgasms resulting from clitoral and vaginal stimulation are physiologically the same, there may be psychological or subjective differences. For example, the context of sexual intercourse includes a partner to whom one may be emotionally attached, whereas masturbation is often (but not always) done without the presence of a partner.

Sexual Attitudes

The Sexual Double Standard. Historically, women's sexuality was discouraged and denied, especially outside of marriage. The social construction of norms about female and male sexuality is nowhere seen more clearly than in this **sexual double standard,** *which allowed and even encouraged premarital sex for men, but not for women.*

As premarital sex became more acceptable, the double standard has evolved into a belief that casual sexual activity is acceptable for men, but that women's sexual experiences should occur only in the context of a serious relationship (Hyde & Durik, 2000). As one example of the double standard, sexually permissive women are perceived by males as more attractive casual dating partners, but as less acceptable partners for long-term relationships (Oliver & Sedikides, 1992).

Gender Differences in Attitudes.   Women generally have less permissive attitudes toward sexual behavior than men (Kennedy & Gorzalka, 2002). In a review of a large number of studies on sexual attitudes and behavior, Mary Oliver and Janet Hyde (1993) found that women reported much more negative attitudes than men about casual premarital sex. Women were moderately less approving than men of extramarital sex and of premarital sex when couples are committed or engaged. They were somewhat more likely to feel anxious or guilty about sex and to endorse the double standard. No gender differences were found in attitudes toward masturbation, however. In general, gender differences in attitudes toward sexual behavior overall narrowed as people got older. These differences also diminished from the 1960s through the 1990s. According to Letitia Anne Peplau (2002), another consistent gender difference in attitudes is women's tendency to emphasize relationships and commitment as a context for sex. This difference has been widely documented among heterosexuals, lesbians, and gay men.

Attitudes Toward Women with Disabilities.   A common assumption is that women with disabilities are asexual beings who have no sex life and do not want one (Crawford & Ostrove, 2003; Dotson et al., 2003). Many women with disabilities have spoken out about the unavailability of adequate counseling on sexuality, birth control, pregnancy, and childbirth (Asch et al., 2001; Olkin & Pledger, 2003). Women with disabilities are less satisfied with their sex lives than able-bodied women and report that they do not get enough touching in their lives (Mestel, 2000). While able-bodied women often resent being treated as sex objects, some women with disabilities resent being treated as asexual objects (Lisi, 1993). The view of women with disabilities as asexual is based on misconceptions about the sexual desires and abilities of women with disabilities. Most individuals with disabilities have the same sexual desires as able-bodied persons. Their ability to perform sexually depends on their adjustment to the physical limitations of their disability and the availability of a helpful partner (Rathus et al., 2005).

Sexual Behaviors

There is considerable consistency between sexual attitudes and sexual behaviors. Those with more permissive attitudes toward premarital, extramarital, or homosexual relations are more likely to have engaged in those behaviors. For example, 75 percent of women and men who say extramarital relations are not at all wrong have had such relations, whereas only 10 percent of those who believe extramarital relations are always wrong have been unfaithful (Smith, 1994). The consistency between sexual attitudes and behaviors may mean that people act in accordance with their attitudes, but it can also mean that people rationalize their sexual activity by adopting matching attitudes. Both may be involved.

In the National Health and Social Life Survey (NHSLS), the most comprehensive study of sexuality in America in the 1990s, researchers surveyed a representative sample of over 3,400 Americans from ages 18 to 59 (Laumann et al., 1994). They found that the vast majority of married Americans reported having sexual relations either a few times per month or two to three times a week, with an average of seven times a month. The frequency of sexual relations declined gradually with age, with 50- to 59-year-olds reporting an average of four to five times a month. The most sexually active women were those ages 25 to 29, 96 percent of whom reported sexual activity during the past year as compared to 59 percent of the 55- to 59-year-old women. Both women and men expressed fairly high levels of satisfaction with marital sex, although women were slightly less satisifed.

Gender Differences. A number of gender differences in sexual activity have been reported, largely corresponding to gender differences in attitudes toward sexuality. Oliver and Hyde (1993) found that men, compared to women, have a higher incidence of intercourse, more frequent intercourse, a greater number of partners, and a younger age at first intercourse. Interestingly, the largest gender difference was in the incidence of masturbation, even though attitudes toward masturbation were the same. The size of this difference is shown in the NHSLS study which found that 7 percent of women but 28 percent of men reported masturbating at least once a week (Laumann et al., 1994). Also, while the great majority of married individuals reported being faithful to their spouses, more men than women said they had engaged in extramarital sex (Smith, 2002). This gender gap is closing, however. In a nationwide survey in 1991, 10 percent of women reported being unfaithful. This figure jumped to 15 percent in 2002, while the percentage for men remained at 22 percent over the same time period (Ali & Miller, 2004).

Letitia Anne Peplau (2002) sums up these differences as indicating that men are more interested in sex than are women. She also contends that assertiveness and dominance are more closely linked to male sexuality than to female sexuality. For example, she notes that men tend to initiate sex in heterosexual relationships and that men are more likely than women to use intimidation or physical force to get an unwilling partner to engage in sex (see Chapter 14). Another, more controversial, gender difference proposed by Peplau and by Roy Baumeister (2000) is that women have greater sexual plasticity, that is, that their sexual beliefs and behaviors are more capable of being shaped and changed by cultural, social, and situational factors. For example, women are more likely than men to engage in sexual behavior that runs counter to their established pattern of sexual desire, that is, heterosexual women having sex with women and lesbians engaging in sex with men (Diamond, 2003b). Women's sexual attitudes and behaviors also seem to be affected more by their education level and by the views of their culture than are men's attitudes and behaviors (Peplau, 2002).

Although gender differences in sexuality are well documented, we also must keep in mind that there are tremendous variations in sexual expression among women of different ages, marital statuses, educational levels, religions, and races/ethnicities. Women who are younger, White, well educated, and have no religious affiliation have more varied sexual practices than other women. For example, they are more likely to have experienced oral and anal sex and to find these acts appealing (Laumann & Mahay, 2002).

Two limitations of research on sexual attitudes and behaviors must be kept in mind. One is the problem of volunteer bias. Many people refuse to participate in surveys of their sexual views and practices. Thus, samples are biased because they include the responses only of those individuals who are willing to discuss their intimate behavior. Such individuals tend to be more sexually permissive and to have more liberal attitudes toward sexuality than nonvolunteers. Therefore, survey results based on volunteer samples may not be representative of the population at large (Rathus et al., 2005).

A second problem is that all the results are based on self-reports, not on direct observations of behavior. It is possible that there are gender differences in reporting behaviors, but few if any differences in sexual behaviors or attitudes. Women may underreport their sexual experiences and men may exaggerate theirs (Oliver & Hyde, 1993). As a result of these two problems, we must take findings regarding gender differences in sexuality with a grain of salt.

Sexual Problems

What constitutes a sexual problem or dysfunction for women? How frequently do such problems occur? These issues are currently topics of vigorous debate among researchers. The research of Masters and Johnson described earlier in the chapter focused on the physiology of sexual response, culminating in orgasm. Anything interfering with this outcome was defined as a sexual problem. Some psychologists argue that emphasizing orgasm reflects the male perspective that sex ends with ejaculation, whereas for many women, orgasm is not the goal or the most important part of sexual activity (Tolman et al., 2003). In this section, we examine changing views of women's sexual problems.

The University of Chicago Study.   In a frequently cited survey of American adults ages 18 to 59 years by University of Chicago psychologists (Laumann et al., 1999), 43 percent of women and 31 percent of men reported experiencing sexual dysfunction. The researchers employed the widely used system for classifying sexual dysfunction in women and men that appears in the Diagnostic and Statistical Manual of the American Psychiatric Association (1994). Four categories are recognized: sexual desire disorders, sexual arousal disorders, orgasmic disorders, and sexual pain disorders. Feminist scholars have criticized this categorization, as we shall see shortly, because it is overly genital and neglects issues of relationships and social context (Hartley & Tiefer, 2003).

In the study by Laumann and his colleagues, the most frequent sexual problem among women was *a lack of desire for sexual activity*, or **inhibited sexual desire.** About one in four women reported having this problem. (Persons who have little interest in sex, but are not concerned by it, are not considered to have the disorder.) About one in seven women reported **sexual arousal disorder,** which involves *insufficient lubrication or a failure to be aroused*. Most women with the disorder also had problems with desire and/or orgasm as well (Williams & Leiblum, 2002). Nearly one in four women reported **female orgasmic disorder,** defined as *experiencing the excitement phase of the sexual response cycle but not achieving orgasm*. If a woman is satisfied with this situation, she is not considered to have an orgasmic disorder. About 7 percent of women reported **dyspareunia,** or *painful intercourse*. Often a physical condition, such as a vaginal infection, sexually transmitted disease, lack of lubrication, or a structural problem, is involved. Psychological factors such as anxiety about sex or prior sexual trauma also may be responsible (Rathus et al., 2005). Another sexual pain disorder documented by Laumann and his colleagues is **vaginismus,** the *involuntary contraction of vaginal muscles*, making intercourse painful or impossible. Vaginismus is often caused by factors such as childhood sexual abuse, rape, a family upbringing that included negative attitudes toward sex and a history of painful intercourse (Rathus et al., 2005).

The researchers found that factors such as age, marital status, ethnicity, education, and economic status were related to the incidence of sexual dysfunction. For women, the prevalence of sexual problems declined as they got older, except for those who reported trouble lubricating. Men, on the other hand, had more problems with age, such as trouble achieving and maintaining an erection and lack of interest in sex. Single, divorced, separated, and widowed individuals showed an elevated risk of sexual problems. Formerly married women, for example, were more likely than married women to experience sexual anxiety and have trouble reaching orgasm. Ethnicity also was associated with sexual problems. White women were more likely to report sexual pain, while Black women more often experienced low levels of desire and pleasure. Latinas, on the other hand, reported lower rates of sexual problems than other women.

Women and men with less education and lower income reported more sexual problems than more highly educated and affluent individuals. For example, women without high school diplomas were twice as likely as college educated women to experience low desire, problems achieving orgasm, sexual pain, and sexual anxiety. Lower levels of household income were associated with an increase in all categories of sexual dysfunction for women, but only in erectile dysfunction (impotence) for men. What might account for this social class difference in sexual problems? Poorer physical and mental health in individuals of lower social status may be a factor, since diminished health is related to problems with sex (Clayton, 2002; Wenzel et al., 2004). Underlying physical conditions that can cause sexual dysfunction include diabetes, heart disease, neurological disorders, side effects of medications, alcoholism and drug abuse, or heavy smoking. Psychological causes of sexual problems include stress or anxiety from work, concern about poor sexual performance, marital discord, or depression. Some of these problems are all too common in the lives of poor women (Brill, 2004; DeUgarte et al., 2004; Tiefer, 2001). Unfortunately, the sociocultural predictors of sexual problems studied by Laumann and his associates were given little attention in the popular and professional media. Instead, they focused on the high incidence of physiological problems, and the need for drug companies to develop medical treatments, such as female Viagra, to treat women's sexual "illnesses" (Driscoll & Groskop, 2003; Hankin, 2004; Hartley & Tiefer, 2003).

In the years since the University of Chicago study, increasing attention has been focused on sociocultural factors in women's sexual problems. For example, a recent telephone survey of women ages 20–65 who were in a heterosexual relationship found that only 24.4 percent reported "marked distress" about their sexual relationship, their own sexuality, or both (Bancroft et al., 2003). This figure was considerably lower than the 43 percent reported by Laumann and his colleagues. Why the striking difference? One possibility is that the telephone study excluded women who did not have a sexual partner, potentially eliminating women with serious sexual problems. But another reason is that this study focused more on psychological than on physical aspects of sex. The researchers found that the best predictors of a woman's sexual satisfaction were her general emotional well-being and her emotional relationship with her partner. Physical aspects of sexual response in women, such as arousal, vaginal lubrication, and orgasm, were poor predictors.

The New View of Women's Sexual Problems.   Along these same lines, a group of therapists and sex researchers called The Working Group recently developed a new view of women's sexual problems that identifies the sociocultural, political, psychological, social, and relational bases of women's sexual problems (Hartley & Tiefer, 2003; Tolman et al., 2003). They define sexual problems as discontent or dissatisfaction with any emotional, physical, or relational aspect of sexual experiences that may arise in one or more of four interrelated aspects of women's sexual lives (see Table 6.1). The New View focuses on the *prevention* of women's sexual problems through tackling the economic, political, and sociocultural root causes of the problems, and not on medical treatment alone (Hartley & Tiefer, 2003).

TABLE 6.1 Women's Sexual Problems: A New Classification

Sexual problems, defined as discontent or dissatisfaction with any emotional, physical, or relational aspect of sexual experience, may arise in one or more of the following four interrelated aspects of women's sexual lives.

I. Sexual Problems Due to Sociocultural, Political, or Economic Factors

A. Ignorance or anxiety due to inadequate sex education, lack of access to health services, or other social constraints:
   1. Lack of vocabulary to describe physical or subjective experience.
   2. Lack of information about sexual biology and life-stage changes.
   3. Lack of information about how gender roles influence men's and women's sexual expectations, beliefs, and behaviors.
   4. Inadequate access to information and services that could provide contraception and abortion, sexually transmitted disease (STD) prevention and treatment, sexual trauma and domestic violence.
B. Sexual avoidance or distress due to perceived inability to meet cultural norms regarding correct or ideal sexuality, including:
   1. Anxiety or shame about one's body, sexual attractiveness, or sexual responses.
   2. Confusion or shame about one's sexual orientation or identity, or about sexual fantasies and desires.
C. Inhibitions due to conflict between the sexual norms of one's subculture or culture of origin and those of the dominant culture.
D. Lack of interest, fatigue, or lack of time due to family and work obligations.

II. Sexual Problems Relating to Partner and Relationship

A. Inhibition, avoidance, or distress arising from betrayal, dislike, or fear of partner, partner's abuse or couple's unequal power, or arising from partner's negative patterns of communication.
B. Discrepancies in desire for sexual activity or in preferences for various sexual activites.
C. Ignorance or inhibition about communicating preferences or initiating, pacing, or shaping sexual activities.
D. Loss of sexual interest and reciprocity as a result of conflicts over commonplace issues such as money, schedules, or relatives, or resulting from traumatic experiences, such as infertility or the death of a child.
E. Inhibitions in arousal or spontaneity due to partner's health status or sexual problems.

III. Sexual Problems Due to Psychological Factors

A. Sexual aversion, mistrust, or inhibition of sexual pleasure due to:
   1. Past experiences of physical, sexual, or emotional abuse.
   2. General personality problems with attachment, rejection, cooperation, or entitlement.
   3. Depression or anxiety.

B. Sexual inhibition due to fear of sexual acts or of their possible consequences, such as pain during intercourse, pregnancy, sexually transmitted disease, loss of partner, loss of reputation.

IV. Sexual Problems Due to Medical Factors

A. Pain or lack of physical response during sexual activity despite a supportive and safe interpersonal situation, adequate sexual knowledge, and positive sexual attitudes. Such problems can arise from:
   1. Numerous local or systemic medical conditions affecting neurological, neurovascular, circulatory, endocrine, or other systems of the body.
   2. Pregnancy, sexually transmitted diseases, or other sex-related conditions.
   3. Side effects of many drugs, medications, or medical treatments.
   4. A medical treatment or diagnostic procedure, such as a hysterectomy or other necessary procedure.

Source: The Working Group on a New View of Women's Sexual Problems. (See Hartley & Tiefer, 2003.)

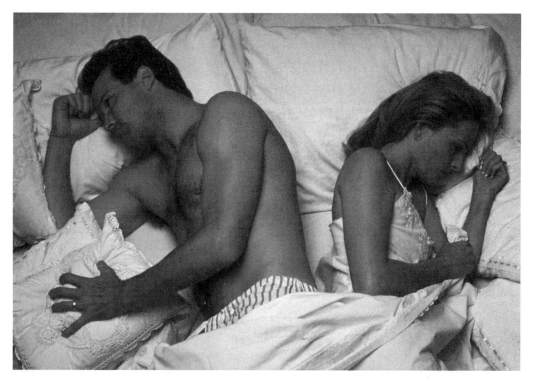

Women's sexual problems may stem from sociocultural, psychological, and relational factors, as well as medical conditions.

Lesbians and Bisexual Women

Before reading this section, try the exercise in Get Involved 6.1. Compare your findings with the information that follows.

Sexual orientation refers to an individual's pattern of sexual and emotional arousal toward other persons (Frankowski, 2004). A **lesbian** is a women who is *emotionally and sexually attracted to other women*, a **gay male** is *attracted to other men*, and a **bisexual** person is *attracted to both men and women* (Frankowski, 2004). It is difficult to estimate the number of women who are lesbian and bisexual because negative attitudes toward homosexuality discourage some individuals from reporting this behavior. In addition, the sexual identities of sexual-minority women may change over time. In the National Health and Social Life survey mentioned earlier, 2 percent of American women *identified* themselves as having a lesbian sexual orientation; 2 to 4 percent reported *engaging in sexual behavior* with women in the past five years; and 8 to 12 percent reported some *sexual attraction* to other women, but no sexual ineraction since age 15. About 1 percent of women reported having a bisexual identity, and 1.4 percent reporting having both female and male partners

---

GET INVOLVED **6.1**

Attitudes Towards Lesbians

Ask two female and two male friends to complete the following exercise:
Our society views some groups of unmarried women as having higher social status or acceptability than other groups of unmarried women. Give each group below a Social Status

Score based on how you think these groups are viewed in our society. Assign each group a score ranging from 1 to 100, with *high* scores indicating *high* status and *low* scores indicating *low* status.

Social Status Score

divorced heterosexual women	_____
never-married homosexual women	_____
widowed heterosexual women	_____
never-married heterosexual women	_____

What Does It Mean?

1. In what ways are your female and male respondents' answers alike? In what ways are they different? Explain the differences and similarities.

2. How does the social status of lesbians compare to that of the three groups of heterosexual women?

3. How would you account for the differences in social status of these four groups of women?

Source: Etaugh & Fulton (1995).

(Laumann et al., 1994). However, a two-year longitudinal study of lesbian and bisexual women found that half of the participants had changed sexual-minority identities more than once in their lives and one-third had done so over a two-year period (Diamond, 2000). In addition, the comprehensive National Longitudinal Study of Adolescent Health found a great deal of fluidity in romantic attractions and relationships over an 18-month period. For example, of the 4 percent of girls who reported bisexual attraction at the beginning of the study, only one-fourth did so 18 months later; the majority of them now reported attraction to and relationships with males (Russell & Seif, 2002).

Bisexual Women

Because most people view sexual orientation as consisting of two categories—heterosexual and homosexual—bisexual individuals tend to be either invisible (Macalister, 2003) or viewed as merely going through a transitional stage between heterosexuality and homosexuality (Rust, 2001a). Women who claim to be bisexual are often told that they are denying their true sexuality, and bisexuality sometimes is seen as a cop-out from commitment to a particular lifestyle or partner (Rust, 2000). Furthermore, bisexuality is often criticized by both heterosexuals and homosexuals as indicating promiscuity, indecisiveness, or immaturity (Morgan, 2002; Mulik & Wright, 2002). The dilemma faced by a bisexual woman was expressed this way:

> *Invisibility is a problem. Few people know we exist because we don't "fit" into either the heterosexual or the lesbian world. When we are open, both worlds judge us.* (Boston Women's Health Book Collective, 1992, p. 214)

One of Claire's students described the following experience in her journal:

> *If I hear "The lesbian's dating a boy?!" one more time . . . So I met a boy and we've started dating, not a big deal to me but obviously to others. My main issue here is pigeon-holing. "I thought you were supposed to be gay," as if I have become a caricature of a human.* (Angelique, age 22)

However, recent research shows that some women and men feel attracted to both sexes simultaneously and may carry on relationships with both men and women at the same time (Reinhardt, 2002). National surveys have found that among women, bisexual attractions are much more common than exclusive attractions to women (4.1 percent versus 0.3 percent), and many bisexuals are more attracted to one gender than the other (Rust 2001b).

Attitudes Towards Lesbians

Heterosexism is *the view that heterosexuality is the norm and that homosexuality is abnormal.* This view often leads to **homophobia,** *negative reactions to homosexuality and irrational fear of homosexuals.* Such reactions are pervasive not only in American society (Harper et al., 2004; Whitley, 2001a), but also in many other parts of the world (see Explore Other Cultures 6.1). In a 2002 survey of American adults,

EXPLORE OTHER CULTURES 6.1
Lesbianism around the World

Lesbians and gay men are discriminated against in varying degrees by laws and social policies around the world. Same-gender sexual behavior still is illegal in more than 70 countries, including many African and predominantly Muslim nations. In these countries, homosexuality may be punishable with prison sentences (for example in Bermuda, Nigeria, and Romania), beatings (India and Pakistan), and death (Iran, Kuwait, and Saudi Arabia) (Ellis, 2002; Kitzinger & Coyle, 2002). Even where homosexuality is not illegal, lesbians and gays often do not "come out" for fear of losing their children, jobs, and social status, or becoming the target of physical or verbal attack (Burn, 2000; Whelehan, 2001).

While Americans have become more accepting of homosexuality in the past few decades, they are less tolerant than citizens of most other advanced democracies in Europe and North America. In France, Britain, Italy, Germany, Czech Republic, and Canada, 75 percent or more believe society should accept homosexuality. Americans, by comparison, are evenly divided on this issue, similar to the views in Latin American countries.

Lesbianism was acceptable in a number of Native American cultures before Western colonization. For instance, women from the Mohave, Maricopa, Cocopa, Klamath, and Kaska tribes could marry other women and make love with other women without stigma (Whelehan, 2001). However, contemporary attitudes of Native Americans, which have been influenced by the dominant American culture, may be less accepting (Amaro et. al., 2002). In the African country of Lesotho, it is not unusual for women to have romantic relationships with each other before and even during heterosexual marriage (Kendall, 1998). However, these relationships occur less often in Lesotho women exposed to Western ideas.

Lesbian experiences vary not only among countries, but also within them. San Francisco, for example, has an active lesbian community, but in most places in the United States, lesbians remain closeted. In countries such as Estonia, where it is acceptable for women to be unmarried or publicly close and affectionate, lesbians are more readily tolerated. Similarly, Thai culture allows two women to live together for extended periods of time, hold hands, hug in public, sleep in the same bed, and even raise a child together, without assuming the relationship is sexual. This makes it possible for lesbians to live together as long as they keep the sexual aspect of their relationship hidden (Burn, 2000).

---

for example, 53 percent felt that sex between adults of the same sex is always wrong, although on a positive note, this was down from 74 percent 15 years earlier (Pew Research Center, 2003). A recent survey of nearly 300,000 first-year college students found that 30 percent believed there should be laws banning homosexual relationships. Interestingly, 38 percent of male students but only 23 percent of females endorsed this statement ("This Year's Freshmen," 2005). A 2003 poll found that, by about a 2-to-1 margin, Americans oppose gay marriage (Pew Research Center, 2003). This view is especially strong among males, Republicans, people with a high degree of religious commitment, older individuals, and those with less education. Another poll found that nearly half of Americans

Lesbian relationships are more accepted in Europe and Canada than in the United States.

opposed adoption rights for lesbian and gay couples. On the other hand, about 75 percent felt homosexuals should have equal rights in employment and housing and supported health insurance and inheritance rights for gay spouses (Kaiser Family Foundation, 2001). Similar attitudes exist in the United Kingdom (Ellis, 2002). Those who believe that individuals cannot change their homosexuality are more sympathetic toward homosexual issues than those who see it as a choice (Leland & Miller, 1998). For a look at a number of factors that influence attitudes toward lesbians and gay men, turn to Learn about the Research 6.1.

LEARN ABOUT THE RESEARCH 6.1

Who Is Homophobic?

Although negative attitudes toward lesbians and gays are prevalent in American society, the degree of homophobia varies markedly from one individual to another and some people are not homophobic at all. Homophobic attitudes are more likely to be found among individuals who are older, less well educated, politically conservative, and from the Midwest, South, and rural areas. Those who hold traditional gender-role attitudes, fundamentalist religious beliefs, and authoritarian right-wing views also have more negative attitudes toward lesbians and gays (Pew Research Center, 2003; Whitley, 2002). Men are more homophobic than women (remember the study of the first-year college students?), particularly toward gay men (Anderson, 2004). Gender differences in attitudes toward lesbians are generally small or absent (Herek, 2000).

What Does It Mean?

1. Individuals with traditional gender role attitudes are also more likely to have negative attitudes toward gays and lesbians. Propose a possible connection between these two sets of attitudes.

2. Why do you think men are more homophobic than women?

3. What steps can be taken by individuals and communities to ensure more equal treatment of lesbians and gays?

Women of Color. People of color hold somewhat more negative attitudes toward homosexuality than do Whites (Whitley, 2001b). Thus, according to Ruth Hall and Beverly Greene (2002), lesbian women of color are in triple jeopardy. They face societal barriers of sexism, racism, and homophobia. In ethnic minority cultures, women who do not adhere to traditional gender roles or who are not subordinate to men are often ostracized. Lesbian members of these communities may be more reluctant to "come out," choosing to remain invisible rather than be rejected (Cole & Guy-Sheftall, 2003; Parks et al., 2004).

Discrimination. Discrimination against lesbians can take many forms. The most virulent form of homophobia is expressed in violent "hate crimes" committed primarily against gay males, mostly by groups of adolescent or young adult males (Federal Bureau of Investigation, 2002; Herek et al., 2002; Mason, 2002). The most frequent forms of harassment experienced by gay and lesbian youth in school are being called names and being ridiculed in front of others (Rivers, 2002). One survey of community college students by Karen Franklin (1998) found that nearly one-quarter admitted to verbally harassing people they thought were gay or lesbian. Among men, 18 percent said they had physically assaulted or threatened to assault gays or lesbians. In a nationwide survey of more than 2,200 lesbians, gays, and bisexuals, three-quarters of the sample reported having experienced prejudice and discrimination based on their sexual orientation. About 75 percent had been verbally attacked and one-third had been the target of physical violence against their person or property (Kaiser Family Foundation, 2001). Similarly, an analysis of seven adolescent health surveys in Canada and the United States found that sexual minority youth were at greater risk for sexual and physical abuse than their heterosexual peers. Up to two in five lesbian and bisexual girls and one in three gay and bisexual boys reported abuse (Saewyc et al., 2004). Even at colleges with strong support groups for gay, lesbian, bisexual, and transgender students, more than one-third of these students say they have been harassed within the previous year, primarily by other students (Rankin, 2003).

Home may not be a safe haven either. Lesbian, gay, and bisexual teens and adults who "come out"—that is, declare their sexual orientation to others—may be rejected by their families. In some cases, they are compelled to leave home and seek survival in the streets (Frankowski, 2004; Markowe, 2002; Rivers, 2002; Savin-Williams & Ream, 2003; Rostosky et al., 2004). Such experiences, not surprisingly, can lead to a reluctance to reveal one's sexual orientation (Rankin, 2003) and to increased levels of emotional stress and psychological problems among harassed individuals (Bailey, 2004; Bolch & Murdock, 2003; Thompson & Johnston, 2004). We shall explore some of these problems more fully in Chapter 13. Despite the stresses faced by many lesbian, gay, and bisexual youth, the good news is that most display strength and resiliency and are often involved in antihomophobia advocacy efforts (Holmes & Cahill, 2004).

Although some states have laws that ban discrimination on the basis of sexual orientation in employment, credit, housing, and public accommodation, many do not. Only one-quarter of employers offer domestic partner health benefits ("Gays Win," 2003). Same-sex marriage is specifically banned in most states; as of this writing it is legal only in Massachusetts, although Vermont and Connecticut give same-sex couples spousal rights (Belluck, 2004; "Partnership Rights," 2004). The Netherlands, Spain, Belgium, and Canada allow same-sex marriages, and Great Britain and the Scandinavian countries permit same-sex couples to register as partners (Garrow, 2004; Hoge, 2002; Lyall, 2005; McLean, 2005). Four states in the United States do not allow lesbian or gay individuals to adopt their partner's child. Only nine states have laws granting this right, which was recently endorsed by the American Academy of Pediatrics. Most other states leave the decision to the courts (Belluck & Liptak, 2004; Thomas, 2003).

Explanations of Sexual Orientation

The origins of homosexuality are complex and controversial (Peplau & Garnets, 2000). A number of psychological and biological theories have been proposed. According to Sigmund Freud (1925/1989), all individuals are initially bisexual. The mother is the original love object for both girls and boys. In heterosexual development, the father becomes the girl's love object, and she substitutes other males for him as she gets older. When the mother remains the love object, lesbian development occurs. Little evidence exists in support of this theory, however. From a learning theory point of view, early positive sexual activity with members of one's own gender or negative sexual experiences with members of the other gender could lead to homosexuality. However, many lesbians and gay males are aware of their sexual orientation before they have engaged in any sexual activity (Carver et al., 2004).

Biological theories focus on genetic or hormonal factors. In one study, 48 percent of identical twin sisters of lesbians were also lesbians, compared with just 16 percent of fraternal twin sisters, and 6 percent of adopted sisters (Bailey et al., 1993). So, sexual orientation appears to be at least partly genetic. But if genetics were the whole story, 100 percent of the identical twin sisters would be lesbian.

Is sexual orientation influenced by sex hormones? In adulthood, there is no link between levels of female and male sex hormones and sexual orientation (Veniegas & Conley, 2000). *Prenatal* sex hormones may be a factor, however. Studies of intersexuality discussed in Chapter 3 pointed to the prenatal influence of androgen on the development of females' sexual orientation. For example, the inner ears of lesbians function more like the inner ears of men than those of heterosexual women (McFadden, 2002). Similarly, finger-length patterns of some groups of lesbians resemble those of men more than those of heterosexual women (Brown et al., 2002; Williams et al., 2000). These findings suggest that high levels of androgens (male sex hormones) during the prenatal period may partially masculinize certain physiological and anatomical characteristics of lesbians, including the brain structures responsible for sexual orientation (Lalumiére et al., 2000; Rahman et al., 2003).

Most likely, complex interactions among genetic, hormonal, and environmental factors determine sexual orientation, and different causal mechanisms may operate for different individuals (Rivers, 2002).

Sexual Activity During Adolescence

Why does it seem that all boys want is sex? (Brenda, age 14)

What happens when I have a boyfriend who wants to have sex and I don't? (Ruth, age 13)

Why is it that when a guy has sex with a girl, he is called a "stud," but the girl is considered a "slut"? (Veronica, age 13; all in Zager & Rubenstein, 2002)

A recent nationwide survey of girls ages 11 to 17 by the American Association of University Women (AAUW) found that sex and pregnancy are the number one issues facing teenage girls today (Haag, 1999). As early as age 12, girls reported being pressured to have sex. This pressure comes not just from boys but also from their girlfriends and the media. Let's take a closer look at sexual activity during adolescence. We'll discuss teenage pregnancy in Chapter 7.

Frequency of Sexual Activity

Most adolescents begin having sexual intercourse in their mid- to late teens. Males become sexually active at younger ages than females and Black female teens typically become sexually active before other female teens (Grunbaum et al., 2004). In addition, adolescent boys, compared to girls, have more sex (including same-sex behavior) and have more sex partners (Savin-Williams & Diamond, 2004). Rates of teenage sexuality reached near-record highs in the late 1980s, but have declined since the early 1990s. For example, the percentage of high school girls who had intercourse decreased from 51 percent in 1991 to 43 percent in 2001 (Centers for Disease Control, 2002c). The decline has been most noticeable among Black females and among males of all ethnicities (Risman & Schwartz, 2002). Efforts to educate young people about safe sex and about the risks of pregnancy and sexually transmitted infections such as AIDS have played a key role in reducing these numbers (Bernstein, 2004; Villarosa, 2003).

Many college students have casual sexual encounters ("hook-ups"), often following alcohol consumption.

Among both female and male college students and young adults, an increasingly common form of sexual activity is the **hook-up,** a *one-time casual unplanned sexual encounter that can range anywhere from kissing to intercourse* (McGinn, 2004; Williams, 2005). Elizabeth Paul and her colleagues (e.g., Paul & Hayes, 2002), for example, found that nearly 80 percent of the students they surveyed had hooked up, usually after consuming alcohol. On average, students had hooked up with 11 different partners during their college years.

Another trend in teenage sexuality involves using the Internet to interact with others (Denizel-Lewis, 2004). The term **cybersex** has several meanings but is often defined as a *social interaction between at least two persons who exchange computer messages for purposes of sexual arousal and satisfaction* (Döring, 2000). There are two feminist views of cybersex, quite different from each other. The victimization perspective focuses on how women and girls as individuals and as a group are harmed by online harassment and virtual rape. In contrast, the liberation perspective argues that cybersex benefits girls and women by allowing them to explore their sexuality freely and more safely (Döring, 2000). Which view do you agree with, and why?

Factors Associated with Sexual Activity

Many factors affect the onset of sexual activity and the risk of becoming pregnant or causing a pregnancy. These include the effects of puberty, family, and peers, as well as individual characteristics. Hormone levels do not predict the onset of sexual behavior in girls, but the observable level of pubertal development—whether they look mature to peers—does (Savin-Williams & Diamond, 2004). One likely reason for this is that the development of breasts, curves, and other secondary sex characteristics may attract sexual attention from males (Zabin & Cardona, 2002).

A recent survey (National Campaign to Prevent Teen Pregnancy, 2003) found that parents are the biggest influence on teenagers' decisions about whether to have sex and friends are next. Parents, however, underestimate their own influence and believe that teenagers' friends play a more important role. Unfortunately, only half of older teen women and just over a third of men this age say that they talked with a parent about birth control before they turned 18 (U.S. Department of Health and Human Services, 2004a).

Teenagers who delay the onset of sexual activity are close to their parents and communicate well with them (Fisher, 2004; Hutchinson et al., 2003; Parera & Suris, 2004; Roche et al., 2005). Their parents are more likely to be married, better educated, have a higher income level, and use firm, consistent discipline (Abma et al., 2004; McNeeley et al., 2002; Zabin & Cardona, 2002). Teenagers who begin sexual activity at a later age are also more apt to be religious, have higher grades in school, be socially mature, have low levels of alcohol and drug use, and, for girls, participate in sports (Bachanas et al., 2002; McCree et al., 2003; Santelli et al., 2003; Rostosky et al., 2004; Steinman & Zimmerman, 2004; Vesely et al., 2004).

An early onset of sexual activity and increased risk of pregnancy are linked to having sexually active or pregnant siblings and peers, having parents with permissive values about sex and a preference for early marriage, and being in a committed dating relationship (East & Jacobson, 2001; Fisher, 2004; Klein et al., 2003; Miller et al., 2001). Girls who have sexual intercourse at an early age, as well as those who fail to use contraceptives, tend to have low self-esteem and little sense of control over their lives (Spencer et al., 2002; Townsend, 2002; Zabin & Cardona, 2002). Sexual and physical abuse in childhood, which may contribute to these negative feelings about oneself, also increase the likelihood of both early sexual activity and early pregnancy (Elliott et al., 2002; Hillis et al., 2004; Miller et al., 2001; Perkins et al., 1998).

The Double Standard

Despite the relaxing of sexual prohibitions over the past few decades, the double standard of sexuality in our society—acceptable for boys, but not girls—remains alive and well. Parents may be willing to condone sexual experimentation in their sons ("Boys will be boys") but rarely sanction it in their daughters. Girls, more than boys, are encouraged to express their sexuality only within the context of a committed, socially approved relationship (Diamond, 2004). Consequently, it is not surprising to find that adolescent girls are more likely than adolescent boys to consider affection a prerequisite for sexual intimacy (Hyde & Durik, 2000). For example, the recent survey of nearly 300,000 first-year college students discussed earlier found that 60 percent of males, but only 35 percent of females agreed with the statement, "If two people really like each other, it's all right for them to have sex even if they've known each other for only a very short time" ("This Year's Freshman," 2005). In addition, there is a positive correlation between expectations for sexual intercourse and the length of relationship for adolescent boys, but not for girls (Werner-Wilson, 1998). Girls' primary reason for having their first sexual intercourse is affection for their partner, whereas boys' main reason is curiosity (Hyde & Durik, 2000).

Sexual Desire

One rarely studied topic in the realm of adolescent sexuality is the sexual desire of teenage girls. When Deborah Tolman (2002) interviewed urban and suburban high school girls, all reported feelings of powerful sexual desire. At the same time, the girls feared the potential of negative consequences of expressing these desires: pregnancy, sexually transmitted infections (STIs), losing respect and reputation, and limiting educational opportunities. Individual girls resolved these "dilemmas of desire" in different ways. Some suppressed their sexual desires, others avoided situations that could arouse sexual feelings, and still others arranged conditions in which they could safely express desire.

Sexual Activity in Midlife

Sexual activity and satisfaction vary among midlife women just as they do among young women. Women who in their earlier years found sexual expression to be fulfilling typically continue to enjoy sex in their middle years and beyond. Other women, whose sexual desires were not strong earlier, may find that their interest diminishes further during middle age. In this section, we examine the sexuality of women in midlife.

Physical Changes

Most women experience a number of physical changes as they enter menopause, some of which may affect sexual activity (Burgess, 2004; Henig, 2004a; Winterich, 2003). Decline in the production of estrogen is responsible for many of these changes. The vaginal walls become less elastic, thinner, and more easily irritated, causing pain and bleeding during intercourse. Decreases in vaginal lubrication can also lead to painful intercourse. Normal acidic vaginal secretions become less acidic, increasing the likelihood of yeast infections.

Various lubricants and moisturizers can ease vaginal dryness. Paradoxically, one of the best remedies is to have more sex! Sexual activity increases blood flow to the vagina, which makes the tissues fuller, and also triggers lubrication (Morris, 2004). Signs of sexual arousal—clitoral, labial, and breast engorgement and nipple erection—become less intense in midlife, and sexual arousal is slower. Most menopausal women, however, experience little or no change in *subjective* arousal. Although the number and intensity of orgasmic contractions are reduced, few women either notice or complain about these changes. Furthermore, slower arousal time for both women and men may lengthen the time of pleasurable sexual activity (Etaugh & Bridges, 2001).

Patterns of Sexual Activity

While some midlife women report a decline in sexual interest and the capacity for orgasm during these years, others report the opposite pattern (Mansfield et al., 1998; S. Rice, 2001). In one study by Phyllis Mansfield and her colleagues (Mansfield et al., 1998), one-fifth of the women reported an increased desire for nongenital sexual expression such as cuddling, hugging, and kissing. The extent of sexual activity in middle-aged women is strongly influenced by past sexual enjoyment and experience. Years of sexual experience can more than make up for any decrease in physical responsiveness (Rathus et al., 2005). Women who have been sexually responsive during young adulthood are most likely to be sexually active as they get older (Etaugh & Bridges, 2001). In addition, both heterosexual and lesbian women who communicate openly with their partners and make changes in their sexual activities to adapt to menopausal changes are more likely than other women to report active and satisfying sex lives (Winterich, 2003).

Many postmenopausal women find that their sexual interest and pleasure are heightened. What are some possible reasons for this? One is freedom from worries about pregnancy (Leary, 1998). This factor may be especially relevant for older cohorts of women for whom highly effective birth control methods were unavailable during their childbearing years. A second reason is the increase in marital satisfaction which often develops during the postparental ("empty nest") years (Etaugh & Bridges, 2005).

Sexual activity decreases only slightly and gradually for women in their forties and fifties. Greater declines may result from physical or psychological changes, however. Physical causes include various medical conditions, surgery, certain medications, and heavy drinking. Hysterectomy does not impair sexual functioning. In fact, recent research has found that following a hysterectomy, women experience improved sexual function, including greater sexual desire, an increase in orgasms, and a drop in painful intercourse (Hartmann et al., 2004; Roovers et al., 2003). For those women who feel that their ability to enjoy sex after a hysterectomy is diminished, counseling can be helpful. Similarly, mastectomy does not interfere with sexual responsiveness, but a woman may lose her sexual desire or her sense of being desired. Talking with other women who have had a mastectomy often helps. One resource is the American Cancer Society's Reach to Recovery program (American Cancer Society, 1999).

Sexual activity and contentment during middle age are more likely to diminish for individuals who have lost their partners (Henig, 2004a). For example, in one nationally representative study of sexuality in Americans age 45 and over, just over half of those polled, but two-thirds of those with sexual partners, were satisfied with their sex lives (AARP, 1999b). While women in their forties and fifties are nearly as likely as men to have a sexual partner (78 percent compared to 84 percent), the "partner gap" between women and men grows in the later years. Among individuals age 75 and older, 58 percent of men but only 21 percent of women have a partner.

Sexual Activity in Later Life

Before reading this section, try Get Involved 6.2. See how your attitudes and those of friends compare to the information in the chapter.

Sexual activity can be as gratifying in the later years as in the younger years (Butler & Lewis, 2002). Unfortunately, as Get Involved 6.2 demonstrates, there are a number of myths and stereotypes about sexuality in later life. Most of today's older Americans grew up at a time when attitudes toward sexuality were more restrictive than they are today, particularly for women (Leiblum & Sachs, 2002; Mares & Fitzpatrick, 2004). Unlike men, many women were taught that they should not enjoy sex and should not initiate it. This "double standard" of sexuality for women and men mentioned earlier in the chapter exists for adults of all ages. Older women also are subjected to the "double standard" of aging discussed in Chapter 2. Thus, compared to older men, women in their later years are perceived as sexually inactive and sexually unattractive (Tariq & Morley, 2003). In a special issue of the *Journal of Social Issues* devoted entirely to sexuality a few years ago, there was not a single word about the sexuality of older women (Goodchilds, 2000). Many older women themselves are self-conscious about their aging bodies (Henig, 2004a). Men tend to choose younger women or women who look young as their sexual partners and mates (Daniluk, 1998; Rathus et al., 2005). Let us examine older women's sexuality—the benefits of sexual activity in later life,

GET INVOLVED **6.2**

Attitudes Toward Sexuality in Later Life

On a scale from 1 (strongly disagree) to 7 (strongly agree) indicate the extent to which you disagree or agree with each of the following statements. Also, ask three female and three male acquaintances who vary in age to respond to these statements.

1. Older people lose their interest in sex and no longer engage in sexual activity.
2. Changes in hormone levels that occur during and after menopause cause women to find sex unsatisfying and unpleasant.
3. Women who are beyond the childbearing years lose their sexual desire and their sexual desirability.
4. In order to have a full and satisfying sex life, a woman must have a male partner.
5. Older women who still enjoy sex were probably nymphomaniacs when they were younger.
6. Older people with chronic illness or physical disabilities should cease sexual activity completely.

What Does It Mean?

Add up the ratings you gave to these six statements. Do the same for each of your respondents. Note that each statement reflects a myth based on folklore and misconceptions. Therefore, the higher the score, the more the respondent holds unfounded beliefs about sexuality in later life.

1. Are there differences between the views of your female and male respondents? Explain your answer.

2. Are there differences between the views of respondents who vary in age? Explain your answer.
3. Could society's attitudes toward aging and the elderly be related to the persistence of these myths about sexuality in later life? Explain your answer.

Source: Doress-Worters & Siegal (1994); Gibson (1996).

sexual behaviors and the factors affecting them, and enhancement of sexual experience in the later years.

Benefits of Sexual Activity in Later Life

Sexual activity can have physical, psychological, and emotional benefits for the elderly (Burgess, 2004). The physical benefits include improving circulation, maintaining a greater range and motion of joints and limbs in arthritic persons, and controlling weight gain (Butler & Lewis, 2002; Leitner & Leitner, 2004). In one study of adults ranging from 60 to 91 years of age, others reported physical benefits of sex included reducing tension and helping one sleep (Doress-Worters & Siegal, 1994).

Sexual activity among the elderly has psychological and emotional benefits as well. It can improve one's sense of well-being, increase life satisfaction, enhance a women's feeling of femininity and desirability, offer an outlet for emotions, and provide a shared pleasurable experience (Leitner & Leitner, 2004). In the later years, sexual activities other than intercourse—oral sex, manual stimulation, caressing— bring pleasure with or without orgasm (Burgess, 2004; Rathus et al., 2005).

Sexual Behavior of the Elderly

Interest in sexual activity remains fairly high throughout adult life, declining only gradually in the later years (Burgess, 2004). In one study of older women and men, 90 percent of those over age 70 expressed a desire for sexual intimacy at least once a week (Wiley & Bortz, 1996). In a Duke University longitudinal study of adults ages 60 to 94, 50 percent of individuals 80 years and older reported still having sexual desires (Leitner & Leitner, 2004).

Some women find sex more satisfying and their attitudes toward sex more positive and open in later life. In one nationwide survey of Americans over age 60, 70 percent of sexually active women said they were as satisfied, or even more satisfied, with their sex lives than they were in their forties (Leary, 1998). Once grown children have left the nest, couples may experience a "second honeymoon" as marital satisfaction increases (Aubin & Heiman, 2004). (See the second vignette at the beginning of the chapter.)

Some elderly individuals desire to be more sexually active than they are currently. In the Leary (1998) survey mentioned above, nearly 40 percent of older women and men wished they had sex more frequently. One reason for this discrepancy between interest and activity, particularly among women, is the lack of a partner (Kilborn, 2004). For example, in the Duke University study mentioned earlier, 24 percent of the females but only 14 percent of the males had ceased sexual activity. The most common reason given by the females for stopping was lack of a male partner; the most common reason given by men was health. It is probably no coincidence that while the incidence of masturbation peaks in the teenage years for males and then declines, the opposite trend applies to women. The lack of available partners for elderly women is a likely explanation for these findings (Belsky, 1999).

Factors Affecting Sexual Behavior

A number of both physical and psychological factors influence sexual behavior in older women.

Physical Factors.   The physical changes in the reproductive system that begin in midlife (see Chapter 7) become more pronounced in the later years, as estrogen levels continue to decline gradually. Physical changes, illness, chronic disabilities, and medication can affect sexuality in later life (Tariq & Morley, 2003). However, even the most serious conditions should not stop women and men from engaging

Sexual activity can be as gratifying in later life as in the younger years.

in satisfying sexual activity (Butler & Lewis, 2002). Heart disease, especially if one has had a heart attack, leads many older adults to give up sex, fearing it will cause another attack. But the risk of this is low. Most people can resume sexual activity in 12 to 16 weeks. Stroke rarely damages sexual function and it is unlikely that sexual exertion will cause another stroke. Arthritis, the most common chronic disability, causes joint pain that can limit sexual activity (Read, 2004). Surgery and drugs can relieve the pain, but in some cases the medications decrease sexual desire. Exercise, rest, warm baths, and changing the positions or timing of sexual activity can be helpful. Medications such as certain antidepressants and tranquilizers also can reduce a woman's sexual desire. However, a physician can often prescribe a different medication without this side effect.

Psychosocial Factors. A person's attitudes toward sex-related physical changes can interfere with sexual activity more than the actual changes themselves. A major psychosocial constraint is the societal view that sexual desire in the elderly, especially elderly women, is abnormal (McGinn & Skipp, 2002; Read, 2004). As a result, older adults who want to fulfill their sexual desires may feel apprehensive and guilty. In addition, many older women feel unattractive and thus may avoid sexual activity with a partner or decide not to seek a new partner if they become widowed or divorced (Burgess, 2004).

Another constraint for residents of nursing homes is that the attitudes of nursing home staff are often not supportive of sexual behavior. Although more nurses are respecting the wishes of their clients for sexual freedom and privacy (Johnson & Scelfo, 2003), many nursing home administrators feel that sexual activity on the part of residents "causes problems," even if the individuals are married. Even masturbation may be strongly discouraged (Beers & Jones, 2004; Butler & Lewis, 2002; Villarosa, 2002a).

Enhancing Sexuality in Later Life

Sexual activity can be more rewarding for older adults if people come to realize that sexual expression is a normal part of life regardless of age. Sex counseling can help remove inhibitions restricting an older person's sexual behavior. Emphasizing the quality of the sexual relationship rather than performance can make sexual experiences more enjoyable for the elderly (Hillman & Stricker, 1994; Leitner & Leitner, 2004). Elderly people who are in supervised living arrangements need to be given opportunities to have private time together for intimate contact (Butler & Lewis, 2002). Health care professionals should provide information and counseling to the elderly regarding the impact of both normal physical changes and medical conditions on sexual functioning (Richardson & Lazur, 1995).

The many older women who are not in an ongoing physical relationship need to feel it is permissible to express their sexuality in whatever way is comfortable for them, whether it be enjoying their fantasies, engaging in masturbation, using a vibrator, or accepting an asexual lifestyle (Butler & Lewis, 2002; Read, 2004). While some older women are celibate because they lack the opportunity to meet partners, other choose to be celibate but still enjoy sensuous experiences:

> *In Colette's novel,* Break of Day, *I discovered celibacy as a strategy for older women who too often see themselves as stripped of identity without a partner. Colette sees age fifty-five as the end of having lovers, but the beginning of an aloneness that is joyous and drenched in sensuality—particularly for the artist in all of us. It is a great gift to be one's self at last.* (Marilyn Zuckerman, a poet in her sixties, in Doress-Worters & Siegal, 1994, p. 88)

SUMMARY

Sexuality

- The external female organs (vulva) consist of the mons pubis, labia majora, labia minora, and clitoris.
- The four phases of the sexual response cycle are excitement, plateau, orgasm, and resolution.
- Women, unlike men, are capable of multiple orgasms.
- Orgasms resulting from clitoral and vaginal orgasm are physiologically the same.
- The sexual double standard condones casual sexual activity for men, but not for women.

- Women have less permissive attitudes toward sexual behavior than men and emphasize relationships as a context for sex.
- There is considerable consistency between sexual attitudes and sexual behaviors.
- Women are less likely than men to engage in most sexual behaviors and to have extramarital sex.
- The four major types of sexual dysfunction are sexual desire disorders, sexual arousal disorders, orgasm disorders, and sexual pain disorders.

- The New View of women's sexual problems focuses on sociocultural, psychological, and relational factors.

Lesbians and Bisexual Women

- Lesbians and gays are attracted to same-sex persons; bisexuals are attracted to both sexes.
- Sexual identities of some sexual minority individuals change over time.
- Homophobia is pervasive in American society. It is most commonly found in older, less-educated, politically conservative males who hold traditional gender-related attitudes and fundamentalist religious beliefs.
- Complex interactions among genetic, hormonal, and environmental factors appear to determine sexual orientation.

Sexual Activity during Adolescence

- Rates of teenage sexuality have been decreasing.
- The onset of sexual activity is influenced by pubertal development and individual characteristics as well as by family and peers.

Sexual Activity in Midlife

- Postmenopausal physical changes can lead to painful intercourse.
- Some women show a decline in sexual interest and capacity for orgasm, while others show the opposite pattern.

Sexual Activity in Later Life

- Sexual activity can have physical, psychological, and emotional benefits for the elderly.
- Interest in sexual activity remains fairly high throughout adulthood, declining gradually in the later years.
- Sexual interest in the elderly is greater than sexual activity. One reason, especially for women, is lack of a partner.
- Physical changes, illness, disability, and psychosocial factors influence sexual behavior in older women.
- Sexuality may be enhanced through counseling, changes in societal attitudes, and greater opportunities for intimate contact.

KEY TERMS

vulva	orgasmic platform	gay male
mons pubis	sexual double standard	bisexual
labia majora	inhibited sexual desire	heterosexism
labia minora	sexual arousal disorder	homophobia
clitoris	female orgasmic disorder	hook-up
vagina	dyspareunia	cybersex
sexual response cycle	vaginismus	
vasocongestion	lesbian	

WHAT DO YOU THINK?

1. Why do you think women generally have less permissive attitudes toward sexual behavior than men do?

2. Why do you think that our society holds negative attitudes toward gays and lesbians?

3. If you were to design a school-based or community-based sex education program, what would you include?

4. What is your position on programs that provide contraceptives to teenagers?

IF YOU WANT TO LEARN MORE

Atkins, D. (Ed.). (2003). *Bisexual women in the twenty-first century*. Binghamton, NY: Harrington Park Press.

Balsam, K. F. (Ed.). (2004). *Trauma, stress, and resilience among sexual minority women: Rising like the phoenix*. Binghamton, NY: Harrington Park Press.

Butler, R. N., & Lewis, M. I. (2002). *The new love and sex after 60*. New York: Ballantine.

Cramer, E. P. (Eds.). (2003). *Addressing homophobia and heterosexism on college campuses*. Binghamton, NY: Harrington Park Press.

Daniluk, J. C. (1998). *Women's sexuality across the life span: Challenging myths, creating meanings*. New York: Guilford.

Haag, P. (1999). *Voices of a generation: Teenage girls on sex, schools, and self*. Washington, DC: American Association of University Women.

Harvey, J. H., Wenzel, A., & Sprecher, S. (Eds.). (2004). *The handbook of sexuality in close relationships*. Mahwah, NJ: Erlbaum.

Kaschak, E., & Tiefer, L. (Eds.). (2002). *A new view of women's sexual problems*. New York: Haworth.

Rathus, S. A., Nevid, J. S., & Fichner-Rathus, L. (2005). *Human sexuality in a world of diversity*. Boston: Allyn & Bacon.

Rose, T. (2003). *Longing to tell: Black women talk about sexuality and intimacy*. New York: Picador.

Tolman, D. L. (2002). *Dilemmas of desire: Teenage girls talk about sexuality*. Cambridge, MA: Harvard University Press.

Travis, C. B., & White, J. W. (Eds.). (1999). *Sexuality, society, and feminism*. Washington, DC: American Psychological Association.

WEBSITES

Disability

Disabled People's International
http://www.dpi.org

Lesbians

Gay/Lesbian Issues
http://gaylesissues.about.com/culture/gayleissues/

7 Reproductive System and Childbearing

I felt godlike—a miracle worker. It was the best moment of my life. I felt my baby's head, then saw his face—I got to cut his cord and put him to my breast. I felt like I did the impossible. I couldn't believe he was finally out into the light. I felt holy. (Boston Women's Health Book Collective, 1992, p. 447)

Giving birth to a child can be one of the major events of a woman's life. Childbirth typically (although not exclusively) occurs during young adulthood, the years from about 20 to 40. In this chapter, we focus on women's reproductive system functioning throughout the lifespan, including menstruation, contraception, abortion, pregnancy, and childbirth. We conclude with an exploration of reproductive functioning in midlife and beyond, looking at menopause and hormone replacement therapy.

Menstruation

The menstrual cycle involves the release of a mature egg or ovum from its surrounding capsule or follicle. The cycle, which occurs in four phases, averages 28 days in length. (*Menstruation* is derived from the Latin word for *month*.) The menstrual cycle is governed by a feedback loop involving two brain structures— the hypothalamus and the pituitary gland—and the ovaries and uterus (Reame, 2001). In this section we explore the biological, psychological, and cultural aspects of menstruation.

The Menstrual Cycle

In the *follicular* phase of the menstrual cycle, Days 4 to 14, low levels of estrogen and progesterone cause the hypothalamus to stimulate the pituitary gland to secrete follicle-stimulating hormone (FSH). This causes the ovaries to increase estrogen production and bring several follicles and their eggs to maturity. Estrogen stimulates development of the endometrium (uterine lining) in order to receive a fertilized egg. Estrogen also signals the pituitary to stop producing FSH and to start producing luteinizing hormone (LH). The LH suppresses development of all but one follicle and egg.

In the second or *ovulatory* phase, about Day 14, LH levels peaks, causing rupture of the follicle and release of the egg near a fallopian tube. During ovulation, some women experience *mittelschmerz* ("middle pain") on the side of the abdomen where the egg has been released.

During the *luteal* phase, LH stimulates the follicle to form a yellowish group of cells called the *corpus luteum* ("yellow body"), which produces large amounts of progesterone and estrogen. These hormones, which reach their peak around Day 20 or 21 of the cycle, cause the endometrium to secrete nourishing substances in the event an egg is fertilized and implanted in the uterine lining. If fertilization does not occur, high progesterone levels cause the hypothalamus to stop the pituitary's production of LH. This causes decomposition of the corpus luteum and a sharp drop in levels of estrogen and progesterone through Day 28.

The fourth phase, *menstruation* (Days 1 to 4), occurs when the low levels of estrogen and progesterone can no longer maintain the uterine lining, which is shed and exits through the cervix (the lower end of the uterus) and vagina as menstrual flow. The low hormone levels trigger the beginning of another cycle. Should the egg be fertilized, however, the hormone levels remain high and a new cycle does not occur.

Changes in the levels of the ovarian and pituitary hormones over the menstrual cycle are shown in Figure 7.1.

Menstrual Pain

Menstrual pain, or **dysmenorrhea,** includes painful abdominal cramps and lower back pain during menstruation. About 55 to 73 percent of women report experiencing menstrual pain each month (Hourani et al., 2004). Women who report high levels of stress in their lives, who are heavier drinkers, and who have poorer self-perceived health are more likely to experience menstrual pain (Hourani et al., 2004; Wang et al., 2004).

After the mid-twenties, the prevalence of reported pain declines, perhaps because of changes brought about by pregnancy (Parent-Stevens & Burns, 2000). The cause of this discomfort is thought to be **prostaglandins,** *hormonelike chemicals secreted by the uterine lining and other tissues as menstruation approaches.* These substances cause uterine contractions, decreased blood flow, and increased sensitivity to pain, which lead to cramping. Adolescents and women who suffer from

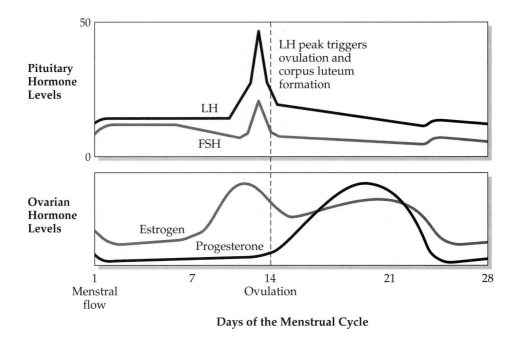

FIGURE 7.1   Changes in hormone levels during the menstrual cycle.

Source: Donatelle & Davis (1998), p. 190. Reprinted with permission from Allyn & Bacon.

severe menstrual pain have unusually high levels of prostaglandins (Golub, 1992). Antiprostaglandin drugs, available both in prescription form and over the counter—such as Motrin, Naprosyn, Anaprox, and Ponstel—help relieve menstrual pain in 80 to 85 percent of women. Aspirin, a mild antiprostaglandin, also is helpful (Chrisler & Johnston-Robledo, 2000; Golub, 1992), as is a low-fat vegetarian vegan diet, which includes grains, legumes, vegetables, and fruits, but no eggs or dairy products (Barnard et al., 2000).

Attitudes toward Menstruation

> *On a recent TV show, the plot involved a man intent on killing a group of female medical students. He wore a T-shirt that read "Don't trust anybody who bleeds for five days and doesn't die." That chilling statement said volumes about a mind-set going back millennia.* (Pam, 49-year-old school teacher)

Throughout history, menstruation has had a "bad press." Menstrual blood has been viewed as having magical and often poisonous powers. Menstruating women have been isolated and forbidden to prepare food or to engage in sexual activity (Kowalski & Chapple, 2000). Menstrual myths and taboos still exist, although in somewhat less extreme form. For example, some adolescent girls and women believe that menstruating women should not exercise, swim, or get a hair permanent (Reame, 2001). In addition, many euphemistic terms are used to avoid the word *menstruation:* "period," "that time of the month," "I've got my friend," "she's on the rag," "the curse," "I'm unwell" (Costos et al., 2002). Have you heard or used other expressions? How many are positive? Many Americans believe that a woman cannot function normally when menstruating, yet there is little evidence that athletic performance, academic performance, problem solving, memory, or creative thinking show meaningful fluctuations over the menstrual cycle (Golub, 1992).

One recent study by Gordon Forbes and his colleagues (Forbes et al., 2003) illustrates that negative attitudes toward the menstruating woman remain strong. College men and women both perceived a menstruating woman, compared to the "average woman," as being more irritable, angry, and sad, and as less energized and less sexy. Men, but not women, also saw her as annoying, unreasonable, "spacey," less nurturing, less reliable and dependable, less creative and intellectually curious, and as more disagreeable and spiteful than other women. Women found some redeeming features in the menstruating woman, viewing her as more maternal, strong, and trustworthy than the average women.

Menstrual Joy

Despite the prevalence of negative attitudes toward menstruation, some women experience their menstrual periods as self-affirming, creative, and pleasurable, and as signifying femininity and fertility (Boston Women's Health Book Collective, 1998; Lee, 2002). Negative expectations about menstruation may influence many women to focus more on its associated unpleasant symptoms. But what would happen if menstruation were portrayed in a more positive light? Researchers in the United States (Chrisler et al., 1994) and in Great Britain (Aubeeluck & Maguire, 2002) studied the effects of presenting positive and negative views on women's reported responses to menstruation. The researchers administered both the Menstrual Joy Questionnaire (MJQ) and the Menstrual Distress Questionnaire (MDQ) to college women (see Get Involved 7.1). The MJQ lists positive feelings that might be experienced before or during menstruation, such as self-confidence, creativity, and power. The MDQ lists negative feelings that might occur at these times, such as irritability, anxiety, and fatigue. The researchers found that women who completed the MJQ before they were given the MDQ reported less menstrual distress and more favorable attitudes toward menstruation than those who received the questionnaires in reverse order. It appears that the way menstruation is portrayed can affect the way women react to their menstrual cycles. Try the questionnaires in Get Involved 7.1 and see whether you find the same results.

Interestingly, the findings that menstruation actually has some positive aspects did not generate a lot of media publicity or subsequent research. According to Margaret Matlin, (2003), this illustrates the **women-as-problem bias,** that is, *psychologists' preference for studying negative aspects of women's lives rather than positive ones.*

During their menstrual periods, some women experience "menstrual joy," a feeling of enhanced creativity and energy.

GET INVOLVED **7.1**

Menstrual Symptoms

Ask six female friends or relatives to complete both parts of the following questionnaire. Give half of them Part I, followed by Part II. Give the other half Part II first, then Part I. The instructions are: *Rate each item on a 6-point scale, using 1 if, shortly before and during your menstrual period, you do not experience the feeling at all; 2, if you experience the feeling slightly; 3, if you experience it moderately; 4, if you experience it quite a bit; and 5, if you experience it intensely.*

Part I Menstrual Joy

Energetic	_____
Affectionate	_____
Cheerful	_____
Creative	_____
Powerful	_____
Self-confident	_____
Active	_____
Sense of well-being	_____

Part II Menstrual Distress

Irritated	_____
Sad	_____
Tense	_____
Moody	_____
Fatigued	_____
Out of control	_____
Anxious	_____
Angry	_____

Add the score for the Menstrual Joy items. Do the same for the Menstrual Distress items.

What Does It Mean?

1. Did individuals who completed the Menstrual Joy items first report less menstrual distress than those who completed the Menstrual Distress items first? If so, why?
2. Why do you think some women have more positive feelings than others before and during their menstrual periods?
3. Why have the negative aspects of menstruation been emphasized much more than the positive aspects?
4. What might be done to focus more on the positive side of menstruation?

Source: Adapted from The Menstrual Joy Questionnaire in J. Delaney, M. J. Lupton, & E. Toth, *The Curse: A Cultural History of Menstruation*, rev. ed. Copyright 1988 by the Board of Trustees of the University of Illinois; based on the Menstrual Distress Questionnaire from Moos (1985).

Premenstrual Syndrome (PMS)

For me, menstrual distress is very real. Every month, the week before my period started, I became a different person. I felt such rage and could not control it. My husband and children suffered verbal and physical abuse for years. I thought I was going insane. In the last 3 years, I have been taking medication and am doing better. I feel like I can take back my life. (Sharah, 35 years old)

For most women, mild to moderate physical and emotional fluctuations are part of the normal menstrual cycle experience. Women may experience breast tenderness, bloating, anxiety, or mood swings that may be annoying but do not disrupt their daily lives (Parent-Stevens & Burns, 2000). A small minority of women, about 3 to 9 percent, experience *symptoms so severe that their normal functioning is impaired for the week of each month preceding menstruation*, as illustrated in Sharah's comments. These women are considered to suffer from **premenstrual syndrome (PMS).** No marked ethnic differences in the prevalence of PMS have been identified (Daw, 2002; Mortola, 2000).

What is PMS?   For years, controversy has swirled around the validity of PMS as a disorder because scientists have not agreed upon its definition. Since 1987, the American Psychiatric Association has included PMS in its diagnostic handbook, labeling it **Premenstrual Dysphoric Disorder (PMDD).** To be diagnosed with PMDD, *a woman must experience multiple symptoms during the week before her menstrual period, including depression, anxiety, mood swings, or anger/irritability. The symptoms must interfere markedly with work or social relationships and must be present only in the premenstrual phase of the cycle* (Grady-Weliky, 2003). Some women physicians feel that the diagnosis of PMDD validates the experiences of a group of women and is thus empowering (Hirshbein, 2003). But other theorists object to treating normal reproductive system functioning in women as a disease. Feminist psychologists such as Joan Chrisler, Paula Caplan, and others believe that PMDD's classification as a psychiatric disorder stigmatizes women as mentally ill, undermines their self-esteem, and feeds into socially constructed stereotypes about women (Cosgrove & Riddle, 2003; Daw, 2002).

For example, a widely held stereotype in North America is that women experience negative moods before their menstrual periods (Chrisler & Johnston-Robledo, 2000). Thus, if a woman feels anxious, sad, irritable, or moody and believes she is in the premenstrual phase of her cycle, she may attribute her feelings to PMS. The role of cultural factors in determining one's reaction to menstruation is further illustrated in a study of Samoan women who were exposed to modern Western culture and subsequently reported increased numbers of menstrual symptoms (Fitzgerald, 1990). Even within the same culture, differences in the life circumstances of individual women may influence their experiences with menstrual symptoms. For example, women who acknowledge high levels of stress related to work, family, or finances report increased severity of PMS (Gallant & Derry, 1995). Biological factors may also be involved. For instance, the brains of women with and without PMS react differently to normal fluctuating levels of estrogen and progesterone (Brody, 1998). It is unclear, however, whether these differences contribute to the development of PMS or result from it.

Treating PMS.   Whether PMS/PMDD is a mental disorder or not, it is important to give help to women who seek it (Daw, 2002). Various treatments for PMS have been tried. While some women report that dietary changes or progesterone supplements provide some relief, these approaches have generally been shown to be ineffective (Grady-Weliky, 2003). Taking daily 1,200-milligram doses of calcium, however, reduces the symptoms of PMS in many women. Vitamin B6 also may provide relief (Daw, 2002). Antidepressants that raise levels of the substance serotonin in the brain—including Prozac, Paxil, and Zoloft—relieve emotional and often physical symptoms in over 70 percent of women with PMS. The anti-anxiety drug Xanax is also effective in more than 70 percent of women with the disorder (Mortola, 2000; Steiner & Born, 2002).

Contraception

The typical American woman marries at age 25 and achieves her desired family size of two children by age 31. She then spends the next 20 years until menopause trying to avoid an unintended pregnancy (Dailard, 2003a). In this section we look at the use of contraception, starting with the teen years.

Contraception in Adolescence

The use of contraceptives, both condoms and long-acting hormonal methods, has increased among sexually active adolescents, especially girls, in recent years, due in part to the growing awareness of the danger of AIDS and other sexually transmitted infections (Santelli et al., 2004). Still, a substantial number of adolescents use contraceptives inconsistently or not at all. About one-fifth of girls ages 15 to 19 and their partners do not use contraceptives the first time they have sexual intercourse (Grunbaum et al., 2004). Many adolescent females wait a year or more after becoming sexually active to seek medical services for contraception. Unfortunately, about half of all adolescent pregnancies occur within 6 months after the onset of sexual activity (American Academy of Pediatrics, 2005).

Many adolescent girls and women resist initiating condom use. There are several reasons for this. Some females do not have enough power and control in their relationship with a male partner to be able to persuade him to wear a condom, particularly if he is reluctant to do so (Gavey & McPhillips, 1999). Also, women may reject condom use because it diminishes their sexual pleasure and disrupts intimacy (Bowleg et al., 2004). For some women, sexual intercourse without condoms may symbolize feelings of trust, commitment, and "true love" in the relationship. For others, taking control of a sexual situation—even if just to introduce a condom—may disrupt their feminine sexual identity and threaten potential rewards they expect in the form of love and protection (Gavey & McPhillips, 1999). Other factors that contribute to lack of contraceptive use in adolescent females include reluctance to acknowledge one's own sexual activity, a sense of invincibility ("*I* won't get pregnant."), and misconceptions regarding use of contraception.

Which individuals are most likely to practice contraception? The older teenagers are when they begin sexual activity, the more likely they are to use contraception. Other factors associated with contraceptive use in high school and college students include being in a committed relationship, having high educational aspirations and achievement, having knowledge about sex and contraception, fearing HIV infection, having good communication and a supportive relationship with parents, discussing contraceptive use with parents and with one's partner, waiting a longer time between the start of a relationship and having sex with that partner, and having high self-esteem and feelings of control over one's life (Sheeran et al., 1999; Manlove et al., 2003; Miller et al., 1998).

Teenagers who attend schools that distribute condoms, compared to teens in schools that don't, are less likely to have ever had sex, or to have had sex recently. Moreover, sexually active youth whose schools give out condoms are twice as likely to use condoms as those who can't get condoms at school (Blake et al., 2003). Unfortunately, however, few high schools in the United States make contraceptives available (Santelli et al., 2003).

Methods of Contraception

The one totally foolproof method of contraception is abstinence. Today, increasing numbers of teenagers are pledging not to have sex before marriage. However, a majority of those who take this virginity pledge do not live up to their vows (Brody, 2004a). Moreover, those teenagers who have taken a virginity pledge are *less* likely to use contraception when they do engage in sexual activity (Bearman, 2004; Manlove et al., 2003).

A wide variety of contraceptive choices are available in addition to abstinence (see Table 7.1). As women's reproductive goals change during their childbearing years, the type of contraception they choose also changes. Birth control pills are most often used by women in their twenties, by unmarried women, and by those with some college education. Tubal ligation is more commonly used by women who are over 34, have previously been married, have less than a high school education, or who are poor. Tubal ligation for women has become far more common than vasectomy has for their male sexual partners (Alan Guttmacher Institute, 2005; National Center for Health Statistics, 2003). Of all these methods, the condom is the only one providing any protection against sexually transmitted infections. In addition to these methods, emergency contraception, or the so-called "morning after pill," is also available. This method, known as Plan B, is typically used when regular contraception ("Plan A") either fails or is skipped. It involves taking high doses of birth control pills within 72 hours after having sex, and then again 12 hours later. This procedure works by delaying ovulation or blocking fertilization of the egg. Currently, Plan B is available only by prescription in the United States ("Birth Control," 2005). The U.S. Food and Drug Administration continues to ban over-the-counter sales of Plan B, even though a few individual states and several Canadian provinces allow it (Donohoe, 2005). Contrary

TABLE 7.1 Effectiveness Rates of Contraceptive Methods

Method	Percent Effectiveness		Disadvantages
	Correct Use	Typical Use	
Birth control pills (combined hormones)	99.9	92.0	Risk of blood clots in smokers over 35
Norplant (implant)	99.9	99.0	Menstrual bleeding
Depo-Provera (injection)	99.7	97.0	Menstrual bleeding
Intrauterine device (placed in uterus)	99.4	99.0	Heavy menstrual flow; cramps; pelvic infections
Diaphragm (cup placed in vagina)	94.0	84.0	Need to insert before intercourse; genital irritation
Cervical cap (cup placed over cervix)	92.0	82.0	Urinary tract infection; high failure rate
Sponge (placed in vagina)	85.0	70.0	Need to insert before intercourse; high failure rate
Spermicide	94.0	71.0	Need to insert before intercourse; genital irritation
Condom (sheath placed over penis)	97.0	85.0	Need to put on before intercourse; may lessen male's sensations; may tear, slip off
Withdrawal (of penis before ejaculation)	96.0	77.0	High failure rate
Rhythm method (fertility awareness)	91.0	75.0	High failure rate
Tubal ligation (cutting and tying fallopian tubes)	99.5	99.3	Slight surgical risk
Vasectomy (cutting and tying sperm-carrying ducts)	99.9	99.8	Slight surgical risk

Source: Adapted from Alan Guttmacher Institute (2004a); Rathus et al. (2005), p. 406, Table 12.1.

to popular belief, providing emergency contraception in advance to teenagers does not result in more unsafe sex practices or in decreased use of condoms or hormonal contraceptives (Gold et al., 2004).

Abortion

Abortion is one of the most commonly performed medical procedures and also one of the most controversial. In the United States, the debate over abortion centers around two opposing views: Abortion as a right and a means for attaining individual freedom and equity for women versus abortion as a threat to morality, the family, and society. These differing attitudes toward abortion in turn stem from different socially constructed beliefs, attitudes, and values about gender roles and female sexuality (Hull & Hoffer, 2001).

The 1973 landmark Supreme Court decision in *Roe* v. *Wade* gave women the legal right to terminate pregnancy by abortion during the first trimester (three months) of pregnancy. It allowed individual states to set conditions for second-trimester abortions and ruled third-trimester abortions illegal except when the mother's life was endangered (Rathus et al., 2005). Since then, a number of restrictions on abortion have been enacted (Donohoe, 2005; Joffe, 2003; Miller, 2004). For example, nearly 90 percent of the states in the United States require parental consent or notification for minors seeking abortion (Adler et al., 2003; Miller, 2004). The United States Congress has barred the use of federal Medicaid funds to pay for abortion except when the mother's life is endangered or in cases of rape or incest. Since poor families rely on Medicaid for health care and few have private health insurance, low-income women now are less able to afford abortion (Borgmann & Weiss, 2003; Donohoe, 2005). Congress also recently banned a specific type of late-term abortion known as dilation and extraction and referred to by critics as "partial birth" abortion ("Frank Talk," 2003).

Nationwide polls conducted 30 years after the *Roe* v. *Wade* ruling have found that public opinion has shifted away from general acceptance of legal abortion toward a more ambivalent acceptance, favoring choice but only under certain conditions (Donohoe, 2005; Joffe, 2003). The proportion of first-year college students believing that abortion should be legal was 54 percent in 2004, a drop of 9 percentage points since 1990 ("This Year's Freshmen," 2005).

Incidence

Over half of pregnancies among American women are unplanned and half of these are terminated by abortion (Alan Guttmacher Institute, 2000). In 2001, over 850,000 women in the United States had abortions (Strauss et al., 2004). Not surprisingly, nearly 90 percent of abortions take place within the first trimester (Strauss et al., 2004). In recent years, the abortion rate has steadily been declining. Teens have shown the most dramatic drop: a 25 percent decrease between 1985 and 2000.

Three-fourths of women obtaining abortions are under 30. Four out of five are unmarried, over half are already mothers, and almost half had a previous abortion. White women account for 54 percent of all abortions, but their abortion *rate* is below that of women of color. Black women are three times as likely as White women to have an abortion (Strauss et al., 2004). Why are abortion rates higher for women of color? Research suggests that they are more likely than White women to become pregnant unwillingly. Cultural pressures may disadvantage minority women in negotiating sexual and contraceptive choices with their male partners (Travis & Compton, 2001).

Methods

The safest and most common method of abortion is **vacuum aspiration,** in which *the contents of the uterus are removed by suction* (David & Lee, 2001). While most American women prefer this surgical procedure, those up to nine weeks pregnant can choose to take certain drugs to induce abortion. Women take mifepristone, the French abortion pill known as RU-486, and 6 to 8 hours later take the drug misoprostol. This procedure, known as a medical abortion, is highly effective when used within the first 49 days of pregnancy (Creinin et al., 2004). Women who choose medical abortion prefer its privacy, naturalness, and avoidance of surgery (Fielding et al., 2002). Currently, more than half of the early abortions in France, Scotland, and Sweden, but only 18 percent in the United States, are done with pills rather than surgically (Finer & Henshaw, 2003; Kolata, 2002a, 2003).

Consequences of Abortion

Abortion is one of the safest medical procedures available. The risk of death from childbirth (1 in 10,000) is about ten times higher than the risk of abortion performed within the first 12 weeks by a health professional (1 in more than 100,000) (David & Lee, 2001; Donohoe, 2005). What about the psychological consequences of abortion? Since abortion is a planned response to an unwanted pregnancy, the woman may experience positive emotions to it, such as feelings of relief or of having made a good decision. On the other hand, negative emotions such as anxiety, regret, or guilt may also arise because of moral and social sanctions against abortion (Bradshaw & Slade, 2003; Travis & Compton, 2001). Brenda Major and her colleagues (Major et al., 1998) found that a woman's reaction to abortion is affected by her particular circumstances, including her coping skills and the degree of social support she has. For example, a woman is more likely to experience postabortion stress if she has little social support from her partner, family, and friends; poorer coping skills; if she blames herself for the pregnancy; and if she has a prior history of depression (Major et al., 2000). The most negative feelings occur *before* the abortion. While some women report mild distress afterward—guilt, anxiety, and regrets—the strongest feeling is one of relief (Adler & Smith, 1998). Research on the long-term psychological aftereffects of abortion has found no link between abortion and subsequent mental health (Donohoe, 2005; Stotland, 2001). When women seek but are *denied* abortions (as was the case in some eastern European countries), their children are more likely than children of mothers who did not seek abortion to feel neglected or rejected, to drop out of school, and to have social problems at work and with friends (David & Lee, 2001).

So far in this chapter, we have focused on the reproductive lives of young women in the United States. For a more global picture, turn to Explore Other Cultures 7.1 and 7.2.

Young Women's Reproductive Lives around the World

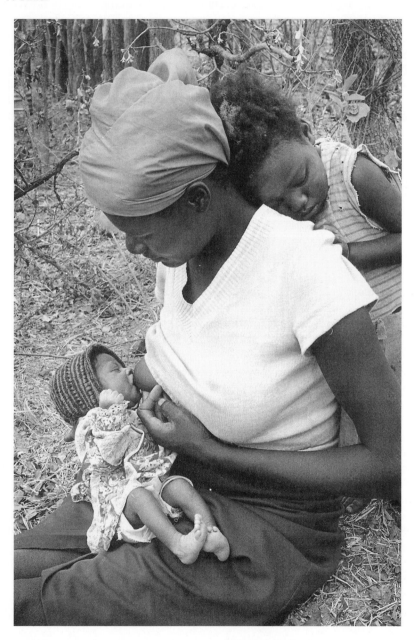

In order for young women throughout the world to best fulfill their future roles as mothers, workers, and leaders, they need improved access to education and to reproductive health services. How are their reproductive health needs currently being met? (We look at education in Chapter 9.) Reports by the Alan Guttmacher Institute (1998, 2002; Singh et al., 2003) gathered information on this question from 49 developing and 6 developed countries around the globe. Here are some of the key findings:

- Up to 60 percent of adolescent births throughout the world are unplanned.
- Contraceptive use by married and unmarried adolescents is greater than in the past, but in most of the world is still low. Among married adolescents, for example, contraceptive use is less than 5 percent in India and Pakistan and under 30 percent in Africa and the Middle East.
- Adolescent childbearing is declining in countries where it had been common, as access to education increases and the advantages of delayed childbearing are recognized. Still, in many parts of the developing world, 40 to 60 percent of women—especially rural adolescents and those with little education—have

their first child before age 20. In the developed world, by contrast, fewer than 1 in 10 have an early first birth.
- Sexually transmitted infections that threaten the lives and health of young women and their newborns are on the rise, particularly in the developing world. For example, in some parts of Africa, nearly 40 percent of pregnant women test positive for HIV (see Chapter 12).
- Sexual relationships that result from force, coercion, and abuse, and cultural practices such as female genital mutilation (see Explore Other Cultures 7.2), and sexual exploitation of young girls and adolescents for commercial gain, endanger the reproductive and mental health of young women.

In most countries, the poorest young women are at greatest risk of poor sexual and reproductive health. A recent study from 12 developing countries in Asia, sub-Saharan Africa, and Latin America found that poor women are more likely than wealthier women to be married and have a child by age 18 and are less likely to use contraceptives, use maternal health services, or know how to protect themselves from HIV (Rani & Lule, 2004).

EXPLORE OTHER CULTURES **7.2**

Female Genital Mutilation

Female genital mutilation (FGM), *the surgical removal of parts of the external female genitalia*, is a major source of reproductive health problems for girls and women in 28 African countries, parts of the Middle East, Malaysia, and Indonesia, and for immigrants of those nations who live in Europe and North America (Kalev, 2004; Lacey, 2004). An estimated 2 million girls and women per year undergo this procedure, usually in early childhood or adolescence. The mildest form of FGM involves removing the clitoris, but usually both the clitoris and labia minora are removed. The most extreme form, known as **infibulation** or pharaonic circumcision, consists of *removing the clitoris, labia minora, and the inner two-thirds of the labia majora, which are then sewn together*. A tiny pencil-sized hole is left for the passage of urine and menstrual flow. The procedure usually is performed by women, often using crude, unsterilized instruments and without anesthesia. Resulting medical problems range from pain and infection through long-term difficulties with urination, menstruation, sexual intercourse, and giving birth (Burney, 2004; Ramsey, 2004).

Why does this practice persist when it is so obviously harmful to women? Girls in these cultures are considered unmarriageable without undergoing FGM. Some people mistakenly believe that the Islamic religion requires it. Others argue that eliminating the source of women's sexual sensations ensures female chastity (Gaines, 2003; Rosenberg, 2004). A 1996 federal law has banned the practice in the United States, and it is condemned by the United Nations and World Health Organization. Women's organizations in Africa are actively involved in efforts to eradicate FGM, which slowly is beginning to lose favor in some African nations (Lacey, 2004; Rosenberg, 2004).

Pregnancy

For much of history, a woman's life was dominated by pregnancy and childbirth. A hundred years ago, death associated with pregnancy and childbirth was a serious threat for women around the globe. In the twentieth century, the risk dropped significantly for women in developed nations, but it continues to pose a major risk for those in developing countries (Maine & Chavkin, 2002; United Nations Population Fund, 2004). For a closer look at this issue, see Explore Other Cultures 7.3.

In the past several decades, the advent of the birth control pill, widespread contraceptive use, and legalized abortion have allowed individuals to plan and control the size of their families (Propp, 2003). The marvels of modern technology make it possible to monitor pregnancy virtually from the moment of conception and render it possible for infertile couples to bear children. In this section, we explore pregnancy, miscarriage, and pregnancy in teenagers.

Pregnancy

Pregnancy begins when an egg and sperm cell unite in the fallopian tube. The fertilized egg begins to divide as it travels toward the uterus, a three- or four-day journey. When it arrives, it implants itself into the thick lining of the uterus. Pregnancy typically lasts 40 weeks and is divided into three trimesters of three months each. A missed menstrual period is often the first indication of pregnancy although simple tests which are available in any drugstore can detect pregnancy within days after conception (Carlson et al., 2004).

Physical Changes.   During pregnancy, the blood volume in the body doubles and the breasts generally increase two bra sizes. The most dramatic change occurs in the uterus, which grows from two ounces to two pounds, not including the placenta or the baby (Curtis & Schuler, 2004; Schulman, 2003). Early signs of pregnancy include breast tenderness, more frequent urination, fatigue and nausea. Nausea and vomiting usually are confined to the first trimester and, despite being called "morning sickness," they can occur anytime during the day (Carlson et al., 2004). Claire and Judith can vouch for the value of eating crackers or toast slowly in the morning before getting up. Ginger and vitamin B6 are also good for reducing nausea (Smith et al., 2004). Food aversions and cravings also may develop (Curtis & Schuler, 2004). For example, Claire couldn't stand coffee or onions, which she normally loved. Many women describe the second trimester as the easiest stage of pregnancy (Carlson et al., 2004). During this phase, most of the nausea and fatigue disappear. By the end of the fifth month, women begin to feel fetal movements ("quickening"). During the third trimester, weight gain and protrusion of the abdomen become quite noticeable. Some of the activities of daily living, such as tying one's shoes, may become a challenge. The expanding uterus exerts increasing pressure on the other internal organs, which may lead to breathlessness, heartburn, and a need for frequent urination (Carlson et al., 2004).

In the past, pregnancy was viewed as an illness, but that is less true today. Most women feel that their pregnancy is a normal and healthy—if somewhat inconvenient—experience. Regular exercise along with good nutrition reduces or eliminates many discomforts (Boston Women's Health Book Collective, 1998). Claire played pool well into her first pregnancy, until her bulging abdomen made it too difficult to bend over the pool table. During her pregnancy with her second child, a summer baby, she swam until the day she gave birth.

EXPLORE OTHER CULTURES **7.3**

Pregnancy-Related Deaths around the World

Women in developed countries rarely die of complications of pregnancy nowadays, but these complications remain the number one cause of death of young women in less-developed parts of the world. For example, the maternal mortality rate is 46 times higher for sub-Saharan Africa than for industrialized nations (920 maternal deaths for every 100,000 live births versus only 20) (United Nations Population Fund, 2004; World Health Organization, 2004). Even within the same geographic area, striking differences exist. Haitian women, for instance, are ten times more likely to die in pregnancy than Dominican women, who live on the same island. And the maternal mortality rate for Russian women is nearly thirteen times higher than that of their Finnish neighbors. Women at greatest risk around the world are those who are poor, live in rural areas, and are members of minority groups. For example, Black women in the United States are four times more likely to die of pregnancy complications than are White women. In Canada, Native women are at greater risk than White women (Maine & Chavkin, 2002). A key factor in these differences in maternal mortality is access to good-quality health care. Black Americans receive poorer health care than White Americans, even when they are of the same socioeconomic status (Saftlas et al., 2000). In developing countries, the low social status of women hampers their access to existing health care services (United Nations Population Fund, 2004; World Health Organization, 2004). Women's lack of power in families and communities gives them little say over decisions that could save their lives

(Murphy, 2003). For example, even where low-cost transportation has been arranged by charitable organizations to increase access to emergency facilities, some husbands refuse to spend scarce resources on their wives, even though they would do so for themselves or their sons (Liljestrand & Gryboski, 2002).

Psychological Changes During Pregnancy.   A woman's feelings during pregnancy vary tremendously depending on such factors as her economic circumstances, her desire to be pregnant, her physical condition, and her childhood experiences (Boston Women's Health Book Collective, 1998; Carlson et al., 2004). At each stage, women sometimes feel positive and sometimes negative. Feelings of being more sensual, potent, creative, and loving may occur. Negative feelings include loss of individuality, worries about whether the baby will be normal, distress at gaining weight and looking awkward, concerns about changes in the couple's relationship, and anxieties about coping with the responsibilities of parenting (Carlson et al., 2004; Ohye et al., 2003; Read, 2004).

Reactions to Pregnant Women.   A pregnant woman elicits a variety of reactions from those around her. Many women have had the experience of having their pregnant abdomen patted by people who would not consider such a gesture with a nonpregnant woman (Bergum, 1997). Research by Hilary Lips (1997) shows that young adults perceive pregnant women as irritable, emotional, and suffering from physical maladies. In addition, surveys show negative attitudes toward and perceptions of pregnant women in the workplace. They may face discrimination in the job interview and are perceived as less competent workers than other women (Bragger et al., 2002; Eastman & Utley, 2004). The discomfort some people feel around pregnant women was made abundantly clear to Claire in the end-of-semester course evaluations filled out by students when she was seven months pregnant. Some made negative comments about her teaching while pregnant; one said "Go home and have your baby." More recently, Claire's daughter-in-law Jen, who worked at a restaurant, told her supervisor that she was pregnant. Over her objections, he promptly reduced her hours (and thus her income) and assigned her to a less desirable shift.

Miscarriage

Miscarriage is the *spontaneous loss of a pregnancy during the first 20 weeks of gestation* (Carlson et al., 2004). At least one in seven known pregnancies results in miscarriage. However, the actual rate may be at least twice that, because a very early pregnancy loss may occur before a woman realizes that she is even pregnant (Springen, 2005).

Most miscarriages are a result of major genetic defects in the embryo or fetus. Others are caused by hormonal imbalances in the mother, structural problems in the uterus or cervix, or diseases of the immune system (Daly, 2005). Following one miscarriage, a woman's chances of having a subsequent normal pregnancy remain quite high. Even after several miscarriages, her chances are still about 60 percent (Carlson et al., 2004).

Until recently, it was assumed that miscarriages were not very stressful to the parents because the embryo or fetus was not yet a "real child." Well-meaning friends and relatives, even to this day, say things such as "It was meant to be" or "You can always have another child." Worse yet, others may say nothing, as though the event had not happened (Leon, 2001). But, in fact, parents start anticipating the birth of their child very early in pregnancy, and so a miscarriage produces grieving and a sense of loss (Daly, 2005; Sanderson, 2004). In addition, women may feel guilty and somehow responsible for the pregnancy loss. They also may feel angry and jealous toward other pregnant women. These feelings may be mingled with anxiety about the possibility of problems occurring in a future pregnancy (Carlson et al., 2004). Women who have been struggling for years with infertility problems, and women who have delayed parenthood into their thirties may be especially devastated when they experience a miscarriage. Fathers grieve too, of course, but their grief typically is of shorter duration and less intense than that of mothers (Leon, 2001).

Listening and responding supportively to the grieving parents can be very helpful (Springen, 2005). Speaking with others who have been through the same experience is often beneficial for the parents. For example, when Claire's daughter Andi miscarried during her first pregnancy at age 39, she found it comforting to talk to her cousin, who had had two consecutive miscarriages before giving birth to a healthy baby.

Teenage Pregnancy

In an AAUW survey of teenage girls, Blacks and Latinas mentioned pregnancy as an issue in their lives more than White and Asian American girls and did so at a younger age. Black and Latina girls described pregnancy as a "choice," which they counseled their peers not to make at an early age. Asian American and White girls described pregnancy as an "accident" and cautioned against the "risks" and "dangers" of sex (Haag, 1999).

Nevertheless, over 800,000 American girls age 15 to 19 become pregnant each year, and most of these pregnancies are unplanned (Alan Guttmacher Institute, 2004b; Dittmann, 2003). As of 2003, Asian American teenagers had the lowest birth rate (1.8 percent), followed by Whites (2.8 percent), Native Americans (5.3 percent), Blacks (6.5 percent), and Latinas (8.2 percent). Since 1991, the birth rate among teenagers has declined, with a bigger decrease among the youngest teenagers (ages 10–14) and an especially big drop among Black adolescents (Hamilton et al., 2004). Among those teens who do have babies, however, the proportion who are unmarried has jumped from 15 percent in 1960 to 89 percent in 2002 (Martin et al., 2003; Downs, 2003). The decrease in teenage births is not a result of abortion, which has declined among teenagers starting in the 1990s. Rather, young people are delaying sex until they are older, having sex less frequently, and using birth control, especially condoms, more often and more responsibly. They are also choosing more effective contraceptive methods, such as long-lasting hormonal implants (Boonstra, 2002; Dailard, 2003b; Ventura et al., 2003). How do pregnancy rates in the United States compare to those in other industrialized nations? For the answer, see Explore Other Cultures 7.4.

Most teenage pregnancies in the United States are unplanned, often with negative consequences for both mother and child.

EXPLORE OTHER CULTURES 7.4

Why Is the Teen Pregnancy Rate So High in the United States?

Despite the decline in births among American teenagers, the United States still has one of the highest teen pregnancy rates among industrialized nations. The U.S. rate is nearly twice that of Great Britain and Canada, and at least four times the rates of France, Germany, and Japan (Boonstra, 2002; Darroch et al., 2001). What could account for this big difference? Are U.S. teenagers more sexually active? Do they begin having sex at an earlier age? Research by Jacqueline Darroch and her associates (2001) found that levels of sexual activity and the age at which teenagers initiated sex did not, in fact, vary appreciably across the countries. The major reason that teen pregnancy is higher in the United States, they found, is that teens' use of contraceptives is higher in other countries, where teenage sexual activity is more accepted and contraceptive services are much more widely available (Alan Guttmacher Institute, 2002a). The differing attitudes toward teenage sexuality in the United States and Europe are reflected in their sex education policies. An "abstinence-only" policy is often emphasized in sex education in the United States, whereas Europeans emphasize informed choice and responsibility (National Campaign, 2003; Roth, 2003). Many European countries have provided comprehensive sex education to all school children for many years. These programs encourage abstinence but also provide information about birth control methods and provide free access to contraceptives (Papalia, 2005).

Consequences of Teenage Pregnancy. The consequences of unplanned teenage pregnancy are often grim. Teenage mothers are likely to live in poverty and to suffer from a lack of psychological and social support. In addition, they typically drop out of school, have less stable employment patterns, and are more likely to be on welfare. Their marriages are less apt to be stable, they are more depressed, and they are more likely to have additional children out of wedlock (Coley & Chase-Lansdale, 1998; Hofferth & Reid, 2002; Kalil & Kunz, 2002; Zabin & Cardona, 2002).

Children born to teenagers have an increased risk of prematurity, birth complications, and death within the first year (Menacker et al., 2004), which may result partly from the young age of the mother and partly from inadequate prenatal care. Pregnant teenagers and mothers are more likely than other women to engage in behaviors which put their unborn babies and young infants at risk. For example, they are more likely to smoke during pregnancy and are less likely to put their infants in the back sleep position, which helps prevent sudden infant death syndrome (Phares et al., 2004). The children of young mothers are also more apt to have emotional, behavioral, and cognitive difficulties, most likely as a result of their impoverished caregiving environment (Coley & Chase-Lansdale, 1998; Hofferth & Reid, 2002), and they are more likely to be abused or neglected (Annie E. Casey Foundation, 1999). In adolescence, children of teenagers show higher rates of school failure, delinquency, and early sexual activity and pregnancy than teens born to older mothers (Coley & Chase-Lansdale, 1998).

Support for Pregnant Teenagers.   Support programs for pregnant teenagers have met with some success in improving the lives of teenage parents and their children (Kaufmann, 1996; Reichman & McLanahan, 2001; Seitz, 1996). Programs include one or more of the following components: family planning services, childcare provisions, education about parenting and job skills, and welfare reform incentives. Teenage mothers who participate in comprehensive programs have fewer children in the long run and are more likely to complete high school and become economically self-sufficient. Their children are healthier, suffer less abuse, have fewer developmental problems, and do better in school (Chira, 1994; Gennetian & Miller, 2002; Seitz, 1996).

Preventing Teenage Pregnancy.   Programs aimed at preventing teen pregnancy have taken various approaches: providing knowledge of sexuality and contraception, teaching abstinence, building decision-making job and social skills, enhancing gender and ethnic pride, and discussing life options (Daniluk & Towill, 2001; DiClemente et al., 2004; Lewin, 2001a). Programs that combine elements of these approaches are the most successful in delaying sexual activity, increasing contraceptive use, and reducing pregnancy (Dailard, 2002; DiClemente et al., 2004; Robin et al., 2004; Schemo, 2000a; Zabin & Cardona, 2002). While an overwhelming majority of American parents favor sex education in school, there is considerable debate on what should be taught, when, and by whom. Many school-based programs focus only on abstinence but are prohibited from mentioning contraception (Ali & Scelfo, 2002; Schemo, 2000b). Unfortunately, this approach has little effect on reducing sexual activity or pregnancy (Lewin, 2001b; Risman & Schwartz, 2002).

Childbirth

Women describe the birth of their first child as a physically and psychologically transforming experience (DiMatteo & Kahn, 1997; also see the vignette at the beginning of the chapter). In Chapter 8, we will examine some of the psychological aspects involved in making the transition to motherhood. In this section, we focus on the biological aspects of childbirth. We also examine postpartum distress, infertility, and assisted reproductive technology.

Stages of Childbirth

In the first stage, the cervix becomes dilated to 10 centimeters (about 5 inches) in diameter, a process that may last from a few hours to a day or more. In the second stage, which lasts from a few minutes to several hours, uterine contractions move the baby through the vagina. At the end of this stage, the baby is born. During the third stage, which lasts from a few minutes to an hour, the placenta detaches from the uterine wall and is expelled. Progesterone and estrogen levels drop dramatically during the second and third stages (Rathus et al., 2005).

Methods of Childbirth

Throughout most of the twentieth century, women gave birth in hospitals, attended by obstetricians using surgical instruments and anesthetics. While use of these medical procedures has saved lives and reduced pain, it also has depersonalized childbearing. Feminists argue that it has taken from women control over their own bodies and, through drugs, denied many women the experience of giving birth (Rathus et al., 2005; Travis & Compton, 2001).

One example of the "medicalization" of the birth process is the **cesarean section** (or C-section). *Incisions are made in the abdomen and uterus and the baby is surgically removed.* C-sections are performed if vaginal delivery is expected to be difficult or threatens the health of the mother or baby—as when the mother's pelvis is small or misshapen, the baby is very large, or the baby is not in the normal birth position ("Cesarean Delivery," 2002). But more pregnant women in the United States and Canada are choosing to deliver this way when there is no medical need (Anderson, 2004; "More Women," 2004). As a result, the cesarean delivery rate is higher in North America than in other industrialized countries. In the United States, the rate rose from 5 percent in 1970 to 25 percent by 1988. Concerns about unnecessary C-sections led to a drop in the C-section rate during the early 1990s, but it has grown to a record high of nearly 28 percent of all births (Martin et al., 2003; Hamilton et al., 2004).

Another example of the medicalization of childbirth is the induction of labor for practical (rather than medical) reasons, such as the convenience of the doctor, hospital, or parents. While the procedure is relatively safe, it increases the risk of C-sections, especially in first-time mothers. The reason is that the cervix may not dilate quickly enough. In the United States, the rate of labor-induced births doubled from 10 to 20 percent during the 1990s, causing some experts to speak out against the practice (Villarosa, 2002b).

Parents now can choose among more family-centered approaches to childbearing. The most popular method in the United States is prepared child birth, or the **Lamaze method.** *Prelabor classes teach the mother to control her pain through relaxation, breathing techniques, and focusing exercises.* A labor coach (usually the husband or partner) provides moral support and coaches techniques of breathing and relaxation during childbirth (Donatelle & Davis, 1998; Torpy, 2002). Others also may serve as a labor coach: a woman's mother, sister, friend or *an experienced and knowledgeable female labor and birth coach* known as a **doula.** Doula comes from the Greek word meaning "woman caregiver of a woman." Studies have found that women who are randomly assigned a doula during labor have less pain and anxiety during labor, need less medication, have fewer C-sections, and have shorter labors and less postpartum depression than women without a doula (Kennell & McGrath, 1993; Kennell et al., 1991; Scott et al., 1999). In addition, women assigned doulas are found to be more sensitive, loving, and responsive to their infants two months later (Gilbert, 1998).

Home birth also has increased in recent years, providing families with familiar settings and enhancing the feeling that the woman and her family are in control. More women are also choosing to deliver in homelike birthing centers outside a hospital. Family members and friends may be present during labor and delivery.

Many hospitals now provide similar family-friendly birthing rooms (Carmichael, 2004). Other aspects of family-centered birth include minimizing the use of anesthesia, using the more natural (and gravity-assisted) sitting position to give birth and eliminating practices such as enemas, shaving of the genital area, and performing an episiotomy, an incision that widens the vaginal opening to allow passage of the baby's head (Kuhn, 2005; Tarkan, 2002).

Using certified nurse-midwives for prenatal care and delivery has also become increasingly popular in the United States. Certified nurse-midwives attended only 1 percent of births in 1975 but now perform about 10 percent of vaginal deliveries (Carmichael, 2004; Pérez-Peña, 2004). Mortality rates are lower and birth weights are higher for infants delivered by nurse-midwives than for those delivered by physicians even though nurse-midwives tend to serve traditionally higher-risk women such as teenage mothers and those with lower income and less education (Lydon-Rochelle, 2004). The most likely explanation for this is that nurse-midwives, compared to physicians, spend more time with patients during prenatal visits, provide more patient education and counseling, and are with their patients throughout labor and delivery (Strong, 2000).

Childbearing after 40

A recent survey by economist Sylvia Hewlett (2002) found that nearly 9 out of 10 young women were confident that they could get pregnant into their forties. Indeed, a growing number of women are having children after the age of 40 (Hamilton et al., 2004). In 2003, over 100,000 U.S. women between 40 and 44, and nearly 6,000 women between 45 and 49 gave birth, a record high. But because fertility begins to decline after age 27, older women have a harder time conceiving. Among women over 40, half will require medical assistance in order to conceive (Brody, 2004b). About 15 to 20 percent of women aged 40 to 42 can become pregnant using their own eggs, compared with fewer than 3 percent of women over 44, as an increasing percentage of their eggs become abnormal (Gibbs, 2002; St. John, 2002). Women over 40 have more miscarriages than younger women, more preterm, low-birth-weight and stillborn babies, higher levels of complications during pregnancy, more chromosomal abnormalities (such as Down syndrome), and are more likely to have cesarean sections (Brody, 2004b; Cleary-Goldman et al., 2004; Jacobsson et al., 2004; O'Connor, 2004). The good news is that almost all older mothers, like their younger counterparts, have healthy babies, and that infant mortality rates are comparable for the two groups (O'Neil, 1999).

A lesser-known fact about midlife pregnancy is that about half of the pregnancies of women over 40 are unintended—a rate second only to teenagers. During perimenopause, the years prior to the end of menstruation, women may grow lax about birth control because they think there is little risk of pregnancy and may believe they have reached menopause. However, a woman's menstrual cycle becomes less regular in perimenopause and she may go several months without a period before having one (Goldberg, 2003).

To find out more about individual women's experiences with pregnancy and childbirth, try Get Involved 7.2.

GET INVOLVED **7.2**

Pregnancy and Childbirth Experiences

1. Briefly interview two women in their twenties, two middle-aged women, and two older women about their experiences with pregnancy and childbirth. It is helpful, but not essential, if you know your respondents fairly well. You may interview your sisters, cousins, friends, mother, aunts, grandmothers, and so on. Keep a record of your respondents' comments.

2. Compare and contrast the responses of the women in the three age groups.

What Does It Mean?

1. In what ways are the pregnancy experiences of the three groups of women different? In what ways are they alike?

2. In what ways are the childbirth experiences of the three groups different? In what ways are they alike?

3. What social and historical conditions may have influenced the pregnancy and childbirth experiences of these three generations of women?

Childbearing in the Later Years

Claire remembers seeing an amusing comic strip several years ago that featured an elderly couple sitting in rocking chairs. The woman, knitting a tiny sweater, was obviously pregnant. Looking at her husband with an irritated expression on her face, she exclaimed "You and your 'once more for old times' sake!'" The humor of the situation was based on the impossibility of an elderly woman's becoming pregnant. But this is no longer a laughing matter.

Early in 2005, Adrianna Iliescu gave birth in Romania to a healthy baby girl. News of the event spread like wildfire around the globe. What made this birth so special? Adrianna Iliescu was 66 years old (Mutler, 2005). Donated sperm fertilized a young woman's donor eggs in a test tube, and the resulting embryos were implanted in Adrianna Iliescu's hormonally readied uterus. Most fertility clinics set an age limit of 50 to 55 for a woman seeking in vitro fertilization, but this was not the case in Romania. Recent breakthroughs in transplanting ovarian tissue and in freezing eggs and embryos further raise the possibility that women may be able to bear children well into their golden years (Grady, 2004c; Kalb, 2004a; Wadyka, 2004).

Controversy swirls around the issue of whether postmenopausal women should be denied help in becoming pregnant (Budd, 2002; "Donor-Egg," 2002; Newman, 2000; Thomas, 2005). Those who support this view cite several reasons: (1) Such pregnancies risk the mother's health; (2) an older mother is less likely than a younger one to live long enough to raise her child to adulthood; (3) it is unnatural and a perverse use of technology that has been widely accepted for younger women for nearly 30 years.

These arguments have been rebutted by others who claim that (1) The complications that could affect the older mother's health also occur in younger

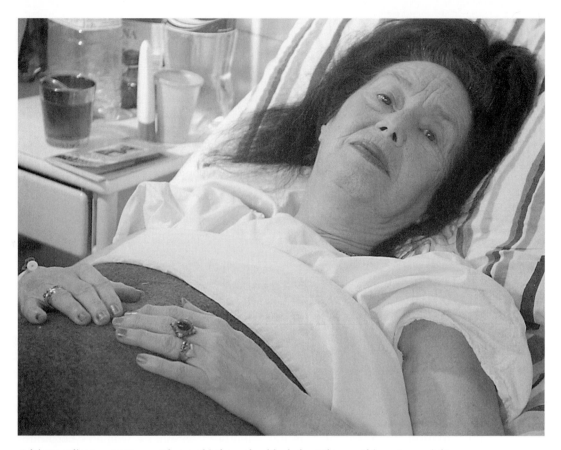

Adrianna Iliescu, age 66, recently gave birth to a healthy baby. Why was this controversial?

women, although less frequently, and are treatable ("Donor-Egg," 2002); (2) Any responsible mother, regardless of age, should make provisions for the care of her child in the event that she dies before the child is grown. Some younger women with severe medical conditions have babies. Should they also be barred from reproducing? (3) If the reproductive technology exists, why shouldn't an older woman take advantage of it? Should older women be denied other medical advances such as coronary bypass surgery? (Claire's mother-in-law had this procedure when she was in her early eighties and lived another twenty years in robust health. She did not, however, contemplate having another child.)

Marcia Angell, a physician and former executive editor of the *New England Journal of Medicine*, believes that both age discrimination and gender discrimination are at the root of society's discomfort about older women's having babies (Angell, 1997). Think of people's reactions to the news of men becoming fathers in their seventies and eighties: comedian Charlie Chaplin, actor Tony Randall, and former U.S. Senator Strom Thurmond, to mention but a few. Rather than disapproval, there is acceptance and even admiration of the sexual prowess of these older men.

Postpartum Distress

During the postpartum period, the first weeks after birth, many women experience some psychological distress. Postpartum distress is widely reported in countries around the world, although it is not universally perceived as an illness requiring the intervention of health professionals (Oates et al., 2004). The mildest and most common form, called **maternity blues** or baby blues, is experienced by up to 80 percent of new mothers. *This mood state, characterized by crying, anxiety, and irritability, typically begins three to four days after childbirth and lasts about two to four days.* Maternity blues are more common following a first birth and may reflect the mother's adjustment to parenthood (Greenberg & Springen, 2001; McDonald, 2003).

One out of eight women have *severe feelings of depression that last for weeks or months after delivery.* These changes, called **postpartum depression,** are characterized by anxiety or panic attacks, loss of interest in daily activities, despair, feelings of worthlessness and guilt, sleep and appetite disturbances, fatigue, difficulty in concentrating, and thoughts of harming oneself or the baby. One or 2 in 1,000 women experience postpartum psychosis, a serious condition that often includes delusions, hallucinations, and thoughts (or deeds) of hurting oneself or the infant (Carlson et al., 2004; McDonald, 2003; Sit, 2004). Andrea Yates, the woman convicted of drowning her five young children in the bathtub, suffered from postpartum psychosis. She explained that Satan told her this was the only way to save the children, because she was a "bad mother" (Johnson & Rust, 2005).

Women are more likely to develop postpartum depression if they are young, poor, less educated, and first-time mothers. Risk factors also include a history of mental illness, previous depression, marital difficulties or other stressful life events, major role changes such as the transition from employed woman to stay-at-home mother, and lack of support from family and friends (Arnold et al., 2002; Nicolson, 2003). In interviews with 35 British and American mothers with postpartum depression, Natasha Mauthner (2002) found that many of the women held idealized cultural constructions of the "perfect mother" that contrasted sharply with their perception that they were not measuring up. It is unclear whether the drastic drop in levels of estrogen and progesterone after birth also plays a role, since symptoms of postpartum depression are not uncommon in mothers of newly adopted children, and also in fathers (Morris, 2002; Whiffen, 2001).

Social support plays an important role in reducing the risk of postpartum depression (Ohye et al., 2003; Ray & Hodnett, 2003). In one study for example, mothers participated with a midwife in a supportive informal counseling session of up to two hours immediately after their child's birth (Lavender & Walkinshaw, 1998). Three weeks after delivery, only 9 percent of the mothers received a high score on a measure of depression, compared with 55 percent of new mothers in a control group who had not been assigned to a counseling session. While support and counseling clearly help prevent postpartum depression, the great majority of women recover from the condition within three to six months without any treatment (Steiner et al., 2003).

Infertility and Assisted Reproductive Technology

Infertility is *the failure to conceive a child after a year of trying* (Smith et al., 2003). About one couple in six in the United States cannot conceive and the likelihood of being infertile increases with age for both women and men (Dunson et al., 2004). In one-third of the cases, the difficulty is traced to the woman, in about 20 percent the problem originates with the man, in another 20 percent both partners have problems and in the remaining cases, the origin is unknown (Centers for Disease Control, 2003a). Causes of infertility in women include blockage of the fallopian tubes, failure of the ovaries to produce eggs, uterine fibroids, and **endometriosis,** *the presence of uterine lining tissue in abnormal locations* (Centers for Disease Control and Prevention, 2003a). A leading cause of infertility in women is polycystic ovary syndrome (PCOS), in which high levels of the hormone testosterone interfere with ovulation (Rebar & DeCherney, 2004). Clues that a woman may have PCOS are the presence of facial hair, acne, unexplained weight gain, and irregular periods (Cedars, 2004; Ehrmann, 2005). Lifestyle factors also play a role in infertility. If a woman is a heavy smoker, consumes large amounts of caffeine, or she or her partner drink heavily, the risk of infertility increases (Hassan & Killick, 2004).

About 15 percent of infertile couples have tried recently developed assisted reproductive technologies (Rebar & DeCherney, 2004). In 75 percent of those cases, couples use IVF or **in vitro fertilization** in which *the couple's own sperm and egg are fertilized in a glass laboratory dish ("in vitro" means "in glass") and the resulting embryo is transferred into the woman's uterus* (Centers for Disease Control and Prevention, 2003a). Louise Brown, born in England in 1978 as a result of IVF, was the first of these so-called test tube babies, now numbering over hundreds of thousands strong worldwide (Guterman, 2003). In 14 percent of infertility treatments, the couples' frozen embryos are used, and in 11 percent, donor eggs are used. Donated eggs typically are used for older women who do not produce eggs or whose eggs are damaged (Centers for Disease Control and Prevention, 2003a; Wright et al., 2004). Older women who use donor eggs from young women can have successful pregnancies at least until their mid-fifties (Heffner, 2004; Wadyka, 2004). In the United States, egg selling is big business. So-called "Ivy League eggs" are in great demand, and ads in campus newspapers offer up to $10,000 for the eggs of college women ("Eggs Shared," 2003). On rare occasions a "donor uterus" is used when a woman can produce eggs but cannot carry a pregnancy to full term. An embryo is produced by IVF using the couple's egg and sperm and is then placed in the donor's uterus. In one well-known case, 53-year-old Geraldine Wesolowski carried a child for her daughter-in-law, who had no uterus, and gave birth to her own grandson (Etaugh & Rathus, 1995).

The "success rate," that is, the percentage of times a live birth results, is about 23 percent for the patient's frozen embryos, 33 percent for IVF, and 47 percent for freshly fertilized embryos from donor eggs (Wright et al., 2004). Babies born after fertility treatments have higher rates of stillbirth, prematurity, low birth weight and birth defects (Jackson et al., 2004). Depending on the procedure used, anywhere from about 25 percent to over 40 percent are multiple births (Wright et al., 2004; Smith et al., 2003). In addition, the treatments are expensive. For example the average cost of a single IVF effort in the United States is about $12,400, and insurance does not usually cover the procedure (Lee, 2005).

Another more controversial approach to infertility, **surrogate motherhood**, involves *paying a woman to be artificially inseminated with the sperm of an infertile woman's husband and giving birth to the child.* About 1,000 infants are born through surrogacy every year in the United States (Graham, 2005). This practice raises a number of social, legal, and financial questions (Graham, 2005; Robinson & Miller, 2004; Scott-Jones, 2001). Can a contract signed before a baby's conception be legally binding after birth? Who are the legal parents? Should the surrogate mother be paid for her services? Some critics argue that surrogate motherhood exploits women physically, economically, and emotionally (Leiblum, 1997). Others believe that surrogate motherhood can benefit all parties as long as the interests of the surrogate mother are protected (Purdy, 1992). Overall, surrogacy appears to be a positive experience for surrogate mothers. These women have often completed a family of their own and wish to help an infertile couple become parents. They generally have a good relationship with the commissioning couple, have few problems handing over the baby, and many maintain contact with the couple and the child (Jadva et al., 2003).

In addition, fears about the impact of surrogacy on the well-being of children and families appear to be unfounded (Golombok et al., 2004). In fact, mothers of children born via a surrogacy arrangement show more warmth towards their babies and are more emotionally involved than in families where the child is conceived naturally. Both the mother and father have better parenting skills than do the parents in nonsurrogate families, and the babies themselves show no differences in their temperament and behavior, when compared with nonsurrogate babies. Nor do there seem to be problems when the surrogate mothers hand over the babies to the mothers who have commissioned the surrogacy.

While some couples wish to have children but cannot, others make a choice not to have children. For a fuller discussion of this issue, see Learn About the Research 7.1.

LEARN ABOUT THE RESEARCH 7.1

Childfree by Choice

My husband and I told family and friends when we married that we didn't want to have children. They kept saying we would change our minds. My parents begged me to change my mind. When I was told at 25 years old during a cancer scare that I was sterile, . . .

I joyfully announced to my hubby that we would no longer have to use birth control. I thought that the announcement of my "God"-given sterility would end the baby nag . . . but no—people began to tell me it was my duty to adopt, encouraged me to get on the fertility treatment treadmill, said they would pray for me, told me miracle baby stories or looked at me with pity. (40-year-old woman, in *Ms.*, 2004, p. 6)

More than at any other time in history, women and men in the industrialized world are deciding not to have children. Europe's population has been falling since 1998 as the birth rate there has continued to decline. At this rate, Europe will have 90 million fewer people by 2050 (Elder, 2003). Demographers predict that almost 25 percent of American women born between 1956 and 1973 will not have children (Burkett, 2000).

The decision to not have children is facilitated by the availability and legality of effective forms of birth control, the women's movement's emphasis on women's right to make choices in their lives, and the wider participation of women in the labor force (Caplan, 2001; Gillespie, 2003). However, the decision not to have children—to be childless or "childfree"—goes against the traditional gender norms of almost all cultures. Women who make this choice are often criticized as shallow, selfish, deviant, and unfeminine (Gillespie, 2003; Taylor & Taylor, 2003). They may be marginalized, given unsolicited advice,

and pressured by others to have children (Daniluk, 1999; Letherby & Williams, 1999).

Why do women choose not to have children? The reasons are many. Interviews of one group of intentionally childfree women between 40 and 78 years old found that the women wanted autonomy, self-expression, education, economic independence, and opportunities for a better life (Morell, 1993). Other women simply do not enjoy children, believe that they would not make good parents, or want a flexible lifestyle that would be hampered by children (Dierbeck, 2003). Still others perceive motherhood to be a sacrifice and a burden, involving loss of time, energy, and ultimately, identity (Gillespie, 2003).

One recent study by Debra Mollen Baker (2003) of intentionally childfree women found that several had shown a resistance to traditional gender roles while growing up, with half describing themselves as tomboys. While most of these women did not experience abusive or neglectful childhoods, some detected that their mothers were dissatisfied or ambivalent about their parental role. These women tended to value at least some traditionally masculine activities and values and felt more supported by their fathers than their mothers in their decision to not have children.

What Does It Mean?

1. Are the terms "childless" and "childfree" exact synonyms? In what ways do they differ in meaning?
2. In what way could a mother's dissatisfaction or ambivalence about parenting

influence her daughter's decision about whether to have children?
3. What can be done to increase society's acceptance of women who decide not to have children?

Reproductive Functioning in Midlife and Beyond

Declining estrogen production results in menopause, one of the most obvious biological events of women's middle years, and also hastens the development of osteoporosis.

Menopause

Menopause is the *cessation of menstrual periods for a full year*. For most American women, menopause occurs between the ages of 44 and 55, with an average age of 51. Smokers reach menopause up to 2 years earlier than nonsmokers (Avis et al., 2002). Menopause occurs because of the decline in the number of ovarian follicles (egg-producing cells), which results in a decline in the production of both estrogen and progesterone. Some estrogen continues to be produced after menopause by the adrenal glands and fat cells (Sherwin, 2001). *The three to nine years preceding the beginning of menopause*, known as the **perimenopause**, are marked by increasing irregularity of the menstrual cycle and variations in the amount of menstrual flow (Kuczynski, 2002b). As we shall see, the way in which a woman experiences menopause reflects a host of physiological, psychological, and cultural factors (Rossi, 2004).

Physical Symptoms.   The frequency and severity of physical symptoms associated with menopause vary widely among women. In fact, the *only* symptom that all menopausal women experience is the end of menstruation. In North America, the most commonly reported symptom is the **hot flash**, *a sudden feeling of heat that spreads over the body, usually lasting four to ten minutes that is often accompanied by perspiration* (Stearns et al., 2003). Surveys report that anywhere between 50 and 80 percent of menopausal women experience hot flashes. For example, in a recent nationwide study of adult Americans by the MacArthur Foundation, half of the postmenopausal women surveyed reported having no hot flashes at all, only 25 percent said they had hot flashes at least once a month, and 12 percent reported having them almost daily (Rossi, 2004). Some women will have hot flashes for a few months, some for a few years, and many not at all. Hot flashes at night (sometimes called *"night sweats"*) can interfere with the sleep of some menopausal women, but most women find hot flashes to be only a minor inconvenience (Butler & Lewis, 2002; Grady, 2002a).

Loss of estrogen also causes thinning of the vaginal lining and decreased vaginal lubrication. These changes can lead to painful sexual intercourse and also make the vagina more prone to infection. Headaches, fatigue, joint and muscle pains, and tingling sensations are other physical symptoms that are occasionally reported (Schulman, 2003; Sommer, 2001). Women who smoke may experience more severe symptoms (Centers for Disease Control, 2002b). The most serious physical consequence of menopause, osteoporosis, is discussed in Chapter 12.

Women in different ethnic and cultural groups vary in the kinds and degree of menopausal symptoms they report. Asian American women experience fewer symptoms than Black, Latina, or White women (Avis et al., 2002).

Psychological Reactions.   It is popularly believed that menopausal women are more likely to display such psychological symptoms as depression, irritability, or mood swings. There is no evidence, however, that these or other psychological symptoms are more prevalent among menopausal women. Some women may feel irritable or tired, but these feelings may be linked to disruptions in sleep caused by hot flashes (Avis et al., 2002; Avis, 2003; Sommer, 2001).

Even if some women do show heightened psychological distress during the menopausal years, this cannot be attributed solely to biological processes. Changes in social roles that occur in midlife (see Chapter 11) may be largely responsible for increased distress. Women not only are confronting their own aging during this time but may also be coping with stressful changes in the family: the illness or death of a spouse, divorce or separation, difficult teenagers, children who are preparing to leave home, and/or aging parents who require care (Avis et al., 2002).

Attitudes toward Menopause.   Popular images and stereotypes of menopausal women are overwhelmingly negative in North America. Menopause continues to be defined in the medical and psychological literature by a long list of negative symptoms and terms such as "estrogen deprivation" and "total ovarian failure" (Derry, 2002). The popular press reinforces the notion of menopause as a condition of disease and deterioration that requires treatment by drugs (O'Grady, 2003). Even Gail Sheehy's (1991) bestselling book *The Silent Passage*, which attempts to shatter negative myths about menopause, describes it as a "lonely and emotionally draining experience" (p. 14).

Not surprisingly, women express more positive attitudes toward menopause when it is described as a normal life transition than when it is described as a medical problem (Gannon & Ekstrom, 1993). A woman who expects menopause to be unpleasant is apt to focus on its negative aspects. For example, women with a negative attitude toward menopause are more likely to report vaginal dryness, decreased sexual interest, and negative mood (Collins, 1997).

Most middle-aged American women, however, minimize the significance of menopause as only a temporary inconvenience. Many look forward to menopause as marking the end of menstruation and childbearing (Ayubi-Moak & Parry, 2002; Walter, 2000). In the MacArthur Foundation survey mentioned earlier, the majority of postmenopausal women reported feeling "only relief" when their menstrual periods stopped, while only 2 percent said they experienced "only regret" (Rossi, 2004). Postmenopausal women have more positive attitudes toward menopause than younger middle-aged women, with young women age 35 or less holding the most negative views of all (Gannon & Ekstrom, 1993; Sommer et al., 1999).

Attitudes toward menopause also differ according to a woman's ethnic and cultural background. For example, a recent study of over 16,000 Asian American, Black, Latina, and White women found that Black women had the most positive attitudes toward menopause whereas Asian American women were least positive (Sommer et al., 1999). Across ethnic groups, better-educated women held more positive views.

What are women's experiences with and attitudes toward menopause in non-Western societies? Take a look at Explore Other Cultures 7.5.

EXPLORE OTHER CULTURES 7.5

Menopause: Symbol of Decline or of Higher Status?

Women in non-Western cultures often have menopausal experiences and attitudes very different from those reported by Western women, indicating that menopausal symptoms are at least in part socially constructed. For example, Japanese and Indonesian women are much less likely than women in Western cultures to report hot flashes or other physical symptoms (Sowers, 2000; Steiner et al., 2003), and among Mayan women, hot flashes are virtually unknown (Feldman, 2000). Women of high social castes in India and Lakota Sioux women in the United States report very few negative symptoms, and menopause is in fact an eagerly anticipated event. Why might that be? When these women reach menopause, they are freed from menstrual taboos and are able to participate more fully in society (Feldman, 2000; Sherwin, 2001; Winterich, 2003). No wonder they experience few negative menopausal symptoms! In Western cultures, on the other hand, aging does not confer higher status on a woman but rather lowers it. It is thus not surprising that there are more complaints about "symptoms" in such a youth-oriented culture (Sowers, 2000).

Women of high social castes in India look forward to menopause which frees them from menstrual taboos and allows them full participation in society.

Hormone Replacement Therapy

Hormone replacement therapy (HRT) is *a medical treatment that replaces hormones whose levels drop after menopause.* Women who have had their uterus removed can take estrogen alone, while those who still have their uterus are advised to take a combination of estrogen and synthetic progesterone (progestin) in order to protect against uterine cancer.

The combined estrogen-progestin pill relieves the menopausal symptoms of hot flashes, night sweats, insomnia, and vaginal dryness. It helps prevent osteoporosis and reduces the risk of colon cancer. However, the recent Women's Health Initiative study found that it also increases the risk of heart attack, stroke, blood clots, breast and ovarian cancer, gallbladder disease, and dementia (Cushman et al., 2004; Peterson et al., 2004; Schneider, 2004; Nelson, 2004). The use of estrogen alone also increases the risk of stroke and dementia and fails to protect against heart disease, although it does not increase the risk of breast cancer and protects against hip fractures ("Estrogen Therapy Woes," 2004; Hulley & Grady, 2004; Klein & Rapp, 2004).

Which women should use HRT after menopause? That decision must be based on each woman's evaluation of the benefits and risks to herself (see Table 7.2) given her personal and family medical history (Kolata, 2004b; Nelson, 2004). Some women whose quality of life suffers because of extreme hot flashes or vaginal atrophy are electing to use HRT. However, they are now advised to take the lowest dose that provides relief, and for the shortest time possible (Berger, 2004; Carlson et al., 2004; Col et al., 2004). Some women should definitely *not* use hormones. These include women who already have had cancer of the breast or uterus, chronic liver disease, or diabetes. Women should *consider* avoiding hormones if they have migraine headaches, gallbladder disease, uterine fibroid tumors, high blood pressure, seizure disorders, blood clots, stroke, or family history of stroke (Berger, 2004; Carlson et al., 2004; Col & Komaroff, 2004; "New Risks," 2004).

Alternatives to Standard Hormone Replacement Therapy. The usual dose of estrogen given in HRT is 0.625 milligram. However, lower doses may confer similar

TABLE 7.2   Benefits and Risks of Combined Hormone Replacement Therapy

Benefits	Risks
• Ends hot flashes	Increases risk of heart attack and stroke
• Relieves vaginal dryness and atrophy	Increases risk of ovarian cancer
• Delays bone loss	Increases risk of uterine cancer if estrogen is taken without progesterone
• Increases bone density	Increases risk of gallbladder disease
• Decreases risk of colon cancer	Increases risk of breast cancer
• May decrease risk of Parkinson's disease	Increases risk of dementia
	Increases risk of urinary incontinence

Sources: Grodstein et al. (2003); Grodstein et al. (2004); Yaffe (2003); Nelson (2004).

benefits in building bones and relieving hot flashes and vaginal dryness, while lowering risks (Duenwald, 2002; Lindsay et al., 2002). An alternative approach is the use of synthetic estrogens that have some of the benefits but fewer of the risks of natural estrogen. One such hormone, raloxifene, appears to offer some protection against heart disease among women with elevated risk of the disease (Barrett-Connor et al., 2002). It also *reduces* the risk of breast cancer (Cummings, 1999).

Lifestyle modifications, especially those involving exercise and dietary modifications, appear to be beneficial in reducing menopausal symptoms. For example, women who exercise regularly have a lower incidence of hot flashes than women who do not (McMillan & Mark, 2004). Limiting or eliminating caffeine, alcohol, and spicy foods also reduces the frequency of hot flashes. Consuming foods and herbs that contain estrogen-like substances, such as soy products, wild yams, flaxseed, and black cohosh may also be helpful (Col & Komaroff, 2004; Krebs et al., 2004; McMillan & Mark, 2004), although the evidence is mixed (Pradhan & Bachmann, 2003; Tarkan, 2004). Known as **phyto-estrogens,** these *plant foods do not contain estrogen but affect the body in a similar manner.* Phyto-estrogens are many times weaker than pharmaceutical estrogens and may not help women experiencing severe effects of menopause. Furthermore, there is as yet no evidence that these estrogen substitutes provide the same long-term benefits against osteoporosis that estrogen provides (North American Menopause Society, 2003).

SUMMARY

Menstruation

- The menstrual cycle is regulated by hormones, brain structures, and reproductive organs.
- Attitudes toward menstruation remain somewhat negative, despite evidence that physical and psychological performance does not change meaningfully over the menstrual cycle.
- Some women experience menstrual joy, a feeling of heightened creativity and energy.
- Only a small minority of women experience the symptoms of premenstrual syndrome (PMS). However, a majority believe they suffer from the disorder.

Contraception

- Contraceptive use has increased among adolescents, but many use contraceptives sporadically or not at all.
- The type of contraception chosen by women changes as their reproductive goals change.

Abortion

- Most abortions occur within the first trimester by means of the vacuum aspiration method.
- Early abortion is physically safe and generally has no negative psychological aftereffects.

Pregnancy

- Physical effects of pregnancy include nausea, fatigue, and weight gain.
- Women have both positive and negative feelings during pregnancy.
- People may react negatively to a pregnant woman.
- Most miscarriages result from genetic defects in the embryo or fetus.
- The teenage pregnancy rate is higher in the United States than in most industrialized nations, but the teenage birth rate is declining, probably due to increased condom use.
- Teen pregnancy has serious economic, social, and medical costs.

- Programs stressing abstinence, contraception, and life skills can delay sexual activity and reduce pregnancy rates.

Childbirth

- The three stages of childbirth are dilation of the cervix, birth of the baby, and expulsion of the placenta.
- Rates of cesarean delivery and induction of labor are high in the United States.
- Family-centered approaches to childbearing include the Lamaze method, home birth, birthing rooms and centers, and use of midwives.
- Older women have more difficulty conceiving but generally have healthy babies.
- Many women experience maternity blues shortly after giving birth. A small percentage experience the more severe postpartum depression and postpartum psychosis.
- About 15 percent of infertile couples have tried reproductive technologies, such as in

vitro fertilization, frozen embryos, donor eggs, and surrogate motherhood.

Reproductive Functioning in Midlife and Beyond

- Menopause, caused by a decrease in estrogen production, causes hot flashes and vaginal dryness but is not linked to heightened psychological distress.
- Menopausal experiences and attitudes differ across ethnic and cultural groups.
- Middle-aged women usually have positive attitudes toward menopause.
- Benefits of hormone replacement therapy (HRT) include decrease in menopausal symptoms and decrease in the risk of osteoporosis and colon cancer.
- Risks of HRT include increased risk of heart attack, stroke, breast cancer, ovarian cancer, gall bladder disease, and dementia.
- Alternatives to HRT include synthetic estrogens and phyto-estrogens.

KEY TERMS

dysmenorrhea
prostaglandins
women-as-problem bias
premenstrual syndrome (PMS)
premenstrual dysphoric disorder (PMDD)
vacuum aspiration
female genital mutilation

infibulation
miscarriage
cesarean section
Lamaze method
doula
maternity blues
postpartum depression
infertility
endometriosis

in vitro fertilization
surrogate motherhood
menopause
perimenopause
hot flash
hormone replacement therapy
phyto-estrogens

WHAT DO YOU THINK?

1. If a friend of yours unexpectedly became pregnant, what factors might influence her decision about whether or not to terminate the pregnancy?

2. Why do you think that even though many college students have heard about

the risks of sexually transmitted diseases, including HIV infection, they fail to use condoms regularly or to engage in other self-protecting behaviors? What actions could be taken to make more of your friends engage in "safer sex" practices?

3. Do you favor or oppose school-based education programs that provide contraceptives to teenagers? Support your answer.

4. Who is the baby's real mother—the surrogate mother who conceived and carried the baby or the wife of the man who fathers the baby? Is motherhood primarily

a biological or psychological concept? Explain your answers.

5. Should women in their fifties and sixties have babies? Why or why not?

6. In your opinion, why do young women have more negative views of menopause than middle-aged women?

IF YOU WANT TO LEARN MORE

Aronson, D., Clapp, D. N., & Hollister, M. R. (Eds.). (2001). *Resolving infertility*. New York: Harper Resource.

Chrisler, J. C. (Ed.). (2004). *From menarche to menopause: The female body in feminist therapy.* New York: Haworth.

Laflamme, L. M. (2001). *Rites of passage: A celebration of menarche.* New York: Synchronicity Press.

Love, S. (1998). *Dr. Susan Love's hormone book: Making informed choices about menopause.* New York: Random House.

Mauthner, N. S. (2002). *The darkest days of my life: Stories of postpartum depression.* Cambridge, MA: Harvard University Press.

North American Menopause Society (2003). *Menopause guidebook: Helping women make informed healthcare decisions through perimenopause and beyond.* Cleveland, OH: Author.

Ussher, J. M. (2005). *Managing the monstrous feminine: Regulating the reproductive body.* Hampshire, UK: Psychology Press.

Wingood, G. M., & DiClemente, R. J. (Eds.). (2002). *Handbook of women's sexual and reproductive health.* New York: Kluwer Academic/Plenum.

WEBSITES

Sexuality & Reproductive Health

About Go Ask Alice!
http://www.goaskalice.columbia.edu/

Contraception

About Go Ask Alice!
http://www.goaskalice.columbia.edu/
Planned Parenthood: Your Contraceptive Choices
http://www.plannedparenthood.org/pp2/portal/medicalinfo/birthcontrol/

Pregnancy and Childbirth

Reproductive Health
http://www.cdc.gov/reproductivehealth/index.htm

Childbirth
http://www.childbirth.org
Pregnancy & Child Health Resource Centers
http://www.mayoclinic.com/findinformation/healthylivingcenter/index.cfm

Infertility

Infertility Resources
http://www.ihr.com/infertility

Menopause

North American Menopause Society
http://www.menopause.org

CHAPTER

8 Relationships

A middle-aged lesbian couple had been together for 15 years when their daughter was born. To celebrate the joyous occasion, they held a naming ceremony attended by their closest friends. The nonbiological mother held the baby and presented her with her full name consisting of her given name and each of her parents' surnames. Then each parent lit a candle and made a wish for their baby girl. Following this, they expressed their feelings for one another and for the new family they had created. (Muzio, 1996)

Last Sunday, Ashley and I went over to my mom's house and we made applesauce together. It was really fun because it was all three of us and I used to do that with my mom when I was a kid . . . And we were just working together doing all the different parts of the applesauce and conversing. And it was just a real regular time. We were all acting like friends, but at the same time there was that bond there—that grandmom, mom, daughter thing. It was neat. (Denise, age 38, in Fingerman, 2001, p. 66)

These vignettes portray women's experiences with interpersonal relationships in different parts of the life cycle. In this chapter we explore the nature of women's close relationships—including friendships, romantic relationships, marriage and other long-term relationships, unattached lifestyles, and motherhood. We end the chapter by examining women's relationships in the later years with their siblings, adult children, grandchildren, and parents.

Friendships

Close relationships are essential to good mental health and well-being. Friends, in particular, are a major source of support and self-esteem throughout our lives (Collins & Feeney, 2004). Let's take a closer look at gender differences in friendships, starting in adolescence and moving through the adult lifespan.

Friendship in Adolescence

Starting in childhood and throughout life, our closest friends tend to be people of our own gender. Even though romantic attachments increase during adolescence, most teenagers still choose members of their own gender as best friends (Hartup, 1993). Starting in early adolescence, girls report greater satisfaction with their same-gender friendships than do boys (Thomas & Daubman, 2001). They also report more positive friendship quality and closeness (Rose, 2002; Rose & Asher, 2004).

Intimacy, the sharing of thoughts and feelings with someone else, is a key characteristic of adolescent friendships (American Psychological Association, 2002; Brown, 2004). Girls' relationships are more intimate than those of boys (Compian & Hayward, 2003; Sanchez-Hucles, 2003). Girls show greater increases in intimacy from early to late adolescence, they report more self-disclosure and emotional support, and they spend more time with their friends than do boys (Black, 2000; Quatman & Swanson, 2002; Rose, 2002).

Girls tend to have a few very close friends, whereas boys are more likely to have larger, less intimate friendship groups (deGuzman et al., 2004; Markovits et al., 2001). Boys' friendships focus on shared group activities, mostly sports and competitive games. Girls' friendships, on the other hand, are more apt to emphasize self-disclosure and emotional support (Winstead & Griffin, 2001). In the words of one adolescent girl,

> I've had a best friend for about five years now, and she pretty much knows everything about me. I'd probably turn to her for all of my problems because she's always helped me out and always gave me the right answers for everything. (Commonwealth Fund, 1997, p. 19)

Studies of ethnically and socioeconomically diverse adolescents have found friendship patterns that differ somewhat from those commonly seen among White, middle-class adolescents (Brown et al., 1999). For example, Julia Duff (1996) found differences in how upper- and middle-class suburban White girls and poor and working-class urban girls of color describe their closest friendships with other girls. Whereas 95 percent of the White girls reported competition as an aspect of their friendships, only 38 percent of girls of color did so. Similarly, the White girls were five times as likely to report feeling "used" by a close friend and were nearly three times as likely to indicate that jealousy was an issue. Other research suggests that differences in adolescent girls' friendship patterns may be more strongly related to social class than to ethnicity. In one study (Gallagher & Busch-Rossnagal, 1991), for example, middle-class Black and White girls were more likely to disclose beliefs and attitudes to their friends than were Black and White girls of lower socioeconomic status.

Friendship in Adulthood

Both women and men highly value their friendships. These close relationships provide mutual support and encouragement as well as interpersonal intimacy. However, it seems clear that, as in adolescence, women care about their close friends more than men do (Bank & Hansford, 2000). Furthermore, women and men achieve closeness with their friends somewhat differently. Women are described as operating "face to face," by sharing thoughts and feelings, whereas men develop closeness "side by side," by sharing activities with their friends (Sanchez-Hucles, 2003).

The greater emphasis on emotional expressiveness shown by women is reflected in several ways. Both adult and adolescent females disclose more to their friends and reveal more intimate information than males do (Black, 2000; Sanchez-Hucles, 2003; Sheets & Lugar, 2005). When helping a friend with a problem, women are also more likely than men to express greater empathic understanding of their friend's problem (George et al., 1998).

The emotional support shown in heterosexual female friendships is a particularly important quality of lesbian friendships as well, since lesbians are frequently subjected to antagonism in their social environment. The reinforcement and empathy that are part of close relationships in this "family of choice" can help lesbians cope with prejudice from the broader society (Green, 2004). Social support can also help them develop and maintain their lesbian identity (Stanley, 2002).

How can we account for gender differences in emotional intimacy and expressiveness in friendships? Consistent with our assumption that gender is socially constructed, experiences and attitudes shape orientations toward friendship. As we saw in Chapter 4, parents are more likely to encourage emotional expression in their daughters and discourage it in their sons, and females and males carry these messages into their peer relationships. Furthermore, because emotional expression is viewed as a female trait and many males think of gay men as having feminine traits, males might associate emotional closeness between males with homosexuality, a perceived connection that can be threatening and might steer men away from expressing emotions to their male friends (Sanchez-Hucles, 2003).

Although most of the research on adult friendship has focused on same-sex friends, some recent studies have examined cross-sex friendships (Monsour, 2002). These friendships are similar in many ways to same-sex friendships but also offer some unique benefits. Female-male friends provide each other with insider perspectives and other-sex companionship and also sensitize each other to gender differences in communication style. Feminine men have more cross-sex friendships than masculine men, and masculine women have more cross-sex friendships than feminine women (Reeder, 2003).

Friendship in Later Life

Friends provide the emotional support and companionship that sustain women as they meet the challenges, changes, and losses of later life. Because so many married women eventually lose their spouses through death or divorce, most women grow old in the company of other women (Doress-Worters & Siegal, 1994; Monsour, 2002). In later life, women are more engaged with friendships and social networks than are men and are more likely both to give and to receive emotional support (Canetto, 2003). Friendships among older women enhance physical and mental health and contribute to continued psychological growth (Patrick et al., 2001). Older women's close friends tend to be about the same age and socioeconomic status, have the same social and ethnic background, and live close to each other (Rawlins, 2004).

Social class influences the way in which friendships are made and maintained. Elderly middle-class women often make friends through membership in an association. The main basis of such friendships is shared interest of the group and its activities. Working-class and poor women are more likely to choose relatives as close friends and to provide concrete and practical assistance to each other (Sanchez-Hucles, 2003).

Women's social involvement with their friends includes both home- and community-based activities. The most common social activity of older women and their close friends is getting together for conversation. Frequent topics of discussion include reminiscing about memorable events involving their spouses, children, and careers (Rawlins, 2004).

Women and their friends also help one another with transportation, shopping, and running errands (Adams, 1997). Those who perceive an equal give-and-take in their relationships with friends are more content and happy with the friendships (Roberto, 2001). Long-term friends contribute to a sense of continuity and connection with the past. Over time, friends can come to be considered as family, further increasing one's sense of connectedness (Lewittes, 1989).

For some lesbians, friendships function as an extended family (Knickmeyer et al., 2002). Many midlife and older lesbians who came out during a period that was more hostile toward lesbianism than is true today were not accepted by their families. For them, and for other lesbians who have been rejected by their families of origin, friendships serve this familial role. And because most lesbians have not been married and have not created a traditional family, these social networks of friends can be an important source of support to midlife and older women (Grossman et al., 2000; Orel, 2002).

Friends provide emotional support and companionship for women as they grow older.

Romantic Relationships

The process of looking for a suitable partner preoccupies many of us during our teen and young adult years. In this section, we look at some features of this process. What qualities do women and men look for in a potential partner? How do they act in dating situations? How do they gauge their partner's interest in having sex?

Importance of Physical Attractiveness

What do females and males look for in a romantic partner or mate? People are often attracted to potential mates whom they perceive as loving, supportive, and secure in their relationships (Klohnen & Luo, 2003). Women prefer men who display self-assurance and stand up for themselves with other men, but who also exhibit warmth and agreeableness (Gangestad et al., 2004). Although both genders also value physical attractiveness, men put more emphasis on looks than women do (Fletcher et al., 2004; Geary, 2002). Personal advertisements written by women and men are good illustrations of this gender difference. Consider this hypothetical ad: "Attractive, slender blonde seeking financially stable partner." Who comes to mind, a woman or a man? Studies show that heterosexual women's and men's ads complement one another. Women are more likely to offer physical attractiveness and ask for financial stability. On the other hand, men are more apt to ask for physical attractiveness, including specific facial and bodily features (e.g., blue eyes, long legs, thin) and offer financial security (e.g., Gonzales & Meyers, 1993; Willis & Carlson, 1993). The personal ads of gays and lesbians similarly show that gay men are more interested in the attractiveness of their partners than are lesbian women (Hatala & Prehodka, 1996). Lesbians also are less likely than heterosexual females to offer attractiveness as an attribute, perhaps because they are less likely to base their relationships on physical appearance (Kimmel, 2002; Smith & Stillman, 2002b).

This great value placed on physical appearance has unfortunate consequences for heterosexual women. Not only can it contribute to a distorted body image and eating disorders (see Chapters 4 and 13), but it also denigrates women by placing more importance on superficial characteristics than on behaviors and accomplishments. Emphasizing characteristics beyond a person's control (e.g., facial attractiveness) rather than qualities that are achievable (e.g., conscientiousness) can lower self-esteem (Hamida et al., 1998).

Because of the double standard of aging (see Chapter 2), midlife women are much more dissatisfied with their appearance than midlife men (Halliwell & Dittmar, 2003; McConatha et al., 2002). Consequently, they are more likely than men to use age concealment techniques, such as liposuction, face lifts, tummy tucks, and eyelid surgery (Barrett, 2004; Gorman, 2004). The latest rage is Botox, a diluted poison that is injected into the brow muscles, paralyzing them temporarily and causing wrinkles to vanish. Of the more than 1 million people who get Botox injections each year, the vast majority are White, middle-aged women (Gorman, 2004; Kuczynski, 2002a). Moreover, women feel pressured to seek out

Midlife women are more likely than midlife men to use age-concealment techniques.

surgery at younger ages than a decade ago, often beginning with their eyelids in their mid- or late thirties, and moving through a series of cosmetic surgeries over the next few decades (Merkin, 2004).

The emphasis on physical appearance has a particularly negative impact on women with disabilities. These women are less likely than nondisabled women to be perceived as attractive and desirable and may even evoke reactions of repulsion and rejection. Not surprisingly, the resulting poor self-image and fear of rejection can lead women with disabilities to avoid social and intimate relationships (Crawford & Ostrove, 2003; Hanna & Rogovsky, 1991).

EXPLORE OTHER CULTURES **8.1**
What Do People in Other Cultures Look for in a Mate?

David Buss (1994) and his colleagues have studied the characteristics that adults in 37 cultures prefer in potential mates. In all cultures, men valued physical attractiveness more highly than did women. They also preferred younger mates and mates with housekeeping and cooking skills. Women in 36 of 37 cultures, however, valued "good earning capacity" more than men did and they preferred older mates. Still, there was a great degree of consistency in the preferences of women and men. Both ranked "kind and understanding" as most important, followed by "intelligent," "exciting personality," and "healthy." Despite these overall similarities, cultural differences occurred on almost all items. The largest cultural difference

was found for chastity, which was considered to be unimportant by northern Europeans, but very important in China, India, and Iran. What might account for these cultural differences? Alice Eagly and her colleagues (Eagly et al., 2004) reexamined the 37 cultures and found that women's preference for older mates with resources and men's preference for younger women with domestic skills and intact virginity were most pronounced in societies in which women's status was low. These differences decreased as societies became more egalitarian. In other words, gender differences in the characteristics that people prefer in mates reflect the extent to which women and men occupy different roles in a given society.

The results reported in this section were based on U.S. samples. What do females and males in other cultures look for in a romantic partner or prospective mate? See Explore Other Cultures 8.1.

Perception of Sexual Interest

How do young adults determine sexual interest of their partner? In heterosexual relationships both males and females interpret certain nonsexual behaviors as cues that one's partner is interested in sex. For example, some young adults believe that asking someone out on a date indicates the requester is interested in having sex (Mongeau et al., 1998). Also, some assume that how much a partner spends on a date influences how far things go sexually—a belief held more strongly by Blacks than Whites (Ross & Davis, 1996).

In general, however, men are more likely than women to perceive sexual interest in nonsexual behaviors (Dion & Dion, 2001; Nelson & LeBoeuf, 2002). For example, college men are more likely than college women to attribute sexual characteristics (e.g., sexy, promiscuous) to women they observe or converse with (Tomich & Schuster, 1996) and to interpret a female's nonsexual behaviors, such as asking out a male (Mongeau et al., 1998), giving him a hug or a pat (Afifi & Johnson, 1999), or flirting with him (Henningsen, 2004) as an indication that she is interested in having sexual intercourse with him. Explanations of these gender differences range from differential socialization to greater readiness toward sexual arousal in men (Dion & Dion, 2001). Whatever the cause, can you identify problems stemming from the cues men use to perceive sexual interest? Unfortunately, the sexual meaning men give to many nonsexual behaviors can lead to a misunderstanding of women's desires and to possible sexual aggression.

Almost all of the research on dating has focused on nondisabled women and men. Persons with disabilities face other issues in dating relationships. To examine some of these issues for women with disabilities, see Learn about the Research 8.1.

LEARN ABOUT THE RESEARCH 8.1

Dating Issues for Women with Physical Disabilities

Because previous research had shown that women with physical disabilities are considered asexual and not acceptable as romantic partners, Diana Rintala and her colleagues examined dating issues experienced by women with and without disabilities. Their national sample included 475 women with disabilities (average age, 41.5) and 425 nondisabled women (average age, 38). These women responded to mailed questionnaires.

There were some differences in the dating histories of these groups of women. Women who were disabled before their first date began dating approximately two and one-half years later than nondisabled women. However, there was no difference in the percentage of women with or without disabilities who had ever had sex with a man, although somewhat fewer women with disabilities reported having had sex with a woman.

The findings indicated several differences between these two groups of women in

issues related to dating. Compared to nondisabled women, the women with disabilities were less satisfied about their dating frequency and perceived more problems trying to attract dating partners. They were also more concerned about both physical obstacles in the environment and societal barriers to dating, including people's assumptions that women with disabilities are uninterested in or unable to have sexual intimacy. Last, women with disabilities experienced more personal barriers to dating, such as pressure from family members not to date and low frequency of getting out of the house to socialize.

Based on these findings, the authors suggest several interventions that might improve the dating experiences of women with disabilities. Some of these are (1) removal of physical barriers in public places, (2) educating the public about disability and sexuality, and (3) educating families about the appropriateness of dating for women with disabilities.

What Does It Mean?

1. Rintala and her colleagues offered some general forms of intervention. What specific strategies could be used to educate the public about disability and sexuality and to change families' feelings about the appropriateness of dating? What solutions other than those presented here might improve the dating situation for women with disabilities?

2. This investigation focused on women only. Do you think men with disabilities experience similar problems? Explain your answer.

Source: Rintala et al. (1997).

Dating

Onset of Dating. Mixed-gender peer groups start to form during early adolescence. These groups are central to the emergence of dating and romantic relationships that begin to blossom at this time (Collins, 2003; Furman, 2002; Roisman et al., 2004.). Dating serves a variety of purposes apart from its obvious role as a courting ritual that can lead to serious commitment and marriage. Dating can help one learn how to establish intimacy with other individuals. It can develop new interests in sports or hobbies, serve as an opportunity for sexual experimentation, enhance a teenager's social status and popularity, and help forge a sense of identity (Gallagher, 2001; Sanchez-Hucles, 2003; White et al., 2001).

Since the beginning of the century, the age when U.S. adolescents start dating has decreased. Many girls now begin to date at age 12 or 13, and many boys at 13 or 14. Some children start as early as age 10 (Jarrell, 2000). About one-quarter to one-third of 13- to 15-year-olds have been involved in a romantic relationship, compared to nearly half of 15- to 17-year-olds, and 70 percent or more of 18- to 20-year-olds (Brown, 2004).

You will recall from Chapter 6 that the age when sexual activity begins depends on a number of factors. Many of these same factors are related to the age at onset of dating. For example, Black teenagers begin both dating and sexual activity earlier than White and Latina/o adolescents. Other factors related to early dating include early age at puberty, being poor, and not having a strong religious identity (Bingham et al., 1990; Compian & Hayward, 2003; Miller & Moore, 1990). Girls from divorced or stepparent families initiate dating and sexual activity earlier than girls whose parents are married.

Young people usually bring to their early dating encounters a set of beliefs regarding how they should behave in order to appeal to the other gender and maintain the relationship. The advice passed along to girls by girlfriends, mothers, older siblings, and the media frequently includes such helpful hints as massaging the boy's ego, bringing up subjects that he enjoys talking about, admiring his accomplishments (but not mentioning yours), and being understanding, but not too assertive or confrontational. A boy, on the other hand, learns to "take care" of a girl he dates by making the arrangements, being chivalrous (opening the door, helping her put her coat on), paying for the date, and taking her home (Boynton, 2003; Maccoby, 1998; Rose, 2000). Notice how traditionally gender-typed these dating expectations are.

Dating Scripts. Suzanna Rose and Irene Hanson Frieze (1993) explored this subject in greater detail by studying the expected **dating scripts** and actual dating behavior of college students on a first date. A dating script is a *culturally developed sequence of expected events that guide an individual's behavior while on a date.* (The task they used is described in Get Involved 8.1. Try it with some of your friends.) Students' expected dating behaviors and their actual behaviors were very similar. Some aspects of the dating script were the same for females and males. These included worrying about one's appearance, talking, going to a show, eating, and

GET INVOLVED **8.1**

Dating Scripts of Women and Men

Complete the following task from the study by Rose and Frieze (1993, p. 502). Then ask two unmarried female and two unmarried male undergraduates to do the same.

From the perspective of your own gender, list the actions which a woman (use the word "man" *for male participants) would typically do as she (he) prepared for a first date with someone new, then met her (his) date, spent time during the date, and ended the date. Include at least 20 actions or events which would occur in a routine first date, putting them in the order in which they would occur.*

What Does It Mean?

1. What elements of a dating script were shared by your female and male respondents?
2. In what ways were the dating scripts gender-stereotypical?
3. How do your results compare to those of Rose and Frieze (1993) described in the text?
4. Based on your knowledge of gender stereotypes, gender-related attitudes, and socialization experiences, what might account for the differences in the dating scripts of females and males?
5. Do you think that the degree of traditional gender-stereotypical behavior in dating scripts would be the same on a fifth date as on a first date? Explain your answer.

---

kissing goodnight. Many of the elements of the date, however, were strongly gender-stereotypical. Males were the initiators. They asked for and planned the date, drove the car and opened doors, and started sexual interaction. Females, on the other hand, reacted to what men did: being picked up, having doors opened, and responding to sexual overtures. They also focused more on the private domain, such as concern about appearance and enjoying the date (Rose & Frieze, 1993). Dating scripts of lesbians and gay males are similar in many respects to those of heterosexuals, but they are not as strongly gender-typed (Rose & Zand, 2002).

Gender-Related Behaviors and Roles in Dating Relationships

Given the strong societal emphasis on women's physical attractiveness, it is understandable that college women, more than men, put a lot of time into getting ready for dates (Laner & Ventrone, 1998). This behavior is consistent with the heterosexual romantic script whereby women try to look attractive to men who, in turn, compete for their attention (Boynton, 2003).

Are there other gender-based behaviors that characterize romantic relationships? Although young adults' beliefs about appropriate behaviors and roles for women have become more egalitarian over time (Spence & Hahn, 1997; Twenge, 1997a), we have just seen that females and males still have traditional expectations about heterosexual dating. Consistent with societal stereotypes, college women will "try to act very feminine" when they want to impress a man (Sherman & Spence, 1997, p. 270), and college men like a woman "who dresses in feminine styles" and who "is soft and feminine" (Sherman & Spence, 1997, p. 269). We also see the operation of stereotypes in people's construction of appropriate behavior for males on a first date. Consistent with the stereotype of male agency, many college students expect males to play the more active role by planning the date and carrying out these plans, and a sizable minority believe men should pay for the date (Laner & Ventrone, 1998; Ross & Davis, 1996).

These views about appropriate dating behaviors reflect not only the stereotype of the communal female and the agentic male but also suggest that heterosexual romantic relationships are characterized by a continuing power imbalance between women and men (Laner & Ventrone, 1998). Does research evidence support this assumption of greater male power? Studies of late adolescents and young adults report wide variations in respondents' perceptions of the distribution of power in their heterosexual relationships. Judgments of equality were found in 29 to 79 percent of samples (Galliher et al., 1999; Sprecher & Felmlee, 1997) with variations reflecting the gender of the perceiver, differences among the samples in different studies, and types of power examined. Thus, some dating couples view their relationships as egalitarian, at least in terms of certain types of power, whereas others perceive a power imbalance. When there is inequality, who is seen as having more control? Consistent with males' greater power in society, couples are more likely to view males than females as the powerful partner (Sprecher & Felmlee, 1997). The status and value attached to males in North America might provide men with interpersonal resources to control outcomes in their romantic relationships with women. Moreover, men are more likely than women to view the male as the more powerful partner, possibly reflecting men's greater endorsement of a masculine power ideology (Sprecher & Felmlee, 1997).

Recent Trends in Dating

As more individuals remain single for longer periods of time, or become single as a result of divorce, elaborate partnering "markets" to help people in their quest for companionship and sex have developed in major cities, according to research by Edward Laumann and his colleagues (2004). His research team interviewed over 2,000 adults in four Chicago neighborhoods, including those with largely Black, Hispanic, or gay populations. They found that the partnering markets operate differently for women and men. Women, for example, were less likely than men to meet a partner through institutions such as work or church as they got older, making it harder to find someone. One reason for this is that men in their forties often sought women who were at least five to eight years younger. Neighborhoods and cultures also influenced the ways in which people found partners. In Hispanic neighborhoods, for example, family, friends, and the church played a more important role in meeting partners than in other areas. Young, upper-income individuals on the city's north side were more apt to find partners at school or work. Gay men surveyed were more likely to look for short-term relationships, while lesbians usually sought long-term partners.

Another contemporary way to meet a potential partner is to visit online dating sites. A growing number of singles—over 45 million in 2002—now subscribe to these services (Harmon, 2003; Mahoney, 2003). As of 2004, more than 800 dating sites were available (Williams, 2004). Online dating is rapidly shedding its image as a last resort for losers or a meeting ground for casual sex, as word spreads of successful long-term relationships that began online. Not surprisingly, traditional "dating scripts" still apply, at least in the sense that men almost always send the first e-mail message and rarely respond when a woman does so (Harmon, 2003).

Not only are there more single Americans than ever before, but more of them are middle-aged or elderly. Many older singles are either dating or looking for someone to date, according to a recent survey by AARP (2003). Interestingly, one-third of the women (like most men) prefer to date younger individuals. Older singles have more realistic dating expectations than younger ones. Few of them expect or want dating to lead to marriage. Instead they are looking for someone to talk to and do things with. And, like their younger single counterparts, many older adults are looking for partners or companions online (Sidener, 2004).

On the other hand, some singles report that the increased pressure to date encouraged by the barrage of Web sites, matchmaking services, books on attracting a mate, and reality television shows (*The Bachlorette, Average Joe*) is leading to "dating fatigue" (Zernike, 2003a). More people are dropping out of dating services, spending less time compulsively looking for people to date, and becoming more comfortable with not being part of a couple.

Committed Relationships

Committed relationships can take several different forms. Among heterosexuals, the most common type of committed relationship by far is marriage. Cohabitation (i.e., living together) has increased in recent years, often as a prelude to marriage. Lesbians and gay men also form committed relationships, although they are unable to legally marry in most of the United States. In this section, we examine these forms of committed relationships.

Marriage

Most women view marriage positively, although some variation occurs across ethnic groups. Specifically, Latinas are more oriented toward marriage than either Black or White women, and Black women show less interest than do women of other ethnic groups (Tucker & Mitchell-Kernan, 1995). How can these differences be explained? Latina women's commitment to marriage might reflect the strong value placed on family in Latina/o culture (Tucker & Mitchell-Kernan, 1995), while the more negative attitude of Black women might be because they see few financial benefits from marriage, given the high unemployment rate of Black men (Schwartz & Rutter, 1998).

Marriage Rates.   High marriage rates indicate the continuing value placed on marriage in our society. In 2002, 84 percent of White, 74 percent of Latina, and 62 percent of Black women 18 years or older were married or had been married at some point, with percentages for men at 74 percent, 63 percent, and 60 percent, respectively (U.S. Census Bureau, 2003). However, these rates reflect a slight decline over time and a rise in the age of first marriage. For example, the percentage of ever-married females dropped from 81 percent in 1990 to 79 percent in 2002 and the corresponding decline for males was 74 to 72 percent (U.S. Census Bureau, 2003c). Also, in 2003 the median age at first marriage was 25.3 for women and 27.1 for men, an increase of approximately four years since 1970 (Fields, 2004). This increase in age of marriage is due in part to changes in economic conditions, leading both women and men to desire some degree of financial security before embarking on a long-term commitment. In addition, as more women pursue higher education and careers, they tend to marry later (Riche, 2003; Settersten et al., 2005). Women with disabilities are less likely to marry and are more likely to marry later in life than men with disabilities or nondisabled women (Asch et al., 2001). The vast majority of Americans marry individuals of their own race. However, during the past 25 years the number of interracial marriages has increased, comprising about 1.7 percent of all married couples in 2003 (Fields, 2004; U.S. Census Bureau, 2003c).

Nature of the Relationship.   Not surprisingly, emotional expressiveness is very important for marital satisfaction. Disclosure of personal information to one's spouse and a willingness to express positive feelings about him or her lead to happier marriages (Culp & Beach, 1998; Vangelisti & Daly, 1997). Wives also tend to be happier and more satisfied when their husbands display an understanding of the relationship, perhaps because it reflects an interest in her (Acitelli, 1992) and/or a willingness to work on the marriage.

Consistent with the social construction of females as emotionally expressive and concerned about the feelings of others, women are more involved than men in maintaining this important emotional communication (e.g., Steil, 2001). They are more likely to try to listen to their spouses and make them feel loved (Lynch, 1998). In addition, wives provide better support on days when their husbands experience greater stress than they do. By contrast, when wives experience more stress, their husbands display a mixture of support and negativity (Neff & Karney, 2005). Among White newlyweds, wives communicate more with their husbands about themselves and their relationship than husbands communicate with their wives. However, this difference does not characterize Black newlyweds, possibly because Blacks do not endorse the cultural prohibition against men's emotional expressiveness as much as Whites do (Oggins et al., 1993).

Based on these gender differences in social-emotional involvement, one might expect that women's marital outcomes would be less positive than men's.

In fact, several studies do show that men experience greater marital satisfaction than women (e.g., Lasswell, 2002; Steil, 2001); however, other research shows no gender difference in marital satisfaction (e.g., Lucas et al., 2003). Further research is needed before firm conclusions can be drawn.

Whether or not men experience more satisfaction from their marriages than women do, it is clear that marriage provides women and men with many benefits. Both married women and men are happier than their unmarried counterparts, a relationship found in 42 nations around the globe (Diener et al., 2000). Moreover, married individuals, especially those in good relationships, are mentally and physically healthier (DeVaus, 2002; Gallo et al., 2003; Kiecolt-Glaser & Newton, 2001). They show a lower incidence of risky and antisocial behavior and greater financial success and stability (Johnson et al., 2004). This "marriage benefit" is smaller for women than for men, however, and is possibly even nonexistent, according to some researchers. People in strained, unhappy relationships usually fare worse medically than happily married individuals. Furthermore, marital stress affects women's health more than men's (Lerner, 2002).

Why are people in good marriages happier and healthier than single individuals? One obvious answer is the emotional support they receive from their spouse, although, as we have seen, women provide more support than they receive. Second, married couples often benefit financially because they have a combined household and, frequently, two incomes. Third, married people may be physically healthier than their nonmarried counterparts because spouses tend to encourage health-promoting behaviors in one another (DiMatteo, 2004; Gallo et al., 2003; Kantrowitz, 2004). It is also possible, of course, that individuals with positive personality traits and healthier lifestyles are more likely to attract a mate in the first place (Johnson et al., 2004).

Marriage in Later Life.   As life expectancy has increased, so has the incidence of long-term marriages. About one marriage in five now lasts at least 50 years (Birchler & Fals-Stewart, 1998). Since women typically marry older men and outlive them and since men are more likely to remarry following widowhood or divorce, many more men than women are married in later life (Smith & Baltes, 1999). Among Americans age 65 to 84, only 45 percent of women are married, compared with 74 percent of men. For people 85 and over, the percentages are much lower, especially for women: Only 12 percent of women and 58 percent of men are married (U.S. Census Bureau, 2003c).

Marriage appears to provide numerous benefits in later life, particularly for men. Married people, especially men, live longer. As noted above, they also have better mental and physical health and more economic resources than unmarried people (Kinsella & Velkoff, 2001). The majority of older people rate their marriages as happy or very happy, with men more satisfied than women. In part, marital satisfaction in later life probably reflects the selective survival of marriages that did not end in divorce (Huyck, 1995). In one longitudinal study of couples married between 50 and 69 years (Field & Weishaus, 1992), many respondents reported increased satisfaction and feelings of closeness in old age.

What factors contribute to a successful long-term marriage? In a survey of couples who had been married for 45 to 64 years, respondents said that the most important reason for the success of their marriage was involvement in an intimate relationship with someone they liked and enjoyed being with. Other important factors were commitment to the partner and to the institution of marriage, humor, and agreement on a wide variety of issues (Lauer et al., 1995).

Cohabitation

Cohabitation, *the state in which an unmarried couple lives together*, has dramatically increased in the United States over the last several decades. Over 40 percent of women ages 15 to 44 have lived with an unmarried male partner and 9 percent are cohabiting now (Booth & Crouter, 2002; Simmons & O'Connell, 2003). In Europe, marriage rates are plummeting and an estimated 50 percent of 25- to 34-year-olds are cohabiting (Kantrowitz, 2004).

For many couples, cohabitation serves as a trial marriage. In fact, the majority of first marriages and remarriages follow a period of cohabitation (Smock & Manning, 2004). A recent study found that most high school seniors view cohabitation as a desirable way for couples to determine before marriage whether they are compatible (Smock & Manning, 2004). For some couples, especially divorced or widowed persons, cohabitation is seen as an alternative to marriage and may involve having children (Raley & Wildsmith, 2004). Some women may be attracted to cohabitation because it provides freedom from traditional marital sex roles (J. Rice, 2001). Still other cohabiting women mention finances, convenience, and housing needs as the main reasons for moving in with a partner (Sassler, 2004).

Despite its popularity, not all people are in favor of cohabitation. One factor related to a willingness to cohabit is lower religiosity (Dush et al., 2003; Smock & Manning, 2004), perhaps because cohabitation is counter to the teachings of many religions. Furthermore, women who hold more liberal sexual views and less traditional gender attitudes have more positive views of cohabitation (Huffman et al., 1994). Clearly, this lifestyle is inconsistent with traditional views about premarital chastity for women and is less likely than marriage to enable fulfillment of traditional gender roles.

How happy are cohabiting couples and how do they feel about their relationship? Cohabitors tend to be happier than single individuals who are not living with a partner, but not as happy as married couples (Stack & Eshleman, 1998). In addition, cohabitors who do not expect to marry report less emotional commitment to their partner and feel less positive about their relationship than engaged or married cohabitors (Brown & Booth, 1996; Kline et al., 2004; Nock, 1995). Interestingly, there is some evidence that the differences between married and cohabiting couples' satisfaction and level of commitment are greater among Latinas/os than Blacks or Whites (Nock, 1995). Perhaps the strong value on family within Latina/o culture creates greater problems for Latina/o cohabiting couples.

Other comparisons show that married individuals who previously cohabited have more problems than those who did not. In fact, couples who cohabit prior to marriage are more likely than noncohabitors to get divorced (Dush et al., 2003). This does not necessarily mean that cohabitation fosters marital instability. Possibly, these findings result from a **selection effect** whereby *the attitudes of individuals who cohabit are more accepting of divorce and less committed to marriage than the attitudes of noncohabitors* (Smock & Manning, 2004).

Lesbian Relationships

Contrary to popular stereotypes, lesbians and gay men are as likely as heterosexuals to be part of a couple. Lesbian couples are more likely than gay men to be in a lasting, marriage-like relationship (Galliano, 2003). For example, nearly two-thirds of the gay couples who have married in Massachusetts have been women (Bellafante, 2005). Close to 75 percent of lesbians are in committed relationships (Bohan, 1996). Many are in long-term relationships of 20 years or more and symbolic signs of commitment, such as an exchange of rings, are common (Bryant & Demian, 1994). Lesbians are likely to meet their partners through friends or feminist or lesbian activities and are very unlikely to meet them at bars or through personal ads (Bryant & Demian, 1994).

In mid-twentieth century many lesbians adopted rigid male (butch) and female (femme) gender-related behaviors and roles. These roles were criticized

Lesbian couples are more likely than gay men to be in a lasting, marriage-like relationship.

during the feminist movement of the 1960s, based on concerns about sexism inherent in traditional gender expectations (Peplau & Beals, 2001; Smith & Stillman, 2002a). The last 20 years has seen a reemergence of the butch and femme experience for some lesbian women (Levitt & Hiestad, 2004). Even so, lesbian relationships tend to be egalitarian, with household activities, decision-making tasks, and other relationship behaviors based more on individual skills and interests than on rigid gendered conceptions of appropriate behaviors. In fact, lesbian relationships are characterized by more equality of power and a more equal division of paid and unpaid labor than are either heterosexual or gay relationships (Patterson et al., 2004; Peplau & Beals, 2001; Sanchez-Hucles, 2003; Solomon et al., 2004). Interestingly, bisexual women who have had relationships with partners of both genders report more conflicts over power in their heterosexual than in their same-gender relationships, in part because of dissatisfaction with the power balance in heterosexual relationships (Weinberg et al., 1994).

Most lesbians are involved in sexually exclusive relationships (Peplau & Beals, 2001). Although they engage in less frequent sex than either heterosexuals or gays (Bohan, 1996), they engage in considerable nongenital physical expression, such as hugging and cuddling, and are as satisfied with their sexual relationships as are heterosexual and gay couples (Littlefield et al., 2000; Patterson, 2000). In addition, some lesbians are involved in a **Boston marriage,** which is a *nonsexual romantic relationship between two lesbians* (Rothblum & Brehony, 1991). The partners feel love and affection for one another and consider themselves a couple. They are accepted by the lesbian community, which is rarely aware of the nonsexual nature of the relationship.

Although lesbians are generally satisfied with their relationships, lesbian couples experience a variety of unique stressors. First, the coming-out process can be problematic (Patterson, 2000). Conflicts can arise when one partner is more open about her sexual orientation than the other partner. Second, close same-gender friendships, which are common for women, might be threatening to the partners of lesbian women in these friendships (Bohan, 1996). Third, lesbians must cope with the frequent lack of societal acceptance of their relationship (Bohan, 1996). Fourth, lesbian couples frequently face economic difficulties, in part because their income is based on the earnings of two women and women tend to earn less than men (see Chapter 10) and because many lesbian couples are denied domestic partner insurance benefits typically awarded to married individuals ("Gays Win," 2003). Fifth, lesbian women are often denied custody of their children and may be prohibited from adopting their partner's child (Belluck & Liptak, 2004).

On a more positive note, lesbian couples report feeling less lonely than heterosexual married women (Grossman et al., 2001). Some writers suggest that lesbian couples are advantaged compared with heterosexual wives because they are more likely to have a partner with whom they expect to grow old, to share similar life expectancy, to be less threatened by changes in physical appearance, and to have accumulated their own financial resources through employment (Huyck, 1995).

Choosing to be in a relationship or to start a family can be especially problematic for disabled lesbians. They must deal with double stereotypes that do not see them either as possible partners or parents (O'Toole & Bregante, 1993).

Despite the stressors faced by lesbian couples, lesbians do not differ from heterosexual women in how much they love their partner (Bohan, 1996). Lesbians are as satisfied with their relationships as are heterosexuals (Kurdek, 1998; Patterson, 2000), and their satisfaction is based on similar factors. For example, both lesbians and heterosexuals feel better about their relationships when they and their partners share equal power and decision making, equal commitment to the relationship, and similar interests and backgrounds (Peplau & Beals, 2001). In addition, the quality of lesbians' relationships is dependent on their degree of openness about their sexual orientation. Lesbians who are open, especially to family and friends, tend to perceive their relationship more positively than those who are not in part because approval from one's family is highly related to relationship satisfaction (Caron & Ulin, 1997). Perhaps not surprisingly, lesbian couples who chose civil unions in Vermont when that option became available recently are more open about their sexual orientation than those not seeking that option (Solomon et al., 2004).

Aging lesbians must confront the triple obstacles of sexism, ageism, and homophobia (Jones, 2001). Older lesbians who faced prejudice and discrimination during more hostile times often hid their identities and their relationships with other women (Butler, 2004; Klinger, 2002). Even now, because of social constraints, they may not openly acknowledge the nature of their relationship. Unfortunately, this secrecy has led to the near invisibility of the elder lesbian and gay population, and to reduced access to health services.

Elderly lesbians in long-term committed relationships typically provide each other with a mutual support system and the economic benefits of sharing resources and a home (Roberto, 2001). Having had to cope with the social stigma of homosexuality, many lesbians and gays may be better prepared than heterosexuals to cope with the stigma of aging (Kimmel, 2002; Orel, 2002).

Unattached Lifestyles

When people marry, they don't always live happily ever after. Some divorce, others lose their spouses or same-sex partners through death. A small percentage of women never marry at all. In this section we examine various unattached lifestyles: divorce, singlehood, widowhood, and loss of a same-sex partner.

Divorce

Most couples probably do not walk down the aisle with expectations of splitting up. Nevertheless, approximately 40 percent of all American marriages end in divorce, although divorce rates have decreased somewhat in recent years (Hurley, 2005). Although separation and divorce are most likely to occur within the first 10 years of marriage, marriages can dissolve at any point in the life cycle (Hurley, 2005). Marriages end for numerous reasons—including incompatibility, communication problems, infidelity, substance abuse, and physical violence.

While divorce occurs throughout the population, divorce rates vary across ethnic groups and educational levels. Asian Americans have the lowest divorce rates in the United States and Native Americans have the highest. Black and Latina women are more likely to be separated than other women (Kreider & Simmons, 2003). In addition, college-educated individuals are less likely to divorce than those without college degrees (Hurley, 2005).

Women with disabilities are more likely than nondisabled women or men with disabilities to be divorced (Asch et al., 2001; Kilborn, 1999). Not surprisingly, both financial pressure and interpersonal problems can be contributing factors. If the spouse with a disability is unable to continue working, or if the nondisabled partner must quit work to care for her or his spouse, the couple might experience considerable financial strain. In addition, psychological reactions, such as anger or moodiness, on the part of either spouse or stress stemming from an overload of responsibilities for the nondisabled partner can damage the quality of the relationship. Consistent with the social construction of females as caregivers and the resultant socialization of girls to be responsive to the emotional needs within a relationship, wives are less likely than husbands to leave a spouse who has a disability (Kilborn, 1999).

Effects of Divorce on Women and Their Children.

Although divorced mothers view themselves as better parents than do mothers in high-conflict marriages, single parenting after a divorce can be highly stressful (Hetherington & Kelly, 2002). The breakup of a marriage produces numerous stressors for custodial parents and their children. Not only must both deal with strong emotional reactions, such as grief, anger, and guilt, but also their daily routines often involve major adjustment. Financial pressures can require the mother to begin or extend her employment, there can be major modifications in household responsibilities, and the family might have to change residence.

Given these and other stressors associated with parental divorce, children tend to experience a variety of emotional and behavioral problems in the immediate aftermath (Hetherington & Kelly, 2002; Hetherington, 2004; Wolchik et al., 2002), but most rebound within two years and are as psychologically healthy as children from two-parent homes. In fact, a meta-analysis comparing children from divorced and nondivorced families concluded that differences are very small and that children in conflict-ridden intact families experience lower levels of psychological well-being than do children in divorced families (Amato & Keith, 1991b). Another recent meta-analysis found that children in joint-custody arrangements following divorce are as well-adjusted as children in two-parent families (Bauserman, 2002).

Divorced women also experience initial problems followed by satisfactory adjustment. Immediately following the breakup, it is common for divorced women to experience higher levels of depression and distress than married women. These negative reactions are greatest in the first few years after the divorce and decline somewhat over time (Lasswell, 2002), with few long-term effects on women's psychological adjustment (Amato & Keith, 1991a; Thabes, 1997). Not surprisingly, other life conditions can affect a woman's adjustment to divorce. For example, studies suggest that Latinas experience more distress than White women, perhaps due to the triple burdens stemming from racism, sexism, and economic hardship (Parra et al., 1995). However, Black mothers show a greater sense of personal mastery following divorce than White mothers (McKelvey & McKenry, 2000), possibly because African American culture provides these women with greater coping skills to deal with the adversities of divorce.

Many women experience a dramatic decline in family income after divorce, which places them in a significantly worse financial situation than divorced men (Kilborn, 2004). Divorced mothers are nearly twice as likely as divorced fathers to live in poverty. Fewer than two-thirds of divorced mothers with children under 21 are awarded child support, and less than half of these receive full child support on a regular basis (U.S. Census Bureau, 2003a). White mothers are more likely than other groups to receive child support and other assets (Steil, 2001). But regardless of ethnicity, divorced women with low income and low occupational status are at risk for distress and depression (Keyes & Shapiro, 2004).

Despite the problems resulting from a breakup, divorce can represent a positive means of reacting to a neglectful, conflict-ridden, or abusive relationship, and women do not feel more upset after a divorce than they did in their high-conflict marriages. Although initially they experience depression and distress, women tend to be happier two years postdivorce than they were during the last year of their marriage. Further, divorced women are likely to be less depressed than women in unhappy marriages (Hetherington & Kelly, 2002).

In addition to relief from leaving a conflict-laden marriage, many women report a variety of positive psychological outcomes—greater feelings of independence and freedom, the ability to meet the challenges of living without a spouse; and to function as a single parent, which can produce a new sense of competence (Hetherington & Kelly, 2002). Moreover, they report greater life satisfaction than women who have never married (Frazier et al., 1996).

Coping with Divorce. What factors help women cope with the strains of divorce? According to Gina Bisagni and John Eckenrode (1995), employment can facilitate adjustment because it provides an identity outside of women's marital role. In their study, paid work was found to serve as a meaningful outlet—an avenue for productivity and a source of positive distraction and social support for divorced women. Consequently, it was associated with an increase in divorced women's self-esteem and a decrease in their feelings of distress. A teacher, commenting on how helpful it was to have the distraction of her job, stated, "Work filled my time and diverted my mind. . . . I was very busy with my job. It kept my mind off things for a while" (Bisagni & Eckenrode, 1995, p. 581). And a clerical worker described the social support she received from her job: "My coworkers really do care. Like when I was going through the divorce, they really wanted to know if I was okay, without trying to pry. . . . If I wasn't working here, if I couldn't talk to my coworkers, I probably would've gone to professional help a lot longer" (Bisagni & Eckenrode, p. 580).

Social support from family and friends is also vitally important in helping divorced women cope (Pinquart, 2003). Women who have a social network of friends and relatives to help them deal with the ramifications of divorce are less depressed in the years following the marital breakup (Jenkins, 2003; Thabes, 1997). In one study of divorced women, 96 percent of the Latina respondents and 78 percent of the White respondents stressed the importance of family members during the divorce (Parra et al., 1995). Romantic partners are another source of support; women who are in a romantic relationship tend to feel less depressed than those who are not (Thabes, 1997).

Single Women

Although some women become single at least for a period of time as a result of the end of a marriage, others never marry. Approximately 3.6 percent of women and 3.8 percent of men in the United States age 75 and over have never married (U.S. Census Bureau, 2003c). Women with disabilities are more likely than nondisabled women or men with disabilities to remain single (Asch et al., 2001; Hanna & Rogovsky, 1991).

While marriage is still viewed as the expected lifestyle, today there is more freedom in, acceptance of, and support for single lifestyles than in the past. Still, single women continue to be portrayed negatively in the media and are widely perceived as odd, social outcasts who lead barren, disappointing lives (Fraser, 2002; Hoban, 2002; Israel, 2002). How do never-married heterosexual women feel about being single today? Evidence shows that many are ambivalent about their marital status. On the one hand, they miss the benefits of steady companionship and feel sad about growing old alone, but at the same time, they enjoy their freedom, independence, and opportunities for self-development (AARP, 2003; Reynolds & Wetherell, 2003). Increasing numbers of single women are signing up for housewarming and birthday registries, having decided not to wait for marriage to request the china, crystal, and appliances they wish to own (Zernike, 2003a). Others are not only purchasing a home instead of renting but are also buying a second, vacation home (Cohen, 2003).

The absence of a marital partner does not mean that single women are lacking social relationships. As we have seen, some date (AARP, 2003) or are in committed romantic relationships, and many spend considerable time with nonromantic significant others, such as relatives, friends, and neighbors (Pinquart, 2003; Zernike, 2003a). In the words of one woman: "It would be nice to be in a relationship, but I don't really need that. My life is fine the way it is. And my life is full of love" (Boston Women's Health Book Collective, 1998, p. 187).

One disadvantage of being a single woman in midlife is that single women are expected, more so than their married sisters, to provide caregiving for aging parents, even at the expense of their own careers. Moreover, the single woman is less apt to have a caregiver for herself when this is needed, and as a result she is more likely to be institutionalized (Gottlieb, 1989).

On the plus side, never-married women typically have developed skills in independent living and in building support systems that stand them in good stead as they get older (Gottlieb, 1989; Newtson & Keith, 2001). Compared with married women, the never-married older woman is better educated, in better health, places a great deal of importance on her job, is less likely to be depressed and commit suicide, values her freedom and autonomy, and has close connections with both siblings and other interpersonal supports (Gottlieb, 1989). The workplace is a significant source of friends for single women, and in retirement these women go on to form new friendships with neighbors or members of organizations to which they belong (Doress-Worters & Siegal, 1994). Single older women have also learned to cope in their earlier years with the "stigma" of not being married and so are better able to deal with the effects of ageism in their later years. Most older, single women are satisfied with their lives and seem at least as happy as married women (Newtson & Keith, 1997; Paradise, 1993).

Widowhood

Despite the increasing divorce rate, most marriages are terminated not by divorce, but by the death of a spouse. In most countries of the world, women are much more likely to become widowed than men, since women not only have a longer life expectancy but also tend to marry men older than themselves (Kinsella & Velkoff, 2001). As of 2002, there were 11.4 million widows but only 2.6 million widowers in the United States, a ratio of more than 4 to 1. About 61 percent of women over the age of 75, but only 21 percent of men the same age, are widowed (U.S. Census Bureau, 2003). Black women are widowed at a younger age than White women (Bradsher, 2001).

Remarriage rates are much higher for widowers than for widows in many countries of the world (Kinsella & Velkoff, 2001; Walter, 2003). In the United States, for example, by two years after the death of a spouse, 61 percent of men are in a new romantic relationship, and 25 percent are remarried. The figures for women, on the other hand, are only 19 percent and 5 percent, respectively (Wortman et al., 2004). Consequently, elderly women are three times as likely to live alone as are elderly men (Fields, 2004).

One obvious reason for the much lower remarriage rate of women is that unmarried older women greatly outnumber unmarried older men. In 2002, for instance, unmarried women aged 65 and over in the United States outnumbered unmarried men in that age category by more than 3 to 1 (U.S. Census Bureau, 2003c). Furthermore, since men tend to marry women younger than themselves, the pool of potential mates expands for an older man but shrinks for an older woman. In addition, widowed women are much less likely than widowed men to be interested in forming a new relationship. Widows point out that they value their independence and enjoy their freedom. Moreover, they are not eager to resume the domestic responsibilities of a long-term relationship. Many do not relish the idea of becoming a caregiver for an older man, having, in some cases, already experienced the stresses of caring for a terminally ill partner (Beers & Jones, 2004; Wortman et al., 2004).

Four months after her husband of 42 years died, Verna hit an emotional low. "I told myself I have two choices. I can sit home, mourn, complain and cry, or make a new life in which I would learn to smile and be happy again in my own activities such as volunteering and starting a social life with new friends who aren't couples. (Arney, 2001)

Reaction and Adjustment to Widowhood.   Widowhood is one of the most stressful of all life events. The surviving spouse must not only cope with the loss of one's life partner but also adjust to a new status as a widowed person (Utz et al., 2004). During the first year after their husband's death, widows show poorer mental and physical health than longer term widows (Wilcox et al., 2003). Most elderly widowed individuals adjust to their spouse's death within two to four years, although feelings of loneliness, yearning, missing their partner, and lowered life satisfaction remain for extended periods of time (Cutter, 1999; Lucas et al., 2003; Wisocki, 1998). As many as 10 to 20 percent of widows, however, experience long-term problems, including clinical depression, abuse of alcohol and prescription drugs, and increased susceptibility to physical illness. Among these are women with a prior history of depression, those whose marriages were less satisfactory, those whose husbands' deaths followed the deaths of other close relatives and friends, and those who depended on their husbands for most social contacts (Cutter, 1999).

Other factors—age, the degree of forewarning of the spouse's death, and financial, social, and personal resources—also affect a woman's reaction to widowhood (Bradsher, 2001; Michael et al., 2003). Studies comparing the mental and physical health of older widows and older married women generally have not found any differences between these groups (O'Bryant & Hansson, 1995). Younger widows, on the other hand, initially experience greater difficulties in coping with their situation (Michael et al., 2003). One reason for the greater distress experienced by young widows may be the greater likelihood that the husband's death was unexpected. Although younger individuals experience greater distress following their partner's death, the length of recovery is greater for older people (Michael et al., 2003).

Widowhood often results in a substantial reduction in financial resources for women, not only because the husband's income ceases, but also because considerable expenses may be incurred during the husband's final illness (Hungerford, 2001; McGarry & Schoeni, 2003). Elderly women, especially those living alone, are more likely than elderly men to live in poverty (Jenkins, 2003).

Loneliness is another problem faced by widows. About 70 percent of elderly widows live alone (Fields & Casper, 2001). Having the social support of family, friends, and neighbors to stave off loneliness helps to alleviate the psychological and physical effects of loss-related stress (Jenkins, 2003; Laditka & Laditka, 2003; Pinquart, 2003; Zettel & Rook, 2004). Women friends who are themselves widowed can be particularly supportive (Belsky, 1999). Interestingly, research has found more loneliness among women who have lived with a spouse for many years than among women who live alone (Cohler & Nakamura, 1996).

The death of a spouse takes a heavier toll on men than on women. Widowed men suffer more psychological depression, psychiatric disorders, physical illnesses, and have higher death rates and suicide rates than widowed women (Canetto, 2003; Ray, 2004; Wisocki & Skowron, 2000). This may be due to the fact that women are more apt than men to admit a need for social support, to benefit from that support, and to have broad social networks with relatives and friends, including other widows (Antonucci et al., 2001; Nagourney et al., 2004; Ray, 2004).

The experiences of widowhood are vividly portrayed in a recent longitudinal study of over 4,300 older Australian widows by Susan Feldman and her colleagues (Feldman et al., 2000). The concerns of the widows were not restricted just to the experience of bereavement and loss but also involved the challenges of daily life, including financial and social matters. Recent widows worried about managing their personal finances and coping with financial hardship. Another common theme was the need to keep busy. Relationships to family, friends, neighbors, and social groups became especially important. Many women displayed an attitude of courage, strength, and resilience as they coped with the challenges of their new life. In the words of one woman, who had been widowed for four years,

> *I felt desolate and despairing [when he died]. . . . I have managed to survive and lead a comfortable and quite interesting (albeit at times a rather lonely) life. I am pleased that I have adjusted, and I handle all of my affairs. I shall never get over the loss, but I have lived to see the day.* (Feldman et al., 2000, p. 164)

This realization that they have withstood an event that seemed insurmountable appears to enhance the self-esteem of widowed women (Carr, 2004).

Keep in mind that our knowledge of widows has been obtained primarily from older women, most of whom had traditional marriages. When the young women of today become widows, they will be more likely than the current population of widows to have had a different set of life experiences, including a college education and a job or career that will better prepare them for a healthy adjustment to widowhood (Etaugh & Bridges, 2005).

Loss of a Same-Sex Partner

Lesbians and gay men may encounter unique problems when their partner dies. They may not be eligible for survivor benefits and in the absence of a will, they may have no claim to the partner's estate that they have helped to build (Peplau & Beals, 2001). Loss of a same-sex partner is especially stressful if the relationship was not publicly acknowledged, but even when the relationship is open, friends, family, and work colleagues may not comprehend the severity and nature of the loss (Fullmer et al., 1999; Walter, 2003).

> *Recently, I vacationed with friends who had been friends also with my deceased partner-in-life. A guest arrived with slides of earlier vacations, including pictures of my lover. I objected that if I had been a man who had been recently widowed, they surely would have asked if I would object to showing the pictures. One friend responded she wanted*

very much to see them. She blanched when I suggested that she might feel differently after the death of her husband. Clearly, she thought that my relationship to Karen differed from her marriage; she evidently also thought my love differed from her friendship with Karen only by degree. Heterosexuals really do not understand what lesbians feel for their partners, even when they know us well. All of these friends had known Karen and me as lovers and had sent me bereavement condolences when Karen died. (in Doress-Worters & Siegal, 1994, p. 145)

Motherhood

One of the most intimate relationships a woman can experience is her relationship with her child. Consistent with the assumption that motherhood serves as a major source of fulfillment for women, many women view bearing and/or rearing their children as the most meaningful experience of their lives (Josselson, 1996). In the words of one mother, "For the first time I cared about somebody else more than myself, and I would do anything to nurture and protect her" (Boston Women's Health Book Collective, 1992, p. 488).

This does not mean, however, that parenting leads exclusively to positive emotions. Instead, as Yael Oberman and Ruthellen Josselson (1996) point out, mothers experience a swirl of opposing emotions. Motherhood can bring a great sense of power and joy accompanied by a tremendous burden of responsibility and guilt. As one woman said, "The first month was awful. I loved my baby but felt apprehensive about my ability to satisfy this totally dependent tiny creature. Every time she cried I could feel myself tense up and panic" (Boston Women's Health Book Collective, 1998, p. 511). Motherhood can produce an expansion of personal identity as well as the loss of self. Mothers can feel exhilarated by their new role yet resent or mourn the loss of other aspects of their lives that might now diminish, such as involvement in work or community activities, or even commitments to friendships, which necessarily change (Hayt, 2002).

Stereotypes of Mothers

Despite the multidimensionality of women's actual experiences of motherhood, people tend to impose a "good mother" stereotype on them. The good mother stereotype is socially constructed as a warm, forgiving, generous, nurturing, person who is able to meet all her children's needs and who puts their needs before her own (Fleming, 2002; Douglas & Michaels, 2004). Unfortunately, as Kathy Weingarten and her colleagues (Weingarten et al., 1998) point out, no mother is able to consistently meet either her own standards or the standards of others, and all suffer at least occasionally because of this idealized image. One mother complained, "I didn't know how to change a diaper any more than my husband did. In fact, I may have been more nervous about it, since I was 'supposed' to know how" (Boston Women's Health Book Collective, 1998, p. 511). Popular childrearing books do little to dispel this notion. One recent study examined the degree to which 23 current popular childrearing books portrayed the "new image" of the involved father (Fleming & Tobin, 2005). Only 4 percent of paragraphs mentioned fathers. In addition, the father's role was portrayed as predominantly ancillary to the mother's and was often depicted as voluntary and negotiable.

The good-mother image perpetuates feelings of inadequacy and guilt in women as they strive to achieve "perfect motherhood" (Warner, 2005). It also can lead people to blame mothers for their children's problems (Douglas & Michaels, 2004; Miller-Day, 2004) because the social construction of the mother role, more than the father role, assumes an all-knowing, self-sacrificing, always-caring parent. This may explain why a man who harms or even kills his own children barely makes the local news, whereas when Andrea Yates drowned her five children (see Chapter 7), she received international attention (Barash, 2002).

The good mother stereotype illustrates the **motherhood mandate,** *the societal belief that women should have children and that they should be physically available at all times to tend to their young children's needs* (Russo, 1979). This view of motherhood was very evident in North America before the women's movement in the 1960s and 1970s, but recent decades have seen a dramatic increase in the employment of women, including those with children (see Chapter 11). Does this mean that the motherhood mandate has waned? Many researchers believe it has come back in a different form. According to Betty Holcomb (1998), an editor of *Working Mother*, the 1990s witnessed "the birth of a new mystique about motherhood" (p. 48), evidenced by the media's glorification of middle-class mothers who leave the workplace to become full-time homemakers, combined with the contradictory denigration of women on welfare who stay home with their children. Susan Douglas and Meredith Michaels (2004) criticize the "new momism" in which the mother is expected to devote her entire being, all the time, to her children.

In addition to communal qualities, there are numerous demographic characteristics included in the societal image of the good mother. According to researchers (Franzblau, 2002; Johnston & Swanson, 2003a; Weingarten et al., 1998), the good mother is expected to be middle-class, heterosexual, married, not too old, and to have a job that does not prevent her from spending "adequate" time with her children. The more a mother deviates from this image, the more devalued she is and the less likely her own mothering practices and experiences are seen as valid. In the words of a homeless mother: "People definitely think we're not good mothers—just for the fact that we're homeless, we're not good mothers" (Koch et al., 1998, p. 62).

A recent content analysis of contemporary women's magazines by Deirdre Johnston and Debra Swanson (2003b) found mixed messages that could undermine the confidence of both employed and stay-at-home mothers. Women were almost always portrayed as full-time homemakers, but these women were frequently shown as overwhelmed, confused, and interested only in superficial topics. When employed mothers were shown, their focus was on whether employment jeopardized family relationships.

Like many other research findings, the motherhood stereotype reflects the primarily White middle-class viewpoint about White middle-class mothers.

A look at some images of Black mothers as viewed by both the White dominant culture and the Black community gives us a different picture of motherhood. According to psychologist Elizabeth Sparks (1998), three stereotypes of Black mothers have been prominent in the last several decades. The **matriarch stereotype**, an image of Black women constructed by Whites, applies to *the Black mother who not only works outside the home and thus fails to adequately fulfill the mother role, but who also antagonizes her male partner to the point that he chooses to leave the family.* This stereotype leads Whites to attribute blame for many societal problems, including unemployment, teenage pregnancies, and a high crime rate to Black mothers. A second image held by Whites is that of the **welfare mother stereotype**, a view of *the Black mother who is lazy, sexually promiscuous, uninvolved emotionally in her children, and unable to socialize her children toward hard work.* According to Sparks, a third stereotype of the Black mother is one that has been embraced by Blacks. This is the **superwoman stereotype** and refers to an *idealized image of a Black woman who sacrifices her own needs for those of her children and family while contributing to her family's economic security and working to advance the Black community.*

These three images ignore societal conditions and assume that the individual has total responsibility for her own outcomes (Sparks, 1998). They disregard the harsh realities of poverty and prejudice that characterize the lives of many Black families and greatly limit women's opportunities and choices regarding goals and lifestyle. This disregard can result in blaming mothers who do not fulfill the superwoman image. Furthermore, because many Black women have internalized the ideal image of the superwoman, some blame themselves for what they perceive as a personal failure and feel guilty and worthless.

Single Mothers

In the last several decades there has been a significant increase in the percentage of single-parent, mother-headed families. Whereas in 1970 approximately 12 percent of families were maintained by a mother only, this figure increased to 26 percent in 2003, including 47 percent of Black, 25 percent of Latina, 14 percent of White, and 13 percent of Asian families. By comparison, only 6 percent of households are maintained by a single father (Fields, 2004). Who are these single mothers? Approximately two-thirds are White, and most have one or two children. Furthermore, they tend to be very poor. Nearly half of all households below the poverty line are headed by single mothers (Bridges, 2003/2004). As Table 8.1 shows, about one-third of female-headed families with dependent children live in poverty, and this number is significantly greater among Black and Latina families than White families. Note that single-father families of all ethnicities are much less likely to be poor. *The increasing percentage of women living below the poverty line* is referred to as the **feminization of poverty**.

Although there are several types of single mothers, including teen parents and divorced mothers, the most rapidly increasing category is the never-married adult. Whereas in 1960 only 4 percent of single mothers had never been married, in 1998 that figure increased to 40 percent (Popenoe & Whitehead, 1999). These

TABLE 8.1   **Poverty Status of Single-Parent Families in 2002**

Ethnicity	Single-Mother Families % Below the Poverty Level	Single-Father Families % Below the Poverty Level
All ethnic groups	32	16
Black	40	26
Latina/o	40	22
White	26	11

Source: Fields (2004).

never-married women include unmarried women living with an other-gender or same-gender partner, women who are not in relationships and who choose to become parents, and unmarried women who are raising their child alone but did not choose this lifestyle (Fields, 2004; Wark, 2005).

What are some of the problems experienced by single mothers? Given the high proportion of single mothers living in poverty and the lower earnings of women compared to men (see Chapter 10), it is not surprising that financial problems are a major source of stress. Also, because they are frequently juggling housekeeping, childrearing, and employment responsibilities, single mothers have to deal with problems involving time and the coordination of activities (Hertz & Ferguson, 1998).

How do women cope with the responsibilities of single motherhood? One important factor is social support. Studies of both White middle-class (Hertz & Ferguson, 1998) and Black and White low-income mothers (Olson & Ceballo, 1996) found that support from family and friends is crucial. This support can come in the form of backup help when there is an emergency, regular assistance with transportation to and from day care, and the watchful eye of a neighbor while the mother is at work.

Suzanne Randolph (1995) discusses several strengths of Black families and communities that help Black single mothers cope more effectively. Because Blacks have a long history of maternal employment, single mothers have numerous role models for managing the stressors of coordinating these roles. **Extended families**, in which *at least one other adult family member resides in the same household as the mother and her children* and **augmented families**, in which *adult nonrelatives live with the mother and her children* are family structures in the Black community that can be helpful to single mothers. These families offer additional role models for the children and provide substitute caregivers when the mother is at work or is tending to other responsibilities outside of the home. Because extended families are frequently involved in childrearing in Latina/o and Native American as well as Black families (Coll et al., 1995), they can be helpful to single mothers in these communities as well.

Social support is one of the factors that is critical in promoting positive educational performance and behavior in children of single mothers. A recent study found that in the presence of favorable maternal characteristics, such as education and positive expectations of the child, along with social and economic resources supportive of parenting, children of single mothers did as well behaviorally and academically as children in two-parent homes (Ricciuti, 2004b). The findings were similar for Black, Latina, and White children. Unfortunately, many single mothers lack the social, economic, or parenting resources that promote good parenting.

Lesbian Mothers

Although North American society tends to think of families from a heterosexual perspective, a lesbian sexual orientation is not inconsistent with motherhood. In fact, an estimated 10–14 million children in the United States are raised by lesbian or gay parents (Patterson & Friel, 2000). The majority of these children were born into previous heterosexual marriages; however, a growing number of lesbians choose to involve children in their lives after they have identified as lesbians. These women make use of artificial insemination, maternal surrogacy, adoption, or foster care (Johnson & Piore, 2004; Morris et al., 2002).

Because custody battles involving lesbian mothers frequently focus on the psychological adjustment and parenting styles of lesbian mothers, numerous studies have examined lesbians in their motherhood role (Morris et al., 2002; Tasker 2002). These studies show that lesbian mothers are similar to heterosexual mothers in self-esteem and psychological adjustment (Golombok et al., 2003). This similarity between lesbian and heterosexual mothers is particularly noteworthy when we consider that lesbian mothers face stressors not experienced by heterosexual parents. The intensified social disapproval frequently encountered by lesbian mothers makes them feel more isolated (Bohan, 1996). Some lesbians face rejection by their families of origin when they decide to parent (Dominus, 2004; Gartrell et al., 2000; Johnson & O'Connor, 2002). Furthermore, unlike the heterosexual community, the lesbian community is not structured around children, and this, too, can add to lesbians' sense of isolation (Bohan, 1996).

While lesbian women do not differ from heterosexual women in nurturance or commitment to their children, they do raise their daughters and sons in a less gender-stereotypic manner (Patterson, 2000; J. Rice, 2001). As models of gender-related behavior, they are less traditional than heterosexual mothers (Carrington, 2002). For example, partners are more likely to equally share financial and family responsibilities and be involved in feminist activities. Lesbian mothers also are less likely to purchase gender-stereotyped toys for their children and have less traditional gender-related expectations for their daughters.

Recent research on lesbian donor insemination families shows that the quality of children's relationship with the social mother is comparable to that with the biological mother (Vanfraussen et al., 2003). Moreover, unlike fathers in heterosexual families, the social mother is as involved in the child's activities as is the biological mother.

Just as the research on lesbian mothers finds few differences from heterosexual mothers, scores of studies show few differences between children raised by lesbian mothers and those raised by heterosexual mothers. Reviews of this research conclude that children from lesbian and heterosexual families are similar in psychological adjustment, self-esteem, moral adjustment, relationships with their peers, and cognitive functioning (Johnson & O'Connor, 2002; Patterson, 2000; Stacey & Biblarz, 2001; Wainwright et al., 2004). In addition to psychological adjustment, researchers have focused on the gender-related development of children raised in lesbian families. Not surprisingly, given that lesbian mothers raise their children in a less gender-stereotypic manner than heterosexual parents, their children, especially daughters, are less likely to have stereotyped notions of masculine and feminine behavior and more likely to aspire to occupations that cross traditional gender lines (Fulcher et al., 2003; Stacey & Biblarz, 2001). Also, adult children of lesbian mothers, like those of heterosexual mothers, have a gender identity consistent with their biological sex and are no more likely to have a lesbian, gay, or bisexual orientation (Dominus, 2004; Patterson, 2000; Wainwright, Russell, & Patterson, 2004). See Learn about the Research 8.2 to examine the psychological and social outcomes of adults raised by lesbian mothers.

Mothers with Disabilities

The traditional view held by society is that women with disabilities are psychologically unable to cope with the demands of pregnancy, childbirth, and childrearing (Hwang, 1997; Olkin, 2003). However, there is no evidence that disabled mothers are less capable parents than nondisabled women (Hwang, 1997). Through the Looking Glass (TLG) is a non-profit organization that provides services and training to prospective and new parents with disabilities.

The Postparental Period

Since my boys left, I have started dedicating my time to worthy causes that I enjoy. I volunteer at the hospital, spend a few hours a week at a retirement home, and I joined a women's group. My husband and I also are planning a vacation. We haven't done that—just the two of us—in a long time. These changes are good for me. Sure I still miss the boys, but they're growing up now. It's part of life, so you make the best of it. (55-year-old woman)

Motherhood, as we have seen, is an important aspect of identity for most women. How do mothers experience the **postparental period,** that is, *the period of a parent's life when children no longer live in the parent's home?* Considerable evidence indicates most women react quite positively to this "empty nest" period. Women in midlife frequently feel that the postparental period provides new opportunities for self-development (Clay, 2003). Some women pursue new careers, others further their education, and others provide service to their communities.

LEARN ABOUT THE RESEARCH 8.2

Adult Children of Lesbian Mothers

Most of the research on the effects of lesbian mothers on children has focused on school-age children. Fiona Tasker and Susan Golombok expanded on this research by examining the experiences of young adults who had been raised by lesbian mothers and comparing these to the experiences of their counterparts reared by heterosexual mothers. The researchers restricted the heterosexual sample to adults whose mothers had been single for some period while raising them in order to compare two groups of children whose mothers differed in sexual orientation, but not in the presence of a man in the household. Twenty-five children of lesbian mothers and 21 children of heterosexual mothers were interviewed.

The findings showed no difference in the psychological well-being of the two groups of adult children. Moreover, adults raised by lesbian mothers were no more likely than those in heterosexual families to have experienced same-gender sexual attraction. However, there was a difference in sexual experimentation. Of those who reported some same-gender interest, children raised by lesbian mothers were more likely than children in heterosexual families to have been involved in a same-gender sexual relationship. These relationships ranged from a single incident of kissing to cohabitation. All of the respondents in both groups had also experienced at least one heterosexual relationship. Having a lesbian mother may thus broaden the adolescent's view of acceptable sexual behavior possibilities. However, the finding that 23 of the 25 young adults raised by lesbian mothers identified themselves as heterosexuals suggests that consideration of same-gender sexual relationships does not lead to a lesbian or gay sexual identity.

In regard to childhood peer relationships, slightly more of the adults raised in lesbian rather than heterosexual families recalled having been teased about their sexuality. However, the percentage who reported this teasing was low; it included 11 percent of the children of lesbian mothers compared to 4 percent of the children raised by heterosexual mothers.

What Does It Mean?

1. The respondents from heterosexual families had been raised by mothers who had been single for some period of time during the respondent's childhood. Do you think differences between the two groups would have been more pronounced if the adult children of heterosexual mothers had come from homes with both a mother and father? Explain your answer.
2. Prepare an argument in support of or in opposition to lesbian motherhood. Refer to the findings of this study, other material from this chapter, theories of gender typing (see Chapter 3), and any other information that you believe is relevant.
3. Do you think that adults raised by lesbian mothers, versus those reared by heterosexual mothers, differ in the way they raise their own children? Explain your answer.

Source: Tasker & Golombok (1997).

There is no evidence that disabled women are less capable mothers than other women.

And, because children can be a source of tension in any marriage, women often report higher marital satisfaction once their children have left home (Cavanaugh & Blanchard-Fields, 2006).

Of course the postparental period is not experienced the same way by all women. Some women, who are reluctant to let go of their parenting role, may perceive this period as stressful and as a time of loss (Van Steenhouse, 2002). Mothers who are employed during the childrearing years establish an identity in addition to their motherhood role, and this can ease the difficulty of relinquishing parenting responsibilities (Lippert, 1997). On the flip side of the coin, more adult children are either leaving home later or returning home in their twenties and thirties for financial or personal reasons (Buss, 2005; Cohen et al., 2003; E. Spragins, 2003). Between 1970 and 2000, the percentage of 24- to 34-year-olds living with parents or grandparents increased by 50 percent. While the numbers are fairly small overall—about 14 percent—the trend is most visible in large expensive cities such as New York, where the figure jumps to 30 percent (Lewin, 2003). The return to the nest of these older children can be stressful for some parents and may disrupt plans to move or retire. To find out more about experiences of the postparental period, try Get Involved 8.2.

GET INVOLVED **8.2**
Women's Experiences during the Postparental Period

Interview two midlife women whose children have left home. Choose any women available to you, such as relatives, neighbors, classmates, and the like. However, if possible, select one woman whose last child left home within the year and another whose children have been gone for several years. Ask each to identify (1) any positive and/or negative experiences. Also, ask each to indicate (2) any changes in her employment role (e.g., started a new job, increased her work hours), community service, and/or leisure activities as a result of her children's departure, and to indicate (3) whether she perceives these changes as primarily positive or primarily negative.

What Does It Mean?

1. How would you characterize the experiences of your two interviewees? Did they mention more positive or negative experiences? How do their experiences compare to the postparental outcomes reported in the text?

2. What changes, if any, did they make in their life roles? How did they feel about these changes?

3. Were there any differences in the experiences of the woman whose children recently left home and the woman whose children left years earlier? If yes, how do you explain these differences?

4. Do you think the postparental experiences of these midlife women will differ from the future experiences of today's young adults? Why or why not?

Relationships in the Later Years

As women get older, they experience several changes in their family relationships. Earlier in the chapter, we saw that marriages may end as a result of divorce or death. Bonds with siblings often become stronger as one gets older. In addition, new life enters the family in the form of grandchildren and great-grandchildren. Role reversal often occurs as aging women become caregivers for their even older parents. In this section, we will explore these changes.

Siblings

Most older Americans have at least one living sibling. Because women live longer, a surviving sibling is often a sister (Treas & Spence, 1994). Sisters and brothers play a unique role in the lives of older people, drawing on the shared experiences of childhood and most of the lifespan (McKay & Caverly, 2004). Feelings of closeness and compatibility among siblings increase throughout the course of adulthood and are generally strong in later life (Roberto, 2001; Scharf et al., 2005). Sibling bonds vary across ethnic groups, with older Blacks relying more on siblings for assistance than do their White or Latina/o counterparts (Bedford, 1995). Relationships with sisters are emotionally closer than those with brothers, and the bond between sisters is particularly close (Canetto, 2003). The closer women and men over 65 are to their sisters, the fewer symptoms of depression they have. This is especially true for recently widowed women. For rural aged women, life satisfaction is higher if they simply have a sister living nearby, regardless of the amount of contact they have (Bedford, 1995).

The closeness of the sibling bond in later life is illustrated in the following comment:

> *I have two sisters who live upstairs. People are always surprised that we get along so well, living in the same house. My sisters never go out without coming by to ask me if they can get me anything. We weren't always like that. We were too busy with our own lives. Now we try hard to help each other.* (a 70-year-old widow, in Doress-Worters & Siegal, 1994, p. 134)

Adult Children

Women are typically described as the family "kinkeepers," maintaining the bonds between and within generations. They typically organize family communication and their children are more apt to confide in them than their fathers (Hendrick, 2001; Lefkowitz & Fingerman, 2003). Adult daughters maintain closer ties to their parents than do sons. During adolescence, the mother-daughter relationship is often characterized by both closeness and emotional conflict. Closeness typically increases once the daughter leaves home to attend college (Smetana et al., 2004). The positive link between grown daughters and their mothers can be enormously satisfying, as shown in recent surveys of older women and their middle-aged daughters (Fingerman, 2001; Miller-Day, 2004; Moen, 1996). Close mother-daughter ties include satisfying interactions, a history of little conflict, few control issues, and many opportunities for informal contact (Blieszner et al., 1996; Lefkowitz & Fingerman, 2003). In the words of four mothers;

> *She has been awfully good to me in every way, when I'm sick and when I'm well, when I'm in a good humor and when I'm in a bad humor.*

> *I can reason with [my daughter] and she understands me. We just sit down and talk it over. We never have an argument. Not that we're perfect, but it's just not necessary.*

> *We go for lunch. We go shopping. . . . I may go three or four days or a week and not see her, but we talk. I feel like that starts my day.* (Blieszner et al., 1996, pp. 13–18)

> *She tells me about her work and sometimes her problems, which includes me in her world. It makes me happy.* (Fingerman, 2001, p. 60)

While some older women (and men) live with their adult children, this is the least preferred residential choice for elderly people (Bould & Longino, 2001). Elderly Americans strongly prefer living alone even when in declining health. Most would rather have "intimacy at a distance" than live with relatives. Half of elderly parents do, however, live within 10 miles of an adult child (Usdansky, 2000). Elderly women who live alone report high levels of psychological well-being and appear to be doing as well as, or even better than, older women who live with a spouse (Michael et al., 2001). Informal and formal caregiving systems in the community contribute to this well-being by enabling older persons to remain at home longer. The elderly usually first seek care from the informal system of family, friends, and neighbors (Family Caregiver Alliance, 2003). When informal sources cannot meet their needs, older individuals turn to the services of organizations and professionals, such as Meals on Wheels, van service for the disabled, home aides, and visiting nurses (Shapiro, 2001).

Nearly one in ten elderly men and two in ten elderly women reside with their adult children, siblings, or other relatives (AARP, 1999), usually because of increasing infirmity. Living with an adult child is more prevalent among ethnic minority elderly than among Whites in the United States, and this living arrangement is also common in developing countries (Bongaarts & Zimmer, 2002; Kinsella & Velkoff, 2001). (For a closer look see Explore Other Cultures 8.2.)

In the United States, older Asian Americans are most likely to live with their children. Blacks and Latinas/os are less likely to live with their children than Asian Americans, and Whites are least likely to do so (Armstrong, 2001). As we saw earlier, older ethnic minority women play key roles in their family networks by providing economic, social, and emotional support to their adult children and grandchildren. Poor Black households are predominantly organized around women, with older women at the center. Males are more directly involved in Latina/o and Native American households and families. Still, women in these groups enjoy greater prestige, respect, and domestic authority as they grow older (Armstrong, 2001; Padgett, 1999).

EXPLORE OTHER CULTURES **8.2**
Living Arrangements for Elderly Women and Men

In the United States, half of all women aged 75 and older live alone, in contrast to less than one-fourth of men in the same age category. Looked at another way, close to 80 percent of all U.S. adults 75 and over who live by themselves are women (Fields, 2004). Figures for Canada and Great Britain are comparable to those for the United States, and a similar pattern is found in most other developed countries. In most Asian countries, however, the situation is quite different. About 75 percent of elderly women and men live with relatives, many of them in three-generation households (Ofstedal et al., 2003). Multigenerational families also remain common in rural parts of Eastern Europe, including Russia, Poland, and Romania. Even so, older women in these countries still are two to three times as likely as older men to live alone (Mercer et al., 2001).

In developing countries, relatively few older women and men live alone. In some of these countries, it is traditional for an older woman to live with her eldest son. This arrangement is commonly found in some African countries and in several Asian nations, including China, India, Pakistan, and Bangladesh (U.S. Census Bureau, International Database, 1995, 1997). You may recall from Chapter 4 that these Asian countries place a much higher value on sons than daughters, resulting in abortion of female fetuses and greater neglect of female children. Can you see the link between these practices and the sons' obligation to care for parents in their old age?

Grandchildren

> *The greatest gift I ever received was my grandmother. My grandmother has been the backbone of my life since I was 18 months old, when I began living with her. My grandmother put her life on hold so that I could become the best I could be.* (Sharoia Taylor, age 16, in AARP, 2004, p. 11)

The stereotyped portrayal of a grandmother is often that of an elderly, white-haired woman providing treats for her young grandchildren. However, grandmothers do not fit into any one pattern. While more than 75 percent of Americans over age 65 are grandparents, some people become grandparents as early as their late twenties. About half of women experience this event by age 47, and some spend half of their lives as grandmothers (Etaugh & Bridges, 2005; Sheehy, 2002). Nowadays, many middle-aged grandmothers are in the labor force and may also have responsibilities for caring for their elderly parents (Velkoff & Lawson, 1998). Thus, they may have less time to devote to grandparenting activities. On the other hand, more grandmothers are taking on the responsibility of raising their grandchildren, as we will see later in the chapter. Grandmothers' involvement with their grandchildren depends on a number of factors, including geographical distance, the grandmother's relationship with her grandchild's parents, and the grandmother's physical and mental health (Roberto, 2001).

Earlier in the chapter, we noted that the ties between family generations are maintained largely by women. One example of this is that grandmothers tend to have warmer relationships with their grandchildren than do grandfathers. The maternal grandmother often has the most contact and the closest relationship with grandchildren (Walther-Lee & Stricker, 1998). In some parts of the world, in fact, the presence of a grandmother may spell the difference between life and death for her grandchildren (see Explore Other Cultures 8.3).

An old song proclaims, "Over the river and through the woods to grandmother's house we go." Nowadays this isn't always the case. As more parents separate and divorce, they may refuse to let grandparents see their grandchildren. An estranged parent may deny children access to their grandparents as a means of punishing the spouse. Some grandparents have confronted this situation by suing for visitation and legal rights to grandchildren (Henderson, 2005; Olsen, 2002; Sanger, 2000). As a result, many states now have laws allowing grandparents to petition courts to continue seeing their grandchildren after their child's marriage ends through divorce or death. In some states, grandparents can petition even when a married child just wants to keep the grandparents and children apart (Hafemeister & Jackson, 2000; Lewin, 1999).

EXPLORE OTHER CULTURES 8.3

Grandmothers: The Difference between Life and Death

According to anthropologist Kristen Hawkes and her colleagues (cited in Angier, 1999), postmenopausal women have helped ensure the survival and fitness of their grandchildren since prehistoric times. These women, no longer reproductively active themselves, are able to invest their energies in providing for the physical and psychological health of grandchildren and other young relatives. Hawkes and her colleagues studied the present-day Hadza hunter-gatherers of Northern Tanzania and found that older women gather more edible plant foods than any other members of the group. Nursing Hadza women, unable to provide for their older children while tending their infants, rely not on their mates but on these postmenopausal women relatives—their mothers, aunts, or elderly cousins—to make sure that the older children are well fed. The presence or absence of a grandmother often makes the difference between life or death for grandchildren in other subsistence cultures as well. Recently, anthropologists Ruth Mace and Rebecca Sear (cited in Angier, 2002) found that in rural Gambia, the presence of a maternal grandmother doubled the survival rate of her toddler grandchildren. However, the presence of a paternal grandmother (the father's mother) made no difference in the children's survival. Even more surprisingly, the presence of the father didn't either! Similar results have been found in parts of rural India and Japan as well (Angier, 2002). Why do you think the role of the maternal grandmother is especially important?

Providing Care and Support for Grandchildren.   During their grandchild's infancy and preschool years, grandmothers often provide the children's parents with considerable emotional support, information, help with child care and household chores, and to a lesser degree, financial support (Black et al., 2002). Nearly one half of all grandmothers in the United States provide this help on a regular basis (Baydar & Brooks-Gunn, 1998). For example, over 20 percent of all preschoolers whose mothers work or are in school are looked after by their grandparents, usually a grandmother (U.S. Census Bureau, 2004b). Some baby-boomer grandmothers (such as Claire's sister) are retiring from their careers to become paid nannies for their grandchildren (Alexander, 2004). The grandmother's role in lending economic, social, and emotional support for her children and grandchildren is more active in many ethnic minority groups than among Whites. For example, Asian American grandparents are more likely than other groups to care for their grandchildren whose mothers are employed (K. Smith, 2002). Latina women are the most influential and important source of social support for their young adult daughters with children (Ginorio et al., 1995). The advice and opinions of Latina grandmothers often are sought in major family decisions (Facio, 2001). Both Native American and Black grandmothers are significant figures in the stability and continuity of the family (John et al., 2001; Johnson et al., 2003; Ralston, 2001). In one study of low-income multiracial Hawaiian children who had an absent or incapacitated parent, the nurturance and guidance of grandparents was a key factor in the children's well-being as they grew to adulthood (Werner & Smith, 2001; Werner, 2004).

In some parts of the world, grandmothers spell the difference between life and death for their grandchildren.

For some children, grandparents are part of the family household. The number of grandparents living in homes with grandchildren has doubled since 1970 to 5.8 million in 2002 (U.S. Census Bureau, 2004b; Simmons & Dye, 2003), including 8 percent of Black, Native American, and Latina/o adults, 6.4 percent of Asian American adults, and 2.5 percent of White adults. Some of the increase results from an uncertain economy and the growing number of single mothers, which has sent young adults and their children back to the parental nest (Lugalla & Overturf, 2004). In other cases, elderly adults are moving in with their adult children's families when they can no longer live on their own. New immigrants with a tradition of multigenerational households have also swelled the number of such living arrangements (Lugalla & Overturf, 2004). The arrangement benefits all parties. Grandparents and their grandchildren are able to interact on a daily basis. The grandparents often assume some parenting responsibilities, which makes it possible for single teenage mothers to stay in school (Gordon et al., 2004).

Raising Grandchildren. Increasing numbers of grandparents now find themselves raising their grandchildren on their own. Of the 5.8 million grandparents living in a household with a grandchild, over 40 percent *are raising their grandchildren without a parent present*. About two-thirds of these **skip-generation parents** are grandmothers. Grandparents become full-time caregivers for their grandchildren for a number of reasons: parental illness, child abuse, substance abuse, and psychological or financial problems (Sanchez-Hucles, 2003; Waldrop, 2004). In some developing countries, parents migrate to urban areas to work, while grandparents remain behind and raise the grandchildren (Yardley, 2004). The AIDS epidemic has also increased the number of grandparents who are raising grandchildren in many nations, including the United States (Knodel et al., 2003; UNAIDS, 2004). Children reared by their grandparents fare well relative to children in families with one biological parent. They also show little difference in health and academic performance relative to children raised in traditional families (Thomas et al., 2000).

The belief that caregiving grandmothers are primarily poor ethnic women of color is a myth. Parenting grandmothers can be found across racial and socioeconomic lines (Harm, 2001). About half the grandparents raising grandchildren are White, 29 percent are Black, 17 percent are Latina/o, 3 percent are Asian American, and 2 percent are Native American. Black women who are raising their grandchildren, compared to White women, report feeling less burdened and more satisfied in their caregiving role, even though they are generally in poorer health, dealing with more difficult situations, and dealing with them more often alone (Pruchno, 1999).

Rearing a grandchild is full of both rewards and challenges (Waldrop, 2004). While parenting a grandchild is an emotionally fulfilling experience, there are psychological, health, and economic costs. A grandmother raising the young child of her drug-addicted adult daughter may concurrently feel ashamed of her daughter; anxious about her own future, health, and finances; angry at the loss of retirement leisure; and guilt about her own parenting skills (Harm, 2001; Williamson et al., 2001). Moreover, grandparents primarily responsible for rearing grandchildren are more likely than other grandparents to suffer from a variety of health problems, including depression, diabetes, high blood pressure, heart disease, and a decline in self-rated physical and emotional health. Furthermore, they tend to delay seeking help for their own medical problems (Gibbons & Jones, 2003; Lee et al., 2003; Ruiz et al., 2003).

Grandparents raising grandchildren are often stymied by existing laws that give them no legal status unless they gain custody of the grandchild or become the child's foster parents. Each of these procedures involves considerable time, effort, and expense. Yet without custody or foster parent rights, grandparents may encounter difficulties in obtaining the child's medical records, enrolling the child in school, or becoming eligible for certain forms of financial assistance (Beltran, 2004; Haskell, 2003). For example, the welfare grant that a low-income grandmother collects on her grandchild's behalf is only a fraction of what she would receive if she were to become the child's foster parent (Bernstein, 2002). In most instances, grandchildren are ineligible for coverage under grandparents' medical insurance, even if they have custody (Ellin, 2004a). In some cases, states ignore the significant expenditures made by caretaker grandparents when calculating the grandparents' eligibility for Medicaid ("Grandparents Raising Grandchildren," 2002). Consequently, many grandparent caregivers face significant financial challenges (Fuller-Thomson & Minkler, 2003).

Parents

While more elderly women are becoming caregivers of their grandchildren, caregiving is increasingly occurring at the other end of the age spectrum as well. As more Americans join the ranks of the "oldest old" (85 and older), growing numbers of elderly "children" find themselves taking care of their parents. Nearly half of all caregivers of the "oldest old" are daughters. Daughters-in-law and granddaughters play a substantial role as well (Katz et al., 2000; Usdansky, 2000).

The elderly caregiver may herself have some health problems (National Council on Family Relations, 2003; Vitaliano et al., 2004; Vitaliano et al., 2003) and is facing her own aging. The sight of her parent becoming more frail and dependent may conjure up a frightening and saddening vision of what is in store for her. Elderly daughters sometimes feel angry and guilty at the sacrifices involved in looking after a parent.

> *My grandmother lived to be almost one-hundred-and-two years old, and my mother cared for her until she was ninety-seven and had to go into a nursing home. Now my mother obviously feels it is her turn, which it is. I am the real problem here, for I have led a very active life and cannot seem to adjust to this demanding and devastating situation. I do not know what to hope for and am almost overcome with the inevitable guilt at my resentment and anger. I have no one to talk to.* (a 72-year-old woman, in Doress-Worters & Siegal, 1994, p. 208)

Some caregiving daughters have a different philosophy, enjoying the time spent with their parent(s). One 72-year-old woman described taking public transportation every day to visit her 99-year-old father. They would chat about their family and she did his grocery shopping. Although she had developed asthma and was not in the best of health, she looked forward to her daily visits (Bennet, 1992).

Ethnic minority groups provide more care for aging family members than Whites do, and they also feel more guilty about the amount of care given. Among Asian Americans, 42 percent help care for older relatives, compared to 34 percent of Latinos/as, 28 percent of Blacks, and 19 percent of Whites (AARP, 2001). One of Claire's Black students described how her family takes care of its sick or elderly members rather than putting them in nursing homes. Her widowed 76-year-old grandmother, for example, cared for her frail great-grandmother for many years until the older woman died at the age of 102.

We have been discussing older women's relationships with family and friends. To explore this topic on a more personal level, try Get Involved 8.3.

GET INVOLVED **8.3**

Interview with Older Women

Interview two women age 65 or older. It is helpful, but not essential, if you know your respondents fairly well. You may interview your mother, grandmothers, great-aunts, great-grandmothers, and so on. Keep a record of your respondents' answers to the questions below. Compare and contrast the responses of the two women.

1. What is one of the nicest things to happen to you recently?
2. How would you describe your relationship with your children?
3. Do you have any sisters and brothers? How would you describe your relationship with them?

4. What do you like about being a grandparent? (if applicable)
5. What types of activities do (did) you enjoy with your grandchildren?
6. Tell me about your best friends and the kinds of things you enjoy doing together.
7. What do you like about your current living situation?
8. What do you dislike about it?
9. In general, what are your feelings on nursing homes?
10. How do you feel about the life you've led?
11. As an experienced woman, what tidbit of wisdom could you pass on to me?

What Does It Mean?

1. How would you characterize the relationships of your interviewees with their adult children? Do they appear to be closer to their daughters than to their sons? If so, why?
2. What kinds of relationships do your interviewees have with their grandchildren? Have either or both participated in child-care activities with their grandchildren? How do their experiences compare to those reported in the text?
3. Were there any differences in the relationships of these women with their sisters as compared to their brothers? If yes, how do you explain these differences?
4. How does the discussion in this chapter help you understand your respondents' attitudes toward their current living situation and toward nursing homes?

SUMMARY

Friendships

- Girls' friendships are more intimate than those of boys. Girls tend to have a few close friendships whereas boys have larger, less intimate friendship groups.
- Both college women and men like to talk to their friends about the other gender. However, women's conversations more than men's focus on interpersonal issues.
- Emotional closeness is important to the friendships of both heterosexual and lesbian women but is more central to women's than men's friendships.
- Gender socialization and heterosexual males' perceived connection between emotional closeness and homosexuality are two explanations for the gender difference.
- Friendships among older women enhance physical and mental health.

Romantic Relationships

- Heterosexual women are more likely than heterosexual men to value a romantic partner's financial stability and less likely to place importance on physical attractiveness. Similarly, lesbian women put less emphasis on physical attractiveness than gay men do.
- Heterosexual and gay men put more emphasis on the physical attractiveness of a potential partner than heterosexual and lesbian women.
- Middle-aged women are more likely than middle-aged men to use age-concealment techniques.
- Romantic relationships are commonly characterized by traditional gender-related behaviors and roles. When there is a power imbalance, the male is generally viewed as the more powerful partner.
- The age when adolescents start to date has decreased.
- Many dating behaviors are strongly gender-stereotypical.
- Men are more likely than women to perceive nonsexual behaviors, such as a female asking out a male, as indicative of sexual interest.

- Current dating trends include development of urban "partnering markets," online dating services, dating among older singles, and resisting pressures to date.

Committed Relationships

- Most women and men marry, but the age of marriage has gone up in recent years.
- Emotional expressiveness contributes to marital well-being, and wives are more involved than husbands in maintaining this emotional communication.
- Women and men who are married are happier and healthier than their unmarried counterparts.
- More men than women are married in later life. Couples often report increased marital satisfaction with age.
- Cohabitors who do not intend to marry tend to be less satisfied with their relationships than married individuals, in part because of the absence of legal commitment.
- Married couples who previously cohabited are more likely to get divorced. This might be accounted for by a selection effect.
- Most lesbians are in committed, egalitarian, sexually exclusive relationships. Although many experience stressors not encountered by heterosexuals, they are similar to their heterosexual counterparts in their relationship satisfaction.
- Older lesbians in committed relationships provide each other with a mutual support system and shared economic benefits.

Unattached Lifestyles

- About 40 percent of U.S. marriages end in divorce.
- Divorce is associated with stressors for both women and their children.
- Despite initial emotional problems, both women and children tend to effectively adjust.
- Divorced women are generally less depressed than those in unhappy marriages.
- Employment and social support help women cope during the postdivorce period.

- Single women report mixed feelings about being unattached. Some regret the absence of a steady partner, some are satisfied living alone, and some become involved in romantic relationships. Many are very involved in social networks of relatives, friends, and neighbors.
- Single women have skills in independent living and in building support systems.
- Women are more likely than men to be widowed but are much less likely to remarry.
- Reaction to widowhood depends on several factors including age, degree of forewarning of the spouse's death, and financial and social resources.
- Loss of a lesbian partner may be very stressful.

Motherhood

- Stereotypes of mothers, including the good mother stereotype, the matriarch, welfare mother, and superwoman images of Black mothers, can lead to blaming mothers and mothers' self-blame if something goes wrong or if the mothers deviate from the ideal stereotype.
- Two major challenges faced by single mothers are financial problems and numerous responsibilities. Social support, as well as extended and augmented families, can help single mothers cope.

- Lesbian and heterosexual mothers are similar in mothering style and adjustment. Children reared in lesbian and heterosexual families are similar in their psychological and social adjustment and their sexual orientation.
- Most women report positive feelings about the postparental period. Women who were employed during the childrearing years find it easier to relinquish the parental role.

Relationships in the Later Years

- Feelings of closeness among siblings increase during adulthood, and the sister-sister bond is especially strong.
- Older women generally have positive relationships with their adult daughters.
- Unmarried elderly adults, most of whom are women, prefer living alone. Living with an adult child is the least popular choice, especially among Whites.
- The closeness of the grandparent-grandchild relationship depends on many factors.
- Visitation rights for grandparents is a growing social issue.
- More grandparents than ever live in multi-generation households, particularly in ethnic minority groups.
- Increasing numbers of grandmothers are rearing their grandchildren.
- Growing numbers of elderly adults, especially women, are caregivers of their parents.

KEY TERMS

dating scripts
cohabitation
selection effect
Boston marriage
motherhood mandate

matriarch stereotype
welfare mother stereotype
superwoman stereotype
feminization of poverty
extended families

augmented families
postparental period
skip-generation parents

WHAT DO YOU THINK?

1. The text discusses several negative consequences of the strong emphasis placed by men on a romantic partner's appearance. Can you think of other negative ramifications of this strong value? What kind of societal changes might contribute to a deemphasis on physical attractiveness in romantic attraction?

2. Letitia Peplau (1998) contends that research on lesbian and gay couples can help dispel biased stereotypes. What are some common stereotypes about lesbian couples? How can scientific research be made public and accessible so that these stereotypes can be altered? Do you think there should be an attempt to eradicate these stereotypes as well as other unfavorable attitudes? Explain your answer.

3. Do you agree with Holcomb's (1998) contention that there has been a resurgence of praise for women who give up their careers for full-time motherhood? If so, how can society reconcile the contradictory assumptions that full-time motherhood is desirable for middle-class mothers, but that poor mothers should combine employment with parenthood? How do you think people react to middle-class mothers who choose to continue their employment? How do they react to fathers who opt for full-time parenting? Explain each of your answers.

4. What are the advantages and disadvantages of grandparents rearing their grandchildren?

5. Are elderly widows better off living alone? With family members? In a retirement community? Why?

6. More single women are deliberately choosing to have and rear children on their own. Are they being selfish? Explain your answer.

IF YOU WANT TO KNOW MORE

Clunis, D. M., Fredriksen-Goldsen, K. I., Freeman, P. A., & Mystrom, N. (2004). *Lives of lesbian elders: Looking back, looking forward.* Binghamton, NY: Harrington Park Press.

Coll, C. G., Surrey, J. L., & Weingarten, K. (1998). *Mothering against the odds: Diverse voices of contemporary mothers.* New York: Guilford.

Coyle, A., & Kitzinger, C. (Eds.). (2002). *Lesbian and gay psychology: New perspectives.* Oxford, UK: Blackwell.

Douglas, S., & Michaels, M. (2004). *The mommy myth: The idealization of motherhood and how it has undermined women.* New York: Free Press.

Florsheim, P. (2003). *Adolescent romantic relations and sexual behavior: Theory, research, and practical implications.* Mahwah, NJ: Erlbaum.

Fridstein, M. (1997). *Grandparenting: A survival guide.* Glenwood Springs, CO: Tageh Press.

Ginsburg, G. D. (2000). *Widow to widow: Thoughtful, practical ideas for rebuilding your life.* New York: Perseus.

Laumann, E. O., et al. (2004). *The sexual organization of the city.* Chicago: University of Chicago Press.

Miller-Day, M.A. (2004). *Communication among grandmothers, mothers, and adult daughters: A qualitative study of maternal relationships.* Mahwah, NJ: Erlbaum.

Warner, J. (2005). *Perfect madness: Motherhood in the age of anxiety.* New York: Riverhead Books.

Weeks, J., Heaphy, B., & Donovan, C. (2001). *Same-sex intimacies: Families of choice and other life experiments.* New York: Routledge.

WEBSITES

Lesbian Mothers

Lesbian Mothers Support Society
http://www.lesbian.org/lesbian-moms/

Living Arrangements

Senior Living Alternatives
http://www.senioralternatives.com/

Caregiving

National Alliance for Caregiving
http://www.caregiving.org

Grandparents

http://www.aarp.org/grandparents

9 Education and Achievement

You might recall from the opening vignette in Chapter 1 that when Judith applied to graduate school in 1965 she was told that several psychology graduate programs had higher admission standards for female applicants than male applicants. The unofficial explanation for this discriminatory practice was the need to limit the number of female students because they were more likely than men to drop out of lengthy graduate programs for marriage and/or childrearing. This view that women would or should not pursue both family life and a career was evident, also, in the comment of a male graduate student who asked why Judith wanted a doctorate given that, at some point, she hoped to get married and have children. Similarly, when she did later get married, a female cousin suggested she now give up her Ph.D. aspirations and become a mother instead.

This perceived dichotomy between career and family might seem strange today. The cultural milieu has changed dramatically since the 1960s. Today the majority of college women want to have it all—both a career and a family (e.g., Davey, 1998; Hoffnung, 2004). On the other hand, some women today experience conflicts between their career goals and their commitment to relationships. As educational psychologist Sally Reis states:

> *Smart ambitious young women come to college with all these big plans, but then they fall in love, and all their priorities change. It happens during college, in terms of the workload they take. It happens as they graduate, and many put off graduate school to feed the relationship. Maybe they work to support their partners, or they follow them. Then once they have children, those original goals are pushed far off.* (quoted in D'Arcy, 1998, p. F3)

In this chapter we set the framework for understanding women's experiences in the workplace. First, we examine females' educational expectations, values, attainments, and college experiences. Next we explore young women's career aspirations, issues related to career counseling, and their plans regarding coordination of their careers with family life. Then we turn to influences on their career choices and gender bias in the hiring process.

Women's Educational Values, Attainment, and Campus Experience

As we discuss in more detail in Chapter 10, men earn higher salaries than women (U.S. Census, 2004a) and occupy higher positions in their jobs (Fassinger, 2001). Further, more men than women achieve prominence in domains such as politics, literature, and the professions. It has been suggested that these discrepancies indicate that women, compared to men, place a lower value on education and have a lower level of educational attainment. Does the evidence support these assumptions? In this section, we examine women's educational values, attainments, and experiences on the college campus.

Educational Values

To answer the question about values, Barbara Bank (1995) examined females' and males' reasons for seeking a bachelor's degree. Her results showed that female and male respondents placed a similar value on college education and reported similar explanations for desiring a degree. Both mentioned enjoyment, determination, and skill, as well as career plans, occupational prestige, and financial rewards. Furthermore, in a study of Black and White college students, Lawrence Ganong and his colleagues (Ganong et al., 1996) found no differences between women and men in their expectations about the level of education they will achieve and the likelihood they will be professionally successful. Thus, the evidence indicates that women and men have similar educational values and expectations. Now we turn to their actual educational experiences.

Educational Attainment

In the United States, 85 percent of females and 84 percent of males graduate from high school (U.S. Census Bureau, 2005a). Until the mid-90s, men earned the majority of bachelor's degrees each year, but women now surpass men (Peter & Horn, 2005).

You can see in Table 9.1 that within each ethnic group, women obtain the majority of associate's, bachelor's, and master's degrees and, except for Asian Americans, at least half of all doctoral degrees. White and Latina women still earn a minority of the professional (e.g., medical, dental, law) degrees. However, both doctoral and professional levels of education have experienced a dramatic change in the participation of women. For example, in 1965 women obtained only 12 percent of doctoral and 4 percent of professional degrees (U.S. Census Bureau, 2003b), compared to the 2001 figures of 46 percent and 45 percent, respectively ("The Nation:

TABLE 9.1 Degrees Conferred by Ethnicity and Gender, 2001–2002

Type of Degree	Ethnicity									
	Asian Americans		Blacks		Latinas/os		Native Americans		Whites	
	women	men	women	men	women	men	women	men	women	men
Associate's	57%	43%	66%	34%	60%	40%	66%	34%	59%	41%
Bachelor's	55	45	66	34	60	40	60	40	57	43
Master's	54	46	71	29	62	38	62	38	61	39
Doctorate	46	54	62	38	55	45	63	37	50	50
Professional	52	48	62	38	48	52	50	50	45	55

Source: "The Nation: Students," 2004, p. 22.

Students," 2004). Today, women earn about two-thirds of degrees in veterinary medicine and pharmacy, formerly male-dominated fields. They also earn nearly half of law degrees, and over 40 percent of medical degrees (Cox & Alm, 2005).

This high level of educational attainment by women is, unfortunately, more true of nondisabled women than of women with disabilities. Women with disabilities also have less education than men with disabilities (Fulton & Sabornie, 1994) and are less likely to graduate from high school or attend college (Hanna & Rogovsky, 1991). Furthermore, they are less likely than males with disabilities to receive occupationally oriented vocational training that can provide them with the skills needed in the job market (Wagner, 1992).

So far, we have been discussing educational attainment of girls and women in the United States. In developing societies, many girls are unable to attend school at all, or attend for just a few years before they drop out (Larsen & Verma, 1999). For a closer look at this serious problem, see Explore Other Cultures 9.1 and 9.2.

EXPLORE OTHER CULTURES **9.1**

Educating Girls Worldwide: Gender Gaps and Gains

What is the state of education for girls around the world? A study of 132 developing and developed nations (Population Action International, 1998) reports both good news and bad news. The good news is that between 1985 and 1995, access to education improved worldwide, particularly for girls at the secondary (high school) level. More than half the countries studied now have no gender gap, including the United States, where 99 percent of girls and boys go to school.

The bad news is that 51 countries still have serious gender gaps, with 75 million fewer girls than boys in school. Two out of every three children without even a primary school education are girls (Slaughter-Defoe et al., 2002). Gender disparities are greatest in South Asia, the Middle East, and sub-Saharan Africa, where, not surprisingly, male literacy rates far surpass those of females (Nussbaum, 2004). In most countries, girls from poor families are less likely to attend school than those from wealthier households (Rani & Lule, 2004). In Africa and Latin America, increasing numbers of unmarried girls are dropping out of school because of unplanned pregnancy.

School policies often require the expulsion of pregnant girls. Another reason that girls leave school earlier than boys is to work the land. In Africa, girls and women do 80 percent of the agricultural work, although they own just 1 percent of the farmland (Smith, 2005). Moreover, the AIDS epidemic in Africa is forcing many girls to leave school to support the family and care for the sick. (See Chapter 12.)

Educating girls has many benefits. The more years of education, the fewer, healthier, and better educated are their subsequent children. In addition, empowering women through literacy can enhance their voice in family affairs and reduce gender inequality in other areas (Ibrahim, 2004/2005; Larson & Wilson, 2004; Nussbaum, 2004). How can girls' enrollment in school be increased? Strategies suggested by the World Bank ("Gender Equality," 2003) and other organizations include

> Build more schools, especially in rural areas of developing countries.
> Lower the costs to families of educating their daughters.

Educate parents about the importance of educating daughters as well as sons.

Provide programs to prevent teenage pregnancy.

Encourage teen mothers to stay in school.

Attach day-care centers to schools to look after young children, allowing their older sisters to attend school.

Recruit more female teachers.

EXPLORE OTHER CULTURES 9.2

The Oppressive Educational Climate under Taliban Rule

In 1996, the ultraconservative Islamic Taliban regime took over in Afghanistan. It promptly banned education for girls and women and fired the female teachers. This was a severe blow in a country where only 4 to 10 percent of women can read compared to a literacy rate of 40 percent for males (Waldman, 2002). For the five years of Taliban rule, almost no females saw the inside of a classroom, although some courageous women secretly taught small groups of girls in their homes, and some girls were home-schooled by their parents (Dominus, 2002). One rare exception occurred 18 months before the regime ended, when the personal female physician of the four wives of the Taliban's supreme leader was given permission to set up a nursing school for women (Onishi, 2002b). Following a strict set of rules, the young women traveled each day in a bus with black windows to the school entrance reserved for them. They could not talk to the male nursing students, who were in a separate wing, or leave the building. They were not allowed to wear makeup. Above all, they were forbidden to look at pictures of the human body. One student was found with such a picture and was promptly expelled (Onishi, 2002b). With the end of Taliban rule, women and girls eagerly flocked back to the classroom, despite attempts by Islamic militants to damage or destroy some of their schools (Rohde, 2002). Hundreds of women's literacy classes formed in neighborhood houses as women gathered to learn to read and write (Gall, 2002). Yet even in the "new" Afghanistan, the educational picture still is far from rosy. In 2004, the Afghan Supreme Court banned married women from attending high school classes. Moreover, because a rise in banditry and rape has made roads unsafe even in daylight, many girls do not dare go to schools (Kristof, 2004). This problem is particularly acute in rural areas, where only 31 percent of girls are enrolled in school, compared with 62 percent of boys (UNICEF, 2004).

Campus Climate

Julie Zeigler arrived at Duke University in 2003 to work on a doctorate in physics. Instead, she left in 2004 with only a master's because of a hostile atmosphere towards women that female graduate students and faculty say has existed for years. These

In 2001, for the first time in five years since the Taliban took control of the country, this girls' school in Afghanistan reopened.

women report that male physicists have kissed and grabbed them, ignored them, refused to take them seriously and greeted their comments and questions with hostility. (Wilson, 2004)

The gender biases in elementary and high school (Chapter 4) continue into college and graduate school. Female students often experience a **chilly climate** in the classroom and elsewhere on campus, in which *faculty members display different expectations for women students, or single them out or ignore them* (Hall & Sandler, 1982; Sands, 1998; Shepela & Levesque, 1998). Some faculty members use sexist language, tell sexist jokes, or suggest that women are less able to learn the material. Other biases include rarely covering material by female authors or theorists, seldom using examples containing women, and portraying women only in traditional roles (Myers & Dugan, 1996). Eventually, this chilly atmosphere can negatively affect women's feelings of self-worth and confidence. The impact may be even greater for ethnic minority women, lesbian and bisexual women, and women with disabilities. They may be the target of blatant sexist, racist, homophobic, and other prejudicial acts, such as placing signs on residence hall room doors that bar members of certain groups. Or, they may experience more subtle humiliations, such as a professor's sexual or racial humor.

Female faculty members can also experience a chilly climate, especially if they are mothers. Many female professors report that they felt treated like valued colleagues until they had children. After that, they felt their colleagues' assessment of their competence and commitment began to decline. For example, when a male faculty member spends the day at home to do research, it's assumed he did just that. But the same action by a female faculty member may be construed as taking time off to be with the baby (Williams, 2002).

The chilly climate for women is another reflection of the gender inequality of power in North American society. Sexist treatment of women on campus, whether blatant or subtle, reflects a greater value attached to males and serves to maintain an already existing power imbalance. Furthermore, this treatment reinforces constructions of women as inferior or less valued than men.

Single-Gender Institutions. Given the existence of an uncomfortable climate on some mixed-gender campuses, it is not surprising that several scholars (AAUW, 1998b; Gross, 2004; Reid & Zalk, 2001; Watson et al., 2002) point to the benefits of single-gender high school and college environments for women's academic and personal development. M. Elizabeth Tidball and her colleagues note, for example, that graduates of women's colleges compared to female graduates of mixed-gender institutions report greater satisfaction with all aspects of their college experience except the social life (Tidball et al., 1999). Furthermore, women's colleges provide more leadership opportunities for women students, higher achievement expectations for them, and more female role models within the faculty and administration (Reid & Zalk, 2001). As an example of the last point, 87 percent of the presidents of women's colleges in 1997 were women compared to 16 percent of the presidents of mixed-gender institutions (Tidball et al., 1999).

Other benefits of women's high schools and colleges are the greater likelihood of close student-faculty relations, increased self-confidence, less sexism, and more female class participation (Duncan et al., 2002; Gross, 2004; Reisberg, 2000; Umbach et al., 2004). Also, women's college graduates are more likely than graduates of mixed-gender institutions to pursue male-dominated fields, such as the physical

Some educators believe that women's colleges provide a more effective educational environment for female students.

sciences and mathematics, to reach high levels of achievement in their careers and, for both reasons, to earn higher salaries (Reid & Zalk, 2001; Tidball et al., 1999).

Despite these positive findings, it should be noted that not all researchers draw the same conclusions about the value of women's colleges. Faye Crosby (in Gose, 1995), for example, claims that studies of women's colleges have been flawed in that many have compared students at highly selective women's institutions to students at less selective mixed-gender colleges and universities. Recent research shows that women do as well or better in small, selective, liberal arts colleges as in women's colleges (Epstein & Gambs, 2001). Furthermore, some scholars believe that isolation from men in the college environment can hinder women's academic development and that segregation of women reinforces the stereotype that they are low achievers and need special help (Epstein & Gambs, 2001).

The Academic Environment for Women of Color.   Not surprisingly, the climate for female students of color on college campuses is more problematic than that for White women. Some women of color experience primarily White campuses as unwelcoming and unsupportive (Hackett et al., 1992), and Black students who drop out of college are more likely than Whites to attribute their college withdrawal to frustration and a lack of social and academic support (Allen, 1996). Moreover, some of the students examined in a study by Crawford and MacLeod (1990) reported instances of racist comments on the part of their professors. For example, one female student stated that a male "instructor makes sexual and racial 'jokes' and comments that I find offensive. There has {sic} been repeated allusions to the 'stupidity' of Native Americans and the inferiority of cultures other than his own" (Crawford & MacLeod, 1990, p. 119).

Claude Steele (Steele, Spencer et al., 2002; Jaffe, 2004) suggests that "stereotype threat" (discussed in Chapter 5 in relation to women) can also seriously affect the college experience of students of color. He contends that Black students' awareness of the societal devaluation of Black people creates a pressure to defy negative stereotypes about ability. According to Steele, in addition to concern about their own academic performance, Black students must deal with the possibility that their poor performance will confirm the inferiority of their ethnic group in the eyes of others. In an attempt to feel less vulnerable, they may downplay the importance of achievement to their self-esteem.

Another problem for some students of color is that they experience the individualism prominent in academic life as inconsistent with the collectivistic values of their culture. The individualistic value system of Western, primarily North American and European, cultures emphasizes personal achievement, independence, and individual uniqueness. The collectivistic values of Asian, Native American, and Latina/o cultures, on the other hand, stress the importance of the group, including the family, the community, and the work team. This competitive style of college education can be uncomfortable for these students. Native Americans, for example, have difficulties adjusting to the competitive climate (Canabal, 1995; LaFromboise et al., 1990). As one Native American senior stated, "When I was a child I was taught certain things, don't stand up to your elders, don't question authority, life is precious, the earth is precious, take it slowly, enjoy it. And then you go to college and you learn all these other things and it never fits" (Canabal, 1995, p. 456).

Although the clash between individualism and collectivism can produce conflicts for some students, Angela Lew and her colleagues (Lew et al., 1998) note that these value systems can coexist. These researchers examined the achievement values of Asian American students and found that some students adopted both sets of values; they saw individual achievement as a way to fulfill both personal and family goals. Lew and her associates suggest that internalization of both value systems can be helpful because it enables the student to function effectively in two different cultural environments. Of course, it may be easier for some students than for others to integrate and reconcile the disparate sets of values.

The Academic Environment for Working-Class and Poor Women.   Research on working-class and poor women's adjustment to college life is very limited. However, one interesting study (LePage-Lees, 1997) of high-achieving women from working-class or poor families found that many of these women felt they had to hide their backgrounds from others in order to achieve during undergraduate and graduate school. Also, they felt their socioeconomic backgrounds put them at an intellectual disadvantage, that other students were better prepared and more intelligent. One respondent said: "People now think the only issue is ethnicity, and I still think that economic level is an important issue regardless of ethnicity. Economics doesn't explain everything but it explains a lot" (p. 380).

Another type of poor woman with special needs and difficulties in the college environment is the woman on welfare. Those who decide to better themselves and their children through their own higher education anticipate and receive many benefits. However, they also face numerous obstacles. As Erika Kates (1996) points out, these women must cope with child-care responsibilities, transportation costs, reductions in federal assistance, and other difficulties. On the positive side, higher education is an important route to a reasonable income and greatly reduces reliance on federal aid (e.g., Kates, 1996). The story of Pauline illustrates the obstacles and benefits. This Black woman attended college at age 17 but dropped out after falling in love. She then had three children and was deserted by the children's father. Once her youngest child was in child care, she began community college as a welfare recipient. While in school she faced several obstacles; however, Pauline successfully completed college and then found a job in her town's school department (Kates, p. 550).

Women with Disabilities and the Physical Campus Environment.   The institutional environment we have discussed thus far focuses on behavioral issues. Women with disabilities face not only these issues but must also cope with challenges in bureaucracy and the physical environment. According to Lillian Holcomb and Carol Giesen (1995), women with disabilities on college campuses face obstacles such as inadequate funding of support services, old buildings not designed to be barrier-free, and campus grounds made inaccessible by not having curb cuts.

G E T   I N V O L V E D   **9.1**

Does Your Campus Have a Hospitable Environment for Women?

Answer the questions presented below and ask three female students the same questions. If possible, select interviewees who vary in ethnicity, physical ability/disability, and/or sexual orientation.

1. Did you ever hear a professor tell a sexist or racist "joke" during or outside of class?
2. Did you ever hear a professor make a derogatory comment about a student's gender, ethnicity, physical disability, or sexual orientation? If yes, indicate the nature of that comment.

3. Do you feel that women and men receive the same degree of encouragement and support from their instructors? If not, explain.
4. Do you feel that women of color, women with disabilities, and lesbian women receive the same degree of encouragement and support from their instructors as White, nondisabled, heterosexual women? If not, explain.
5. Do you experience any conflict between the values that characterize this campus and the values of your cultural group?

What Does It Mean?

1. Did you find any evidence of sexism, racism, bias against women with disabilities, and/or prejudice against lesbians? If yes, do you think these experiences affect the educational process of students who are targets of these behaviors? Why or why not?
2. Did you find any evidence of differential support for students because of their gen-

der, ethnicity, physical ability, or sexual preference? If yes, do you think this can affect the educational process of students who receive less support? Why or why not?
3. Did you note any conflict between campus and cultural values? If yes, is this conflict similar to that described in the text?

In addition, they can experience increased burdens in the time needed to engage in activities such as traversing an inaccessible campus or using Braille to study.

Use the survey in Get Involved 9.1 to assess the academic climate on your campus.

Women's Work-Related Goals

In an address to the graduating class of a women's college, feminist author Gloria Steinem noted a major difference between the goals of her generation of female college graduates in 1956 and those of young women today: "I thought we had to marry what we wished to become. Now you are becoming the men you once would have wanted to marry" (in Goldberg, 1999, G3). This quote suggests that college women are striving for—and attaining—high-achievement goals; they are no longer living vicariously through the accomplishments of their husbands.

In the following discussion we see that women do, indeed, have high aspirations. However, we also see that there continue to be some differences in the career goals of females and males.

Career Aspirations

There are few differences in the career aspirations of women with and without disabilities (DeLoach, 1989) and among women of different ethnicities (Arbona & Novy, 1991). However, there is some evidence that Black college women expect success more than White women do (Ganong et al., 1996). In addition, Asian American college women are more likely than White college women to aspire toward male-dominated and more prestigious occupations (Leung et al., 1994). One explanation is that although Asian culture values traditional gender roles, Asian American families encourage their daughters to pursue nontraditional prestigious occupations associated with social recognition (Leung et al., 1994).

Research has shown that high school girls and boys generally aspire to careers that are equal in prestige (Watson et al., 2002) and that college women are as motivated as college men to pursue a career and to achieve success in their field (Hoffnung, 2004). During high school and college, however, women sometimes lower their aspirations, major in less prestigious, often female-dominated, career fields and, therefore, eventually end up in lower-level careers (Hoffnung, 2004; Lips, 2004; Mau, 2003; VanLeuvan, 2004). See Learn about the Research 9.1 to

LEARN ABOUT THE RESEARCH 9.1
The Illinois Valedictorian Project

The Illinois Valedictorian Project followed a group of 46 female and 35 male 1981 high school valedictorians as they proceeded through college and into adulthood. Seventy-two were White, five were Black, three were Mexican American, and one was Asian American. While in high school, 21 percent of the women and 23 percent of the men rated their intelligence as far above average. After two years of college, however, only 4 percent of the women but 22 percent of the men said their intelligence was far above average. By senior year, not a single woman reported her intelligence in this category, while 25 percent of men did. Yet the women had maintained a grade-point average of 3.7 on a 4-point scale throughout college, compared to 3.6 for the men. By the sophomore year in college, women had lowered their career aspirations

more than men. The women expressed persistent concerns about combining career and family, leading six of them to abandon plans for medical school. Two-thirds of the women valedictorians, but none of the men, planned to reduce or interrupt their employment to accommodate childrearing.

In 1991, six years after college graduation, both women and men were pursuing careers in the male-dominated fields of science, business, and the professions of law, medicine, and college teaching. However, a substantial proportion of women (but not men) were employed in the traditionally female fields of precollege teaching, nursing, physical therapy, and secretarial work. A few were employed in nonprofessional positions or were working as full-time homemakers.

What Does It Mean?

1. What do you think accounts for the drop in women's intellectual self-confidence during the college years?
2. What can be done to prevent this from happening?

3. Why do you think some women maintained their original career aspirations while others changed or reduced theirs?

Source: Arnold (1993).

read more about this phenomenon. Then let us take a closer look at factors that influence young women's career aspirations.

Women are more likely to seek and earn degrees in academic disciplines that focus on people, such as communication, education, psychology, and social sciences (Gravois, 2005; Lips, 2004). (See Table 9.2.) Interestingly, girls who believe in the altruistic value of math and science have more interest in, and more positive attitudes toward, these fields than do other girls (Weisgram & Bigler, 2004). What might account for this? One explanation is that, as we saw in Chapter 4, girls are socialized toward communal behaviors. Consistent with the social construction of women as caring and nurturant, they are encouraged to develop a strong interest in and concern for other people.

Table 9.2 also shows that relatively few female students aspire toward computer and information sciences, engineering, and physical sciences. Even those qualified college women who venture into the sciences and engineering are more likely than college men to drop out of these programs (Lips, 2004; Smith, 2001; Steele, James et al., 2002). For example, among biology majors with A averages, 80 percent of the women, compared to 60 percent of the men, change majors. In the physical sciences, these percentages are 69 percent of women versus only

TABLE 9.2   Bachelor's, Master's, and Doctoral Degrees, 2002, in Selected Fields by Gender

Educational Field	Bachelor's Degree		Master's Degree		Doctorate	
	women	men	women	men	women	men
Biological/life sciences	61%	39%	58%	42%	45%	55%
Business & management	50	50	41	59	38	62
Communications	64	36	65	35	59	41
Computer & information sciences	28	72	33	67	21	79
Education	77	23	76	24	66	34
Engineering	21	79	21	79	18	82
English	69	31	68	32	59	41
Mathematics	47	53	42	58	29	71
Physical sciences	42	58	42	58	27	73
Psychology	78	22	77	23	67	33
Social sciences & history	52	48	52	48	41	59

Source: "The Nations Students" (2004). U.S. Department of Education (2004).

1 percent of men, and in engineering 71 percent compared to 18 percent (Selingo, 1998). This is unfortunate, given the high status and high pay associated with these careers and given the need for additional qualified scientists (American Association of University Women, 2004).

What accounts for women's continued low participation rate in these academic areas? As we saw in Chapter 5, the possibility that females are less mathematically or scientifically skilled can be ruled out. We also noted in that chapter that parents and teachers are less likely to encourage the development of math or science skills in girls than boys. We saw that gender differences in attitudes toward and interest in science emerge as early as elementary school (AAUW, 2004), with girls becoming less confident of their ability to do well in math and science and subsequently avoiding advanced course work in math, chemistry, and physics. In addition, stereotypes of scientists as "nerds" who are obsessed with technology, but who have little interest in people, conflict more with the gender roles of women than of men (Beyer et al., 2004). The dearth of female role models and insufficient faculty encouragement may be other factors that play an important role in steering women away from careers in the sciences (VanLeuvan, 2004).

In addition, female students who do choose to major in math, science, and engineering report higher levels of discrimination than either women in female-dominated majors, such as arts, education, humanities, and social sciences, or men in any major (J. Steele et al., 2002). Female graduate students in science and engineering have even been told by male professors that women do not belong in those fields (e.g., Hollenshead et al., 1996).

Career Counseling

Historically, several problems have been related to career counseling for women. Until the 1960s women were largely invisible to career counselors, because women were not viewed as pursuing careers. In the 1960s and 1970s, career counselors tended to steer girls and women toward traditionally female careers and away from male-dominated occupations (Betz, 1994). Although there is now greater acceptance of females' pursuit of traditionally male occupations, counselors, teachers, and parents continue to show gender-biased attitudes toward career choices (Betz, 1994; Phillips & Imhoff, 1997). Many girls are discouraged from taking advanced math and science courses or from choosing high-status professions dominated by males. Gender bias also permeates vocational interest inventories and aptitude testing (Betz, 1994).

What can career counselors do to support, encourage, and expand the career aspirations of young women? Nancy Betz (1994) suggests that counselors should help women in the following four areas: (1) dealing with realistic concerns, such as managing career and family roles; (2) obtaining necessary education, training, and job-hunting skills; (3) locating support systems, mentors, and role models; and (4) dealing with discrimination and sexual harassment, if necessary. Cherry Greene and Wanda Stitt-Gohdes (1997) recommend that career counselors increase young women's awareness of career opportunities in the traditionally male skilled trades. Career counselors also need to become aware and understand that both woman's and men's views and needs are shaped by culture, ethnicity, social class, sexual orientation, and disability (Niles, 2003; Tang, 2003). For example, Carla McCowan and Reginald Alston (1998) suggest that counselors working with Black college women set up mentoring programs that pair them with Black professionals in order to expose them to information about career options and to help them develop realistic goals.

Work-Family Expectations

> *My plan is to get a job after graduate school and hopefully marry. After a few years of establishing myself in my career, I plan to have two children. After a short maternity leave, I plan to work part time, and hope my husband will too, so one of us can always be home. When I told my boyfriend this, he said he hasn't even considered how to balance work and family, and he was astonished that my plans for the future are all mapped out.* (Erika, 21-year-old college senior)

The vast majority of college women nowadays desire marriage, motherhood, and a career (Davey, 1998; Hoffnung, 2004). For example, in Michele Hoffnung's (2004) survey of senior women at five different American colleges, 96 percent planned to have a career, 86 percent planned to marry, and 98 percent planned to have children (See Learn About the Research 9.2 for a study of Canadian women's plans.) If you are interested in both employment and parenthood, have you considered how you would like to combine these? Research shows that most college women, like Erika, want to work before they have children and interrupt their employment for some period during their children's early years (e.g., Bridges & Etaugh, 1996; Schroeder et al., 1992). The majority of male students, however, are like Erika's boyfriend and are much less likely to think about connections between career and family goals (Konrad, 2003; Mahaffy & Ward, 2002).

Although most college women want to interrupt their employment for child-rearing, Black college women want to discontinue their employment for a shorter period of time than White women do. For example, Judith and Claire found that Black women want to return to employment when their first child was approximately 2½-years-old, whereas White women want to delay employment until their child was approximately 4 (Bridges & Etaugh, 1996).

Why do Black college women prefer an earlier return to employment after childbirth? One factor is that White college women are more likely than their Black peers to believe that maternal employment is harmful to young children (Bridges & Etaugh, 1996; Murrell et al., 1991). For example, Whites are more likely than Blacks to think that continuous maternal employment produces negative outcomes for children, such as low self-esteem, feelings of neglect, and lack of maternal guidance (Bridges & Etaugh, 1996). The more positive attitude of young Black women might, in turn, be related to Black women's long history of combining the roles of mother and provider (Galliano, 2003). Audrey Murrell and her colleagues (Murrell et al., 1991) found that college-educated Black women had a stronger work orientation and a more intense commitment to professional goals than White women.

LEARN ABOUT THE RESEARCH 9.2

Young Women's Preferred and Expected Patterns of Employment and Childrearing

E. Heather Davey (1998) assessed the views of Canadian college and noncollege young women regarding their preferences and expectations for combining employment and childrearing. Respondents were given a choice of three options: leaving work before the birth of the first child, working until the birth of the first child and working again after the youngest child reaches an age deemed appropriate by the respondent, or working continuously, with maternity leaves as needed.

She found that only a small minority either wanted or expected to leave employment before motherhood. Interestingly, there was a difference in preferences for and expectations about the other two options. Although 50 percent desired a long interruption of employment, only 29 percent expected to follow this pattern. Furthermore, whereas 46 percent wanted to work continuously, taking maternity leaves as needed, 59 percent expected to do so. The researcher points out that this last pattern more realistically conforms to current employment trends and she suggests that the more realistic expectations shown by these young women reflect their increasing awareness of economic realities.

What Does It Mean?

1. What are other explanations of the discrepancies between these women's preferred and expected employment-childrearing patterns?
2. Do you think there are differences between young men's preferred and expected employment-fatherhood patterns? Explain your answer.

3. Do you think it would be useful for young women thinking about their careers to have realistic expectations about how they will combine the employment and parenting roles? If yes, what can be done to guide young women toward a realistic appraisal of their future roles?

Source: Davey (1998).

Along these same lines, evidence suggests that college-educated Black women are more likely than their White counterparts to be encouraged by their parents to consider an occupation as essential to success (Higginbotham & Weber, 1996). Together, this body of research indicates that employment may be a more integral aspect of Blacks' construction of women's roles than it is for Whites.

Some educated women of color face another role-related problem: finding an appropriate mate within one's ethnic group. Evidence suggests that uneducated Native American men are reluctant to marry college-educated women (LaFromboise et al., 1990) and that Native American college women fear they will not be able to marry Native men (Medicine, 1988). Similarly, Black college women express the desire to marry a person of equal or greater educational and occupational status. However, because, they earn a higher proportion of every type of higher education degree than Black men, they may be frustrated in this desire (Ganong et al., 1996).

Black college women prefer an earlier return to employment after childbirth than do White women.

Work-Family Outcomes

In the previous section, we saw that the great majority of college women expect to "have it all": career, marriage, and motherhood. How do these expectations relate to actual career and family outcomes? In order to explore this question, Michele Hoffnung (2004) surveyed women seniors at five northeastern colleges and then followed them up seven years later.

Career remained the major focus for the women throughout their twenties. Not quite half had married, and most had not yet started a family. Marital status was unrelated to educational attainment and career status seven years out from college graduation. The few women who had become mothers, however, had fewer advanced degrees and lower career status than other women. They typically chose more traditional careers that took less time to train for, such as teacher or physical therapist. These women also held more traditional attitudes towards women's rights, roles, and responsibilities and were more likely to come from families with lower socioeconomic status.

In college, women of color had lower expectations for marriage than White women did and, in fact, they were less likely to be married seven years later. Their educational attainments were equal to those of White women and their careers had higher status. These findings are consistent with research we looked at in the previous section suggesting that college-educated women of color have very high career motivation (Bridges & Etaugh, 1996; Murrell et al., 1991).

Salary Expectations

Consistent with a tendency to have less prestigious career aspirations than men do, women expect lower salaries in their jobs. Kenneth Sumner and Theresa Brown (1996) asked college students in a variety of majors to give their salary expectations. Students' assessments of their entry-level incomes were closely linked to their college major. Given that salaries tend to be higher in male-dominated occupations than in female-dominated occupations (Lipson, 2001), it is not surprising that students in male-dominated majors expected higher starting salaries than did those in female-dominated fields. However, when asked to indicate their peak salaries, students revealed large gender differences regardless of major. Males in male-dominated, female-dominated, and gender-neutral majors expected higher peak salaries than women in these fields did. For example, in male-dominated majors, males expected an average of $67,500 whereas females expected only $48,600, and in female-dominated majors, the averages were $55,600 for men and $34,000 for women.

Why do women expect lower salaries? One possibility is that women know that females earn lower salaries than males and base their own salary expectations accordingly (Heckert, 2002). Another possibility is that women lower their salary expectations because they place importance on making accommodations in their job to fulfill their family obligations (Heckert, 2002; Jackson et al., 1992). A third possibility is that women are more likely than men to believe they deserve less (Yoder, 2003) (see Chapter 10).

Influences on Women's Achievement Level and Career Decisions

Although this chapter focuses on education and achievement, it is essential to note that achievement goals can be satisfied in diverse ways. Raising a well-adjusted and loving child, providing emotional and physical support to a spouse recovering from a stroke, and helping the homeless in one's community are only a few of the numerous forms achievement can take that are independent of education and occupation. However, despite the diversity of achievement directions, researchers have focused primarily on the traditional areas of education and occupation, and if we define achievement in this manner, it appears that women have achieved less than men. As we noted at the beginning of this chapter, more men than women attain the highest educational levels, aspire to the most prestigious careers, and hold high positions within their occupational fields. Now we examine possible internal and external influences on women's achievement level and occupational decisions. First, we look at their orientation to achievement in general and the personality traits that might be related to their career decision making. Then, we explore social and cultural influences on young women's educational and occupational pursuits.

Orientation to Achievement

For several decades psychologists attempted to explain women's lower achievement compared to men's as due, in part, to their orientation to achievement.

Achievement Motivation. One explanation was that females' **achievement motivation,** that is, their *need to excel,* was lower than males'. However, early studies by David McClelland and others on which this conclusion was based used a male-biased theoretical framework. Achievement was defined primarily in ways applicable to men's lives and emphasized competition and mastery in such areas as school, jobs, and sports. But achievement can also occur in other domains, such as the personal or interpersonal areas (Basow, 2001).

At the present time, researchers believe that women and men are similarly motivated to achieve (Hyde & Kling, 2001). However, gender socialization practices of families, peers, teachers, and others teach youngsters not only the importance of achievement, but also the "appropriate" direction it should take for their gender. For example, girls tend to learn that, if they have children, they should be the primary caregiver. Consequently, they may adjust their achievement goals in order to meet this expectation.

Fear of Success. Another view of women's lower achievement in comparison to men's came from Matina Horner (1972), who proposed that women want to achieve but have a **fear of success,** that is, *a motive to avoid situations of high achievement.* Horner contended that women were concerned about the negative social consequences that can result from success, especially social rejection and loss of femininity. This suggestion might seem strange as you read this book at the beginning of the twenty-first century. However, in the 1970s and 1980s this idea was embraced by many scholars who studied females' fear of success.

To test her concept of the fear of success, Horner devised the following statement: *After first-term finals, Anne/John finds herself/himself at the top of her/his medical school class.* She asked college women to write a paragraph about Anne and college men to write about John. Approximately two-thirds of the women wrote negative stories with themes such as Anne's physical unattractiveness, her inability to have romantic relationships, rejection by her peers, and her decision to transfer into a less prestigious occupation. Most of the stories told by the men about John, on the other hand, reflected positive outcomes.

Although Horner believed these results indicated a motive to avoid success on the part of women, subsequent research points to a different conclusion. It now appears that these stories did not reflect women's fear of high-achieving situations in general, but rather their awareness of negative consequences that can occur when individuals violate gender stereotypes. Medicine, especially in the 1970s when Horner performed her study, was strongly dominated by men. Thus it is likely that females' negative stories reflected their concern about the problems individuals face in gender-atypical occupations, rather than their desire to avoid a high level of achievement (Hyde & Kling, 2001). A subsequent study showed that both women and men wrote negative stories about a successful woman in medicine *and* a successful man in nursing (Cherry & Deaux, 1978). Furthermore, considerable evidence now shows that women and men do not differ in their fear of success (Mednick & Thomas, 1993). Consequently, psychologists today do not believe that women's lower level of educational or occupational achievement can be accounted for by their fear of success.

Achievement Attributions. A third explanation given for gender differences in levels of achievement is that females and males make different **achievement attributions,** that is, *explanations about their good and poor performance.* In general, people are *more likely to attribute positive events to their own internal traits, such as their ability or effort, whereas they tend to attribute negative events to external causes such as task difficulty or bad luck.* This **self-serving attributional bias,** like self-esteem (see Chapter 4), is linked to healthy psychological adjustment and happiness (Mezulis et al., 2004). In other words, taking responsibility for good performance (e.g. "I did well on the test because I know the material"), but attributing poor performance to external factors (e.g., "I failed the test because it was unfair"), enables a person to maintain a good self-image. On the other hand, the reverse pattern— blaming yourself for failure while not taking credit for your successes—could lead to an unwillingness to persevere in a challenging situation and to low self-esteem.

A recent meta-analysis by Amy Mezulis and her colleagues (Mezulis et al., 2004) shows that females, but not males, show a marked decline in the self-serving attributional bias starting in early adolescence. (Reread the section on self-esteem in Chapter 4, and note the similar, and possibly related, decline.) These gender differences in attributions of performance are small, however (see reviews by Mednick & Thomas, 1993; Whitley et al., 1986) and are associated with the type of performance situation. For example, in male-stereotyped domains, such as mathematics, males attribute success to ability more than do females, but in female-stereotyped domains, such as languages or English, the reverse pattern occurs (Beyer, 1997; Birenbaum & Kraemer, 1995). Similarly, women are more likely to attribute failure to lack of ability on a math test than on a verbal test, whereas men show the reverse tendency (Kiefer & Shih, 2004).

Achievement Self-Confidence. Another internal barrier that has been used to explain women's lower achievement in comparison to men's is their lower self-confidence. Many studies show that males are more self-confident in academic situations than females. For example, girls tend to underestimate their grades, ability level, and class standing whereas boys tend to overestimate theirs (Beyer, 1999; Eccles, 2001). Mary Crawford and Margo MacLeod (1990) also found that when asked why they don't participate in class discussion, college women's responses reflected questionable confidence in their abilities, such as "might appear unintelligent in the eyes of other students" and "ideas are not well enough formulated" (p. 116). Men's reasons, on the other hand, focused on external factors, as in "have not done the assigned reading" or participation might "negatively affect [their] grade" (p. 116). Other research suggests that even among high achievers in the sciences, fewer women than men believe their scientific ability to be above average (Sonnert & Holton, 1996).

Females do not show lower levels of confidence in all situations, however. Studies indicate that females' confidence is lower than males' in male-linked tasks, such as mathematics, but not in female-linked tasks, such as language, arts, music, and social skills (Beyer et al., 2002; Eccles, 2001; Jacobs et al., 2002; Watt, 2004). Females' confidence is also higher when performance estimates are made privately rather than publicly (e.g., Daubman, Heatherington, & Ahn, 1992). Research by Kimberly Daubman and her colleagues (Daubman & Sigall, 1997; Heatherington et al., 1993) suggests that in some situations, what appears to be lower self-confidence (e.g., publicly predicting lower grades for oneself) might really reflect women's desire to be liked or to protect others from negative feelings about themselves.

Conclusion.   Early conclusions that women have lower aspirations than men because they are not as highly motivated to excel and because they fear the negative consequences of success have not been supported. Although some evidence exists for gender differences in achievement attributions and self-confidence, these differences are not observed in all situations. Furthermore, as is the case with all types of psychological gender differences, the differences are small and do not apply to all females and males. Thus, most social scientists point to other factors to help explain different career aspirations and attainment levels of women and men.

Personality Characteristics

Are personality characteristics related to women's career aspirations? The answer is "yes." Women who choose male-dominated careers are more likely than those who pick female-dominated careers to be competitive, autonomous, and instrumental and to have less traditional gender attitudes (Hutson-Comeaux et al., 2002; Phillips & Imhoff, 1997). In addition, women who choose nontraditional skilled labor jobs in the trades have high self-esteem and are less concerned about other people's judgments of their career choice (Greene & Stitt-Gohdes, 1997).

Another personality factor related to career choice is the individual's **self-efficacy,** that is, *the belief that one can successfully perform the tasks involved in a particular domain*. Individuals with high self-efficacy for a particular field are more likely to aspire toward that field as a career (Eccles, 2001). For example, while females tend to have lower self-efficacy in mathematics and science than males (Bandura, 2002; Beyer et al., 2002a, 2002b) (see Chapter 5), those women who select careers in science or engineering have high self-efficacy for mathematics (e.g., Farmer, 1997) and low levels of math anxiety (Chipman et al., 1992). Furthermore, females, compared to males, have higher self-efficacy for health-related professions and female-dominated skilled labor occupations. These gender differences, in turn, correspond to differences in occupational choice.

Sexual Orientation

For some lesbians, the career decision-making process can be complicated by sexual identity formation. Many lesbians become aware of their sexual identity during late adolescence or adulthood, at the same time that they are selecting a career. According to Ruth Fassinger (1995), the overlap of these two processes can complicate career development. Lesbians might put career selection on hold as they explore their sexuality and intimate relationships. Also, as a result of coming out, many lose the family support that can be beneficial to the career-selection process.

In addition, lesbians' career choices might be directly affected by their perception of the occupational climate for lesbians and gays. Whereas some lesbians select occupations they perceive as employing large numbers of lesbians and gays in order to experience an environment in which there is safety in numbers (Morrow et al., 1996), lesbians who are closeted or anxious about their sexual identity might steer away from these occupations (Fassinger, 1995). Occupations that are oppressive for lesbians and gays (e.g., teaching and the military) might also not be considered, thus narrowing lesbians' field of choices (Fassinger, 1995).

On the positive side, Fassinger (1995) notes that lesbians tend to be less traditional in their attitudes about gender than are heterosexual women. Consequently, they tend to consider a broader range of occupational options including those that are nontraditional for women.

Social and Cultural Factors

Although some internal characteristics are related to individuals' career choices, career decisions are made within a sociocultural context in which the attitudes of significant people and the values of one's culture contribute to career selection as well. Support and encouragement from parents are very important. The same-sex parent appears to have the greatest effect on career expectations of adolescents (Whiston & Keller, 2004). One longitudinal study of female high school seniors, for example, found that attachment to the mother contributed to high career aspirations five years later (O'Brien et al., 2000). Among female college students, those with plans for a nontraditional career are more likely than other women to have a mother with a nontraditional career and a father who supports their career choice (Whiston & Keller, 2004). High-achieving Black and White women report receiving considerable family support for pursuing their highly prestigious careers and being strongly influenced by their families' values regarding the benefits of hard work (Richie et al., 1997; Simpson, 1996). For example, a Black female attorney whose father was a janitor, commented: "They wanted me to have a better life than they had. For all of us. And that's why they emphasized education and emphasized working relationships and how you get along with people and that kind of thing" (Higginbotham & Weber, 1996, p. 135).

In addition to social support, cultural values play a role in women's career development. According to McAdoo (in Higginbotham & Weber, 1996), many Black families believe that college education and professional attainment are family, as well as individual, goals. Moreover, there is evidence that high-achieving Black women who move up from their lower social-class backgrounds feel a sense of obligation to their families. In one study (Higginbotham & Weber, 1996), almost twice as many Black as White upwardly mobile women expressed this sense of familial debt. A Black occupational therapist said: "I know the struggle that my parents have had to get me where I am. I know the energy they no longer have to put into the rest of the family even though they want to put it there and they're willing. I feel it is my responsibility to give back some of that energy they have given to me. It's self-directed, not required" (p. 139). In contrast, here is the comment of a White library administrator: "Growing up in a family, I don't think it's that kind of a relationship—that's their job. I feel that way with my son. I certainly love him but I don't want him ever to be in a position to think he owes me" (p. 140).

Another cultural value shown by Black women is their concern for their communities. Many successful Black women are committed to ending both sexism and racism in the workplace and community (Richie et al., 1997) and see their achievements as ways of uplifting Black people (Collins, in Higginbotham & Weber, 1996). As expressed by a high-ranking Black female city official: "Because I have more opportunities, I've got an obligation to give more back and to set a positive example for Black people and especially for Black women. I think we've got to do a tremendous job in building self-esteem and giving people the desire to achieve" (Higginbotham & Weber, 1996, p. 142).

Many high-achieving Latina women receive family encouragement and have a supportive social network. However, some experience a conflict between traditional cultural values that guide them toward family-oriented goals and other socialization factors that encourage high educational and career attainment (Gomez et al., 2001; Kitano, 1998).

Conflicting values also are evident in the experiences of educated Native American women. Although research on Native Americans' achievement goals is sparse, it suggests that family and community members often try to discourage Native women from attending college. Consequently, those that persist in seeking a college education feel they are going against their culture (Kidwell, in LaFromboise et al., 1990).

To more directly learn about family and cultural influences on women's career goals, perform the interviews described in Get Involved 9.2.

In addition to cultural variations across ethnic groups, values associated with social class can influence career decisions. According to Constance Flanagan (1993), working-class families, who hold more traditional gender attitudes than middle-class families, also see less value in academic achievement. Thus, lower-class women who have an interest in school and a willingness to be independent of their families are likely to become invested in employment immediately after high school whereas middle-class women with those attributes are apt to seek higher education.

Job-Related Characteristics

Individuals vary in the benefits they want from working in a particular job, and these benefits can play a role in guiding career selections. Research shows that college women and men both strongly value interesting or challenging work, a

GET INVOLVED **9.2**

Family and Cultural Values about Education and Career Goals

Interview two female students who vary in ethnicity. Select your interviewees from any two of the following ethnic groups: Asian American, Black, Latina, Native American, and White. Inform them you are exploring connections between women's family and cultural values and their education and career goals.

First, ask each respondent to indicate her college major, career goal, and expected educational attainment (i.e., highest educational degree). Second, ask her to evaluate the degree to which her family's values support her specific educational aspirations and career goals. Third, ask her to evaluate the degree to which her specific educational aspirations and career goals were influenced by her ethnic or national cultural values.

What Does It Mean?

1. Did you find any differences among respondents in the extent to which they received support from their families? If yes, refer to information presented in the text or to your own ideas and explain these differences.

2. Did your respondents report that their goals were influenced by their values? Is the information you obtained consistent with the material presented in the text? If not, explain the discrepancies.

sense of personal fulfillment, a good salary, and an opportunity for advancement (Bridges, 1989).

However, college females and males differ in the importance they attach to other job-related attributes, which can account for some of the differences in their occupational choices. A meta-analysis by Alison Konrad and her colleagues (Konrad et al., 2000) found that differences were relatively small but were generally consistent with gender roles and stereotypes. For example, males were somewhat more likely to value earnings, promotions, freedom, challenge, leadership, and power. Females were more apt to value interpersonal relationships and helping others. One striking exception to this pattern was in traditionally masculine occupations, where women rated most masculine-typed job characteristics as highly or more highly than men did. One possible explanation is that women who enter traditionally masculine occupations have particularly strong preferences for masculine-typed job attributes and outcomes.

Another gender difference in job values is the greater emphasis women place on good, flexible working hours and ease of commuting (Konrad et al., 2000). This gender difference probably reflects women's belief that mothers should stay home and care for infants, a value that is expressed during many stages of females' lives. For example, high school girls report a greater willingness than boys do to make occupational sacrifices for their future families (Jozefowicz et al., in Eccles et al.,

1999). Furthermore, a sample of rural women indicated that they assessed occupational alternatives according to how easily a particular job would accommodate their role as mother (Vermeulen & Minor, 1998).

Regardless of the type of job, women's ratings of the importance of several job characteristics rose during the 1980s and 1990s. These include job security, power, prestige, feelings of accomplishment, task enjoyment, and using one's abilities. It is possible that as gender barriers to opportunity declined, women's aspirations rose to obtain previously unavailable job attributes (Konrad et al., 2000).

Entering the Workplace

We have seen that a variety of personal, social, and cultural factors contribute to women's career choices. Once they have made their selections, do women run into any obstacles in the workplace? In Chapter 10 we look into women's experiences on the job, but we begin here by examining the hiring process.

Antidiscrimination laws prohibit the use of gender (as well as ethnicity, national origin, or age) as a determinant in hiring or in other employment decisions. However, gender-based and other forms of discrimination still occur (Padavic & Reskin, 2002). Both gender and ethnic discrimination in hiring have been reported in studies of Black and White female professionals and managers (Richie et al., 1997; Weber & Higginbotham, 1997). As an example of this bias, Rhea Steinpreis and her colleagues (Steinpreis et al., 1999) sent a job resume to psychology academicians and asked them to evaluate the quality of the work-related experience that was presented. Although the resumes were identical, those who were told the applicant was a man evaluated the credentials more positively and indicated a greater willingness to hire than did their colleagues who were told the applicant was a woman. Along the same lines, female job candidates or candidates described as having feminine traits (regardless of biological sex) are considered best suited for jobs dominated by women. Men, or applicants described as having masculine traits, are judged as best suited for male-dominated occupations (Kleyman et al., 2004).

Although gender discrimination can influence hiring decisions, it does not occur in all situations. Not surprisingly, one factor that influences evaluation of job applicants is the gender dominance of the occupation. A recent meta-analysis (Davison & Burke, 2000) found evidence of a promale bias for male-dominated jobs and a profemale bias for female-dominated jobs.

Another factor that affects bias in hiring decisions is the amount of information provided about the applicant. Gender bias is most likely when little information is provided about the candidate's qualifications. In this situation, the gender of the applicant is highly salient and can give rise to stereotyped impressions and decisions. On the other hand, when the candidate's academic and employment records are presented, her or his qualifications strongly influence the evaluator's impression (Davison & Burke, 2000).

S U M M A R Y

Women's Educational Values, Attainment, and Campus Experience

- College women and men have similar values and expectations about their educational attainment.
- Women obtain the majority of associate's and bachelor's degrees whereas men earn the majority of doctoral and professional degrees.
- The campus climate can be problematic for some women. They may experience sexism in the classroom and many perceive the academic environment as hostile and demeaning.
- Women of color, poor women, and women with disabilities experience additional problems on campus.

Women's Work-Related Goals

- College women generally aspire to less prestigious careers than college men. Few women decide to enter the physical sciences or engineering.
- Career counselors can do several things to support and expand women's career aspirations.
- Most college women envision their futures as involving employment, marriage, and motherhood. Many plan to interrupt their employment for childrearing.
- Women have lower salary expectations than men. Possible explanations are women's knowledge that females earn less than males, their willingness to accommodate their jobs to their family life, and their belief that they deserve less.

Influences on Women's Achievement Level and Career Decisions

- There is no evidence that women have less motivation to achieve than men do or that women stay away from high-achieving situations because they fear success.
- Gender differences in attributions for performance are very small and are more likely to occur when making attributions in gender-stereotypic domains.
- Women display less self-confidence than men, especially in relation to male-linked tasks and when estimates of one's performance are made publicly.
- Women with nontraditional gender-related traits or attitudes are more likely to aspire toward male-dominated careers.
- Women's feelings of self-efficacy for particular occupational fields are related to their aspirations for those fields.
- Lesbians' career decisions are sometimes influenced by their perceptions of the job climate for lesbians and gays.
- Family support and family and cultural values can influence women's career development.
- Job-related characteristics valued more highly by males include a good salary, promotions, and opportunity for advancement.
- Characteristics valued more strongly by females than males are interpersonal relationships and helping others. However, women in male-dominated occupations highly value masculine-typed job qualities.

Entering the Workplace

- There is some evidence of gender discrimination in hiring, especially when the job is dominated by the other gender.

K E Y   T E R M S

chilly climate
achievement motivation

fear of success
achievement attributions

self-serving attributional bias
self-efficacy

WHAT DO YOU THINK?

1. Discuss your opinion about the relative advantages and disadvantages for women of attending a women's college versus a mixed-gender college.

2. This chapter discusses several issues faced by women of color and women with disabilities on college campuses. Select two or three of these concerns and suggest institutional procedures that could address these problems and improve the academic climate for these groups.

3. Many women who desire both employment and motherhood want to interrupt their employment for childrearing. What can explain this? As part of your answer, discuss the extent to which gender differences in power (see Chapter 1) and gender socialization (see Chapter 4) explain this.

4. The traditional conception of achievement as the attainment of high academic and occupational success has been criticized as reflecting the achievement domains of men more than of women. Do you agree with this criticism? Give a rationale for your answer. Also, if you agree, suggest other indices of success that would reflect women's achievement more accurately.

5. Discuss the relationship between gender stereotypes and common career choices of young women and men. Also, several changes have occurred in the educational attainment and career aspirations of women over time. Show how a changing social construction of gender has contributed to this.

IF YOU WANT TO LEARN MORE

Datnow, A., & Hubbard, L. (2002). *Gender, policy, and practice: Perspectives on single-sex and coeducational schooling.* New York: Routledge.

Davis, S. N., Crawford, M., & Sebrechts, J. (Eds.). (1999). *Coming into her own: Educational success in girls and women.* San Francisco: Jossey-Bass.

Farmer, H. S. (Ed.). (1997). *Diversity and women's career development: From adolescence to adulthood.* Thousand Oaks, CA: Sage.

Gmelch, S. B. (1998). *Gender on campus: Issues for college women.* New Brunswick, NJ: Rutgers.

Howes, E. V. (2002). *Connecting girls and science: Constructivism, feminism, and science education reform.* New York: Teachers College Press.

Josselson, R. (1996). *Revising herself: The story of women's identity from college to midlife.* New York: Oxford University Press.

Katz, M. (1996). *The gender bias prevention book: Helping girls and women to have satisfying lives and careers.* Northvale, NJ: Jason Aronson.

Tolley, K. (2002). *The science education of American girls: A historical perspective.* New York: Routledge.

WEBSITES

Education

American Association of University Women
http://www.aauw.org

Women with Disabilities

Disabled People's International
http://www.dpi.org

CHAPTER

10 Employment

When I got my offer, I was so thrilled and honored, I accepted my job immediately. I didn't even think to bargain. Maybe we lack self-confidence, so we undersell ourselves. (Martha West, law professor, in Fogg, 2003, p. A14)

When a man leaves, he is getting the golden parachute to enjoy the good life. When a woman leaves of her own accord, they say 'Well, she couldn't take the pressure' . . . I'll say the unspoken: A lot of companies are still more comfortable with a White man in the job. (John Challenger, chief executive of Challenger, Gray, & Christman, a Chicago firm that tracks chief executives, in Stanley, 2002)

A couple of times in my career, someone would tell me that I couldn't do something. I would just tell myself that I wasn't going to talk to that person anymore, and I went ahead and did it anyway . . . I tell other women that persistence pays, and that if you can't work through a problem, to go around it. (Christine King, chief of AMI Semiconductor, in King & Olsen, 2002)

We're still climbing Mount Everest, and we're maybe halfway up . . . There are pockets [of success], and there always have been. And what's exciting is there are more pockets of success now. (Megan Smith, MIT graduate, former chief executive of a dot.com, now in business development at Google, in Hafner, 2003)

In this chapter we examine the nature of women's employment. We begin with an overview of why women work, how many women work, what kinds of jobs they have, the challenges they face in job advancement and becoming leaders, the salaries they receive, and their job satisfaction. We then focus on the status of older women workers. Next, we consider procedures and policies that can improve the work environment for women. Finally, we turn to retirement and economic issues facing older women.

In our exploration of these topics, we use the terms *employment* and *work* interchangeably, so it is important that we clarify their meaning. According to Irene Padavic and Barbara Reskin (2002), the term *work* refers to activities that produce a good or a service. Thus, it includes all sorts of behaviors, such as cooking dinner, mowing the lawn, writing a term paper, teaching a class, fixing a car, volunteering in a nursing home, or running a corporation. The kind of work that we cover in this chapter is work for pay, a major focus of the lives of women (and men) in terms of both time and personal identity. However, our focus on paid employment does not imply that this form of work is more valuable than other types of productive activities. Our society would not function without the unpaid labor that contributes to family and community life.

Women's Decision to Work, Employment Rates, and Occupational Choices

Which women decide to work? What percentage are employed? What occupations do they choose? Let's discuss each of these issues.

Decision to Work

"If you had enough money to live as comfortably as you'd like, would you prefer to work full time, work part time, do volunteer-type work, or work at home caring for the family?" (Families and Work Institute, 1995, p. 54). Two national surveys asking this or a similar question in the 1990s yielded a variety of opinions. Approximately 50 percent of women reported they would desire employment even if it were not financially necessary, and 50 percent reported they would not want to work (Boxer, 1997; Families and Work Institute, 1995). Furthermore, these studies showed that several factors contribute to women's decision to work or not under this circumstance. One factor is age. As we will see in Chapter 11, child-care responsibilities continue to be viewed as primarily women's domain. Therefore, it is not surprising that women in the 25- to 34-year-old age group tend to be least likely to desire employment. Instead, many of these women want to stay home and care for their families (Families and Work Institute, 1995).

Other factors that differentiate between women who would and would not prefer employment are education and salary. The Families and Work Institute study (1995) showed that a desire for employment was strongest among the most educated and highly paid women in the sample: 58 percent of the college-educated respondents and 65 percent of those earning at least $50,000 desired paid work. Possibly these women were more likely than less-educated or lower-paid women to see their jobs as careers important to their personal identities and to have more psychologically rewarding experiences at work.

Employment Rates

Women's labor force participation has increased dramatically in recent decades, especially among mothers of young children (Halpern, 2005). Whereas in 1970 only 30 percent of married women with children under age 6 were in the labor force, by 2004 this number had increased to 62 percent (U.S. Bureau of Labor Statistics, 2005; U.S. Census Bureau, 2003c). Among all individuals age 16 years and older, 59 percent of White women and 62 percent of Black women are employed compared to 74 percent of White men and 67 percent of Black men (U.S. Bureau of Labor Statistics, 2005). Women with disabilities have lower employment rates than either men with disabilities (Olkin, 2003) or nondisabled women (Strauser et al., 2002).

What accounts for the influx of women into the workplace? Several factors have contributed (DiNatale & Boraas, 2003). First, the women's movement provided encouragement for women to consider other role options in addition to the homemaker role. Second, women's current higher level of educational attainment (see Chapter 9) has better prepared them for careers that provide greater challenge, stimulation, and a sense of accomplishment. Women with higher levels of education are more likely to be employed and to return to work more rapidly after giving birth (Downs, 2003). Third, many women must work for financial reasons. Today, few middle-class families can afford home ownership, adequate health insurance, and a middle-class lifestyle on one income (Halpern, 2005). In working-class families, two incomes are often needed to remain above the poverty line (Casper & King, 2004). Nearly half of married working women earn half or more of their family's income (AFL-CIO, 2004). When single women with children are included, over 60 percent of working women earn at least half of the family income and about one-third earn virtually all of it. Economic necessity is particularly great for women who are single heads of households, since they comprise half of all families living in poverty in the United States (Casper & King, 2004; Proctor & Dalaker, 2002). In 2002, 23 percent of all families with children were headed by an unmarried mother, and 73 percent of these mothers were employed (U.S. Census Bureau, 2003c). Unfortunately, for poor women who are heads of households, the employment opportunities are greatly limited, and numerous obstacles block the way to employment. Read Learn about the Research 10.1 for an exploration of employment issues for sheltered homeless and low-income women.

Occupational Choices

One way to examine the occupational choices of women and men is to look at the occupations that employ the fewest number of women and those that employ the greatest number of women. The 20 occupations with the lowest percentage of women are in just four major groups sometimes called "hard hat" occupations: construction; installation, maintenance, and repair; production; and transportation and material moving. The 20 occupations with the greatest concentration of women are similarly clustered in just a few groups, principally health care, office and administrative work, teaching, and caring for young children (Weinberg, 2004).

LEARN ABOUT THE RESEARCH 10.1

Employment Decision Making of Sheltered Homeless and Low-Income Single Mothers

The passage of state and federal welfare reform programs in 1996 increased employment rates and reduced poverty rates among poor, single mothers. However, earning enough to support a family continues to be problematic for these women and their employment options remain very limited. A low-wage earner who has left the welfare system may earn too much to be eligible for benefits such as Medicaid and food stamps, yet be too poor to afford health insurance or adequate food. Thus, many former welfare recipients are more financially strapped than before (Clampet-Lundquist et al., 2004; Costello & Wight, 2003). In addition, much of the low-income work available occurs in evening or night shifts, creating scheduling and child-care problems for families (Hawkins & Whiteman, 2004).

In order to understand both the obstacles to and positive influences on the employment of poor mothers, Margaret Brooks and John Buckner (1996) interviewed 220 homeless mothers living in shelters and 216 housed mothers on welfare. Most of these women were White, Latina, or Black, the majority had never been married, and they had an average of two children.

Among those respondents who had been employed during the preceding five years, nearly 40 percent had worked in service occupations, primarily food service and cashier jobs. This figure is higher than the percentage of women in general who work in these occupations. Because these jobs are frequently of limited duration, pay low wages, provide little opportunity for advancement, and offer limited benefits, they do not readily lead to self-sufficiency.

Having a high school diploma or GED and a primary female caregiver who had been employed during the respondent's childhood were more common among women who had worked. On the other hand, one characteristic more prominent among women who did not work was difficulty speaking or understanding English.

Given their living and financial conditions, these women experienced numerous barriers to employment. The greatest were child care and family responsibilities. The majority of respondents reported the need for child-care assistance in order to be able to seek employment. In addition, more than one-quarter expressed the need for transportation and job training.

The authors concluded their study by stating:

> Until work opportunities for low-skilled individuals are created, until women receive job training and education, and until affordable, quality child care is available, the task of becoming self-supporting will remain a daunting one for single mothers. Welfare reform that ignores these needs is fraught with peril for thousands of families and our society as a whole. (p. 536)

What Does It Mean?

1. How can some of the problems raised by this study be addressed by government, the private sector, educational institutions, or other societal institutions? Be specific.
2. What can poor women do to ensure that their children have better opportunities?

3. Most of the research on women's achievement and career aspirations has focused on middle-class women. Which factors examined in Chapter 9 do not appear to be relevant to the lives of poor women? Explain your answer.

Source: Brooks & Buckner (1996).

Another way of looking at occupational segregation is to determine the **index of segregation**, *the proportion of workers of either gender who would have to change their occupations in order to achieve equal gender representation across all occupations.* This figure would be 0 if every occupation employed equal numbers of each gender and it would be 100 if every occupation employed only one gender. In 1997 the index was about 50 percent. In other words, 50 percent of all workers of one gender would have had to shift to jobs dominated by the other gender in order to attain equal gender representation across the workplace (Gutek, 2001).

Occupational segregation has declined considerably since the 1970s (Gutek, 2001). Women have increased their numbers in both managerial and professional jobs, and now hold half of these positions. However, a closer look at the gender distribution within professions overall shows significant differences in the types of occupations pursued by women and men. In 2004, 79 percent of dietitians and nutritionists were women compared with only 14 percent of architects and engineers. In addition, although more women have entered the relatively high-paying skilled trades (e.g., as carpenters, plumbers, and electricians), they still comprise a very small percentage of these workers (U.S. Bureau of Labor Statistics, 2005). Women remain segregated in so-called "pink-collar" fields. Nearly 30 percent of female employees work in just 10 occupations. Most of these are low-status, low-paying service jobs such as receptionist, cashier, restaurant server, nursing aide, and cook (AAUW Educational Foundation, 2003). Thus, the workplace continues to be characterized by significant gender segregation, with men tending to dominate the most prestigious occupations such as medicine, engineering, and banking (Cleveland et al., 2005).

Furthermore, more employers today are cutting costs by hiring part-time or temporary workers, who are paid less and have minimal or no benefits. Women are more likely than men to hold these jobs, whose flexibility may fit well with a woman's family obligations (American Psychological Association, 2004b; Marler & Moen, 2005).

The workplace is segregated not only by gender but also by ethnicity. More Whites than Blacks and Latinas/os are employed in high-status and high-paying managerial or professional occupations and more ethnic minorities than Whites hold service jobs (U.S. Census Bureau, 2003c). However, the ethnic differences among women are not as great as the gender differences. For example, secretarial work and cashiering are among the four most common jobs for Asian American, Black, Latina, and White women (Padavic & Reskin, 2002).

Gender Differences in Leadership and Job Advancement

The news that Brian Williams would succeed Tom Brokaw as the evening news anchor on NBC News in 2004 prompted TV analysts to note that while women have made huge gains in television news, the anchor remains a male bastion. (Rutenberg, 2002)

Despite the success of a handful of big-name female directors like Penny Marshall, Nora Ephron, and Jane Campion, little has changed for women directors in 15 years. "They call it the 'boy wonder syndrome.' After these guys do their first big picture, they take on a presence larger than life. This doesn't happen for women." (Martha Lauzen, in Kennedy, 2002)

Women constitute only 17 percent of opinion writers at The New York Times, *10 percent at* The Washington Post, *28 percent at* U.S. News & World Report, *23 percent at* Newsweek, *and 13 percent at* Time. *Overall, only 24 percent of nationally syndicated columnists are women and they tend to be White and right wing.* (Ashkinaze, 2005)

Leadership Positions

Women make up nearly half of the paid labor force of the United States and about half of those are in managerial positions. Yet the higher up one goes in an organization, the scarcer women become. For example, women constitute only 16 percent of Fortune 500 corporate officers, 12 percent of board directors, 14 percent of U.S. senators, 15 percent of congressional representatives, 16 percent of state governors, 24 percent of college and university presidents, and 2 percent of high-level military officers. The situation for women of color is even worse. Similar small proportions of women in high positions exist in other nations (American Council on Education, 2005; Center for American Women and Politics, 2005; Indvik, 2004; Wellington & Giscombe, 2001; M. C. Wilson, 2004). Out of 184 countries, the United States ranks fifty-ninth—just above Sierra Leone—in women's participation in the lower or single legislative body of the country. Women make up just 15 percent of the U.S. House of Representatives. Sweden is near the top of the list, with 45 percent, while Bahrain, Kuwait, Saudi Arabia, and the United Arab Emirates are at the bottom with 0 percent women (Inter-Parliamentary Union, 2005). Even in female-dominated fields, men dominate at the top ranks. For example, about 97 percent of school superintendents are men (Fassinger, 2001).

The concept of the **glass ceiling** refers to *invisible but powerful barriers that prevent women from advancing beyond a certain level.* Some also suggest the existence of a **sticky floor** in traditional women's jobs, meaning *women have little or no job ladder, or path, to higher positions* (Gutek, 2001). Clerical work is an example of an occupation with little room for growth. Furthermore, some women report experiencing a **maternal wall,** in which they *get less desirable assignments and more limited advancement opportunities once they have a child* (Nelson & Burke, 2002).

Barriers That Hinder Women's Advancement

What prevents women from reaching positions of leadership? We turn now to the role of mentors, social networks, and discrimination.

Mentors and Social Networks. A **mentor** *is a senior-level person who takes an active role in the career planning and development of junior employees.* Mentors help their

Indonesia's President Megawati Sukarnoputri, right, met with New Zealand Prime Minister Helen Clark in Jakarta in 2002. More women around the world are assuming positions of political power, although their numbers remain small.

mentees develop appropriate skills, learn the informal organizational structure, meet appropriate people, and have access to opportunities that enable them to advance. Consequently, mentoring has positive effects on job satisfaction, promotion, and career success (Allen & Eby, 2004; Heyl, 2005; Williams-Nickelson, 2005).

Women employees may have difficulty in identifying an appropriate mentor. The limited number of women in senior-level positions makes it hard for a woman to find a female mentor. In addition, men may be reluctant to mentor young women (Gutek, 2001; McCann, 2004). One male manager had this to say (Nicolau, in the Federal Glass Ceiling Commission, 1995a, p. 28): "It's always going to be tough to figure out how to treat the women, but now it's worse and I'd rather not be in a mentoring relationship with them."

A second vehicle for advancement that is limited for women and people of color is access to informal social networks. These networks can provide information about job opportunities as well as opportunities to meet important members of the organization. Furthermore, they offer social support and can serve as an important step in developing a mentoring relationship with a senior-level person. Networking is strongly related to women's jobs and life satisfaction (Auster, 2001). However, White male reluctance to deal with women and people of color means these groups are less likely than White men to be invited to informal social events (e.g., golf outings, lunches) or to be included in informal communication networks (Fassinger, 2001; Harway, 2001). In addition, women are more likely to have child-care responsibilities right after work, which limits their opportunities for after-hours socializing with male colleagues (Allen, 2004). The frustration this can produce was expressed by a Black female administrator in higher education who said, "Unless you are able to deal with the old White boy network you will continue to face obstacles and barriers" (Ramey, 1995, p. 116). One way for women to become part of a network is to join local or national organizations such as the National Association for Female Executives and the American Association of University Women (AAUW), attend events, and meet people (Eddleman et al., 2003).

Discrimination.   Another factor limiting the job advancement of women and ethnic minorities is discrimination, that is, unfavorable treatment based on gender or ethnicity. Recently settled lawsuits against major corporations and brokerage firms including Wal-Mart, Morgan Stanley, Merrill Lynch, Boeing, and Abercrombie & Fitch reveal major sex and ethnic inequities in pay and promotion (Greenhouse, 2004; "Major Companies," 2004; McGeehan, 2004). For example, brokerage firms have been found to take away women's clients and commissions, give them pay cuts and demotions following maternity leave, and refuse to supply them with study materials that help male brokers earn their licenses (Antilla, 2002).

Gender discrimination is alive and well in higher education as well. For example, the more prestigious the university, the fewer women it has on the faculty and in tenured positions (Wilson, 2004b). Those women who do get hired at major research universities often experience discrimination. At the Massachusetts Institute of Technology (MIT), the most prestigious science and engineering university in the United States, a study in the late 1990s found that women were disadvantaged not only in promotions and salary but also in research grants, appointments to important committees, types of teaching assignments, and even in the size of their research laboratories. Furthermore, not one woman had ever served as head of a science department (Rimer, 2005; Zernicke, 2001). As a result of the report, several women scientists received salary increases, research funds, and larger or improved laboratories, but three years later, many women at MIT still felt marginalized (Smallwood, 2002). For example, in one engineering department, women were rarely asked to serve on search committees when new faculty were hired. The small inequities which may seem insignificant in isolation accumulate over time to create an unfair and hostile environment for women (Fassinger, 2001). With the fall 2004 hiring of Susan Hockfield as MIT's first female president (Lawler, 2004), will the status of women improve at the university? Time will tell.

Experiences of gender discrimination at work are related to more negative relationships with supervisors, and coworkers, along with lower levels of organizational commitment and job satisfaction (Bond et al., 2004; Murray, 2003). Moreover, discrimination may affect women more negatively than men. For women, perceiving and experiencing discrimination is associated with negative psychological symptoms, such as increased anxiety and depression, and lowered self-esteem. Among men, however, the perception and experience of discrimination is unrelated to well-being (Schmitt et al., 2002). A more subtle form of discrimination is **patronizing behavior,** in which *supervisors give subordinates considerable praise while withholding valued resources such as raises and promotions.*

Such behavior has a more negative effect on the performance of female workers than male workers (Vescio et al., 2005).

Let's now look at three factors that help explain why women experience discrimination in the workplace: stereotypes, cultural differences, and perceived threat.

Stereotypes.   One important factor is the operation of gender stereotypes. The successful manager is seen as having male gender-stereotypic traits, such as ambition, decisiveness, self-reliance, and strong commitment to the work role; hence, reliance on traditional gender stereotypes will lead to the conclusion that a woman is not qualified (Cleveland et al., 2005; Diekman et al., 2004; Masser & Abrams, 2004; Willemsen, 2002). Across a wide variety of settings, women are presumed to be less competent than men and less worthy to hold leadership positions (Carli & Eagly, 2001; Fielden & Cooper, 2002; Ridgeway, 2001). A review of studies in the United States, Germany, the United Kingdom, China, and Japan by Virginia Schein (2001) reveals that individuals in these nations, especially men, perceive men to be more qualified managers. Madeline Heilman's (2001) review of research on leadership in organizations shows that the success of female managers is devalued or is attributed to external factors rather than to the woman's competence. When women are perceived to be as competent as men, they are often viewed as violating gender stereotypes that require women to be communal. As a consequence people, especially males, often dislike highly competent and agentic women and dismiss their contributions (Carli, 2001; Eagly & Karau, 2002; Heilman et al., 2004; Masser & Abrams, 2004). Women also are more negatively evaluated when they adopt less pleasant aspects of masculine style of leadership, that is, an autocratic, punitive, nonparticipative approach (Atwater et al., 2001; Eagly et al., 1992). In the words of a male corporate vice president "With a male executive there's no expectation to be nice. He has more permission to be an ass. But when women speak their minds, they're seen as harsh" (Banerjee, 2001). In order to be influential, women therefore must combine agentic qualities such as competence and directness with communal qualities such as friendliness and warmth (Carli & Eagly, 2001).

Unfavorable gender stereotypes of women are most likely to operate when the evaluators are men (Carli, 2001; Padavic & Reskin, 2002). In one study, for example, female college students perceived female managers as high in agentic traits, but male college students did not (Deal & Stevenson, 1998). In fact, male respondents characterized female managers very negatively, viewing them as bitter, easily influenced, hasty, nervous, passive, and shy. Given that more than half of all managers and administrators are men and that men dominate higher-level management positions, many female workers are evaluated by men and, therefore, face the possibility of similar stereotype-based judgments and decisions.

Negative gender stereotypes also are more likely to operate when women perform in a male domain. In such settings, women are less likely than men to be selected as leaders, to receive positive evaluations for their leadership, or to be liked (Eagly et al., 1992; Heilman et al., 2004).

The operation of negative stereotyping when women work in male-related jobs or use masculine styles is clearly illustrated by the experience of Ann Hopkins (see Chapter 2). Ms. Hopkins was an extremely competent, high-achieving accountant who did not receive her earned promotion to partner because her employers claimed she was not sufficiently feminine. Apparently Ann Hopkins was punished for her masculine style in a male-dominated field. According to Alice Eagly and her colleagues (Eagly et al., 1992) female managers "pay a price" for intruding in men's domains, in terms of either their leadership position or their leadership style.

Cultural Differences.   In addition to gender stereotypes, the perception of cultural differences between the evaluator and subordinate can influence discrimination in the workplace. Differences between White male managers and females or people of color can create tension that managers attempt to avoid. As one corporate manager stated: "What's important is comfort, chemistry, relationships, and collaborations. That's what makes a shop work. When we find minorities and women who think like we do, we snatch them up" (Federal Glass Ceiling Commission, 1995a, p. 28). His need to emphasize minorities and women suggests that he thinks achieving rapport with these groups is less likely to occur than rapport with other White men.

Perceived Threat.   A third factor influencing discrimination in the workplace is the perception of threat. Many White middle and upper-middle managers view the career progression of women or people of color as a direct threat to their own advancement. "If they are in, there's less of a chance for me. Why would I want a bigger pool? White men can only lose in this game. I'm endangered" (Federal Glass Ceiling Commission, 1995a, p. 31). In one study of a large Canadian federal agency, 126 male managers estimated the number of women at their level in their department and indicated their perception of whether men in management are disadvantaged relative to women (Beaton et al., 1996). As you might expect, the more women were estimated to be in a department, the greater the perception that women pose a threat to men. Similarly, women view women's gains in power more positively than men do (Diekman et al., 2004). Not surprisingly, groups that are disadvantaged by the present hierarchy are more likely to approve of social change.

What do all of the barriers against the advancement of women and people of color have in common? Consistent with one of our major themes, these obstacles are clear reflections of power differences in the workplace. White men have higher status and more resources; that is, they have higher organizational power. Although there has been progress in recent years, men continue to have the ability to control opportunities and decisions that have major impact on women and ethnic minorities. On the positive side, however, as more and more women and people of color enter higher-status occupations and gradually advance within these fields, they will acquire greater organizational resources, thus contributing to a reduction in this power inequality.

Women as Leaders

We have seen that women face more barriers to becoming leaders than men do, especially in male-dominated fields (Eagly & Karau, 2002). How do women and men actually behave once they attain these positions? In other words, what are their leadership styles? And are women and men equally effective as leaders?

Leadership Style.   One dimension of leadership is **task orientation**, which *focuses on getting the job done*, versus **interpersonal orientation**, which is *concerned with the morale and welfare of others*. A second dimension is a **democratic style**, which *encourages others to participate in decision making*, versus an **autocratic style**, which *discourages participation* (Eagly & Johannesen-Schmidt, 2001). A third aspect of leadership is a **transformational** versus a **transactional** style. Transformational leaders *set high standards and serve as role models by mentoring and empowering their subordinates*. Transactional leaders *clarify workers' responsibilities, monitor their work, reward them for meeting objectives, and correct their mistakes.*

A meta-analysis by Alice Eagly and Blair Johnson (1990) found only small gender differences in leadership style. Women were somewhat more democratic and interpersonal, whereas men were somewhat more autocratic and task oriented. Differences were larger in laboratory research than they were in actual organizational settings. Recent research shows that women are more transformational and that men are more transactional (Eagly & Johannesen-Schmidt, 2001; Eagly et al., 2003). Male managers are less likely than female managers to reward good performance and are more likely to pay attention to workers' mistakes, wait until problems become severe before attending to them, and be absent and uninvolved in critical times.

Effectiveness.   A meta-analysis by Alice Eagly and her colleagues (Eagly et al., 1995) found no difference in the overall effectiveness of female and male leaders in facilitating accomplishment of the goals of their group. Men were judged more effective in the military, a male-dominated area, whereas women were viewed as more effective in female-dominated domains. More recent research, however, shows that women's more transformational style and greater use of rewards for good performance are linked to higher ratings of effectiveness (Eagly & Johannesen-Schmidt, 2001). Along these same lines, a five-year study of the leadership skills of over 2,400 female and male managers found that female managers were rated significantly better than their male counterparts by their supervisors, themselves, and the people who worked for them (Pfaff & Associates, 1999). These differences extended both to the communal skills of communication, feedback, and empowerment and to agentic skills such as decisiveness, planning, and setting standards.

Gender Differences in Salaries

> *Women, want to earn more than men? Here's how: Clean up hazardous waste! Install telecommunications lines! Otherwise, forget it.*

This clearly fictitious job ad is based on real data released recently by the U.S. Census Bureau on the salaries of hundreds of jobs (Weinberg, 2004). In the two jobs mentioned above, women earned slightly more than men, on average. For three other jobs, they earned the same: meeting planners, cafeteria workers, and construction helpers. In the other 500 jobs, women earned less.

In this section, we look at the gender gap in salaries and explore reasons for this difference.

Comparative Salaries

Although the earnings gap between women and men has declined over the last few decades, in 2004 women still earned only 80 cents for each dollar men earned. Men who work full time earn a median weekly salary of $713, compared to $573 for women (U.S. Bureau of Labor Statistics, 2005). Women of color fare even more poorly than White women (except for those with college degrees, as we'll see shortly). Among full-time year-round workers, White women earn 70 percent of what White men earn, but these figures drop to 63 percent for Black women, 58 percent for Native American women, and 53 percent for Latinas (Caiazza et al., 2004). Similarly, women with disabilities have lower earnings than their male counterparts and earn only 69 percent of what women in general earn (Yoder, 2000). In addition, the gender gap in pay increases with age. In 2001, women age 55 to 64 earned 68 percent of the salary of men the same age. Women age 25 to 34, on the other hand, were paid 86 percent of the wages of men of comparable age (U.S. Census Bureau, 2003c). Why are older women's earnings depressed? For one thing, older women have spent less time in the labor force than younger women. Also, many started working when employers were free to discriminate in pay between women and men doing the same work. Even now, nearly 45 years after the passage of the 1963 Federal Equal Pay Act, the legacy of once-legal salary discrimination remains (Bosworth et al., 2001).

Although women of color make less than White women on average, Black women with bachelor's degrees earn slightly more than similarly educated White women (U.S. Census Bureau, 2005a) What are possible reasons for these differences? For one thing, minority women, especially Blacks, are more likely to hold two jobs or work more than 40 hours per week. In addition, Black professional women tend to return to the work force earlier than others after having a child. Also, employers in some fields may give extra financial incentives to hire young Black professional women.

Given that the majority of employed women provide at least half of their families' income and that a sizable minority of families are headed by employed single women, the gender gap in wages has important implications for families. Not only is it detrimental to the financial well-being of many families, both two-parent and single-parent, but it also places more women than men at risk of poverty (DeNavas-Walt et al., 2004; Lipson, 2001).

To get a more detailed picture of the gender gap, let's examine wage differentials within selected occupations. In 2004, the ratio of female-to-male earnings was 80 percent for software engineers, 73 percent for lawyers, and 85 percent for pharmacists (U.S. Bureau of Labor Statistics, 2005). Even in occupations that employ primarily women, women's salaries are lower than men's. In 2004, female nurses earned 87 percent as much as male nurses, and, among secretaries and administrative assistants, women earned 92 percent of what men earned (U.S. Bureau of Labor Statistics, 2005). As we saw earlier, these wage discrepancies are smaller for younger women than for older ones (Luciano, 2003).

What is the cumulative effect of the gender pay gap? Unfortunately, it is far from trivial. For the average woman with a bachelor's degree, the wage gap translates into $900,000 over her lifetime (Day & Newburger, 2002). For poor, single mothers the earnings gap poses an additional set of problems. Many unmarried women who are employed do not earn enough to support their families. In fact, there is evidence that if single mothers were paid the same as men, who are comparable in education and number of hours worked, the poverty rate for their families would be reduced by 50 percent (AFL-CIO and the Institute for Women's Policy Research, 1999). Instead, these women are at high risk for both welfare and homelessness.

Not surprisingly, most studies show that women believe their salaries are not commensurate with the value of their work or their abilities and experience. Regardless of their age, ethnicity, occupation, or income, women believe that the most necessary change in the workplace is better pay (Castro, 1997). Although most studies show that employed women tend to be dissatisfied with their salaries, recall that women have lower salary expectations than men do (see Chapter 9). Do you think these lower expectations can have an impact on satisfaction? Turn to Learn about the Research 10.2 for some intriguing perspectives on this question.

Reasons for Differences in Salaries

Several factors have been offered as explanations of the pay differential. In considering these reasons, keep in mind the societal power differential in the workplace.

Gender Differences in Investments in the Job.   According to the **human capital perspective,** *salaries reflect investments of human capital (e.g., education and work experience) and because of their family responsibilities, women, relative to men, reduce their investment in their education and jobs* (Hattery, 2001). That is, women are paid less than men because they have less training and put less time into their careers. Does the evidence support this viewpoint?

We look first at the influence of educational background. If educational differences could explain salary differences, females and males with comparable levels of education should earn similar wages. The reality is that at every level of educational attainment, from high school to master's degree, Black, Latina, and White women earn less than men in the same ethnic group (Peter & Horn, 2005; U.S. Bureau of Labor Statistics, 2005). It is disheartening that male high school dropouts earn almost as much as women with two-year college degrees, and that the average salary of women with a college degree is over $25,000 less than the earnings of male

LEARN ABOUT THE RESEARCH 10.2

How Do Women Perceive Their Wages?

Salary expectations are closely related to perceptions of entitlement. That is, the higher the salary a person feels entitled to, the higher the salary the person expects. In addition, several scholars contend that salary satisfaction is influenced by the consistency between actual salary and salary believed to be deserved (Bylsma & Major, 1994; Jackson et al., 1992). One study (Bylsma & Major, 1994) showed that, women, compared to men, feel they deserve lower pay and are more likely to feel satisfied with objectively lower earnings. What could possibly explain women's feelings of lower pay entitlement?

According to Linda Jackson and her colleagues (Jackson et al., 1992), women perceive lower salaries as fair salaries. These researchers suggest that, as a result of differ-ential socialization, women and men have different attitudes toward money, which affect their views of a fair wage.

Another explanation is that women and men have different perceptions of personal entitlement because they have different standards of comparison (Gutek, 2001; Hogue & Yoder, 2003). People tend to evaluate what they deserve by comparing themselves to similar others. Because women's salaries have historically been lower than men's, the standard women use to judge entitlement is lower than the standard used by men. This lower comparison standard then influences women to feel they deserve less than men feel they deserve. Consequently, they are satisfied with lower pay.

What Does It Mean?

1. Jackson and her colleagues suggest that women have lower standards than men for fair salaries. Additionally, they claim that this might be because women and men have different attitudes toward money. First, show how different views about money could lead to different perceptions of fair salaries. Then, use information from any chapters in the text to formulate an argument that either supports or refutes the assumptions of gender differences in perceived fairness and attitudes toward money.

2. Use material from any chapters in the text to frame an argument that either supports or refutes Bylsma and Major's claim that women and men have different perceptions of what they deserve and that these differences are due to different comparison standards.

3. Bylsma and Major contend that the lower comparison standards and feelings of entitlement are applicable to any less-powerful group. If this assumption is correct, can you suggest ways to counteract the influence of lower comparison standards?

---

college graduates (U.S. Census Bureau, 2004a). College-educated Black women earn only $1,500 more than White male *high school* graduates (AAUW, 2002). Over-all, a bachelor's degree increases a man's lifetime earnings by $1.1 million but adds only $600,000 to a woman's earnings (Day & Newburger, 2002).

What about investment of time on the job? Women spend an average of 36 hours per week at work compared to men's 42 hours (U.S. Bureau of Labor

Statistics, 2005), and time at work does play some role in the wage gap (Padavic & Reskin, 2002; Tischler, 2004). Another indicator of time investment is the interruption of employment. Because of their childbearing and childrearing responsibilities, women are more likely than men to temporarily leave employment (Avellar & Smock, 2003). However, employment interruptions are becoming less common because there is a greater dependence on two incomes, thus shortening parental leaves, and because women are having fewer children. For example, a survey of senior managers (Korn/Ferry, in the Federal Glass Ceiling Commission, 1995a) found that only one-third of the women in their study had ever taken a leave, most leaves were for less than six months, and excluding interruptions for maternity, men took more leaves than women.

So, do differences in investment help explain pay differences? According to Padavic and Reskin (2002), human capital differences were a major source of the gender wage gap in the 1970s but that influence is now minimal. One study found that educational background and number of hours worked per week did not account for the salary difference between women and men in the beginning stages of business management careers (Tsui, 1998). Also, an examination of school psychologists demonstrated gender differences in salaries despite similarities in work experience and time spent at work (Thomas & White, 1996). Studies that have taken into account all human capital differences show that these differences explain only 50 to 75 percent of the gender wage gap (AFL-CIO & the Institute for Women's Policy Research, 1999). In other words, 25 to 50 percent of the salary difference cannot be explained by differences in educational background and time commitment. Let's look at other possible factors.

Occupational and Job-Level Distribution.   A major factor contributing to both gender and ethnic differences in pay is the difference in jobs held by women and men and by individuals in different ethnic groups (Lips, 2003; U.S. Bureau of Labor Statistics, 2005). We saw earlier in this chapter that women and people of color are less likely than White men to attain higher-level, higher-paying positions. Women tend to be congregated in female-dominated occupations, and these occupations are at the low end of the salary scale. According to the National Committee on Pay Equity, the greater the number of women or people of color in an occupation, the lower the wages (Lipson, 2001). As an example, child-care workers earn a lower hourly wage than car washers or parking lot attendants (Weinberg, 2004).

Why do occupations employing mostly women pay less than those employing mostly men? One answer is that women's occupations are devalued relative to men's (Lips, 2003). In Chapter 3 we saw that people more highly value males and male-related attributes. In the workplace this value difference gets translated into employers' higher evaluation of male-dominated jobs and job-related skills associated with men (Cohen & Huffman, 2003). For example, physical strength, which characterizes men more than women, is highly valued and well compensated in metal-working jobs. Nurturance, a trait associated with females, on the other hand, is not highly valued. Consequently, occupations that rely on caregiving, such as child care, are on the low end of the pay scale (Padavic & Reskin, 2002).

Salary Negotiations.   Another reason for the gender gap in salaries is that women are less likely than men to initiate salary negotiations and are more willing to accept whatever salary is offered by their employer (Babcock & Laschever, 2003). For example, in Linda Babcock's survey of recent Carnegie Mellon graduates who had master's degrees, only 7 percent of the women but 57 percent of the men had negotiated their salaries. Moreover, those who negotiated raised their salaries by an average of $4,053 (Ellin, 2004b). Even when women do negotiate, they don't fare as well as men. When negotiating a starting salary or a raise, men receive an average 4.3 percent more than the initial offer, whereas women receive only 2.7 percent more (Eddleman et al., 2003).

Why are women less likely to bargain when setting their starting salaries or raises? One factor is that women are generally less comfortable than men with self-promotion. Starting in childhood, boys are encouraged to talk about their achievements, whereas girls are taught to be polite, compliant, modest, and not to brag (Frankel, 2004; Rapp, 2003). This makes some women feel that negotiating brands them as selfish troublemakers (Conrad, 2005). In addition, women are more likely to believe that employers will notice and reward good performance without being asked (Ellin, 2004b; Fogg, 2003). Another related factor, as we saw in Learn About the Research 10.2, is that women often underestimate their worth. In addition, men may overestimate theirs. For example, a recent study of business students by Lisa Barron (cited in Ellin, 2004b) found that 71 percent of the men indicated they were entitled to more money than other job applicants, whereas 70 percent of women believed they were entitled to a salary equal to that of other candidates. For tips on negotiating your salary, see Table 10.1.

Wage Discrimination.   One key factor in the gender gap in salaries is **wage discrimination,** *differential payment for work that has equal or substantially similar value to the employer.* Unequal pay scales were once considered justifiable by employers on the basis that women work only for "extras" or "pocket money" or that women

TABLE 10.1   Tips on Effectively Negotiating Salaries

1. Find out salary information for comparable jobs by using Websites, contacting professional associations, talking to colleagues, using your college's placement office.
2. Assess the value of your skills and work experience using the same resources mentioned in item 1.
3. During negotiations, indicate that salary is important to you.
4. Negotiate things other than salary: benefits, perks, job title, responsibilities, and so on.
5. Be persistent and willing to compromise. If the hiring individual says "no," don't simply accept this. Ask "How close can you come to my offer?"
6. Role-play salary negotiations with experienced colleagues, or job counselors at your college.

Sources: Ellin (2004b), Frankel (2004), Kolb & Williams (2003).

can function with less money than men can (Padavic & Reskin, 2002). Since passage of the 1963 Federal Equal Pay Act, however, unequal pay for equal work has been illegal. Nevertheless, because wage discrimination laws are poorly enforced, equal pay legislation has not guaranteed equality (AAUW, 2002; National Science Foundation, 2003). It should not be surprising, therefore, that thousands of women have filed discrimination claims (Padavic & Reskin, 2002), and settlements have been made for women employed in a range of occupations.

Another troubling finding is that *women with children earn significantly less than childless women, even when they have comparable education, work experience, and job characteristics*. This phenomenon, known as the **motherhood penalty**, averages about a 5 percent reduction in salary per child (Avellar & Smock, 2003). What can account for the motherhood penalty? Researchers suggest two possibilities. One is that mothers may be less productive on the job than nonmothers because the latter can spend more of their nonemployment time in refreshing leisure, rather than in exhausting housework and child care. Alternatively, employers may discriminate against mothers in terms of job placement, promotion, or pay levels within jobs (Budig & England, 2001). In support of this view, outstanding employees who are mothers are perceived as less professionally competent than those who have no children (Etaugh & Poertner, 1992). Once again, as we saw in Chapter 2, social roles influence gender stereotypes.

Discriminatory policies contribute to ethnic differences in pay as well as to gender differences. For example, a study conducted by the Fair Employment Council of Washington sent out pairs of Black and White women, matched in work experience and backgrounds, to apply for the same advertised jobs. Not only did more White than Black women receive job offers, but they were also more likely to be offered a higher starting salary (Bendick, in Frye, 1996). What are wages and working conditions like for women in developing nations? For a closer look, read Explore Other Cultures 10.1.

Now that you are familiar with some of the problems experienced by women in the workplace, perform the interviews in Get Involved 10.1 to gain firsthand knowledge about women's experiences with wage or promotion discrimination, and with other forms of gender-biased treatment.

Women's Job Satisfaction

Earlier in this chapter, we saw that women and men congregate in different jobs and that the most prestigious occupations employ more men than women. We also noted that women's job levels and salaries are generally lower than men's. Do these gender differences in occupational dimensions correspond to differences in job satisfaction?

Gender Differences in Satisfaction

Given the existence of the glass ceiling, it is not surprising that women express less satisfaction than men about their promotional opportunities (Chiu, 1998;

EXPLORE OTHER CULTURES 10.1
Girls and Women in the Global Factory

The fact that women's work worldwide is frequently unpaid or underpaid is closely linked to women's lower power and status (Burn, 2000). In many developing countries in Africa, Central America, and Asia, thousands of women and girls as young as 8 work for low wages 15 or more hours a day, everyday, in **sweatshops**—*businesses that violate safety, wage, and child labor laws* (International Labour Organization, 2004). Health problems are common in these factories due to harsh working conditions such as poor ventilation, exposure to chemicals, and repetitive motion. Shawn Burn (2000) points out that most of the clothes, shoes, toys, and electronics purchased by North Americans were likely manufactured by women working in sweatshops in nations such as Bangladesh, Burma, China, the Dominican Republic, Haiti, Honduras, Indonesia, Guatemala, Malaysia, Mexico,

Nicaragua, the Philippines, and Vietnam. In Bangladesh, for example, the young female workers are paid an average of 1.6 cents for each $17 baseball cap with a Harvard logo that they sew (Hayden & Kernaghan, 2002). These women laborers seldom question their working conditions, having grown up in male-dominated households where they have learned to be subservient and dutiful (Cairoli, 2001). In addition, they often are unaware of their rights and are afraid of losing their jobs if they assert themselves. The efforts of the International Labour Organization, along with women's increasing union membership and the work of women activists around the world, have produced some progress in passing laws to improve women's work conditions, producing greater implementation of these laws, and educating women about their rights (Burn, 2000).

Many of the clothes, shoes, toys, and electronics purchased by North Americans are manufactured by women working in Asian or Latin American sweatshops.

Lyness & Thompson, 1997). More than three-quarters of the women in the Families and Work Institute sample (1995) discussed earlier in this chapter indicated concern about insufficient opportunities for women to get ahead or to grow. However, research on gender differences in overall job satisfaction provides mixed results. Although numerous studies show that women are less satisfied than men (Chiu, 1998; Singh et al., 1995), there are many exceptions. Some investigations indicate no gender differences in overall job satisfaction (Lyness & Thompson, 1997; Mason, 1995; Weeks & Nantel, 1995), whereas others show higher satisfaction in some occupations among females than among males (Mason, 1995). The fact that women are not consistently less satisfied than men suggests that many factors contribute to the overall satisfaction gained from one's job. Job and salary level are two sources. Social support from peers and supervisors is also strongly related to job satisfaction (Bond et al., 2004). Ellen Auster (2001) suggests that a number of other factors are associated with women's midcareer satisfaction:

1. having children, which seems to serve as a counterbalance to work pressures (see Chapter 11);
2. for ethnic minority women, developing a broad social network that crosses racial/ethnic boundaries;
3. having employment gaps (for example, parental leave) that are voluntary and supported by the organization;
4. using flexible options, such as job-sharing and flextime (see Chapter 11);
5. having mentors in one's career;
6. networking (that is, developing relationships that have the potential to assist in one's career);

7. having balanced proportions of women and men within one's work unit;
8. experiencing lower levels of sex bias and discrimination;
9. having family-friendly organizational policies such as parental leave, day care, and fitness activities (see Chapter 11);
10. having opportunities for autonomy, creativity, training, development, and advancement within a context of job security;
11. having lower stress levels.

Factor Influencing Lesbians' Job Satisfaction

Increasing numbers of organizations have adopted antidiscrimination policies that include sexual orientation, although these are still in the minority (Button, 2001). Unfortunately, many lesbian, gay, and bisexual employees experience workplace discrimination based on their sexual orientation (Lyons et al., 2003). Such discrimination is related to lower levels of job satisfaction and organizational commitment and higher levels of psychological distress (Lyons et al., 2003; Ragins & Cornwell, 2001). Thus, the decision of whether or not to come out is a major concern for lesbian workers. Potential benefits of coming out include the development of a positive identity, enhanced self-esteem, and self-acceptance (Kolchakian & Fassinger, 2003). On the negative side, lesbian and bisexual women fear that sexual identity disclosure might precipitate workplace discrimination, including job loss, salary reduction, or harassment (Ragins & Cornwell, 2001). This fear is not without some basis in fact. Lesbian, gay, and bisexual individuals earn less than their heterosexual counterparts and are often fired or passed over for promotion because of their sexual orientation (Harper et al., 2004). As one example, a college presidency offered to a woman was withdrawn when the board of trustees found out that she was a lesbian (Reid & Zalk, 2001). Lesbian women of color experience an extra burden because they risk adding homophobia to the gender or ethnic prejudice which they might already experience (Gallor, 2003). Given the possible risks of coming out in the workplace, it is not surprising that the majority of lesbians do not disclose their sexual identity at work (Ragins & Cornwell, 2001).

The Older Woman Worker

After Helen Martinez's children were grown, she found employment as a secretary with a large corporation. Eventually, she was promoted to executive secretary, a position she held for several years. Helen decided to retire when her husband did. He was 65; she was 61. They did some traveling and joined a local senior citizens group. After 8 years, her husband died. Helen found that her Social Security benefits and the income from her pension were barely enough to support her. At the age of 70, she decided to go back to work for her old firm. She works 2½ days a week, running a job bank. Now 79, she does not plan to retire again unless forced to by poor health.

Dr. Marguerite Vogt, age 88, has been a dedicated molecular biologist for 70 years. Her many accomplishments include her groundbreaking research on the polio virus that led to the development of the polio vaccine. Dr. Vogt, who works at the Salk Institute in San Diego, continues to spend 10 hours a day, 7 days a week, in her laboratory. "I like it here," she says. If I were to stay at home, I'd be bored." (Angier, 2001)

Helen Martinez is typical of many women workers who enter or reenter the labor force in later life. Marguerite Vogt, on the other hand, is an example of older women workers who have been employed continuously throughout their adult lives. In this section, we examine the varying experiences of older women workers.

Employment Rates

Labor force participation of middle-aged and older women has increased sharply over the past three decades. Two-thirds of married women and 70 percent of unmarried women age 45 to 64 now are in the labor force. Over the age of 65, about 14 percent of single women, 11 percent of married women, and 10 percent of widowed and divorced women are employed (U.S. Census Bureau, 2003c). During the same 30-year period, by contrast, men have been retiring earlier. By 2002, only 84 percent of 45- to 64-year-old married men were in the workforce, compared to 91 percent in 1970. Similarly, the participation rate of married men 65 and over dropped from 30 to 19 percent (U.S. Census Bureau, 2003c). As a consequence of these changes, which hold across all ethnic groups, the proportion of paid workers 45 and over who are women is higher than ever before.

Why Do Older Women Work?

Older women work for most of the same reasons as younger women. Economic necessity is a key factor at all ages. In addition, feeling challenged and productive and meeting new coworkers and friends give women a sense of personal satisfaction and recognition outside the family (Choi, 2000; Doress-Worters & Siegal, 1994). Active involvement in work and outside interests in women's later years appear to promote physical and psychological well-being. Work-centered women broaden their interests as they grow older and become more satisfied with their lives. Employed older women have higher morale than women retirees, whereas women who have never been employed outside the home have the lowest (Perkins, 1992).

Entering the Workforce in Later Life

Many older women have been employed throughout adulthood. For some—working-class women, women of color, and single women—economic necessity has been the driving force. A few women overcame great obstacles to become pioneers in fields almost completely dominated by men. But for many women who are now in later life, a more typical pattern has been movement in and out of the labor force in response to changing family roles and responsibilities (Choi, 2000; Doress-Worters & Siegal, 1994).

Many older women have been employed throughout adulthood, while others enter or reenter the labor force in later life.

Some women decide to reenter the labor force after their children are grown, or following divorce or the death of their spouse. The prospects of entering or reentering the labor force after 25 or 30 years may be daunting to some women who wonder if they have the skills to be hired. Older women should not overlook the wealth of relevant experience they have accumulated through their home-making, childrearing, and volunteer activities.

Age Discrimination in the Workplace

Earlier in the chapter, we discussed gender discrimination in employment. As women get older, they also confront age discrimination in the workplace. Because many women enter or reenter the workforce when they are older, they face age discrimination at the point of hiring more often than men do (Rayman et al., 1993). The reasons for age discrimination and the age range during which it occurs differ for women and men. Women's complaints filed with the Equal Employment Opportunity Commission primarily concern hiring, promotion, wages, and fringe benefits. Men more often file on the basis of job termination and involuntary retirement (Rayman et al., 1993).

Women also experience age discrimination at a younger age than men (Rife, 2001). This is another example of the "double standard of aging" discussed in Chapter 2. Women are seen as becoming older at an earlier age than men (Kite & Wagner, 2002; Sherman, 2001). Our society's emphasis on youthful sexual attractiveness for women, and the stereotype of older women as powerless, weak, sick, helpless, and unproductive create obstacles for older women who are seeking employment or who wish to remain employed (Perkins, 1992).

Changing the Workplace

We have seen that women continue to be more heavily congregated in lower-status occupations, to have limited opportunities for advancement, to earn lower salaries than men, and to be targets of biased behavior. What can be done to continue improvements in the work environment that have begun during the last few decades?

Organizational Procedures and Policies

Pay Equity.   We have seen that equal pay legislation has not eliminated the gender or ethnicity wage gaps. As long as women and men or Whites and people of color are segregated in different occupations, it is legal to pay them different wages. One way of narrowing these earnings gaps is **pay equity,** *pay policies based on workers' worth and not their gender or ethnicity* (AAUW, 2002). Pay equity would require that employees in different jobs that are similar in skill, effort, and responsibility receive comparable wages.

Affirmative Action.   Think of what affirmative action means to you. To what extent do you characterize affirmative action as a set of procedures that ensures equitable treatment of underrepresented individuals or, alternatively, as a policy that fosters preferential treatment and reverse discrimination? Affirmative action goals and procedures are highly misunderstood. Let's examine the legal conception of affirmative action as well as typical misconceptions of its meaning.

Affirmative action in employment refers to *positive steps taken by a company, institution, or other type of employer to ensure that the workplace provides equal opportunity for all* (Crosby et al., 2003). That is, affirmative action involves deliberate actions that facilitate the recruitment and advancement of historically underrepresented workers. To achieve equity, these procedures involve weighing candidates' qualifications as well as group membership. Is this definition consistent with your conception of affirmative action?

Perceptions of affirmative action are often unfavorable (Hing et al., 2002). According to Jennifer Eberhardt and Susan Fiske (1998), many people attribute the achievements (e.g., job attainment, promotion) of less powerful individuals (e.g., women, people of color) to group-based preferential treatment but ascribe the accomplishments of more powerful individuals (e.g., White males) to merit. Consequently, they think that affirmative action results in reverse discrimination that hurts qualified White males in favor of unqualified women or people of color. Contrary to these misperceptions, Eberhardt and Fiske claim that the recruitment and promotion of unqualified individuals and the reliance on group membership only, without consideration of qualifications, are highly unusual and illegal practices. Furthermore, the U.S. Department of Labor (n.d.) reports that accusations of reverse discrimination comprised less than 2 percent of the 3,000 discrimination cases filed in federal court between 1990 and 1994 and that few of these were upheld as legitimate claims.

Despite criticisms of its practices, affirmative action has played an important role in reducing gender inequity in the workplace (Crosby et al., 2003), and there is evidence that it has done so without negatively affecting performance, productivity, or company profits (Murrell & Jones, 1996). Its success in bringing more women into the workplace and increasing the gender similarity in occupations, job levels, and salaries is likely to result in even further reductions in gender imbalances in the future.

One drawback of affirmative action is that it produces ambiguity about the basis for selection of targeted individuals (Crosby et al., 2003). Both targets and coworkers might be unsure about the extent to which employment decisions are influenced by gender and ethnicity versus background and performance. However, this problem can be greatly reduced by making clear that both merit and group membership influence the selection of targets.

What kind of actions would be most effective in improving the workplace for women? The exercise in Get Involved 10.2 explores this issue.

Other Organizational Procedures. Improvements for women and other underrepresented groups must also involve changes in the workplace itself. It is essential for employers to develop a work environment that values diversity and to back up this attitudinal climate with well-publicized antidiscrimination policies. Managers and other workers can be sensitized about both subtle and blatant forms of prejudice and discrimination in the work environment and can learn that the employer will not tolerate any form of discrimination. This can be accomplished through workshops aimed at increasing awareness of how stereotypes operate in evaluating and treating less powerful individuals, including women, people of color, lesbians and gays, and people with disabilities. A nationwide study of the effectiveness of policies such as these found that antidiscrimination policies were highly successful in protecting lesbian and gay workers from discrimination (Ragins, 1998).

GET INVOLVED **10.2**

Ways to Make the Workplace Better for Women

Listed below are six factors that can contribute to an improvement in women's opportunities and experiences at work. Indicate how important you think each would be to making the workplace better for women in the future by rank ordering these from 1 to 6. Give a 1 to the factor you think would be most beneficial to improving future conditions for women, give a 2 to the factor you consider would be next most helpful, and so on. Also, ask a woman who differs from you in ethnicity to do the same.

__ 1. women's hard work
__ 2. the efforts of feminists to improve conditions for women
__ 3. women's past contributions that demonstrate their value as workers
__ 4. laws that make it less likely for employers to discriminate
__ 5. greater number of women who know how to succeed in the workplace
__ 6. a workplace that is more responsive to women's needs

What Does It Mean?

Factors 1, 3, and 5 (Set A) all point to actions on the part of working women. Factors 2, 4, and 6 (Set B) reflect adaptations resulting from political/social activism, legal mandates, and adaptations within the workplace. Determine the number of items in each set that you included among your top three items. Do the same for your other respondent.

Konek and her colleagues asked a large number of career women to rank these influences and found that these women ranked the items in Set A higher than those in Set B. The researchers interpreted this as an emphasis on individualism, a belief that one's success is due to one's own efforts.

1. Did your answers match the responses of the study's respondents? If yes, was the reason the same? That is, do you value self-reliance and hard work more than external changes that provide increased opportunities?

2. Make the same comparison for your other respondent. Do her answers reflect an emphasis on individualism?

3. Did you notice any differences between the answers given by you and your other respondent? If yes, is it possible that these differences reflect a different emphasis on individualism versus collectivism?

4. Which actions mentioned in the text but not included on this list would be effective? Additionally, are there other strategies that might be beneficial?

Source: Based on Konek et al. (1994).

Another strategy, recommended by the Federal Glass Ceiling Commission (1995b), is for organizations to identify employees with high potential, including women and people of color, and provide them with career development opportunities, such as specialized training, employer-sponsored networks, and job assignments that expand their experience and organizational visibility. Equally important, the commission stresses, is that senior management clearly communicate throughout the organization its firm commitment to a diverse workforce.

In order to facilitate reporting of complaints, organizations also should make use of clear, well-publicized procedures for filing and evaluating claims of discrimination. Organizations that enact such procedures and ensure that claims can be filed without fear of recrimination produce more favorable work environments for women (Stokes et al., 1995).

Strategies for Women

Although organizational efforts have more far-reaching effects, there are several actions that women can take as they either prepare themselves for employment or attempt to improve their own situation while in the workplace. Beth Green and Nancy Russo (1993) suggest that women can benefit from workshops or work-related social networks that arm them with information that can help them better understand and fight against discriminatory practices in the workplace.

A useful strategy for women who experience discrimination is to join together with others who are experiencing similar inequities. Reporting a shared problem can, in some situations, receive both attention and a commitment to institutional change. Remember how a collective effort by women in the School of Science at the Massachusetts Institute of Technology led to improvements in salary, research money, and laboratories.

Retirement

Much of what we know about the effects of retirement is based on studies of men, despite the steady increase in women in the workplace over the past 60 years. This bias reflects the assumption that retirement is a less critical event for women than for men because of women's lesser participation in the labor force and their greater involvement in family roles. But almost half of workers now are women, and retirement has equally important consequences for them (Kim & Moen, 2001b). In this section, we examine factors that influence women's decision to retire, their adjustment to retirement, and their leisure pursuits in retirement. Conduct the interviews in Get Involved 10.3 to learn about the work and retirement experiences of individual older women.

The Retirement Decision

The decision to retire depends upon many factors including health, income, occupational characteristics, and marital and family situations (Choi, 2000). When men retire, they are leaving a role that has typically dominated their adult years. They are more likely than women to retire for involuntary reasons, such as mandatory retirement, poor health, or age. Women, on the other hand, are more apt to retire for voluntary, family-related reasons, such as the retirement of one's husband or the ill health of a relative (Canetto, 2003; Hyde, 2003).

Compared to men, women arrive at the threshold of retirement with a different work and family history, less planning for retirement, and fewer financial

GET INVOLVED **10.3**

Interview with Older Women: Work and Retirement

Interview two women, age 65 or older. It is helpful, but not essential, to know your interviewees fairly well. You may interview your mother, grandmothers, great-aunts, great-grandmothers, and so on. Keep a record of your interviewees' responses to the questions below. Compare and contrast the responses of the two women.

1. (If employed) How are things going in your job?
2. Have you reached most of the goals you set for yourself in your life?

3. When do you plan on retiring? (or when did you retire?)
4. What are some of the day-to-day activities that you look forward to after retirement (or that you've enjoyed since retirement)?
5. How will (did) retirement change you and your lifestyle?
6. How will you adjust (or how have you adjusted) to these changes?
7. In general, how would you describe your current financial situation?
8. What do you think of the Social Security system?

What Does It Mean?

1. How do the work and/or retirement experiences of these women compare with the experiences of older women reported in this book?

2. Are the financial situations of your respondents similar or different to those of older women described in the text? In what ways?

resources (Butrica & Uccello, 2004; Carp, 2001b; Kim & Moen, 2001a, 2001b). As noted earlier, women typically experience greater job discontinuity. They may have had fewer opportunities to obtain personal career goals and may therefore be more reluctant to retire. Given their more discontinuous employment history and their employment in lower-paid jobs, women are not as likely as men to be covered by pension plans, and their Social Security benefits are lower (Bethel, 2005). Many older women workers with low salaries choose to continue to work as long as they can. These women may not be able to afford the luxury of retirement because of economic pressures, such as inadequate retirement income or sudden loss of a spouse. Widowed and divorced women are more apt than married women to report plans for postponed retirement or plans not to retire at all (Duenwald & Stamler, 2004). A growing number of women continue to work after their husbands retire. In 2000, 11 percent of all couples involving a man 55 or over consisted of a retired husband and an employed wife (Leland, 2004).

In addition, women who have strong work identities have more negative attitudes toward retiring than those with weaker work identities. Professional women and those who are self-employed, who presumably have strong work identities, are less likely than other women to retire early. Martha Graham, for example, danced until age 76 and then kept choreographing for another 20 years. Georgia O'Keeffe continued to paint into her nineties (Springen & Siebert, 2005). Older professional women do not often make systematic plans for their retirement, nor do they wish to do so (Etaugh & Bridges, 2005; Heyl, 2004). Working-class women and men, on the other hand, are more likely to view retirement as a welcome relief from exhausting or boring labor (Gross, 2004a).

We have seen why some women may delay their retirement. Why do others retire early? Poor health is one of the major determinants of early retirement. Since aging Black women and men tend to be in poorer health than aging Whites, they are likely to retire earlier (Bound et al., 1996). Health is a more important factor in the retirement decision for men than for women—especially unmarried women—among both Blacks and Whites (Hatch & Thompson, 1992; Honig, 1996). This gender difference may result from the fact that, unlike married men, married women in poor health may withdraw early from the labor force or do not enter it in the first place. Early withdrawal or nonparticipation in the workforce is enabled by having a provider husband and by societal expectations that employment is optional for women.

Women's role as primary caregiver is another factor contributing to their early retirement. Of the 2.2 million people who provide unpaid home care to frail elderly individuals, nearly three-quarters are women (Canetto, 2001). Elder care responsibilities often result in increased tardiness and absenteeism at work, as well as health problems for the caregiver (Mor-Barak & Tynan, 1995). Because most businesses do not offer work flexibility or support to workers who care for elderly relatives, more than 20 percent of women caregivers reduce their hours or take time off without pay. Of those who continue to work, more than 8 percent are forced to retire earlier than planned (Perkins, 1992). Also, women whose husbands are in poor health are more likely to retire than women whose husbands enjoy good health (Talaga & Beehr, 1995).

Some women, of course, simply want to retire, whether to spend more time with a partner, family, or friends; to start one's own business; to pursue lifelong interests; or to develop new ones.

> *I haven't regretted retiring. I didn't quit my job through any dissatisfaction with the job or the people but I just felt that my life needed a change. I noticed that after working an eight-hour day I didn't have much steam left for a social life and fun. It's been pleasant spending these years doing what I want to do because I spent so many years accommodating myself to other people's needs and plans.* (a woman in her seventies, in Doress-Worters & Siegal, 1994, p. 183)

Adjustment to Retirement

Retirement has long been seen as an individual—primarily male—transition. But now, couples must increasingly deal with two retirements, according to Phyllis Moen and her colleagues (Moen et al., 2001). In their study of 534 retired couples, these researchers found that retirement was a happy time for the couples. But the transition to retirement, defined as the first two years after leaving a job, was a time of marital conflict for both women and men. Wives and husbands who retired at the same time were happier than couples in which the spouses retired at different times. Marital conflict was highest when husbands retired first, perhaps because of uneasiness with the role reversal of a working wife and a stay-at-home husband. Not only does the situation pose a potential threat to the husband's role as provider, but it can also lead to disagreements over the division of household labor (Mares & Fitzpatrick, 2004).

Although both genders typically adjust well to retirement, women may take longer to get adjusted (Etaugh & Bridges, 2005). Newly retired women report lower morale and greater depression than newly retired men (Moen et al., 2001). Men seem to enjoy the freedom from work pressure when they retire whereas women appear to experience the retirement transition as a loss of roles. Because women are not under the same socially prescribed pressures to be employed as are men, those who *do* work, whether out of financial need or commitment to their job, may find it more difficult to stop working (Szinovacz, 1991).

For both men and women, a high level of life satisfaction in retirement is generally associated with having good health, adequate income, and a high activity level (Fitzpatrick & Vinick, 2005; Kim & Moen, 2001a, 2001b). Financial factors may account for the fact that Black retirees have lower levels of life satisfaction than White retirees and that Black women are less satisfied than Black men (Krause, 1993). Marital status is a contributing factor as well. Married people have more positive retirement attitudes and higher retirement satisfaction than unmarried retirees. Retired women, particularly unmarried ones, are more involved with friends, family, organizations, and volunteer work than are retired men or lifelong housewives (Carp, 2001b; Dorfman, 1995; Etaugh & Bridges, 2005). These social contacts are important for the life satisfaction of retired women, particularly those who are unmarried (Dorfman & Rubenstein, 1993; Reeves & Darville, 1994). For women who have never married, retirement can represent an especially significant transition. Although work assumes a greater importance in their lives than in the lives of never-married men and other women, most never-married women appear to be satisfied with retirement. Still, many develop second careers after retirement, or continue to work part time (Rubinstein, 1994).

We shall see in Chapter 11 that multiple roles often have positive consequences for women who are employed. What is the effect of multiple role identities on older retired women? Pamela Adelmann (1993) compared Black and White women age 60 and over who considered themselves retired only, homemakers only, or both. Women who called themselves both retired and homemakers had higher self-esteem and lower depression than women identified with only one role, especially the homemaker role. Apparently, multiple-role identities continue to benefit women even after retirement. For a closer look at the influence of major life changes such as illness, marital transition, and death of loved ones on adaptation to retirement read Learn about the Research 10.3.

LEARN ABOUT THE RESEARCH **10.3**
Do Major Life Events Influence Adaptation to Retirement?

Many elderly adults are exposed to at least one of the following major life events requiring adjustment: divorce; major injury or illness experienced by oneself, the spouse, or other family members; the death of one's spouse, child, other family members, or friends; moving to another dwelling or another town; and moving in with a child, other family member, or friend. How do these events affect one's adaptation to retirement? Do women and men react differently to these events? To find out,

Maximiliane Szinovacz and Christine Washo (1992) surveyed people who had retired from state jobs in Florida within a five-year period. Women reported experiencing more major life events than men, particularly during the period preceding retirement. Recent retirees who had been exposed to two or more major life events were found to be adapting less well to retirement. Women were much more adversely affected than men.

What Does It Mean?

1. Why do retired women experience more major life events than men?
2. Why do you think the women retirees were more affected by major life events

than were men? Think about some of the factors that influence women to retire in the first place.

Leisure Activities in Retirement

Leisure or free time in later life is a fairly recent social phenomenon. In 1900, the average work week was over 70 hours. Most adults died by their mid-forties, and worked until their death. Until the Social Security Act of 1935, retirement was not a reality for most Americans. The economic safety net provided by Social Security, along with increased life expectancy, have given older Americans the opportunity for retirement and, consequently, an increased amount of free time (Stanley & Freysinger, 1995).

Gender Differences. Women and men, regardless of age, vary in the nature of leisure activities they prefer. Elderly women are more likely than elderly men to participate regularly in social activities, baking and canning, sewing and quilting, collecting, and reading. Elderly males are more frequent participants in vigorous or moderate physical activity, yard work, spectator sports, hunting, and fishing. Elderly women and men show little difference in activities such as walking, crafts and painting, cards, and bingo (Mobily, 1992). In retirement, women are more likely than men to integrate their spheres of leisure activity, bringing together their worlds of friends, home, and hobbies (Hanson & Wapner, 1994).

Women's leisure activities often bring together their worlds of friend, home, and hobbies.

Much of the research on leisure activities for the elderly has focused on middle-class Whites and has been studied largely from a male perspective. Very little is known about the context and meanings of leisure for aging, usually poor, minority women. Katherine Allen and Victoria Chin-Sang interviewed 30 retired Black women whose average age was 75. Work had largely dominated the lives of the women. Most of them had worked domestic and service jobs. When asked how their experience of leisure had changed since retirement, most women replied that they had none in the past. The women considered leisure time in older age to be time to relax or to work with and for others as they chose. The church and the senior center provided important contexts for their leisure activities (Allen & Chin-Sang, 1990).

Factors Affecting Leisure Activity.   One factor influencing participation in leisure activity is age. A longitudinal study of women and men at age 54 and again at 70 found that the frequency of women's leisure activity involvement was less likely than that of men to be affected by increasing age. Men's participation in all categories of leisure activity declined between the ages of 54 and 70. On the other hand, women's informal social, home, spectatorship, travel, and hobbies/crafts activities showed no change over the 16-year period. Only their participation in sports and volunteering/formal organizations declined (Stanley & Freysinger, 1995). For another look at the relationship between age and leisure activity, try the exercise in Get Involved 10.4.

Other variables affecting leisure involvement are the amount of free time, transportation, and information on and availability of leisure programs. Some elderly people (usually the poor, because they have to, and the more educated and

GET INVOLVED **10.4**

Leisure Activities of Elderly and Young Women

1. Make three columns with the following headings:

   | Young Women's Current Activities | Older Women's Current Activities | Older Women's Past Activities |

2. Briefly interview three young adult females about their current leisure activities. List the most common activities in the first column.

3. Briefly interview three women ages 65 or older about their current leisure activities and about their leisure activities when they were in their early twenties. List their most common current activities in the second column, and their most common leisure activities when they were young adults in the third column.

What Does It Mean?

1. How do the leisure activities of the older women compare with the leisure activities of older women reported in this book?
2. How similar are the current leisure activities of the older women to those when they were young women?
3. Are the leisure activities of the older women when they were young adults more similar to their current activities, or to the activities of the young adult females you interviewed? In what way?
4. Based on this exercise, would you predict that young women's leisure activities in later life would be more similar to their present activities or to those of today's older women? Explain your answer.

Source: From Leitner & Leitner (1996). Reprinted with permission from The Haworth Press.

affluent, because they want to) continue to work long after the age of 65. Additionally, caring for ill family members, a responsibility usually assumed by women, can severely curtail the amount of available free time. Women, more than men, may be affected by the availability of transportation services, information about recreational facilities and programs, and the availability of such programs. In one study, women were more likely to list the following as obstacles to recreation participation: lack of partners, family commitments, lack of information, lack of transportation, and physical difficulties (Riddick, 1993). The last of these obstacles is likely to become an even greater problem in the future. Because those over 85 (a majority of them women) are the fastest growing segment of the population, increasing emphasis will need to be given to providing and adapting leisure services for the moderately impaired or low-functioning elderly (Leitner & Leitner, 2004).

Varieties of Leisure Activity. There are many paths to fulfilling leisure activities for women in later life. Some older women devote themselves to pursuits which they had little time for in their younger years. Think of Grandma Moses, for example, who took up painting late in life and became an internationally acclaimed artist. Then there are the increasing number of elderly adults who are taking college courses and participating in Elderhostels (Tyre, 2002). Other older women become volunteer workers in a wide variety of community settings: schools, hospitals, museums, churches, and service organizations, including the Peace Corps (Gross, 2004a; Lowell, 2004). Devotion to volunteering remains strong until very old age. Twenty-three percent of people 75 and older are still volunteering, compared with only 4 percent who continue to be employed (Commonwealth Fund, 1993b). Volunteer service provides a number of benefits for the elderly, including increased life satisfaction (Beers & Jones, 2004; Morrow-Howell et al., 2003). In one recent study, older African American women who volunteered as tutors in elementary schools showed improved physical activity, social interaction, and cognitive stimulation compared to a control group of nonvolunteers (Fried et al., 2004).

Whatever a woman's situation as she ages, there is usually some way in which she can serve as an **advocate,** *a person who plays an active role in making changes in her life, the lives of others, and in society* (Dowling, 2001). For example, women can and do join and actively participate in any of a number of organizations that advocate for the rights of older persons or specifically for older women. The American Association of Retired Persons (AARP), with over 24 million members, is a powerful advocacy group. The Gray Panthers, a smaller, more activist group, was founded by Maggie Kuhn following her forced retirement at age 65. The Older Women's League (OWL) focuses on social policies affecting midlife and older women (Doress-Worters & Siegal, 1994). Some older women have been political and social activists for most of their lives and do not let their age slow them down. For example, Doris "Granny D" Haddock walked across the United States when she was 90 to raise awareness of finance reform. In 2004, at age 93, she undertook a 15,000 mile road trip to encourage working women to vote (Bridges et al., 2003/2004). Then there are sisters Carrie and Mary Dann, now in their 70s, who have fought for over 30 years to keep the U.S. government from seizing tribal lands (Bridges et al., 2003/2004).

Becoming an activist can transform the life of an older woman. Take the case of Rosemary Bizzell, a widow and grandmother of eight. Prior to joining OWL in 1981, she had never been involved in community affairs. Within three years, she had risen to prominence in the city council and in state government. In her words,

My self-image as an older woman has improved tremendously in spite of much rejection in job hunting. Apparently I was supposed to count my blessings and not expect to advance. Well, becoming involved in OWL has certainly challenged me. I cannot thank the OWLs enough for opening up a whole new world for older women. I am proud of the opportunity to be part of it. (in Doress-Worters & Siegel, 1994, p. 436)

Economic Issues in Later Life

After I've paid the rent, I pay the phone bill. My burial plot is all paid for, and I have just a little insurance for my grown children. Then there's my health. My doctor refused

Medicaid—after 15 years—and now I have to pay him $27 out of every check. Then it takes $2.50 to do the laundry—you've got to keep your linens clean. I try to buy the cheapest things. I always make my own milk from powder. I only buy bread and chicken, and those no-name paper articles, but it still adds up. If I need clothes, I go across the street to the thrift shop. I watch for yard sales—if you see something for half a buck, there's a Christmas present. If I have 80 cents, I can go to the Council on Aging for a hot lunch. But the last two weeks of the month are always hard. You just can't make it. I'm down to my last $10, and I've got more than two weeks to go. (a woman in her seventies, cited in Doress-Worters & Siegal, 1994, pp. 191–192)

At every age, women are more likely to live in poverty than men, and poverty rates are higher for ethnic-minority women than for their White counterparts (Caiazza et al., 2004; DeNavas-Walt et al., 2004). But financial insecurity can be an even greater problem for older women, who are nearly twice as likely as older men to live in poverty (Jenkins, 2003). In this section, we examine reasons for the precarious financial condition of many older women. We then turn to actions that young women can take to ensure a more secure financial future when they retire.

Poverty

What factors account for the relatively high poverty rates of older women? Their lower lifetime earnings and reduced time in the labor force adversely affect eligibility and benefits from Social Security and pensions (Ellin, 2002). Women also are less likely to have accumulated income from savings and investments. The net result is that the income gap between women and men increases in retirement (Porter et al., 1999). U.S. women age 65 and older have an average income of $11,000, only 55 percent of the $19,168 income of men the same age (Crenshaw, 2002).

Another factor associated with poverty is marital status. About 20 percent of single older women in the United States live in poverty and are poorer than their counterparts in other industrialized nations (WISER, 2002). Formerly married women (i.e., widows or divorced women) are worse off financially than older women who have never married (Canetto, 2003). Among married women, however, only 5 percent are below the poverty line (Jenkins, 2003). But a married woman is just a heartbeat away from widowhood. The income from a husband's pension is usually reduced considerably or eliminated when he dies, greatly increasing his widow's risk of plunging into poverty. Since women usually marry older men and outlive them, there is a high likelihood that they will live alone on a meager income as they grow older. The costs of a husband's illness and burial may seriously deplete the couple's savings, leaving the widow in a precarious economic state (Canetto, 2003). The longer an older woman lives, the further her assets must stretch. This situation helps explain why the very oldest women have the highest poverty rates (WISER, 2002). Figure 10.1 illustrates a recent analysis of the percentage of older unmarried women and men who live below the poverty level.

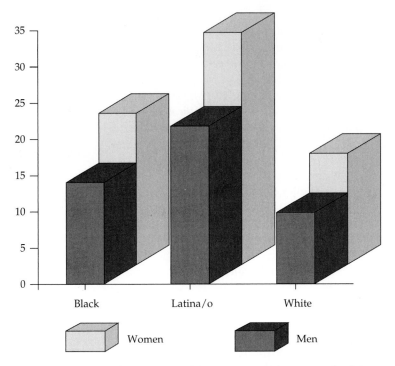

FIGURE 10.1 Percentage of Older Black, Latina/o, and White Women and Men below the Poverty Level in 2003.

Source: Butrica & Uccello (2004).

For a closer look at the economic status of older women in other parts of the world, read Explore Other Cultures 10.2.

Retirement Income: Planning Ahead

It is difficult for young women to look ahead to their retirement years. However, information in this chapter makes it clear that women must take steps early in their adult life to make plans to improve their financial security in retirement. Until fairly recently, retirement planning and money management were thought to be best left to husbands (AARP, 1995). As a result, many women of all ages have relatively little understanding of what retirement planning entails. It is never too early to start thinking about the issues involved. See Table 10.2 for guidelines on how to start planning for retirement *now*.

First, you need to know that a secure retirement is based on a three-legged stool consisting of Social Security, pension income, and individual savings. As we have seen, all three are linked to a woman's lifetime earnings, work history, and marital status (Costello & Wight, 2003).

EXPLORE OTHER CULTURES **10.2**

Economic Status of Older Women

In richer (i.e., developed) countries, the elderly can more easily afford to retire because of Social Security systems or pensions. In the United States and New Zealand, for example, only about 10 percent of women aged 65–69 are in the labor force (Kinsella & Velkoff, 2001). As in the United States, however, these benefits are often inadequate for women since they penalize the female-dominated activities of homemaker, part-time employee, domestic worker, and agricultural worker. In several countries, even women who have worked for much of their adult lives receive smaller pensions than men. In one study, women's benefits as a proportion of men's were 64 percent in the United States, 77 percent in France and Switzerland, and 85 percent in Sweden. However, at least five developed countries provide equal benefits for women and men: Australia, New Zealand, Great Britain, Germany, and the Netherlands (Mercer et al., 2001).

In developing nations, the economic situation for older women is much more grim than in developed countries. Social Security and pension plans are often nonexistent. Therefore, elderly women and men must continue working. In Rwanda, for example, nearly three-quarters of women between 65–69 remain economically active (Kinsella & Velkoff, 2001). The low status of women in developing countries can have devastating effects in later life. For example, in most of sub-Saharan Africa, women do not have land rights or property rights. A husband typically allocates his wife a plot of land to work on to produce food for the family. But if he dies, she no longer has the right to that land or even to the family's house. The land and house are taken over by the husband's family, and she often is evicted and left destitute ("Africa's Homeless Widows," 2004; LaFraniere, 2005a).

In developing countries, elderly women and men must continue working because there are no Social Security or pension benefits.

TABLE 10.2 Retirement Planning for Women

1. Establish your own savings and checking accounts.
2. Learn about your payroll benefits, such as health insurance, pension plan, and Social Security.
3. Set up an emergency fund worth three to six months' salary.
4. Learn about financial planning by taking a course or finding a financial advisor.
5. Consider setting up an IRA.
6. Carry enough insurance to cover loss of life, health, home, and earning power.
7. Make a will.
8. Set up a **durable power of attorney,** *a document which authorizes someone to manage your financial affairs should you become incompetent.*

Sources: Fisher & Shelly (2002), Orman (2001).

Social Security. Social Security benefits are the major source of income for many elderly adults, especially those who are poor. Social Security provides 40 percent of total income for the elderly population as a whole, but 70 percent of the total income for those who live in poverty (AARP, 1999a). Moreover, Social Security benefits keep about a third of the nation's elderly from sinking into poverty and also narrow the income disparities between older women and men (Porter et al., 1999). Without Social Security, about 53 percent of elderly women and 41 percent of men would be poor. With it, however, these figures are reduced to 15 percent and 8 percent, respectively, cutting the gender gap from 12 to 7 percentage points.

About 60 percent of Social Security recipients over 65 and 72 percent of those over 85 are women. Over 40 percent of single older women and over 60 percent of single Black and Latina women receive 90 percent of their income from Social Security. Almost 20 percent of all older women rely on Social Security as their *only* source of income (Bethel, 2005; Older Women's League, 2002). Heavy reliance on Social Security can be a financial nightmare. For example, the average Social Security benefit for retired female workers in 1999 was $8,364 a year, only $364 above the federal poverty threshold for older adults (Hinden, 2001).

Worker Benefits. The Social Security system, inaugurated in 1935, was designed to serve the traditional family of that time, which included a breadwinner father, a homemaker mother, and children. Most of today's families do not fit that mold, since the majority of women are in the labor force. Women's different work patterns mean that they are disadvantaged by a Social Security system designed to reward male work histories that often include many uninterrupted years in a relatively high-paying job (Older Woman's League, 2002).

Ethnic minority women, who tend to be concentrated in lower-paying jobs and to have higher unemployment rates, receive even lower benefits than White women. Because they are more likely than White women to be employed "off the books" where benefits do not accrue, theirs are the lowest of all, while those of White men are the highest. Moreover, many women (75 percent of Whites and 61 percent of Blacks) apply for their benefits early, at age 62, because they need the income. But doing so reduces benefits to 80 percent of their normal amount (Feldstein, 1998).

Spousal Benefits.   A lifelong homemaker has no Social Security protection in her own name. She is eligible to receive a spousal benefit equal to half of her husband's benefit if they have been married for at least 10 years. A divorced woman is also eligible to receive half of her ex-husband's benefit if they were married for at least 10 years. If the marriage did not last 10 years, however, she receives no compensation. If a divorced woman remarries, she automatically forfeits her right to her former husband's spousal benefit. A widow receives 100 percent of her husband's benefit, although she is ineligible for any benefits until she is 60. If she applies for benefits at age 60 rather than waiting until age 65, however, her benefits are reduced to 72 percent of her normal widow's benefit (Social Security Administration, 2002).

Dual Entitlement.   Married women who are wage earners have **dual entitlement** but are, in effect, penalized as well. *They qualify for Social Security benefits based on both their own and their husband's work history.* But these women receive the higher of the two benefits to which they are entitled; they do not receive both. Dually entitled women often are eligible for higher benefits based on their husband's work record than on their own. Over 60 percent of retired, wage-earning wives draw benefits based on their husband's work records. They would have been entitled to these benefits even if they had never worked a day in their lives! Thus, the Social Security contributions that married women make as workers seem unnecessary and unfair (Feldstein, 1998; Institute for Women's Policy Research, 2005; Social Security Administration, 2002).

Pensions.   The second leg of the retirement stool—private pensions—can be an important source of income for women. But relatively few women have income from pensions. In the late 1990s, only 26 percent of U.S. women aged 65 and older received pension income compared with 48 percent of men (Kinsella & Velkoff, 2001). The average pension benefit paid to women is also less than half that paid to men (Bethel, 2005). Black and Latina women are less likely than White women to receive any pension income (Costello & Wight, 2003). Why do so few women receive pension benefits? Let us briefly examine some reasons for this.

Work Patterns.   As with Social Security, private pension plans are designed for employees who follow the traditional male work pattern of long continuous years of employment in higher-paying jobs. Women not only work less continuously and in lower-paying jobs, but they are also more likely to work at jobs that have low pension coverage (service jobs, nonunion jobs, small businesses). Moreover, women are much more likely than men to work in part-time or temporary jobs, which have little or no pension coverage (Costello & Stone, 2001; Ossofsky, 2000).

Vesting.   Women's shorter job tenure also makes it more difficult for them to receive pensions because of a practice known as **vesting.** *The vesting period is the number of years of participation in a company plan that is required to be eligible for a pension.* The majority of plans require five years on the job in order to be vested. However, the average job tenure for a woman is only 3.8 years compared with 5.1 years for men (Ossofsky, 2000).

Nonportability.   Women also are disadvantaged because of **nonportability** of pension plans. This means that *most traditional pension plans cannot be taken from one job to another.* This practice affects women more than men, since women are more likely to change jobs frequently. Even if a woman has worked enough years to be vested in a pension plan, she may lose a large portion of her pension benefits if she changes jobs. The reason is that the pension is based on her wages as of the date she leaves the plan. Inflation will severely reduce the value of her benefit by the time she reaches retirement age (Older Women's League, 1998).

Spousal Benefits.   As with Social Security benefits, a woman is more likely to receive spousal pension benefits as a wife, widow, or divorcée than she is from her own experience as a worker. Widows typically receive a benefit of half the amount the couple received when the husband was alive. Divorced women, too, can receive similar survivor's pension benefits when their former husband dies. On the other hand, she does not automatically receive any of his pension benefits following divorce. Many women do not realize that if they divorce, the divorce settlement can be written to include a share of their husband's pension (Hoffman, 2002; Uchitelle, 2001).

Savings and Investments.   The third leg of the retirement stool is income from savings and investments. Nearly 70 percent of retirees have some income from assets, such as interest on savings accounts. Older minority women are much less likely to have such income (25 percent of Black women and 33 percent of Latina women). Asset income averages only a few hundred dollars a year for both women and men and is thus not a major income source (Rix, 1990).

Investments can be a source of income for retirement. Women are much more cautious investors than men (Little, 2005) and are more likely to invest in conservative options such as bonds, certificates of deposit, and money-market accounts that pay lower returns than stocks. Although women tend to take fewer risks in the stock market, they do slightly better than men. Why? According to financial expert Jane Bryant Quinn (2001), women trade less, and those who trade less do better.

SUMMARY

Women's Decision to Work, Employment Rates, and Occupational Choices

- Approximately half of women would prefer to work even if they had no financial need. This percentage is higher among highly educated and more highly paid women and lower among women of childbearing and early childrearing age.
- More than 60 percent of women 16 years and older, including those who are married and have young children, are employed. Economic necessity is a major reason for women's employment.
- Although the last several decades have seen a decrease, gender and ethnic segregation in the workplace continues to be highly prevalent. The most prestigious occupations are dominated by White men.

Gender Differences in Leadership and Job Advancement

- Women and people of color are less likely than White males to attain high positions in their occupations.
- Barriers that hinder women's advancement include the glass ceiling, shorter job ladders, limited availability of mentors, exclusion from informal social networks, and discrimination.
- Discriminatory treatment is due, in part, to the operation of gender stereotypes, cultural differences between managers and subordinates, and White males' perception of threat.
- Women are presumed to be less capable leaders than men. Males often express dislike for highly competent and agentic women.
- As leaders, women tend to be more democratic, interpersonal, and transformational, and less autocratic, task oriented, and transactional than men.

Gender Differences in Salaries

- Women earn 80 percent of what men earn. The gender discrepancy is even greater between women of color and White men.

These income differences result from several factors, including gender differences in job investments, in occupations, in job levels, and in salary negotiation, as well as discrimination.
- Women tend to be dissatisfied with their incomes, although under some circumstances, they express less pay dissatisfaction than men.

Women's Job Satisfaction

- Findings regarding women's and men's overall satisfaction with their jobs are mixed, but women are less satisfied with their advancement opportunities than men are.
- One factor contributing to job satisfaction for lesbian women is the organizational climate for lesbians and gays.

The Older Woman Worker

- Increased numbers of middle-aged and older women are in the labor force. Economic necessity is a key reason.
- Employment among older women promotes physical and psychological well-being.
- Women face age discrimination in the workplace at a younger age than men.

Changing the Workplace

- Organizational strategies that can improve the workplace for women and people of color include implementation of pay equity, establishment of clearly defined affirmative action policies and procedures, and maintenance of an organizational environment characterized by sensitivity to diversity.

Retirement

- Women's retirement decisions depend on many factors.
- Women earning low wages tend to delay retirement, as do professional and self-employed women. Older women with caregiving responsibilities tend to retire early.

- The decision to retire is influenced by individual, family, economic, and occupational factors.
- The transition to retirement is a time of marital conflict, especially when husbands retire first.
- Satisfaction in retirement is associated with having good health, adequate income, high activity level, and contact with friends and relatives.
- Older women and men differ in the nature of their preferred leisure activities.

Economic Issues in Later Life

- Older women, especially minorities, are more likely than older men to be poor or near-poor.
- The poverty rate is greater for very old women and for unmarried women.
- Because women, compared with men, spend less continuous time in the workforce, and are in more low-paying jobs, their eligibility for and benefits from Social Security and pensions suffer. Women also have less income from savings and investments than do men.
- Preretirement planning in young adulthood can improve women's financial security during later life.

KEY TERMS

index of segregation
glass ceiling
sticky floor
maternal wall
mentor
patronizing behavior
task orientation
interpersonal orientation

democratic style
autocratic style
transformational style
transactional style
human capital perspective
wage discrimination
motherhood penalty
sweatshops

pay equity
affirmative action
advocate
durable power of attorney
dual entitlement
vesting
nonportability

WHAT DO YOU THINK?

1. The Families and Work Institute survey showed that approximately one-half of female respondents would like to work even if they had no financial need to work. What kinds of rewards, other than financial, are provided by employment? How does gender socialization affect the particular values women attach to work? Explain your answers.

2. Why do you think many people have negative impressions, including misconceptions, of affirmative action? Incorporate information about stereotypes, gender socialization, gender differences in

power, and/or any other material related to this course.

3. This chapter discussed several procedures for improving the workplace for women and people of color. What other actions can be undertaken by employers or individuals in these groups to decrease gender and ethnicity inequities in the work environment?

4. How might greater gender equity in the workplace change the current social construction of gender? Would this, in turn, influence the gender acquisition of gender-related traits, behaviors, roles, and/or the

career goals of future generations of females? Explain your answers.

5. Given the substantial influx of women into the labor force in the past several decades, the proportion of retired working women to lifelong homemakers will continue to increase among elderly women. What are the implications of this?

6. What can be done to help ease the "feminization of poverty"?

7. What are some implications of the older woman's greater economic insecurity?

8. What is meant by the statement that elderly minority women are in "triple jeopardy." Provide and discuss examples.

IF YOU WANT TO KNOW MORE

AAUW Educational Foundation. (2003). *Women at work*. Washington, DC: Author.

Aitchison, C. (2004). *Gender and leisure: A socialcultural nexus*. New York: Routledge.

Babcock, L., & Laschever, S. (2003). *Women don't ask: Negotiation and the gender divide*. Princeton, NJ: Princeton University Press.

Calasanti, T. M., & Slevin, K. F. (2001). *Gender, social inequalities, and aging*. Walnut Creek, CA: AltaMira Press.

Cleveland, J., Stockdale, M., & Murphy, K. (2000). *Women and men in organizations: Sex and gender isues at work*. Mahwah, NJ: Erlbaum.

Hall, P. (2002). *The bonus years: Women and retirement*. New York: Miranda Press.

Johnson, J. (2002). *Getting by on the minimum: The lives of working-class women*. New York: Routledge.

Milligan, E. (2001). *A woman's guide to a secure retirement*. New York: Alpha Books.

Nelson, D. L., & Burke, R. J. (2003). *Gender, work, stress, and health*. Washington, DC: American Psychological Association.

Parker, P. S. (2005). *Race, gender, and leadership: Reenvisioning organizational leadership from the perspectives of African-American women executives*. Mahwah, NJ: Erlbaum.

Rosser, S. V. (2004). *The science glass ceiling: Academic women scientists and the struggle to succeed*. New York: Routledge.

Valian, V. (1999). *Why so slow? The advancement of women*. Boston: MIT Press.

WEBSITES

Women in the Workplace

Women's Bureau of the U.S. Department of Labor
http://www.dol.gov/dol/wb

Lesbians in the Workplace

Gay Workplace Issues
http://www.nyu.edu/careerservices/students/diversity/page_four.html

Pay Equity

AFL-CIO: Working Women Working Together

http://www.aflcio.org/women

Retirement and Economic Issues

AARP (formerly, American Association of Retired Persons)
http://www.aarp.org/
Gender and The Social Security System
http://www.owl-national.org/gender
http://www.socialsecuritymatters.org/

The beginning of my academic career in the early 1970s coincided with early parenthood. My daughter was less than 1 year old when I started working as an assistant professor of psychology and my son was born two years later. Although I adored my children, loved being their mother, and got enormous satisfaction from my career, juggling the two roles was often stressful. To this day, I can vividly recall the anxiety and confusion that erupted when my daughter or son woke up too sick to go to their caregiver's home or when both were of school age and school was canceled because of snow (a frequent occurrence in our New England community). Also, I remember being plagued by worry that my commitment to my children was preventing me from devoting sufficient time and energy to my career and that my employment was somehow hurting my children. Interestingly, however, I don't recall ever feeling that my husband's job was damaging our children or that being a father was hindering his job advancement. (Judith Bridges)

Historically, women and men had different roles within the family. Men were the economic providers and women the caregivers and homemakers. However, the traditional family comprising children, a provider-father, and a stay-at-home mother is relatively rare today (American Psychological Association, 2004b). Whereas 57 percent of children in 1960 were raised in this type of household, only about 14 percent of children are now at home full-time with their mothers (Hattery, 2001). As we saw in Chapter 10, the majority of women, including married women with children, are now employed. Not only are more married women working, but they are also working longer hours than women did a generation ago (Jacobs & Gerson, 2001). Consequently, there has been a major transformation in women's roles.

Today's young women are involved in a challenging balancing act between the demands of completing their education, beginning their professional lives, finding a partner, and having children. Some women postpone or even forego marriage and/or children in favor of work or career, others leave the workplace or opt for part-time employment while their children are young, and still others are combining family and full-time careers (Riche, 2003; Wallis, 2004).

This chapter explores issues related to the coordination of women's multiple responsibilities in the domestic and employment domains. We begin with a look at attitudes toward their family and employment roles. Then we examine the impact of women's employment on the division of labor in the home as well as the challenges, costs, and benefits of balancing family and work. We explore employer resources that facilitate this coordination and consider strategies women use to manage family and work responsibilities. We conclude with a discussion of midlife transitions in family and work roles.

Attitudes toward Women's Family and Employment Roles

Although the traditional view of the male provider-female homemaker was once seen as the expected and desirable family type, most adults today do not perceive it as ideal. In 1977, 66 percent of American adults believed that husbands should be providers and wives full-time homemakers. However, in the late 1990s that figure dropped to 40 percent (Cherlin, 1998; Smith, 1999). In the recent nation-wide survey of first-year college students mentioned earlier in the book, only 21 percent believed that married women should be full-time homemakers. Just 16 percent of the women endorsed that view, compared with 27 percent of the men ("This Year's Freshmen," 2005).

Role of Ethnicity

Individuals of diverse ethnic backgrounds support employment of women. In one large-scale survey (Taylor et al., 1999) Black, Mexican American, and White respondents all endorsed the belief that women and men should contribute to their family's finances. However, a sizable minority of the Black and Mexican American respondents, especially those who were recent immigrants, indicated that despite the expectation of joint financial contribution, men should maintain the primary financial responsibility for their family. Possibly, this belief is an attempt to maintain male dignity in a society that makes it difficult for ethnic minority men to fulfill their provider role responsibility (Taylor et al., 1999).

Role of Motherhood

Although North Americans tend to accept women's employment role, their approval of this role varies greatly depending on the presence and age of a woman's children. For example, a national survey (Smith, 1999) found that the overwhelming majority of adults from Canada and the United States approve of women working full time if they have no children or if their children are gone from the home. However, they are much less supportive of full- or even part-time employment for mothers of preschoolers. Several polls in recent years have found that by ratios of 3 or 4 to 1, Americans believe that women with young children should stay at home with them (Lewin, 2001b; Sylvester, 2001). For a closer look at attitudes toward maternal employment in other industrialized nations, see Explore Other Cultures 11.1.

Personal Aspirations

What plans do college women have for balancing work and family? Most college women desire both a career and motherhood but want to discontinue their employment for a period of time during their children's early years (e.g., Davey, 1998; Schroeder et al., 1992). Judith and Claire (Bridges & Etaugh, 1996) found that, on average, Black college women want to interrupt their employment until their child is approximately 2½ years old, while White women want to wait until their child is approximately 4 years old.

These personal preferences are consistent with college women's general attitudes about combining motherhood and employment. The majority of college

EXPLORE OTHER CULTURES **11.1**
Attitudes toward Married Women's Employment: A Cross-cultural Perspective

Judith Treas and Eric Widmer (2000) examined attitudes toward married women's employment in 23 largely Western and industrial countries. Almost everyone agreed that married women should work, preferably full time, before they had children. Support for full-time work was almost as high after children were grown. Mothers of preschoolers were expected either to stay home or work only part time. These with school-age children were expected to work only part time. Despite this general consensus, nations also showed some difference in attitudes. Basically, three different nation clusters were identified: the "work-oriented," "family accommodating," and "motherhood-centered." The work-oriented cluster consisted of Canada, East Germany, Israel, the Netherlands, Norway, Sweden, and the United States. Whatever the life-course stage, this cluster's respondents were the least likely to recommend that married women stay home.

Unlike other clusters, they favored part-time employment for mothers of preschoolers. These countries had more egalitarian gender-role attitudes than the other nations in the study and perceived fewer conflicts between women's work and family roles. The "family accommodating" cluster (Australia, Austria, West Germany, Great Britian, Italy, Japan, New Zealand, Northern Ireland, and Russia) put less emphasis on maternal employment. They expected mothers to stay at home with preschoolers and work only part time not only when their children reached school age, but even after they were grown. The "motherhood centered" cluster (Bulgaria, the Czech Republic, Hungary, Ireland, Poland, Slovenia, and Spain) endorsed full-time employment before and after marriage, but staying at home with preschoolers and even to some extent, with school-age children. Not surprisingly, this group had the most traditional gender-role attitudes.

---

women (and men) believe that mothers *should* stay home with their baby for at least the first few months (Novack & Novack, 1996), so it is not surprising that both college women and men evaluate mothers who resume full-time employment after a brief maternity leave more negatively than mothers who interrupt their employment until their children are in school (Bridges & Etaugh, 1995). Furthermore, college students and employed women perceive these full-time employed mothers as less communal than mothers who reduce their work hours after their baby's birth (Etaugh & Folger, 1998; Etaugh & Moss, 2001).

Although college women tend to have negative attitudes toward early maternal employment, there is some variation in these beliefs. One key moderating factor is the employment history of young women's own mothers. White women's attitudes toward employed mothers are more positive the younger they were when their own mothers got involved in paid work (Novack & Novack, 1996), and the longer their mothers worked during their own childhood, the earlier they want to return to employment after childbearing (Bridges & Etaugh,

GET INVOLVED **11.1**

How Do College Students Evaluate Employed Mothers?

For this activity, based on a study by Judith and Ann Marie Orza (1993), ask four traditional-aged female students to read a brief description of a mother and indicate their impression of her on several rating scales. Give two participants Description A, followed by the rating scales, and two participants Description B, followed by the same scales.

Description A: Carol is a 34-year-old married woman with a 7-year-old child in second grade. Carol is employed full time as a newspaper reporter. She worked as a reporter before her child was born and then resumed working full time at the end of her six-week maternity leave.

Description B: Carol is a 34-year-old married woman with a 7-year-old child in second grade. Carol is employed full time as a newspaper reporter. She worked as a reporter before her child was born and then resumed working full time when her child was in first grade and thus in school all day.

Now indicate how much you like and respect Carol by completing the following two rating scales:

| like her very little | 1 2 3 4 5 6 7 | like her very much |
| respect her very little | 1 2 3 4 5 6 7 | respect her very much |

What Does It Mean?

Calculate the average rating for each respondent. A high score reflects a positive evaluation of the mother and a low score shows a negative evaluation. Next, average the responses given by the two respondents who read the description of the continuously employed mother (Description A) and average the scores of the two who read the paragraph about the mother who interrupted her employment (Description B).

1. As discussed in the text, this study found that mothers who take a brief maternity leave are more negatively evaluated than those who interrupt their employment. Did you find the same results? If yes, give reasons for this finding.

2. Describe any socialization experiences that might be associated with young women's personal beliefs about a brief maternity leave versus interrupted employment.

3. This study on attitudes toward maternal employment and others presented in the text examined traditional-aged college students. Do you think that older women would have different impressions? Explain your answer.

Source: Based on Bridges & Orza (1993).

1996). Adolescent and young adult children whose mothers were employed during their childhood do not feel they were neglected and actually appreciate the effort their mothers undertook to help provide for the family (Gerson, 1999). Consistent with the assumption that gender is constructed in part from interpersonal experiences, it seems likely that positive experiences with an employed mother early in their childhood lead women to consider the combination of motherhood and employment as acceptable female role choices that are not harmful to children. Try the Get Involved 11.1 activity to examine attitudes toward employed mothers at your college or university.

Division of Household Labor

Increasing numbers of women and men have substantial household obligations along with major work responsibilities. What is the relative importance of work and spousal and parental roles in the lives of women and men? Do the husbands of employed women contribute more to unpaid child care or housekeeping labor than the husbands of nonemployed women? Has this changed over time? Are women and men satisfied with this division of labor? We now explore these questions and others related to the division of family responsibilities.

Importance of Work and Family Roles for Women and Men

Rachel Cinamon and Yisrael Rich (2002) examined the importance of spousal, parental, and work roles for married and employed professional women and men. Among the women, 40 percent put equal emphasis on family and work, 44 percent put more emphasis on family, and just 16 percent put more emphasis on work. Men, on the other hand, were less likely to put equal emphasis on family and work (34 percent), or to put more emphasis on family (32 percent). They were more likely than women to place more emphasis on work (33 percent). Based on these results, what might you predict about the division of household labor between women and men? Read on to see if you were right.

Women's Housework and Child Care

Studies published in the 1970s and the 1980s showed that husbands increased their household labor very little when their wives were employed. Although husbands have increased their housework participation somewhat since the 1970s and wives have reduced theirs, men's contribution to household labor still does not equal that of women (American Psychological Association, 2004b; Bond et al., 2003; Greenhaus & Parasuraman, 2002; Hook, 2004). In 1965, American women did 40 hours of housework a week, compared to 12 for men. Now, according to a recent study, women average 27 hours and men average 16. Interestingly, Japanese men perform only 4 hours of housework a week, while Swedish men put in 24 hours (Johnson, 2002). According to a 1997 survey in the United States, among employed couples with no children, wives spend about 5 more hours per week performing housework than their husbands do, but among employed couples with children, the combined housework and child care gap jumps to 17 hours (Goldstein, 2000). Also, although research shows greater husband involvement in household and child-care duties in Black, compared to White, families (Coltrane, 2000; Sanderson & Thompson, 2002), employed women still perform a disproportionate share of these responsibilities in Black, Latina/o, and White families (Bureau of Labor Statistics, 2004). Women still assume the main responsibility for traditional female chores, such as cooking, cleaning, and shopping, whereas men have more responsibility for traditional male chores such as yard work, repairs, and car maintenance (Bureau of Labor Statistics, 2004; Coltrane, 2000). Note that the tasks done by women are generally performed one or more times per day or week, while those by men are done only periodically.

Regardless of their employment role, women continue to perform most child-care activities, including feeding and bathing young children, attending school conferences and sports events, helping with homework, disciplining, taking children to the doctor, and arranging for substitute care when there is a school vacation or a child is sick (Laflamme et al., 2002; Milkie et al., 2002; Renk et al., 2003). In lesbian families, couples are likely to share both child care and household tasks (J. K. Rice, 2001).

Although most women perform the bulk of their families' caregiving and household responsibilities, variations occur in the relative balance of household labor, and some husbands and wives equally share these tasks. As might be expected, women in **traditional couples**, in which *the husband is employed and the wife is a full-time homemaker*, provide a higher proportion of household labor than women in couples in which both partners are employed (Dancer & Gilbert, 1993; Perry-Jenkins et al., 1992).

Among two-income couples, there is evidence of variations in the division of household labor according to the spouses' investment in their work role. **Dual-career couples**, those in which *both partners have received considerable training for their work, are strongly invested in their job and consider their job as highly relevant to their personal identity* tend to share housework responsibilities more equally than do **dual-earner couples**, couples in which *both partners are employed but have less personal investment in their jobs than do career-oriented individuals*. This difference has been observed among Asian Americans (Espiritu, 1997), Latinas/os (Pesquera, 1993), and Whites (Dancer & Gilbert, 1993).

Why is domestic role sharing greater among dual-career than dual-earner couples? One possibility is that the allocation of household duties is based at least in part on spouses' own gender attitudes. People with careers are generally more highly educated than other workers, and more educated individuals tend to hold more nontraditional gender attitudes (Brewster & Padavic, 2002). Another possibility is that career women who are highly committed to their jobs may expect greater household participation from their partners (Dancer & Gilbert, 1993).

Caring for Aging Parents

Increasing numbers of women currently fulfill another caregiving role in addition to raising their children. They provide care to aging parents and other relatives who need assistance with daily living tasks such as cooking, bathing, financial management, transportation to doctors, and shopping. As with child caregiving, women provide the majority of this care (Brody, 2004; National Alliance for Caregiving, 2004; Sarkisian & Gerstel, 2004). In fact, it has been estimated that women can expect to spend 18 years providing care to an elderly parent (Older Women's

Housework and child care are more equally shared in dual-career couples.

League, 2001), a period of time roughly comparable to that devoted to childrearing. Although men also provide assistance, female caregivers may spend as much as 50 percent more time providing care than male caregivers (Family Caregiver Alliance, 2003).

The average female caregiver is age 46, married, and works outside the home. She is likely to be a daughter, but daughters-in-law and granddaughters play a substantial role as well (Katz et al., 2000; National Alliance for Caregiving, 2004). The financial impact of caring for elderly relatives is considerable. One national survey found that one-third of women decreased work hours, and nearly one-third passed up a job promotion, training, or assignment. Some women took a leave of absence or switched from full-time to part-time employment. Still others quit their jobs or retired early (Family Caregiver Alliance, 2003). Taking time out of the labor force for caregiving places an additional strain on women's retirement income. In addition, caregivers of elderly parents may also have less time for family and friends, further increasing emotional strain (National Alliance for Caregiving, 2004). No wonder caregivers of older relatives are more likely than noncaregivers to show higher levels of depression, anxiety, hostility, and stress (Michelson & Tepperman, 2003; Raschick & Ingersoll-Dayton, 2004).

Leisure Time

With all the time women are spending on child care, elder care, and employment, is there any time left for leisure? It is no surprise that employed mothers have less leisure time than nonemployed mothers (Bureau of Labor Statistics, 2004; Cherlin & Krishnamurthy, 2004). Feminists point out that the concept of leisure is different for women and men, with women experiencing less time for leisure in their lives than men. A common focus of women's leisure, according to this perspective, is the combining of family obligations with leisure opportunities. A woman may perceive the family's leisure as her leisure and vice versa. The home is the most common place in which women's leisure occurs. In this way, leisure can sometimes be combined with household chores. Women may often "double up" their activities and may be engaging in a leisure activity such as watching TV, while at the same time doing housework, such as cooking or mending. Thus, much of women's leisure time may be fragmented rather than occurring in large blocks of time (Bittman & Wajcman, 2000; Mattingly & Bianchi, 2003; Wearing, 1998). Even after retirement, women have less time for leisure than men, since they continue to remain more occupied with domestic chores and family responsibilities (Bernard & Phillipson, 2004). For example, we saw in Chapter 8 that many older women have caregiving responsibilities for grandchildren, ailing spouses, or parents.

Women's Perceptions of the Division of Family Labor

Although women perform about two-thirds of the total household labor, only about one-third of them rate their division of labor as unfair (Coltrane, 2000). What might account for this apparent paradox between women's heavier workload and their sense of satisfaction about the allocation of domestic responsibilities? Possibly, women are satisfied because their gender socialization has led them to believe that both childrearing and household work are in women's domain. Based on this construction of the female role, there might not be any discrepancy between what they expected and what they experienced. Also, if women do not assume most of what they consider to be women's work, they might feel guilty. Additionally, some women might compare their own household responsibility to that of other women, rather than to their husband's responsibility (Major, 1993) and, therefore, not see themselves as unfairly burdened.

For those women who feel that the division of domestic labor is unfair, the perceived inequity does not stem from the amount of time they spend on household tasks, but from their *share* of the total time spent by the couple (Coltrane, 2000). In research involving Asian American, Black, Latina, Middle Eastern American, and White wives, the more time wives spent relative to their husbands', the more likely they were to view the allocation of family responsibilities as unfair and to feel dissatisfied with it (Stohs, 2000; Van Willigen & Drentea, 2001).

Explanations of the Division of Family Labor

What factors account for women's disproportionate share of child care and house-keeping duties? This section considers three possible answers to this question.

Time Constraints. One explanation for the unequal division of household labor is that domestic responsibilities are allocated on the basis of each spouse's time availability. Consistent with this view, full-time homemakers, who have more time available, spend more time in household tasks than do employed women (Coltrane, 2000). Furthermore, the more hours wives spend in paid work, the less time they expend in housework (Coltrane, 2000).

Although spouses' time availability is to some extent related to the amount of time they invest in household labor, some patterns of domestic involvement are inconsistent with this explanation. First, even when comparing spouses with comparable work hours, mothers spend more time than fathers caring for their children (Aldous et al., 1998). Second, while researchers typically find that the more time fathers spend on their jobs, the less time they devote to parenting and housework, some studies find no relationship (Coltrane, 2000). Thus, it appears that time availability plays some role but cannot alone adequately explain the allocation of domestic responsibilities.

Relative Power. Another possible answer to our question is that women's disproportionate share of household labor results from their lower degree of marital power (Coltrane, 2000; Hook, 2004). According to this view, power in marriage depends, in part, on work-related resources, such as occupational prestige and income. The more resources one partner has in relation to the other, the greater that partner's influence (i.e., power) over the other. Because people tend to dislike household chores and to assign them little prestige, the person with the greater resources will use his or her power to limit engagement in these tasks.

Does research support this view? Evidence indicates that the discrepancy in husbands' and wives' resources explains women's participation in household labor more than it explains men's participation. The lower a woman's occupational status (Pittman & Blanchard, 1996) and earnings (Steil & Weltman, 1991) relative to her husband's, the more housework and child care she performs. However, a power discrepancy does not necessarily affect a husband's involvement in household labor. Although men who have less resource power than their wives have a somewhat greater child-care responsibility than men who have less power (Steil & Weltman, 1991), the relative degree of husbands' and wives' resources is unrelated to husbands' participation in housework (Pittman & Blanchard, 1996).

This finding may be due to the definition of marital power as the relative degree of work-related resources, which might not fully capture the meaning of marital power. Society's assumption of male power is so firmly rooted in the social construction of gender that it is not easily dismantled by resource equality. Even when wives and husbands bring similar work resources to the marriage, the impact of our expectations about males' higher status, value, and power remain. Janice Steil and Karen Weltman (1991) found that among professional couples in which wives earned significantly more than their husbands, neither husbands nor wives evaluated the wife's career as more important than the husband's. Furthermore, despite their lower income, husbands maintained greater financial decision-making power. Marital power is apparently influenced by more than occupational resources; men's participation in housework doesn't increase when they have fewer occupational resources than their wives because they maintain other forms of power.

Gender Attitudes.   A third explanation for the division of household labor is that the unequal distribution reflects spouses' personal beliefs about appropriate gender roles (Coltrane, 2000; Hook, 2004). People construct images of the roles expected for each gender, and this construction guides their own behavior. According to this view, many couples, including dual-income couples, have internalized the traditional gender beliefs that managing children and the home is *primarily* the wife's responsibility and that husbands should be the *main* financial providers. These views reflect strong societal norms, and many individuals who are socialized into these beliefs as a result of observation in the home, assigned chores, and media depictions of gender roles may be hard pressed to deviate from them.

Consistent with this explanation, men who have nontraditional attitudes about family roles spend more time doing housework than those with traditional views (Coltrane, 2000), whereas women with nontraditional beliefs spend less time in household labor than women who have traditional attitudes (Rowley, 1999). Moreover, college students with traditional gender-role attitudes are more likely to find it acceptable for a man to contribute less to household chores (Swearingen-Hilker & Yoder, 2002).

Family-Work Coordination

Women's Experiences with Parental Leave

Although we have seen that young college women would like to discontinue their employment for some period of time after the birth of their baby, most women do not follow that pattern. In 2002, 55 percent of married women with infants 1 year or under were employed (Downs, 2003).

The high employment rate of mothers with infants points to the importance of adequate parental leave policies, and three-quarters of Americans favor paid maternity leave (Smith, 1999). Parents would benefit from leave policies that provide sufficient time to adjust to parenthood and for biological mothers to recuperate from the physical stresses of pregnancy and birth. Incredibly, the United States is one of the few industrialized countries in the world without a national policy requiring paid parental leave. (See Explore Other Cultures 11.2.) In North America there is a stark contrast between Canada, which provides 17 weeks of paid leave, and the United States, which has no federal legislation governing leave with pay. The only federal law mandating parental leave in the United States is the Family and Medical Leave Act, which is applicable only to workplaces with

EXPLORE OTHER CULTURES 11.2
Parental Leave Policies around the World

Paid and job-protected maternity leaves from work were first established over a century ago in Europe to protect the health of mothers and their newborn infants. Beginning in the 1960s, these policies have expanded to also cover paternity leaves in most industrialized nations and several developing countries (Kamerman, 2000a, 2000b). The European Union adopted a minimum 14-week maternity leave in 1992 and a 3-month parental leave in 1998. Most developed countries far exceed this minimum, however, providing an average of 10 months leave (Waldfogel, 2001). The Scandinavian countries have the most generous policies. In Sweden, which far outspends the United States on family benefits (Ozawa, 2004), parents receive 80 to 90 percent of their salary during a 15-month child-care leave (Burn, 2000). Germany provides a 14-week leave at full salary, another two years at a modest flat rate and a third unpaid year. In over half the 129 countries providing paid leaves, including many developing nations in Africa, Asia, and Latin America, the parent gets 80 to 100 percent of wages during the leave period (Burn, 2000; Kamerman, 2000a, 2000b). The United States offers the briefest leave of any industrialized nation (12 weeks) and is among only a handful with an unpaid leave. Australia and New Zealand are two other countries with unpaid leave, but their leaves are a full year long (Kamerman, 2000a, 2000b). Why do you think the United States lags so far behind other nations?

50 or more employees, thus covering only 55 percent of the workforce. It allows workers (women and men) in those companies to take up to 12 weeks of *unpaid* leave for medical conditions or family responsibilities, including the birth or adoption of a child (Waldfogel, 2001). Although some American women are eligible for at least partial-pay maternity benefits through policies of their employer or state, many women take shorter leaves than they would like to take because their families cannot afford their loss of income.

What other factors are related of the length of a woman's parental leave? Women with higher levels of education return to work more rapidly after giving birth and are more likely to return to work full time than women with less education (Downs, 2003). Women with more nontraditional attitudes about combining employment and parenting also expect to resume working sooner (Lyness et al., 1999). In addition, pregnant women who perceive their employers as supportive of employees' family needs are more committed to their organizations and expect an earlier return to employment after childbirth (Lyness et al., 1999). Possibly, the belief that the employer is sensitive to work-family issues contributes to a greater comfort at work and an expectation that family responsibilities will be accommodated.

Roseanne Clark and her colleagues (Hyde et al., 1995) examined the relationship between the length of maternity leave and mothers' mental health. They found that leave time was not related to psychological state unless the mother experienced other stressors, such as marital problems or an unrewarding job. If these difficulties were present, mothers with shorter leaves were more depressed

4 months after childbirth than those with longer leaves. However, by 12 months after the birth, this effect disappears (Klein et al., 1998).

How does parental leave affect women's experiences on the job? A 1991 survey of over 4,000 employed mothers found that more than two-thirds said their boss supported their taking time off after the birth of their baby and felt their leave did not negatively affect their career (Marshall, 1998), while one-third felt they were treated less favorably after their leave and approximately half believed that people at their job view women who take maternity leave as less committed to their work. (Remember the chilly climate experienced by women faculty members with members with babies described in Chapter 9?) Although the evidence is mixed, it suggests that using family leave may, in fact, be harmful to one's career, and more so to the careers of men than women. Male employees who take leave for birth or care of a sick parent are viewed as less committed to the organization than men who do not take leave or women who take leave for the same reason (Wayne & Cordeiro, 2003). Stay-at-home fathers often find a stigma attached to their decision, especially when they return to the workforce after a period at home. Some employers, for example, question whether staying at home is a cover for "couldn't find work" (Dunham, 2003).

Women's Experiences Balancing Family and Work

Do you think balancing family and work involves both costs and rewards? What kind of costs and rewards might stem from juggling these roles? Consider these questions, then try Get Involved 11.2 to explore your personal expectations of this issue.

When Judith and Claire (Bridges & Etaugh, 1996) asked White and Black college women to respond to the items presented in Get Involved 11.2, we found that these students estimated that the benefits would be greater than the costs (70 percent versus 55 percent). Although the White and Black students had similarly viewed the probability of benefits, the White students estimated a higher likelihood of negative outcomes from working during motherhood than did the Black students (58 percent versus 49 percent). The long history of Black women's employment (Hattery, 2001) may contribute to their more positive attitude toward maternal employment. These different views held by Black and White women show that these attitudes are socially constructed from individuals' experiences and do not inevitably arise from one's gender.

In actuality, the effects of performing family and work roles are complex and encompass both negative and positive aspects. Because of this, it is important to examine women's actual experiences associated with these roles as well as explanations of these outcomes.

Concerns.   Previously we saw that employed women perform the bulk of child care and housework duties. Understandably, one major concern expressed by these family-work jugglers is simply finding the time to adequately fulfill all their responsibilities (DeGroot & Fine, 2003; Families and Work Institute, 1995).

GET INVOLVED **11.2**

What Psychological Experiences Do You Think You Will Have If You Combine Employment and Motherhood?

Pretend that you have two children and a spouse/partner employed full time outside of the home. Given these circumstances think about the experience you might have if you, also, were employed full time outside the home throughout your childrearing years. For each of the following possible consequences of employment during parenthood, estimate the probability, from 0 percent to 100 percent, that you would experience that outcome.

___1. higher self-esteem
___2. more guilt feelings

___3. greater feeling of missing out on your children's developmental progress (e.g., first steps)
___4. greater self-fulfillment
___5. greater number of conflicting demands
___6. greater intellectual stimulation
___7. more resentment from spouse/partner
___8. more anxiety about your child
___9. more mental exhaustion
___10. greater degree of pride
___11. more social stimulation
___12. more irritability
___13. more conflict with your spouse/partner
___14. more approval from other people

What Does It Mean?

Items 2, 3, 5, 7, 8, 9, 12, and 13 are possible costs and items 1, 4, 6, 10, 11, and 14 are possible benefits of employment for mothers. For each of these two sets of outcomes, calculate the average probability that you reported. First, add up the eight probabilities you specified for the costs and divide that total by 8. Then, sum the probabilities you estimated for the six benefits and divide that total by 6. After calculating your averages, read the text's presentation of the findings of this study.

1. Compare your expectations to those reported in the text. Are they similar? If not, can you think of reasons for any observed differences?
2. Do you think your expectations will influence your decision about the timing of your employment and childbearing?
3. Do you think your answers would have differed if you were the other gender? Refer to material on gender attitudes and gender socialization to explain your answer.

Source: Based on Bridges & Etaugh (1996).

Another primary issue is arranging for good child care. "If I did not find good care, I simply would not work" (Snyder, 1994, p. 166). "I currently would like a different job but can't get too serious about looking because I don't care to take my children out of the center we currently use" (Snyder, 1994, p. 165). Comments like these illustrate the central importance that child care has for employed women. Not surprisingly, worries about child care can lead to high levels of stress for employed mothers (Googins, 1991).

Costs.   As we saw earlier in this chapter, women carry most of the responsibility related to child care and housework. As might be expected, many women, especially mothers, experience **role strain,** that is, *stress stemming from one's roles.* In the words of one employed mother of an infant, "Everything was a compromise. When I went to work, I felt like I should be at home. And when I was at home, I thought I left in the middle—all of these management meetings would be going on and I'm like up and out of there. And everybody's looking around like, 'Where's she going?'" (Hattery, 2001, p. 58). Role strain can stem from **role overload,** *role demands that exceed one's available time and/or energy,* and/or **interrole conflict,** *incompatible demands stemming from two or more roles.* Role overload can occur, for example, when, after 9 hours of work and commuting, a mother does her family's laundry, cooks dinner, washes the dishes, and supervises her children's homework. Interrole conflict, on the other hand, would occur if a mother wants to attend her child's band concert at school but is expected to chair an important business meeting scheduled for the same time. Women in two-career families often experience the dual pressures of performing well in fast-paced demanding careers and performing well in their roles as mothers, increasing their risk of both physical and emotional exhaustion (Luthar & Sexton, 2004). Florence Denmark and her colleagues (Denmark et al., 1996, p. 108) describe family-work role strain like this: "Between work and family, women face competing demands on their attention. Some days they may feel they cannot accept one more demand on their time. Too much stress and they are like a balloon ready to pop." In fact, the more role strain women experience, the greater their depression and stress and the lower their job and life satisfaction (Bird & Rogers, 1998; Kossek & Ozeki, 1998).

What produces role strain? According to the **scarcity hypothesis,** *excessive role responsibilities deplete the individual's limited supply of time and energy and, consequently, can lead to stress.* When individuals have more responsibilities than they have time or energy for handling them, or when they are overwhelmed by conflicts between their role responsibilities, they can experience frustration, fatigue, or other indications of stress (Barnett, 2001).

Estimates of the percentage of employed women who experience role strain vary from 40 percent (Galinsky & Bond, 1996) to over 80 percent (Carlisle, 1994). This large range is to be expected because experiences related to family-work balancing can be influenced by numerous factors, not the least of which is the presence of children. The wife and worker roles alone are not related to role overload or conflict. It is the addition of the mother role to the worker role that creates women's role strain (Ray & Miller, 1994). Also, the less their husbands are involved in child care and domestic chores, the more likely it is that employed mothers experience stress or depression (Kiecolt-Glaser & Newton, 2001).

As we stated above, mothers' perceptions of the quality of their child-care arrangements are crucial to their level of role strain. One study showed that professional women were more likely than blue-collar or clerical women to report better child-care arrangements and to be able to forget about family issues while at work (Burris, 1991). Possibly, their greater comfort about their children's care enabled them to focus on work without the intrusion of family concerns.

Although men are not immune to either role overload or interrole conflict, considerable evidence demonstrates that employed married women are more likely than employed married men to experience both of these and that this gender difference holds across several ethnic groups, including Whites (e.g., Berger et al., 1994; Duxbury & Higgins, 1994), Blacks (McLoyd, 1993), and Latinas/os (Berger et al., 1994). The social construction of women as the major caregivers and homemakers and the construction of men as the primary providers means that women's family and work roles are parallel to one another whereas men's are simultaneous. Women's employment is seen as *additional to* their family role, whereas men's employment is viewed as *part of* their family role (Simon, 1995). This leads to greater role strain for women than for men (Kiecolt-Glaser & Newton, 2001; Sachs-Ericsson & Ciarlo, 2000).

In addition to role strain, lesbian role jugglers must face other problems as well. For example, their coworkers and/or supervisors might disapprove of their choice of intimate partner, making the work environment uncomfortable. Furthermore, the lack of insurance benefits available for lesbian families can produce economic pressures (Fassinger, 1995).

Benefits.   Juggling family and work can lead to role overload and interrole conflict, but it can also bring numerous rewards, including higher self-esteem, greater respect from others, and greater economic security (Auster, 2001; Barnett & Hyde, 2001). As one professional woman put it: "I feel that I would be a much better mother if I combined motherhood with employment. I think I would be more fulfilled and feel a sense of accomplishment about my life" (Granrose & Kaplan, 1996, p. 47). Indeed, even though employed mothers are more likely than unemployed mothers to report they "always feel rushed," they are also more likely to say that they get "a great deal" or "a very great deal" of satisfaction from their family lives (Cherlin & Krishnamurthy, 2004).

The benefits of multiple role coordination are explained by the **enhancement hypothesis** (Barnett, 2001; Barnett & Gareis, 2000). According to this perspective, *each additional role provides a new source of self-esteem, social approval, social status, and other benefits.* Successfully applying the different skills required by different roles can lead to achievements in many areas. Consequently, family-work balancers can develop competence in numerous domains and experience greater personal pride and fulfillment.

Aside from any rewards associated with managing several roles, women can benefit by using one role to buffer strains associated with another (Barnett & Hyde, 2001); that is, positive or neutral events in one role can reduce the psychological impact of negative events in another role. A 35-year-old professional woman describes it like this: "Sometimes I have a really rough day at work and then I come home and these two little kids run to the door. My older daughter says 'I'm really glad you got picked to be my mother.' Then, I forget the day at work" (Crosby, 1991, p. 103). Similarly, daughter caregivers who enjoy their jobs are less likely to feel stressed by the demands of caring for an ailing parent than are women whose work is less satisfying (Martire & Stephens, 2003).

Faye Crosby (1991) discusses three reasons why buffering helps psychological well-being. First, involvement in more than one role offers the opportunity for a time-out, giving the family-work juggler an opportunity to distance herself from the problems in one role while she engages in another role. For instance, a mother who is upset about her child's lack of achievement in school can put that worry aside while she focuses on her employment responsibilities.

Second, challenges in one role help put into perspective worries associated with another role. For example, a woman who is very bothered about interpersonal conflicts with her coworkers might view this problem as less important when faced with her husband's serious illness. When his health improves, she might continue to view the interpersonal tension at work as minor.

Third, buffering helps protect women's self-esteem. Positive or even neutral events in one role can help restore self-esteem that has been damaged by negative events in another role. Thus, the disappointment of not receiving a promotion at work can be mitigated by a mother's feelings of competence as she helps her child successfully cope with a bully at school.

In addition to benefits earned while juggling family and work roles, there is evidence of long-term positive outcomes. Longitudinal research shows that among women who graduated from college in the 1960s, those who combined family and employment roles in early adulthood have more positive role experiences in middle age and experience greater midlife well-being than do other women (Vandewater et al., 1997).

Gender Attitudes and Family-Work Balancing Experiences. The effects of women's employment on their well-being are related, in part, to their gender attitudes. Employed women with nontraditional attitudes report more benefits than women with traditional beliefs (Marshall & Barnett, 1993). In addition, nonemployed mothers with nontraditional views tend to be more stressed than those with traditional beliefs. For example, mothers who want to work outside the home but are full-time homemakers are more depressed than full-time homemakers who do not want to be employed (Aube et al., 2000). When women's roles are consistent with their attitudes about appropriate roles, they experience better psychological outcomes.

Ethnic Comparison of Family-Work Balancing Experiences. Few studies have examined the outcomes of family and work roles for women in different ethnic groups, but available limited research points to similar reactions in ethnically diverse women. Latina and White women managing multiple roles report comparable degrees of role overload and distress (Berger et al., 1994). A similar study of Black and White middle-class women found no ethnic differences in the personal costs or benefits related to respondents' family and work roles (Bridges & Orza, 1996).

Effects of Mothers' Employment on Children

The majority of infants and preschool children in the United States spend time in the care of paid caregivers (Brauner et al., 2004). Yet, as we have seen, most Americans do not favor employment for mothers with preschoolers. Furthermore, some pediatricians and psychologists caution mothers about the dangers of nonmaternal care. Does research support this advice?

It appears that it is not scientific evidence, but the gender-role belief that women belong at home that fuels the argument against nonmaternal child care. In actuality, most researchers conclude that maternal employment and nonmaternal care are not harmful. Although a few early studies suggested some negative social and achievement-related effects of nonfamily care during the baby's first year, recent research shows no added risks for children's social, academic, or emotional development nor for their relationships with their mothers, even during infancy (Erel et al., 2000; Gennetian & Miller, 2002; Howes & Aikins, 2002; NICHD Early Child Care Research Network, 2002). Ellen Galinsky's (2001) interviews with more than 1,000 children in grades three to twelve found that children's perceptions of their mothers' parenting abilities were not related to whether their mothers worked outside the home.

In fact, children may benefit from maternal employment. For one thing, girls and boys whose mothers are employed develop less stereotypical attitudes about gender roles than children with nonemployed mothers (Hoffman & Youngblade, 2001; Riggio & Desrochers, 2005). Because the employment role is seen as an agentic role and because maternal employment frequently necessitates nonstereotypical structuring of household responsibilities among both parents and children, employed mothers often serve as less traditional role models than do full-time homemakers. Both female and male college students with employed mothers have more egalitarian views toward sharing household and child-care tasks than students with nonemployed mothers (Cunningham, 2001; Riggio & Desrochers, 2005). In addition, adolescent girls whose mothers are employed tend to have higher educational and career aspirations than their counterparts with nonemployed mothers.

Are there other benefits of out-of-home child-care programs? The answer to this question is complex and depends, in part, on the consistency between a particular program and childrearing behaviors and values in the home; on characteristics of the child, such as social class; and on the quality of the program, as measured by variables such as the amount of teacher training and the staff-to-child ratio. What is clear is that high-quality care provides significant emotional and intellectual benefits to children, especially those from disadvantaged homes (e.g., Fuller et al., 2002; Loeb et al., 2004; Marshall, 2004; McClelland et al., 2003; NICHD Early Child Care Research Network, 2002). Both better academic performance and a reduction in adolescent social problems, such as teen pregnancy and delinquency, are associated with high-quality care for children from disadvantaged backgrounds (Reynolds et al., 2001). Research also links the quality of child care to children's well-being, social-emotional development, cognitive growth, and subsequent adjustment (NICHD, Early Child Care Research Network, 2003; Phillips & Adams, 2001; Votruba-Drzal et al., 2004).

Our exploration of the effects of maternal employment on children's development and our discussion of benefits that might result from this employment do not

High-quality day care provides significant emotional and intellectual benefits to children.

imply that full-time homemaking is detrimental to children's development. What is important is the consistency between a mother's role (employed or not employed) and her belief about the value of maternal employment for her children. Mothers whose roles match their own attitudes are likely to be more effective parents. A mother who is dissatisfied with her role is less likely to display the type of positive parenting characteristics that can lead to good outcomes for her children (Harrison & Ungerer, 2002; Hoffman & Youngblade, 2001; Lerner et al., 2002).

Interestingly, most research on the effects of parental employment on children has focused on maternal employment. Many scholars (e.g., Silverstein, 1996) claim there is no evidence for an instinct that makes women better suited to parenting than men; nonetheless, the social construction of gender leads us to conceptualize parenting within the female gender role. This is so ingrained in our thinking that there has been much less investigation of fathering than mothering (Silverstein & Phares, 1996) Furthermore, because employment is identified more closely with the father role than the mother role, there has been little research on children's outcomes associated with paternal employment. Feminist author Betty Friedan has identified our mother-centered focus on parenting as a problem and encourages psychologists to do more research on fathering (Murray, 1999).

However, even graduate students, the voice of future psychology, continue to frame their investigations of parenting within a mother-focused perspective (Silverstein & Phares, 1996).

Effects of Wives' Employment on the Marital Relationship

Since employment of wives and mothers represents a departure from traditional gender roles, does it have implications for the marital relationship? Research has produced inconsistent findings on this question. Some studies have found that women's employment increases the incidence of divorce, while others show no such effect (Sayer & Bianchi, 2000). Data from the comprehensive National Survey of Families and Households shed light on the reason for this discrepancy. Women's employment does not affect the likelihood of divorce among couples who are happily married. However, it is a factor in ending unhappy marriages (Schoen et al., 2002). Can you think of a reason for this? According to the economic opportunity hypothesis, employment gives women the resources to leave an unhappy marriage (Schoen et al., 2002). How about the alternative hypothesis that a woman's employment *causes* a rift in the marital relationship? Let us examine some of the research that relates women's employment to the marital satisfaction of both wives and husbands.

Does a man's sense of well-being depend on whether the wife views her employment as an essential aspect of her identity (as a career) versus as a means of earning a living (as a job)? Terri Orbuch and Lindsay Custer (1995) examined this question in study samples of Black and White men married to homemakers, career-oriented wives, or job-oriented wives. Their results showed that husbands of homemakers had the lowest well-being and husbands of women who viewed their employment as a job had the highest. How can these findings be explained? According to Orbuch and Custer, one possibility is that husbands of job-oriented wives benefited from the financial support of a working wife but didn't experience the potentially greater challenge to their traditional role associated with a career-oriented spouse. Consistent with this explanation, men experience a decline in well-being when their wives' share of the family household income increases (Rogers & DeBoer, 2001).

Turning to wives' feelings about their marriage, satisfaction is related, in part, to the consistency between wives' roles and their gender-related attitudes. In interviews with married women, Maureen Perry-Jenkins and her colleagues (Perry-Jenkins et al., 1992) found that employed women who were uncomfortable about their work role experienced less marital satisfaction than those who wanted to work outside the home, and were less satisfied than full-time homemakers. It appears that positive outcomes can accrue from either full-time homemaking or from combining family and work. What is more important than the actual roles is the attitude toward those roles.

Studies of the relationship between women's employment and wives' and husbands' sexual satisfaction show parallel findings. Janet Shibley Hyde and her colleagues (Hyde et al., 2001) studied the association between employment and the sexual experiences of more than 500 heterosexual women and their husbands or intimate partners and found that neither women's employment status nor the number of hours they spent at work was related to their sexual frequency or enjoyment. What was important was the quality of their jobs. Both women and men reported greater sexual satisfaction when they had more rewarding work experiences. This could be because positive experiences in the workplace help couples more fully enjoy their sexual relationship or because a satisfactory sex life contributes to enjoyment on the job. Or, it may be that neither domain influences the other, but that well-adjusted adults lead lives that are satisfying in many domains, including work and sexual relationships.

Solutions to Family-Work Balancing Difficulties

As we have seen, the numerous rewards that can accrue from combining family and work roles do not eliminate the challenges jugglers face in managing their roles. What approaches can help reduce these difficulties?

Resources Offered by Employers.   Given the kinds of information we have examined in this chapter, it is not surprising that a 1999 national survey of workers in the United States found that 97 percent said balancing family and work is their most important concern, taking precedence over issues such as job security and salary ("W/F Balance," 1999). Organizational resources play a key role in helping parents coordinate their family and work roles (Burke, 2004). One way is by offering paid family leave, discussed earlier.

A second family-friendly benefit is flexible work hours (American Psychological Association, 2004b; Frone, 2003). **Flextime,** *flexible work scheduling that allows the employee to choose the arrival and departure time within a set of possible options offered by the employer,* can enable parents to better accommodate their work hours to their children's regular child-care or school schedules and to deal with unforeseen and unscheduled family demands. One recent poll of over 750 organizations found that over half of them offered flextime and nearly one-third offered compressed work weeks (Taylor, 2001). Flexible and compressed work schedules are associated with reduced work-family conflict, lower absenteeism, greater job satisfaction, and higher productivity (Cascio & Young; 2005; Cook et al., 2002), benefiting both employees and employers.

A third option that would help some workers is telecommuting. The increasing use of technology in the labor force makes this option to work from home attractive to certain types of workers (Begun, 2002). In 2000, 43 percent of large employers let their employees work from home at least some of the time, up from 33 percent the year before (Ligos, 2001).

Fourth, employer help with child care would ease a major burden faced by employed parents. Child-care assistance programs can include referral services and day-care subsidies as well as on-site day care and backup day care when

Telecommuting is a family-friendly option that allows employees to work from home.

families have emergencies (Frone, 2003; Halpert, 2002). Fifty percent of workers sampled in a national survey desired on-site care, which would enable them to spend some time with their children during the course of the work day as well as to more easily transport them to and from day care ("W/F Balance," 1999). Given that child care is one of employed parents' greatest worries, the strong need for additional safe, affordable child-care options for infants and preschool children must be addressed (Costello & Wight, 2003). Parents also need assistance with care of older children (Lerner et al., 2002). School programs that provide before- and after-school care would not only provide safe and stimulating activities for children but would also reduce parental worry and eliminate the need for parents to coordinate multiple daily child-care arrangements.

Finally, elder-care benefits would help many of the 15 million workers who provide care for older relatives. About one-fifth of companies in the United States now provide referral services on care to the elderly (Jackson, 2002).

Unfortunately, family-friendly benefits such as flexible hours, telecommuting, on-site child care, and elder-care benefits are offered primarily by large companies, yet the majority of workers are employed by small companies. Furthermore, companies that employ better-educated, highly skilled workers are more likely to offer these benefits than companies with a primarily unskilled labor force (AAUW Educational Foundation, 2003; Friedman, 2001; Stier, 2000).

Support from Other People.   Enlisting the aid of others to reduce their domestic burden can be effective for some family-work jugglers (Frone, 2003). Women who have the financial resources can purchase services they would otherwise perform, such as housecleaning and meal preparation. Other women rely on the assistance of family members. Women's well-being is positively related to their husbands' greater participation in child care and housework (Galinsky & Bond, 1996; Ozer, 1995) as well as to husbands' emotional support (Matire et al., 1998). Keep in mind, however, that support from husbands or male partners is frequently construed as "help," not as a shared responsibility, underscoring the social construction of different and unequal roles for women and men.

Some employed couples work alternating shift schedules in order to share the child-care duties, thus reducing or eliminating the need for nonparental care. For a close look at the gender attitudes of some working-class couples who use this strategy, turn to Learn about the Research 11.1.

LEARN ABOUT THE RESEARCH **11.1**

How Do Working Class Couples with Alternating Shifts Reconcile Their Own Roles with Their Traditional Gender Attitudes?

We saw in Chapter 10 that nonstandard shift work often creates scheduling and logistical problems for families (Hawkins & Whiteman, 2004). Nonstandard schedules are linked with lower marital satisfaction and with marital instability, especially in families with children (Presser, 2004).

When two parents work different shifts, this creates transitions termed **tag-team parenting** (Daly, 2004), in which *parents hand off the child-care responsibilities to each other as they come and go from work.* This arrangement clearly represents a departure from traditional gender roles. How do working-class couples with alternating shifts reconcile these more fluid roles with their traditional gender attitudes?

Francine Deutsch and Susan Saxon (1998) interviewed 23 primarily White working-class couples who had traditional views about parental, marital, and employment roles. These couples alternated their work shifts, so that one parent would be able to take care of the children while the other parent worked outside the home. Husbands worked an average of 46 hours per week in blue-collar occupations, such as custodian and electrician, and wives worked an average of 33 hours per week in a variety of jobs, including clerical worker and food service worker.

Some of the couples handled the inconsistency between their gender attitudes and their own roles by modifying their traditional views. For example, one woman commented, "When we first married, Larry felt like I was there to be his wife, to do the dishes, to clean the house, to take care of the kids. Things have changed since then. We're more equals. It's more like I'm his wife, not his slave" (p. 344).

Other ways that these couples handled inconsistencies between their attitudes and roles was to maintain the belief that their family roles still reflected three core elements of traditional gender roles. First, they continued to hold the view that the husband was the primary provider. As one husband said, "I have to work and I have to be the breadwinner" (p. 349). Second, these couples, especially the husbands, did not view the worker role as a primary aspect of the mother's identity. Instead they saw it as a financial necessity. One husband said, "I think it would be great if she could be home all the time. . . . Right now she's really got no choice because we need the money, but if it were her decision . . . and she wanted to stay home, hey great" (p. 350). Interestingly, however, many of the wives viewed their jobs as providing rewards beyond the financial one. As one woman said, "I look forward to 5:30 every night . . .

taking off in the car by myself. . . . I love my job . . . I love doing the paperwork and working with numbers . . . anyone asks me a question, 9 out of 10 times I have an answer for them and it's wonderful. I feel very successful" (p. 351). Third, these mothers and fathers saw the mother as the primary caregiver. One mother stated it like this, "As much as we try to do everything 50/50, if Jimmy gets hurt and he cries, I think I'm the one that should take care of him" (p. 356).

The authors conclude that these couples were able to reconcile potentially discrepant attitudes and role behaviors by viewing their roles as constrained by financial considerations and maintaining their beliefs that the husband was still the primary breadwinner and the wife, the primary caregiver.

What Does It Mean?

1. The couples examined in this study were primarily White and working class. Do you think middle-class couples or couples with different ethnicities might reconcile their attitudes and roles in a different way? Give reasons for your answer.

2. What are the advantages and disadvantages to the children of parents who work alternating shifts?
3. What are the advantages and disadvantages to the marriage of alternating shifts?

Source: From Deutsch & Saxon (1998).

Personal Coping Strategies.   Unfortunately, some women receive no support from others, or the help they do receive is insufficient. Under these circumstances, women use several personal strategies to manage their numerous role responsibilities. One is to negotiate with their employer about reduced hours (Frone, 2003). Women who reduce their work hours as a means of coping with family and work responsibilities report both benefits and costs. They experience greater satisfaction at home and less work-family conflict than women employed full time. However, at work, they report less career opportunity and work success (Hill et al., 2004).

Another strategy for women is to change their perceptions of their responsibilities (Frone, 2003). They might, for example, lower their standards for housecleaning or accept the possibility that a promotion might take longer to achieve. Many employed women utilize this strategy at least to some extent. As we saw earlier in this chapter, employed mothers spend fewer hours doing housework than do stay-at-home mothers.

GET INVOLVED **11.3**

Women's Experiences Coordinating Family and Work Roles

Interview two employed mothers. If possible, select mothers who have children under 6. However, if not possible, interview mothers with children of any age. Ask each to talk about the following experiences: (1) time problems, if any, performing all of their responsibilities; (2) conflicts, if any, between demands from different roles; (3) problems, if any, arranging for child care; (4) psychological benefits they receive from their mother role; (5) psychological benefits they receive from their work role; (6) personal coping strategies and/or employer benefits that have helped them deal with any time problems, conflicts, or child-care difficulties; and (7) additional employer benefits they would find beneficial.

What Does It Mean?

1. What new information did you learn from these mothers' experiences that you did not learn from the text?
2. Did the responses of these women enhance your understanding of the costs and benefits of balancing motherhood and employment? Explain your answer.
3. Which solution do you think is the most effective for dealing with family-work balancing? Explain your answer.
4. Which family-work balancing hypothesis best accounts for these mothers' experiences? Explain your answer.

A third approach women use to coordinate family and work roles is to put in extra time in order to handle all role responsibilities (Frone, 2003). This approach can be very difficult and exhausting, and women who use it are sometimes referred to as "supermoms." A fourth strategy used by college-educated women is to devote themselves to their careers and then take time off to be stay-at-home mothers while their children are young (Frone, 2003). This option, however, is seldom realistic for single mothers or for women whose husbands do not earn a sizable income (Hill et al., 2004). The exercise in Get Involved 11.3 will help you gain firsthand information about women's experiences balancing family and work roles.

Midlife Transitions in Family and Work Roles

Many women who currently are in their middle adult years go through a process of life review, that is, an intensive self-evaluation of numerous aspects of their lives (Etaugh & Bridges, 2005). They reexamine their family and occupational values and goals, evaluate their accomplishments, and sometimes consider new career directions. Some make transitions to different jobs during their middle adult years while others begin their paid work role at this point in their lives.

Because of the many societal gender-role messages encountered by the current cohort of midlife women, some have followed traditional roles early in adulthood and continued these roles at midlife while others began their adult lives committed to traditional roles but made changes in their middle adult years. Still others deviated from traditional expectations by committing themselves to careers in early adulthood. Because each of these patterns of choices can be fulfilling (Vandewater & Stewart, 1997), many women are satisfied with their life paths and, therefore, make no changes at midlife.

Given changing societal standards about appropriate roles for women, it is not surprising that one characteristic theme in the life reviews of midlife women today has been the search for an independent identity. Ravenna Helson (1992) has noted that for many women, the need to rewrite the life story in middle age is related to the lessening of the dependence and restriction associated with marriage and motherhood as children grow up. Thus, many heterosexual women attempt to affirm their own being, independent of their husbands, through graduate education, beginning a career, or switching careers (Helson, 1992; Shellenbarger, 2004; Stewart & Vandewater, 1999). Lesbian midlife women, however, generally do not experience major transitions at midlife. Many are not mothers and have not experienced the role constraints characteristic of traditional heterosexual marriages. Therefore, they are not aiming to redefine themselves as separate from significant others. Furthermore, they already have a strong sense of self due to years of defining themselves independently of others' expectations and fighting hostility directed toward the lesbian community, and most have considered work an important part of their identity throughout their adult lives (Etaugh & Bridges, 2005).

Satisfaction with Life Roles

For many midlife women, paid work is a significant predictor of psychological well-being (Vandewater et al., 1997). Middle-aged women who are involved in either beginning or building their career are both psychologically and physically healthier than women who are maintaining or reducing their career involvement (Etaugh & Bridges, 2005). Women who have attained the occupational goals they set for themselves in young adulthood also have a greater sense of life purpose and are less depressed in midlife than those who fall short of their expectations (Carr, 1997). Furthermore, satisfaction with work predicts a general sense of well-being: the more satisfied women are with their jobs, the better they feel in general (Vandewater et al., 1997).

For other women, being a full-time homemaker or student can be associated with the same degree of psychological well-being as that experienced by women who are employed (McQuaide, 1998). Midlife homemakers whose life goal was this domestic role have a comparable sense of purpose in life to women who aspired toward and achieved an occupational role. Not surprisingly, however, women who are involuntarily out of the workforce, due to forced early retirement or layoff, are not as satisfied with midlife as women with a chosen role

(Etaugh & Bridges, 2005). Thus, there are multiple routes to well-being in midlife, and it appears that a key factor influencing midlife role evaluation is not a woman's *role* per se but fulfillment of her *preferred role* (Carr, 1997).

Regrets about Life Direction

Although some midlife women are satisfied with traditional roles, others are distressed about missed educational or occupational opportunities. Some middle-class women, who as young adults devoted themselves solely to marriage and motherhood, in midlife voice regrets about their earlier traditional decisions. Abigail Stewart and Elizabeth Vandewater (1999) examined regrets experienced by women who graduated in the mid-1960s from either Radcliffe College or the University of Michigan. The concerns reported by these women centered on dis-appointment about not pursuing a more prestigious career, marrying before establishing a career, and not returning to work after having children. Stewart and Vandewater found that the experience of regret was not necessarily associ-ated with reduced psychological adjustment. Instead, the crucial factor appeared to be acting on these regrets to effect life changes. The women who acknowledged their regrets and made modifications based on these regrets experienced greater psychological well-being at midlife than those who had regrets but did not use those as a basis for altering their life direction.

Why did some women have regrets but not act on them? Interestingly, it was not the presence of external constraints, such as the number of children they had, that seemed to prevent these women from making goal-related changes. Instead, it was the tendency to focus on negative life events; to engage in self-pity, moodiness, and negativism. These women seem to have been constrained by personality characteristics rather than external obstacles.

Making Changes

Pursuing a new direction at midlife involves making significant changes in one's life role during the middle adulthood years. A midlife woman who chooses to switch direction at this point must be willing to leave one long-term role (e.g., full-time homemaking or career) that has been a significant part of her identity and proceed down a new and as yet unfamiliar path. In so doing, she is leaving a role to which she has devoted considerable time and energy during her adult years. What are the psychological experiences of women who begin a work role or alter occupational directions in midlife?

Let's look at Stewart and Vandewater's (1997) sample of 1964 Radcliffe College graduates who made major work-related changes in midlife. After an ear-lier, full-time commitment to the traditional roles of wife and mother or to tradi-tional female jobs, such as elementary or secondary school teaching, they realized there was a broader set of options available to them and decided to follow a new career interest or return to an earlier interest that they had never pursued. What precipitated their new directions? For many, the women's movement made a strong impact on their midlife development by raising their awareness of the increasing possibilities open for women and, consequently, changing the way they constructed the female role. As they described it: "[The] women's movement taught me that I could be a doer and not a helper" and "[The] women's movement and political activism of the '60s led me to law school" (p. 404). These women were happy about the changes they made and felt a sense of accomplishment and pride. However, despite new directions suggested by the increasing societal acceptance and encouragement of women's diverse roles, making these significant life changes was often difficult.

Midlife Transitions: A Cautionary Note

We saw in Chapter 1 that generalization on the basis of one type of respondent can lead to false conclusions about individuals who are not represented in the sample. For at least two reasons the research findings presented here are relevant to a very specific group of midlife women and should not be extended to other females. First, the respondents in these studies reflect a homogeneous educational and socioeconomic group of women. They were primarily White, highly educated, middle-class women. The midlife experiences of women of color, less-educated women, and poor women are vastly different. Large variations in the options available to different groups of women can affect their aspirations and opportunities during both early adulthood and at midlife. For example, poor women may feel so constrained by poverty that significant change and growth at midlife appears outside the realm of possibility.

Second, the midlife experiences discussed here must be placed in their historical context. As social constructions of gender have evolved over time, women have experienced differing perceptions of their options. Women examined in the studies reported here were in their middle adult years at the beginning of the twenty-first century. Consequently, the gender-based social climate that shaped their development was different from the societal attitudes influencing the lives of future generations of midlife women. For example, today's midlife women were exposed to traditional and flexible gender role expectations at different points in their lives. Thus, it is likely that they experienced more regrets about previous traditional choices than future generations of midlife women will. Because there are greater options for young women today than there were in the 1960s and 1970s when current midlife women were making life choices, it is possible that fewer young women today will find the need to make significant revisions in their life paths during middle age (Stewart & Ostrove, 1998). Today's elderly women have also experienced different constructions of women's roles than have current midlife women. Because they were in midlife before the major societal role changes discussed here, they did not experience the career and role opportunities encountered by today's midlife women and, consequently, were not faced with decisions about major role changes.

SUMMARY

Attitudes toward Women's Family and Employment Roles

- The majority of North Americans approve of women's employment. However, only half believe mothers of preschool children should work.
- Most college women want to combine a career with motherhood. However, they would like to interrupt their employment for childrearing and believe mothers should stay home for a period of time.
- Students more negatively evaluate mothers who continue their employment after the birth of their baby than mothers who interrupt their employment for childrearing.

Division of Household Labor

- Women perform most of the child care and housekeeping duties in the family. This pattern exists across ethnic groups.
- Equal distribution of these responsibilities is more likely in dual-career than in dual-earner or traditional couples.
- Women provide the majority of care for aging parents and other elderly relatives.
- Much of women's leisure time is fragmented into small blocks of time.
- Women tend to be satisfied with the division of labor, although they perform the greater share.
- One reason may be that women have been socialized to view household duties as their domain. They might also view their obligations as fair compared to those of other women.
- Explanations for the unequal division of labor focus on time constraints, relative power, and gender attitudes. There is more support for the latter two than for the first.

Family-Work Coordination

- The United States is one of the few industrialized countries that does not have federal legislation mandating paid parental leave.

- Women take shorter parental leaves if they are more highly educated, have nontraditional attitudes toward combining employment and parenting, and perceive their employers as family-friendly.
- Women across ethnic groups experience role strain as well as numerous benefits from multiple role juggling.
- Role strain can be explained by the scarcity hypothesis; benefits, such as self-esteem and approval from others, can be explained by the enhancement hypothesis.
- Another benefit of engaging in both family and work roles is that one role can buffer strains associated with the other.
- Most research shows no negative effects of maternal employment on children.
- Day care, even during infancy, does not hinder the child's social, academic, or emotional development. Furthermore, it can help improve school performance and reduce the social problems of children from low-income homes.
- Children with employed mothers have less stereotypical attitudes about gender roles than children of full-time homemakers.
- Positive psychological feelings, good parenting, and marital satisfaction are more likely when a woman feels comfortable about her role, whether as a full-time homemaker or employed wife and mother.
- Employer resources, such as flextime, telecommuting, and child-care assistance; and husbands' participation in family responsibilities and provision of emotional support can help women more effectively manage their multiple demands.
- Personal adjustments, such as altering one's role definitions, changing one's perceptions of responsibilities, and attempting to perform all role duties, are types of strategies women use to balance their family and work roles.

Midlife Transitions in Family and Work Roles

- Many women go through a life review during their middle adult years.

- Because those who are in midlife at the beginning of the twenty-first century were exposed to traditional gender-role expectations during their early years and to flexible gender roles later, many women now seek an identity independent of their husband's.
- Some midlife women are satisfied with either the career or traditional paths they have followed.

- Other women experience regrets about previous traditional role choices, and some of these women choose to make significant changes in their life direction.

KEY TERMS

traditional couples
dual-career couples
dual-earner couples
role strain

role overload
interrole conflict
scarcity hypothesis

enhancement hypothesis
flextime
tag-team parenting

WHAT DO YOU THINK?

1. Use any theory of gender typing (see Chapter 3) to explain the current division of household labor as presented in the text. Would this theory predict a greater equality of child care and household responsibility in the future? Explain your answer.

2. Recall that women seem to be satisfied with an unequal division of household labor. Do you agree with the explanations given in the text? Are there other factors that can account for this phenomenon? Explain your answers.

3. Explain why young Black women, compared to White women, desire an earlier return to employment after they have children. Refer to material in previous chapters and any other information that addresses the question.

4. Women now experience more role strain than men. Do you think this will change in the future? Explain your answer.

5. Does any of the material in this chapter have public policy implications related to parental leave? That is, does it point to the need for new parental leave legislation? Explain your answer.

6. Discuss the origins and implications of the widespread conceptualization of parenting as a female role. What benefits to mothers, fathers, and children would stem from a more inclusive view of parenting?

IF YOU WANT TO KNOW MORE

Chira, S. (1998). *A mother's place: Taking the debate about working mothers beyond guilt and blame.* New York: HarperCollins.

Crouter, A. C., & Booth, A. (Eds.). (2004). *Work-family challenges for low-income parents and their children.* Mahwah, NJ: Erlbaum.

Dunne, G. A. (Ed.). (1998). *Living "difference": Lesbian perspectives on work and family life.* Binghamton, NY: Haworth Press.

Friedman, S. D., & Greenhaus, J. H. (2000). *Work and family—Allies or enemies?* New York: Oxford University Press.

Halpern, D. F., & Murphy, S. E. (Eds.). (2004). *From work-family balance to work-family interaction: Changing the metaphor*. Mahwah, NJ: Erlbaum.

Hattery, A. (2001). *Women, work, and family: Balancing and weaving*. Thousand Oaks, CA: Sage.

Kossek, E. E., & Lambert, S. J. (2005). *Work and life integration: Organizational, cultural, and individual perspectives*. Mahwah, NJ: Erlbaum.

Poelmans, S. A. Y. (2005). *Work and family: An international research perspective*. Mahwah, NJ: Erlbaum.

Schindler-Zimmerman, T. (Ed.). (2002). *Balancing family and work: Special considerations in feminist therapy*. New York: Haworth.

Wearing, B. (1998). *Leisure and feminist theory*. Thousand Oaks, CA: Sage.

Williams, J. (2001). *Unbending gender: Why family and work conflict and what to do about it*. New York: American Psychiatric Society.

WEBSITES

Family-Work Coordination

Catalyst
http://www.catalystwomen.org/
Institute for Women's Policy Research
http://www.iwpr.org/

Work and Family: National Partnership for Women and Family
http://www.nationalpartnership.org/
Work and Family Connection
http://www.workfamily.com
Sloan Work and Family Research Network
http://www.bc.edu/wfnetwork

12 Physical Health

Physical health is not just a biological phenomenon, but a social one as well. It involves both individual behaviors and lifestyles and societal systems. As viewed from a feminist perspective, women's health and health care are linked to inequalities in assessment, treatment and access to care, and lack of research on health topics relevant to women in general and to ethnic minority women (Travis & Compton, 2001).

In this chapter, we examine issues in women's health and health care. We start by focusing on health services. Next, we turn to sexually transmitted infections, including AIDS, which has become the scourge of adolescent and young women worldwide. We then explore disorders which tend to affect women in the middle and later years: reproductive system disorders, osteoporosis, heart disease, and breast cancer. We continue with a discussion of women's health later in life. We close by focusing on ways to promote good health.

Health Services

About 10 years ago, Dr. Annette Stanton, a professor of psychology at the University of Kansas, attended a university reception with a colleague. She reacted strongly when her colleague referred to a recent study concerning the connection between heart disease and caffeine consumption, which had received a great deal of media coverage. "I guess our hearts are safe if we have a cup of coffee," he said. "Your heart may be safe; I have no idea about the safety of my heart! That study was conducted on over 45,000 men," retorted Dr. Stanton. (adapted from Stanton, 1995, p. 3)

Only a decade or so ago, little was known about many aspects of women's health. Women were routinely excluded as research participants in large studies designed to examine risk factors and potential treatments for various diseases. Even the first clinical trials to examine the effects of estrogen on heart disease were conducted solely on men! Scientists gave two principal reasons for confining medical experiments to men. First, women's monthly hormonal fluctuations "complicated" research results. Second, potential ethical and legal problems might arise from experimenting on women who would later bear children. The "male is normative" assumption (see Chapter 2) played a role as well (Dan & Rosser, 2003; Roth, 2003; World Health Organization, 2004).

In any case, the recognition that women had a number of poorly understood medical problems and that diseases sometimes affect women and men in radically different ways has increasingly led health researchers to include women in their studies (Pinn, 2003). Under the leadership of the first woman Surgeon General, Bernardine Healy, the federal government established an Office of Research on Women's Health, and the National Institutes of Health (NIH) now requires the inclusion of women in federally funded medical research (Sarto, 2004; Simon et al., 2005). However, although more women are being studied, men continue to be the focus for much of the research on the leading cause of death among both women and men: heart disease (Hayes et al., 2003). Few studies include elderly women, even though heart disease is common in this group (Mosca et al., 2004). In addition, women, older people, and ethnic minorities are underrepresented in recent research on two of the leading causes of cancer death: lung cancer and colorectal cancer (Murthy et al., 2004). Other health issues of ethnic minority women have also not been sufficiently explored (Mosca et al., 2004).

Basic research on the biomedical differences between women and men remains a low priority at NIH (Simon et al., 2005). Moreover, medical researchers often ignore the requirement that they analyze their data to see if women and men respond differently to a given treatment (Hayes et al., 2003). In addition, women are still underrepresented in studies to establish standard doses of new medications. This omission can have serious consequences, since women, especially older women, may have adverse effects from unnecessarily high drug doses, which have been established using male body weight as the standard (Anderson, 2005; Correa-de-Araujo, 2005).

In addition, gender biases still exist within the health care delivery system, leading to differences in the way health professionals interact with women and men and to differences in the care women and men receive (Travis & Compton, 2001). In this section, we examine issues of gender discrimination in health services.

The Physician-Patient Relationship

Sexism in the physician-patient interaction is well documented. Feminist analysis of the interaction between female patients and male physicians describe it as paternalistic, with women patients treated as subordinates. Male physicians frequently trivialize women's experiences by interrupting female patients and making jokes in response to their concerns. Physicians belittle women's health complaints by attributing them to psychosomatic factors (Canetto, 2003; Wilkinson & Ferraro, 2002). For example, women's pain reports are taken less seriously than men's and they receive less aggressive treatment for it. Women's pain reports are more likely to be dismissed as "emotional" and thus not "real" (Wartik, 2002). This stereotype may account for the fact that women consistently receive more prescriptions for tranquilizers, antidepressants, and anti-anxiety drugs than men (Canetto, 2003; Correa-de-Araujo et al., 2005; Curtis et al., 2004).

Sexist views of women are perpetuated in medical journal advertisements and medical textbooks as well. For example, anatomy and physical diagnosis textbooks have considerably fewer illustrations of women than men, and most of these are in the sections on reproduction (Mendelson, in Levison & Straumenis, 2002). Similarly, 80 percent of recent cardiovascular drug ads in medical journals feature men only, even though heart disease is the number one killer of both women and men. When women are included, they tend to be younger than the average age of women with heart disease. In addition, the women are predominantly White, even though the rate of heart disease for African American is 72 percent higher than for White women (Ahmed et al., 2004). Moreover, most physicians depicted in medical journal ads are White males while most of their patients are portrayed as White women. Female patients are also much more likely than male patients to be shown nude or provocatively dressed (Hawkins & Aber, 1993; Metzl, 2003). Elderly female patients often are portrayed as disheveled, disoriented, and needing medication for sleep or depression, thus perpetuating both ageist and sexist stereotypes (Hawkins & Aber, 1993).

A nationwide survey of women's health by the Commonwealth Fund (1993a) found that women are much more likely than men to change physicians because they are dissatisfied (41 percent of women compared to 27 percent of men). The major reason women change their doctors is communication problems. One-fourth of women (compared to 12 percent of men) report that they are "talked down to" or treated like a child by a physician. Moreover, 17 percent of women (compared to 7 percent of men) have been told that a medical condition they felt they had was "all in their head." Female physicians are more likely than male physicians to establish interpersonal rapport with their patients and to provide them with information (Bertakis et al., 2003; Cooper-Patrick et al., 1999; Roter et al., 2002). They also spend more time with their patients and tend to focus on them as people rather than on the procedures they need (Brukner, 2003; Steinhauer, 1999). Patients of female physicians report a greater willingness to reveal personal problems such as family violence or sexual abuse (Clancy, 2000). Not surprisingly, both women and men express more satisfaction with women physicians (Bertakis et al., 2003; Coulter et al., 2000).

Type and Quality of Care

Discrimination based on gender affects not only interpersonal aspects of health care, but also the type and quality of care that women receive. When we look at medical conditions that affect both women and men, women often receive less adequate care even when the severity of the condition is the same for both. As we shall see later in this chapter, women with heart disease receive less aggressive treatment than men (Godfrey, 2005). Women are also not as likely as men to receive kidney dialysis or a kidney transplant (Canetto, 2001; Clancy, 2000). This is especially true for ethnic minority women (Canetto, 2003).

Biases exist even in childhood. For example, girls who are growing too slowly are referred to specialists only half as often as boys (Grimberg et al., 2005). While it is true that boys tend to suffer greater social consequences if they are short, slow growth may be a sign of underlying disease. The failure of doctors to send small girls for closer examination can mean that serious problems go undetected.

Ageism presents older women with a double whammy. For one thing, they are less likely than younger women to receive Pap smears or mammograms. In 2000, for example, 43 percent of women age 75 and over had not had a Pap smear within the past two years and 39 percent had not had a mammogram during that time period. The corresponding figures for women in their fifties and early sixties were 16 percent and 21 percent, respectively (National Center for Health Statistics, 2003). In addition, physicians often attribute an older woman's chronic ailments to natural aging and consequently they are less apt to treat her for these conditions. For example, despite the fact that urinary incontinence, which affects more women than men, can be treated effectively using medical or behavioral means, many health professionals dismiss it as an inevitable part of the aging process (Pasupathi & Löckenhoff, 2002).

Women of Color and Health Care

Women of color are more likely than White women to be poor and uninsured (United States Census Bureau, 2003c). Latinas have the highest uninsurance rate of any group of women (DeNavas-Walt et al., 2004). Because the lack of health insurance is often a financial barrier to seeking preventive health care, women of color and poor women are less likely to get the medical care they need (Behbakht et al., 2004; Liao et al., 2004). In particular, women of color have often lacked access to preventive health services such as Pap smears, mammograms, and cholesterol screening (Liao et al., 2004; Ryerson et al., 2005). Furthermore, experiences with prejudice, language barriers, or culturally inappropriate health care cause many women of color to visit the doctor less frequently than White women do (Buki et al., 2004; "Making the Grade," 2004). In the words of one lower-income Latina woman "They don't understand my language, my culture, my issues" (Clemetson, 2002, p. A12). Breast cancer and cervical cancer screening rates are especially low among certain Latina subgroups, particularly poor Mexican and Dominican women. For many of these women, personal barriers such as fear, shame, and embarrassment prevent them from seeking screening (Behbakht et al., 2004; Garbers et al., 2003).

The good news is that the number of ethnic minority women receiving mammograms and Pap smears has risen substantially during the past decade (Ryerson et al., 2005). The bad news is that even when their insurance and income are the same, racial and ethnic minorities in the United States often receive health care of lower quality than Whites (Stolberg, 2002). In addition, poor women receiving Medicaid assistance have different reproductive health benefits than women with employment-based health insurance. Poor women on Medicaid receive mandated coverage of contraceptives, unlike working- and middle-class women. On the other hand, working- and middle-class women often have mandated coverage for infertility treatments which Medicaid does not cover. The result is a policy that discourages poor women from having children (Lott & Bullock, 2001).

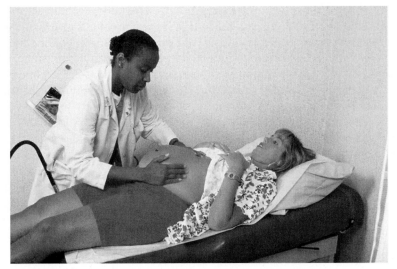

Female physicians are more likely than male physicians to establish rapport with their patients.

White women use both prescription and over-the-counter medications at a somewhat higher level than women of color (National Center for Health Statistics, 2004). One possible reason for this is that ethnic minority women may be more likely to encounter special difficulties procuring and using medications. Language differences and cultural differences in perceptions of illness can make communicating with the doctor especially problematic. As a result, ethnic minority women may have greater difficulty following a prescribed regimen (Torres et al., 2004).

Lesbian Health and Health Care

There is some evidence that lesbian and bisexual women may be at increased risk for certain health problems. These risks do *not*, however, arise simply from having a particular sexual orientation. Rather, certain risks may be more prevalent among lesbians because of lifestyle factors. For example, lesbian and bisexual women may face heightened risks of breast and ovarian cancer because they are less likely than heterosexual women to experience the hormonal changes associated with pregnancy and because they are more likely to smoke and consume alcohol (Case et al., 2004; Fish & Wilkinson, 2003; "Lesbian Community," 2004; Waitkevicz, 2004).

The social stigma attached to homosexuality also contributes to elevated health risks for lesbians by reducing access to health care (Bauer & Wayne, 2005; Brotman et al., 2003; Carlson et al., 2004). Surveys have found that many lesbians avoid going to the doctor for routine checkups—especially gynecological exams—because they feel uncomfortable talking about issues that may reveal their sexual orientation and consequently elicit negative reactions from the physician (Clark - et al., 2003; Marrazzo, 2004; Waitkevicz, 2004). In the words of one young woman, "If you lie, then you may not get the information you need to take care of yourself. And if you come out, your doctor may become really uncomfortable with you" (Thompson, 1999, p. A25). Lesbians also tend to limit their visits to doctors because they are less likely to have health insurance, since lesbians generally cannot share spousal benefits. Even for lesbians who do have coverage, managed health care plans often limit women's ability to choose lesbian-friendly health care providers. The reduced access to health care that results from fear of discrimination and from financial barriers puts lesbians at greater risk for preventable illnesses and makes them more likely to die from diseases that are treatable if detected early (Bradford & White, 2000; "Lesbian Community," 2004; Sved, 2001). Surveys of the health care choices of lesbians have found preferences for female practitioners, holistic approaches, preventive care and education, and woman-managed clinics (Lucas, 1992; Sved, 2001; Trippet & Bain, 1992).

Health Insurance

We have seen that women of color are more likely than White women to lack health insurance. Another group with a high rate of uninsurance are women in their late fifties and early sixties. Millions of these midlife women do not receive employer-based health insurance and are not yet eligible for Medicare benefits, which begin at age 65. Currently, one in seven women age 60–64 has no health insurance (OWL, 2004).

Let us now look at the kinds of insurance programs available to U.S. adults and see how they affect women. The types of insurance programs available to U.S. adults can be grouped into public plans (Medicare, Medicaid) and private plans (fee-for-service and managed care).

Medicare. **Medicare**, established in 1965, is the *federal program designed to provide medical care for those who are over 65 or permanently disabled, regardless of income.* Medicare covers less than half of medical costs and it does not cover most long-term care, or home and supportive care. These limitations affect women disproportionately because they have more, and more complex, medical conditions than men. In addition, some physicians do not accept Medicare patients because the reimbursement is low (AARP, 2005; Iglehart, 2002; Jacoby, 2002).

Medicaid. **Medicaid**, established the same year as Medicare, is a *combined state and federal program designed to provide medical care for the needy of any age.* As with Medicare, many health care providers refuse to see Medicaid recipients because of low reimbursement rates (Iglehart, 2003). These patients have no choice but to rely on clinics and emergency rooms.

Individuals with high medical bills who do not qualify for Medicaid *ultimately become eligible once they have depleted most of their financial resources and assets.* This process, called **spending down**, is most common among residents of nursing homes, most of whom are women (Beers & Jones, 2004; Meyer & Bellas, 1995).

Women rely more heavily than men on both Medicaid and Medicare because they are more likely to be poor and because they live longer (Older Women's League, 2000). Women are less likely than men to have insurance through their own employer since they are more likely to work in temporary or part-time jobs or in occupations that do not provide health insurance benefits. A woman who is covered under a spouse's plan risks losing coverage in the event of divorce, death, or the spouse's retirement (Older Women's League, 2004).

Private Insurance Plans.   The majority of Americans are covered by private health insurance provided by their own employer or the employer of a family member. One of the two types of private plans is **fee-for-service insurance** (also known as indemnity insurance). *The insurer pays part of the cost (usually 80 percent) for specified services, including hospitalization (up to a certain limit) and diagnostic services, but not preventive care* (AARP, 2002a, 2002b).

The second type of private insurance is **managed care**, which has become the leading means of financing health care (AARP, 2002a, 2002b). Managed care *provides services to members for a flat fee and emphasizes preventive care and early detection of disease more than fee-for-service plans do*. Health maintenance organizations (HMOs) and preferred provider organizations (PPOs) are the most common types of managed care. Providing inexpensive screening procedures such as mammograms and Pap tests makes the services affordable for many women. It is therefore not surprising that women in managed care are more likely than those in fee-for-service plans to receive Pap smears and colon-cancer screening (Katzenstein, 1999). Moreover, women over 65 in HMOs are more likely than fee-for-service patients to have had their cancers diagnosed at an earlier stage (Riley et al., 1999). However, managed care often limits access to specialists and reduces treatment options for many women, particularly older women who frequently have many chronic ailments requiring treatment by different specialists. Limited finances often prevent elderly women from seeing the physicians or purchasing the medications not covered by their managed care insurance (AARP, 2002a, 2002b; Older Women's League, 2004). Moreover, women enrolled in HMOs are more likely to report not getting needed care and having difficulties reaching their physician when needed. Women in HMOs are also less satisfied with their physicians than those not in HMOs (Collins & Simon, 1996).

Older women may view health and health care differently than younger women. To compare how these two groups view health issues, try Get Involved 12.1.

Sexually Transmitted Infections (STIs)

Sexually transmitted infections (STIs) have reached epidemic proportions, especially among young Americans ages 15–24. Over 9 million of the nearly 19 million new cases of STIs diagnosed in the United States in 2000 affected teens and young

GET INVOLVED 12.1

What Women Say about Their Health

Answer the following questions, which were included in a nationwide poll (Elder, 1997). Then ask two young adult women and two women age 65 or older to answer the same questions.

1. Whom would you trust more to be your doctor, a woman or a man, or would you trust them equally?
2. Which presents the more serious risk, heart disease or breast cancer?
3. How would you describe your health: excellent, good, fair, or poor?

4. In general, who has more health problems, men or women?
5. Who handles being sick better, women or men?
6. Whose complaints do doctors take more seriously: men's, women's, or about the same for both?
7. How often do doctors talk down to you? Most of the time, some of the time, hardly ever, or never?
8. Where do you get most of your medical information: doctors, television, newspapers and magazines, or the Internet?

What Does It Mean?

1. How do the responses of the older women compare with the information presented in the chapter?
2. How do the responses of the older women compare with the responses of your college-age friends? How can age account for these differences?

3. Can you think of any factors other than age that might account for any differences between the responses of the two groups of women?

---

adults (Weinstock et al., 2004). We will first give an overview of STIs (see Table 12.1) and then turn to AIDS, the most life-threatening of the STIs.

Overview of STIs

The most common STI in the United States today is chlamydia, followed by gonorrhea (Carlson et al., 2004). Rates of gonorrhea and chlamydia are extremely high among teenagers in the United States, compared to European nations, perhaps because those nations have more widespread and intensive prevention policies and provide better access to STI health care (Miller et al., 2004; Panchaud et al., 2000). If untreated, STIs can have serious consequences. Chlamydia and gonorrhea can lead to chronic pain, pelvic inflammatory disease, stillbirth, infertility, and even death (Altman, 2004a; Shih et al., 2004). In addition, the human papilloma virus that causes genital warts increases the risk of cervical cancer (Boonstra, 2004). People with syphilis, gonorrhea, chlamydia, or herpes are more likely than others to become infected with the AIDS virus, in part because they have open sores that allow the virus to enter the body (National Institutes of Health, 2004).

TABLE 12.1   Major Sexually Transmitted Infections (STIs)

STI	Mode of Transmission	Symptoms	Treatment
Gonorrhea	Vaginal, oral, or anal sex, or from mother to newborn during delivery	In women, vaginal discharge, burning urination, irregular menstrual periods	Antibiotics, e.g., ceftriaxone
Chlamydia (Most common STI)	Vaginal, oral, or anal sex, or from mother to newborn during delivery	In women, painful urination, lower abdominal pain, vaginal discharge	Antibiotics, e.g., doxycycline azithromycin
Syphilis	Vaginal, oral, or anal sex, or touching an infectious chancre (sore)	Initially, hard, round painless chancre (sore)	Antibiotics, e.g., penicillin, tetracycline
Genital herpes	Vaginal, oral, or anal sex; most contagious during active outbreaks	Painful sores around genitals, thighs, buttocks	Acyclovir (Zovirax) promotes healing but isn't a cure
Trichomoniasis	Sexual contact	In women, yellowish odorous vaginal discharge; itching, burning in vulva. Often, no symptoms	Metronidazole (Flagyl)
Genital warts	Sexual and other contact, such as infected towels, clothing	Painless warts on genital area or anus, or in vagina, cervix, or rectum	Cryosurgery (freezing), burning, surgical removal
Acquired immune deficiency syndrome (AIDS)	Sexual contact; infected blood transfusions; mother to fetus during pregnancy or through childbirth or breastfeeding	Fever, weight loss, fatigue, opportunistic infections such as rare forms of cancer and pneumonia	No cure. Antiretroviral drugs like AZT may delay progress of the disease

Source: Rathus et al. (2005), pp. 533–535, Table 16.1. Reprinted with permission from Allyn & Bacon.

STIs have a disproportionate impact on women. They are transmitted more easily to women than to men and are more difficult to diagnose in women (Altman, 2004a; National Institutes of Health, 2004). In addition, women may be at high risk of STIs because of social and cultural norms that dictate that women do not decline sexual intercourse with their partners or insist on the use of condoms (Pettifor et al., 2004). Factors that enhance a woman's risk for contracting STIs include being under 25, using condoms inconsistently, being sexually active at an early age, having sex frequently and with multiple partners, and using drugs or alcohol. Black and Latina females are at higher risk than White females (National Institutes of Health, 2004; Upchurch et al., 2004). Because the risk of woman-to-woman sexual transmission of STIs is small, the prevalence of STIs in lesbians is fairly low (Wingood & DiClemente, 2002). It is not zero, however, contrary to the beliefs of many lesbian women (Marrazzo et al., 2005).

One factor behind the rapid increase in STIs is that the majority of American women have relatively little knowledge of STIs and even less concern about contracting one. In one poll, for example, women and men were asked to name the two most common STIs. Only 13 percent of women named the human papilloma virus and only 3 percent mentioned trichomoniasis. Yet these two diseases account for about two-thirds of the new cases of STIs that occur annually in the United States (Dogar, 1999). Moreover, many women and adolescent girls are not very comfortable communicating with their partners or doctors about STIs (Ginty, 2000; Vastag, 2001). For more on this subject, see Learn about the Research 12.1.

AIDS

Acquired immunodeficiency syndrome (AIDS) is *caused by the human immunodeficiency virus (HIV)*. The most devastating of all the STIs, it is now the leading cause of death in Africa and the fourth leading cause of death worldwide (Bellamy, 2004). While the overall number of AIDS cases in the United States began to drop

---

LEARN ABOUT THE RESEARCH **12.1**

Knowledge and Communication about Sexually Transmitted Infections

In 1997, a telephone survey was conducted with a national sample of women from 18- to 44-years old who had been to a new gynecologist or obstetrician for the first time within the previous year (Lewin, 1997). Only 3 percent of the women believed they were at risk for sexually transmitted infections. When asked what STIs they were aware of, less than one-quarter could name chlamydia, the most common STI. Most of the women did not know that chlamydia and other STIs increased susceptibility to HIV infection. Only 15 percent of the women discussed STIs other than AIDS with their physician, and just 3 percent raised the topic themselves. HIV and AIDS were discussed in 21 percent of the visits, but only 2 percent of patients initiated the topic. Most women believed it was up to the physician to bring up the subject. Yet physicians are reluctant to broach the subject, for fear of offending their patients (Ginty, 2000). A recent survey found that fewer than one in 10 women ages 25–34 were advised by their gynecologist to get an STI test, despite the prevalence of many STIs in this age group (Salganicoff et al., 2003).

What Does It Mean?

1. Why do you think that most obstetricians and gynecologists do not discuss STIs with their patients?
2. What actions can be taken to better educate women about STIs? What do we need to teach young people in school on this topic?
3. What can be done to increase communication between a woman and her reproductive health care provider?

in the mid-90s, cases of HIV infection and AIDS among individuals of color have continued to increase. Women—particularly women of color—are the fastest-growing group of Americans infected with HIV. Heterosexual sex has become the leading method of transmission for women both in the United States and abroad (Ojikutu & Stone, 2005). For a closer look at the global AIDS epidemic, see Explore Other Cultures 12.1.

AIDS is the sixth leading cause of death in America for women age 25 to 34, but the leading cause of death for Black women in that age group (Anderson & Smith, 2004). Women accounted for nearly 30 percent of new HIV infections in the United States in 2000–2003 ("Diagnosis of HIV/AIDS," 2004). While many are young, low-income women of color who live in urban areas, the incidence of HIV-infected rural White women is also on the rise (Wingood & DiClemente, 2002). Black and Latina women, who constitute less than a quarter of American women, make up more than two-thirds of women with AIDS in the United States ("Diagnosis of HIV/AIDS," 2004; National Institutes of Health, 2004). Over 60 percent of American women with AIDS are Black, nearly one-fifth are White, and nearly one-fifth are Latina. Why are Black women at heightened risk for AIDS? According to researchers, one factor is the lower number of economically viable and available Black men, which may lead Black women to take more sexual risks in order to attract a partner (Cowley & Murr, 2004; Villarosa, 2004).

Women, especially those of color, are sicker at the time of diagnosis with HIV or AIDS and die more quickly than men with the disease (Villarosa, 2004). Why are women often diagnosed at a later stage of HIV than men? For one thing, women generally are viewed as being at low risk for the disease and so they and their physicians may overlook signs of HIV infection that they exhibit. Second, women usually serve as caregivers for family members and, increasingly, as breadwinners. As a result, they may delay seeking health care for themselves until they are very ill. Finally, many HIV-infected women live in poverty and do not have access to health care (Carlson et al., 2004; Cowley & Murr, 2004).

Decisions about childbearing can be difficult for HIV-infected women (Clark et al., 2004). Without any intervention, the chances of passing the virus to their children are 20 to 25 percent (Santora, 2005). In industrialized countries an infected woman who takes antiretroviral drugs during pregnancy, has a cesarean delivery, and who avoids breastfeeding has only about a 1 to 2 percent chance of infecting her child. But in developing countries, complex antiretroviral drug regimens are unavailable, and avoidance of breastfeeding is not a realistic option for most women (Coovadia, 2004). Consequently, many women with HIV must wrestle with the fact that their children may be infected and may also be motherless at a young age (Ciambrone, 2003). It is helpful for HIV-infected women to share dilemmas such as this with a support group (Wingood & DiClemente, 2002). Many of these women feel isolated and have not disclosed their illness out of fear of rejection and ostracism (Feist-Price & Wright, 2003; Herbert & Bachanas, 2002). Often, a support group may be a woman's first opportunity to meet other women with HIV or AIDS and to receive help in locating government-subsidized sources of anti-HIV medication (Cowley & Murr, 2004).

EXPLORE OTHER CULTURES **12.1**

The Global AIDS Epidemic

An estimated 40 million people worldwide, nearly half of them women, are infected with HIV (UNAIDS, 2004). Sub-Saharan Africa, with 10 percent of the world's population but two-thirds of the world's HIV/AIDS sufferers, is the most severely affected region. There, 60 percent of those infected are women (Cohen, 2004). Nearly 40 percent of pregnant women in parts of Botswana and 25 percent of those in South Africa have HIV (UNAIDS, 2003, 2004).

Adolescent girls and young women of childbearing age in Africa are two to five times more likely to develop HIV/AIDS than their male counterparts for a variety of biological, social, and economic reasons (Marton, 2004; UNAIDS, 2004). Many adolescent women marry older men, who have likely had several previous sexual partners. At the same time, cultural resistance to condom use is high. Moreover, most adolescents in sub-Saharan Africa do not know how to prevent AIDS (Bankole et al., 2004). These factors result in high rates of sexually transmitted infections, which increase chances of HIV transmission. In addition, the poverty, economic dependency, and low status of women render them powerless to protect themselves against unsafe or unwanted sex. In South Africa, for example, Kristin Dunkle and her colleagues (Dunkle et al., 2004) found that women with violent or controlling male partners are at increased risk of HIV infection. Abusive men were more likely to be infected themselves and imposed risky sexual practices on their partners. Sadly, the proportion of infected women is rapidly expanding in other parts of the world as well, particularly Eastern Europe and Central and Southeast Asia (Cohen, 2004; "The Feminization

of AIDS," 2004; UNAIDS, 2004). In India, where the vast majority of females with HIV are infected by their husbands, women who challenge their spouses by asking them to use condoms risk domestic violence. Those who contract HIV from their husbands may be abandoned by their families. Some then become sex workers to survive, further spreading the disease (Marton, 2004). Unfortunately, the majority of women and men in Africa, Asia, and Latin America—including those in countries with high rates of HIV— believe that they are at little or no risk of infection (Stephenson, 2002). Even those girls and women who do not contract HIV are deeply affected by the epidemic, since the burden of caring for the sick usually falls on them. Girls are often withdrawn from school to care for ailing parents or younger siblings, or to earn an income (United Nations Population Fund, 2004).

A handful of developing countries have had some success in slowing the spread of HIV through AIDS education and condom promotion, and in providing greater access to HIV treatment for those who are infected (UNAIDS, 2005). In sub-Saharan Africa, for example, Uganda and Zambia appear to be reversing their widespread epidemics (UNAIDS, 2003; United Nations Population Fund, 2004). In Thailand, the first nationwide program in a developing country to prevent transmission of HIV from mothers to newborns has been highly successful (Altman, 2002). Still, nine out of ten people who need HIV treatment are not being reached. Without treatment, 5 to 6 million people in developing countries will die of AIDS every two years (UNAIDS, 2004).

Adolescent girls and young women account for nearly 60 percent of Africans with HIV/AIDS.

The best way to prevent AIDS is to practice "safer sex," that is, avoid unprotected sex with multiple partners and always use latex condoms during sexual intercourse (Carlson et al., 2004; Crosby et al., 2003). The good news is that in recent years, American teenagers have shown improvement in these HIV-related sexual risk behaviors (Smith, 2003). Unfortunately, many young people, including college students, still fail to engage in safer-sex practices. Factors underlying these risky sexual behaviors include a perceived low risk of infection and negative attitudes toward condom use (Rathus et al., 2005).

AIDS in Older Women.   Whatever a woman's age, if she is sexually active, she is at risk for contracting sexually transmitted diseases, including HIV. Since older women are generally viewed as sexually disinterested and inactive, they are less likely to be given information about safer sex practices (Levy et al., 2003). Few educational and prevention programs target this age group (Altschuler et al., 2004).

Today, however, over 16,000 cases of AIDS among women aging 50 and older have been diagnosed, and the number of new cases per year is growing steadily (National Center for Health Statistics, 2004). In the mid-1980s, most AIDS cases among women in that age group were caused by blood transfusions. Now, heterosexual contact is the leading cause (Mack & Ory, 2003; McNeil, 2004). One factor putting older women at increased risk during heterosexual contact is the increased thinning of the vaginal tissues and the decrease in lubrication after menopause. These conditions can lead to small skin tears or abrasions during sexual activity that increase the chance of HIV entering the bloodstream (Levy et al., 2003). Another factor in the rise of HIV in the elderly is the increase in sexual activity fueled by Viagra, but without a corresponding increase in condom use (Zablotsky & Kennedy, 2003).

Older women who have HIV infection may have a harder time than infected younger women in obtaining a correct diagnosis and treatment. Physicians do not expect to see AIDS in older women (McNeil, 2004), and therefore they are more likely to make a late diagnosis or a misdiagnosis. Symptoms of AIDS resemble those of various age-related diseases including Alzheimer's, which is one of the most common misdiagnoses (McNeil, 2004). Women of this age group are also less likely to think of themselves as being at risk for AIDS, and so they may not think to ask for an HIV test (Zablotsky & Kennedy, 2003). Failure to diagnose HIV early can have serious consequences at any age since it is harder to arrest the disease when it becomes more advanced. But older adults with HIV are even more likely to deteriorate rapidly because of their already weakened immune system (Levy et al., 2003).

HIV infection takes an enormous emotional toll on older women, many of whom live alone and are already trying to cope with physical, economic, and personal losses. While today's younger women are used to talking more freely about sexual problems, this is difficult for many older women. They feel ashamed and may suffer alone, avoiding telling friends and family (Fowler, 2003). Some avoid intimate contact with grandchildren, such as kissing on the lips, for fear of endangering the youngsters. Those women who join therapy groups often find them to be a great source of emotional support (Ciambrone, 2003).

Reproductive System Disorders

Sexually transmitted infections are not the only diseases that can affect the reproductive system. We now turn to other disorders including benign (noncancerous) conditions such as endometriosis and fibroid tumors, as well as various cancers.

Benign Conditions

Endometriosis is a chronic and sometimes extremely painful condition in which the *lining of the uterus (endometrium) migrates and grows on pelvic structures, such as the ovaries, fallopian tubes, and bladder*. Nearly 7 percent of women are affected. Endometriosis can cause pelvic and menstrual pain and heavy bleeding. Severe endometriosis is a major cause of infertility (Carlson et al., 2004).

Up to three out of four women will develop **fibroid tumors**, which are *noncancerous growths of the uterus*, at some time in their lives. Fibroids are not dangerous, but they can cause severe pelvic pain, heavy bleeding, and possibly infertility and miscarriage. They occur more often in Black women than in White women (Carlson et al., 2004).

Cancers

Endometrial or uterine cancer is the most common cancer of the female reproductive tract and is often characterized by vaginal bleeding. It occurs most often in postmenopausal women, in obese women, and in smokers (Carlson et al., 2004; Viswanathan et al., 2005). Although it is more common in White women than in Black women, Black women are more likely to die from it. Because most cases are detected early, this is one of the most curable cancers of the reproductive system, with a five-year survival rate of 96 percent for localized uterine cancer (American Cancer Society, 2004).

Cancer of the **cervix**, *the lower end of the uterus*, is the third most common cancer of the female genital system, after uterine and ovarian cancer (Gingrich, 2004). In the United States, it has a five-year survival rate of more than 90 percent in its early stages (Feldman, 2003). Black, Latina, and Native American women, however, have a much higher death rate, probably because their more limited access to medical care prevents early diagnosis and treatment (Gingrich, 2004; Jemal et al., 2004). Factors that increase the risk of cervical cancer include smoking, obesity, early age at first intercourse, multiple sex partners, extended use of oral contraceptives, and infection with human papilloma virus (HPV), the common virus that causes genital warts (American Cancer Society, 2004; Smith et al., 2003). The **Pap smear**, *an inexpensive and effective screening technique*, has been used for over 50 years to identify precancerous changes in the cervix. The test has slashed cervical cancer deaths by 75 percent and saved tens of thousands of lives (Boonstra, 2004; Feldman, 2003). Of those women who develop cervical cancer in the United States, about half have never had a Pap smear (Boonstra, 2004). Women should start getting an annual Pap test by age 21 or three years after the onset of sexual activity, whichever comes first. If a woman 30 or older has had three normal test results in a row, the interval can increase to every two to three years (Gingrich, 2004). At that age, combining the Pap test with screening for HPV can save even more lives. Unfortunately, only 80 percent of women have Pap smears at least once every three years. Women who are poor, uninsured, less educated and elderly are least likely to get regular Pap tests (Behbakht et al., 2004; Ryerson et al., 2005). The good news is that a recently developed vaccine protects women against HPV and may virtually eliminate cervical cancer over the next several decades (Grady, 2004d).

Ovarian cancer received increased attention after the comedian Gilda Radner (1990) and the editor-in-chief of *Harper's Bazaar*, Liz Tilberis (1998), wrote books about their courageous fight against the disease, which ultimately killed them. Ovarian cancer is a major killer of women, accounting for 25 percent of all reproductive system cancers, but half of all deaths from these cancers. It is a so-called "silent killer" because its symptoms usually do not appear until the cancer is in an advanced stage. At that stage, the five-year survival rate is only 15 to 30 percent, and 72 percent when detected at the intermediate stage (American Cancer Society, 2004; Breedlove & Busenhart, 2005; Goff et al., 2004). Fortunately, a newly developed diagnostic test may be able to detect ovarian cancer in its early stages (Breedlove & Busenhart, 2005). One in 70 women will have ovarian cancer during their lifetimes ("Genetic Testing," 2004). Immediate family members of ovarian, breast, or colon cancer patients and women who take fertility drugs or hormone replacement therapy are at increased risk. However, bearing children, breastfeeding, and taking birth control pills are protective factors (Glud et al., 2004; Patlak,

2003; Petitti, 2003; Victory et al., 2004). Use of aspirin or acetaminophen (marketed as Tylenol) also reduces the risk of ovarian cancer (Troisi & Hartge, 2000; UPI, 2004).

Hysterectomy

Each year, over 600,000 women in the United States undergo a **hysterectomy**, the *removal of the uterus* (Kuppermann et al., 2004). By age 60, more than one in three American women have had their uterus removed, one of the highest rates in the world (Carlson et al., 2004). For years, many critics have questioned the high rate of hysterectomy in this country. While removal of the uterus is considered appropriate in cases of cancer of the uterus, cervix, or ovaries, these situations account for only a small fraction of the total (Carlson et al., 2004). Endometriosis, heavy menstrual bleeding, and chronic pelvic pain are other common reasons for hysterectomy (Torpy et al., 2004). But the most common reason is the presence of fibroid tumors (Carlson et al., 2004). Because Black women are more likely than White women to have fibroid tumors, their hysterectomy rates also are higher (Keshavarz et al., 2002). Other less invasive procedures, such as *blocking blood flow to the fibroids* (a procedure called **fibroid embolization**), are now available to women (Altman, 2004b).

These less invasive procedures may have fewer negative psychological effects than hysterectomy. For example, Jean Elson (2004) interviewed 44 women, ages 24 to 69, whose uterus had been removed for benign conditions. All the women reflected on their gender identity following surgery. Their reactions ranged all the way from "Now I feel like a fake woman" to "I have always been . . . the same person" (Ayoub, 2004, p. A18). Most of the women did not miss menstruation much, but they missed the potential to have children. This was true whether or not they already had children and even if they never intended to have them (Ayoub, 2004).

Another common practice, which has been heavily criticized, is the removal of the ovaries along with the uterus, even when the ovaries are normal and healthy. Physicians who carry out such surgery contend that when a women is in her mid-40s or older, the ovaries' major function is over and that removing them forestalls the possibility of ovarian cancer (Carlson et al., 2004). Can you see the sexist bias in this argument? Could one not equally argue that the prostate and testes of middle-aged men should be removed to prevent cancer of these organs?

Osteoporosis

Osteoporosis is an *excessive loss of bone tissue in older adults which results in the bones becoming thinner, brittle, and more porous.* Osteoporosis affects about 10 million Americans, 80 percent of them women (Grady, 2004b). But the seeds of osteoporosis are sown in adolescence. For females, 95 percent of bone mass is reached by age 17, and peak bone mass by age 25 (Brody, 2003c; Prendergast & Dalkin, 2004). At age 30, gradual bone loss begins. The rate of bone loss accelerates sharply for 10 years after

Osteoporosis increases after menopause and can lead to disabling and even fatal fractures.

the onset of menopause, as estrogen levels drop (Brody, 2003b). Each year, more than 1.3 million fractures related to osteoporosis occur in the United States. One in three women over 80 years of age will have a fracture of the hip during her lifetime. These fractures can be crippling and painful and can cause permanent loss of mobility. Moreover, 15 to 20 percent of patients with a hip fracture die of complications such as blood clots and pneumonia (Strewler, 2004).

Risk Factors

Some women are more likely to develop osteoporosis than others. For a list of risk factors, see Table 12.2. Postmenopausal women with one or more of these risk

TABLE 12.2   Risk Factors for Osteoporosis

Biological Factors

- Gender: Women's risk is greater because their bones are smaller and lighter
- Age: After age 30, bone loss begins
- Menopause: Drop in estrogen levels increases bone loss
- Thin, small-framed body
- Ethnic background: White, Latina, Asian American, and Native American women are at higher risk than Black women, who have heavier bone density
- Family history of osteoporosis (older relatives who have had fractures or spinal curvature)

Lifestyle Factors

- Diet low in calcium and vitamin D
- High salt intake, leading to excretion of calcium
- Lack of physical activity
- Smoking
- Excessive alcohol and caffeine consumption

Medical Factors

- Medical history of rheumatoid arthritis, liver disease, thyroid disorder
- Eating disorders
- Certain medications: diuretics, steroids, anticonvulsants

Sources: Gourlay & Brown (2004); National Osteoporosis Foundation (2004); Raisz (2004).

factors, and all women over 65, should consider getting a bone density test, which can detect even a small loss of bone mass (Lewiecki, 2004).

Prevention and Treatment

A look at Table 12.2 indicates some ways to build and keep as much bone as possible. Increasing calcium intake during childhood, adolescence, and young adulthood is the most effective way of building denser bones. In order to suppress bone loss, the National Institutes of Health recommends consumption of 1,300 milligrams of calcium per day for adolescents, 1,000 milligrams for women 19 to 50, and 1,200 milligrams for postmenopausal women. Good sources of calcium include low-fat and nonfat milk, cheese, and yogurt; tofu; dark-green leafy vegetables such as kale and turnip greens; and canned sardines and salmon (with the bones) (U.S. Department of Health and Human Services, 2004b).

Unfortunately, adolescents consume far less calcium than they should, and their calcium intake has been declining over the past 30 years. Teenage girls now drink 50 percent more soft drinks and one-third less milk than they did in 1977 (O'Neil, 2003). The result is that only 14 percent of adolescent girls consume adequate amounts of calcium (Brody, 2003a). In addition, most women consume only about half the daily amount of calcium they need. Calcium supplements are good additional sources, especially those containing calcium carbonate (found in Tums and Rolaids) or calcium citrate (found in Citracal). The body can absorb up to 500 milligrams of calcium at a time so if a person takes 1,000 milligrams per day, it should be divided into two doses (U.S. Department of Health and Human Services, 2004b).

Calcium cannot be absorbed without vitamin D. Many women do not get the 800 international units of vitamin D per day shown to sharply decrease the likelihood of osteoporosis and bone fractures. Milk fortified with vitamin D and sunlight are two of its best sources. As little as 15 minutes per day in the sun helps the body produce Vitamin D (Brody, 2003a). Still, most adults may need dietary supplements in order to prevent vitamin D deficiency (U.S. Department of Health and Human Services, 2004b).

Diet is only part of the equation, however. Exercise is very important in increasing bone mass during adolescence and young adulthood (Lloyd et al., 2004) and in slowing bone loss after menopause. The exercise should be weightbearing, such as brisk walking, low-impact aerobics, or lifting weights. Even everyday activities such as climbing stairs, walking the dog, doing yard work, or playing actively with children can be beneficial. It is never too late to start exercising and a little bit of physical activity is better than none (Beers & Jones, 2004; Cassel, 2002; U.S. Department of Health and Human Services, 2004b).

Decreasing or eliminating smoking and decreasing consumption of alcohol and most sources of caffeine are good not only for strong bones but may also confer many other health benefits, as we shall see later in the chapter. Drinking black or green tea, however, seems to strengthen bones (Wu et al., 2002).

Estrogen helps build and maintain strong bones. Estrogen replacement therapy starting in perimenopause and continuing after menopause slows bone loss, increases bone mass, and reduces the incidence of fractures (Banks et al., 2004; U.S. Department of Health and Human Services, 2004b). However, because hormone replacement therapy now is known to increase the risk of heart attack, stroke, and breast cancer (see Chapter 7), it is no longer considered an option for preventing osteoporosis (Prendergast & Dalkin, 2004). Fortunately, other medications can help a woman strengthen her bones.

Drugs called bisphosphonates, such as alendronate (marketed as Fosamax), increase bone mass and decrease the risk of hip and spinal fractures. **Raloxifene,** a *synthetic estrogen* marketed as Evista, also increases bone density in postmenopausal women and reduces the risk of spinal fractures. It is not, however, as effective as natural estrogen or alendronate in building bone mass. Tamoxifen, used to treat and prevent breast cancer, maintains bone mass and is a good choice for women with estrogen-sensitive cancer. Another option is calcitonin, but it is the least powerful of the bone builders (Brody, 2003c; Kolata, 2003; Solomon & Dluhy, 2003).

Heart Disease

Heart disease is a major health threat for both women and men around the world (Mitka, 2004) and the number one killer of American women. More women in the United States die of heart disease than from all forms of cancer combined, including breast cancer (Stoney, 2003). Furthermore, women's death rate from heart disease has been increasing while that of men is declining (Hayes et al., 2003). Yet women show a devastating lack of awareness of the risks of heart disease. Most women perceive breast cancer as a far greater threat to their health than heart disease. Although nearly 30 percent of American women die from heart disease annually, only 10 percent fear it as their greatest health risk. Conversely, only 4 percent will die of breast cancer, even though 22 percent of women fear dying from it (Society for Women's Health Research, 2005). While awareness that heart disease is the top killer of women has grown since 2000, awareness of risk factors for the disease remains low, particularly for women younger than age 45 and for ethnic minority groups (Mosca et al., 2004).

Gender Differences

Heart disease in women becomes apparent about 10 years later than in men. Illness and death from heart disease increase dramatically in women after menopause, due partly to declining estrogen levels. By age 75, a woman has a greater risk of heart attack and heart disease than a man her age (Brody, 2005). Women are more likely than men to die after a heart attack (Kalb & Springen, 2004; King et al., 2004). If they survive, they are more likely to have a second attack (Hong et al., 2003). Since women are older than men when they develop heart disease, their prognosis is poorer (Kalb & Springen, 2004). But women are more likely than men to die after treatment for heart disease, even when they are equally old and ill ("Heart Attacks," 2002).

Risk Factors

Some risk factors for heart disease are unchangeable. In addition to gender and age, these include ethnicity and family history. The death rate from heart attack is higher for Black women than White women, who, in turn, are much more likely to die from heart disease then are Latina, Native American, and Asian American women. In addition, the risk of heart disease and stroke increases if close family members have had these diseases ("Disparities in Premature Deaths," 2004; Jha et al., 2003; Lloyd-Jones et al., 2004; Newton et al., 2000).

Major risk factors over which women have control include physical inactivity, smoking, being overweight, having a poor diet, and using hormone replacement therapy (Col & Komaroff, 2004; Paynter et al., 2004). Women who have none of these factors have a much lower risk of heart disease than other women. Even young women, who have a low rate of heart disease, should begin controlling these risk factors early in life (Daviglus et al., 2004; McGill & McMahan, 2003).

Inactivity is a major risk factor in heart disease and stroke. Sedentary women are nine times more likely to die from cardiovascular disease than women who are very active. Women benefit from vigorous exercise such as aerobics, running, biking, or swimming for at least 30 minutes, three to four times a week. But even moderate everyday activities such as a brisk walk, gardening, household chores, and climbing stairs for a total of 30 minutes on most days provide health benefits (American Heart Association, 2004; Beers & Jones, 2004; Blair & Church, 2004; Slentz et al., 2004). Unfortunately, more than 80 percent of American women are sedentary or do not engage in any regular physical activity. In addition, women become even less active as they get older, when they most need the cardiovascular benefits of exercise (Kimm et al., 2002; U.S. Census Bureau, 2003c).

High blood pressure (hypertension) is another major risk factor for heart attack and the most important risk factor for stroke (Hong et al., 2003). By their sixties, at least half of all women—but nearly 80 percent of postmenopausal Black women—have high blood pressure (Newton et al., 2000). Latinas and Asian-American women, on the other hand, have lower than average rates (Carlson et al., 2004). Reducing salt intake, losing weight (if overweight), exercising, eating a fiber-rich diet, and taking medication (if needed) can bring blood pressure under control (Carlson et al., 2004; Streppel et al., 2005).

Women with *diabetes* are more likely to have a heart attack or stroke than are nondiabetic women. Diabetes may be delayed by controlling blood sugar, eating less saturated fat, staying physically active, and maintaining a normal weight (American Heart Association, 2004; Beers & Jones, 2004). Being *overweight* also increases the risk of both heart attack and stroke. Overweight individuals are more likely to develop high blood pressure, high cholesterol levels, and diabetes (Hong et al., 2003). The good news is that dropping just 10 percent of one's body weight can lower cholesterol, blood pressure, and the risk of diabetes (Grady, 2003).

Smoking is a powerful risk factor for heart disease and stroke in women. A woman who smokes is two to six times as likely to have a heart attack as a non-smoker and is more apt to die from the heart attack (Canto & Iskandrian, 2003). Smoking is especially harmful in women because it decreases estrogen's protective effects and can cause menopause to occur about two years early. Half of all heart attacks in middle-aged women are attributed to smoking, and the vast majority of women who develop heart disease before age 50 are smokers (Olson & Warren, 2000). The good news is that chances of dying from heart disease are cut in half within a year of quitting smoking and are as low as a nonsmoker's chances within 15 years after stopping (American Heart Association, 2002).

Diet also is important in reducing the risk of heart disease and stroke. A heart-healthy diet—sometimes called "the Mediterranean diet"—is rich in vegetables and fruits, whole grains, nuts, monounsaturated oils (olive, canola), and protein derived from fish, beans, low-fat or nonfat dairy products, lean meats,

Being overweight increases a woman's risk of heart attack, stroke, breast cancer, and diabetes.

and poultry (American Heart Association, 2004; Brody, 2003c; Mozafarrian et al., 2005). Drinking black or green tea also appears to protect against heart disease, especially in women. In addition, women who consume one alcoholic drink per day are less likely to suffer a heart attack or stroke than women who do not drink (Rehm et al., 2002). Red wine may be especially beneficial (Brody, 2003b).

Hormones also affect heart disease. Older forms of *birth control pills*, which contained high levels of estrogen and progestin, increased women's risk of heart disease and stroke. Newer versions of the pill contain lower hormone doses and actually decrease the chances of these diseases (Victory et al., 2004). As noted earlier in the chapter, *hormone replacement therapy* increases the risk of heart disease in postmenopausal women.

Men with aspects of so-called Type A personality—particularly anger, hostility, and time urgency/impatience—are more prone to develop high blood pressure and heart disease (Smith, 2003; Williams et al., 2003), but women do not show this association (Eaker et al., 2004). Several recent studies, however, show that, for both women and men, depression is strongly associated with getting heart disease and with dying from it (see review by Frasure-Smith & Lespérance, 2005). Since women are more likely than men to be depressed (see Chapter 13), this factor increases women's risk. In addition, women who are divorced, widowed, or unhappily married have a higher risk of heart disease than women who are satisfied with their marriages (Troxel et al., 2005).

Diagnosis and Treatment

The management, diagnosis, and treatment of heart disease in women are poorly understood and often carried out in an inconsistent manner. The result is that women receive poorer care (Godfrey, 2005; Travis, 2005). Women with heart disease often do not receive the aggressive treatment from physicians that men do (Carlson et al., 2004; Kalb & Springen, 2004; Vaccarino et al., 2005). For one thing, physicians often miss the signs of heart disease and heart attack in women because women are less likely to show the "classic" symptom of chest pain and are more apt than men to show symptoms such as nausea, dizziness, shortness of breath, sweating, chest pressure or heaviness, unusual fatigue, sleep disturbance, back or abdominal pain, heartburn, heart palpitations, or just an odd, unwell feeling. Women may be misdiagnosed as simply suffering from indigestion, muscle pain, stress, or anxiety (Godfrey, 2005; Krantz et al., 2004; Schoenberg et al., 2003). In addition, women are often believed to be less threatened by heart disease or less responsive to treatment, both of which are untrue (Travis & Compton, 2001; Welty, 2001). In one recent online survey of 500 randomly selected physicians, women at risk of developing heart disease were more likely than men to be assigned to a low-risk category. They were less likely to be advised to change their living habits and to take medications to help prevent heart attacks (Brody, 2005). Even when women experience the classic symptom of pain, they are more reluctant than men to seek medical care, believing that they would be "wasting the doctor's time" (Richards et al., 2002). Sometimes they ignore the symptoms because they are too busy taking care of everybody else (Kalb & Springen, 2004; Schoenberg et al., 2003).

When women do show up at the emergency room with the classic heart attack symptoms, they are less likely then men to be admitted for evaluation (Washington & Bird, 2002). Furthermore, they are not as likely than men to receive one of the most important diagnostic heart tests, the angiogram, which can show blockage in coronary arteries (Krantz et al., 2004). Women heart patients also are less likely to receive cholesterol-lowering drugs, devices such as pacemakers, or stents (to open clogged arteries), or treatments such as angioplasty (also used to clear arteries) or coronary bypass surgery. And in the critical hours following a heart attack, fewer women are given clot-dissolving drugs (Carlson et al., 2004; Kalb & Springen, 2004; Stoney, 2003) and they wait longer than men to receive an emergency angioplasty to open blocked arteries ("Women & Heart Health," 2005). Do these gender differences occur because physicians hesitate to give risky procedures to women, who are older and more ill than men when they are diagnosed? This may be part of the answer. But even when women and men are the same age and have identical symptoms and conditions, women are less likely to receive these treatments (Knox & Czajkowski, 1997). Moreover, they are less often given aspirin, which aids in dissolving blood clots, or beta-blockers, which protect against future heart attacks (Kalb & Springen, 2004). Women also get fewer referrals for cardiac rehabilitation programs following heart attacks, even though they benefit from therapy at least as much as men do (Krantz et al., 2004; Stoney, 2003; "Women & Heart Health," 2005). In addition, women are often underrepresented in studies designed to test the effectiveness of such programs (Bittner & Sanderson, 2003).

Psychological Impact

The psychosocial health of women following a heart attack or coronary bypass surgery is worse than that of men (Brukner, 2003). Women are more anxious and depressed, return to work less often, take longer to recuperate physically, and resume their sex lives later than men. In spite of their poorer heath, women resume household activities sooner than men and are more likely to feel guilty that they cannot quickly resume the chores they once did (Carlson et al., 2004; Epstein, 2001; Knox & Czajkowski, 1997). Women's poorer psychosocial functioning after heart attack and heart surgery can take a toll on their well-being, productivity, and quality of life. In addition, the greater depression experienced by women after heart attack or heart surgery is associated with a greater risk of death and of second heart attacks. Health care providers need to become aware of the potential difficulties faced by women with heart disease and to take steps to enhance the recovery of their female patients (Carlson et al., 2004; Knox & Czajkowski, 1997).

Breast Cancer

As we noted earlier, women fear breast cancer more than any other disease including heart disease, the top killer of women (Kalb & Springen, 2004). Yet breast cancer is not even the number one cancer killer of women. That dubious distinction falls to lung cancer (National Center for Health Statistics, 2003). One out of every eight women will develop breast cancer at some time in her life (Carlson et al., 2004). Although this statistic sounds frightening, it represents a lifetime risk. At age 40, only 1 in 217 women develops breast cancer. At age 50, the risk increases to 1 in 54 women and at age 70, it rises to 1 in 14. Only for women who are 90 years and older is the risk 1 in 8.

The majority of women in whom breast cancer is diagnosed—70 percent—do not die of the disease. Moreover, the death rate from breast cancer has been dropping in recent years as a result of earlier detection and improved treatments (American Cancer Society, 2004). As of 2003, the five-year survival rate for women with localized breast cancer was 97 percent. Even if the cancer has spread to lymph nodes, 79 percent of women will be alive five years later. If it invades bones or other organs, the rate drops to 23 percent (American Cancer Society, 2004).

Why is the prospect of getting breast cancer so terrifying? According to Jane Brody (1999) and Ellen Ratner (1999), both breast cancer survivors and authors, the extensive publicity given to the disease in recent years in order to stimulate research and raise women's awareness has created the misleading impression that breast cancer is more common and more deadly than it actually is. In addition, while only a small number of women die of breast cancer in their 30s and 40s, their untimely deaths may trigger greater alarm than the heart attack deaths of a far greater number of women later in life.

Risk Factors

Age, as we have just seen, is the greatest risk factor for breast cancer. In fact, 70 percent of women who develop breast cancer have no risk factors other than age (Smith et al., 2000).

Ethnicity and *social class* are also risk factors. White women are slightly more likely than Black women to get breast cancer overall, but Black women are far more likely to die from it (Jemal et al., 2004; National Center for Health Statistics, 2003). Part of the reason is that Black women are poorer. Low-income women, regardless of race, are diagnosed later, receive lower quality of care, and are more likely to die of breast cancer than other women (Adams et al., 2004; Bradley et al., 2002). But in addition, the tumors of Black women appear to be faster growing and more malignant. Even when Black and White women wait the same amount of time to see a doctor after they first detect signs of breast cancer, the Black women's cancers are already more advanced (American Cancer Society, 2004; Royak-Schaler et al., 2003; Vastag, 2003).

Family history of breast cancer—especially in one's mother, sister, or daughter—is another risk factor, accounting for 5 to 10 percent of breast cancers (Carlson et al., 2004). A small percentage of women with a family history of breast cancer have unusually high risk—60 to 85 percent—as a result of inheriting one of two breast cancer genes, BRCA-1 and BRCA-2. Inherited breast cancer occurs at younger ages, is more likely to affect both breasts, and often appears in multiple family members, including men, over several generations. The genes are more common in Jewish women of Eastern European origin than in other groups (Grady, 2002b, 2003; Wooster & Weber, 2003).

Age, ethnicity, and family history are risk factors women cannot change. Other factors over which they have little or no control include *early age at menarche, late age at menopause, late age at first birth* (after 30), and *having no or few children*. All these events lengthen the amount of time women's breast tissue is exposed to high levels of estrogen, which can stimulate growth of breast cancer cells (American Cancer Society, 2004; Michels & Willett, 2004).

Women can reduce their risk of breast cancer by making certain lifestyle choices. One of these choices is not *smoking* (Al-Delaimy et al., 2004; Cerhan et al., 2004). Consumption of two or more *alcoholic* drinks per day also increases the risk of developing breast cancer (Horn-Ross et al., 2004).

The role of *fat consumption* in breast cancer is controversial. Most studies have found no link between overall fat intake and incidence of breast cancer (Holmes & Kroenke, 2004). Some research, however, has shown that the *type* of fat is important ("Breast Cancer," 2003; Menendez et al., 2005; Wolk et al., 1998). Monounsaturated fat (olive oil, canola oil) may reduce the risk of breast cancer, whereas polyunsaturated fat (corn, safflower, and soybean oil) and animal fat may increase it. *High-carbohydrate diets*, especially those high in refined sugars, also are linked to greater risk of breast cancer (Cerhan et al., 2004; Romieu et al., 2004).

The more *weight* a woman gains during adulthood, the greater are her chances of developing breast cancer (Cerhan et al., 2004; Feigelson et al., 2004). Body fat produces estrogen which can help breast cancer grow. One way to reduce fat is to engage in *physical activity*. Strenuous exercise in adolescence and young adulthood can delay onset of menstruation or interrupt it. This lowers a woman's overall exposure to estrogen, possibly inhibiting development of breast cancer. Even among premenopausal and postmenopausal women, physical activity reduces breast cancer risk, most likely because it reduces body fat (Cerhan et al., 2004; Holmes & Kroenke, 2004). Use of *birth control pills* does not increase breast cancer risk in White or Black women, even among those who started taking the pill early in life (Marchbanks et al., 2002). However, we have seen that *hormone replacement therapy* does increase risk (American Cancer Society, 2003). To assess your risk of breast cancer, try Get Involved 12.2.

Detection

Despite recent research that questions the usefulness of breast self-examination (Springen & Fragala, 2002), the American Cancer Society recommends that women age 20 and older do a monthly breast self-examination about a week after their menstrual period ends (during menstruation breasts have normal lumps) (Smith & Saslow, 2002). Figure 12.1 provides instructions. Many women do not examine their breasts, partly out of fear of finding a lump. (Keep in mind that 80 to 90 percent of all lumps are noncancerous.) This is unfortunate, because a substantial portion of breast cancers are found during self-examination, particularly among women under 50 (Zuger, 1998). A major reason for this is that mammograms are less effective at detecting tumors in dense young breast tissue (Kalb, 2004b). Women with dense breast tissue are encouraged to use ultrasound to help find early breast cancer (Elliott, 2004). All women should also have a clinical breast exam by a health professional every three years from ages 20 to 39 years and annually from age 40 onward (American Cancer Society, 2003).

A **mammogram,** *a low-dose X-ray picture of the breast*, detects small suspicious lumps up to two years before they are large enough to be felt. Most experts believe that regular mammogram screening is a potential life-saving tool, particularly for women over 50 (Ryerson et al., 2005). Despite recent debates about whether mammograms actually help reduce breast cancer deaths (Consedine et al., 2004; Schwartz et al., 2004), medical experts and major health organizations such as the American Cancer Society and the National Cancer Institute continue to recommend a yearly mammogram for women over 40 (Elmore et al., 2005). Nationwide, the number of women who are screened continues to increase. Now, nearly 75 percent of eligible women have had a mammogram in the last year or two (Sherman, 2002). However, women with low income or less

GET INVOLVED **12.2**

Assessing Your Risk Breast Cancer

Read each question below and circle the number in the parentheses following your response. Then give the questionnaire to female friends and relatives, including both young and older women.

1. Age group: a. under 40 (1) b. 40-49 (5) c. 50 and over (10)
2. Ethnicity: a Asian (1) b. Latina (1) c. Black (2) d. White (3)
3. Family history: a. None (1) b. Mother, sister daughter with breast cancer (3)
4. Your history: a. No breast disease (1) b. Previous breast cancer (10)
5. Age at menarche: a. Late (1) b. Early (2)
6. Age at menopause: a. Have not reached menopause (1) b. Reached menopause before 50 (2) c. Reached menopause after 50 (3)
7. Pregnancy: a. first pregnancy before 30 (1) b. first pregnancy at age 30 or older (2) c. No pregnancy (3)
8. Smoking: a. Never smoked (1) b. Am a light smoker (2) c. Am a heavy smoker (3)
9. Drinking: a. Have one or fewer drinks a day (1) b. Have two or more drinks a day (2)

Individual numbers for specific questions should not be interpreted as an exact measure of relative risk, but the totals give a general indication of your risk.

10. Physical activity: a. Engage in vigorous physical activity (1) b. Engage in moderate amount of physical activity most days (2) c. Engage in little or no physical activity (3)
11. Weight gain in adulthood: a. Little or none (1) b. About 8–10 lbs (2) c. More than 10 lbs (3)
12. Do a monthly breast self-exam: a. No (0) b. Yes (Subtract 1)
13. Have had a normal clinical breast exam by a health professional: a. No (0) b. Yes (Subtract 1)
14. Have had a normal mammogram: a. No (0) b. Yes (Subtract 1)

Total: _____

Under 14 shows low risk; 14–22 means moderate risk; over 22 indicates high risk.

What Does It Mean?

1. How did breast cancer risk vary with the age of your respondents?
2. Did you find age differences in the use of early detection procedures?
3. What advice can you give to your respondents who have moderate to high risk of breast cancer?

---

than a high school education, who have more limited access to affordable health care, are more likely to delay the onset of screening (Colbert et al., 2004) or not get screened at all (Ryerson et al., 2005). Some women avoid mammograms because they fear the pain or discomfort of the procedure itself, while others fear receiving a breast cancer diagnosis (Consedine et al., 2004).

Since breast cancer typically strikes after age 50, some women and their doctors may ignore early warning signs, such as a self-detected small lump, assuming

How to Examine Your Breasts

Do you know that 95% of breast cancers are discovered first by women themselves? And that the earlier the breast cancer is detected, the better the chance for a complete cure? Of course, most lumps or changes are not cancer. But you can safeguard your health by making a habit of examining your breasts once a month – a day or two after your period or, if you're no longer menstruating, on any given day. And if you notice anything changed or unusual – a lump, thickening, or discharge – contact your doctor right away.

How to Look for Changes

Step 1
Sit or stand in front of a mirror with your arms at your side. Turning slowly from side to side, check your breasts for
- changes in size or shape
- puckering or dimpling of the skin
- changes in size or position of one nipple compared to the other

Step 2
Raise your arms above your head and repeat the examination in Step 1.

Step 3
Gently press each nipple with your fingertips to see if there is any discharge.

How to Feel for Changes

Step 1
Lie down and put a pillow or folded bath towel under your left shoulder. Then place your left hand under your head. (From now on you will be feeling for a lump or thickening in your breasts.)

Step 2
Imagine that your breast is divided into quarters.

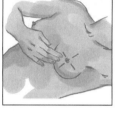

Step 3
With the fingers of your right hand held together, press firmly but gently, using small circular motions to feel the inner, upper quarter of your left breast. Start at your breastbone and work toward the nipple. Also examine the area around the nipple. Now do the same for the lower, inner portion of your breast.

Step 4
Next, bring your arm to your side and feel under your left armpit for swelling.

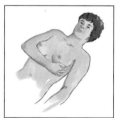

Step 5
With your arm still down, feel the upper, outer part of your breast, starting with your nipple and working outwards. Examine the lower, outer quarter in the same way.

Step 6
Now place the pillow under your right shoulder and repeat all the steps using your left hand to examine your right breast.

FIGURE 12.1 Doing a Breast Self-Examination

Source: From American Cancer Society (1997). Reprinted with permission.

it's only a benign cyst. Consequently, young women tend to be diagnosed when their disease has progressed further (Leibson-Hawkins, 2004).

Treatment

When breast cancer is diagnosed, several treatment options are available. For many years, the standard treatment was **radical mastectomy,** *the removal of the*

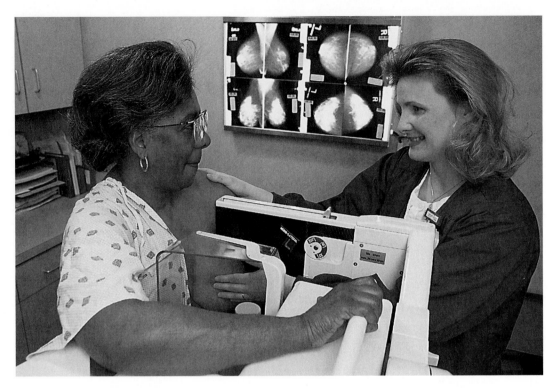

Women over the age of 40 should receive a yearly mammogram.

breast, underlying chest wall, and underarm lymph nodes. Because of disfigurement and side effects, it now is rarely done. **Modified radical mastectomy** involves *removal of the breast and underarm lymph nodes* and **simple mastectomy,** *removal of the breast only.* In **lumpectomy,** also known as partial mastectomy or breast-conserving surgery, only *the lump and some surrounding tissue are removed.* Lumpectomy is almost always followed by several weeks of radiation. For small tumors in the early stages of disease, lumpectomy followed by radiation is as effective in terms of 20-year survival as mastectomy (American Cancer Society, 2004).

Chemotherapy may be used to kill cancer cells that the surgeon was not able to remove. An alternative drug is the estrogen blocker tamoxifen, which cuts rates of breast cancer recurrence by as much as half, and helps *prevent* breast cancer among women at high risk for the disease (Piccart-Gebhart, 2004; Underwood, 2004). Combining tamoxifen with standard chemotherapy is more effective than either by itself (Grady, 2005). A new class of drugs called aromatase inhibitors may work even better than these treatments in preventing breast cancer recurrence (Coombes et al., 2004; Morandi et al., 2004; Piccart-Gebhart, 2004). Another drug, Herceptin, shrinks tumors in women who have a certain type of fast-growing cancer or whose advanced breast cancer is not responsive to other treatments (Raymond & Cowley, 2005).

Psychological Impact

The diagnosis of breast cancer and the surgery that often follows causes depression, anxiety, and anger in most women (Andersen & Farrar, 2001; Smith & Saslow, 2002). If the cancer recurs at some point after treatment, women may experience even higher levels of distress. Concerns about bodily appearance can be substantial for women who have had breast surgery. Lumpectomy has a more positive effect on body image and sexual functioning than mastectomy (Compas & Luecken, 2002).

Individual differences in reactions to breast cancer vary considerably. Young women appear to be affected more negatively than middle-aged or older women. They are more likely to have to deal with disruptions in family life and careers, as well as problems with fertility and sexual functioning. Consequently, they show greater declines in social functioning, mental health, and quality of life (Kroenke et al., 2004). But regardless of age, women with a "fighting spirit," higher levels of hostility, and those who voice their fears and anxieties survive breast cancer longer than those who show passive acceptance, stoicism, emotional inhibition, feelings of hopelessness, or denial of facts about the cancer (Compas & Luecken, 2002; Ray, 2004; Revenson, 2001).

The importance of support groups in helping women cope with cancer cannot be underestimated. David Spiegel and his colleagues (Spiegel et al., 1989; Spiegel, 1998) found that after attending weekly group therapy sessions for a year, women with advanced breast cancer showed less emotional distress and more adaptive coping responses than women who had been assigned to a control group. A 10-year follow-up found that the women in group therapy had lived on average twice as long (36.6 versus 18.9 months from entry in the study to death) as women in the control group. One reason for this is that psychological intervention can increase levels of an antibody that fights breast cancer tumors (Andersen & Emery, 1999). While social support does not always improve survival rates, it can enhance quality of life, mood, energy levels, and tolerance of chemotherapy and reduce depression and pain (Andersen & Emery, 1999; Goodwin et al., 2001; Nagourney, 2004). Overall, psychosocial interventions that focus on reducing stress, increasing knowledge and improving coping skills give breast cancer patients a greater sense of control, improved body image and sexual functioning, reduced distress, and greater adherence to their prescribed course of therapy (Dittman, 2003; Smith & Saslow, 2002; Taylor et al., 2003).

Physical Health in Later Life

In this section, we examine factors contributing to women's health in later life. We also explore gender differences in **mortality** (*death rates*) and in **morbidity** (*illness*), look at disability in old age and, finally, discuss the conditions that promote good health.

Gender Differences in Mortality

Women are sicker; Men die quicker. This old saying sums up what is often referred to as the **gender paradox:** *women live longer than men, but in poorer health* (Crimmins et al., 2002; Goldman & Hatch, 2000).

The female-male mortality gap begins before birth. While 115 males are conceived for every 100 females, the rate of miscarriage and stillbirth is higher for males. Although about 105 live males are born for every 100 live females, more male babies die in infancy (Arias, 2004) and thereafter throughout life. Starting with the 40 to 44 age group, women outnumber men (U.S. Census Bureau, 2005). Between ages 65 and 69, only 81 males survive for every 100 females. Between ages 80 and 84, the ratio is down to 53 to 100, and by age 100, women outnumber men four to one (Cavanaugh & Blanchard-Fields, 2006; Jones, 2003).

At the turn of the twentieth century, life expectancy in the United States was about 51 years for women and 48 years for men. Since then, the gender gap has widened. Life expectancy at birth now is about 80 for women and 5½ years less for men. The gender gap exists for both Blacks and Whites. White women tend to outlive White men by five years (80.5 versus 75.4) and Black women, on average, outlive Black men by nearly seven years (76.1 versus 69.2) (Hoyert et al., 2005). Why do women outlive men? Some explanations focus on biological factors, others on lifestyle behavioral differences.

Biology. One biological explanation is that women's second X chromosome protects them against certain lethal diseases—such as hemophilia and some forms of muscular dystrophy—that are more apt to occur in individuals (i.e., men) who have only one X chromosome. Another biological reason for women's greater longevity is their higher estrogen levels, which seem to provide protection against fatal conditions such as heart disease (Belsky, 2001). In addition, women have a lower rate of metabolism, which is linked to greater longevity. Another suggestion is that women's immune systems are more robust than men's, making men more susceptible to contracting certain fatal diseases (Gaylord, 2001; Perls & Fretts, 1998).

Lifestyle Behaviors. One lifestyle factor accounting for the gender gap in mortality is that males are more likely than females to engage in potentially risky behaviors such as smoking, drinking, violence, and reckless driving. They also may be exposed to more hazardous workplace conditions (Bogg & Roberts, 2004; Grunbaum et al., 2004; Vyrostek et al., 2004). Table 12.3 shows that accidents and unintentional injuries are the third leading cause of death of males, but the seventh leading cause for females. Cirrhosis, caused largely by excessive drinking, is the tenth most common cause of death for males but does not appear on the "Top Ten" list for females.

TABLE 12.3   Ten Leading Causes of Death for Females and Males in 2002

Rank	Women	Men
1	Heart disease	Heart disease
2	Cancer	Cancer
3	Cerebrovascular diseases (stroke)	Unintentional injuries
4	Chronic lung disease (asthma, bronchitis)	Cerebrovascular diseases (stroke)
5	Alzheimer's disease	Chronic lung disease (asthma, bronchitis)
6	Diabetes	Diabetes
7	Unintentional injuries	Pneumonia and influenza
8	Pneumonia and influenza	Suicide
9	Kidney disease	Kidney disease
10	Septicemia (infection of the blood)	Chronic liver disease and cirrhosis

Source: National Center for Health Statistics (2004).

Smoking.   As women's lifestyles have become more similar to men's so have some of their health behaviors. For example, while the frequency of men's smoking has declined over the past 40 years, that of women has increased since the 1930's and remains high among women aged 18–24 (Stewart et al., 2004). One-quarter of women in the United States and more than one-quarter of high school girls currently smoke. The prevalence of smoking varies widely across ethnic groups. Among women, Asian-Americans have the lowest rates (7 percent), followed by Latinas (11 percent), Blacks (19 percent), and Whites (22 percent). Native-American women have a much higher rate than any other group: 41 percent (Centers for Disease Control, 2004).

The result of women's increase in smoking and men's decrease is that smoking-related deaths from lung cancer have declined for men but have soared 600 percent for women (Grady, 2004a), surpassing breast cancer as the leading cause of cancer deaths among women. Smoking also is a key factor in the rise of chronic lung disease and stroke as a cause of death in women (Kurth et al., 2003; Mokdad et al., 2004; National Center for Health Statistics, 2004).

Teenage girls are drawn to smoking for many reasons, including an attempt to express independence, curb appetite, reduce stress, and display "adult" behavior (Chesley et al., 2004; Fulkerson & French, 2003; "Making the Grade," 2004). Young women are heavily targeted by the tobacco industry, which has intentionally designed cigarettes to promote smoking in women (Carpenter et al., 2005; Henningfield et al., 2005; Patel et al., 2004) In response to one advertiser's slogan, "You've come a long way baby," Claire reminds her students, "Yes, your rates of lung disease are getting closer to men's."

Another behavioral difference contributing to women's longevity is that women make greater use of preventive health services and are more likely to seek medical treatment when they are ill (Lethbridge-Cejku et al., 2004; McGlynn et al., 2003; National Center for Health Statistics, 2004). This may help explain why women live longer than men after the diagnosis of a potentially fatal disease. Women's greater tendency to visit the doctor's office suggests that they are more health conscious than men. Women generally know more than men about health, do more to prevent illness, are more aware of symptoms, are more likely to talk about their health concerns, and ask doctors more questions during visits (Elder, 1997; Levine, 2004; "Women Heed Warnings," 1998).

Women also outlive men because of their more extensive social support networks involving family, friends, and formal organizational memberships. Involvement in social relationships is related to living longer, perhaps because social ties reduce the impact of life stresses or convince us to increase our health-producing behaviors (Giles et al., 2005; McGinnis & Foege, 2004; Ray, 2004).

Social Class and Ethnic Differences

Women live longer than men regardless of social class and ethnic membership. Nevertheless, there are differences in longevity among women of different social classes and ethnic groups, as well as across cultures (see Explore Other Cultures 12.2).

Social Class. Around the world, women and men with higher incomes and more education have longer life expectancies and better health (Mannheim Research Institute, 2005; Marmot, 2003; Schneiderman, 2004). Some of this

---

EXPLORE OTHER CULTURES **12.2**

Health Report Card for Women around the World

Women outlive men in almost every nation. In over half of developed countries, women's life expectancy is at least 80 years, an average of seven years more than men (Kinsella & Velkoff, 2001; National Center for Health Statistics, 2004). In developing countries, on the other hand, women outlive men by only three years. Women live longest in Japan—an average of 84 years—but live only until 43 years, on average, in Uganda. Longevity has increased for both sexes in almost all nations, with the exception of some African countries that have been devas-

tated by HIV/AIDS (Mercer et al., 2001). Death in childbirth partially accounts for the smaller female advantage in longevity in developing countries ("World Health Day," 2005). In some countries, however, the smaller difference also is a result of selective abortion and neglect of female children (see Chapter 14). Access to better health care helps account for the larger longevity differences between females and males in developed countries (Cavanaugh & Blanchard-Fields, 2006).

difference can be accounted for by a higher incidence of risk factors such as smoking, obesity, high blood pressure, and physical inactivity among the poor and working class. People with lower incomes are less able to afford decent medical care or even adequate food and experience higher levels of chronic stress as a result of such experiences as financial difficulties and job loss. The combination of all these factors shortens life expectancy and increases rates of illness and disease (American Cancer Society, 2004; Chen, 2004; Schneiderman, 2004).

Ethnicity.   Health risks and mortality rates for women vary by ethnic group (see Table 12.4). Mortality rates from all of the major causes of death (except car accidents, chronic lung disease, and suicide) are higher for Black women than for White women. Black, Latina, and Native American women are more likely than White women to die of diabetes. Asian American women, compared to White women, have lower mortality rates from heart disease; stroke; lung, breast and cervical cancer; cirrhosis; and chronic lung disease (Li et al., 2003; National Center for Health Statistics, 2004). Black women have the shortest life expectancy of any group and Asian Americans the longest ("Making the Grade," 2004). Differences in mortality rates for women of different ethnic groups are related to their economic status throughout their lives. Blacks and Native Americans, for example, have high mortality rates and low lifetime family incomes, while Asian Americans have some of the highest family incomes and lower mortality rates (Torrez, 2001).

Gender Differences in Illness

Although they live longer than men, women have more chronic conditions that cause suffering but do not kill. This is true in every country in which these statistics have been gathered, including developing nations (Beers & Jones, 2004;

TABLE 12.4   Leading Causes of Death for Females by Ethnicity, 2002

Rank	White	Black	Native American	Asian/Pacific Islander	Latina
1	Heart disease	Heart disease	Cancer	Cancer	Heart disease
2	Cancer	Cancer	Heart disease	Heart disease	Cancer
3	Stroke	Stroke	Unintentional injuries	Stroke	Stroke
4	Chronic lung disease	Diabetes	Diabetes	Diabetes	Diabetes
5	Alzheimer's disease	Kidney disease	Stroke	Unintentional injuries	Unintentional injuries

Note: Native American includes American Indian and Alaskan Native females.
Source: National Center for Health Statistics (2004).

Mannheim Research Institute, 2005; Mathers et al., 2002). Women have higher rates of chronic fatigue syndrome, fibromyalgia, thyroid conditions, migraine headaches, anemia, urinary incontinence, and more than 80 autoimmune disorders such as rheumatoid arthritis, Crohn's disease, multiple sclerosis, and lupus (Carlson et al., 2004; Fairweather & Rose, 2004; Holroyd-Leduc & Straus, 2004; National Institutes of Health, 2004). American and Canadian women are less likely than their male counterparts to rate their health as excellent and more likely to describe it as good or fair (Sanmartin et al., 2004).

These statistics do not mean, however, that women are more likely than men to develop health problems. Women spend 64 of their years in good health and free of disability, compared with only 59 years for men. But because women live longer than men, it is women who more often live many years with chronic, often disabling illnesses (Altman, 1997; Crimmins et al., 2002). Keep in mind that a person may have one or more chronic diseases without being disabled. The key issue is whether the chronic condition restricts daily life or reduces the ability to take care of oneself (Bee, 2000).

Disability

As you might expect, the chance of developing a disability increases with age. About 18 percent of women ages 16 to 64 but 43 percent of women aged 65 and over have at least one functional limitation ("Women and Disability," 2004). The degree of disability resulting from chronic conditions is assessed by measuring how well individuals can carry out two groups of activities: (1) **activities of daily living (ADLs)**, which include *basic self-caring activities such as feeding, bathing, toileting, walking, and getting in and out of a bed or chair*; and (2) **instrumental activities of daily living (IADLs)**, which *go beyond personal care to include preparing meals, doing housework, shopping, doing laundry, attending social activities, using the telephone, taking medications, and managing money* (Unger & Seeman, 2000). Older women are more likely than older men to have some difficulty with both ADLs and IADLs (National Center for Health Statistics, 2004).

Among women ages 65 to 74, 6 percent need help with ADLs such as bathing and dressing, while 18 percent need assistance with IADLs such as shopping and household chores (Campbell et al., 1999). In the 85 and over age group, 23 percent of women require help with ADLs, compared to only 12 percent of men ("How Healthy," 2003). African American women are more likely than other women to report chronic and/or disabling conditions, followed by Native American, White, and Latina women. Asian American women are only half as likely as other women to suffer from disabilities (Canetto, 2003; Carlson et al., 2004; Kelley-Moore & Ferraro, 2004). As you might imagine, life satisfaction is often lower for women who have serious health problems. Over 40 percent of women with disabilities report lower life satisfaction, compared with 18 percent of women with fair or poor health and 6 percent of all women (Commonwealth Fund, 1993a). But chronic illness need not prevent a woman from enjoying her life. In the Women's Health and Aging study, 35 percent of women with moderate to severe disabilities reported a high sense of happiness and personal mastery and low levels of anxiety and depression (Unger & Seeman, 2000).

Promoting Good Health

It is a mistake simply to equate getting older with getting sicker. Throughout life, women can take active steps to maintain good health and decrease the impact of any health problems that develop. Lifestyle choices involving physical activity, good nutrition, not smoking, and moderate alcohol use can promote longevity and good health (Knoops et al., 2004; Rimm & Stampfer, 2004).

In this section we examine practices that promote good health. For a closer look at some of these factors in elderly women, see Learn about the Research 12.2.

LEARN ABOUT THE RESEARCH 12.2
Good Health Habits and Longevity

The relationship between good health habits and longevity was demonstrated dramatically in the Alameda County Study, a large-scale longitudinal investigation conducted in Alameda County, California (Breslow & Breslow, 1993; Kaplan, 1992). At the beginning of the study, the researchers asked each of the nearly 7,000 randomly chosen adults about their health practices. In a follow-up study done 18 years later, five good health behaviors were found to predict lower rates of death among the participants: keeping physically active, not smoking, drinking moderately, maintaining normal weight, and sleeping seven to eight hours a night. The most unexpected finding was that being involved in close relationships was as powerful a predictor of life expectancy as good health practices. Women and men who followed the greatest number of good health practices and who were most involved in social networks were least likely to die over the 18 years of the study. Moreover, these individuals were only half as likely to develop disabilities.

Another more recent study suggests that both social activities and other nonstrenuous "productive" activities such as cooking, shopping, gardening, and volunteering may be just as important as physical activity in helping elderly people live longer (Glass et al., 1999). The findings, based on nearly 3,000 women and men age 65 and over living in New Haven, Connecticut, showed that physical, social, and productive activities produced similar benefits in increasing longevity.

What Does It Mean?

1. In this chapter, we have seen that women are more health conscious than men. Why do you think that is? What are the implications for women's greater longevity?
2. How can more women and men be encouraged to develop good health habits?
3. Teenagers and young adults are less likely to engage in good health practices than are middle aged and older adults. What might account for this difference?
4. How would you explain the findings that social and productive activities increase longevity?

Physical Activity and Exercise

Most people are pantywaists. Exercise is good for you. (Emma "Grandma" Gatewood, age 67, the first person to hike the entire 2,170 miles of the Appalachian Trail three times, quoted in Snell, 2002)

Physical Benefits.   The numerous health benefits of physical activity have been well documented. Regular physical exercise is linked with a reduction in the incidence of heart disease, stroke, breast cancer, colon cancer, ovarian cancer, hypertension, diabetes, obesity, and osteoporosis (Balakar, 2005; Beers & Jones, 2004; National Center for Health Statistics, 2004; Slentz et al., 2004). Even among individuals who cannot achieve ideal weight, exercise reduces the risk of health decline (He & Baker; 2004; Hu et al., 2004)

In the later years, physical activity enhances the range of motion of joints which can help arthritics maintain normal functioning (Carlson et al., 2004; Hughes et al., 2004). It also helps maintain the muscle strength, balance, and flexibility needed to perform activities of daily living (Ballard et al., 2004). Exercise programs designed to improve balance and increase flexibility and strength in elderly women and men reduce the likelihood of falls, improve walking speed, and decrease reports of pain and disability (Beers & Jones, 2004; Chang et al., 2004; Gill et al., 2002). Even the very old can benefit from exercise. Maria Fiatarone and her colleagues (Fiatarone et al., 1994) conducted a study with 100 women and men whose average age was 87 (about one-third were in their 90s). Half worked out for 45 minutes three times a week on leg-strengthening machines. The program improved walking speed, stair-climbing ability, and overall level of physical activity. Four individuals were able to discard their walkers for canes.

Older women and men tend to approach physical activity in different ways. Men do more structured activities such as formal exercise, whereas older women keep physically active by going out on a regular basis and doing things they enjoy (walking, gardening, playing with grandchildren). Both styles are linked to health benefits (Strawbridge et al., 1993).

Psychological Benefits.   Women are more likely than men to exercise not only for physical fitness, but also for the psychological benefits it provides (AARP, 2002a). Regular exercise promotes a sense of well-being, feelings of accomplishment, happiness, and increased self-esteem. It also decreases tension, anxiety, depression, and anger (Ensel & Lin, 2004; Menec, 2003; Netz et al., 2005; Nagourney, 2005; Penninx et al., 2002). Exercise improves physical appearance by developing and toning muscles and reducing body fat. Feeling good about personal appearance enhances self-esteem. Regular physical activity can develop increased abilities in one's favorite recreational activities, which also can improve self-esteem (Donatelle, 2002). Furthermore, physically active older adults outperform the sedentary elderly on tests of memory, reaction time, reasoning, attention, planning ability, mental speed, and mental flexibility. These findings suggest that regular participation in exercise improves cognitive functioning in later life (Colcombe &

Kramer, 2003; Kramer & Willis, 2002; Weuve et al., 2004; Yaffe et al., 2001). An alternative explanation, of course, is that smart people may exercise more because they are aware of its benefits!

Factors Linked to Women's Activity Levels.   Inactivity increases with age for both women and men. The proportion of American women who say they never exercise almost doubles, from 24 percent for those under 29 to 43 percent for those 75 and older. Only one-third of women over 65 show appropriate activity levels. In addition women of all ages are less apt to exercise than men (Lee, 2003; Nomaguchi & Bianchi, 2004; U.S. Census Bureau, 2003c).

Latina, Native American, Asian American, and Black women and girls exercise less than White women and girls (Grunbaum et al., 2004; King, et al., 2000; Liao et al., 2004). Much of this ethnic difference may be accounted for by differences in educational and income levels. Ethnic minority women are more likely to live in poverty and have lower income and educational levels than White women. The proportion of women who engage in exercise rises as educational and income levels increase. Over half of women who live in poverty and nearly two-thirds of those without a high school education do not exercise. By comparison, only one-quarter of women with incomes at least four times above the poverty level and about one-third of women with some college education do not exercise (Schoenborn & Barnes, 2002; Wilcox et al., 2003).

One explanation for the low levels of physical activity among older women is the stereotype that exercise is increasingly seen as inappropriate as a person ages. This stereotype applies even more strongly to women than to men because of the societal expectation that at all ages, women are less physically active than men (Travis & Compton, 2001). In addition, the social construction of gender dictates that women are the primary caregivers and managers of home and family. Taking time away from domestic responsibilities to indulge in personal leisure may cause some women to feel selfish or guilty. In addition, the caregiving duties that many older women perform may sap their energy and make them too tired to be physically active (King et al., 2000).

Older women must not only overcome sexist and ageist views about appropriate physical behavior in later life (Porzelius, 2000) but must also combat chronic health problems that inhibit many older people from exercising. Arthritic pain and urinary incontinence, chronic conditions that are much more prevalent in older women than in older men, may serve as deterrents to physical activity. Other barriers include the absence of a companion and the lack of convenient transportation to a safe and affordable exercise facility. In addition, some women feel that they are too old to improve their physical condition, fear that exercise may lead to injury or death, or believe that the declines of aging cannot be reversed (Wilcox et al., 2003). Unfortunately, the issue of attractive exercise programming for older women has been largely overlooked by exercise specialists, yet another example of the relative invisibility and lack of power of older women (King et al., 1998; Travis & Compton, 2001).

Nutrition

As we have seen, good nutrition is a key factor in promoting health. Regardless of age, a healthful diet includes lots of vegetables, fruits, and whole grains, moderate amounts of protein, and sparing use of fats, oil, and sugar (Carlson et al., 2004; Johnson, 2004).

But a woman's nutritional needs also vary over her lifespan. During puberty, for example, calorie requirements rise to at least 2,200 per day for the average girl, and more if she is physically active. Calcium intake is especially important to ensure maximum bone growth. Pregnant women need about 300 extra calories a day to attain the recommended weight gain of 22 to 27 pounds. Breastfeeding women require extra fluids, calcium, protein, and 500 more calories per day than prior to pregnancy. By menopause, women need only about two-thirds of the calories required when they were 20, plus increased consumption of calcium and vitamin D (Carlson et al., 2004; Johnson, 2004).

Many older women who live independently do not consume sufficient amounts of one or more essential nutrients. The reasons for these deficiencies include difficulty getting to stores, insufficient income to buy wholesome foods, medications that interfere with absorption of nutrients, chronic conditions that restrict people to bland diets low in certain nutrients, problems with chewing, and loss of appetite. Poor appetite can result from illness, inactivity, diminished senses of taste and smell, depression, or eating alone (Brody, 2001). Adequate intake of calcium and vitamin D is very important for older women in order to minimize the onset and severity of osteoporis. But few women consume the 1,200–1,500 milligrams recommended during the menopausal and postmenopausal years (North American Menopause Society, 2003). In addition, older people do not absorb vitamin D as readily as they did when younger. Thus, nutritionists recommend that elderly women take vitamin supplements to make sure that their dietary needs are met (Carlson et al., 2004; Johnson, 2004).

SUMMARY

Health Services

- Women are increasingly being included in health research. Unfortunately, they continue to be treated with less respect within the health care system and receive poorer medical care than men.
- Women of color are more likely than White women to be poor, uninsured, and lack medical care.
- Lesbians may have elevated health risks, in part due to reduced access to health care.
- Women rely more heavily than men on Medicare and Medicaid.

- Managed care insurance plans have both advantages and disadvantages for women.

STIs

- Sexually transmitted infections (STIs) are transmitted more easily to women than to men and are harder to diagnose in women.
- Women, especially those of color, are the fastest-growing group of Americans with HIV.
- HIV infection in older women is less often diagnosed and treated correctly than in younger women.

Reproductive System Disorders

- Benign disorders of the reproductive system include endometriosis and fibroid tumors.
- Uterine and cervical cancers have higher survival rates than ovarian cancer.
- The Pap smear is an effective screening device for cervical cancer.
- American women have one of the highest hysterectomy rates in the world.

Osteoporosis

- Osteoporosis, the loss of bone tissue, increases after menopause and can lead to disabling and even fatal fractures.
- Building and maintaining bone mass is enhanced by increasing calcium intake; decreasing use of alcohol, caffeine, and tobacco; increasing physical activity; and taking estrogen or certain medications.

Heart Disease

- Heart disease, the leading killer of women, increases dramatically after menopause.
- Women develop heart disease later than men and are twice as likely to die of it.
- Risk factors for heart disease include gender, age, ethnicity, family history, smoking, physical inactivity, high cholesterol levels, high blood pressure, diabetes, and being overweight.

- Women with heart disease receive less aggressive treatment than men.

Breast Cancer

- One in eight women will develop breast cancer, but survival rates have been increasing.
- Risk factors include age, ethnicity, family history, drinking, smoking, weight gain, and inactivity.
- Many women do not do monthly breast self-exams or get regular mammograms.
- For small early tumors, lumpectomy with radiation is as effective as mastectomy.
- Support groups helps women cope with cancer.

Physical Health in Later Life

- At every age, women report more illness and use of health care services than men, yet women consistently outlive men.
- Both biological factors and lifestyle differences are responsible for women's greater longevity.
- Health risks and mortality rates for women differ by social class and ethnic group.
- Older women are more likely than older men to have some difficulty with various activities of daily living.

Promoting Good Health

- Practices that promote good health include physical activity and good nutrition.

KEY TERMS

Medicare
Medicaid
spending down
fee-for-service insurance
managed care
acquired immunodeficiency
   syndrome (AIDS)
endometriosis
fibroid tumors

cervix
Pap smear
hysterectomy
fibroid embolization
osteoporosis
raloxifene
mammogram
radical mastectomy
modified radical mastectomy

simple mastectomy
lumpectomy
mortality
morbidity
gender paradox
activities of daily living
   (ADLs)
instrumental activities of
   daily living (IADLs)

WHAT DO YOU THINK?

1. Why do you think women's heart disease risks were largely ignored until fairly recently? What actions can individuals take to help improve this situation? What actions can members of the medical community take?

2. How can knowledge of risk factors for diseases in older White women and older women of color help us in prevention and early detection of these diseases? How can high risk factors be reduced for both groups?

3. Why do you think there is a difference between mammogram screening rates for women who differ in socioeconomic status? What actions could be taken to change these disparities?

4. Of the health conditions mentioned in this chapter, which ones can you prevent? Which ones can you delay? What actions can you take now to protect yourself from these problems? Which of these are you currently doing, and why?

IF YOU WANT TO LEARN MORE

Banks, M. E., & Kaschak, E. (Eds.). (2003). *Women with visible and invisible disabilities: Multiple intersections, multiple issues, multiple therapies.* New York: Haworth.

Ciambrone, D. (2004). *Women's experiences with HIV/AIDS: Mending fractured selves.* New York: Haworth.

Carlson, K. J., Eisenstat, S. A., & Ziporyn, T. (2004). *The new Harvard guide to women's health.* Cambridge, MA: Harvard University Press.

Gallant, S. J., Keita, G. P., & Royak-Schaler, R. (Eds.). (1997). *Health care for women: Psychological, social and behavioral influences.* Washington, DC: American Psychological Association.

Goldberg, N. (2002). *Women are not small men: Strategies for preventing and healing heart disease in women.* New York: Ballantine.

Goldman, M. B., & Hatch, M. C. (Eds.). (2000). *Women and health.* New York: Academic Press.

Northrup, C. (1998). *Women's bodies, women's wisdom.* New York: Bantam Books.

Ratner, E. (1999). *The feisty woman's breast cancer book.* New York: Hunter House.

WEBSITES

Health Care and Health Issues: General

The AMA Women's Health Information Centre
http://www.ama-assn.org/
New York Times articles on women's health and excerpts from the Harvard Guide to Women's Health and the American Medical Women's Association Women's Complete Health Book
http://www.nytimes.com/women
The National Women's Health Information Center
http://www.4woman.gov
Iris Cantor Women's Health Center
http://www.cornellwomenshealth.com
The Society for Women's Health Research
http://www.womenshealthresearch.org/

http://www.fda.gov/womens/tttc.html
http://www.womensorganizations.org/
http://www.nwhn.org/
http://www.cdc.gov/health/womensmenu.htm

Disability

Disabled People's International
http://www.dpi.org
National Organization on Disability
http://www.nod.org
American Association of Persons with Disabilities
http://www.aapd-dc.org

Heart Disease

American Heart Association
http://www.amhrt.org

American Heart Association
http://www.americanheart.org/

Cancer

American Cancer Society
http://www.cancer.org
National Ovarian Cancer Coalition (NOCC)
http://www.ovarian.org
The Susan G. Komen Breast Cancer Foundation
http://www.komen.org

Arthritis

Arthritis Foundation
http://www.arthritis.org

National Institute of Arthritis and
Musculoskeletal and Skin Diseases
http://www.niams.nih.gov

Diabetes

American Association of Diabetes Educators
http://www.diabeteseducator.org
National Institute of Diabetes and Digestive
and Kidney Diseases
http://www.niddk.nih.gov

Lesbian Health

Lesbian Health Research Center
http://www.lesbianhealthinfo.org

13 Mental Health

I was diagnosed with anorexia nervosa in my sophomore year of high school. I was always the bigger one of my friends and my boyfriend, at the time, would always tell me he liked the fact that I was chubby. I would see all the stick-skinny models and actresses on TV and feel completely disgusted with myself. At one point during my fight with anorexia, I weighed about 35 pounds less than was healthy for my height and I was very sick. It is so scary to look in a mirror and see fat when you are actually skin and bones. It ruined my relationship with so many loved ones and I still don't have regular menstrual cycles. (Stephanie, college junior, age 20)

It happened one Saturday night [at] a Greek restaurant . . . Suddenly I began to feel as if the walls were edging in. My palms grew damp, my heart drummed, my stomach churned. I had only one thought: If you don't get out of this restaurant immediately, you are going to faint or die. I mumbled that I didn't feel well and raced for the door . . . I began to avoid restaurants, but then my panic [appeared] in other venues . . . My world shrank to a thin corridor of safe places. (Anndee Hochman, 2004, pp. 99, 100)

Overall, rates of mental illness are almost identical for women and men. There are, however, striking gender differences in the prevalence of specific mental disorders. Women have higher rates of eating disorders, depression, and anxiety disorders. Men are more likely to have personality and substance abuse disorders (Carlson et al., 2004). In this chapter, we focus not only on pathology, however, but also on mental *health* and the factors that promote it. We begin the chapter by looking at two key factors that are associated with good mental health: social support and optimism. We then explore mental health in childhood and adolescence, followed by a discussion of eating disorders and substance abuse. Next, we explore anxiety disorders, depression, and suicide. We then discuss mental health issues of lesbians and of older women. We close with a look at the diagnosis and treatment of psychological disorders.

Factors Promoting Mental Health

Social Support

A substantial body of research indicates that both receiving and giving social support plays an important role in maintaining good mental health and helping people cope with stressful life events (Antonucci et al., 2002; Brown et al., 2003; Diener & Seligman, 2004; Shaw et al., 2004; Sugisawa et al., 2002). This association is especially strong for females. For example, girls are more likely than boys to seek social support following stressful events, and this support appears to play a more protective role for girls than for boys (Jackson & Warren, 2000; Llabre & Hadi, 1997). Similarly, a recent study found that women who feel more loved and supported by their friends, relatives, and children are at less risk for major depression. Among men, however, level of social support is unrelated to the risk of depression (Kendler et al., 2005).

Tend and Befriend.   Women also use social support as a coping aid more readily than men do. Shelley Taylor and her colleagues (Taylor et al., 2000, 2002, 2003) have proposed that women often respond to stress by tending to themselves and their children and by forming ties with others (the "tend and befriend" response). Men, in contrast, are more likely to show aggression or escape. This so-called "fight or flight" response was proposed by psychologists 60 years ago to explain how both men and women react to stress. That view, however, was heavily based on studies of males (Azar, 2000; Goode, 2000) and was just assumed to apply to females (yet another example of the "male as normative"). But Taylor and her colleagues found many studies that supported their model. For example, Rena Repetti's research (cited in Taylor et al., 2000) showed that mothers returning home after a stressful day at the office were more caring and nurturant toward their children, while stressed fathers were more likely to withdraw from their families or incite conflict. What stimulates these different behaviors in females and males? Taylor and her colleagues suggest that hormonal differences are partly responsible, but they and others are quick to reject the idea that gender stereotypes are biologically hard-wired. Alice Eagly (cited in Goode, 2000), for example, points out that the gender difference could be a result of cultural conditioning that prepares females from an early age for the role of caregiver and nurturer.

Women are more likely than men to use social support to cope with stress.

Optimism: "The Power of Positive Thinking"

Question: "Do you know the difference between an optimist and a pessimist?"
Answer: The first one sees the glass as half full, while the second sees it as half empty.

You may have heard this saying before, but did you also know that optimism can actually be good for your health? An optimistic outlook—the expectation that good rather than bad things will happen—has been linked to a variety of positive mental and physical health outcomes (Giltay et al., 2004; Jones et al., 2004; Peterson, 2000; Schnieder, 2001). A recent study by Deborah Jones and her colleagues (2004), for example, found that optimism appeared to protect women from some of the health risks associated with depression. Another intriguing finding by Karen Matthews and her associates (2004) is that middle-aged women with an optimistic outlook on life are less likely to show the beginning of heart disease than are pessimists.

Mental Health in Childhood and Adolescence

Compared to boys, girls show fewer adjustment problems in childhood. Girls, however, are more likely than boys to first manifest psychological difficulties during the adolescent years (Becker, 2001; Costello et al., 2003). Stress levels increase for both genders during these years. However, the patterns of stress girls encounter may leave them more vulnerable to emotional disorders, such as depression, than do those experienced by boys (Broderick & Korteland, 2002). We shall explore these stresses later in the chapter.

Internalizing Disorders in Girls

Adjustment problems that are more common in girls and women, such as depression, anxiety, and social withdrawal, are often labeled "internalizing problems" (Graber, 2004; Hasebe et al., 2004). Later in the chapter, we discuss these disorders in greater detail. Internalizing disorders are harder to detect and easier to overlook than the externalizing problems more often shown by boys and men: aggression, conduct disorders, antisocial behaviors, and attention deficit hyperactivity disorder (ADHD). Early socialization of girls and boys into gender-typed behaviors may be responsible for these differences in the expression of distress (Andreasen, 2005; Hoffmann et al., 2004; Hoglund & Leadbeater, 2004).

Externalizing Disorders in Girls

Ironically, girls with externalizing disturbances are rarely studied because of the notion that these are "male" problems (Pepler et al., 2004; Prinstein & LaGreca, 2004; Serbin et al., 2004). This stereotype persists despite the fact that acts of violence by teenage girls are on the increase. Large national surveys show that 15 to 30 percent of girls have committed a serious violent offense, such as aggravated assault, by age 17 (Lamberg, 2002). Girls who show externalizing problems, compared to other girls, exhibit deficits in social, emotional, and communication skills and elevated rates of substance use and risky sexual behavior (Bierman et al., 2004;

Prinstein & LaGreca, 2004; White, 2001). Moreover, these girls are more likely to have difficulties as adults. For example, longitudinal studies in Sweden (Wangby et al., 1999), New Zealand (Fergusson & Woodward, 2000), and Canada (Serbin et al., 2004) found that girls with externalizing problems in childhood and early adolescence were at greater risks of all types of maladjustment in late adolescence and adulthood than were those without such problems. They had higher rates of educational failure, juvenile crime, substance abuse, mental health problems, pregnancy, and poor parenting skills. On the other hand, there was little or no relationship between having internalizing problems during adolescence and later maladjustment (Wangby et al., 1999).

Eating Disorders

The prevalence of eating disorders among women has increased dramatically since the 1980s, paralleling the increase in girls' and women's body dissatisfaction that we discussed in Chapter 4 (Reijonen et al., 2003; Society for Adolescent Medicine, 2003). In this section, we examine types of eating disorders, their likely causes, and their treatment.

Types of Eating Disorders

Three major types of eating disorders have been identified. They are anorexia nervosa, bulimia nervosa, and binge eating disorder. Stephanie, one of Claire's students, described her battle with anorexia in the first vignette at the beginning of the chapter.

Anorexia Nervosa.   The defining characteristics of **anorexia nervosa** are *a refusal to maintain a minimal normal body weight (defined as 85 percent of ideal weight), intense fear of gaining weight, a distorted body image (feeling fat even when too thin), and amenorrhea* (lack of menstruation) in females. Anorexic individuals diet, fast, and exercise excessively in order to lose weight (Reijonen et al., 2003; Walsh, 2004). Unlike "normal" dieters, anorexics may lose 25 percent of their original body weight. Many of them share self-starvation tips and "thinspiration" messages on so-called "pro-ana" Websites (Chesley et al., 2003; Orenstein, 2005; Pollack, 2003). One recent survey of teens diagnosed with eating disorders at Stanford University's children's hospital found that 40 percent had visited "pro-ana" Websites (Irvine, 2005). Unfortunately, dramatic weight loss can cause osteoporosis, hormone abnormalities, dangerously low blood pressure, and damage to vital organs (Miller et al., 2005; Misra et al., 2004; Morris, 2004b). Approximately 10 percent of anorexics die from the physical complications of self-starvation or from suicide (Keel, 2005; Morris, 2004b).

Girls and women account for more than 95 percent of cases of anorexia nervosa. About 1 to 4 percent of female adolescents and young adults suffer from the disorder (Henig, 2004b; McDonald, 2003). While anorexia is often thought of as a White, middle-class or upper-class disease, its incidence is increasing among

Singer Karen Carpenter is shown here with her brother a year before her death at age 32. She died of cardiac arrest resulting from anorexia nervosa.

women of color and poor women (Jacobi et al., 2004; Keel, 2005; Reijonen et al., 2003; Striegel-Moore et al., 2003). Although the peak period for anorexia is adolescence (Currin et al., 2005), females can become anorexic at virtually any age. It is no longer rare for 10- and 11-year-old girls or even those as young as 7 to have the disorder (Daw, 2001; Gardner et al., 2000). In addition, a growing group of women in their thirties, forties, and fifties are developing eating disorders. Many of these women have likely been overly concerned with weight and body image throughout their lives. The midlife trigger for the eating disorder may be the 10- to 15-pound weight gain that typically occurs during menopause. Sometimes, losing a spouse, dealing with a troubled child, or even having a child leave for college can set off eating problems (Morris, 2004b).

Young women with physical disabilities also have an elevated risk of developing symptoms of eating disorders. These women may be more vulnerable because their disabilities often involve body-image disturbances, they feel lack of control resulting from needing assistance from others, and they may focus on weight maintenance to sustain mobility (Gross et al., 2000).

Bulimia Nervosa. The primary features of **bulimia nervosa** are *recurrent episodes of uncontrolled binge eating, followed by purging activities aimed at controlling body weight.* Purging activities include self-induced vomiting, exercise, extreme dieting or fasting, and the abuse of laxatives, diuretics, or enemas (Henig, 2004b; Walsh, 2004). One young woman, bulimic since the age of 9, graphically describes her binge-purge cycles:

> *At my lunch break, I would eat a quarter-pounder with cheese, large fries, and a cherry pie. Then I would throw up in the antiseptic-scented bathroom, wash my face and go back on the floor, glassy-eyed and hyper. After work, I would buy a quarter-pounder with cheese, large fries, and a cherry pie, eat it on the way home from work, throw up at home with the bathtub running, eat dinner, throw up, go out with friends, eat, throw up, go home, pass out.* (Hornbacher, 1998, p. 91)

Individuals with bulimia seem to be driven by an intense fear of weight gain, and a distorted perception of body size similar to that seen in anorexics. Unlike anorexics, however, bulimics often maintain normal weight (Carlson et al., 2004). Although usually not life-threatening, bulimia can cause intestinal and kidney problems, as well as extensive tooth decay because of gastric acid in the vomited food. Bulimia also may result in an imbalance of electrolytes, the chemicals necessary for the normal functioning of the heart (Alexander et al., 2000; Keel, 2005).

As with anorexia nervosa, young women account for more than 90 percent of the cases of bulimia (McDonald, 2003). About 1 to 4 percent of females in late adolescence and early adulthood have bulimia. The typical onset is in late adolescence (Henig, 2004).

Binge Eating Disorder. This disorder is characterized by recurrent binge eating and the absence of compensatory weight-control efforts. It is the most common of the eating disorders, has a later onset, and is often associated with obesity (Keel, 2005; Walsh, 2004).

Causes of Eating Disorders

Biological, psychological, and cultural factors all seem to play a part in the development of eating disorders (Keel, 2005; Littleton & Ollendick, 2003; Reijonen et al., 2003). Let us consider each of these in turn.

Biological Factors.   One line of biological evidence comes from comparing identical twins (who share the same genetic material) with fraternal twins (who share only half). An identical twin is much more likely than a fraternal twin to develop an eating disorder if her co-twin also has the disorder (Jacobi et al., 2004; Walsh, 2004). While this research suggests the existence of a genetic predisposition toward eating disorders, these findings could also reflect identical twins' highly similar social and cultural environments. Another biological consideration is that anorexics and bulimics have low levels of serotonin, a mood- and appetite-regulating chemical in the brain. However, these chemical imbalances may result *from* the eating disorder rather than cause it (Jacobi et al., 2004).

Psychological Factors.   Certain psychological characteristics also put young women at higher risk for eating disorders. These include low self-esteem, high levels of anxiety, depression, perfectionism, conscientiousness, competitiveness, obsessive-compulsive thoughts and behaviors, difficulty in separating from parents, strong need for approval from others, and perceived lack of control in one's life (Cohen & Petrie, 2005; Jacobi et al., 2004; Keel, 2005; Stice et al., 2004). Eating disorders may also reflect family problems. For example, parents of anorexics are overly nurturant and overprotective and place undue emphasis on achievement and appearance. Families of bulimics are more hostile, conflicted, and disorganized, as well as less nurturant and supportive than families of anorexics or normal adolescents (Halmi, 2000). Another risk factor for eating disorders is sexual or physical abuse (Jacobi et al., 2004; Polivy & Herman, 2002).

Cultural Factors.   Some feminists view eating disorders as drastic attempts to attain the reed-thin ideal of beauty that has been socially constructed by a patriarchal society (e.g., Piran, 2001). The impact of the media in transmitting this message is illustrated dramatically in Anne Becker's study of adolescent girls living in Fiji (reported in Goode, 1999b). For details, read Explore Other Cultures 13.1.

In North America, the effect of cultural pressures to be thin is perhaps seen most vividly among girls and young women who are involved in sports. The incidence of disordered eating (ranging from excessive dieting to anorexia or bulimia) among female athletes is estimated to be as high as 62 percent, far greater than the estimate of 3 percent among the general population of girls and young women (Arnold, 2004). *The combination of disordered eating accompanied by amenorrhea and premature bone loss, or osteoporosis* (discussed in Chapter 12), is sometimes referred to as the **female athlete triad** (Ireland & Nattiv, 2003). The prevalence of this condition appears to have grown along with girls' participation in dance and performance sports such as gymnastics and figure skating, in which a slim figure is

EXPLORE OTHER CULTURES **13.1**
Cultural Pressure to Be Thin

When interviewed by Ann Becker in 1995, just as television was introduced to Fiji, only 3 percent of girls reported they vomited to control their weight. In 1998, 15 percent reported the behavior. Similarly, 29 percent scored highly on a test of eating-disorder risk in 1998 compared with just 13 percent in 1995. The more television the girls watched, the more likely they were to diet and to report feeling "too big or fat." Several girls mentioned that they wanted to look like the Western women they saw on television shows (Becker et al., 2002). The study does not conclusively prove that television helps cause eating disorders. Still,

Becker notes that the increases are dramatic in a culture that traditionally has equated a robust, nicely rounded body with health and that considers considerable weight loss ("going thin") a sign of illness.

A similar cultural shift is taking place in West and Central Africa where the big, voluptuous woman has been considered the ideal of female beauty. In Nigeria, for example, brides are sent to fattening farms before their weddings. But in 2001, tall, slim, Agbani Darego of Nigeria won the Miss World title. Since then, Nigerian girls and young women clamor to be thin (Onishi, 2002a).

considered ideal (Parsons & Betz, 2001; Powers, 2002). Athletes competing at an elite (that is, highly competitive national, or international) level are at greatest risk (Smolak et al., 2000). Claire's student Betsy, who spent several years at a strict, elite ballet academy, described the pressure to stay thin:

> *Standing at the barre, the ballet master would poke and pull at your body. The professionals would stand outside between rehearsals always holding a cigarette. All the young students concluded that smoking, in replacement of food, made you thinner. Although I never started smoking, I started consuming orange juice . . . and that's all. At slumber parties on the weekends, I made sure that my friends thought I loved food, and saw me devour the pizza. I also made sure that they didn't see me get rid of it in the bathroom afterward.*

Treatment of Eating Disorders

Eating disorders are difficult to cure. Cognitive-behavioral therapy, which helps people to change both their behaviors and the way they think about themselves and others, seems to be more effective than other forms of therapy for bulimia and binge-eating disorder. Antidepressants are also of use in treating these disorders (Gowers & Bryant-Waugh, 2004; Keel, 2005; Walsh, 2004). Family therapy, which elicits the parents' aid in getting the client to eat and then gradually returns control of eating to the client, shows promise in the treatment of anorexia (Gowers & Bryant-Waugh, 2004; Hsu, 2004; Keel, 2005). Antidepressants help prevent relapse once the anorexic client returns to normal. They are not effective in reversing anorexic symptoms, however (Gowers & Bryant-Waugh, 2004; Walsh, 2004).

Anorexia is particularly resistant to a wide range of interventions (Walsh, 2004). Regardless of type of treatment, only about 46 percent of anorexics fully recover, about one-third show improvement, and 20 percent remain chronically ill (Keel, 2005). In follow-up studies, up to two-thirds of treated anorexic patients continued to show disturbed attitudes toward food, weight, and body shape (Wentz et al., 2001). Treatment for bulimia tends to be more successful. About half of women diagnosed as bulimic show full recovery five to ten years later, while 30 percent show some symptoms and 20 percent still have the full-blown disorder (Keel, 2005). Binge-eating disorder has a more favorable prognosis than either anorexia or bulimia, with a recovery rate of about 80 percent five years after treatment and a low relapse rate (Russell & Carr, 2003).

Substance Use and Abuse

Until recently, substance use was considered primarily a male problem, and much of the research dealing with abuse of alcohol and other drugs was carried out on males. This oversight has led to inadequate diagnosis and treatment of women with substance abuse disorders (Canterbury, 2002). In this section, we concentrate on substance abuse issues in women.

Alcohol

Incidence.   Both in adolescence and adulthood, females are less likely than males to use alcohol and to be heavy drinkers (Cheng et al., 2004; Johnston et al., 2004). Overall, about 8 percent of women and 17 percent of men have been diagnosed with alcohol problems, a male-to-female ratio of over 2 to 1 (Greenfield, 2002). *However, while women's alcoholism starts later than men's alcoholism, it progresses more quickly*, a pattern called **telescoping** (Stoffelmayr et al., 2000). Native American women have higher rates of alcohol use than women in other ethnic groups (Mail et al., 2002). White women have the next highest rate of drinking, followed by Black women and Latinas. Asian American women have lower rates of alcohol use than other groups of women (Centers for Disease Control and Prevention, 2002a).

Problem drinking in young women has been increasing at an alarming rate both in the United States and the United Kingdom (Fletcher, 2005; Naimi et al., 2003). For example, U.S. college women are now almost as likely as college men to engage in **binge drinking,** defined as *having five drinks in a row for men or four in a row for women at least once in the last two weeks*. Half of college men and 41 percent of college women are binge drinkers (Wechsler et al., 2002). Heavy drinking is especially prevalent among sorority women (Mohler-Kuo et al., 2004). Sadly, the gender gap in drinking has disappeared among young adolescents: Female and male ninth graders are equally likely to drink (41 versus 40 percent) and to binge drink (20 versus 21 percent) (National Center on Addiction and Substance Abuse, 2002). One possible explanation is an increase in alcohol advertising targeting teenage girls. In the past few years, advertising for low-alcohol drinks such as wine coolers and alcoholic iced teas has increased in national magazines, but especially in those read primarily by adolescent girls (Jernigan et al., 2004).

Health Consequences.   Women have more body fat, less water, and less of the enzyme that breaks down alcohol than men do. As a result, they have higher levels of alcohol in their blood even when they consume the same amount of alcohol per unit of body weight (National Institutes of Health, 2003; Springen & Kantrowitz, 2004). For example, 3 ounces of alcohol consumed by a 120-pound woman has a greater effect on her than the equivalent 6 ounces of alcohol consumed by a 240-pound man has on him. One consequence is that women develop cirrhosis of the liver, hepatitis, heart disease, and brain damage at lower levels of alcohol intake than men. Prolonged heavy drinking also increases the risk of breast cancer, osteoporosis, and infertility (National Institutes of Health, 2003; Prendergast, 2004; Springen & Kantrowitz, 2004). In addition, college women who drink heavily increase their risk of being sexually assaulted (Mohler-Kuo et al., 2004).

Drinking alcohol during pregnancy can lead to **fetal alcohol syndrome (FAS),** *a disorder characterized by mental retardation, growth deficiencies, facial deformities, and learning and behavioral problems.* FAS is the third most common birth defect and the leading preventable cause of mental retardation in the United States (Kvigne et al., 2004). Even light drinkers risk having children with **fetal alcohol effect (FAE)**, *a milder but still serious form of FAS* (Carroll, 2003; Schneider et al., 2004; "Surgeon General's Advisory," 2005). Unfortunately, 20 to 38 percent of women of childbearing age binge drink at least once a month, potentially exposing fetuses early during the first trimester before the women realizes she is pregnant (Naimi et al., 2003). Sadly, a woman who binge drinks during pregnancy triples her child's odds of having drinking-related problems in young adulthood (Baer et al., 2003).

Risk Factors.   Children of alcoholic parents or siblings have increased rates of alcoholism (Cheng et al., 2004). Genetic factors may play about as strong a role for daughters as for sons, although findings are mixed (Bouchard, 2004; National Institute on Alcohol Abuse and Alcoholism, 2003). Adolescents whose parents and peers consume alcohol and tolerate its use are more likely to start drinking at an early age which places them at higher risk for later alcohol-related problems (Jersild, 2002; Misra, 2001; National Institutes of Health, 2003). Women who were sexually abused in childhood, or who had emotional or behavioral problems early in life are also at greater risk for later alcohol problems. Divorced and single women are more likely than married or widowed women to drink heavily and to have alcohol-related problems (National Institutes of Health, 2003). Women who are heavy drinkers also are more likely than other women to be depressed, anxious, and to report stressful life events (King et al., 2003; Springen & Kantrowitz, 2004).

Treatment.   Society has set up several double standards for women and men. The double standard of aging was described in Chapter 2 and the double standard of sexuality was discussed in Chapter 6. There is also a double standard with regard to drinking. Heavy drinking in men is often expected and seen as normal, whereas heavy drinking in women is strongly criticized. As a result, women tend to hide or deny their alcohol use, making them less likely to seek help and to be more seriously ill before the disease is diagnosed (Canterbury, 2002; National Institutes of Health, 2003). Moreover, physicians ask more questions about alcohol use and give more advice and information to male than to female problem drinkers (Liu et al., 1999). One study (Brown et al., 1995), for example, found that only one-third of women who had a checkup during the past year were asked about their drinking patterns. For women over 65, the rate dropped to one-sixth. (Older women are particularly invisible, as we have seen.) Twelve-step alcoholism treatment programs such as Alcoholics Anonymous have been criticized for being based exclusively on research with alcoholic men. Alternative programs, such as Women for Sobriety, focus on the special issues and needs of women with drinking problems (Canterbury, 2002; Wartik, 2001). Although these programs have shown some success in treating alcohol disorders in women, they are in short supply (Windle & Windle, 2002).

Illegal Substances

Incidence.   Use of illegal substances such as marijuana, cocaine, heroin, hallucinogens, and steroids varies by gender and ethnic group. Among women, use is highest among Native Americans, followed by White, Latina, Black, and Asian American women. Regardless of ethnicity, however, males have higher rates of illegal drug use than females both in adolescence and adulthood. Males also use illegal drugs more heavily than females do (Compton et al., 2004; Johnston et al., 2005). One possible reason for the gender gap is that drug use among girls and women is less acceptable in our society. Recently, the gender gap in substance use has decreased as a result of a steeper decline in use among males than among females (Johnston et al., 2005). One disturbing trend, for example, is an increase in the use of anabolic (muscle-building) steroids by preteen and adolescent girls (Johnson, 2005; Johnston et al., 2005). According to health experts, some teenage girl athletes are moving away from a preoccupation with thinness toward a lean, more muscular look, a trend labeled "reverse anorexia" (Adler, 2004; Nyad, 2004). Unfortunately, not only does steroid use expose females to the same severe health risks as boys (e.g., heart, liver, and skin diseases), but it also may damage their ability to bear children (Adler, 2004; Kolata, 2002b).

Typically, individuals who use illegal substances use more than one and also use or abuse alcohol. In girls and women, the problem is compounded because they are more likely than men to both use and misuse prescription drugs, such as tranquilizers, antidepressants, and sleeping pills (Marecek & Hare-Mustin, 1998; Merline et al., 2004).

Treatment.   As with treatment for alcohol problems, women in drug abuse treatment programs have different needs than men in treatment. A successful program for women often depends on meeting these different needs, according to Christine Grella, who found that women in women-only drug treatment programs were more than twice as likely to complete treatment as women in mixed-gender programs ("UCLA Study," 2000).

Anxiety Disorders and Depression

Nearly one in four Americans will have an anxiety disorder in their lifetime and nearly one in five will develop major depression (Kornstein & Wojcik, 2002; Pigott, 2002). Women are at greater risk than men for both disorders. In this section, we first review anxiety disorders. We then turn to depression and its all-too-frequent outcome: suicide.

Anxiety Disorders

Almost everyone feels anxious now and again. When you have to give a speech in class, for instance, it is normal to feel anxious. But when anxiety is irrational, excessive, and persists over several months, it is called an anxiety disorder (Carlson et al., 2004). Most anxiety disorders occur two to three times as frequently in women as in men (Mahler, 2003; Pigott, 2002).

Generalized anxiety disorder is characterized by *excessive worry and anxiety about a variety of life situations or events.* Many people experience physical symptoms as well. It is one of the most common anxiety disorders, with about 8 percent of women developing it at some time in their lives (Piggott, 2002). The difference between ordinary worrying and generalized anxiety disorder is that the level of concern is excessive, resulting in distress and interfering with everyday functioning (Mahler, 2003).

Panic disorder is marked by *sudden unpredictable attacks of intense anxiety accompanied by a pounding heart, dizziness, sweating, shortness of breath, and trembling.* A person having an attack has a sense of impending doom, losing control, or dying ("Anxiety Disorders," 2002). As shown in the second vignette at the beginning of the chapter, panic disorder can lead to **agoraphobia**, a *fear of being in public places where escape might be difficult if one were suddenly incapacitated* (*agora* is the Greek word for "marketplace") (Cahill & Foa, 2001). Agoraphobia, by far the most common phobia, will be experienced by about 9 percent of women during their lifetimes (Piggott, 2002).

Agoraphobia is just one of a group of anxiety disorders known as a **specific phobia**, a *fear of a specific object, such as a spider, or a specific situation, such as being in public places, or flying.* Roughly 14 percent of women develop a specific phobia at some time in their life (Piggott, 2002). Specific phobias usually start in childhood. Social construction of gender-specific attitudes and behaviors may account for the higher prevalance of these phobias in females than in males. Expression of fear and anxiety is more socially acceptable in girls and women than in boys and men, who are discouraged from displaying these emotions (Mahler, 2003; Merikangas & Pollack, 2000).

Depression

I have been immobilized, unable to formulate thought or action. Can't get out of bed most of the time. I feel terrible—hopeless, joyless, exhausted, lost. (Sondra, age 48, cited in "Depression & Women," 2003, p. 1)

Incidence.   **Depression** is *characterized by prolonged depressed moods and loss of pleasure in most activities* ("Depression & Women," 2003). Higher rates of depression among females first appear in early adolescence and continue into adulthood (Gilbert, 2004; Kilpatrick et al., 2003). A recent longitudinal study of Canadian teenagers by Nancy Galambos and her colleagues (2004) found that by late adolescence, 25 percent of females had experienced an episode of major depression. Across many nations, cultures, and ethnicities, women are about twice as likely as men to suffer from depression (Mannheim Research Institute, 2005; Nolen-Hoeksema & Keita, 2003). Although the incidence of depression is lower among Whites than among Blacks and Latinas/os, the 2:1 gender ratio holds across all three groups (Freeman et al., 2004; Nolen-Hoeksema, 2002). Moreover, women are more likely than men to suffer an anxiety disorder along with their depression (Mahler, 2003).

What are the stresses of adolescence that are linked to higher rates of depression in girls than in boys? Karen Rudolf and Constance Hammen (1999) found that teenage boys were more likely to complain of stressful situations such as doing poorly in school, getting sick, moving to a new school, getting in trouble with the police, or other events unrelated to interpersonal problems. Girls, on the other hand, experienced most of their stress from relationship problems, including fights with peers, siblings, or friends. Girls reported more symptoms of depression in response to stress than boys did. Their symptoms included being sad, feeling like crying, and feeling alone and unloved. Because girls have closer, more intimate relationships with family and friends than boys do, disruptions and conflicts in these relationships can lead to depression and distress (Graber, 2004; Kendler et al., 2005).

Theories.   Many theories have been offered to explain the gender difference in depression. Gender differences in help-seeking behavior or willingness to report symptoms have been ruled out as possible reasons (Hankin & Abramson, 2001). One explanation is biological, linking depression to hormonal changes that occur during the menstrual cycle, the postpartum period, and menopause. As we saw in Chapter 7, however, menopause is not associated with an increase in depression. In Chapter 7, we also noted that direct relationships between menstrual and postpartum hormonal changes and depression are weak, temporary, and far from universal (Nolen-Hoeksema, 2002). One biological factor that *is* strongly linked to depression is having a low level of the neurochemical serotonin. Men produce more serotonin than women do, possibly making women more susceptible to depression (Cahill, 2005).

A second possible explanation is that stressful life events may precipitate depression, and that women's lives are more stressful than men's. Women are more likely than men to have low social status, undergo economic hardship, face discrimination in the workplace, experience marital and family strains, and be subjected to domestic violence, sexual abuse, and sexual harassment (Belle & Doucet, 2003; Elliott, 2001; Greenglass, 2002; Koss et al., 2003). Research has documented that economic hardship, family-based strains, childhood sexual abuse, sexist discrimination, and neighborhood violence are indeed contributing factors to depression in women (Adler & Snibbe, 2003; Ewart & Suchday, 2002; Kilpatrick et al., 2003; Lennon et al., 2002; Rickert et al., 2000; Stoppard & McMullen, 2003).

A third proposed explanation is that the feminine role makes women more vulnerable to depression by making them feel helpless and powerless to control aspects of their lives (Nolen-Hoeksema, 2002). Females are expected to be less competent and more in need of help than males. Their efforts and achievements are more likely to be ignored or devalued. The sense that one's actions do not count can lead to a feeling of "learned helplessness," which in turn is linked to depression. In support of this view, girls and women with more masculine behavior traits are less likely to experience depression than those with more feminine traits (Lengua & Stormshok, 2000; Obeidallah et al., 1996).

A fourth theory known as *silencing the self* (Jack, 2003) is based on the assumption that women are socialized to place a high value on establishing and maintaining close relationships. According to this view, women defer to the needs of others, censor their self-expression, repress anger, and restrict their own initiatives, which increases their vulnerability to depression.

Susan Nolen-Hoeksema (2003) has proposed a fifth theory based on the way that females and males respond when they are depressed. She and other researchers have found that when adolescent girls and women are depressed, they focus on their inner feelings and try over and over again to analyze the causes and consequences of their depression. This so-called *ruminative style* leads to more severe and longer-lasting depressed moods. Adolescent boys and men, on the other hand, tend to engage in activities to distract themselves when they are depressed (Mor & Winquist, 2002; Nolen-Hoeksema, 2003; Rose, 2002). Try Get Involved 13.1 to see whether you find differences in the way women and men respond when they are depressed.

These explanations of depression are not mutually exclusive. Indeed, several of these factors most likely are involved (Hankin & Abramson, 2001). For example, one large-scale study of adults suggests that women are more likely than men to get caught in a cycle of despair and passivity because of a lower sense of control over important areas of life, compounded by more chronic strain caused by women's lesser social power. In the study, chronic strain led to more rumination, which in turn increased feelings of powerlessness and depression (Nolen-Hoeksema et al., 1999).

Depression in Later Life.   Depression among the elderly can be the result of medical illness and disability and in turn can contribute to heart disease and earlier onset of death (Lyness, 2004; Schulz et al., 2000). Major clinical depression affects 15 to 20 percent of elderly adults in the United States. Higher rates of depression are found among medically ill, unmarried, socially isolated, homebound, or functionally impaired older adults (Ciechanowski et al., 2004; Mannheim Research Institute, 2005).

These statistics may be underestimates, however, because most depressed elderly are undiagnosed and untreated (Burns, 2004; Ciechanowski et al., 2004;

GET INVOLVED **13.1**

How Do Women and Men Respond to Depression?

For this activity, ask one young adult woman, one young adult male, one middle-aged woman, and one middle-aged male to complete the following survey.

What do you do when you're feeling depressed?

Instructions: Everyone gets depressed—sad, blue, down in the dumps—some of the time. People deal with being depressed in many different ways. For each item, please circle the number that best describes what you *generally* do when you are *depressed*. Choose the most accurate response for *you*, not what you think "most people" would say or do. There are no right or wrong answers.

	Never or Almost Never	Sometimes	Often	Always or Almost Always
1. I try to figure out why I am depressed	1	2	3	4
2. I avoid thinking of reasons why I am depressed	1	2	3	4
3. I think about how sad I feel	1	2	3	4
4. I do something fun with a friend	1	2	3	4
5. I wonder why I have problems that others do not	1	2	3	4
6. I think about all my short-comings, faults, and mistakes	1	2	3	4
7. I think of something to make myself feel better	1	2	3	4
8. I go to a favorite place to distract myself	1	2	3	4
9. I think about why I can't handle things better	1	2	3	4
10. I do something that made me feel better before	1	2	3	4

What Does It Mean?

Before adding up each respondent's scores for the ten items, reverse the points for items 2, 4, 7, 8, and 10. That is, for a rating of 1 (never or almost never), give 4 points; for a rating of 2, give 3 points, and so on. Then sum the points for the ten items for each respondent. Higher scores reflect greater rumination.

1. Are there differences between your female and male respondents in how they react when they are depressed? If so, how do you account for differences?
2. Did your young adults respond differently from your middle-aged adults? Account for any differences.
3. Did your results support Susan Nolen-Hoeksema's findings regarding how women and men respond when they are depressed? Account for any differences.

Source: Adapted from Butler & Nolen-Hoeksema (1994).

Lyness, 2004). Studies of older adults who committed suicide as a result of depression have found that while 75 percent had visited a doctor within a month of their deaths, only 25 percent of those individuals were diagnosed as being depressed (Goleman, 1995). Older adults do not always experience the classic symptoms of depression: sleeplessness, fatigue, low energy, loss of appetite, guilt feelings, and depressed mood. Rather, depressed elderly individuals may show anxiety, malaise, confusion, and physical complaints (Holroyd, 2002; Pasupathi & Löckenhoff, 2002; Rudolph & Burt, 2003). Some symptoms, such as sudden irritability and fault finding, or pessimism and little hope for the future, may be dismissed as typical personality changes that accompany aging. Even the classic symptoms of low energy, loss of appetite, or loss of interest in former sources of enjoyment may be seen by doctors simply as characteristics of a frail older person (American Psychological Association, 2004a). Furthermore, some health professionals may feel that depression in the elderly is "normal" because of medical, financial, or family difficulties or the losses that come with age (Ciechanowski et al., 2004; "Depression Across the Lifespan," 2003). While it is true that health problems among older adults may contribute to symptoms of depression (Wrosch et al., 2004), most older people confront their problems without becoming clinically depressed. In fact, elderly adults have a lower prevalence of psychological disorders than younger adults (American Psychological Association, 2004a). Sometimes, depression in the elderly is a side effect of medications given for conditions such as heart disease. A change in medication frequently gets rid of the depression (McCoy, 2002).

When depressed older adults are correctly diagnosed and treated, they improve at the same rate as younger patients ("Depression Across the Lifespan," 2003). Unfortunately, older women are less likely than younger women to receive psychotherapy, and women 75 and over are more likely to receive no treatment at all (Glied, 1998).

Suicide

Incidence.   Across all ages and ethnic groups in the United States, men are four times more likely than women to commit suicide, whereas women are two to three times more likely than men to attempt it (Kaslow et al., 2004). White women and men have higher suicide rates than individuals in other ethnic groups. White males having the highest rate at every age except 15–24, when Native American males exceed them (National Center for Health Statistics, 2004). The lower suicide rates among Black women are thought to be related to the protective factors of extended family networks and religious faith (Chaudron & Caine, 2004). For a look at gender differences in suicide across cultures, see Explore Other Cultures 13.2.

Suicide in Adolescence and Young Adulthood.   Among adolescents and young adults aged 15–24 years, suicide is the third leading cause of death for both males and females (National Center for Health Statistics, 2004; Torpy, 2005). Basic risk

EXPLORE OTHER CULTURES 13.2

Gender Differences in Suicide: A Global Phenomenon

In nearly all countries, men are more likely than women to commit suicide. In industrialized nations, the male-to-female suicide ratio ranges from 2:1 in the Netherlands to 5.4:1 in the Russian Federation (Chaudron & Caine, 2004). The ratios for the United States and Canada are 3.59 and 3.28:1, respectively (Pampel, 1998). One study that included 70 countries, both developed and developing, found higher suicide rates among men in all nations except China and Papua New Guinea (Canetto & Lester, 1995). In another study of 29 nations (Lester & Yang, 1998), higher divorce rates were associated with higher suicide rates. Interestingly, this association was stronger for men than for women, in line with findings that marriage seems more beneficial for men than for women (see Chapter 8). Across cultures, unemployment is also more strongly associated with suicide and acceptance of suicide among men than among women (Helgeson, 2002). For women, suicide is more closely linked to their social and economic status. In nations where women's status is low, such as China, India, and parts of Turkey, their suicide rates are relatively high (Canetto & Lester, 1995; Frantz, 2000; "Suicide," 2004). In

fact, suicide rates for girls and women in rural areas of China, Singapore, and India and in Southeastern Turkey are as much as twice that of boys and men (Aaron et al., 2004; Frantz, 2000; Kim & Singh, 2004). One of the differences between women's suicide in the West and in developing countries is the method used. Women in Western countries usually swallow pills or slash their wrists, which are treatable events. In Asia, however, women ingest highly lethal insecticides, hang themselves, or set themselves on fire (Aaron et al., 2004).

Why are young Asian women committing suicide at such a high rate? A major factor seems to be cultural and gender conflicts that are made more intense as these traditional agricultural societies are transforming themselves into industrial societies. Many girls are still forbidden to go to school or to work and they are forced into arranged marriages which may be abusive or unhappy (Kristof, 2004b; Moreau & Yousafzai, 2004). At the same time, they are exposed through movies and television to a more prosperous, egalitarian life which is denied to them. Such lack of control of one's life may lead to despair and suicide (Frantz, 2000).

---

factors for adolescent suicide in both sexes include depression, exposure to suicide or suicide attempts by family or friends, substance or alcohol abuse, and having guns in the home. Social factors are more strongly associated with having suicidal thoughts for girls than for boys. In particular, girls who are socially isolated from peers are more likely to think about suicide than are girls with strong social networks (Bearman & Moody, 2004).

Suicide in Later Life.   Risk factors associated with suicide in the elderly are the death of a loved one; physical illness; uncontrollable pain; the specter of dying a prolonged death that harms family members emotionally and financially; fear of institutionalization, social isolation, and loneliness; and major changes in social

Maggie Kuhn, who founded the Gray Panthers after her forced retirement at age 65, illustrates the active role older women can play as advocates for social change.

roles, such as retirement. As in adolescence, those who abuse alcohol and other drugs, are depressed, or suffer from other mental disorders are also at high risk (Goode, 2003a; Kaslow et al., 2004; Roscoe et al., 2003; McCloud et al., 2004).

On a positive note, remember that most older people with health and other problems cope well with the changes of later life and do not become depressed or suicidal (Beers & Jones, 2004). Many continue to lead active and productive lives. In the words of Maggie Kuhn, an older-woman activist:

> *Old age is not a disaster. It is a triumph over disappointment, failure, loss, illness. When we reach this point in life, we have great experience with failure. I always know that if one of the things that I've initiated falters and fails, it won't be the end. I'll find a way to learn from it and begin again.* (Kuhn, 1991, p. 214)

Mental Health of Lesbians

Until 1973, the American Psychiatric Association (1994) classified homosexuality as a mental disorder. It took nearly another 30 years for the American Psychological Association to adopt Guidelines for Psychotherapy with Gay, Lesbian, and Bisexual Clients ("Guidelines," 2000). These guidelines urge psychologists to understand how prejudice, discrimination, and violence pose risks to the mental health and well-being of lesbian, gay, and bisexual clients.

Stresses

In Chapter 6, we discussed the widespread nature of prejudice and discrimination against lesbians, gays, and bisexuals in the United States and other Western nations. Such homophobia can cause considerable stress in the lives of lesbians, gays, and bisexuals and increase the risk of physical and psychological problems (Frankowski, 2004; Meyer, 2003; Warner et al., 2004). Let us look at these stress-related difficulties, and some coping mechanisms that can help.

Problems and Coping Mechanisms

Compared to heterosexual teens, lesbian, gay, and bisexual adolescents have higher rates of substance abuse, poor school performance, truancy, running away from home, risky sexual behavior, conflicts with the law, depression, and suicidal thoughts (Bailey, 2004; Bearman & Moody, 2004; Consolacion et al., 2004; D'Augelli, 2002; Goodman et al., 2005; Wichstrom & Hegna, 2003). In addition, lesbians report higher rates of problem drinking than heterosexual women, and their rates, unlike those of other women, do not decline with age (Hill, 2000; King et al., 2003; Klinger, 2002). Several studies have found that compared to heterosexual individuals, lesbians, gays, and bisexuals show higher rates of anxiety disorder, depression, and suicide (Case et al., 2004; Warner et al., 2004).

On a more positive note, many lesbians, gays, and bisexuals develop effective coping responses which are linked to good mental health. These include accepting one's homosexuality, having a good social support network, and being active in the lesbian and gay community (Bowleg et al., 2004; David & Knight, 2002; Meyer, 2003; Szymanski et al., 2001). Having family and friends who acknowledge and support their sexual identity is another key factor linked to the well-being of lesbians (Beals & Peplan, 2005). Lesbians, gays, and bisexuals are also more likely than heterosexuals to seek psychological counseling (Balsam et al., 2004; King et al., 2003; Meyer, 2003). About three-quarters of lesbians have used mental health services compared with anywhere from 14 to 29 percent of heterosexual women (Morris, 1998; Solarz, 1999). Therapists who treat lesbians, gays, and bisexuals are most effective when they are well informed about LGB issues and are sensitive to the needs of this population (Klinger, 2002).

Mental Health of Older Women

> As my hair grays, my skin wrinkles, and my fat redistributes, I can't take it all too sorrowfully. I have had a productive youth and have accomplished enough during it to provide a dozen people with material for my birthday roast. Milestone birthdays of middle age are wonderful when you have made positive choices, managed the unexpected, learned from the storms and sorrows, but still find yourself emotionally and physically whole. (Pam, on the occasion of her fiftieth birthday)

In this section, we look at the mental health of women as they get older. First we focus on gender differences. We then concentrate on the vital older woman.

Gender Differences

The psychological health of women tends to improve as they get older (Jones & Meredith, 2000; Kessler et al., 2004; Mroczek, 2000). For example, in one study of African Americans, Chinese Americans, Norwegians, and American nuns (Gross et al., 1997), older women showed fewer negative emotions and more emotional control than younger women. Still, older women, compared to older men, experience more frequent negative emotions and a lower sense of well-being (Canetto, 2001; Steffens et al., 2000). However, gender differences in depression decline or even disappear by age 80 because men's depression rates increase sharply after age 60, while those of women remain the same or decrease (Barefoot et al., 2001; Canetto, 2001; Freeman et al., 2004; Kasen et al., 2003). Similarly, women's neurotic tendencies decline as they age, but this is not the case for men (Srivastava et al., 2003).

The Vital Older Woman

In my sixties, I found my first taste of freedom. My earlier life was spent living according to other people's expectations of me: my parents, my husband, my family. When your family doesn't need you anymore, that's frightening, but freeing. There's time to explore and contemplate what you've learned so far. And there's a duty to send out some of those messages so that other people can benefit from all the difficult lessons you've learned. (Anna Kainen, 1995, age 82, writer)

Women, speak out. Stand up for what you believe. Go back to that teenage person you were, who wanted something very badly, then go out and get it. This is a time in your life when there's nothing and no one standing in your way. (Elizabeth Watson, 1995, age 82, theologian and environmental activist)

We have examined a number of challenges faced by many older women: declining health, financial problems, and the loss of loved ones. But this does not mean that the later years of a woman's life are filled with frustration and despair. Many older women cope successfully with the challenges that old age brings. They don't just *endure* old age; they *enjoy* it.

One of the characteristics of older women who adjust well to later life is the ability to integrate agency and communion (Hubbs-Tait, 1989). You will recall from Chapter 2 that agency refers to such attributes as independence, activity, competitiveness, self-confidence, ambition, and assertiveness. Communion (emotional expressivity) includes such characteristics as affection, compassion, kindness, gentleness, being helpful to others, and awareness of the feelings of others. As we noted in Chapter 3, those individuals who combine both sets of characteristics are referred to as androgynous. Aging androgynous women show better adjustment, greater feelings of mastery, and higher self-esteem than women who show only the stereotypically feminine traits of communion (Frank et al., 1985; Livson, 1983). It may surprise you to learn that most older women cope with life stresses more effectively than younger women.

Older women in general accept their lives as having been well spent (Hubbs-Tait, 1989). Elderly Black women express significantly more contentment with their lives than elderly White women, even though Blacks are more disadvantaged socioeconomically and perceive their health as worse than Whites do (Johnson, 1994). How can we explain this? Many aging minority women are able to draw on psychological, social, and cultural strengths which ease their transition to old age. They have spent their lives marshaling scarce resources to cope with everyday demands and these coping strategies pay off later on as self-reliance. Strengths also arise from family, church, community networks, and shared ethnic identity (Mattis, 2002; Padgett, 1999; Yoon & Lee, 2004). In addition, White women may have expectations of life in the later years that are unrealistically high.

Diagnosis and Treatment of Psychological Disorders

The diagnosis and treatment of psychological disorders in women have often been topics of controversy. Feminist researchers and theorists point out that diagnosis and treatment are conducted by a predominantly male psychiatric culture, using a medical model of psychological illness and viewing many aspects of female behavior as pathological (Blehar & Norquist, 2002). Let's take a closer look at diagnosis and treatment of women's psychological disorders.

Gender Bias in Diagnosis

Is there a double standard of mental health for women and men? In a classic study, Inge Broverman and her colleagues (Broverman et al., 1970) reported that mental health professionals gave similar descriptions for a "healthy" adult (gender unspecified) and a "healthy" male. A "healthy" woman, however, was seen as less healthy in several ways: more submissive, more excitable in minor crises, more emotional, more illogical, more easily hurt, more sneaky, and less independent.

Over the years, other researchers have repeated this study with mixed results. One meta-analysis found less bias in later studies than in earlier ones (Smith, 1980). Others have found that gender bias in diagnosis is alive and well. A recent study found that counselors-in-training continue to have different standards of mental health for women and men, and that "healthy women" are viewed differently than "healthy adults" (Seem & Clark, 2004).

Other research has found that therapists are influenced by deviations from traditional gender roles. In one study (Waisberg & Page, 1988), for example, female patients who showed "masculine" symptoms (alcohol abuse or antisocial personality) were rated as more seriously disturbed than males with the same symptoms. Similarly, male patients with "feminine" symptoms (anxiety or depression) were viewed as more disturbed than females with these symptoms. Drug treatment was more likely to be recommended for females, especially by male therapists. In another study (Robertson & Fitzgerald, 1990), therapists viewed one of two videotapes in which the same male actor discussed having symptoms of depression such as sleeplessness, poor appetite, and boredom. In one video, the male was portrayed in the traditional role of sole breadwinner with a full-time homemaker wife. In the other video, the employment and domestic roles of the husband and wife were reversed. Therapists rated the nontraditional male as less masculine and, more importantly, as more depressed than the traditional male. A recent meta-analysis of 42 studies (McGorty, Iyer, & Hunt, 2003) found that professionals were more likely to diagnose and treat anxiety when it occurred in women and were more likely to diagnose and treat antisocial behavior when it occurred in men. These results suggest that individuals are judged as more psychologically disturbed when they violate traditional gender expectations. For more about gender biases in diagnosis, see Learn about the Research 13.1.

LEARN ABOUT THE RESEARCH 13.1
What Is "Normal"? Gender Biases in Diagnosis

Some psychologists (e.g., Worell & Johnson, 2001) argue that the definitions of "normal" that guide psychological diagnoses are socially constructed by the dominant cultural group (i.e., White heterosexual males) and reflect stereotypical notions of gender, race/ethnicity, and sexuality. To test this view, Jill Cermele and her colleagues (Cermele et al., 2001) analyzed the depiction of women and men in the Casebook that accompanies the **Diagnostic and Statistical Manual IV,** the *standard classification system used in the United States.* The researchers found that the Casebook (Spitzer et al., 1994), which provides case studies to guide the clinician, does indeed contain stereotyped descriptions of women and men.

Men's personality traits were much more likely to be described in positive ways (e.g., charming, friendly, engaging) than in negative ways, whereas females were more often described negatively (e.g., frightened, sad, helpless). In addition, there were more than three times as many negative physical descriptions of women (e.g., disheveled, pale, obese) than of men, who were more often described positively (e.g., tall, handsome, healthy). Women were also more apt to be infantilized (e.g., described as tiny, childlike, frail, and girlish). In addition, they were more often referred to in terms of sexual behavior (e.g., seductive, flirtatious), even when these behaviors had nothing to do with the diagnosis.

What Does It Mean?

1. How might constructing women as different from men influence clinicians in diagnosing mental illness?

2. What can psychologists do to address biases in their notions of what constitutes normalcy and mental illness?

Gender Bias in Psychotherapy

Gender bias also exists in psychotherapy. It may take the form of fostering traditional gender roles (e.g., "be a better wife"), telling sexist jokes, not taking violence against women seriously, and seducing female clients (American Psychological Association, 1975). In one study (Fowers et al., 1996), for example, over 200 clinical psychologists were asked to recommend strategies that would best help hypothetical females and males with identically described problems. The psychologists indicated that male clients could best be helped by increasing their instrumental (traditionally masculine) actions, whereas females could benefit more by enhancing their expressive (traditionally feminine) behaviors. Moreover, therapists are more likely to see women's emotional problems as internally caused (intrapsychic) than they are to regard men's emotional problems in this way, and they may fail to perceive the external stresses of women's lives (Marecek & Hare-Mustin, 1998; Worell, 2001).

Therapy Issues for Women of Color and Poor Women

Women of color and poor women face a number of external stresses which can cause or intensify mental health problems: racism, poverty, culturally approved subordinate status, and living in contexts of violence and chronic strain (Gilbert & Rader, 2001; Wyche, 2001). Unfortunately, financial constraints and time and transportation problems prevent many poor women from seeking help. In addition, people of color are underrepresented in the mental health professions, so that members of these groups often have a therapist who does not know their culture or speak their language. Nonminority providers may apply racial stereotypes to their minority patients instead of seeing them as individuals. Moreover, they can be insensitive to the social and economic conditions in which women of color and poor women live (Bernal et al., 2002; Jackson & Greene, 2000; Lennon et al., 2002; Wyche, 2001). One reason for this is that clinical psychology literature does not contain adequate coverage of ethnically diverse populations. For example, a recent analysis of the leading scholarly clinical psychology journals found that only 29 percent of the articles included ethnic minority populations, and only 5 percent focused specifically on these populations (Iwamasa et al., 2002).

Types of Therapy

Traditional Therapies.   Traditional psychotherapies are based on a medical model in which emotional pain is viewed as a "disease" which must be "treated" by an expert. This leads to a therapeutic relationship marked by an imbalance of power between therapist (often male) and patient (often female). In addition, the individual's emotional problems are seen as having internal, not external causes. The goal of therapy is to promote the person's adjustment to existing social conditions (Worell & Remer, 2003).

Feminist therapy strives toward an egalitarian therapist–client relationship based on mutual respect.

Nonsexist and Feminist Therapies.   According to **nonsexist therapy,** *women and men should be treated equally and viewed as individuals*. In addition, there is less of a power imbalance between therapist and client. Nonsexist therapy is similar to traditional therapies, however, in its focus on internal causes of psychological problems. **Feminist therapy** on the other hand, *emphasizes the role of social, political, and economic stresses facing women as a major source of their psychological problems* (Worell & Remer, 2003). Feminist therapists focus on issues of oppression, such as sexism, racism, and heterosexism (Moradi et al., 2000). They encourage women to become psychologically and economically independent and to try to change a sexist society rather than adjust to it. Another principle of feminist therapy is that therapists should not be more powerful than their clients but should build egalitarian relationships with them. One vehicle for doing so is **counselor self-disclosure**, *the imparting of personal information about the life experiences of the therapist to the client* (Remer & Oakley, 2005). In addition, feminist therapy stresses awareness of the ethnic and cultural differences between client and therapist (Sparks & Park, 2000; Szymanski, 2003; Worell & Remer, 2003). Feminist therapy is a philosophy underlying therapy rather than a specific therapeutic technique, and it can be integrated with other treatment approaches (Marecek, 2001).

SUMMARY

Factors Promoting Mental Health

- Social support enhances mental health.
- Females seek and use social support more than males do.
- In reaction to stress, women more often show the "tend and befriend" response, whereas men are more likely to exhibit "fight or flight" behavior.
- Optimism is linked to positive mental and physical health.

Mental Health in Childhood and Adolescence

- Stress levels increase for girls and boys during adolescence. Much of girls' stress stems from relationship problems and is linked to higher rates of depression.
- Externalizing problems in girls are less common than internalizing problems, but are more likely to be associated with adult maladjustment.

Eating Disorders

- Anorexia nervosa is marked by severe weight loss and fear of being overweight.
- Bulimia nervosa is characterized by cycles of binging and purging.

- Biological, psychological, and cultural factors are involved in these disorders, which occur most often in adolescent girls.
- Adolescent girls are less likely than boys to use most illegal drugs.
- Stress levels increase for girls and boys during adolescence. Most of girls' stress stems from relationship problems and is linked to higher rates of depression.
- Externalizing problems in girls are less common than internalizing problems but are more likely to be associated with adult maladjustment.

Substance Use and Abuse

- Women are less likely to be heavy drinkers than men, but binge drinking is increasing in college women.
- Women's alcoholism starts later than men's, progresses more quickly, and is diagnosed at a more advanced stage.
- Drinking in pregnancy can cause FAS or FAE. Women are less likely than men to use most illegal drugs.

Anxiety Disorders and Depression

- Anxiety disorders are more common in women than men. These include panic disorders and specific phobias.

- Depression is twice as common in women as in men. Possible explanations for this difference include biological factors, stressful life events, learned helplessness, self-silencing, and women's ruminative style in responding to depression.

Mental Health of Lesbians

- Homophobia can cause considerable stress in the lives of lesbians, gays, and bisexuals, resulting in a variety of psychological problems.

Mental Health of Older Women

- The psychological health of women improves as they get older.
- Older women who cope successfully with aging tend to integrate agency and communion.
- Some older women continue their careers; others become volunteers, or advocates for social causes.

Diagnosis and Treatment of Psychological Disorders

- Gender bias exists in diagnosis and treatment of psychological disorders.
- Women of color face external stresses, which can intensify mental health problems and prevent them from seeking help.
- Traditional psychotherapies are marked by a power imbalance between therapist and client, and focus on internal causes of emotional problems.
- Nonsexist therapy treats women and men equally.
- Feminist therapy is nonsexist, encourages equal power between therapist and client, and focuses on societal causes of women's problems.

KEY TERMS

anorexia nervosa
bulimia nervosa
female athlete triad
telescoping
binge drinking
fetal alcohol syndrome (FAS)

fetal alcohol effect (FAE)
generalized anxiety disorder
panic disorder
agoraphobia
specific phobia
depression

Diagnostic and Statistical
    Manual IV
nonsexist therapy
feminist therapy
counselor self-disclosure

WHAT DO YOU THINK?

1. If you became aware that a friend of yours had an eating disorder, what steps could you take to try to help?

2. Why do you think our society is less tolerant of drinking in women than in men?

3. In your opinion, why are women more likely than men to suffer from anxiety disorders and depression?

4. Why do you think that U.S. males are more likely to commit suicide than females, whereas females are more likely to attempt it?

5. How might stereotypes about women and men affect the way psychotherapists work with female and male clients?

IF YOU WANT TO LEARN MORE

Ballou, M., & Brown, L. S. (2002). *Rethinking mental health and disorder: Feminist perspectives.* New York: Guilford.

Brown, D. R., & Keith, V. M. (Eds.). (2003). *In and out of our right minds: The mental health of African American women.* New York: Columbia University Press.

Comas-Díaz, L., & Greene, B. (Eds.). (1994). *Women of color: Integrating ethnic and gender identities in psychotherapy.* New York: Guilford.

Enns, C. Z. (2004). *Feminist theories and feminist psychotherapies: Origins, themes, and diversity* (2d ed). New York: Haworth.

Gillem, A. R. (2004). *Biracial women in therapy: Between the rock of gender and the hard place of race.* New York: Haworth.

Hendricks, J. (2003). *Slim to none: A journey through the waste-land of anorexia treatment.* New York: Contempory Books.

Hornbacher, M. (1998). *Wasted: A memoir of anorexia and bulimia.* New York: Harper Perennial.

Kopala, M., & Keitel, M. A. (Eds.). (2003). *Handbook of counseling women.* Thousand Oaks, CA: Sage.

Levine, M. P., & Smolak, L. (2005). *The prevention of eating problems and eating disorders: Theory, research, and practice.* Mahwah, NJ: Erlbaum.

Nolen-Hoeksema, S. (2003). *Women who think too much: How to break free of overthinking and reclaim your life.* New York: Holt.

Ritter, K. Y., & Terndrup, A. I. (2002). *Handbook of affirmative psychotherapy with lesbians and gay men.* New York: Guilford.

Slater, L., Daniel, J. H., & Banks, A. E. (2003). *The complete guide to mental health for women.* Boston: Beacon Press.

Stoppard, J. M., & McMullen, L. M. (Eds.). (2003). *Situating sadness: Women's depression in social context.* New York: New York University Press.

Sue, D. W., & Sue, D. (2003). *Counseling the culturally diverse.* New York: Wiley.

Taylor, S. (2003). *The tending instinct.* New York: Henry Holt.

Worell, J., & Goodheart, C. (Eds.). (2005). *Handbook of girls' and women's psychological health.* New York: Oxford University Press.

Worell, J., & Remer, P. (2003). *Feminist perspectives in therapy: Empowering diverse women.* Hoboken, NJ: Wiley.

WEBSITES

Mental Health

Mental Health Net: Self-help Resources Index
http://www.cmhc.com/
National Mental Health Association
http://www.nmha.org
Suicide Prevention Action Network
http://www.spanusa.org

Eating Disorders

http://www.mirror-mirror.org/

Alcohol and Substance Abuse

National Institute on Drug Abuse
http://www.nida.nih.gov

Vital Older Women

Older Women's League—OWL
http://www.owl-national.org/
Older Adult Consumer Mental Health Alliance
http://www.oacmha.com

14 Violence Against Girls and Women

Ronnie Falco, a computer science graduate of prestigious Stanford University, began a successful career as a software designer, work that she loved. Unfortunately, however, due to the frustrating interactions she had with her male colleagues, her computer career was short-lived. Her coworkers did not look at her when they spoke to her, directed questions at male colleagues even when she had greater expertise, and seemed to resent her successful solutions to problems. Consequently, after 10 years in the computer industry, Ronnie Falco left and went into the health field. (Piller, 1998)

I suffered at home for over 20 years watching my father try to kill my mother. It was unbelievably frightening to me, and I feel it's taken a terrible toll on me which is still going on. I'm talking about depression, relationship problems, you name it, my life feels like a mess. Living in that situation was horrific. I used to see the carving knife on the landing, and my father would chase my mother upstairs with it. I would hide her in my bedroom and put the chest of drawers against the door, and I'd tell her to get into my bed. Then I'd go out of my bedroom to take the knife off him. That happened dozens and dozens of times in my life. It's beyond words to describe this situation. My father never actually killed my mother, but the constant threat was almost as bad because I never knew what he'd do. I felt I could never go out—that I had to stay at home with my mother because who knew what would happen if I went out and left her alone. To put this on a child destroys you. (Susan, mid-thirties, in Russell, 2001, p. 132)

In this chapter, we focus on negative experiences that girls and women can encounter in personal relationships at school and on the job. We start with sexual harassment at school and in the workplace. We then turn to a bleak aspect of childhood for all too many girls: sexual abuse and others forms of violence and neglect. Next, we look at the disturbing violent side of some relationships, with an examination of dating violence, rape, including date rape, and intimate partner violence. We conclude with an examination of elder abuse.

Sexual Harassment at School

Sexual harassment in an educational setting includes *unwelcome verbal or physical behavior of a sexual nature when (a) submission to or rejection of the behavior forms the basis for decisions about the student (e.g., admission, grades); or (b) the behavior creates an intimidating, hostile, or offensive study environment.* Sexual harassment at school unfortunately is widespread around the globe (DeSouza, 2003). In most cases, boys harass girls, rather than the other way around. Ethnic minority girls, students with disabilities, and lesbian, gay, and bisexual students are more likely to be sexually harassed than their peers (Reid & Zalk, 2001; Smith, 2001). Sexual harassment by peers is much more common than sexual harassment committed by teachers, but students are much more distressed when the harasser is a teacher (Timmerman, 2003).

Elementary and Secondary School

Reports of student sexual harassment are on the rise among junior and senior high school students. In a 2001 survey by the American Association of University Women (AAUW), about half of girls said they had received sexual comments or looks (see Figure 14.1). Nearly half reported being touched, grabbed, or pinched in a sexual way. Two-thirds of girls, but less than one-third of boys, said they were upset after being harassed. Nearly one-third of the girls reported that the

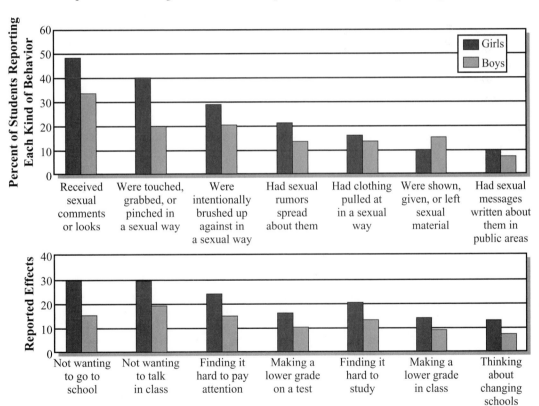

FIGURE 14.1   Percentage of Junior and Senior High School Students Who Reported Experiencing Unwelcomed Sexual Behavior at School "Often" or "Occasionally," and Its Effects

Source: *Data from* American Association of University Women (AAUW, 2001).

unwanted activity made them not want to go to school or talk in class. Girls who are harassed are also more likely to experience academic difficulties, physical symptoms (e.g., headache, digestive upset), interpersonal relationship problems, and negative psychological outcomes such as feeling self-conscious, embarrassed, anxious, afraid, less confident, confused about who they are, and unpopular (DeZolt & Hull, 2001; Duffy et al., 2004; Murnen & Smolak, 2000; Nishina & Juvonen, 2005; Timmerman, 2003). A troublesome finding is that teachers rarely intervene, even when they are aware of serious incidents of sexual harassment. Instead of considering sexual harassment to be serious misconduct, school authorities too often treat it as harmless instances of "boys will be boys" (AAUW, 2001).

That attitude may be changing, however. A landmark decision in 1999 by the U.S. Supreme Court ruled that any school or college receiving federal funds must protect students from severe and pervasive sexual harassment by other students. The case involved 10-year-old LaShonda Davis, who was subjected to five months of unwanted sexual touching and taunting by a male classmate. Despite repeated complaints and pleas for help, school officials took no action. As the harassment continued, LaShonda Davis's grades declined, she became increasingly despondent, and wrote of suicide. At that point her mother sued the school district for their failure to respond, a suit upheld by the Supreme Court after five years of litigation ("Students and Sexual Harassment," 1999).

The College Campus

Although sexual harassment was legally defined earlier in the chapter, there are wide variations in people's conceptions of harassing behaviors. Before reading this section, perform the exercise in Get Involved 14.1 to examine the behaviors and situations that you and your acquaintances classify as sexual harassment.

Research shows there are gender differences in the tendency to classify behaviors such as those listed in Get Involved 14.1 as sexual harassment. Women perceive more situations as harassing than men do (Rotundo et al., 2001), and they are harsher in their judgments of the harasser (Sigal et al., 2005). Whether an individual perceives a behavior as harassment also depends, in part, on the role relationship between the harasser and target. When students are targets, behaviors are more likely to be seen as harassment if they are performed by a professor than by another student (e.g., Bursik, 1992). Did you find these two patterns when you performed the Get Involved activity?

The questions in Get Involved 14.1 raise two controversial issues related to power. One is whether sexual harassment by definition is restricted to behaviors performed by a person with authority (e.g., a professor) over a target (e.g., a student). The other is whether a sexual relationship between individuals who differ in power, as in a professor-student relationship, constitutes sexual harassment even if the student gives consent. In the first issue, the crucial criteria are (1) the target perceives the behavior as unwelcome, and (2) the unwanted behavior creates a hostile or offensive atmosphere for the target. If these conditions are met, it is not necessary that the perpetrator have power over the target (e.g., Fitzgerald, 1996).

GET INVOLVED **14.1**

What Constitutes Sexual Harassment on Campus?

Check each of the following items that you believe is a form of sexual harassment if experienced by a student. Then ask one female student and one male student to do the same.

_____comments on personal appearance by a student

_____comments on personal appearance by a professor

_____unwanted letters or phone calls of a sexual nature from a student

_____unwanted letters or phone calls of a sexual nature from a faculty member

_____unwanted sexually suggestive looks or gestures from a student

_____unwanted sexually suggestive looks or gestures from a faculty member

_____offensive sexually suggestive stories or jokes told by a student

_____offensive sexually suggestive stories or jokes told by a faculty member

_____inappropriate staring by a student that causes discomfort

_____inappropriate staring by a faculty member that causes discomfort

_____unwelcome seductive remarks or questions by a student

_____unwelcome seductive remarks or questions by a faculty member

_____unwanted pressure for dates by a student

_____unwanted pressure for dates by a faculty member

_____unwanted leaning, touching, or pinching by a student

_____unwanted leaning, touching, or pinching by a faculty member

_____unwanted pressure for sexual favors by a student

_____unwanted pressure for sexual favors by a faculty member

_____nonforced sexual relationship between a faculty member and a student

_____nonforced sexual relationship between two students

_____forced sexual intercourse by a student

_____forced sexual intercourse by a faculty member

What Does It Mean?

Separately sum the behaviors you classified as sexual harassment if performed by a student and those seen as sexual harassment if performed by a faculty member. Do the same for each of your respondents.

1. Compare the number of behaviors seen as harassment if performed by a student to those if performed by a faculty member. Is there a difference in your answers or in those of your respondents? Try to explain any differences you might have found. Are these differences consistent with the evidence presented in the text?

2. Is there any difference in the number of behaviors seen as harassment by your female and male respondents? If yes, does it match the difference presented in the text? What do you think can explain this?

Source: Based on Shepela & Levesque (1998).

There is greater controversy surrounding the second issue. Does a romantic relationship between a professor and student constitute sexual harassment, regardless of whether it is consensual? One view is that as long as the student is an adult and expresses willingness to enter into a sexual relationship with a professor, that relationship is acceptable. Male students are more likely than female students to subscribe to this view (L'Armand et al., 2002). Another perspective is that whenever a formal power differential between two people is present, a sexual relationship involves some degree of coercion because the target is not really in a position to freely consent or refuse. According to this viewpoint, *any* sexual behavior directed at a student by a professor is harassment (Fitzgerald, 1996). Some schools have gone so far as to forbid any consensual sexual relationship between students and faculty, while others merely suggest that such relationships are a bad idea (Bartlett, 2002). What is the policy at your school?

Incidence of Sexual Harassment.   The frequency of sexual harassment on college campuses is hard to assess for a number of reasons. Not only do few students submit formal complaints of harassment, but surveys of harassment experiences also show that the incidence varies from campus to campus. Also, the frequency of sexual harassment varies according to the specific type of unwanted conduct and the nature of the power relationship between the harasser and the target. Despite these problems, however, we can draw certain conclusions from recent surveys. First, most students indicate that females are more likely than males to be sexually harassed (Cochran et al., 1997; Kalof et al., 2001). Second, women are more likely to experience subtle forms of harassment, such as unwanted sexually suggestive jokes or body language, than they are to encounter more blatant forms, such as unwanted sexual advances, although the latter do occur (e.g., Cortina et al., 1998; Shepela & Levesque, 1998). Third, students are more likely to experience unwanted sexual behaviors by other students than by faculty members (e.g., Cochran et al., 1997; Shepela & Levesque, 1998).

What about the experiences of doubly oppressed groups of women? Lesbian and bisexual women are more likely than heterosexual women to experience sexual harassment (Cortina et al., 1998). Among ethnic minority groups, incidence rates are highest for Black and Latina women, lowest for Asian American women, and in between these extremes for White women (Cortina et al., 1998).

College women have reported harassment not only in the academic environment, but also within collegiate sports. Since the passage of Title IX (see Chapter 4), the dramatic growth in women's participation in athletics has been accompanied by a sharp decrease—from 90 percent to under 50 percent—in the percentage of female coaches of women's sports (Gill, 2001). At the same time, female student athletes are also experiencing a rising incidence of harassment by their (usually male) coaches (Heywood, 1999).

Responses to Sexual Harassment.   What do people do when they experience sexual harassment? Caroline Cochran and her associates (Cochran et al., 1997) examined the responses of students, faculty, and staff to unwanted sexual attention. Their results showed that the most common response was to ignore the behavior (60 percent). Avoidance of the harasser and talking to others about the harassment were other common reactions. Only 5 percent filed a formal complaint. Unfortunately, this lack of formal response hinders attempts to reduce the frequency of harassment. See Table 14.1 for recommended ways to reduce sexual harassment on campus.

TABLE 14.1   Recommended Procedures for Reducing Sexual Harassment on Campus

Michele Paludi (1996) has made several recommendations about actions students can take to ensure that a campus environment is free of sexual harassment. Here is a sampling of these.

1. Find out whether your campus has policies and procedures for dealing with sexual harassment.
2. Establish a Sexual Harassment Awareness Week during which campuswide activities related to sexual harassment take place. These events can include activities such as plays, movies, and group discussions about sexual harassment.
3. Establish a peer educators program. Peer educators can provide both information to the campus community at large and support to those who have been harassed.

Source: Based on Paludi (1996).

Sexual Harassment in the Workplace

Analogous to the definition of sexual harassment in academic settings, the legal definition of **sexual harassment in the workplace** is *unwelcome verbal or physical behavior when (a) submission to, or rejection of the behavior forms the basis for work-related decisions* (**quid pro quo harassment**), *or (b) the behavior creates an intimidating, hostile, or offensive work environment* (**hostile environment**) (Fitzgerald et al., 2001). Examples of quid pro quo harassment would be the offer of a promotion in exchange for sex and the threat of a layoff if sex were refused. The hostile environment form of harassment is illustrated by the experience of Ronnie Falco, the software engineer described in the vignette at the beginning of the chapter. In Louise Fitzgerald's widely used three-part model of sexual harassment, *quid pro quo* harassment is labeled **sexual coercion.** She divides the *hostile environment* category into two types of behavior: **Gender harassment** is insulting, hostile, and degrading behavior, but not for the purpose of sexual activity (i.e., "the put down"); **unwanted sexual attention** is unwelcome and offensive behavior of a sexual nature (i.e. "the come on") (Street et al., 2003).

Incidence

How common is sexual harassment in the workplace? Although few incidents reach the legal standard of harassment (Fitzgerald et al., 2001), unwanted sexual behaviors in the workplace are commonplace. Virtually all large-scale studies of sexual harassment have concluded that a large proportion of women experience some form of sexual harassment in the workplace (Cleveland et al., 2005). Most commonly, harassment takes the form of sexual remarks and jokes (Auster, 2001; Bell et al., 2002). Although sexual coercion is relatively rare, it does occur. Frequently, the victims are relatively uneducated, and desperately in need of work. Several particularly disturbing cases have involved Latina immigrant farm workers and food packers in the United States who have been forced to have sex with their supervisors or risk being fired, deported, given more physically demanding work, or receiving a cut in pay (Clarren, 2005; Simon, 1998).

Although any woman in any work situation might experience harassment, there are certain factors associated with the greater likelihood of its occurrence. We now turn to an examination of these.

Occupational Characteristics Related to Sexual Harassment.   Sexual harassment is more common in male-dominated blue-collar occupations, such as auto work, firefighting, law enforcement, custodial work, skilled repair, construction, and transit, than in other male-dominated, female-dominated, or gender-balanced jobs (Bell et al., 2002; Fassinger, 2001; Sadler et al., 2004).

To investigate the job climate for women in different occupations, Phyllis Mansfield and her colleagues (Mansfield et al., 1991) examined female workers in two male-dominated (blue-collar) jobs and one traditional female-dominated job (school secretary). Among their respondents, 60 percent of the tradeswomen and 36 percent of the transit workers, compared to only 6 percent of the school secretaries, reported experiencing sexual harassment (Mansfield et al., 1991). Moreover, the blue-collar workers were more likely than the clerical employees to feel isolated and to perceive their supervisors and coworkers as sexist and disrespectful. Also, not surprisingly, they expressed less job satisfaction.

In another study of women in blue-collar occupations, Janice Yoder and Patricia Aniakudo interviewed and surveyed 22 Black female firefighters about their experiences on the job. These researchers found that nearly all these women were subjected to unwanted sexual behaviors including teasing and jokes, suggestive looks, deliberate touching, and unwelcome pressure for dates. In addition to sexual harassment, they reported isolation, lack of support, hostility, and hypercritical training, as well as racism. Consider one woman's experience: "No one really talked to me. It was difficult the first, I'd say, 6 months, because I was basically alone. I'd walk in and everything would get quiet. I'd go to eat; everybody leaves the room . . . I've been on the job now 7 years, and there're still guys that don't talk to me" (Yoder & Aniakudo, 1999, p. 141). Another woman described her first interaction with her White male captain as follows: "The first day I came on, the first day I was in the field, the guy told me he didn't like me. And then he said: 'I'm gonna tell you why I don't like you. Number one, I don't like you cuz you're Black. And number two, cuz you're a woman'" (Yoder & Aniakudo, 1999, p. 140).

Another historically male-dominated field associated with a high incidence of sexual harassment and sexual abuse is the military. To mention one glaring recent example, almost a quarter of the female cadets who graduated from the U.S. Air Force Academy in 2003 were sexually assaulted at the academy and 12 percent were victims of attempted rape. In addition, nearly 70 percent of female cadets reported experiencing sexual harassment at the academy. Many cadets did not initially report the incidents because they feared ostracism, humiliation, and reprisals (Young, 2003). Female cadets, who make up about 18 percent of the student body,

Sexual harassment in the workplace can take many forms.

report being warned by older students about a culture of rape and harassment that victims must accept without complaint if they want to remain at the academy. In the words of one student "They tell you to expect getting raped, and if it doesn't happen to you, you're one of the rare ones. They say . . . if you want to graduate, you don't tell" (Janofsky & Schemo, 2003, p. YT 1). In addition, a recent investigation of women soldiers on active duty found that over 100 servicewomen in Iraq, Kuwait, and Afghanistan reported being sexually assaulted or raped by fellow troops over the previous 18 months (Schmitt, 2004).

Why is sexual harassment of women more common in male-dominated blue-collar occupations and the military than in other jobs? One possibility is that because these fields are strongly associated with the male gender stereotype, male-related physical attributes and skills are highly salient in the performance of these jobs. For example, the investigation of the Air Force Academy scandal suggests that male cadets felt that women slowed them down and were bad for morale (Janofsky & Schemo, 2003).

In addition to the type of occupation, another job characteristic that affects the likelihood of harassment is an organization's standards about acceptable behavior (Gutek, 2001). Theresa Glomb and her colleagues (Glomb et al., 1999) interviewed both nonacademic and academic female university employees about their sexual harassment experiences. These researchers found a positive relationship between their respondents' perceptions that the work environment was tolerant of sexual harassment and their experiences with harassment. Not surprisingly, employers' and supervisors' attitudes regarding the appropriateness and seriousness of harassment can set the tone for behavior in the workplace.

Target Characteristics Related to Sexual Harassment.   Sexual harassment tends to target certain groups more than others. One key characteristic is gender. Women are far more likely than men to be targets and are more likely to report finding these experiences distressing (Gutek, 2001; Ménard et al., 2003; Street et al., 2003), Women are more likely than men to feel frightened and degraded, whereas men are more likely to feel flattered by these behaviors (Koss et al., 1994).

Age and marital status are two other target characteristics associated with harassment. Younger or unmarried women are more likely than older or married females to be harassed (Gutek & Done, 2001). This is possibly because younger and single women are seen as more powerless and vulnerable than their older or married counterparts.

Lesbian women are another group at higher risk (Brogan et al., 2003; Gutek & Done, 2001). If their sexual identity is not known, they are seen as single women; thus, their risk goes up for that reason. Alternatively, if they are open about their identity, antilesbian prejudice can increase the likelihood that they will be targets of harassment.

Several researchers have examined the incidence of sexual harassment among women of different ethnic groups and have found mixed results (Gutek & Done, 2001; Shupe et al., 2002). Studies of women in the military have found that White women report the fewest harassment experiences followed by Asian American women, Latinas, and Black women. Native American women report the highest levels of harassment (Bergman & Drasgow, 2003). Audrey Murrell (1996) notes that ethnic stereotypes of Black women as permissive and hypersexual, Latinas as submissive and hypersexual, and Asian American women as submissive might increase the likelihood that these women are seen as suitable targets for harassment. In addition, she suggests that the marginalization of women of color within the work environment can lower their perceived power, further increasing their risk for harassment.

Characteristics of Offenders.   The picture that emerges from research on harassers is that the way these men construct gender might serve as a foundation for their harassing behaviors. Specifically, harassers tend to have negative attitudes toward women, hold traditional gender attitudes, and perceive sexual relationships as manipulative and exploitative (Gutek & Done, 2001; Ménard et al., 2003). That is, the most likely offenders appear to be traditional men who do not view women as equals.

Consequences

There is considerable evidence that serious psychological and physical consequences for women can result from sexual harassment, including decreased self-esteem, lowered life satisfaction, anger, fear, depression, anxiety, interpersonal difficulties, headaches, gastrointestinal problems, sleep disturbances, high blood pressure, disordered eating, substance abuse, and sexual problems. Additionally, women can experience undesirable job-related outcomes, including reduced job satisfaction, decreased morale, increased absenteeism, and a decline in organizational commitment (Bond et al., 2004; Cleveland et al., 2005; Fitzgerald, 2003). Even if a woman has not experienced sexual harassment herself, just working in an organizational environment that is hostile toward women can have negative effects on her sense of well-being (Miner-Rubino & Cortina, 2004).

Do women who acknowledge they have been harassed have more negative outcomes than those who do not? Louise Fitzgerald and her colleagues (Magley et al., 1999; Munson et al., 2001) found that women who were targeted with unwelcome sexual behaviors had negative psychological and physical reactions whether or not they labeled their experience as harassment. The authors note that women might not realize certain behaviors fit the definition of harassment or, alternatively, they might want to avoid the label of victim. The lack of labeling unwanted sexual acts as harassment does not, however, affect the consequences of those behaviors. It is the experiencing of these behaviors on the job, and not the labeling of them as harassment, that leads to unpleasant psychological and physical outcomes.

Explanations

How can we account for the occurrence of sexual harassment in the workplace? According to **sex-role spillover theory** (Gutek, 2001), *in workplaces with unequal concentrations of women and men, gender is a highly salient attribute. Consequently, in these environments men respond to female employees more as women than as workers. That is, they allow gender roles to spill over into the workplace and to influence their interactions with female workers.* The high incidence of sexual harassment among blue-collar workers supports this theory and points to the importance of an employment context in which male-related physical attributes are very prominent (Ragins & Scandura, 1995). In this type of situation harassment reflects a restrictive construction of gender that specifies separate behaviors and roles for women and men. This inflexibility results in viewing women not as competent workers but as targets of male-female interactions.

The **power theory** of sexual harassment states that *sexual harassment is seen as an abuse of power to gain sexual favors or to reinforce the imbalance in power* (Gutek & Done, 2001). Because society accords greater power to men than to women, men generally have more power in the workplace, and some men abuse this power for sexual ends (e.g., Kurth et al., 2000). Consistent with this theory, women are more upset by unwanted sexual advances from high-status men than from low-status men (Bourgeois & Perkins, 2003). The male-dominated blue-collar occupations, where sexual harassment is most frequent, provides a good example of power theory. According to Fiske and Glick (1995), men in these occupations hold most of the power for several reasons. First, men historically view the blue-collar workplace as their own territory. Second, they are in the majority. Third, they view the few women who enter these occupations as being on probation. Fourth, the generally male supervisors support male workers' power. Fifth, men's overall greater physical strength is an important attribute for most blue-collar jobs. Sixth, men have higher status in society in general. These factors not only maintain a power imbalance in which men are more likely to harass but also contribute to an organizational climate in which the negative effects of sexual harassment tend to be minimized and in which complaints about harassment might not be seen as serious.

Women's Responses

> *After we, a mostly female staff, facilitated the removal of our harassing principal, we had a long group lunch together. We all shared our personal experiences with that man. The shocking thing was that most of the staff had been targeted at one time or another over an 18-year period, and that each of us thought we were the only one and that it was our fault.* (Holly, 50-year-old school teacher)

How do women respond to sexual harassment? Louise Fitzgerald and her colleagues (Fitzgerald et al., 2001) propose a two-category framework that classifies the large variety of responses to sexual harassment as either internally focused or externally focused. **Internally focused responses** are *responses that attempt to manage the emotions and cognitions associated with the incident(s).* For example, ignoring the situation, minimizing the event, or blaming oneself are adjustments that aim to reduce negative emotions or thoughts about the situation. **Externally focused responses**, on the other hand, are *responses that attempt to solve the problem.* Examples are avoiding the harasser, asking him to stop, or seeking organizational assistance. Filing a complaint or lawsuit are rare responses (Magley, 2002).

Most women who are sexually harassed do not confront the perpetrator or report the event, as in Holly's example at the beginning of this section. Why is this? For one thing, sexually harassed women frequently experience guilt, shame, and embarrassment as a result of their harassment (Koss et al., 1994), their fear of retaliation, or humiliation. They also desire to maintain harmony in the workplace (Riger, 2000). In addition, there are social costs to confronting the perpetrator, including fear of retaliation (Shelton & Stewart, 2004). These fears are often justified. Women who report their harassment often experience negative outcomes, such as lowered job evaluations, humiliation, and both physical and psychological health problems (Cortina & Magley, 2003; Ormerod et al., 2003).

Latina women are more likely than White women to avoid or not report the harasser. This may stem from several elements in Hispanic culture, including respect for individuals of higher status, emphasis on harmonious ingroup relations, and a greater adherence to traditional gender roles which fosters more tolerance of sexual harassment and discourages women from discussing sexual topics (Cortina, 2004; Wasti & Cortina, 2002).

Violence Against Girls

> *Violence against women is a pervasive problem that encompasses physical and sexual abuse perpetrated against a woman or female child by persons known or unknown to her, including but not limited to, spouses, partners, boyfriends, fathers, brothers, acquaintances,*

or strangers. . . . At least one woman in three globally is beaten, coerced into sex, or otherwise abused in her lifetime. . . . Because of incidents of nonfatal intimate assaults that occur each year in the U.S. . . . violence is a women's health concern, a human rights issue, and a major public health problem. (Koss et al., 2003, pp. 130–142).

Tragically, both girls and women are victims of violence. In this section, we focus on two forms of violence that are especially likely to be perpetrated against girls: child sexual abuse, and infanticide or neglect.

Child Sexual Abuse

Sexual abuse of children is viewed by many as among the most heinous of crimes (Rathus et al., 2005). While definitions vary, a typical definition of **child sexual abuse** *includes both contact and noncontact sexual experiences in which the victim is below the age of consent and the abuser is significantly older or in a position of power over the child* (Barnett et al., 2005). Sexually suggestive language or exhibitionism are examples of noncontact experience, while contact abuse may range from kissing, fondling, and sexual touching to oral sex and vaginal or anal intercourse. The most recent development in child sexual abuse is exploitation through the Internet. Children may be propositioned online for sexual activity, exposed to various forms of sexually explicit material, or experience online harassment (Barnett et al., 2005).

Incest is a form of child abuse. **Incest** *may be defined narrowly as sexual contact between a child and a close blood relative or other family member.* Incest may be particularly devastating emotionally to a child. It involves a loss of trust in and deep sense of betrayal by the abuser and perhaps other family members—especially the mother—whom the child may perceive as failing to provide protection (Rathus et al., 2005).

Incidence. The incidence of child sexual abuse is difficult to pinpoint precisely. One recent official report estimated that approximately 240,000 children annually were victims of *substantiated* sexual abuse (Barnett et al., 2005). Because many cases of abuse are never reported, this figure is unfortunately quite conservative. An estimated 20 percent of girls and 5 percent of boys are abused during childhood (Villarosa, 2002c). Black, Latina, Native American, and White women report similar rates of child sexual abuse (Koss et al., 2003; Wyatt et al., 2002).

For both females and males, most sexual abuse is committed by a family member or a family friend, takes place at home, and occurs more than once. The large majority of cases involve a female victim and a male perpetrator (Barnett et al., 2005; Villarosa, 2002c), a blatant illustration of the power differential between females and males. In the recent scandal involving child sexual abuse by Catholic clergy, the focus has been on priests who abused boys (Banerjee, 2005). But in fact it is far more common for priests to commit sexual acts with girls and women then with boys and men (Dillon, 2002).

The most frequently reported and publicized type of incest is between a daughter and her father or stepfather, but surveys indicate that brother-sister incest may actually be more common (Rathus et al., 2005). In one study of college students, for instance, 39 percent of the women and 21 percent of the men reported an incestuous relationship with a sibling of the other gender, while just 4 percent reported such a relationship with their father (Finkelhor, 1990). These figures for sibling incest are much higher than the reported incidence of sexual abuse mentioned above. Perhaps brother-sister incest is less likely to be perceived or reported as sexual abuse.

Few girls and even fewer boys tell anyone about being sexually abused. When girls talk to anyone about it, they are most likely to confide in their best friend or their mother (Commonwealth Fund, 1997). Why do so few children talk about being sexually abused? For one thing, they are relatively powerless, and they may fear retaliation from the abuser. Second, the offender is often a trusted and beloved adult whom the youngster may be reluctant to accuse. In addition, the child may feel embarrassed, humiliated, and responsible for encouraging or allowing the abusive behavior to occur (Daniluk, 1998). Claire knows this from personal experience. As she walked home from school one day at age 12, a nicely dressed man who introduced himself as a doctor began chatting with her about the possibility of baby-sitting for his two young sons. He became increasingly graphic about the details of bathing them. When they reached her apartment building, he began fondling her breasts ("My boys don't have anything like this") until she broke away and ran upstairs, flushed with shame and guilt. It was days before she was able to tell her best friend and weeks before she told her mother. Until this moment, she has told no one else, and even now it is difficult for her to write these words.

Consequences.   Sexual abuse can result in devastating consequences for children, not only in the short term, but also well into their adult lives (Sachs-Ericsson et al., 2005). Girls are more likely than boys to be sexually abused and they are more adversely affected by it (Sanchez-Hucles & Hudgins, 2001; White et al., 2001). Sexually abused children are more likely than other children to be depressed, anxious, or angry, to have behavioral and school problems, to show aggression and bullying, to feel ashamed, and to have low self-esteem (Barnett et al., 2005; Feiring et al., 2002; Spataro et al., 2004; Trickett & Gordis, 2004). Many sexually abused children show symptoms of posttraumatic stress disorder (PTSD) including fears, nightmares and sleep disturbances, and "flashbacks" of the traumatic event (Frieze, 2005; Margolin & Gordis, 2004). Inappropriate sexual behavior directed toward themselves or other children and adults is also a common childhood reaction to sexual abuse (LeTourneau et al., 2004; Margolin & Gordis, 2004).

Adolescents who were sexually abused in childhood show earlier sexual activity, have more sex partners, and are more likely to become pregnant (Koenig et al., 2004; Noll et al., 2003; Vigil et al., 2005). They are also more likely than other teenagers to have eating disorders, be depressed, use drugs and alcohol, begin drug use at an early age, and try to injure themselves or commit suicide (Barnett et al., 2005; Kilpatrick et al., 2003; Ompad et al., 2005; Repetti et al., 2002; Tyler, 2002).

In adulthood, victims of child sexual abuse continue to be more anxious, depressed, and angry; to have interpersonal problems and impaired self-concept;

to feel isolated, stigmatized, and distrustful; to have sexual and substance-abuse problems; to have medical problems such as chronic pelvic pain, chronic headaches, and gastrointestinal problems; and to be more suicidal. They also are more likely to have experienced further sexual assault or physical abuse as adults (Kendall-Tackett et al., 2003; Koss et al., 2003; Messman-Moore & Long, 2003; Ullman & Brecklin, 2003; Whiffen & MacIntosh, 2005). More than a third of the women in state prisons and jails have been sexually or physically abused as children, twice the rate of child abuse reported by women overall ("High Percentage," 1999). In one maximum security facility for women, more than half had been sexually or physically assaulted in childhood (Dittmann, 2003). Estimates of child sexual abuse among women on welfare range from 25 to over 40 percent (DeParle, 1999). The effects of sexual abuse are greatest when the abuser was someone close to the child; when the abuse was frequent, severe, and continued over a long period of time; when force was used; and when vaginal, oral, or anal penetration occurred (Barker-Collo & Read, 2003; Hulme & Agrawal, 2004; Koss et al., 2003).

Treatment. Healing from childhood incest and other forms of sexual abuse is a long and arduous process (Faria & Belohlavek, 1995; Godbey & Hutchinson, 1996). Group or individual psychotherapy helps women break their silence, gain perspective and realize they are not alone, relinquish feelings of responsibility for the abuse, and grieve for what they have lost (Bass & Davis, 1994; Boston Women's Health Book Collective, 1998; Price et al., 2001). Ultimately, therapy can improve survivors' self-esteem and their ability to have intimate relationships.

The effectiveness of treatment for victims of child sexual abuse depends on several factors (Barnett et al., 2005). For example, one study evaluated the outcome of group therapy for 65 women who had been sexually abused by their fathers, stepfathers, or another close male relative (Follette et al., 1991). Women with the best treatment outcomes were those who had more education, had experienced only fondling and not oral sex or intercourse, and had lower levels of distress and depression prior to treatment.

Therapy programs for sexually abused children and adolescents are also available. A comprehensive approach is usually recommended. This may involve play therapy or art therapy for very young children; group therapy for adolescents; individual therapy for the child and each parent; marital therapy for the parents; and family therapy (Cohen & Mannarino, 1998; Lutzker et al., 1999; Rathus et al., 2005). Cognitive behavioral therapy that specifically focuses on the abuse appears more effective than other treatments (Ramchandani & Jones, 2003; Saywitz et al., 2000).

Prevention. Increasing numbers of schools are offering sexual-abuse prevention programs. According to one survey, about two-thirds of children in the United States have participated in such programs (Davis & Gidycz, 2000). The programs help children learn what sexual abuse is, how they can protect themselves from it, and what they should do if they experience actual or potential abuse (Renk et al.,

2002). Children are taught to distinguish between "good" touching, such as an affectionate pat on the back, and "bad" touching. They are also encouraged to tell someone about any abuse that does occur. Children who participate in comprehensive school-based programs are more likely to use effective strategies such as refusing, running away, or yelling when confronted by a potential abuser, and they are more apt to report incidents to adults (Davis & Gidycz, 2000; Rathus et al., 2005).

In addition, all 50 states have enacted laws designed to inform communities of the presence of known sex offenders who have been released from prison. These laws are collectively referred to as Megan's Law, after a 7-year-old girl who was raped and murdered in 1994 by a male neighbor who had recently completed a prison sentence for child sexual abuse (Frieze, 2005; Trivits & Repucci, 2002).

Infanticide and Neglect

Sadly, cultural attitudes that devalue females in many parts of the world lead to practices that have harmful and even deadly effects on female infants and girls. To learn more, see Explore Other Cultures 14.1 and 14.2. You also may wish to reread Explore Other Cultures 7.2 on female genital mutilation.

EXPLORE OTHER CULTURES 14.1
Where Are the Missing Girls in Asia?

Women around the world normally give birth to about 105 boys for every 100 girls. But according to recent census figures, there are 119 boys born in China for every 100 girls. In some Chinese villages, as many as 134 boys are born for every 100 girls (Yardley, 2005). In India, the ratio is 113 boys for every 100 girls from birth to age 6. In some areas, there are over 150 boys for every 100 girls (Hudson & den Boer, 2004). An estimated 100 million girls and women who should be alive in these two countries today and another 3 to 7 million in Pakistan are simply "missing" (Dugger, 2001; Glenn, 2004; Kristof, 2002). In societies where the preference for sons is strong, such as China, India, and Pakistan, discrimination and abuse toward female children can take extreme forms such as infanticide, in which the newborn girl is suffocated, drowned, or abandoned (Carmichael, 2004; Lee, 2004). In addition, girls in India, Pakistan, and China are often victims of neglect, not fed as well, vaccinated as often, or taken to the doctor as quickly when ill (Baghdadi, 2005; Bairagi, 2001; Dugger, 2001; Kristof, 2002). Poor families in China and India often view their daughters as a burden, leading them to sell their baby girls for as little as $20 (Bonner, 2003; Kennedy, 2004; Rosenthal, 2003). With the advent of ultrasound, abortion rates of female fetuses have soared in both India and rural China (Rohde, 2003; Rosenthal, 2003). In India, for example, radiologists travel from one rural clinic to another, toting their compact ultrasound machines. Even Indians living abroad in the United States and Canada are bombarded by ads in the newspaper *India Abroad* asking "Desire a son?" and "Pregnant? Wanna know the gender of your baby right now?" (Sachs, 2001).

The extreme preference for sons in these countries stems from the tradition that sons, not daughters, care for aging parents as well as carry on the family name and occupation. In China, the pressure for sons is intensified by family planning laws that limit couples to one or two children (Yardley, 2005). In India, a girl is viewed as a burden who requires a costly dowry when she marries, leaving her parents with nothing or even a debt (Rohde, 2003). Moreoever, the Hindu religion requires that a father's last rites must be carried out by his son (Kennedy, 2004).

What are the consequences of having a disproportionate number of males in the population? Scholars in both Asia and the West are concerned that the surplus of unattached men could trigger sex-related crimes such as rape, prostitution, abduction of women, and forced marriages as well as other violent crimes and social disorder (Hudson & den Boer, 2004; Tai, 2004). As a result, the Chinese government recently made selective sex abortions a criminal offense (Yardley, 2005).

EXPLORE OTHER CULTURES **14.2**

Girls for Sale: The Horrors of Human Trafficking

About 1 million women and girls worldwide are lured into leaving their homeland each year and forced into prostitution or menial work in other nations. Many are duped with the promise of good jobs in wealthier countries, only to find themselves bound by contracts that immediately place them in enormous debt. Some are forced into unpaid and often inhumane servitude as domestics or nannies (Ehrenreich & Hochschild, 2002; Perlez, 2004). But most are forced to work as prostitutes, literally as sexual slaves, in order to pay off their debt (Cockburn, 2003; Gaines, 2003; Kristof, 2005). Countries that are poor, have high unemployment, and lack women's rights show the most human trafficking, defined as the practice of buying and selling people for profit. Heavy trafficking occurs in East Asia, Africa, Central and Eastern Europe, and Latin America (Herman & West, 2003; "Putting the Sex Trade on Notice," 2004). Sex trafficking is not just a problem of poor countries, however. The United States has become a major importer of sex slaves. It is estimated that there are between 30,000 to 50,000 sex slaves in captivity in the United States at any given time, many from Thailand, India, Cambodia, Russia, and Ukraine (Landesman, 2004). Up to one-third of sex-trafficking victims from Russia and Ukraine are college students, often responding to ads for work abroad as a nanny, a model, or an exotic dancer (MacWilliams, 2003). But the typical age of trafficking victims is dropping. It is not uncommon to find girls as young as 13—or even 8 or 9—caught in the tragic net of sexual slavery (Herman & West, 2003; Landesman, 2004). One reason for this is that men who seek out prostitutes are looking for young girls in order to minimize their risk of exposure to HIV (Cohen, 2005).

Dating Violence

A darker and rarely mentioned side of high school dating relationships is physical aggression toward a dating partner. Dating violence among high school students cuts across socioeconomic boundaries and is occuring with alarming frequency.

Many girls and young women around the world have been lured into sexual slavery.

Incidence of Dating Violence

Studies show that anywhere from 9 percent to 65 percent of adolescents report having had at least one experience of physical aggression in a dating relationship, ranging from being hit, shoved, and slapped to being punched, choked, threatened with a weapon, and forced to engage in sexual activity (Barnett et al., 2005). Females typically engage in the milder forms of violence, such as hitting and slapping, whereas boys engage in more serious acts of violence (Hickman et al., 2004; Noland et al., 2004). Most studies, perhaps surprisingly, find that males are more likely than females to report being victims of dating aggression (Hickman et al., 2004; Lichter & McCloskey, 2004; Noland et al., 2004).

One possible explanation of these findings is that females underreport aggression and/or that males overreport it. Males might overreport their victimization in order to rationalize their own aggression (e.g., "She hits me, so I hit her back"). Another possibility is that females *are* actually more aggressive in their dating relationships. Girls are more likely than boys to report using violence as self-defense, or in retaliation for sexual assault, which is more commonly committed by males (Hickman et al., 2004; White, Donat et al., 2001).

Who Engages in Dating Violence?

Certain factors increase the likelihood that high school students will inflict dating violence. One of the strongest predictors of dating aggression for both girls and boys is being the recipient of dating violence (Fitzpatrick et al., 2004; Hendy et al., 2003; White, Donat et al., 2001). This finding supports the self-defense explanation. Believing that dating violence is justifiable is another strong predictor for both females and males. (Interestingly, both genders are more accepting of dating violence in females.) Holding traditional gender-role attitudes is also linked to dating violence for both sexes (Fitzpatrick et al., 2004; Lichter & McCloskey, 2004). In addition, dating violence is more prevalent among adolescents who were abused as children (Wolfe et al., 2004), whose parents were violent toward each other (Hendy et al., 2003), or who engaged in adolescent sibling violence (Noland et al., 2004).

Moreover, female victims of dating violence are more likely than nonvictims to show risky sexual behavior, to have negative sexual self-perceptions, to have been pregnant, attempted suicide, shown disordered eating behavior, engaged in substance abuse, and suffered from low self-esteem (Lewis & Fremouw, 2001; Offman & Matheson, 2004; Omar & Griffith, 2004; Silverman et al., 2004). Other warning signals that a young couple's relationship may turn violent include possessiveness, controlling behavior, unpredictable mood swings, and antisocial behavior (Furman, 2002; Kelley, 2000). Sadly, these factors continue to be involved in violent adult relationships (Schumacher & Leonard, 2005), as we shall see later in the chapter. The fact that young women who experience dating violence in high school are at greater risk for sexual victimization during college highlights the need to implement programs early in the teen years to curtail such violence (Russell et al., 2003; Silverman et al., 2001; Wolfe et al., 2003). High school interventions such as the Safe Dates program reduce the incidence and severity of dating violence (Foshee et al., 2004).

Rape

During spring break of my senior year in high school, I went to San Padre Island with my girlfriends. One night, we went to a bar and somehow got split up. I had no money and didn't know the way back. Some guys said they'd take a cab with me. They got off at their hotel and told me to come to their room while they called my friends. I was scared to go in but I did. One big guy started to force himself on me. I fought him off and he finally stopped. He didn't actually rape me but he violated my body and my trust. He walked me to my hotel acting like nothing had happened. I never told anyone what went on. I felt people would blame me for losing my friends at the bar and being stupid. (Melinda, 20-year-old college junior)

The definition of **rape** varies across states. However, a common legal definition is *sexual penetration of any bodily orifice against the victim's will, obtained by physical force, the threat of force, or while the victim is incapable of giving consent because of* *mental illness, mental retardation, or intoxication* (Bachar & Koss, 2001). The incident described above by Melinda fits the definition of an attempted rape. First, this student clearly communicated her nonconsent and, second, the size differential between the female student and the perpetrator provided him with the physical force necessary to proceed against her will.

Incidence

In the United States, a woman is raped every two minutes (Buddie & Miller, 2001). Between 15 and 25 percent of women will be raped during her lifetime and the prevalence of rape or attempted rape is especially high in college women (Karjane et al., 2002; Ullman, 2002). Women with disabilities also have an elevated risk of being sexually assaulted (Martin et al., 2004). One of the difficulties in obtaining a "true" rate of rape is that the measurement of sexual victimization is not consistent. For example, questionnaires often use terms such as *unwanted, nonvoluntary, forced,* and *coerced* as though they were synonyms, when in fact these terms have different meanings (Hamby & Koss, 2003).

Few studies have included large numbers of people of color. Furthermore, methodological problems, such as ethnic differences in willingness to report rape, make ethnic comparisons difficult. Given these limitations, the available evidence suggests that the rape rate is very high among Native Americans (Söchting et al., 2004) and is more prevalent among Whites than among Latinas/os or Asian Americans, who have the lowest (Arellano et al., 1997; Merrill et al., 1997; Urquiza & Goodlin-Jones, 1994). Comparisons of Blacks and Whites, however, show inconsistent findings. Some indicate a higher prevalence of rape among Black than White women (Grunbaum et al., 2004; Rozee & Koss, 2001), whereas others suggest either the reverse pattern or no ethnic difference. Regardless of ethnic variations in the prevalence of rape, however, perpetrators tend to be of the same ethnicity and social class as their victims (George & Martinez, 2002).

Acquaintance Rape

Numerous studies have shown that the most frequent form of rape differs from the type of incident typically conceptualized as rape. Many people view "real rape" as being committed by a stranger in a dark alley. In fact, before the 1980s, there was no term for rape committed by a nonstranger. But in 1982, an article published in *Ms.* magazine reported evidence of a common, but undiscussed *form of rape,* called "date rape," *that involves perpetrators and victims who know each other* (Warshaw, 1988). Since that time date rape—or the more inclusive term, **acquaintance rape**—has been used to refer to rape by a nonstranger. Subsequent research indicates that in 8 out of 10 rape cases, the victim knows the perpetrator, who often is a casual or steady dating partner (National Center for Injury Prevention and Control, 2005; "Sexual Assault Awareness," 2005). Furthermore, it is estimated that 8–14 percent of women have been raped by a spouse or cohabiting partner (Bennice & Resick, 2003), and the majority of these women are raped more than once by their spouse (Peacock, 1998). "Often he would rape me while I was still sleeping in my bedroom. I would wake with him inside me. He wouldn't stop even after I asked him to" (p. 229).

Although a large proportion of women have had incidents consistent with the legal definition, few actually label their experience as rape, especially if they are raped by an acquaintance (Kahn, 2004; Kahn et al., 2003; Karjane et al., 2002; Peterson & Muehlenhard, 2004). How can this be explained? According to Mary Koss and Hobart Cleveland (1997), women believe that rape is rare, whereas sexual aggression is common and therefore harmless. Thus, women downplay the negative aspects of their experience by emphasizing what they view as relatively normal sexual aggression, or what some people refer to as "seductive behavior." In fact, there is a good deal of overlap in students' definitions of "rape" and "seduction" (Littleton & Axsom, 2003). Another view (Phillips, 2000) is that the woman blames herself for the experience, and at the same time feels responsible for protecting her partner and the relationship. She therefore reframes the situation as being not violent or abusive. Many women (as well as men) are not aware of the broad range of behaviors that constitute rape. Thus, not surprisingly, victims of acquaintance rape who do not acknowledge they have been raped have a narrower definition of rape than those who do acknowledge their victimization. When the assault involves a boyfriend, if the woman is impaired by alcohol or drugs, if the act involves oral or manual sex, or if the woman is verbally rather than physically coerced, she is unlikely to label the situation as rape (Abbey et al., 2004; Kahn et al., 2003; Kahn, 2004; Peterson & Muehlenhard, 2004).

Like Melinda, in the vignette opening this section, few victims of acquaintance rape report their assault to the police (Bachar & Koss, 2001; Buddie & Miller, 2001). One reason is that they frequently engage in self-blame for putting themselves into a risky situation or for failing to communicate their intentions more clearly. They might also not want to go through the highly embarrassing procedures involved in a police investigation and might be aware of widespread lack of support for rape victims (Koss & Cleveland, 1997).

Factors Associated with Acquaintance Rape

What accounts for the high incidence of acquaintance rape?

Sexual Script.   Koss and her colleagues (e.g., Koss & Cleveland, 1997; Koss et al., 1994) contend that the social construction of the roles of men and women in male-female sexual situations provide a social context in which acquaintance rape can occur. This traditional **sexual script** is *a socialized set of expected behaviors characterized by an aggressive male who initiates and pushes for sexual activity and a gatekeeping female who sets the limits.* That is, instead of encouraging similar behaviors and goals, gender socialization teaches males to use any strategy in their pursuit of sexual intercourse and teaches females they are supposed to control men's sexual impulses.

Interpreting roles in this sexual script can lead to rape for a number of reasons. First, some men take the initiator role to the extreme and engage in sexual aggression. Second, as discussed in Chapter 8, men frequently infer sexual interest when it is not intended (e.g., Dion & Dion, 2001). As sexual initiator, a man's misperception of his partner's nonsexual behaviors as sexual interest can fuel his sexual aggressiveness (Bondurant & Donat, 1999). Third, the differing roles within the sexual script can set the framework for misunderstanding because the male assumes the female will attempt to limit sexual activity as part of her role. If a woman does not resist a man's sexual advances, both women and men assume that she is agreeing to have sex (Anderson et al., 2004). But if she says "no," a man might misinterpret this response as token resistance that really means "yes," leading him to disregard her objections to sex.

To examine the actual frequency of token resistance to sex, Charlene Muehlenhard and Carie Rodgers (1998) asked college women and men to describe real situations, if any, in which they told a sexually willing partner that they didn't want to have sex although, in actuality, they intended to have sexual intercourse with that partner. Only 14 percent of the women respondents described situations that reflected token resistance to a man who had been a previous sexual partner and less than 2 percent reported token resistance to a man with whom they had never had intercourse. Furthermore, although a common stereotype about sex is that women, but not men, engage in token resistance, Muehlenhard and Rodgers found no significant differences in the percentages of women and men who described experiences with token resistance. Consequently, these researchers concluded that, "Although both women and men sometimes engage in token resistance to sex, most do not. All refusal should be taken seriously. Engaging in sex with someone who does not consent is rape" (p. 462).

Characteristics of Sexually Aggressive Men.   Sexually aggressive men, including both rapists and those who use verbal coercion to gain sexual activity, are more likely than nonaggressive men to have witnessed or experienced family violence (Chapple, 2003). Furthermore, they are more likely to hold stereotypical attitudes about gender roles, feel hostility toward women, and be physically aggressive in other situations. They are also more likely to believe in **rape myths** (Christopher & Kisler, 2004; Forbes et al., 2004; Mosher & Danoff-Burg, 2005; Murnen et al., 2002). These are *false beliefs about rape that are widely held and that serve to justify male sexual aggression against women* ("Sexual Assault Awareness," 2005). Some of the most prevalent rape myths are that women lead men on and therefore deserve to be raped, that women often make false accusations of rape, and that no woman can be raped against her will.

As might be expected, men tend to endorse these myths more than women do (e.g., Kennedy & Gorzalka, 2002; Nunes et al., 2004; White & Robinson Kurpius, 2002). Also, Black (Johnson et al., 1997), Latino (Cowan, 2000), and Asian American (Kennedy & Gorzalka, 2002) men more strongly believe rape myths than do White men. Black men's greater acceptance of beliefs supportive of rape might be related to a long history of racist law enforcement, which has made it even more difficult for Black women than for White women to report rape or to obtain legal justice (Bryant-Davis, 2003). The endorsement of these beliefs by

---

GET INVOLVED **14.2**
Gender and Rape Myths

Ask two female and two male acquaintances to indicate their degree of agreement with each of the following four statements about rape, from *strongly disagree* (1) to *strongly agree* (7). If possible, select participants from different ethnic groups.

_____ 1. Women often provoke rape.

_____ 2. Women enjoy rape.

_____ 3. Women frequently falsely claim they have been raped.

_____ 4. Only men who are psychologically disturbed engage in rape.

What Does It Mean?

Sum the four ratings for each respondent. The scores can range from 4 to 28, with higher scores reflecting greater acceptance of rape myths. After scoring each person's answers, average the scores of the two females and those of the two males.

1. Compare the scores of the females and males. Did your male respondents express greater acceptance of rape myths than your female respondents did? If yes, explain. If no, indicate possible reasons why your respondents did not reflect the typically found gender difference.

2. If you tested men of different ethnicities, did you note any difference in their scores? If yes, is this difference consistent with that presented in the text? Was there a difference between women respondents of different ethnicities?

3. Which of these four statements received the greatest degree of agreement from your respondents and which received the least agreement? Give possible reasons for these findings.

4. What do you think influences the development of these rape myths?

5. How do you think rape myth acceptance can be reduced?

Latino and Asian American men, on the other hand, may be due to the strong commitment to patriarchy in these cultures (Cowan, 2000; Mori et al., 1995). To get firsthand knowledge about rape myth acceptance, try Get Involved 14.2. Then, to learn more about attitudes toward rape victims in other cultures, read Explore Other Cultures 14.3.

Characteristics of Victims. Few characteristics differentiate women who are more likely to be raped from those who are less likely. Any woman can be raped. However, the majority of acquaintance victims are between the ages of 12 and 24 (Bachar & Koss, 2001). Moreover, as we saw earlier in this chapter, women who are raped are more likely than nonvictimized women to have been sexually abused in childhood and/or adolescence (Söchting et al., 2004), possibly because early victimization can contribute to feelings of self-blame and powerlessness. Victims of acquaintance rape are also more likely than other women to have suffered previous physical aggression from their partner (Rickert et al., 2004).

EXPLORE OTHER CULTURES 14.3

Attitudes toward Rape Victims Around the World

How are rape victims viewed in cultures outside the United States? Madhabika Nayak and her colleagues (Nayak et al., 2003) and researchers led by Colleen Ward (cited in Best, 2001) examined cross-cultural attitudes toward rape victims by interviewing university students from 17 countries. Relatively favorable attitudes were found in the United Kingdom, the United States, Germany, and New Zealand, while less favorable views were expressed in Turkey, Mexico, Zimbabwe, India, Japan, Kuwait, and Malaysia. Having read Chapters 2 and 3 about cross-cultural differences in gender-role attitudes, can you see a recurring pattern in these findings regarding attitudes toward rape victims? In those countries with more egalitarian views of women, attitudes toward rape victims are more positive, whereas rape victims are more likely to be stigmatized in countries where women's status is much lower than that of men. Some cultures have social and legal customs that sanction severe punishment of women in response to infractions of family "honor" (Vandello & Cohen, 2004). For example, under Muslim law, victims of rape are subjected to severe punishments, including imprisonment, public flogging, and death. Little distinction is made between forced and consensual sex. Men are rarely convicted in rape cases, but women who report a rape are often charged with adultery, which is considered a crime more serious than murder (Dowden, 2002; Mydans, 2002). Each year, hundreds of "honor killings" occur in Islamic cultures, in which girls or women are killed, often by male members of their own families, for perceived breaches of chastity (Arsu, 2005; Husseini, 2003; Sengupta, 2003; Tavernise, 2004). During the recent brutal Taliban regime in Afghanistan, many women from ethnic minority groups were sold as sex slaves and forced to wed Taliban soldiers who soon abandoned them. The abductions are considered such a great dishonor that most of the victims' families now shun them (McGirk & Plain, 2002).

Alcohol Consumption.   There is considerable evidence that alcohol consumption by the perpetrator and the victim increases the risk of both sexual coercion and rape or attempted rape (Abbey et al., 2004; Adams-Curtis & Forbes, 2004; Mohler-Kuo et al., 2004; Ullman, 2003). In part, this is because alcohol interferes with the ability to detect danger as well as resist more promptly (Söchting et al., 2004). Furthermore, when men drink, they may be more likely to misperceive women's drinking as a sign of sexual interest (Abbey et al., 2004).

Effects of Rape

Rape survivors may be psychologically plagued by fear, anxiety, self-blame, powerlessness, depression, and long-term mistrust of men (Bachar & Koss, 2001; Christopher & Kisler, 2004; Coid et al., 2003; Frazier, 2003), whether they are victims of acquaintance rape or stranger rape. Some symptoms, such as self-blame and powerlessness, may be more common among acquaintance victims. As shown in one college student's emotional reaction to rape by her resident advisor, "I wouldn't

Alcohol consumption increases the risk of sexual coercion and rape.

even admit it to myself until about 4 months later when the guilt and fear that had been eating at me became too much to hide and I came very close to a complete nervous breakdown. I tried to kill myself, but fortunately I chickened out at the last minute" (Warshaw, 1988, pp. 67–68). Women with a prior history of emotional and

Amina Lawal, with her baby, is pictured in 2002 shortly after an Islamic court sentenced her to death by stoning for committing adultery. After a two-year appeal process that received international attention, she was pardoned.

behavioral problems have greater difficulty than other women in recovering from rape (Koss & Figueredo, 2004). Women who are victims of gang rape, which involve multiple perpetrators, also have more severe physical and emotional consequences than women who experience a single rape (Sadler et al., 2005).

Some rape victims also develop physical health problems, such as chronic headaches and back pain, eating disorders, and sleep disturbances (Bachar & Koss, 2001; Wasco, 2003). Some may experience reproductive problems, such as painful menstruation and irregular periods, as well as sexual problems, including diminished sexual activity, interest, and enjoyment (Barnett et al., 2005; Campbell et al., 2003). Some rape survivors, especially those who were assaulted by someone they knew, show increases in risky sexual behavior (Campbell et al., 2004; Upchurch & Kusunoki, 2004). Others abuse drugs and alcohol or attempt suicide (Ullman, 2004). Rebecca Campbell and her colleagues (Campbell et al., 2004) point out that many rape survivors are further victimized by insensitive treatment from police, prosecuting attorney, doctors, and mental health personnel. Placing unnecessary blame on rape survivors adds to the trauma of the original sexual assault and may hamper recovery.

L E A R N   A B O U T   T H E   R E S E A R C H   14.1

Positive Life Changes Following Sexual Assault

In the aftermath of traumatic events, some individuals may experience positive as well as negative life changes as a result of trying to come to terms with these events (Tedeschi et al., 1998). Patricia Frazier and her colleagues (2004) have been doing a longitudinal study of 171 women who experienced sexual assault, in order to assess the factors which best predicted positive life changes during the women's recovery process. Positive life change was measured by asking participants to rate the extent to which specific aspects of their lives had changed since the assault. Items dealt with one's self (e.g., "My ability to take care of myself"); relationships (e.g., "My relationships with family"); life philosophy or spirituality (e.g., "My sense of purpose in life"); and empathy (e.g., "My concern for others in my similar situation"). Participants rated each item on a 5-point scale ranging from "much worse now" to "much better now." Higher scores indicated positive change. The participants, who were between 16 and 52 years old (mean age, 27), filled out questionnaires at two weeks, two months, six months, and one year after the assault.

One of the factors most strongly related to positive change was social support, which, as we have seen, is related to good mental health. A second factor related to positive change, called "approach coping," involved trying to view the stressful event differently and expressing emotions about it (as opposed to avoiding people and acting as if nothing had happened). In addition, those who relied on their religious faith to cope reported more positive change. Finally, survivors who perceived that they had control over their recovery process were more likely to show positive life changes.

What Does It Mean?

1. Based on these results, what suggestions could you offer to a friend of yours who had just experienced sexual assault?

2. This study focused on women only. Do you think that the results would be similar for men who are survivors of sexual assault? Explain your answer.

Despite the many negative effects of rape, many survivors report positive life changes following sexual assault that help them cope with the event. For a closer look, see Learn About the Research 14.1.

Rape Prevention

Many rape education programs exist, most of them focusing on changing attitudes such as rape myths or increasing women's self-protection (Christopher & Kisler, 2004; Söchting et al., 2004; Ullman, 2002). While education can help women learn how to communicate better with male partners or how to avoid high-risk situations, it is basically men's behaviors that must be changed if rape is to be prevented (Barnett et al., 2005). Because attitudes supportive of rape and the sexual script are learned at a young age, rape education programs should also begin early (Abbey et al., 1996).

In addition to rape education, institutions must develop effective procedures for dealing with complaints. Women who report a rape must be assured that their claim will be fairly investigated and that if guilt is determined, the perpetrator will receive appropriate sanctions (Koss & Cleveland, 1997).

Theories of Rape

How can rape be explained? Our examination focuses on three theories that posit different mechanisms to account for rape.

Evolutionary Theory. **Evolutionary theory** (also known as sociobiology) *applies the principles of natural selection and its goal of reproductive survival to an understanding of social behavior, including rape. According to this theory, rape has evolved because in ancestral environments it was one strategy males could use to ensure their genes would be passed on to future generations.* From an evolutionary perspective, it is to males' reproductive advantage to mate often and with numerous partners because they have abundant sperm, do not have to spend any time gestating offspring, and cannot be sure of paternity of offspring. Thus, although evolutionary theorists believe that rape is inappropriate, they argue it has evolved as one method for achieving reproductive success (Thornhill & Palmer, 2000). To support this view, they point out that forced copulations have been observed in a variety of animal species, and that females of childbearing age are the most likely rape victims (Thornhill & Palmer, 2000).

Some critics, on the other hand, contend that it is not appropriate to draw conclusions about rape by observing nonhuman species because human behavior is more complexly determined (LaFrance, 2001b). Furthermore, Anne Fausto-Sterling (1992) argues that when the term "rape" is applied to other species, its meaning is altered; it no longer reflects a violation of the victim's will because will is an essentially human construct. She also maintains that so-called rape in animals does not have the same implications for females of these species as it does for human females for whom rape arouses fear and influences behavioral choices.

Others question the basic tenet of the theory that frequent copulation with multiple partners is reproductively effective for men. Natalie Angier (1999) argues that a continuous relationship with one woman might be as reproductively successful as promiscuous mating. Marianne LaFrance (2001b) notes that although the majority of rape victims are young women of childbearing age, there are numerous rapes of young children. Furthermore, the observations that some men rape wives and dating partners with whom they have also had consensual sex and that most men do not rape are not consistent with this assumption that the purpose of rape is reproduction (de Waal, 2002).

Feminist Theory. A different perspective is offered by **feminist theory**, *which contends that rape is rooted in the longstanding and pervasive power imbalance between women and men* (Malamuth, 1996). Men have greater legal, economic, and political power, which provides them with more power in interpersonal situations. Men use rape as one mechanism to control women and maintain their dominance.

Support for feminist theory at the societal level is provided by evidence that urban areas with greater gender equality in economic, legal, and political power have lower rape rates than do urban areas with less gender equality (Peterson & Bailey, 1992; Whaley, 2001). Moreover, a man's endorsement of male dominance and restricted rights for women is strongly connected to his acceptance of rape myths (e.g., Anderson et al., 1997).

Social Learning Theory. **Social learning theory** provides a third perspective to the phenomenon of rape. As discussed in Chapter 3, this theory *contends that social behaviors are learned through observation and reinforcement. This includes learning both attitudes supportive of rape and sexually aggressive behaviors* (Frieze, 2005). The theory assumes, for example, that men can develop attitudes supportive of rape or sexually aggressive behaviors via media depictions of sexuality and violence. The theory further holds that their sexual aggressiveness can be reinforced by the widespread acceptance of rape myths which blame the victim and excuse the perpetrator, and by the traditional sexual script which encourages males to be aggressive in sexual situations.

Both of these assumptions have received some research. Consistent with the hypothesized influence of observational learning, Barongan and Hall (1995) found that, for some men, exposure to misogynous rap music increases their aggressive feelings toward women. Several studies have also shown that experience with pornography is related to greater sexual aggressiveness (Frieze, 2005). However, this relationship could reflect either an effect of pornography on sexual aggressiveness or the possibility that sexually aggressive men choose to view violent pornography. In support of the importance of reinforcement, men who more strongly accept rape myths tend to be more sexually aggressive (e.g., Malamuth et al., 1991).

Intimate Partner Violence

> *I have had glasses thrown at me. I have been kicked in the abdomen, kicked off the bed, and hit while lying on the floor—while I was pregnant. I have been whipped, kicked, and thrown, picked up and thrown down again.* (Boston Women's Health Book Collective, 1998, p. 162)
>
> *I was pretty much in a cage . . . He didn't let me use the phone . . . didn't let me go out . . . took away all of my freedom.* (Zink & Sill, 2004, p. 33)

Acts of violence against women, sad to say, are usually committed by their male partner (Barnett et al., 2005). **Intimate partner violence,** also known as battering, or domestic violence, refers to *physical and psychological abuse committed by an intimate partner, that is, a spouse, romantic partner, or a former spouse/partner.* As illustrated in the first vignette of this section, intimate partner violence can range from moderate forms of physical abuse, such as slapping or throwing objects at the victim, to severe forms, including beating and using a weapon (Frieze, 2005). Psychological abuse includes overt attempts to dominate, isolate, and control, as well as more subtle actions that undermine the victim's self-esteem (Kwong et al., 2003;

Sousa et al., 2003). This type of abuse is depicted in the second vignette that opened this section. In some cases of domestic violence, the woman abuses her partner, sometimes in self-defense (Krahé et al., 2003; Newby et al., 2003; Serran & Firestone, 2004). The vast majority of cases, however, involve the male partner as the batterer (HELP Network, 2003). Furthermore, men's attacks on women are likely to be more severe than women's attacks on men (Archer, 2004; HELP Network, 2003), resulting in nearly 2 million injuries and nearly 1,300 deaths each year (National Center for Injury Prevention and Control, 2003). Over one-third of all murders of American women are committed by intimate partners, compared to only 4 percent of men's murders (Rothman et al., 2005).

Incidence

Like rape, intimate partner violence is an underreported crime, but, it is estimated that at least 2.5 million women are abused each year (Walker, 2001). In one recent study, about half of women seeking health care at emergency departments or primary care clinics in the Midwest reported having experienced physical and/or emotional abuse at some point in their lives. One in four women reported severe physical or sexual abuse. Only one-quarter of the women had ever been asked about abuse by a health care provider. Most, however, said they would reveal abuse if asked in a nonhurried, concerned manner (Kramer et al., 2004).

Violence in lesbian relationships occurs about as often as in heterosexual couples (Potoczniak et al., 2003; Tolou-Shams et al., 2002; Wolfe, 2002). However, lesbians are less likely to abuse their partners than are gay men (Tjaden & Thoennes, 2000). Similar to violence in heterosexual relationships, this abuse can be both physical and emotional (Leland, 2000b; West, 2002).

Role of Disability, Social Class, and Ethnicity

Disability, poverty, and ethnicity are all factors in intimate partner violence. Women with physical disabilities experience abuse at about the same rate as nondisabled women, but their abusive relationships continue for a longer period of time (Asch et al., 2001; "Health & Wellness," 2004; Olkin, 2003). They are also abused by a wider variety of people, such as health care providers or attendants, in addition to partners or family members. Poorer women and those with less education report the highest rates of physical abuse (Farmer & Tiefenthaler, 2004; Koss et al., 2003; Kramer et al., 2004). Black women are more likely than White women to be victims of domestic violence (HELP Network, 2003) and they are more severely abused (West, 2002). Black women, however, are more likely than other women to fight back against sexual assault. In one study of poor, urban women (Fine & Weis, cited in Fine & Carney, 2001), abused Black women were more likely than abused White women to secure orders of protection, call the police, go to a shelter, throw the batterer out of the house, or report the incident to brothers and fathers who might confront the abuser.

The Asian American community has the lowest reported rates of intimate partner violence of any other ethnic group (Tjaden & Thoennes, 2000), but this could be an underestimate of its actual occurrence. Asian Americans emphasize the family over the individual, the strong value placed on the male as the authority in the family, and the belief that family affairs must be kept private. These reasons may keep Asian American women from seeking assistance for their abuse, and those who do report it are likely to meet with considerable disapproval in their communities (Ho, 1990).

The relatively few studies of the incidence of domestic violence among Latinas/os in the United States have produced a mixed picture. Some studies show a high incidence of violent spousal behavior compared to other ethnic groups, while others do not (Ceballo et al., 2004). Methodological problems, such as lumping together all Latina/o subgroups, may be responsible for these inconsistencies.

Little research is available on abuse of Native American women. However, recent findings indicate their rate of intimate partner violence is the highest of all ethnic groups (Tjaden & Thoennes, 2000; Wahab & Olson, 2004). This may be related to both alcohol abuse and patriarchal beliefs introduced by the Westernization of Native peoples (Allen, 1990).

Things are no better in other parts of the world, as you'll see in Explore Other Cultures 14.4.

EXPLORE OTHER CULTURES **14.4**

Intimate Partner Violence Around the World

Sadly, violence against women by their male partners occurs in all countries, regardless of economic class and religion (Amnesty International, 2004; Malley-Morrison, 2004; Xu et al., 2005). Recent data from Australia, the United States, Canada, Israel, and South Africa, for example, show that one-third to 70 percent of female murder victims are killed by their husbands or boyfriends (HELP Network, 2003; World Health Organization, 2002). In addition, thousands of women each year are victims of dowry-related killings or are disfigured by acid thrown in their faces by rejected suitors in Bangladesh, Colombia, India, Nigeria, and Pakistan (UNIFEM, 2003). In sub-Saharan Africa and in the patriarchal Arab societies of the Middle East, women themselves often consider wife beating to be justified under certain circumstances, such as disobeying one's husband. Furthermore, they blame women for the beating, believe that women benefit from the violence, and oppose assistance for battered women from governmental agencies (Amowitz et al., 2004; Haj-Yahia, 2002; LaFraniere, 2005).

To make matters worse, the criminal justice system may take crimes of violence against ethnic minority or immigrant women less seriously than those committed against majority women. For example, the longstanding ill treatment of the Roma (formerly called Gypsy) people in the Czech Republic and Croatia have made Roma women reluctant to report crimes of violence to the police. In some countries, the legal system downplays attacks on minority women, attributing them as part of the group's culture (UNIFEM, 2003).

Risk Factors

The need for power and control and the belief that men have the right to punish their female partners play an important role in men's domestic violence (Barnett et al., 2005; Stith et al., 2004). Alcohol and drug abuse by batterers in both heterosexual and lesbian relationships is also common (Boles & Miotto, 2003; Dixon & Browne, 2003; UNIFEM, 2003). Violent husbands are more likely than other husbands to display poor problem-solving and communication skills, high levels of anger and hostility, antisocial behavior, and low self-esteem. Occupational and marital stresses are also associated with intimate partner violence (Barnett et al., 2005; Cano & Vivian, 2003; Hilton & Harris, 2005; Stith et al., 2004). Not surprisingly, male batterers and abused women are more likely than other men and women to have witnessed violence between their parents or experienced physical or sexual abuse in childhood (Aldridge & Browne, 2003; Delsol & Margolin, 2004; Dixon & Browne, 2003; Schafer et al., 2004). This does not mean that all adults with a history of violence will be involved in an abusive relationship, or that all those involved in domestic violence have a history of family battering (Hines & Saudino, 2002). However, these findings do suggest that observing a parent commit violence gives boys the message that violence is a means for handling anger and conflict and influences the development of negative attitudes toward women. For women, the early experience of family violence can provide a similar message that aggression is a "normal" aspect of close relationships. It can also make it more difficult for the abused girl to learn how to accurately screen people and situations for danger (Koss et al., 1994).

Effects of Intimate Partner Violence

The effects of abuse include a wide variety of both physical and psychological problems. Health problems include physical injuries and reproductive difficulties (HELP Network, 2003). Abused women may also suffer psychological problems such as lower self-esteem, depression, anxiety, drug and alcohol abuse, eating disorders, posttraumatic stress disorder, and suicide attempts (National Center for Injury Prevention and Control, 2003; Ozer et al., 2003; Pimlott-Kubiak & Cortina, 2003). Furthermore, psychological abuse has as great an effect on women's physical and mental health as does physical violence (Kramer et al., 2004), perhaps because it involves continual humiliation and the destruction of one's identity. Moreover, the health problems caused by physical and psychological abuse may keep women from obtaining or keeping employment, which can keep them financially dependent on the abuser (Riger & Staggs, 2004). Children who observe parental violence also suffer psychological trauma, as illustrated by Susan's anguished comments at the beginning of the chapter.

Leaving the Abusive Relationship

Many people wonder why abused women don't leave their batterer. However, one of the greatest barriers to leaving is financial concern, as many women do not have the economic resources to provide for their family. Another major obstacle is fear of retaliation (Anderson & Saunders, 2003; Barnett et al., 2005). Batterers can interpret women's attempt to leave as a loss of control and their violence can accelerate. As one battered woman reported, "The very first time that I attempted to leave he tried to choke me with the sheets to the point where I turned blue" (Sorenson, 1996, p. 129). Many older women have stayed in abusive marriages because they were socialized to remain with their husbands regardless of circumstances (Zink et al., 2004). Disabled women may also be more likely than other women to stay in an abusive relationship, especially if their job or transportation opportunities are limited, or if their only alternative living arrangement is in an institution (Warshaw, 2001). In addition, women with more conservative religious beliefs tend to stay in abusive relationships longer than other women. Very religious strains of Judaism, Christianity, and Islam sometimes make it difficult for women to escape such relationships. In addition, both the batterer and the victim may misinterpret religious texts to justify the abuse. Muslim American women have been faced with an increase in domestic violence since the terrorist attacks on September 11. This abuse has largely been unreported in the past, but women are even more hesitant to come forth than before September 11 because of fear of deportation (Childress, 2003).

Theories of Intimate Partner Violence

Two theories presented as explanations of rape are also useful in understanding intimate partner violence. As discussed previously, feminist theory emphasizes gender power imbalance as a destructive factor in men's interactions with women. When applied to battering, it contends that men use violence against women as a means to maintain their power and status (Walker, 2001). Social learning theory, with its focus on observation and reinforcement, posits that domestic violence is a learned behavior that can develop from observing violence within the family and from receiving reinforcement for aggressive acts (Barnett et al., 2005).

Interventions

In the past 25 years, a body of laws has developed concerning domestic violence. These include mandatory arrest of the abuser (Sontag, 2002) and orders of protection that prohibit the abuser from coming near or contacting the woman (Barnett et al., 2005). The development of shelters for abused women has been another key intervention (Frieze, 2005). Feminist therapy (discussed in Chapter 13) is a useful tool for helping to reempower the battered woman. Another helpful intervention for battered women suffering from posttraumatic stress disorder (PTSD) is cognitive trauma therapy (Kubany et al., 2004). This treatment includes exploring the trauma; PTSD education; stress management; exposure to reminders of the abuse and abuser; self-monitoring of negative self-talk; cognitive therapy for guilt; and modules on self-advocacy, assertiveness, and how to identify perpetrators. Women receiving this therapy show large reductions in PTSD symptoms, depression, and guilt and substantial increases in self-esteem (Kubany et al., 2004). Programs also have been designed to treat the batterer either alone or with his partner. They deal with attitudes toward women and toward violence against women, as well as anger management (Frieze, 2005; Wathen & MacMillan, 2003). Unfortunately, the effects of such programs in preventing further violence are modest (Babcock et al., 2004; Cattanco & Goodman, 2005; Ferris, 2004; Gondolf, 2004).

Elder Abuse

> *A handyman befriends his elderly customer and gets her to pay his bills and deed her home to him.* (Sklar, 2000)
> *A woman withdraws large sums from her ailing parents' bank account to pay for her own expenses, including cars and trips.* (Sklar, 2000)
> *A crack-addicted man physically batters his elderly aunts if they do not give him money for his next fix. Eventually, they lose their savings and their home and are reduced to begging in the streets.* (Kleinfield, 2004)

Abuse of older adults is an alarming global phenomenon that has received increasing media attention in recent years. At least 4 percent of older adults—over 2 million people in the United States—experience moderate to severe abuse each year (Collins et al., 2000; Voelker, 2002). Patterns of abuse vary little among Blacks, Latinas/os, and Whites (Cavanaugh & Blanchard-Fields, 2006). Older Black women, however, have lower rates of reported sexual abuse than do Latinas and White women (Grossman & Lundy, 2003). Asian Americans are less likely than other groups to perceive situations as abusive and are less likely to seek help (Barnett et al., 2005). For a look at elder abuse in other countries, see Explore Other Cultures 14.5.

Types of Abuse

Elder abuse refers to *physical, psychological, financial, and neglectful acts that harm the health or welfare of an older adult, and that occur within a relationship of trust* (Centers for Disease Control and Prevention, 2003b; see Table 14.2). Financial and psychological abuse are the most commonly reported types of abuse (Illinois Department of Aging, 2000). Financial exploitation of the elderly has been growing at a disturbing rate. Like much elder abuse, most of these crimes are committed by family members and paid household workers or caregivers, as shown in the vignettes at the beginning of this section.

All states now have laws against elder mistreatment, with most mandating that abuse be reported. Yet various studies estimate that only one in every five or more cases is reported (Centers for Disease Control and Prevention, 2003b; Hurme, 2002). One obstacle is denial of the problem. In addition, elderly persons themselves may lack the opportunity and the physical and mental ability to report

A Global View of Elder Abuse

Unfortunately, elder abuse exists around the world (Malley-Morrison, 2004). Recent interviews with elderly people in Argentina, Austria, Brazil, Canada, India, Kenya, Lebanon, and Sweden (World Health Organization, 2002) indicate that while forms of abuse vary across countries, the most common victims are the elderly poor, widows, and childless older women. In Austria, India, Japan, Korea, Lebanon, and Taiwan, elderly women report that family conflict and jealousy lead to neglect and abuse by their daughters-in-law (Malley-Morrison, 2004; World Health Organization, 2002). In Kenya and Brazil, one serious form of abuse is the practice of abandoning older family members in hospitals, especially during times of drought, poor crop yields, or even holidays. A common theme across many cultures is a pervasive lack of respect for the elderly, whether in health, governmental, and commercial institutions or in personal interactions.

abuse. They often fear not being believed, reprisal, abandonment, and institutionalization. Also, the victimized elderly may wish to protect the abuser, who is most often an adult child or a spouse (Beers & Jones, 2004; Collins et al., 2000; Wei & Herbers, 2004).

Who Is Abused and Who Abuses?

The typical victim of elder abuse is a woman over age 75. She often lives at home with adult caregivers but is isolated and fearful. Frequently, she is physically

TABLE 14.2   Types of Elder Abuse

Type of Abuse	Description
Physical and sexual abuse	Hitting, choking, hair pulling, kicking, sexually molesting, confining the person against her or his will
Psychological abuse	Threatening, humiliating, insulting, intimidating the person, forcing the person to do degrading things, treating the person like a child
Financial abuse	Destroying property or possessions, stealing the person's money, denying the person access to his or her money
Neglect	Depriving the person of items needed for daily living (food, warmth, shelter, glasses, dentures, money), inattention, isolation

Sources: Beers & Jones (2004); Collins et al. (2000).

and/or mentally frail and may suffer from cognitive impairments. She is likely to be widowed or divorced (Wei & Herbers, 2004).

Over two-thirds of the abuse is inflicted by children, spouses, or other relatives. The typical abuser is a middle-aged son of the victim. Adult children with mental, alcohol, or drug problems are among the most likely to be abusers. Often, the abuser is the caregiver of the victim and may also be financially dependent upon the victim (Barnett et al., 2005; Hurme, 2002; Wei & Herbers, 2004).

The stress of providing care for an ill relative may contribute to the problem of elder abuse. Some caregivers for an older person who is physically ill or suffers from dementia may express their frustration by becoming abusive (Hurme, 2002). The caregiver may be someone who neither chose to do so nor is able to cope with the financial, interpersonal, and time demands placed on him or her (Barnett et al., 2005).

While acknowledging that caring for an elderly relative can be stressful, one must be careful not to simply "blame the victim" for being abused. (Notice the parallel with inappropriately blaming a woman who has been raped.) The feminist perspective puts elder abuse in a larger social context. From this point of view, elder abuse is part of a spectrum of male violence against women (Whittaker, 1996) that reflects a social context in which men wield more power and dominance over women.

What Can Be Done?

Some of the options that are available to the younger abused woman—deciding to leave a relationship or going to a shelter—are impractical or virtually impossible for most abused elderly. Awareness of the problem is the first step. One encouraging sign is that in 2002, the United Nations recognized for the first time the need to eliminate violence against the elderly, especially women, around the world ("U.N. Offers," 2002). Education and training are essential to alert the general public and professional service providers to the prevalence of elder abuse and neglect. Professionals must learn to recognize the symptoms of abuse, understand the victim's denial, and strengthen the victim's resolve to end the abuse. The public should be encouraged to report any known or suspected case of abuse. Both the public and the victim must know where to turn for help. New laws have been passed in recent years governing the treatment of victims, especially women, that focus on the need for safety, assistance in accessing the courts, and information about the progress of the proceedings. This emphasis on victims' rights should be ensured by legislation at the state and federal levels. Support groups for victims help validate the victims' experiences and provide a sense of empowerment that may enable them to change the power structure of the abusive relationship (Barnett et al., 2005; Schewe, 2002; Voelker, 2002; Wolf, 2001).

SUMMARY

Sexual Harassment at School

- Reports of sexual harassment are increasing among junior and senior high school students.
- Girls are more likely than boys to be sexually harassed by their schoolmates and they are more upset by it.
- Schools are now legally obligated to protect students from severe and pervasive harassment by other students.
- More female than male students experience sexual harassment on campus. Most incidents involve subtle forms of harassment, and most are perpetrated by other students.
- Ethnic and sexual minority students are more likely to experience harassment than are other students.

Sexual Harassment in the Workplace

- It is estimated that up to half of employed women will experience sexual harassment. Sexist remarks and jokes are common forms of harassment; sexual coercion is relatively rare.
- Women in blue-collar occupations and the military are more likely to be targets of harassment than other women.
- This might be due to the high prevalence of both the male gender stereotype and male-related physical traits in these fields.
- According to sex-role spillover theory, sexual harassment occurs because men respond to females in the workplace as women rather than workers. Power theory states that harassment is used by more powerful individuals either to gain sexual favors or to reinforce their position of greater power.
- Most targets of sexual harassment use informal strategies for dealing with the harassment, such as ignoring it or asking the harasser to stop. They rarely file formal complaints or seek legal redress.
- Numerous negative outcomes can stem from sexual harassment.

Violence Against Girls

- The incidence of child sexual abuse may run as high as 20 percent of females and 5 percent of males. Most abuse is committed by a relative or family friend (usually male).
- Sexual abuse can have a devastating impact on the physical and mental health of children, both immediately and in the long term.
- School-based sexual-abuse prevention programs may help children avoid and report abuse. Psychotherapy can help abused children and women heal.
- Countries with strong preferences for boys show elevated rates of abortion, infanticide, and neglect of female children.
- Many girls and young women around the world have been lured into sexual slavery.

Dating Violence

- Substantial numbers of teenagers experience violence in their dating relationships. More males than females report being victims of such violence.

Rape

- An estimated one-quarter of women experience rape, much of it perpetrated by acquaintances.
- Physical aggressiveness, hostility toward women, gender-stereotypical attitudes, and a history of family violence differentiate sexually aggressive men from other men.
- Alcohol consumption increases the risk of sexual coercion and rape.
- Rape victims can experience a variety of emotional and health problems.
- Evolutionary, feminist, and social learning theories attempt to account for rape. Although some support for all three has been reported, there are many criticisms of evolutionary theory.

Intimate Partner Violence

- At least 2.5 million women are victims of domestic violence each year.
- Battering occurs in both lesbian and heterosexual relationships and across ethnic

groups, although it is more frequent among Blacks than Whites.

■ Major risk factors for both perpetrators and victims of domestic violence are a history of family violence and alcohol and drug abuse.

■ Numerous physical and psychological problems can result from victimization, including physical injuries, reproductive difficulties, lower self-esteem, anxiety, and depression.

■ Financial problems and fear of the perpetrator are the primary reasons for remaining in an abusive relationship.

■ Feminist and social learning theories help explain domestic violence.

Elder Abuse

■ Elder abuse can have physical, psychological, financial, and neglect dimensions. At least 4 percent of older adults in the United States are affected, but few cases are reported.

■ The typical victim is a woman age 75 or older who lives with a caregiver. The typical abuser is a middle-aged son who has mental, alcohol, or drug problems.

■ The following are essential in order to combat elder abuse: Educating professionals and the public; reporting abuse cases; passing victims' rights laws; and forming support groups.

KEY TERMS

sexual harassment in an educational setting
sexual harassment in the workplace
quid pro quo harassment
hostile environment
sexual coercion
gender harassment

unwanted sexual attention
sex-role spillover theory
power theory
internally focused responses
externally focused responses
child sexual abuse
incest
rape

acquaintance rape
sexual script
rape myths
evolutionary theory
feminist theory
social learning theory
intimate partner violence
elder abuse

WHAT DO YOU THINK?

1. Some people have criticized the recent U.S. Supreme Court ruling that obligates schools to protect students from severe and pervasive sexual harassment by other students. Some argue that sexual taunting and even touching is a normal rite of adolescence. Others contend that even such apparently innocent gestures as the exchange of Valentine's Day cards by first graders will now be classified as sexual harassment and thus forbidden. What is your position on this issue, and why?

2. Which of the recommended procedures for reducing sexual harassment on cam-

pus do you think would be particularly effective at your school? Can you think of other activities that might be beneficial on your campus?

3. Why are family members often the perpetrators of child sexual abuse? What actions can be taken to prevent such behaviors?

4. Using either the feminist or social learning theory as a framework, discuss societal changes that might lead to a reduction in both rape and intimate partner violence.

5. How can public awareness of elder abuse be increased?

IF YOU WANT TO LEARN MORE

Allen, J. (2002). *Because I love you: The silent shadow of child sexual abuse.* Charlottesville, VA: Virginia Foundation for the Humanities Press.

American Association of University Women. (2001). *Hostile hallways: Bullying, teasing, and sexual harassment in school.* Washington, DC: AAUW Educational Foundation.

Barnett, O., Miller-Perrin, C. L., & Perrin, R. D. (2004). *Family violence across the lifespan: An introduction* (2d ed.). Thousand Oaks, CA: Sage.

Foote, W. E., & Goodman-Delahunty, J. (2005). *Evaluating sexual harassment: psychological, social, and legal considerations in forensic examinations.* Washington, DC: American Psychological Association.

Frieze, I. H. (2005). *Hurting the one you love: Violence in relationships.* Belmont, CA: Thomson Wadsworth.

Grossman, F. K., Cook, A. B., Kepkep, S. S., & Koenen, K. C. (1999). *With the phoenix rising: Lessons from ten resilient women who overcame the trauma of childhood sexual abuse.* San Francisco: Jossey-Bass.

Lalumiere, M. L., Harris, G. T., Quinsey, W. L., & Rice, M. E. (2005). *The causes of rape: Understanding individual differences in male propensity for sexual aggression.* Washington, DC: American Psychological Association.

Lemoncheck, L., & Sterba, J. P. (2000). *Sexual harassment: Issues and answers.* New York: American Psychiatric Society.

Lloyd, S. A., & Emery, B. C. (2000). *The dark side of courtship: Physical and sexual aggression.* Thousand Oaks, CA: Sage.

Losete, D. R., Gelles, R. J., & Cavanaugh, M. M. (2004). *Current controversies on family violence* (2d ed.). Thousand Oaks, CA: Sage.

Malley-Morrison, K. (Ed.). (2004). *International perspectives on family violence and abuse: A cognitive-ecological approach.* Mahwah, NJ: Erlbaum.

Ottens, A. J., & Hotelling, K. (Eds.). (2001). *Sexual violence on campus: Policies, programs, and perspectives.* New York: Springer.

Pickup, F. (2001). *Ending violence against women: A challenge for development and humanitarian work.* Oxford, UK: Oxfam.

Pierce-Baker, C. (2000). *Surviving the silence: Black women's stories of rape.* New York: W. W. Norton.

Russell, D. E. H. (1999). *The secret trauma: Incest in the lives of girls and women* (Rev. ed.). New York: Basic Books.

WEBSITES

Education

American Association of University Women
http://www.aauw.org

Sexual Harassment

Feminist Majority Foundation: Sexual Harassment Hotline Resource List
http://www.feminist.org/911/harass.html

Violence Against Girls

Abuse/Incest Support
http://www.incestabuse.about.com/health/incestabuse/

Rape

National Clearinghouse on Marital and Date Rape
http://members.aol.com/ncmdr/index.html

Intimate Partner Violence

American Bar Association Commission on Domestic Violence
http://www.abanet.org/domviol/home.html
National Center for Injury Prevention and Control
http://www.cdc.gov/ncipc
Family Violence Prevention Fund
http://endabuse.org
Same-Sex Domestic Violence
http://www.xq.com/cuav/domviol.htm
State Reporting Requirements
http://endabuse.org/statereport/list.php3
Stop Abuse For Everyone (SAFE)
http://www.safe4all.org
U.S. Department of Justice
http://www.ojp.usdoj.gov/vawo

Elder Abuse

National Center on Elder Abuse
http://www.elderabusecenter.org

CHAPTER

15

A Feminist Future
Goals, Actions, and Attitudes

Several years ago, before my (Judith's) daughter left for college, I offered advice about her first-semester courses. Although Rachel accepted a few of my recommendations, she rejected my suggestion of a women's studies course, stating that gender was not an important issue. At age 17, she certainly had no idea the route her academic career would eventually take. Despite her initial protestations, Rachel ultimately registered for a women's studies course in order to fulfill a multicultural curriculum requirement, and this course proved to be a transforming experience. It exposed Rachel to research, theory, and ideology that dramatically affected her attitudes and interests. In fact, this course was the basis for her academic journey that began with a double major in sociology and women studies and culminated in a feminist doctoral dissertation in sociology.

We saw in Chapter 1 that science is not value-free, and as Rachel's experience illustrates, neither is teaching. "The process of education is political" (Wyche & Crosby, 1996, p. 5); that is, both subject matter and teaching methods are influenced by the value system of the instructor and the academic community. Applying this to the field of psychology, Kimberly Kinsler and Sue Rosenberg Zalk (1996) contend that "the greatest value of psychology lies in the field's ability to reveal the psychological processes perpetuating social injustices and to correct the social systems that have an unjust impact on the quality of people's lives" (p. 35). Given this political dimension of teaching, we end this textbook with a look at feminist goals for the future.

In Chapter 1 we presented three feminist themes that have recurred throughout this book: gender inequality of power, diversity of women, and the social construction of gender. In this chapter we return to these themes and translate them into goals for the future, consider actions for achieving these aims, and, because these goals have their root in feminist thought, explore the prevalence of feminist beliefs among North American women.

Feminist Goals

Based on the themes in this book, we have chosen four feminist goals for the future. Do you have others that you would add?

Goal One: Gender Equality in Organizational Power

Despite legislation that prohibits gender discrimination in employment (Title VII of the Civil Rights Act of 1964) and educational programs (Title IX, 1972), gender differences in organizational and interpersonal power continue to limit women's advancement in the workplace. Antidiscrimination legislation alone cannot change attitudes, and discriminatory policies are hard to monitor. Therefore, as has been noted throughout this text, men, especially White men, continue to have greater access to economic and political resources than women do. They continue to greatly outnumber women at high levels of management and in political office and to own most of the wealth (Chapter 10).

To combat this inequity, we choose as our first goal for the future greater equality of organizational power. A strong commitment from an organization's top management can help create a culture that promotes the advancement of young women (Costello & Wight, 2003). As more and more women attain levels of power currently held by men, gender equality will begin to affect other areas. Women's accessibility to important mentors and social networks will increase, providing even more promotion opportunities for women. And because job level is one factor determining salaries, women's wages will rise and become more similar to those of men. The close association between sexual harassment and the power imbalance also suggests that a greater power equality will mean less harassment of women.

Goal Two: Gender Equality in Relationship Power

In addition to greater organizational power, men continue to hold more interpersonal power relative to women. For instance, they tend to have more control over a couple's activities on dates and more influence in marriage (Chapter 8). A second goal, therefore, is greater equality in relationship power. Women would benefit by having a greater voice in dating decision making and a more balanced division of household labor. The latter, in turn, could reduce women's role overload and interrole conflict. Furthermore, because both rape and domestic violence are due, at least in part, to male dominance, shared interpersonal power would go a long way to reducing intimate violence against women.

Goal Three: Gender Equality in Power for All Groups of Women

Women are disadvantaged due not only to the gender inequality of power, but also to differences within genders that add extra burdens to the lives of many women. White women are advantaged compared to women of color; middle-class women have more power than working-class or poor women; heterosexual women are privileged in comparison to lesbian women; nondisabled women are more advantaged than women with disabilities; and younger women have more power than their older counterparts. We have seen that ethnic minority women and women with disabilities experience even greater wage inequities than White and nondisabled women (Chapter 10). Furthermore, women of color and lesbian women experience more job discrimination and sexual harassment than White and heterosexual women (Chapters 10 and 14). Thus, a third power goal is to ensure that increases in female power benefit all women, regardless of ethnicity, class, disability/ability, sexual orientation, or age.

Goal Four: Greater Flexibility in the Social Construction of Gender

We have noted throughout the text that gender is socially constructed, that most gender behaviors and roles—such as career choice (Chapter 9), friendship behaviors (Chapter 8), and contribution to household labor (Chapter 11)—are shaped by interpersonal, societal, and cultural expectations and are not constrained by biological sex. In examining some of the mechanisms that influence this construction of gender, we explored stereotypes that reflect societal gender expectations (Chapter 3), theoretical perspectives about the mechanisms whereby children learn the behaviors and roles expected for their gender (Chapter 3), and parental shaping of the behaviors and interests of girls and boys (Chapter 4). We saw that it is not the biological nature of females and males that serves as the major foundation for people's view of gender or their gender-related activities and preferences, but their conception of what it means to be a female or a male in our society today.

Additionally we have seen that power, or rather the imbalance of power, also guides the social construction of gender (Howard & Hollander, 1997). People with more power, who are in dominant positions, are likely to acquire and use different traits and behaviors than people in subordinate positions. Individuals in high-status positions are more likely to display independence, a male gender-related trait that is difficult to embrace if one lacks access to necessary resources in the home, workplace, or social environment. People lacking powerful resources, on the other hand, are more likely to rely instead on emotional connections between people and, consequently, to develop female gender-related traits, such as compassion. Thus, females' and males' development of gender-related traits, behaviors, and roles is constructed via stereotype-based expectations; socialization by parents, peers, and others; and hierarchical status within society.

Unfortunately, a rigid construction of gender is damaging to human potential (Howard & Hollander, 1997; Katz, 1996). It hinders development of our unique talents and interests by guiding us in directions dictated by the social constructs of our biological sex. Judith recalls her days as a new bride when she refused to allow her husband to share the housecleaning, although both she and her husband were employed full time. Her insistence was based on her traditional conception of the "wife" role, a perception that was constructed from television and magazine images and from the roles of many married couples at that time (the 1960s). Her "wife role" behaviors were not based on her own interests, her time availability, or her husband's desires, but solely on her construction of this role from the societal images and social behaviors she observed around her.

A fourth goal for women, then, is greater flexibility in the construction of gender. Flexibility can lead to an expansion in career options, more flexible decisions about work and family dilemmas, greater sexual equality, and numerous other reductions in gender-constrained behaviors that limit choices made by both women and men. Flexibility of gender-related behaviors and roles also has the potential to reduce the prevalence of sexual harassment and acquaintance rape (Chapter 14), both of which are fostered, at least in part, by traditional constructions of the behaviors of men and women. Further, it can enhance communication within heterosexual couples by freeing each partner from constraints expected for her or his gender.

Actions to Achieve These Goals

Research and Teaching

Research and teaching about the psychology of women can play a significant role in achieving feminist goals for several reasons. First, greater knowledge of gender differences in interpersonal and societal power can help clarify the role that power imbalance plays in women's lives. Understanding the extent to which male power influences rape and battering (Chapter 14), serves as the basis for the division of household labor (Chapter 11), and contributes to wage inequities (Chapter 10) means that both female and male students will be aware of the prevalence of male power. A reduction in male dominance cannot occur until more people recognize that it exists (Johnson, 1997). Exposure to this issue within the classroom can increase awareness that can spark the motivation and action necessary for change. The more we (psychologists and students) understand the dynamics and the effects of power differentials, the better armed we are to reduce privilege and its negative consequences for the less powerful.

Second, research and teaching on the psychology of women enlightens us about the way we construct gender in our lives. Scientific investigation gives us a better understanding of the influences on this construction and of the effects our personal images of gender have on our experiences as females or males. Similarly, exploration of these issues in the classroom has the potential to transform. As both women and men learn about the social basis for gender behaviors and roles, they might feel freer to experiment and to make choices that are less traditional but more personally appropriate.

Third, research and teaching about the experiences of diverse women can dispel myths and stereotypes that distort our understanding and reduce tolerance. These activities also foster greater understanding, appreciation, and celebration of our similarities and differences and can empower all females, not only those in the most privileged group. Although recent years have brought a greater inclusion of underrepresented groups in both research and educational curricula to achieve these diversity goals, the field must continue to expand the diversity of its research participants. A more representative body of knowledge can ensure that researchers, instructors, and students do not generalize from one narrow group of females, carrying the implicit message that people in this group are "normal" and any discrepant behaviors, attitudes, or roles on the part of other individuals are "abnormal" (Madden & Hyde, 1998).

Consideration of diverse women's experiences must include a broader scope of topics as well. Research and teaching must address previously underexamined issues, such as employment obstacles for poor women, dating concerns of women with disabilities, experiences of lesbian mothers, outcomes of living in an extended family, and achievement goals of working-class and poor young women. A broader conceptualization of research and teaching topics not only facilitates understanding but can also inform policy interventions. For example, although company-supplied day care might ease the work-family burden of women in white-collar and professional jobs, free temporary child care might be a better resource for women on welfare who are seeking job training. Similarly, principles guiding custody decisions for divorced heterosexual women might not apply to divorced lesbian women. It is only through an examination of questions relevant to all types of women that societal interventions can best address the diversity of women's needs.

Although there is much less information available about ethnic minority women, working-class and poor women, women with disabilities, lesbian and bisexual women, and older women, it is essential that we incorporate the knowledge base that does exist into our teaching. As cogently stated by Ann Marie Orza and Jane Torrey (1995), "Teachers and researchers in the psychology of women share the goal of including and understanding not only both sexes but also the great variety of people who also differ from the middle-class European male in race, class, or ethnicity" (p. 212). "Perhaps the most important task confronting women's studies (and all other studies) at this moment in history is to convey the fact that an individual's psychological makeup cannot be understood except in the context of the particular roles he or she plays in the particular culture and community to which he or she belongs" (pp. 211–212). Without this diversity focus in our teaching, students' "educational experience does not reflect social reality and is therefore derelict in preparing them, regardless of race, culture, ethnicity, sexual orientation, and gender, to function in a culturally pluralistic and global society" (Sue et al., 1999, p. 1066).

Socialization of Children

Another approach to developing greater flexibility in gender construction is the feminist socialization of children. Parents can bring up their children so that preferences and skills, rather than gender, are the defining characteristics that guide development. How can this be achieved? Read Learn about the Research 15.1 to examine Phyllis Katz's perspective on this topic (1996).

What would be the outcomes of gender-flexible upbringing? First, it would expand the range of activities, behaviors, and roles from which the child and, later, the adult could choose. Instead of assuming, for example, that males make dating decisions, pay for dates, and initiate sex (Chapter 8), whichever dating partner was more comfortable with these behaviors could select them. Furthermore, these might vary depending on the circumstances. This, in turn, could lead to more egalitarian relationships because decision making and instrumental behaviors would not be relegated specifically to males. Similarly, women and men would make occupational choices on the basis of skills, interests, and personal needs without consideration of the gender appropriateness of the field (Chapter 10), a process that might lead to greater occupational prestige and salaries for women and to greater job satisfaction for both genders.

LEARN ABOUT THE RESEARCH 15.1
Why and How Should We Raise Feminist Children?

Phyllis Katz asks what it means to raise a feminist child. One answer is the elimination of all gender-related traits, behaviors, and roles, that is, raising children so that gender is irrelevant. Katz contends, however, that this would not be possible. Children are exposed to influences beyond the home. Consequently, even if parents were to treat their daughters and sons identically, these children would continue to be exposed to other people for whom gender would be important.

Instead Katz advocates raising children to be gender flexible, that is, to select activities and behaviors on the basis of "individual likes and skills rather than being bogged down by gender stereotypes" (pp. 333–334). She notes that because much gender learning takes place during the preschool years, several actions by the parents can play an important role. One is role modeling. For example, maternal employment and nontraditional division of household labor by parents can help develop less stereotypic expectations and behaviors in children. Furthermore, the kinds of activities and goals encouraged by the parents can be instrumental. As examples, discouragement of gender stereotypic activities, toys, and future aspirations can be effective. Also, Katz notes that limiting the amount of television their children can watch might be beneficial because there is some evidence that children who watch less television have less stereotypic conceptions of gender.

What Does It Mean?

1. Do you think that the development of gender flexibility is a positive goal? Explain your answer.
2. Katz suggests it might not be possible to eliminate all gender-stereotypic influences on children. Do you agree or disagree? Explain your answer.
3. Regardless of your own opinion about gender flexibility, use the knowledge you have gained from this course to suggest other factors besides parental behaviors that might facilitate its development in children and adolescents.

Source: Katz (1996).

Second, given the higher status of the male role in North American society, gender flexibility would lead boys to develop a greater understanding and respect for behaviors and roles traditionally associated with females. If boys observe their fathers and other influential adult men performing traditional female behaviors, such as washing the dishes and caring for young children and if boys are required to perform these chores, they will be more apt to view the traditional female role as worthy and dignified. The far-reaching implications are, of course, that little boys grow up to be men. The values instilled in them in childhood will influence their own involvement in traditional female activities and increase their respect for others who perform such activities. This greater respect could, in turn, carry over to the workplace, where more familiarity with family-related activities might encourage the initiation and support of additional family-friendly policies.

Third, gender flexibility would minimize the extent to which people view and evaluate others on the basis of a rigid construction of gender. For example,

When children observe their parents performing nonstereotypic behaviors, they are likely to develop a less rigid construction of gender.

girls who play sports would receive the same degree of encouragement as sports-oriented boys (Chapter 4) and women in blue-collar trades would be accepted rather than harassed by their coworkers (Chapter 14). We would evaluate mothers who voluntarily stay home to care for their children or those who elect to work full time in the same way as we would evaluate fathers in these roles. We would have the same reaction to women and men who are fiercely independent and to those who are highly dependent. That is, if our children were brought up with a feminist perspective of equality, their impressions of others would be influenced by their behaviors and roles rather than by the perceived suitability of those behaviors for individuals of one gender or the other, and the choice of roles, for everyone, would be limitless.

Institutional Procedures

Another route for attaining our goals is for institutions to initiate practices that reduce gender inequality and that create hospitable environments for both women and men. In Chapters 10 and 11 we examined organizational procedures that improve working conditions for women (e.g., pay equity, affirmative action) or that facilitate balancing of family and work (e.g., flextime, child-care assistance programs). Institutional initiatives can enhance the quality of life for women in other ways as well. For example, Mary Koss and her colleagues (Koss et al., 1994) propose several institutional interventions that can lower the risk of rape and domestic violence by reducing gender inequality and enhancing flexibility of gender-related behaviors and roles.

First, Koss and her associates emphasize the importance of education. They recommend that violence prevention begin in elementary school, when values about females' and males' roles are beginning to form, and continue through college. Although different topics would be appropriate at various educational levels, the curriculum should include an examination and reconceptualization of gender roles, prevention of substance abuse, and exploration of rape myths. This type of curriculum would expose children, adolescents, and young adults to problems inherent in traditional gender-related behaviors and roles, would make them more sensitive to the experiences and pressures of the other gender, and would make them aware of the nature of and influences on violence against women.

Second, these researchers suggest that the church can be involved in reduction of intimate violence. Because some people acquire their view of marital relationships through religious doctrine, programs aimed at reducing domestic violence can be particularly effective for these individuals, if associated with the church.

Third, Koss and her colleagues point to the need for change in media images. Researchers should advance our understanding about how the media contribute to violence against women and about ways they can be used to reduce this violence.

In addition to the prevention of violence against women, Koss and her colleagues address ways that health care institutions can more effectively treat women who have been victimized. They stress the importance for health care providers to have adequate training in treating the physical and mental health problems that arise from rape and battering. Providers must be sensitive to victims' needs and be able to offer effective medical treatment as well as appropriate referrals for psychological counseling or assistance with lifestyle changes, such as leaving their violent relationship.

Individual Actions

Many women seek to achieve success and better their own lives through individual efforts. In fact, consistent with a traditional North American value system that applauds individualism, many American women place greater emphasis on their own hard work in improving their lives than on women's collective efforts (Boxer, 1997; Konek et al., 1994). These women think that women's personal effort and success today, more than changes in organizational or governmental policies and practices, will lead to better opportunities for future generations of women (Konek et al., 1994), and they are willing to work hard, assert their rights, seek out opportunities for advancement, and make sacrifices if necessary.

Collective Action

Contrary to the individual approach, many feminist psychologists contend that collective action is necessary in order to achieve significant improvement in women's lives (White et al., 2001; Worell, 2001). This does not imply that women should not work hard to attain personal goals. However, it does mean that individual women should strive to empower all women, not just themselves; they should advocate for social change, not just personal betterment. Furthermore, these collective efforts should address the concerns of diverse groups of women.

One woman who has made a difference in the lives of many other women is Catherine Hamlin, an Australian-born surgeon who has spent over 40 years in Ethiopia repairing fistulas, which are seriously ripped tissues resulting from female genital mutilation. She and her husband founded a fistula hospital which has treated thousands of women. In 2003, Dr. Hamlin was named an honorary fellow in the American College of Surgeons (Bridges et al., 2003–2004).

Two other wonderful examples of women who have made a difference are the winners of the Nobel Peace Prize in 2003 and 2004. The 2003 winner is Shirin Ebadi, an Iranian lawyer, judge, writer, and university lecturer who has spent three decades advancing human rights in her country. While many professional women left Iran after the 1979 Islamic revolution, she stayed and became one of Iran's outspoken advocates for the rights of women and children (Alvarez, 2003; Sciolino, 2003). Wangari Maathal, the 2004 Nobel Peace Prize winner, is the first Black African woman to receive the award. She won for her work as the founder and leader of an organization that has fought deforestation of the land and has improved women's lives through education, family planning, and better nutrition (Maliti, 2004).

The feminist movement in the United States, a collective movement aimed at enhancing women's lives, has unfortunately been focused primarily on the needs of White middle-class heterosexual women and has been criticized for failing to address racism, classism, and heterosexism. It seriously lags behind in dealing with unique problems faced by women of color, poor and working-class women, and sexual minority women (Henry, 2004; Mankiller, 2004; Poo & Tang, 2004; White et al., 2001; Worell, 2001). In the words of a Black college instructor and administrator, "Until very recently I did not call myself a feminist . . . even academic feminism did not include me until the 1980s. Feminism in the United States was pretty monolithic, pretty homogeneous . . . and these groups were very, very exclusive in terms of what they considered to be priorities . . . and so until recently, America did not embrace my experiences" (Kmiec et al., 1996, p. 58).

As bell hooks (1990) contends, women who differ in ethnicity and class have certain experiences in common by virtue of their gender. However, racism, classism, heterosexism, and ableism contribute to double and triple jeopardies experienced by women who are not in the privileged group. Fortunately, the efforts of women of color, poor women, and lesbian women have gradually expanded the feminist movement's perspective, and participation by previously excluded groups has increased (Labaton & Martin, 2004). But this expansion of goals and inclusive participation must continue to grow. Attempts to achieve gender equality should concurrently strive to eradicate inequalities based on ethnicity, class, sexual orientation, physical disability/ability, and age. Only the collective efforts of diverse groups of women working together for the elimination of all types of power inequality can provide a brighter future for all girls and women. For a look at women's movements worldwide, see Explore Other Cultures 15.1.

Given that some women ascribe to beliefs in equality but are not oriented toward working for change for others, are there ways to enhance these women's

Wangari Maathal (left) and Shirin Ebadi (right), winners of the Nobel Peace Prize in 2004 and 2003, respectively, were honored for advancing human rights in their countries.

motivation for social activism? Judith Worell (2001) suggests that communication with other women, learning about the experiences and problems of other women, and exposure to varied situations that involve gender discrimination can broaden one's understanding of women's issues and encourage individuals' greater involvement in advocating for women's rights. Taking women's studies courses, experiencing discrimination firsthand, and having a mother who is a feminist are linked to students' participation in collective action (Liss et al., 2004).

EXPLORE OTHER CULTURES 15.1
Women's Movements Worldwide

Until recently, feminist academics from the Western world focused on the largely middle-class women's movements in the United States and Europe. However, women in the non-Western world, many of them poor, have also had a long history of battling for women's rights (Fraser & Tinker, 2004; Rosen, 2001). Because cultures differ, the struggle does not always focus on the same set of issues. For example, family-planning agendas have helped to mobilize Western feminists but may be viewed skeptically by women in developing nations, where having many children confers status or provides a source of family labor (Burn, 2000). The Afghan Women's Bill of Rights, crafted by a group of Afghan women in 2003, has as its first priority the guarantee of an education. Then come health care, personal security, and support of widows, with freedom of speech taking up fifth place. Even these basic rights are still in jeopardy in Afghanistan ("Afghan Women's Rights," 2003). In addition to women's movements that

exist in individual countries, there is also an international women's movement, sometimes called global feminism. This movement advocates the idea that all humans share the same rights, while at the same time it recognizes the diversity of women's lives and cultures. The global feminist movement is working to challenge violence against women, expand the education of girls, support women's reproductive and sexual freedom, and champion women's access to economic independence (Fraser & Tinker, 2004). The United Nations has attempted to play a leadership role in this effort. In 1979, it issued a treaty known as the Convention on the Elimination of All Forms of Discrimination against Women. Out of 181 nations, 170 have ratified the treaty ("Gender Equality," 2003), although about one-third of the ratifiers listed reservations (Burn, 2000). The nonratifying countries include several from the Middle East and sub-Saharan Africa— as well as the "enlightened" United States! (Lafferty, 2003).

These French women are demonstrating to show their support of equal rights for Algerian women.

The Internet has revolutionized the way women organize and act collectively. The use of e-mail, Websites, Listservs, and search engines has improved communication for virtually all groups but has been especially important in linking women's groups, which tend to be small and often isolated from each other (Lee, 2004). One example of the effectiveness of the Internet in bringing women into the political process occurred when President George W. Bush cut off government funding to family planning programs outside the United States even if the money was not going to be used for abortion. *Los Angeles Times* writer Patt Morrison denounced the decision in her column and publicly made a donation to Planned Parenthood in Bush's name. The news spread rapidly via e-mail, and donations totaling half a million dollars poured into Planned Parenthood in the president's name (Lee, 2004).

Do our feminist goals for the future coincide with the perspectives of you and your acquaintances? Try Get Involved 15.1 to explore students' fantasies about their ideal futures.

Feminist Beliefs

We began the text with a discussion of the meaning of feminism, and now we come full circle, back to this topic. Because the goals we have presented and many of the actions taken to achieve these goals are rooted in a feminist perspective, it is important to explore the prevalence and accuracy of feminist beliefs.

GET INVOLVED **15.1**

A Perfect Future Day

Imagine what you would like your life to be like ten years in the future. Write a paragraph describing what your ideal typical day would be like. Also, ask one same-gender and two other-gender students to perform the same exercise.

What Does It Mean?

Read through the four descriptions and record similarities and differences about the following: (1) marital status, (2) presence of children, (3) if married, family responsibilities of each spouse, (4) employment status, (5) if employed, gender dominance of the occupation, and (6) leisure activities.

1. Do the descriptions written by the women differ from those written by the men in relation to these or any other topics? If

yes, use information learned in this course to explain these differences.

2. Are there any current gender-based expectations about interpersonal or societal roles and behaviors that might hinder your own ideal life from becoming a reality? If yes, what kinds of changes do you think would reduce this impediment? Would you be interested in working for this change?

Source: Based on Kerr (1999).

Although some North Americans believe that feminism has had a positive impact on women's attainment of greater economic, political, and legal opportunities (Boxer, 1997; Fassinger, 1994), others have argued that feminists are the root of numerous personal and social problems, and are especially responsible for the decline in the "traditional" North American family (Faludi, 1991; Johnson, 1997). Many feminists are, indeed, disturbed about the subordination of women within *patriarchal* families where husbands hold the power and dictate the activities of wives and children (Johnson, 1997), but they are supportive of egalitarian families in which husbands and wives share power and respect. It is untrue to say that most feminists oppose the notion of the family—they oppose the notion of an unequal family.

Another accusation made by some antifeminists is that feminists hate men. While it is true that many feminists object to male power which has oppressed women in the workplace, government, education, and the home (Johnson, 1997), an objection to male *privilege* should not be confused with an objection to men per se.

Sadly, these antifeminist beliefs not only dangerously distort the truth but also discredit feminist ideology. Given that most North Americans are strongly profamily and that males have high status and respect within society, the depiction of feminists as antifamily male-bashers sets them up for ridicule and makes it easier to dismiss their beliefs as extremist. What are your thoughts on feminism? Perform Get Involved 15.2 to reassess your views.

Feminist Identification

Although support for the women's movement has increased steadily since the mid-1970s, the proportion of American women who identify themselves as feminists remains low (Reid & Purcell, 2004).

GET INVOLVED 15.2

How Do You View Feminism?

Answer the following questions without looking back at the answers you gave in Chapter 1. First, indicate which of the following categories best characterizes your identity as a feminist.

a. consider myself a feminist and am currently involved in the Women's Movement
b. consider myself a feminist but am not involved in the Women's Movement
c. do not consider myself a feminist but agree with at least some of the objectives of feminism

d. do not consider myself a feminist and disagree with the objectives of feminism

Second, on a scale from 1 (strongly disagree) to 6 (strongly agree), indicate the extent to which you disagree or agree with each of the following statements.

1. Women should be considered as seriously as men as candidates for the presidency of the United States.
2. Although women can be good leaders, men make better leaders.

3. A woman should have the same job opportunities as a man.
4. Men should respect women more than they currently do.
5. Many women in the workforce are taking jobs away from men who need the jobs more.
6. Doctors need to take women's health concerns more seriously.
7. Women have been treated unfairly on the basis of their gender throughout most of human history.

8. Women are already given equal opportunities with men in all important sectors of their lives.
9. Women in the United States are treated as second-class citizens.
10. Women can best overcome discrimination by doing the best they can at their jobs, not by wasting time with political activity.

What Does It Mean?

Before computing your score for the ten items, reverse the points for statements 2, 5, 8, and 10. That is, for a rating of "1" (strongly disagree), give 6 points, for a rating of "2," give 5 points, and so on. Then sum the points for the ten items. Note that higher scores reflect greater agreement with feminist beliefs.

1. Compare your feminist identification (Part I) here with your feminist identifica-

tion at the beginning of the course (see Get Involved 1.1). If there has been a change, explain why.
2. Compare your feminist beliefs at the two points in time. If there has been a change, explain why. What specific course material, if any, contributed to this change?

Source: Based on Morgan (1996).

According to recent nationwide polls and studies of college students (Henderson-King & Zhermer, 2003; Hymowitz, 2002) only about 25 percent of American women label themselves as feminists, and the percentage of men is even lower. Furthermore, college women of color and working-class White women are less likely than middle-class White college women to label themselves as feminists (Aronson, 2003; Myaskovsky & Wittig, 1997). As stated earlier, the feminist movement has been dominated by White women, and many women of color feel that feminists do not have an interest in their unique experiences and concerns (Myaskovsky & Wittig, 1997). Some women of color, therefore, have embraced women of color feminism, a form of feminism that addresses racism and other issues of importance to ethnic minority females (see Chapter 1). Rachel Williams and Michele Wittig (1997) see another problem for some women of color—the perception of conflict between the values embraced by their ethnic group and values associated with feminist ideology. These scholars suggest that Asian American and Latina women may feel torn between the more patriarchal belief system of their cultures and the feminist value of egalitarianism.

Interestingly, many women who reject the feminist label, support the goals of feminism (Aronson, 2003; Hall & Rodriguez, 2003; Liss et al., 2001). Alyssa Zucker

(2004) refers to this group of women as "egalitarians." How can these discrepancies between a feminist identification and views about feminist goals be explained? First, women may be concerned about negative images that some people attach to feminism and feminists (Pierce et al., 2003). At a personal level, they might want to avoid a negative self-image which they believe would result from identifying themselves with a term that has negative connotations. At a public level they might fear the social disapproval that could follow from their identification as a feminist (Burn, 2000; Burn et al., 2000). Some of these negative images are illustrated by the following definitions of feminists offered by college students. One student stated, "Feminism is the way females act to lash out at society. They become uptight about men holding doors open for them and yell about equal rights too much!!" (Jackson et al., 1996, p. 690). A different negative image, that of feminists as man-haters, is illustrated by another student's definition of feminism as "opposing the male sex and it's usually rude and crude sarcastic remarks, papers, or books" (Jackson et al., 1996, p. 690). Still others appear to equate feminism with being unfeminine. In support of this view, women who rate themselves high in femininity are more likely to reject the "feminist" label than women who rate themselves high in masculinity (Toller et al., 2004). Thus, it is not surprising to find that college students respond more favorably to a profeminist message when it is presented by a feminine-appearing speaker than by a masculine-appearing speaker (Bullock & Fernald, 2003), a phenomenon referred to as "feminism lite."

A second reason that some women refuse to identify as feminists despite their agreement with many feminist goals is that they do not believe women are oppressed or that economic and political systems need to be changed (Nelson et al., 1997). Although they value equality of power and opportunity, they believe women have already attained this equality. One study of college women (Foster, 1999) found an association between students' belief that women are disadvantaged relative to men and their participation in activities that enhance the status of women (e.g., talking about women's issues with others, attending talks on women's issues, joining protests). Women who perceived fewer gender differences in social conditions were less likely to be involved in activism.

A third reason some women do not label themselves as feminists is because they believe that a feminist identification implies collective action, but they favor individual efforts, rather than group-based actions, for achieving greater power (Cole et al., 2001).

Emergence of Feminist Beliefs

During this class, I feel my eyes have been opened to what not just women in general, but ethnic, young, old, and disabled women go through every day. . . . Before I took this class, I thought I was aware of all the issues women face. Boy, was I wrong! (Shawna, 21-year-old senior)

Before this course, I thought some women made too big a deal over women's rights issues. My eyes have been so opened, and now I am extremely sensitized to gender issues in society. I actively try to educate people on gender inequality of power and social construction of gender. I am really going to try to raise very gender-flexible children. In a way, I feel like I stepped out of the dark into the light. (Jessica, 25-year-old senior)

  It has become customary for the three of us [friends taking the Psychology of Women course] to discuss women's issues at a local coffee shop on Tuesday evenings, not just among ourselves, but our friends as well . . . I have never taken a class that has caused me to engage in so much conversation outside of the classroom. The biggest success of your class is that regardless of how people feel about a certain issue, your class is causing people to talk and more people are becoming aware of issues that wouldn't be discussed otherwise . . . I feel that my eyes have been opened to a world of issues that have always been right in front of me. (Julie, 22-year-old senior)

One important route to feminist consciousness is enrollment in women's studies courses (Cole et al., 2001; Reid & Purcell, 2004; Stake & Malkin, 2003). Women's Studies programs (some are now called Gender Studies) have proliferated since the early 1970s to about 700 today in the United States (Patai & Koertge, 2003). Courses in these programs help foster feminist goals by providing students with the knowledge to transform society (Kravetz & Marecek, 2001; Reid & Zalk, 2001). Similar to the experiences of Shawna, Jessica, Julie (above), and Rachel (chapter-opening vignette), studies have shown that women's studies courses are instrumental in decreasing gender-stereotypic attitudes (Bryant, 2003; Harris et al., 1999; Lovejoy, 1998; Wilson, 1997) and increasing commitment to feminism (Cole et al., 2001; Worell et al., 1999). Furthermore, Jayne Stake and her colleagues (Stake et al., 1994) found that women's studies courses can encourage activism. Their investigations showed that students who took a women's studies course, compared to those who did not, became more active in feminist activities and made more changes in their own roles and/or ways of interacting with others. Moreover, these changes lasted over time (Stake & Rose, 1994). Exposure to feminism in other ways can also give rise to feminist identity. For example, feminists are more likely than other women to have feminists in their family of origin, such as their mother or sister (Zucker, 2004).

A second route toward feminism involves personal experiences women have that make them painfully aware that they live in a sexist society. For example, experiencing sexual harassment or rape is associated with increased support for feminism and women's rights activism (Cole et al., 2001; Zucker, 2004). To assess your own involvement in feminist activism, try Get Involved 15.3.

Men and Feminism

Various men's movements have developed in recent years, partly as a response to the women's movement. The mythopoetic movement started by John Bly (1990) emphasizes men reconnecting with each other through rituals and retreats. Two religiously based movements of the late 1990s are the Promise Keepers, a Christian fundamentalist group, and the Million Man March, a Black men's group. Both of these movements seek to bring men back into the family, certainly a desirable

GET INVOLVED **15.3**

How Involved in Feminist Activism Are You?

Check each of the following eight activities you engaged in during the six months before the beginning of this semester. Then check each activity you engaged in during this semester.

Before	During
___ kept informed on women's rights issues	___
___ talked with others to influence their attitudes about women's rights issues	___
___ signed a petition related to women's rights	___
___ attended a march, rally, or protest related to women's rights	___
___ wrote letters to politicians or newspapers about women's rights issues	___
___ contributed money to a women's rights cause or to politicians who supported such causes	___
___ circulated a petition about a women's rights cause	___
___ worked for a phone bank, letter writing campaign, or political campaign in the cause of women's rights	___
___ participated in other activity related to women's rights	___

What Does It Mean?

1. Has there been an increase in your feminist activities due to this course? If yes, indicate some of the information you learned that contributed to this change.
2. Which of the following types of activities do you believe is the preferable route toward increased rights and opportunities for women: individual effort alone or individual effort combined with collective action? Explain your answer.

Source: Based on Stake et al. (1994).

---

objective. However, the underlying theme is a return to the traditional roles of men as leaders and women as followers (Kimmel, 2001).

Profeminism is another movement consisting of men who support equality of women and men in all spheres of life, both professional and personal. Profeminist men have organized several campus groups in addition to the National Organization for Men Against Sexism, which includes female as well as male members (Kimmel, 2001). One of the most successful profeminist organizations is the White Ribbon

Campaign, which began in Canada in 1991 in response to the mass killing of 14 women engineering students at the University of Montreal by a deranged man. The campaign, whose slogan is "Men, working to end men's violence against women" has now spread to over 30 countries (www.whiteribbon.ca).

Postscript

We end this exploration of women's lives with two cautionary notes. First, when thinking about the material in this text, keep in mind that the knowledge we have about the psychology of women is situated in a particular time in history. It is strongly connected to existing societal attitudes and to current political, economic, and legal events. As a result of economic and attitudinal changes in the last decades of the twentieth century, for example, a major concern for many married mothers in the new millenium is the balancing of work and family, but this issue would have been irrelevant to stay-at-home mothers in the 1960s. We can expect that some of the information presented here will become obsolete over time. In fact, if women are successful in their efforts, if legislative initiatives and workplace policies address gender inequities in power and opportunities, and if gender roles become more flexible, some current problems, such as wage differentials and sexual harassment, will, we hope, be eliminated.

Second, as discussed in Chapter 1, teaching does not take place in an ideological vacuum. Even if not explicitly stated, a particular set of values underlies all scholarly research, textbooks, and course content, and this book is no exception. Our feminist values served as the basis for our examination of the lives of girls and women. Regardless of your own commitment to these beliefs, we hope your exploration of the psychology of women has been an enriching experience and that you have achieved an increased understanding of the negative effects of male privilege, a greater appreciation of women's diversity, and a greater awareness of the role interpersonal and societal forces play in shaping gender-based attitudes, behaviors, and goals. And, we sincerely hope you apply what you have learned from this text and course to other academic interests, career pursuits, your own experiences, and perhaps to societal change.

SUMMARY

Feminist Goals

- Greater gender equality of organizational and interpersonal power would benefit women in several ways by increasing opportunities in the workplace, giving women a greater voice in dating relationships, creating a more equitable division of household labor, and reducing intimate violence. It is essential that increases in women's power benefit all women, regardless of ethnicity, class, disability/ability, sexual orientation, or age.

- The benefits of a flexible construction of gender include behavior and role choices that reflect individual preferences instead of social expectations, as well as a reduction in sexual harassment and acquaintance rape.

Actions to Achieve These Goals

- Several actions can facilitate the achievement of these goals including a diversity-oriented psychology of women that can inform about the role of male privilege and the constraints of rigid gender roles and enhance our understanding of diversity and increase tolerance.
- Raising gender-flexible children would free people to make personally appropriate choices, rather than those based on gender-role expectations. Additionally, it would help foster greater appreciation of women's traditional roles and lessen the tendency to evaluate others on the basis of their conformity to gender expectations.
- Interventions by educational, religious, and health care institutions, as well as the media, can address violence against women.
- Some women believe that they can enhance their own lives more through their individual efforts than as a result of collective action.
- Many feminists believe that improvement of the lives of women requires collective action.

However, the feminist movement has been focused more on the lives of privileged women than on those who experience double and triple jeopardies stemming from racism, classism, homophobia, and/or ableism.

Feminist Beliefs

- North Americans have mixed views about the value of feminism. Some believe it has helped women. Others believe that feminists are responsible for many personal and social problems.
- Only 25 percent of North American women label themselves as feminists. Some of the women who do not identify themselves as feminists support the goals of feminism. Reasons for this discrepancy include negative images of feminists, the assumption that women have already attained power equality, and the belief that feminism implies collective action.
- Women's studies courses tend to decrease students' gender-stereotypic attitudes and increase their commitment to feminism and activism.
- Various men's movements have developed in recent years, including the mythopoetic movement, Promise Keepers, Million Man March, and profeminism.

WHAT DO YOU THINK?

1. The text presented greater equality of power and greater flexibility in the construction of gender as beneficial to girls and women. Do you think there are any disadvantages for females associated with these goals? In what ways would these goals benefit males? In what ways might they be detrimental to males?

2. Which one or more of the various strategies for improving women's lives do you think would be most effective? Explain your answer.

IF YOU WANT TO KNOW MORE

Ens, C. Z., & Sinacore, A. L. (Eds.). (2005). Teaching and social justice: Integrating multicultural and feminist theories in the classroom. Washington, DC: American Psychological Association.

Fraser, A. S., & Tinker, I. (Eds.). (2004). *Developing power: How women transformed international development*. New York: Feminist Press.

Henry, A. (2004). *Not my mother's sister: Generational conflict and third-wave feminism*. Bloomington, IN: Indiana University Press.

Johnson, A. G. (1997). *The gender knot: Unraveling our patriarchal legacy*. Philadelphia: Temple University Press.

Kirk, G., & Okazawa-Rey, M. (2001). *Women's lives: Multicultural perspectives* (2d ed.). Mountain View, CA: Mayfield.

Labaton, V., & Martin, D. L. (Eds.). (2004). *The fire this time: Young activists and the new feminism*. New York: Anchor Books.

Maglin, N. B., & Perry, D. (Eds.). (1996). *"Bad girls"/ "Good girls": Women, sex and power in the nineties*. New Brunswick, NJ: Rutgers University Press.

Naples, N. A., & Desai, M. (Eds.). (2002). *Women's activism and globalization: Linking local struggles and global politics*. New York: Routledge.

Stetson, D. M. (2004). *Women's rights in the U.S.A.: Policy debates and gender roles* (3rd ed.). New York: Routledge.

WEBSITES

Feminism

Feminist Utopia
http://www.amazoncastle.com/feminism/feminism.htm
Women of Color Web
http://www.hsph.harvard.edu/grhf/woc

Advocating for Change

Activist Web Sites for Women's Issues
http://www.research.umbc.ed/~korenman/wmst/links_actv.html
The Ethnic Woman International
http://www.ethnicwomanmagazinecable.com

REFERENCES

Aaron, R., et al. (2004, April 3). Suicides in young people in rural southern India. *The Lancet, 363,* 1117–1118.

AARP. (1995). *Women's issues.* Washington, DC: Author.

AARP. (1999a). *A profile of older Americans: 1999.* Washington, DC: Author.

AARP. (1999b). *Sex—What's age got to do with it?* Washington, DC: Author.

AARP. (2001). *In the middle: A report on multicultural boomers coping with family and aging issues.* Washington, DC: Author.

AARP. (2002a). *Global aging: Achieving its potential.* Washington, DC: Author.

AARP. (2002b). *Health insurance options for midlife adults.* Washington, DC: Author.

AARP. (2003). *Lifestyles, dating and romance: A study of midlife singles.* Washington, DC: Author.

AARP. (2004, Winter). *The GIC Voice,* p. 11.

AARP. (2005). Medicare at 40: Past accomplishments and future challenges. Washington, DC: Author.

AAUW. (1992). *How schools shortchange women: The AAUW Report.* Washington, DC: AAUW Educational Foundation.

AAUW. (1998a). *Gender gaps: Where schools still fail our children.* Washington, DC: AAUW Educational Foundation.

AAUW. (1998b). *Separated by sex: A critical look at single-sex education for girls.* Washington, DC: AAUW Educational Foundation.

AAUW. (2000). *Tech-savvy: Educating girls in the new computer age.* Washington, DC: AAUW Educational Foundation.

AAUW. (2001). *Hostile hallways: Bullying, teasing, and sexual harassment in school.* Washington, DC: AAUW Educational Foundation.

AAUW. (2002). *Pay equity.* Washington, DC: AAUW Educational Foundation.

AAUW. (2003). *Women at work.* Washington, DC: AAUW Educational Foundation.

AAUW. (2004). *Under the microscope.* Washington, DC: AAUW Educational Foundation.

Abbey, A., et al. (2004a). Sexual assault and alcohol consumption: What do we know about their relationship and what types of research are still needed? *Aggression and Violent Behavior, 9,* 271–303.

Abbey, A., et al. (2004b). Similarities and differences in women's sexual assault experiences based on tactics used by the perpetrator. *Psychology of Women Quarterly, 28,* 323–332.

Abbey, A., Ross, L. T., McDuffie, D., & McAuslan, P. (1996). Alcohol and dating risk factors for sexual assault among college women. *Psychology of Women Quarterly 20,* 147–169.

Abma, J. C., Martinez, G. M., Mosher, W. D., & Dawson, B. S. (2004). Teenagers in the United States: Sexual activity, contraceptive use, and childbearing, 2002. National Center for Health Statistics. *Vital Health Stat, 23(24).*

Acitelli, L. K. (1992). Gender differences in relationship awareness and marital satisfaction among young married couples. *Personality and Social Psychology Bulletin, 18,* 102–110.

Acosta, V., & Carpenter, L. (2002). *Status of women as administrators.* Retrieved September 7, 2002 from http://www.aahperd.org/nagws/pdf_files/acosta Administration.pdf

Adams, J., White, M., & Forman, D. (2004). Are there socioeconomic gradients in stage and grade of breast cancer at diagnosis? Cross sectional analysis of UK cancer registry data. *British Medical Journal, 329,* 142.

Adams, K. E. (2003). Patient choice of provider gender. *Journal of the American Medical Women's Association, 58,* 117–119.

Adams, R. G. (1997). Friendship patterns among older women. In J. M. Coyle (Ed.), *Handbook on women and aging* (pp. 400–417). Westport, CT: Greenwood.

Adams-Curtis, L. E., & Forbes, G. B. (2004). College women's experiences of sexual coercion: A review of cultural, perpetrator, victim, and situational variables. *Trauma, Violence, & Abuse, 5,* 91–122.

Adelman, C. (1999). *Answers in the tool box: Academic intensity, attendance patterns, and bachelor's degree attainment.* Jessup, MD: U.S. Department of Education.

Adelmann, P. K. (1993). Psychological well-being and homemaker vs. retiree identity among older women. *Sex Roles, 29,* 195–212.

Ader, D. N., & Johnson, S. B. (1994). Sample description, reporting, and analysis of sex in psychological research: A look at APA and APA division journals in 1990. *American Psychologist, 49,* 216–218.

Adler, J. (2004, December 20). Toxic strength. *Newsweek*, pp. 45–52.

Adler, N. E., Ozer, E. J., & Tschann, J. (2003). Abortion among adolescents. *American Psychologist, 58*, 211–217.

Adler, N. E., & Smith, L. B. (1998). Abortion. In E. A. Blechman & K. D. Brownell (Eds.), *Behavioral medicine and women: A comprehensive handbook* (pp. 510–514). New York: Guilford.

Adler, N. E., & Snibbe, A. C. (2003). The role of psychosocial processes in explaining the gradient between socioeconomic status and health. *Current Directions in Psychological Science, 12,* 119–123.

Afghan women's rights. (2003, September 24). *New York Times*, p. A26.

Afifi, W. A., & Johnson, M. L. (1999). The use and interpretation of tie signs in a public setting: Relationship and sex differences. *Journal of Social and Personal Relationships, 16*, 9–38.

AFL-CIO & the Institute for Women's Policy Research. (1999). *Equal pay for working families: National and state data on the pay gap and its costs.* Washington, DC: Author.

AFL-CIO. (2004). *Ask a working woman survey report.* Washington, DC: Author.

Africa's homeless widows. (2004, June 16). *New York Times*, p. A18.

Ahmed, S. B., et al. (2004). Gender bias in cardiovascular advertisements. *Journal of Evaluation in Clinical Practice, 10,* 531.

Ahrens, J. A., & O'Brien, K. M. (1996). Predicting gender-role attitudes in adolescent females: Ability, agency, and parental factors. *Psychology of Women Quarterly, 20*, 409–417.

Alan Guttmacher Institute. (1998). *Into a new world: Young women's sexual and reproductive lives.* New York: Author.

Alan Guttmacher Institute. (2000). *Induced abortion.* New York: Author.

Alan Guttmacher Institute. (2002a). Teen pregnancy: Trends and lessons learned. *Issues in Brief, 2002 Series,* No. 3.

Alan Guttmacher Institute. (2002b). Women and societies benefit when childbearing is planned. *Issues in Brief, 2002 Series,* No. 1.

Alan Guttmacher Institute. (2004a). *Contraception use.* New York & Washington, DC: Author.

Alan Guttmacher Institute. (2004b). *U.S. teenage pregnancy statistics.* New York & Washington, DC: Author.

Alan Guttmacher Institute. (2005). *Contraceptive use.* New York & Washington, DC: Author.

Al-Delaimy, W. K., et al. (2004). A prospective study of smoking and risk of breast cancer in young adult women. *Cancer Epidemiology Biomarkers & Prevention, 13,* 398–404.

Aldous, J., Mulligan, G. M., & Bjarnason, T. (1998). Fathering over time: What makes the difference? *Journal of Marriage and the Family, 60,* 809–820.

Aldridge, M. L., & Browne, K. D. (2003). Perpetrators of spousal homicide. A review. *Trauma, Violence, & Abuse, 4,* 265–276.

Alexander, E. A., Shimp, L. A., & Smith, M. A. (2000). Obesity and eating disorders. In M. A. Smith & L. A. Shimp (Eds.), *20 common problems in women's health care* (pp. 161–192). New York: McGraw-Hill.

Alexander, K. (2004). Grandma finds a job, looking after junior. *New York Times*, p. E2.

Alfieri, T., Ruble, D. N., & Higgins, E. T. (1996). Gender stereotypes during adolescence: Developmental changes and the transition to junior high school. *Developmental Psychology, 32*, 1129–1137.

Ali, L., & Miller, L. (2004, July 12). The secret lives of wives. *Newsweek*, pp. 47–54.

Ali, L., & Scelfo, J. (2002, December 9). Choosing virginity. *Newsweek*, pp. 61–65.

Allen, B. A. (1996). Staying within the academy. In K. F. Wyche & F. J. Crosby (Eds.), *Women's ethnicities: Journeys through psychology* (pp. 9–26). Boulder, CO: Westview.

Allen, K. R., & Chin-Sang, V. (1990). A lifetime of work: The context and meanings of leisure for aging black women. *Gerontologist, 30*, 734–740.

Allen, M. W. (2004). The role of laughter when discussing workplace barriers: Women in information technology jobs. *Sex Roles, 50,* 177–189.

Allen, P. G. (1990). *Violence and the American Indian woman. The speaking profits us: Violence in the lives of women of color.* Seattle, WA: SAFECO Insurance Company.

Allen, T. D., & Eby, L. T. (2004). Factors related to mentor reports of mentoring functions provided: Gender and relational characteristics. *Sex Roles, 50,* 129–139.

Altman, L. K. (1997, June 22). Is the longer life the healthier one? *New York Times*, p. WH15.

Altman, L. K. (2002, July 7). Drug reduces HIV rates in newborns, Thai study shows. *New York Times*, p. A3.

Altman, L. K. (2004a, February 28). Action on diseases in women is urged. *New York Times*, p. A13.

Altman, L. K. (2004b, November 23). Treating troubling fibroids without surgery. *New York Times*, p. D8.

Altschuler, J., Katz, A. D., & Tynan, M. (2004). Developing and implementing an HIV/AIDS educational curriculum for older adults. *The Gerontologist*, *44*, 121–126.

Alvarez, L. (2003, October 11). Iranian lawyer, staunch fighter for human rights, wins Nobel. *New York Times*, pp. A1, A6.

Amaro, H., et al. (2002). Cultural influences on women's sexual health. In G. M. Wingood & R. J. DiClemente (Eds.), *Handbook of women's sexual and reproductive health* (pp. 71–92). New York: Kluwer Academic/Plenum.

Amato, P. A., & Keith, B. (1991a). Parental divorce and adult well-being: A meta-analysis. *Journal of Marriage and the Family, 53*, 43–58.

Amato, P. A., & Keith, B. (1991b). Parental divorce and child well-being: A meta-analysis. *Psychological Bulletin, 110*, 26–46.

American Academy of Pediatrics. (2005). Adolescent pregnancy: Current trends and issues. *Pediatrics, 116*, 281–286.

American Cancer Society. (1997). *Cancer risk report.* Atlanta: Author.

American Cancer Society. (1999). *For women facing breast cancer.* Atlanta: Author.

American Cancer Society. (2003). *Breast cancer facts & figures 2003–2004.* Atlanta: Author.

American Cancer Society. (2004). *Cancer facts & figures 2004.* Atlanta: Author.

American Council on Education. (2005). *Status report on minorities in higher education.* Washington, DC: Author.

American Heart Association. (2002). *2002 Heart and stroke statistical update.* Dallas: Author.

American Heart Association. (2004). Evidence-based guidelines for cardiovascular disease prevention in women. *Circulation, 109*, 672–693.

American Psychiatric Association. (1994). *Diagnostic and statistical manual of mental disorders.* 4th ed. Washington, DC: Author.

American Psychological Association. (1975). Report of the task force on sex bias and sex-role stereotyping in psychotherapeutic practice. *American Psychologist, 30*, 1169–1175.

American Psychological Association. (2000). Guidelines for psychotherapy with lesbian, gay, and bisexual clients. *American Psychologist, 55*, 1440–1451.

American Psychological Association. (2001). *Publication manual of the American Psychological Association.* 5th ed. Washington, DC: Author.

American Psychological Association. (2002). *Developing adolescents: A reference for professionals.* Washington, DC: Author.

American Psychological Association. (2003). *Women in the American Psychological Association.* Washington, DC: Author.

American Psychological Association. (2004a). Guidelines for psychological practice with older adults. *American Psychologist, 59*, 236–260.

American Psychological Association. (2004b). *Public policy, work, and families: The report of the APA presidential initiative on work and families.* Washington, DC: Author.

Amnesty International. (2004). *It's in our hands: Stop violence against women.* London: Author.

Amowitz, L. L., et al. (2004). Human rights abuses and concerns about women's health and human rights in southern Iraq. *Journal of the American Medical Association, 291*, 1471–1479.

Andersen, B. L. (2002). Biobehavioral outcomes following psychological interventions for cancer patients. *Journal of Consulting and Clinical Psychology, 70*, 590–610.

Andersen, B. L., & Emery, C. (1999, August). *Biobehavioral model of cancer stress: Psychological, behavioral, and biological responses.* Paper presented at the meeting of the American Psychological Association, Boston.

Andersen, B. L., & Farrar, W. B. (2001). Breast disorders and breast cancer. In N. L. Stotland & D. E. Stewart (Eds.), *Psychological aspects of women's health care* (pp. 457–475). Washington, DC: American Psychiatric Press, Inc.

Anderson, D. K., & Saunders, D. G. (2003). Leaving an abusive partner. An empirical review of predictors, the process of leaving, and psychological well-being. *Trauma, Violence, & Abuse, 4*, 163–191.

Anderson, G. D. (2005). Sex and racial differences in pharmacological response: Where is the evidence? Pharmacogenetics, pharmacokinetics, and pharmacodynamics. *Journal of Women's Health, 14*, 19–29.

Anderson, G. M. (2004). Making sense of rising caesarean section rates. *British Medical Journal, 329*, 696–697.

Anderson, I. (2004). Explaining negative rape victim perception: Homophobia and the male rape victim. *Current Research in Social Psychology, 10*, 43–57.

Anderson, K. B., Cooper, H., & Okamura, L. (1997). Individual differences and attitudes toward rape: A meta-analytic review. *Personality and Social Psychology Bulletin, 23*, 295–315.

Anderson, R. N., & Smith, B. L. (2003). *Deaths: Leading causes for 2001.* National Vital Statistics Reports, 52(9). Hyattsville, MD: National Center for Health Statistics.

Anderson, R. N., & Smith, B. L. (2004). *Deaths: Leading causes for 2002.* National Vital Statistics Reports, 53. Hyattsville, MD: National Center for Health Statistics.

Anderson, S. E., Dallal, G. E., & Must, A. (2003). Relative weight and race influence average age at menarche: Results from two nationally representative surveys of U.S. girls studied 25 years apart. *Pediatrics, 111*, 844–850.

Anderson, S. J., & Johnson, J. T. (2003). The who and when of "gender-blind" attitudes: Predictors of gender-role egalitarianism in two different domains. *Sex Roles, 49*, 527–532.

Anderson, V. N., Simpson-Taylor, D., & Herrmann, D. J. (2004). Gender, age, and rape-supportive rules. *Sex Roles, 50*, 77–90.

Andreasen, N. C. (2005). Vulnerability to mental illnesses: Gender makes a difference, and so does providing good psychiatric care. *The American Journal of Psychiatry, 162*, 211–213.

Angell, M. (1997, April 25). Pregnant at 63? Why not? *New York Times*, p. A27.

Angier, N. (1999, February 21). Men, women, sex and Darwin. *New York Times Magazine*, pp. 48–53.

Angier, N. (2001, April 10). A lifetime later, still in love with the lab. *New York Times*, pp. D1, D6.

Angier, N. (2002, November 5). The importance of grandma. *New York Times*, pp. D1, D4.

Angier, N., & Chang, K. (2005, January 24). Gray matter and the sexes: Still a scientific gray area. *New York Times*, pp. A1, A15.

Annie E. Casey Foundation. (1999). *When teens have sex: Issues and trends.* Baltimore, MD: Author.

Antilla, S. (2002). *Tales from the boom-boom room: Women vs. Wall Street.* Princeton, NJ: Bloomberg Press.

Antonucci, T., et al. (2001). Widowhood and illness: A comparison of social network characteristics in France, Germany, Japan, and the United States. *Psychology and Aging, 16*, 655–665.

Antonucci, T. C., et al. (2002). Differences between men and women in social relations, resource deficits, and depressive symptomatology during later life in four nations. *Journal of Social Issues, 58*, 767–783.

Anxiety disorders. (2002, September). Bethesda, MD: National Institute of Mental Health.

Apparala, M. L., Reifman, A., & Munsch, J. (2003). Cross-national comparison of attitudes toward fathers' and mothers' participation in household tasks and childcare. *Sex Roles, 48*, 189–203.

Arbona, C., & Novy, D. M. (1991). Career aspirations and expectations of black, Mexican American, and white students. *The Career Development Quarterly, 39*, 231–239.

Archer, J. (2000). Sex differences in aggression between heterosexual partners: A meta-analytic review. *Psychological Bulletin, 126*, 651–680.

Archer, J. (2002). Sex differences in physically aggressive acts between heterosexual partners. A meta-analytic review. *Aggression and Violent Behavior, 7*, 313–351.

Archer, J. (2004). Sex differences in aggression in real-world settings: A meta-analytic review. *Review of General Psychology, 8*, 291–322.

Archer, S. L. (1992). A feminist's approach to identity research. In G. R. Adams, T. P. Gullotta, & R. Montemayor (Eds.), *Adolescent identity formation* (pp. 25–49). Newberry Park, CA: Sage.

Archer, S. L. (1993). Identity in relational contexts: A methodological proposal. In J. Krogers (Ed.), *Discussion on ego identity* (pp. 75–99). Hillsdale, NJ: Erlbaum.

Arellano, C. M., Kuhn, J. A., & Chavez, E. L. (1997). Psychosocial correlates of sexual assault among Mexican American and white non-Hispanic adolescent females. *Hispanic Journal of Behavioral Sciences, 19*, 446–460.

Arenson, K. W. (2002, July 4). More women taking leadership roles at colleges. *New York Times*, p. A1.

Arias, E. (2004). *United States life tables, 2002.* National Vital Statistics Reports, 53. Hyattsville, MD: National Center for Health Statistics.

Armstrong, M. J. (2001). Ethnic minority women as they age. In J. D. Garner & S. O. Mercer (Eds.), *Women as they age*, 2d ed. (pp. 97–114). New York: Haworth.

Arnett, J. J. (2002). The sounds of sex: Sex in teens' music and music videos. In J. Brown, K. Walsh-Childers, & J. Steele (Eds.), *Sexual teens, sexual media* (pp. 253–264). Hillsdale, NJ: Erlbaum.

Arney, H. T. (2001, May 23). Friends, active social life help turn widow's life around. *Peoria Times-Observer*, p. A8.

Arnold, A. F., et al. (2002). Psychiatric aspects of the postpartum period. In S. G. Kornstein & A. H. Clayton (Eds.), *Women's mental health: A comprehensive textbook* (pp. 91–113). New York: Guilford.

Arnold, K. D. (1993). Academically talented women in the 1970s: The Illinois valedictorian project. In K. D. Hulbert & D. Tickton (Eds.), *Women's lives through time* (pp. 393–414). San Francisco: Jossey-Bass.

Arnold, M. N. (2004, May). *Eating disorder symptomology in college athletes*. Poster presented at the meeting of the American Psychological Society, Chicago.

Aronson, P. (2003). Feminists or "postfeminists"? Young women's attitudes toward feminism and gender relations. *Gender & Society, 17*, 903–922.

Arriaga, X. B., & Foshee, V. A. (2004). Adolescent dating violence: Do adolescents follow in their friends', or their parents', footsteps? *Journal of Interpersonal Violence, 19*, 162–184.

Arsu, S. (2005, May 16). Turks to fight "honor killings" of women. *New York Times*. p. A10.

Asch, A., Perkins, T. S., Fine, M., & Rousso, H. (2001). Disabilities and women: Deconstructing myths and reconstructing realities. In J. Worell (Ed.), *Encyclopedia of women and gender* (pp. 345–354). San Diego: Academic Press.

Ashcraft, M. H. (2002). Math anxiety: Personal, educational, and cognitive consequences. *Current Directions in Psychological Science, 11*, 181–185.

Ashkinaze, C. (2005, Summer). A matter of opinion. *Ms.*, p. 17.

Athenstaedt, U., Haas, E., & Schwab, S. (2004). Gender role self-concept and gender-typed communication behavior in mixed-sex and same-sex dyads. *Sex Roles, 50*, 37–52.

Atwater, L., Carey, J., & Waldman, D. (2001). Gender and discipline in the workplace: Wait until your father gets home. *Journal of Management, 27*, 537–561.

Aube, J., Fleury, J., & Smetana, J. (2000). Changes in women's roles: Impact on and social policy implications for the mental health of women and children. *Development and Psychopathology, 12*, 633–656.

Aubeeluck, A., & Maguire, M. (2002). The Menstrual Joy Questionnaire alone can positively prime reporting of menstrual attitudes and symptoms. *Psychology of Women Quarterly, 26*, 160–162.

Aubin, S., & Heiman, J. R. (2004). Sexual dysfunction from a relationship perspective. In J. H. Harvey,

A. Wenzel, & S. Sprecher (Eds.), *The handbook of sexuality in close relationships* (pp. 477–517). Mahwah, NJ: Erlbaum.

Auster, E. R. (2001). Professional women's midcareer satisfaction: Toward an explanatory framework. *Sex Roles, 44*, 719–750.

Avellar, S., & Smock, P. J. (2003). Has the price of motherhood declined over time? A cross-cohort comparison of the motherhood wage penalty. *Journal of Marriage and the Family, 65*, 597–607.

Avis, N. S. (2003). Depression during the menopausal transition. *Psychology of Women Quarterly, 27*, 91–100.

Avis, N. E., Crawford, S., & Johannes, C. B. (2002). Menopause. In G. M. Wingood & R. J. DiClemente (Eds.), *Handbook of women's sexual and reproductive health* (pp. 367–391). New York: Kluwer Academic/ Plenum.

Awards for Distinguished Scientific Contribution. (1998). *American Psychologist, 53*, 365–372.

Ayalon, H. (2003). Women and men go to university: Mathematical background and gender differences in choice of field in higher education. *Sex Roles, 48*, 277–290.

Ayoub, N. C. (2004, April 2). Nota bene. *Chronicle of Higher Education*, p. A18.

Ayubi-Moak, I., & Parry, B. L. (2002). Psychiatric aspects of menopause: Depression. In S. G. Kornstein, & A. H. Clayton (Eds.), *Women's mental health: A comprehensive textbook* (pp. 132–143). New York: Guilford.

Azar, B. (2000, July/August). A new stress paradigm for women. *Monitor on Psychology*, pp. 42–43.

Babcock, J. C., Green, C. E., & Robie, C. (2004). Does batterers' treatment work? A meta-analytic review of domestic violence treatment. *Clinical Psychology Review, 23*, 1023–1053.

Babcock, L., & Laschever, S. (2003). *Women don't ask: Negotiation and the gender divide*. Princeton, NJ: Princeton University Press.

Bachanas, P. J., et al. (2002). Psychological adjustment, substance use, HIV knowledge, and risky sexual behavior in at-risk minority females: Developmental differences during adolescence. *Journal of Pediatric Psychology, 27*, 373–384.

Bachar, K., & Koss, M. (2001). Rape. In J. Worell (Ed.), *Encyclopedia of women and gender* (pp. 893–903). San Diego: Academic Press.

Badger, K., Craft, R. C., & Jensen, L. (1998). Age and gender differences in value orientation among American adolescents. *Adolescence, 33*, 591–596.

Baer, J. S., et al. (2003). A 21-year longitudinal analysis of the effects of prenatal alcohol exposure on young adult drinking. *Archives of General Psychiatry, 60,* 377–385.

Baghdadi, G. (2005). Gender and medicines: An international public health perspective. *Journal of Women's Health, 14,* 82–86.

Bailey, D. S. (2004, February). Number of psychology PhDs declining. *Monitor on Psychology,* pp. 18–19.

Bailey, D. S. (2004, March). Lowering risk, building resilience. *Monitor on Psychology,* pp. 34–35.

Bailey, J. M., Pillard, R. C., Neale, M. C., & Agyei, Y. (1993). Heritable factors influence sexual orientation in women. *Archives of General Psychiatry, 48,* 1089–1096.

Bairagi, R. (2001). Effects of sex preference on contraceptive use, abortion and fertility in Matlab, Bangladesh. *International Family Planning Perspectives, 27,* 137–143.

Bakalar, N. (2005, May 17). Exercise: Staying active may reduce risk. *New York Times,* p. F6.

Baker, C. N. (2005). Images of women's sexuality in advertisements: A content analysis of black- and white-oriented women's and men's magazines. *Sex Roles, 52,* 13–27.

Baker, D. M. (2003, August). *Childfree women's experience of gender.* Paper presented at the meeting of the American Psychology Association, Toronto.

Baker, D. P., & Jones, D. P. (1993). Creating gender equality: Cross-national gender stratification and mathematics performance. *Sociology of Education, 66,* 91–103.

Baker, N. L. (2001). Prejudice. In J. Worell (Ed.), *Encyclopedia of gender* (pp. 865–877). San Diego: Academic Press.

Baker-Sperry, L., & Grauerholz, L. (2003). The pervasiveness and persistence of the feminine beauty ideal in children's fairy tales. *Gender & Society, 15,* 711–726.

Ballard, J. E., et al. (2004). The effect of 15 weeks of exercise on balance, leg strength, and reduction in falls in 40 women aged 65 to 89 years. *Journal of the American Medical Women's Association, 59,* 255–261.

Balsam, K. F., et al. (2004). Culture, trauma, and wellness: A comparison of heterosexual and lesbian, gay, bisexual, and two-spirit Native Americans. *Cultural Diversity and Ethnic Minority Psychology, 10,* 287–301.

Bancroft, J., Loftus, J., & Long, J. S. (2003). Distress about sex: A national survey of women in heterosexual relationships. *Archives of Sexual Behavior, 32,* 193–208.

Bandura, A. (2002). Social cognitive theory in cultural context. *Applied Psychology: An International Review, 51,* 269–290.

Banerjee, N. (2001, August 10). Some "bullies" seek ways to soften up. *New York Times,* pp. C1, C2.

Banerjee, N. (2005, February 19). Catholic group receives 1,092 new sex abuse reports. *New York Times,* p. A8.

Bank, B. J. (1995). Gendered accounts: Undergraduates explain why they seek their bachelor's degree. *Sex Roles, 32,* 527–544.

Bank, B. J., & Hansford, S. L. (2000). Gender and friendship: Why are men's best same-sex friendships less intimate and supportive? *Personal Relationships, 7,* 63–78.

Bankole, A., Singh, S., Woog, V., & Wulf, D. (2004). *Risk and protection: Youth and HIV/AIDS in sub-Saharan Africa.* New York & Washington, DC: The Alan Guttmacher Institute.

Banks, A., & Gartrell, N. K. (1995). Hormones and sexual orientation: A questionable link. *Journal of Homosexuality, 28,* 247–268.

Banks, E., et al. (2004). Fracture incidence in relation to the pattern of use of hormone therapy in postmenopausal women. *Journal of the American Medical Association, 291,* 2212–2220.

Barash, D. P. (2002, May 24). Evolution, males, and violence. *Chronicle of Higher Education,* pp. B7–9.

Barash, D. P., & Lipton, J. E. (2002). *Gender gap: The biology of male-female differences.* New York: Transaction.

Barefoot, J. C., et al. (2001). A longitudinal study of gender differences in depressive symptoms from age 50 to 80. *Psychology and Aging, 16,* 342–345.

Barker-Collo, S., & Read, J. (2003). Models of response to childhood sexual abuse. Their implications for treatment. *Trauma, Violence, & Abuse, 4,* 95–111.

Barnard, N. D., Scialli, A. R., Hurlock, D., & Bertron, P. (2000). Diet and sex-hormone binding globulin, dysmenorrhea, and premenstrual symptoms. *Obstetrics & Gynecology, 95,* 240–244.

Barnett, O., Miller-Perrin, C. L., & Perrin, R. D. (2005). *Family violence across the lifespan: An introduction.* Thousand Oaks, CA: Sage Publications.

Barnett, R. C. (2001). Work-family balance. In J. Worell (Ed.), *Encyclopedia of women and gender* (pp. 1181–1190). San Diego: Academic Press.

Barnett, R. C., & Gareis, K. C. (2000). Reduced-hours job-role quality and life satisfaction among married women physicians with children. *Psychology of Women Quarterly, 24,* 358–364.

Barnett, R. C., & Hyde, J. S. (2001). Women, men, work, and family. *American Psychologist, 56,* 781–796.

Barnett, R. C., & Rivers, C. (2004). *Same difference: How gender myths are hurting our relationships, our children, and our jobs.* New York: Basic Books.

Baron, R. S., Burgess, M. L., & Kao, C. F. (1991). Detecting and labeling prejudice: Do female perpetrators go undetected? *Personality and Social Psychology Bulletin, 17,* 115–123.

Barongan, C., & Hall, G. C. N. (1995). The influence of misogynous rap music on sexual aggression against women. *Psychology of Women Quarterly, 19,* 195–207.

Barrett, J. (2004, May 10). No time for wrinkles. *Newsweek,* pp. 82, 85.

Barrett-Connor, E., et al. (2002). Raloxifene and cardiovascular events in osteoporotic postmenopausal women. *Journal of the American Medical Association, 287,* 847–857.

Bartlett, T. (2002, April 5). The question of sex between professors and students. *Chronicle of Higher Education,* pp. A8, 9.

Barton, L. (2005, January 5). Celebrities distort girls' search for ideal shape. *The Guardian (London),* p. 7.

Bartsch, R. A., Burnett, T., Diller, T. R., & Rankin-Williams, E. (2000). Gender representation in television commercials: Updating an update. *Sex Roles, 43,* 735–743.

Basow, S. A. (2001). Androcentrism. In J. Worell (Ed.), *Encyclopedia of women and gender* (pp. 125–135). San Diego: Academic Press.

Basow, S. A., & Rubin, L. R. (1999). Gender influences on adolescent development. In N. G. Johnson, M. C. Roberts, & J. Worell (Eds.), *Beyond appearance: A new look at adolescent girls* (pp. 25–52). Washington, DC: American Psychological Association.

Bass, E., & Davis, L. (1994). *The courage to heal.* 3d ed. New York: HarperCollins.

Bauer, G. R., & Wayne, L. D. (2005). Cultural sensitivity and research involving sexual minorities. *Perspectives on Sexual and Reproductive Health, 37,* 45–47.

Bauer, P. J., Liebl, M., & Stennes, L. (1998). Pretty is to dress as brave is to suitcoat: Gender-based property-to-property inferences by 4-year-old children. *Merrill-Palmer Quarterly, 44,* 355–377.

Baumeister, R. F. (2000). Gender differences in erotic plasticity: The female sex drive as socially flexible and responsive. *Psychological Bulletin, 126,* 347–374.

Baumeister, R. F., Campbell, J. D., Krueger, J.I., & Vohs, K. D. (2003). Does high self-esteem cause better performance, interpersonal success, happiness, or healthier lifestyles? *Psychological Science in the Public Interest, 4,* 1–44.

Bauserman, R. (2002). Child adjustment in joint-custody versus sole-custody arrangements: A meta-analytic review. *Journal of Family Psychology, 16,* 91–102.

Bay-Cheng, L. Y., Zucker, A. N., Stewart, A. J., & Pomerleau, C. S. (2002). Linking femininity, weight concern and mental health among Latina, Black and White women. *Psychology of Women Quarterly, 26,* 36–45.

Baydar, N., & Brooks-Gunn, J. (1998). Profiles of grandmothers who help care for their grandchildren in the United States. *Family Relations, 47,* 385–393.

Bayley, T. M., et al. (2002). Food cravings and aversions during pregnancy: Relationships with nausea and vomiting. *Appetite, 38,* 45–51.

Bazzini, D. G., McIntosh, W. D., Smith, S. M., Cook, S., & Harris, C. (1997). The aging woman in popular film: Underrepresented, unattractive, unfriendly, and unintelligent. *Sex Roles, 36,* 531–543.

Beals, K. P., & Peplau, L. A. (2005). Identity support, identity devaluation, and well-being among lesbians. *Psychology of Women Quarterly, 29,* 140–148.

Bearman, P. (2004, March). *Rules, behaviors, and networks that influence STD prevention among adolescents.* Paper presented at the meeting of the National STD Prevention Conference, Philadelphia.

Bearman, P. S., & Moody, J. (2004). Suicide and friendships among American adolescents. *American Journal of Public Health, 94,* 89–96.

Beasley, B., & Standley, T. C. (2002). Shirts vs. skins: Clothing as an indicator of gender role stereotyping in video games. *Mass Communication & Society, 5,* 279–293.

Beaton, A. M., Tougas, F., & Joly, S. (1996). Neosexism among male managers: Is it a matter of numbers? *Journal of Applied Social Psychology, 26,* 2189–2203.

Becker, A. E., et al. (2002). Eating behaviours and attitudes following prolonged exposure to television among ethnic Fijian adolescent girls. *British Journal of Psychiatry, 180,* 509–514.

Becker, D. (2001). Diagnosis of psychological disorders. In J. Worell (Ed.), *Encyclopedia of women and gender* (pp. 336–343). San Diego: Academic Press.

Becker, S. W., & Eagly, A. H. (2004). The heroism of women and men. *American Psychologist, 59,* 163–178.

Bedford, V. H. (1995). Sibling relationships in middle and old age. In R. Blieszner & V. H. Bedford (Eds.), *Handbook of aging and the family* (pp. 201–222). Westport, CT: Greenwood.

Bee, H. L. (2000). *The journey of adulthood,* 4th ed. Upper Saddle River, NJ: Prentice-Hall.

Beers, M. H., & Jones, T. V. (2004). *The Merck manual of health and aging.* Whitehouse Station, NJ: Merck Research Laboratories.

Begun, B. (2002, April 29). Wired for takeoff, all the way to Salt Lake. *Newsweek,* pp. 40–42.

Behbakht, K., et al. (2004). Social and cultural barriers to Papanicolaou test screening in an urban population. *Obstetrics & Gynecology, 104,* 1355–1361.

Belansky, E. S., Early, D. M., & Eccles, J. S. (1993, March). *The impact of mothers and peers on adolescents' gender role traditionality and plans for the future.* Paper presented at the meeting of the Society for Research in Child Development, New Orleans.

Belkin, L. (2000, December 24). The making of an 8-year-old woman. *New York Times Magazine,* pp. 38–43.

Bellamy, C. (2004). Globalization and infectious diseases in women. *Emerging Infectious Diseases, 10,* 2022–2024.

Bell, L. C. (2004). Psychoanalytic theories of gender. In A. H. Eagly, A. E. Beall, & R. J. Sternberg (Eds.), *The psychology of gender* (pp. 145–168). New York: Guilford.

Bell, M. P., Cycyota, C. S., & Quick, J. C. (2002). An affirmative defense: The preventive management of sexual harassment. In R. J. Burke & D. L. Nelson (Eds.), *Gender, work stress and health.* Washington, DC: American Psychological Association.

Bellafante, G. (2005, May 8). Even in gay circles, women want the ring. *New York Times,* pp. ST1, ST7.

Belle, D., & Doucet, J. (2003). Poverty, inequality, and discrimination as sources of depression among U.S. women. *Psychology of Women Quarterly, 27,* 101–113.

Belluck, P. (2004, May 18). Advocates hail a triumph for civil rights. *New York Times,* pp. A1, A21.

Belluck, P., & Liptak, A. (2004, March 24). Gay parents find big legal hurdles in custody cases. *New York Times,* pp. A1, A14.

Belsky, J. K. (1999). *The psychology of aging: Theory, research and interventions.* Pacific Grove, CA: Brooks-Cole.

Belsky, J. K. (2001). Aging. In J. Worell (Ed.), *Encyclopedia of women and gender* (pp. 95–107). San Diego: Academic Press.

Beltran, A. (2004, Spring). Grandparents raising grandchildren face difficult legal decisions. *AARP: The GIC Voice,* pp. 1, 10.

Bem, S. L. (1974). The measurement of psychological androgyny. *Journal of Consulting and Clinical Psychology, 42,* 155–162.

Bem, S. L. (1975). Sex role adaptability: One consequence of psychological androgyny. *Journal of Personality and Social Psychology, 31,* 634–643.

Bem, S. L. (1981). Gender schema theory: A cognitive account of sex typing. *Psychological Review, 88,* 354–364.

Bem, S. L. (1983). Gender schema theory and its implications for child development: Raising gender-aschematic children in a gender-schematic society. *Signs, 8,* 598–616.

Bem, S. L. (1993). *The lenses of gender: Transforming the debate on sexual inequality.* New Haven, CT: Yale University Press.

Benbow, C. P., & Arjmond, O. (1990). Predictors of high academic achievement in mathematics and science by mathematically talented students: A longitudinal study. *Journal of Educational Psychology, 82,* 430–441.

Benbow, C. P., & Stanley, J. C. (1980). Sex differences in mathematical ability: Fact or artifact? *Science, 210,* 1262–1264.

Benefits of regular physical activity. (2000). *Journal of the American Medical Association, 283,* 3030.

Benenson, J. F., Morash D., & Petrakos, H. (1998). Gender differences in emotional closeness between preschool children and their mothers. *Sex Roles, 38,* 975–985.

Benenson, J. F., Nicholson, C., Waite, A., Roy, R., & Simpson, A. (2001). The influence of group size on children's competitive behavior. *Child Development, 72,* 921–928.

Bennet, J. (1992, October 2). More and more, elderly find themselves taking care of their parents. *New York Times,* p. A21.

Bennice, J. A., & Resick, P. A. (2003). Marital rape. *Trauma, Violence, & Abuse, 4,* 228–245.

Berenbaum, S. A. (1999). Effects of early androgens on sex-typed activities and interests in adolescents with congenital adrenal hyperplasia. *Hormones and Behavior, 35,* 102–110.

Berenbaum, S. A. (2000). Psychological outcome in congenital adrenal hyperplasia. In B. Stalber & B. B. Bercu (Eds.), *Therapeutic outcome of endocrine disorders* (pp. 186–199). New York: Springer-Verlag.

Berenbaum, S. A., & Bailey, J. M. (2003). Effects on gender identity of prenatal androgens and genital appearance: Evidence from girls with congenital adrenal hyperplasia. *Journal of Clinical Endocrinology and Metabolism, 88,* 1102–1106.

Berenbaum, S. A., Bryk, K. K., Duck, S. C., & Resnick, S. M. (2004). Psychological adjustment in children and adults with congenital adrenal hyperplasia. *Journal of Pediatrics, 144,* 741–746.

Berger, L. (2000, July 18). A new body politic: Learning to like the way we look. *New York Times,* p. D7.

Berger, L. (2004, June 6). Hormone therapy: The dust is still settling. *New York Times,* p. 1.

Berger, P. S., Cook, A. S., DelCampo, R. L., Herrera, R. S., & Weigel, R. R. (1994). Family/work roles' relation to perceived stress: Do gender and ethnicity matter? *Journal of Family and Economic Issues, 15,* 223–241.

Bergman, M. E., & Drasgow, F. (2003). Race as a moderator in a model of sexual harassment: An empirical test. *Journal of Occupational Health Psychology, 8(2),* 131–145.

Bergum, V. (1997). *A child on her mind: The experience of becoming a mother.* Westport, CT: Bergin & Garvey.

Berk, L. E. (2003). *Child development.* 6th ed. Boston: Allyn & Bacon.

Berk, L. E., Wholeben, B. M., & Bouchey, H. A. (1998). *Instructors resource manual for Berk, L. E. (1998). Development through the lifespan.* Boston: Allyn & Bacon.

Bernal, G., et al. (Eds.). (2002). *Handbook of racial and ethnic minority psychology.* Thousand Oaks, CA: Sage.

Bernard, M., & Phillipson, C. (2004). Retirement and leisure. In J. F. Nussbaum & J. Coupland (Eds.), *Handbook of communication and aging research,* 2d ed. (pp. 353–382). Mahwah, NJ: Erlbaum.

Bernhard, L. A., & Birch, R. W. (2000). Sexuality. In M. A. Smith & L. A. Shimp (Eds.), *20 common problems in women's health care* (pp. 135–160). New York: McGraw-Hill.

Bernstein, N. (2002, August 14). Child-only cases grow on welfare. *New York Times,* pp. A1, A21.

Bernstein, N. (2004, March 7). In a culture of sex, more teenagers are striving for restraint. *New York Times,* pp. A1, A22, A23.

Bertakis, K.D., Franks, P., & Azari, R. (2003). Effects of physician gender on patient satisfaction. *Journal of the American Medical Women's Association, 58,* 69–75.

Best, D. L. (2001). Cross-cultural gender roles. In J. Worell (Ed.), *Encyclopedia of women and gender* (pp. 279–290). San Diego: Academic Press.

Best, D. L., & Thomas, J. J. (2004). Cultural diversity and cross-cultural perspectives. In A. H. Eagly, A. E. Beall, & R. J. Sternberg (Eds.), *The psychology of gender* (pp. 296–327). New York: Guilford.

Best, D. L., & Williams, J. E. (1993). A cross-cultural viewpoint. In A. E. Beall & R. J. Sternberg (Eds.), *The psychology of gender* (pp. 215–248). New York: Guilford.

Bethell, T. N. (2005, July–August). The gender gyp. *AARP the Magazine,* p. 11.

Betts, K. (2002, March 21). The tyranny of skinny, fashion's insider secret. *New York Times,* p. ST18.

Betz, N. E. (1994). Basic issues and concepts in career counseling for women. In W. B. Walsh & S. H. Osipow (Eds.), *Career counseling for women* (pp. 1–41). Hillsdale, NJ: Erlbaum.

Betz, N. E., & Hackett, G. (1997). Applications of self-efficacy theory to the career assessment of women. *Journal of Cancer Assessment, 5,* 383–402.

Beumont, P. (2005, January 9). Alexander the turkey? *Observer (London),* p. 22.

Beyer, S. (1997, June). *Gender differences in causal attributions of imagined performance on English, history, and math exams.* Paper presented at the meeting of the American Psychological Society, Washington, DC.

Beyer, S. (1999). Gender differences in the accuracy of grade expectancies and evaluations. *Sex Roles, 41,* 279–296.

Beyer, S., Riesselmann, M., & Warren, T. (2002, June). *Gender differences in the accuracy of self-evaluations on chemistry, English, and art questions.* Poster presented at the meeting of the American Psychological Society, New Orleans.

Beyer, S., Rynes, K., Chavez, M., Hay, K., & Perrault, J. (2002, June). *Why are there so few women in computer science?* Poster presented at the meeting of the American Psychological Society, New Orleans.

Beyer, S., Rynes, K., & Haller, S. (2004). Deterrents to women taking Computer Science courses. *IEEE Society and Technology, 23,* 21–28.

Bianchi, S. M. (2000). Maternal employment and time with children: Dramatic change or surprising continuity? *Demography, 47,* 401–414.

Biason-Lauber, A., Konrad, D., Navratil, F., & Schoenle, E. J. (2004). A WNT4 mutation associated with Müllerian-duct regression and virilization in a 46, xx woman. *New England Journal of Medicine, 351*, 792–798.

Bierman, K. L., et al. (2004). Early disruptive behaviors associated with emerging antisocial behavior among girls. In M. Putallaz & K. L. Bierman (Eds.), *Aggression, antisocial behavior, and violence among girls: A developmental perspective* (pp. 137–161). New York: Guilford.

Billings, A. C., Halone, K. K., & Denham, B. E. (2002). "Man, that was a pretty shot": An analysis of gendered broadcast commentary surrounding the 2000 men's and women's NCAA Final Four basketball championships. *Mass Communication & Society, 5*, 295–315.

Bingham, C. R., Miller, B. C., & Adams, G. R. (1990). Correlates of age at first sexual intercourse in a national sample of young women. *Journal of Adolescent Research, 5*, 18–33.

Binion, V. J. (1990). Psychological androgyny: A black female perspective. *Sex Roles, 22*, 487–507.

Birchler, G., & Fals-Stewart, W. (1998). Marriage and divorce. In M. Hersen & V. B. Van Hasselt (Eds.), *Handbook of clinical geropsychology* (pp. 449–467). New York: Plenum.

Bird, C. E., & Rogers, M. L. (1998, November). *Does the presence of children in a household lead to increased depression?: An examination of the effects of children on men's and women's depression levels*. Paper presented at the Conference on Work and Family: Today's Realities and Tomorrow's Visions, Boston.

Birenbaum, M., & Kraemer, R. (1995). Gender and ethnic-group differences in causal attributions for success and failure in mathematics and language examinations. *Journal of Cross-Cultural Psychology, 26*, 342–359.

Biro, F. M., et al. (2003). Pubertal maturation in girls and the relationship to anthropometric changes: Pathways through puberty. *Journal of Pediatrics, 142*, 643–646.

Birth control: More & safer choices. (2005, February). *Consumer Reports*, pp. 36–38.

Bisagni, G. M., & Eckenrode, J. (1995). The role of work identity in women's adjustment to divorce. *American Journal of Orthopsychiatry, 65*, 574–583.

Bittman, M., & Wajcman, J. (2000, September). The rush hour: The character of leisure time and gender equity. *Social Forces, 79*, 165–189.

Bittner, V., & Sanderson, B. K. (2003). Women in cardiac rehabilitation. *Journal of the American Medical Women's Association, 58*, 227–235.

Bjorklund, D. F., & Brown, R. D. (1998). Physical play and cognitive development: Integrating activity, cognition, and education. *Child Development, 69*, 604–606.

Black, K. A. (2000). Gender differences in adolescents' behavior during conflict resolution tasks with best friends. *Adolescence, 35*, 499–512.

Black, M. M., et al. (2002). Behavior and development of preschool children born to adolescent mothers: Risk and 3-generation households. *Pediatrics, 109*, 573–580.

Blair, S. N., & Church, T. S. (2004). The fitness, obesity, and health equation. Is physical activity the common denominator? *Journal of the American Medical Association, 292*, 1232–1234.

Blake, S. M., et al. (2003). Condom availability programs in Massachusetts high schools: Relationships with condom use and sexual behavior. *American Journal of Public Health, 93*, 955–962.

Blakemore, J. E. O. (2001, April). *Children's violations of gender norms: Which ones matter?* Paper presented at the meeting of the Society for Research in Child Development, Minneapolis, MN.

Blakemore, J. E. O. (2003). Children's beliefs about violating gender norms: Boys shouldn't look like girls, and girls shouldn't act like boys. *Sex Roles, 48*, 411–419.

Bleeker, M. M. (2003, April). *Children's attraction to math and science: The importance of parents' gender stereotypes and activities*. Paper presented at the meeting of the Society for Research in Child Development, Tampa, FL.

Blehar, M. C., & Norquist, G. (2002). Mental health policy and women. In S. G. Kornstein & A. H. Clayton (Eds.), *Women's mental health. A comprehensive textbook* (pp. 613–627). New York: Guilford Press.

Blieszner, R., Vista, P. M., & Mancine, J. A. (1996). Diversity and dynamics in late-life mother-daughter relationships. *Journal of Women and Aging, 8(3/4)*, 5–24.

Bly, R. (1990). *Iron John*. Reading, MA: Addison-Wesley.

Blyth, M. (2004). *Spin sisters: How the women of the media sell unhappiness and liberalism to the women of America*. New York: St. Martins Press.

Boduroglu, A., et al. (2002, August). *Stereotypes about young and old adults: A cross-cultural comparison*. Paper presented at the meeting of the American Psychological Association, Chicago.

Bogg, T., & Roberts, B. W. (2004). Conscientiousness and health-related behaviors: A meta-analysis of the leading behavioral contributors to mortality. *Psychological Bulletin, 130*, 887–919.

Bohan, J. S. (1996). *Psychology and sexual orientation.* New York: Routledge.

Bohan, J. S. (2002). Sex differences and/in the self: Classic themes, feminist variations, postmodern challenges. *Psychology of Women Quarterly, 26*, 74–88.

Boisnier, A. D. (2003). Race and women's identity development: Distinguishing between feminism and womanism among black and white women. *Sex Roles, 49*, 211–218.

Bolch, M. B., & Murdock, T. B. (2003, August). *The relationship between the school environment and the emotional adjustment of LGB youth.* Paper presented at the meeting of the American Psychology Association, Toronto.

Boles, S. M., & Miotto, K. (2003). Substance abuse and violence. A review of the literature. *Aggression and Violent Behavior, 8*, 155–174.

Bond, J. T., Thompson, C., Galinsky, E., & Protas, D. (2003). *The 2002 national study of the changing workforce.* New York: Families and Work Institute.

Bond, M. A., et al. (2004). Gendered work conditions, health, and work outcomes. *Journal of Occupational Health Psychology, 9*, 28–45.

Bondurant, B., & Donat, P. L. N. (1999). Perceptions of women's sexual interest and acquaintance rape. *Psychology of Women Quarterly, 23*, 691–705.

Bongaarts, J., & Zimmer, Z. (2002). Living arrangements of older adults in the developing world. An analysis of demographic and health survey household surveys. *The Journals of Gerontology Services B: Psychological Sciences and Social Sciences, 57*, S145–S157.

Bongers, I. L., Koot, H. M., van der Ende, J., & Verhulst, F. C. (2004). Developmental trajectories of externalizing behaviors in childhood and adolescence. *Child Development, 75*, 1523–1537.

Bonner, R. (2003, June 23). A challenge in India snarls foreign adoptions. *New York Times*, p. A3.

Bontempo, D. E. (2001, August). *Family relationships and victimization of lesbian, gay, and bisexual adolescents.* Paper presented at the meeting of the American Psychological Association. San Francisco.

Book, A. S., Starzyk, K. B., & Quinsey, V. L. (2001). The relationship between testosterone and aggression: A meta-analysis. *Aggression and Violent Behavior, 6*, 579–599.

Boonstra, H. (2002, February). Teen pregnancy: Trends and lessons learned. *The Guttmacher Report on Public Policy, 5*, 7–10.

Boonstra, H. (2004, March). Comprehensive approach needed to combat sexually transmitted infections among youth. *The Guttmacher Report on Public Policy, 3–4*, 13.

Booth, A., & Crouter, A. C. (2002). *Just living together: Implications of cohabitation for children, families, and social policy.* Mahwah, NJ: Erlbaum.

Bordo, S. (2003, December 19). The empire of images in our world of bodies. *Chronicle of Higher Education*, pp. 86–89.

Bordo, S. (2004). *Unbearable weight: Feminism, Western culture, and the body.* Berkeley: University of California Press.

Borgmann, C., & Weiss, C. (2003, January/February). Beyond apocalypse and apology: A moral defense of abortion. *Perspectives on Sexual and Reproductive Health, 35*, 40–43.

Bornstein, R. F., & Masling, J. M. (2002). *The psychodynamics of gender and gender role.* Washington, DC: American Psychological Association.

Bosacki, S. L., & Moore, C. (2004). Preschoolers' understanding of simple and complex emotions: Links with gender and language. *Sex Roles, 50*, 659–675.

Boston Women's Health Book Collective. (1992). *The new our bodies, ourselves: A book by and for women.* New York: Touchstone.

Boston Women's Health Book Collective. (1998). *Our bodies, ourselves for the new century: A book by and for women.* New York: Touchstone.

Bosworth, B., Burtless, G., & Sahm, C. (2001, August). *The trend in lifetime earnings inequality and its impact on the distribution of retirement income.* Chestnut Hill, MA: Center for Retirement Research at Boston College.

Botta, R. A. (2003). For your health? The relationship between magazine reading and adolescents' body image and eating disturbances. *Sex Roles, 48*, 389–399.

Bouchard, Jr., T. J. (2004). Genetic influence on human psychological traits. A survey. *Current Direction in Psychological Science, 13*, 148–151.

Bould, S., & Longino, C. F. (2001). Women survivors: The oldest old. In J. M. Coyle (Ed.), *Handbook on women and aging* (pp. 210–222). Westport, CT: Greenwood.

Bound, J., Schoenbaum, M., & Waidmann, T. (1996). Race differences in labor force attachment and disability status. *Gerontologist, 36,* 311–321.

Bourgeois, M. J., & Perkins, J. (2003). A test of evolutionary and sociocultural explanations of reactions to sexual harassment. *Sex Roles, 49,* 343–351.

Bowleg, L., Craig, M. L., & Burkholder, G. (2004). Rising and surviving: A conceptual model of active coping among black lesbians. *Cultural Diversity and Ethnic Minority Psychology, 10,* 229–240.

Bowleg, L., Lucas, K. J., & Tschann, J. M. (2004). "The ball was always in his court": An exploratory analysis of relationship scripts, sexual scripts, and condom use among African American women. *Psychology of Women Quarterly, 28,* 70–82.

Boynton, P. (2003). Abiding by the rules: Instructing women in relationships. *Feminism & Psychology, 13,* 237–245.

Boxer, S. (1997, December 14). One casualty of the women's movement: Feminism. *New York Times,* p. WK3.

Brabant, S., & Mooney, L. A. (1997). Sex role stereotyping in the Sunday comics: A twenty year update. *Sex Roles, 37,* 269–281.

Bradford, J., & White, J. C. (2000). Lesbian health research. In M. B. Goldman & M. C. Hatch (Eds.), *Women & health* (pp. 64–78). New York: Academic Press.

Bradley, C. J., Given, C. W., & Roberts, C. (2002). Race, socioeconomic status, and breast cancer treatment and survival. *Journal of the National Cancer Institute, 94,* 490–496.

Bradshaw, Z., & Slade, P. (2003). The effects of induced abortion on emotional experiences and relationships: A critical review of the literature. *Clinical Psychology Review, 23,* 929–958.

Bradsher, J. E. (2001). Older women and widowhood. In J. M. Coyle (Ed.), *Handbook on women and aging* (pp. 112–128). Westport, CT: Greenwood.

Bragger, J. D., Kutcher, E., Morgan, J., & Firth, P. (2002). The effects of the structured interview on reducing biases against pregnant job applicants. *Sex Roles, 46,* 215–226.

Brauner, J., Gordic, B., & Zigler, E. (2004). *Putting the child back into child care: Combining care and education for children ages 3–5.* SRCD Social Policy Report, 18(3).

Breast cancer: The year in review. (2003, 4th quarter). *Frontline: The Susan G. Komen Breast Cancer Foundation Newsletter,* p. 4.

Breedlove, G., & Busenhart, C. (2005). Screening and detection of ovarian cancer. *Journal of Midwifery & Women's Health, 50,* 51–54.

Breitkopf, C. R., & Berenson, A. B. (2004). Correlates of weight loss behaviors among low-income African-American, Caucasian, and Latina women. *Obstetrics & Gynecology, 103,* 231–239.

Brendgen, M., et al. (2005). Examining genetic and environmental effects on social aggression: A study of 6-year-old twins. *Child Development, 76,* 930–946.

Brescoll, V., & LaFrance, M. (2004). The correlates and consequences of newspaper reports of research on sex differences. *Psychological Science, 15,* 515–520.

Breslow, L., & Breslow, N. (1993). Health practices and disability: Some evidence from Alameda County. *Preventative Medicine, 22,* 86–95.

Brewster, K. L., & Padavic, I. (2002). Change in gender ideology, 1977–1996: The contributions of intracohort change and population turnover. *Journal of Marriage and the Family, 62,* 477–487.

Bridges, J. S. (1989). Sex differences in occupational values. *Sex Roles, 20,* 205–211.

Bridges, J. S. (1991). Perceptions of date and stranger rape: A difference in sex role expectations and rape-supportive beliefs. *Sex Roles, 24,* 291–307.

Bridges, J. S. (1993). Pink or blue: Gender-stereotypic perceptions of infants as conveyed by birth congratulations cards. *Psychology of Women Quarterly, 17,* 193–205.

Bridges, J. S., & Etaugh, C. (1995). College students' perceptions of mothers: Effects of maternal employment-childrearing pattern and motive for employment. *Sex Roles, 32,* 735–751.

Bridges, J. S., & Etaugh, C. (1996). Black and white college women's maternal employment outcome expectations and their desired timing of maternal employment. *Sex Roles, 35,* 543–562.

Bridges, J. S., & Orza, A. M. (1993). Effects of maternal employment-childrearing pattern on college students' perceptions of a mother and her child. *Psychology of Women Quarterly, 17,* 103–117.

Bridges, J. S., & Orza, A. M. (1996). Black and white employed mothers' role experiences. *Sex Roles, 35,* 377–385.

Bridges, M. (2003/2004, Winter). Poverty up, women still down. *Ms.,* p. 16.

Bridges, M. et al. (2003/2004, Winter). 50 women who made a difference. *Ms.,* pp. 53–66.

Bridges, S. K., Lease, S. H., & Ellison, C. R. (2000, August). *Predicting women's sexual satisfaction: Implications for the new millennium.* Paper presented at the meeting of the American Psychological Association, Washington, DC.

Brill, M. (2004). Antidepressants and sexual dysfunction. *Sexuality, Reproduction & Menopause 2,* 35–40.

Broderick, P. C., & Korteland, C. (2002). Coping style and depression in early adolescence: Relationships to gender, gender role, and implicit beliefs. *Sex Roles, 46,* 201–213.

Brody, E. M. (2004). *Women in the middle, their parent-care years.* 2d ed. New York: Springer.

Brody, G. H. (2004). Siblings' direct and indirect contributions to child development. *Current Directions in Psychological Science, 13,* 124–126.

Brody, J. E. (1998, January 22). Study challenges idea of PMS as emotional disorder. *New York Times,* pp. A1, A18.

Brody, J. E. (1999a, October 12). Coping with fear: Keeping breast cancer in perspective. *New York Times,* p. D7.

Brody, J. E. (1999b, November 30). Yesterday's precocious puberty is norm today. *New York Times,* p. D8.

Brody, J. E. (2001). Nutrition a key to better health for elderly. *New York Times,* p. D8.

Brody, J. E. (2002, November 19). Adding some heft to the ideal female form. *New York Times,* p. D7.

Brody, J. E. (2003a, January 7). Drink your milk: A refrain for all ages, now more than ever. *New York Times,* p. D5.

Brody, J. E. (2003b, April 22). Options for protecting bones after menopause. *New York Times,* p. D6.

Brody, J. E. (2004a, June 1). Abstinence-only: Does it work? *New York Times,* p. D7.

Brody, J. E. (2004b, May 11). The risks and demands of pregnancy after 20. *New York Times,* p. D8.

Brody, J. E. (2005, April 12). Women struggle for parity of the heart. *New York Times,* p. D7.

Brody, L. R., & Hall, J. A. (2000). Gender, emotion, and expression. In M. Lewis & J. Haviland-Jones (Eds.), *Handbook of emotions,* 2d ed. (pp. 338–349). New York: Guilford.

Brogan, D. J., O'Hanlan, K. A., Elon, L., & Frank, E. (2003, Winter). The hormone therapy dilemma: Women respond. *Journal of the American Medical Women's Association, 58,* 10–19.

Bronner, E. (1998, February 25). U.S. 12th graders rank poorly in math and science, study says. *New York Times,* pp. A1, C20.

Brooks, M. G., & Buckner, J. C. (1996). Work and welfare: Job histories, barriers to employment, and predictors of work among low-income single mothers. *American Journal of Orthopsychiatry, 66,* 526–537.

Brotman, S., Ryan, B., & Cormier, R. (2003). The health and social service needs of gay and lesbian elders and their families in Canada. *The Gerontologist, 43,* 192–202.

Broverman, I. K., Broverman, D. M., Clarkson, F. E., Rosenkrantz, P. S., & Vogel, S. R. (1970). Sex-role stereotypes and clinical judgements of mental health. *Journal of Consulting Psychology, 34,* 1–7.

Brown, B. B. (2004). Adolescents' relationships with peers. In R. M. Lerner & L. Steinberg (Eds.), *Handbook of adolescent psychology,* 2d ed. (pp. 363–394). Hoboken, NJ: Wiley.

Brown, E. R., et al. (1995, October). *Women's health-related behaviors and use of clinical preventive services: A report to the Commonwealth Fund.* Los Angeles: UCLA Center for Health Policy Research.

Brown, L. M., Way, N., & Duff, J. L. (1999). The others in my I: Adolescent girls' friendships and peer relations. In N. G. Johnson, M. C. Roberts, & J. Worell (Eds.), *Beyond appearance: A new look at adolescent girls* (pp. 205–225). Washington, DC: American Psychological Association.

Brown, S. L., et al. (2003). Providing social support may be more beneficial than receiving it: Results from a prospective study of mortality. *Psychological Science, 14,* 320–327.

Brown, S. L., & Booth, A. (1996). Cohabitation versus marriage: A comparison of relationship quality. *Journal of Marriage and the Family, 58,* 668–678.

Brown, W. M., Finn, C. J., Cooke, B. M., & Breedlove, S. M. (2002). Differences in finger length between self-identified "butch" and "femme" lesbians. *Archives of Sexual Behavior, 31,* 123–128.

Browne, B. A. (1998). Gender stereotypes in advertising on children's television in the 1990s: A cross-national analysis. *Journal of Advertising, 27,* 83–96.

Brownlow, S., Rosamond, J. A., & Parker, J. A. (2003). Gender-linked linguistic behavior in television interviews. *Sex Roles, 49,* 121–132.

Brukner, H. (2003). Understanding cardiovascular health in women: It's a two-way street. *Journal of the American Medical Women's Association, 58,* 203–205.

Brumberg, J. J. (1997). *The body project: An intimate history of American girls.* New York: Random House.

Bryant, A. N. (2003). Changes in attitudes toward women's roles: Predicting gender-role traditionalism among college students. *Sex Roles, 48,* 131–142.

Bryant, A. S., & Demian. (1994). Relationship characteristics of American gay and lesbian couples: Findings from a national survey. *Journal of Gay and Lesbian Social Services, 1,* 101–117.

Bryant, J., & Zillman, D. (2002). *Media effects: Advances in theory and research.* Mahwah, NJ: Erlbaum.

Bryant-Davis, T. (2003). Sexual abuse and rape: Thriving after sexual assault. In L. Slater, J. H. Daniel & A. E. Banks (Eds.), *The complete guide to mental health for women* (pp. 154–163). Boston: Beacon Press.

Budd, K. (2002, May/June). Eggbeaters. *AARP*, p. 15.

Buddie, A. M., & Miller, A. G. (2001). Beyond rape myths: A more complex view of perceptions of rape victims. *Sex Roles, 45*, 139–159.

Budig, M. J., & England, P. (2001). The wage penalty for motherhood. *American Sociological Review, 66*, 204–225.

Bukatko, D., & Shedd, J. (1999, April). *Children's evaluations of gender-stereotyped traits, activities and occupations.* Poster presented at the meeting of the Society for Research in Child Development, Albuquerque, NM.

Buki, L. P., Borrayo, E. A., Feigal, B. M., & Carrillo, I. Y. (2004, December). Are all Latinas the same? Perceived breast cancer screening barriers and facilitative conditions. *Psychology of Women Quarterly, 28*, 400–411.

Bullock, H. E., & Fernald, J. L. (2003). "Feminism?" Feminist identification, speaker appearance, and perceptions of feminist and antifeminist messengers. *Psychology of Women Quarterly, 27*, 291–299.

Bullock, H. E., Wyche, K. F., & Williams, W. R. (2001). Media images of the poor. *Journal of Social Issues, 57*, 229–246.

Bumpass, M. F., Crouter, A. C., & McHale, S. M. (2001). Parental autonomy granting during adolescence: Exploring gender differences in context. *Developmental Psychology, 37*, 163–173.

Bureau of Labor Statistics. (2004). *American time-use survey.* Washington, DC: Author.

Burgess, E. O. (2004). Sexuality in midlife and later life couples. In J. H. Harvey, A. Wenzel, & S. Sprecher (Eds.), *The handbook of sexuality in close relationships* (pp. 437–454). Mahwah, NJ: Erlbaum.

Burke, R. J. (2004). Work and personal life integration. *International Journal of Stress Management, 11*, 299–304.

Burkett, E. (2000). *The baby boon: How family-friendly America cheats the childless.* New York: Free Press.

Burn, S. M. (2000). *Women across cultures: A global perspective.* Mountain View, CA: Mayfield.

Burn, S. M., Aboud, R., & Moyles, C. (2000). The relationship between gender, social identity and support for feminism. *Sex Roles, 42*, 1081–1089.

Burney, T. (2004, June 6). Giving treatment, but not stirring shame. *New York Times*, p. WH6.

Burns, A. (2004). Treating depression in later life. *British Medical Journal, 329*, 181–182.

Burris, B. H. (1991). Employed mothers: The impact of class and marital status on the prioritizing of family and work. *Social Science Quarterly, 72*, 50–66.

Bursik, K. (1992). Perceptions of sexual harassment in an academic context. *Sex Roles, 27*, 401–412.

Burt, K. B., & Scott, J. (2002). Parent and adolescent gender role attitudes in 1990's Great Britain. *Sex Roles, 46*, 239–245.

Buss, D. (2005). Sure, come back to the nest. Here are the rules. *New York Times*, p. BU8.

Buss, D. M. (1994). *The evolution of desire: Strategies of human mating.* New York: Basic Books.

Bussey, K., & Bandura, A. (2004). Social cognitive theory of gender development and functioning. In A. H. Eagly, A. E. Beall, & R. J. Sternberg (Eds.), *The psychology of gender,* 2d ed. (pp. 92–119). New York: Guilford.

Butler, L. D., & Nolen-Hoeksema, S. (1994). Gender differences in responses to depressed mood in a college sample. *Sex Roles, 30*, 331–346.

Butler, R., & Lewis, M. I. (2002). *The new love and sex after 60.* New York: Ballantine.

Butler, S. S. (2004). Gay, lesbian, bisexual, and transgender (GLBT) elders: The challenges and resilience of this marginalized group! *Journal of Human Behavior and the Social Environment, 9*, 25–44.

Butrica, B., & Uccello, C. (2004). *How will boomers fare at retirement?* Washington, DC: AARP.

Button, S. B. (2001). Organizational efforts to affirm sexual diversity: A cross-level examination. *Journal of Applied Psychology, 86*, 17–28.

Buysse, J. M., & Embser-Herbert, M. S. (2004). Constructions of gender in sport: An analysis of intercollegiate media guide cover photographs. *Gender & Society, 18*, 66–81.

Bylsma, W. H., & Major, B. (1994). Social comparisons and contentment: Exploring the psychological costs of the gender wage gap. *Psychology of Women Quarterly, 18*, 241–249.

Cadinu, M., Maass, A., Rosabianca, A., & Klesner, J. (2005). Why do women underperform under stereotype threat? Evidence for the role of negative thinking. *Psychological Science, 16*, 572–578.

Cahill, L. (2005, May). His brain, her brain. *Scientific American, 292*, pp. 40–47.

Cahill, S. P., & Foa, E. B. (2001). Anxiety. In R. K. Unger (Ed.), *Handbook of the psychology of women and gender* (pp. 149–156). New York: Wiley.

Caiazza, A., Shaw, A., & Werschkul, M. (2004). *The status of women in the states: Wide disparities by race, ethnicity, and region*. Washington, DC: Institute for Women's Policy Research.

Cairoli, M. Z. (2001). Factory as home and family: Female workers in the Moroccan garment industry. In C. B. Brettell & C. F. Sargent (Eds.), *Gender in cross-cultural perspective*, 3d ed. (pp. 551–564). Upper Saddle River, NJ: Prentice Hall.

Caldera, Y. M., et al. (1999). Children's play preferences, construction play with blocks, and visual-spatial skills: Are they related? *International Journal of Behavioral Development, 23*, 855–872.

Callan, J. E. (2001). Gender development: Psychoanalytic perspectives. In J. Worell (Ed.), *Encyclopedia of women and gender* (pp. 523–536). San Diego: Academic Press.

Calogero, R. M., Davis, W. N., & Thompson, J. K. (2005). The role of self-objectification in the experience of women with eating disorders. *Sex Roles, 52*, 43–50.

Calvert, S. L. (1999). *Children's journeys through the information age*. Boston: McGraw-Hill.

Calvert, S. L., Kondla, T. A., Ertel, K. A., & Meisel, D. S. (2001). Young adults' perceptions and memories of a television woman hero. *Sex Roles, 45*, 31–52.

Campbell, A., Shirley, L., & Candy, J. (2004). A longitudinal study of gender-related cognition and behaviour. *Developmental Science, 7*, 1–9.

Campbell, A., Shirley, L., & Caygill, L. (2002). Sex-typed preferences in three domains: Do two-year-olds need cognitive variables? *British Journal of Psychology, 93*, 203–217.

Campbell, A., Shirley, L., Heywood, C., & Crook, C. (2000). Infants' visual preference for sex-congruent babies, children, toys, and activities: A longitudinal study. *British Journal of Developmental Psychology, 18*, 479–498.

Campbell, L., & Stevenson, C. M. (2002, June). *Preschoolers' use of sex-typed toys and their perceptions of parental expectations*. Poster presented at the meeting of the American Psychological Society, New Orleans.

Campbell, R., Sefl, T., & Ahrens, C. E. (2003). The physical health consequences of rape: Assessing survivors' somatic symptoms in a racially diverse population. *Women's Studies Quarterly, 31*, pp. 90–104.

Campbell, R., Sefl, T., & Ahrens, C. E. (2004). The impact of rape on women's sexual health risk behaviors. *Health Psychology, 23*, 67–74.

Campbell, V. A., et al. (1999). Surveillance for sensory impairment, activity, limitation, and health-related quality of life among older adults—United States, 1993–1997. *Morbidity and Mortality Weekly Report, 48*, (SS08), 131–156.

Campo-Flores, A. (2002, July 1). "Macho" or "sweetness"? *Newsweek*, p. 51.

Canabal, M. E. (1995). Native Americans in higher education. *College Student Journal, 29*, 455–457.

Canetto, S. S. (2001). Older adult women: Issues, resources, and challenges. In R. K. Unger (Ed.), *Handbook of the psychology of women and gender* (pp. 183–197). New York: Wiley.

Canetto, S. S. (2003). Older adulthood. In L. Slater, J. H. Daniel, & A. E. Banks (Eds.), *The complete guide to mental health for women* (pp. 56–64). Boston: Beacon Press.

Canetto, S. S., & Lester, D. (1995). Gender and the primary prevention of suicide mortality. *Suicide and Life-Threatening Behavior, 25(1)*, 58–69.

Cann, A., & Vann, E. D. (1995). Implications of sex and gender differences for self: Perceived advantages and disadvantages of being the other gender. *Sex Roles, 33*, 531–541.

Cano, A. & Vivian, D. (2003). Are life stressors associated with marital violence? *Journal of Family Psychology, 17(3)*, 302–314.

Canterbury, R. J. (2002). Alcohol and other substance abuse. In S. G. Kornstein & A. H. Clayton (Eds.), *Women's mental health: A comprehensive textbook* (pp. 222–243). New York: Guilford.

Canto, J. G., & Iskandrian, A. E., (2003). Major risk factors for cardiovascular disease. Debunking the "only 50%" myth. *Journal of the American Medical Association, 290*, 947–949.

Capaldi, D. M., Kim, H. K., & Shortt, J. W. (2004). Women's involvement in aggression in young adult romantic relationships: A developmental systems model. In M. Putallaz & K. L. Bierman (Eds.), *Aggression, antisocial behavior, and violence among girls: A developmental perspective* (pp. 223–241). New York: Guilford.

Caplan, P. J. (2001). Motherhood: Its changing face. In J. Worell (Ed.), *Encyclopedia of women and gender*, (pp. 783–794). San Diego: Academic Press.

Caplan, P. J., & Caplan, J. B. (1999). *Thinking critically about research on sex and gender*. 2d ed. New York: HarperCollins.

Caprara, G. V., Barbaranelli, C., & Pastorelli, C. (2001). Prosocial behavior and aggression in childhood and pre-adolescence. In A. C. Bohart & D. J. Stipek (Eds.), *Constructive and destructive behavior: Implications for family, school, and society* (pp. 187–203). Washington, DC: American Psychological Association.

Carli, L. L. (2001). Gender and social influence. *Journal of Social Issues, 57,* 725–741.

Carli, L. L., & Bukatko, D. (2000). Gender, communication, and social-influence: A development perspective. In T. Eckes & H. M. Trautner (Eds.), *The developmental social psychology of gender* (pp. 295–332). Mahwah, NJ: Erlbaum.

Carli, L. L., & Eagly, A. H. (2001). Gender, hierarchy, and leadership: An introduction. *Journal of Social Issues, 57,* 629–636.

Carlisle, W. (1994). Sharing home responsibilities: Women in dual-career marriages. In C. W. Konek & S. L. Kitch (Eds.), *Women and careers: Issues and challenges* (pp. 140–152). Thousand Oaks, CA: Sage.

Carmichael, M. (2004, January 26). No girls, please. *Newsweek,* p. 50.

Carmichael, M. (2004, May 10). Have it your way: Redesigning birth. *Newsweek,* pp. 70, 72.

Caron, S. L., & Ulin, M. (1997). Closeting and the quality of lesbian relationships. *The Journal of Contemporary Human Services, 78,* 413–419.

Carp, F. M. (2001a). Living arrangements for midlife and older women. In J. M. Coyle (Ed.), *Handbook on women and aging* (pp. 253–270). Westport, CT: Greenwood.

Carp, F. M. (2001b). Retirement and women. In J. M. Coyle (Ed.), *Handbook on women and aging* (pp. 112–128). Westport, CT: Greenwood.

Carpenter, C. M., Wayne, G. F., & Connolly, G. N. (2005). Designing cigarettes for women: New findings from the tobacco industry documents. *Addiction, 100,* 837–851.

Carpenter, S. (2000, October). Strengthening the voices of women psychologists. *Monitor on Psychology,* p. 57.

Carr, D. (1997). The fulfillment of career dreams at midlife: Does it matter for women's mental health? *Journal of Health and Social Behavior, 38,* 331–344.

Carr, D. (2004a). Gender, preloss marital dependence, and older adults' adjustment to widowhood. *Journal of Marriage and Family, 66,* 220–235.

Carr, D. (2004b). Psychological well-being across three cohorts: A response to shifting work-family opportunities and expectations? In O. G. Brim, C. D. Ryff, & R. C. Kessler (Eds.), *How healthy are we? A national study of well-being at midlife* (pp. 452–484). Chicago: University of Chicago Press.

Carr, J. G., Gilroy, F. D., & Sherman, M. F. (1996). Silencing the self and depression among women. *Psychology of Women Quarterly, 20,* 375–392.

Carrington, C. (2002). *No place like home: Relationships and family life among lesbians and gay men.* Chicago: University of Chicago Press.

Carroll, L. (2003, November 4). Alcohol's toll on fetuses even worse than thought. *New York Times,* pp. D1, D6.

Carter, B., & Elliott, S. (2004, May 26). MTV to start first network aimed at gays. *New York Times,* pp. C1, C8.

Carver, P. R., Egan, S. K., & Perry, D. G. (2004). Children who question their heterosexuality. *Developmental Psychology, 40,* 43–53.

Carver, P. R., Yunger, J. L., & Perry, D. G. (2003). Gender identity and adjustment in middle childhood. *Sex Roles, 49,* 95–109.

Cascio, W. F., & Young, C. E. (2005). Work-family balance: Does the market reward firms that respect it? In D. F. Halpern & S. E. Murphy (Eds.), *From work-family balance to work-family interaction: Changing the metaphor* (pp. 49–63). Mahwah, NJ: Erlbaum.

Case, P., et al. (2004). Sexual orientation, health risk factors, and physical functioning in the Nurses' Health Study II. *Journal of Women's Health, 13,* 1033–1047.

Casey, M. B. (2002). Developmental perspectives on gender. In S. G. Kornstein & A. H. Clayton (Eds.), *Women's mental health: A comprehensive textbook* (pp. 499–514). New York: Guilford.

Cash, T. F., Morrow, J. A., Hrabosky, J. I., & Perry, A. A. (2004). How has body image changed? A cross-sectional investigation of college women and men from 1983 to 2001. *Journal of Consulting and Clinical Psychology, 72,* 1081–1089.

Cash, T. F., & Pruzinsky, T. (Eds.). (2002). *Body image: A handbook of theory, research, and clinical practice.* New York: Guilford.

Cashdan, E. (1998). Smiles, speech, and body posture: How women and men display sociometric status and power. *Journal of Nonverbal Behavior, 22,* 209–228.

Casper, L. M., & King, R. B. (2004). Changing families, shifting economic fortunes, and meeting basic needs. In A. C. Crouter & A. Booth (Eds.), *Work-family challenges for low-income parents and their children* (pp. 55–79). Mahwah, NJ: Erlbaum.

Cassel, C. K. (2002). Use it or lose it: Activity may be the best treatment for aging. *Journal of the American Medical Association, 288,* 2333–2335.

Cassell, J., & Jenkins, H. (Eds.) (1998). *From Barbie to Mortal Kombat: Gender and computer games.* Cambridge, MA: MIT Press.

Castaneda, D. (1996). Gender issues among Latinas. In J. C. Chrisler, C. Golden, & P. D. Rozee (Eds.), *Lectures on the psychology of women* (pp. 167–181). New York: McGraw-Hill.

Castro, I. L. (1997, Spring). Worth more than we earn: Fair pay as a step toward gender equity. *National Forum, 77,* 17–21.

Catsambis, S. (1999). The path to math: Gender and racial-ethnic differences in mathematics participation from middle school to high school. In L. A. Peplau, S. C. DeBro, R. C. Veniegas, & P. L. Taylor (Eds.), *Gender, culture, and ethnicity: Current research about women and men* (pp. 102–120). Mountain View, CA: Mayfield.

Cattaneo, L. B., & Goodman, L. A. (2005). Risk factors for reabuse in intimate partner violence: A cross-disciplinary critical review. *Trauma, Violence, & Abuse, 6,* 141–175.

Cavanaugh, J. C., & Blanchard-Fields, F. (2006). *Adult development and aging.* 5th ed. Belmont, CA: Wadsworth.

Cebello, R., et al. (2004). Domestic violence and women's mental health in Chile. *Psychology of Women Quarterly, 28,* 298–308.

Cedars, M. I. (2004). Polycystic ovary syndrome: What is it and how should we treat it? *Journal of Pediatrics, 144,* 4–6.

Center for American Women and Politics (2005). *Women in elected office 2005.* Retrieved from http://www.cawp.rutgers.edu.

Centers for Disease Control and Prevention. (2000). *All the stages of our lives.* Atlanta: Author.

Centers for Disease Control and Prevention. (2002a). Alcohol use among women of childbearing age—United States, 1994–1999. *Morbidity and Mortality Weekly Report, 51,* 273–276.

Centers for Disease Control and Prevention. (2002b). Annual smoking—attributable mortality, years of potential life lost, and economic costs—United States, 1995–1999. *Morbidity and Mortality Weekly Report, 51,* 300–303.

Centers for Disease Control and Prevention. (2002c). Trends in sexual risk behaviors among high school students—United States 1991–2001. *Morbidity and Mortality Weekly Report, 51,* 856–858.

Centers for Disease Control and Prevention. (2003a). *2001 assisted reproductive technology success rates: National summary and fertility clinic reports.* Atlanta: Author.

Centers for Disease Control and Prevention. (2003b). Nonfatal physical assault-related injuries among persons aged ≥60 years treated in hospital emergency departments—United States, 2001. *Morbidity and Mortality Weekly Report, 52,* 812–816.

Centers for Disease Control and Prevention. (2004). Cigarette smoking among adults—United States, 2002. *Morbidity and Mortality Weekly Report, 53,* 427–430.

Cerhan, J. R., et al. (2004). Adherence to the AICR cancer prevention recommendations and subsequent morbidity and mortality in the Iowa women's health study cohort. *Cancer Epidemiology Biomarkers & Prevention, 13,* 1114–1120.

Cermele, J. A., Daniels, S., & Anderson, K. L. (2001). Defining normal: Constructions of race and gender in the DSM-IV casebook. *Feminism & Psychology, 11,* 229–247.

Cesarean delivery. (2002). *Journal of the American Medical Association, 287,* 2738.

Chang, J. T., et al. (2004). Interventions for the prevention of falls in older adults: Systematic review and meta-analysis of randomised clinical trials. *British Medical Journal, 328,* 680–683.

Chapple, C. L. (2003). Examining intergenerational violence: Violent role modeling or weak parental controls? *Violence and Victims, 18,* 142–162.

Chasteen, A. L. (1998, August). *The role of age and age-related attitudes in perceptions of elderly individuals.* Paper presented at the meeting of the American Psychological Association, San Francisco.

Chaudron, L. H., & Caine, E. D. (2004). Suicide among women: A critical review. *Journal of the American Medical Women's Association, 59,* 125–134.

Chen, E. (2004). Why socioeconomic status affects the health of children. A psychosocial perspective. *Current Directions in Psychological Science, 13,* 112–115.

Cheng, A. T. A., et al. (2004). A 4-year longitudinal study on risk factors for alcoholism. *Archives of General Psychiatry, 61,* 184–191.

Cherlin, A. J. (1998, April 5). By the numbers. *New York Times Magazine,* pp. 39–41.

Cherlin, A. J., & Krishnamurthy, P. (2004, May 9). What works for mom. *New York Times,* p. WK13.

Cherney, I. D., & Ryalls, B. O. (1999). Gender-linked differences in the incidental memory of children and adults. *Journal of Experimental Child Psychology, 72,* 305–328.

Cherry, F., & Deaux, K. (1978). Fear of success versus fear of gender-inappropriate behavior. *Sex Roles, 4,* 97–101.

Chesley, E. B., et al. (2004). Longitudinal impact of weight-related intentions with the initiation and maintenance of smoking among adolescents. *Journal of Adolescent Health, 34,* 130.

Chesley, E. B., Alberts, J. D., Klein, J. D., & Kreipe, R. E. (2003). Pro or con? Anorexia nervosa and the Internet. *Journal of Adolescent Health, 32,* 123–124.

Childress, S. (2003, August 4). 9/11's hidden toll. *Newsweek,* p. 37.

Chipman, S. F., Krantz, D. H., & Silver, R. (1992). Mathematics anxiety and science careers among able college women. *Psychological Science, 3,* 292–295.

Chira, S. (1994, September 20). Teen-age mothers helped by Ohio plan, study finds. *New York Times,* p. A12.

Chiu, C. (1998). Do professional women have lower job satisfaction than professional men? Lawyers as a case study. *Sex Roles, 38,* 521–537.

Chodorow, N. J. (1990). *Feminism and the psychoanalytic theory.* New Haven, CT: Yale University Press.

Choi, N. G. (2000). Determinants of engagement in paid work following Social Security benefit receipt among older women. *Journal of Women & Aging, 12,* 133–154.

Chrisler, J. C., & Ghiz, L. (1993). Body image issues of older women. In N. D. Davis, E. Cole, & E. D. Rothblum (Eds.), *Faces of women and aging* (pp. 67–75). New York: Harrington Park Press.

Chrisler, J. C., & Johnston-Robledo, I. (2000). Motherhood and reproductive issues. In M. Biaggio & M. Hersen (Eds.), *Issues in the psychology of women* (pp. 199–226). New York: Kluwer.

Chrisler, J. C., Johnston, I. K., Champagne, N. M., & Preston K. E. (1994). Menstrual Joy: The construct and its consequences. *Psychology of Women Quarterly, 18,* 347–387.

Christopher, F. S., & Kisler, T. S. (2004). Sexual aggression in romantic relationships. In J. H. Harvey, A. Wenzel, & S. Sprecher (Eds.), *The handbook of sexuality in close relationships* (pp. 287–309). Mahwah, NJ: Erlbaum.

Ciambrone, D. (2003). *Women's experiences with HIV/AIDS. Mending fractured selves.* Binghamton, NY: Haworth Press.

Ciechanowski, P., et al. (2004). Community-integrated home-based depression treatment in older adults. *Journal of the American Medical Association, 291,* 1569–1577.

Cillessen, A. H. N., & Mayeux, L. (2004). From censure to reinforcement: Developmental changes in the association between aggression and social status. *Child Development, 75,* 147–163.

Cinamon, R. G., & Rich, Y. (2002). Gender differences in the importance of work and family roles: Implications for work-family conflict. *Sex Roles, 47,* 531–541.

Clampet-Lundquist, S., et al. (2004). "Making a way out of no way": How mothers meet basic family needs while moving from welfare to work. In A. C. Crouter & A. Booth (Eds.), *Work-family challenges for low-income parents and their children* (pp. 203–241). Mahwah, NJ: Erlbaum.

Clancy, C. M. (2000). Gender issues in women's health care. In M. B. Goldman & M. C. Hatch (Eds.), *Women & health* (pp. 50–64). New York: Academic Press.

Clark, M. A., et al. (2003). The cancer screening project for women: Experiences of women who partner with women and women who partner with men. *Women & Health, 38,* 19–33.

Clark, R. A. (1998). A comparison of topics and objectives in a cross section of young men's and women's everyday conversations. In D. J. Canary & K. Dindia (Eds.), *Sex differences and similarities in communication: Critical essays and empirical investigations of sex and gender in interaction* (pp. 303–319). Mahwah, NJ: Erlbaum.

Clark, R. A., Maupin, R. T., Jr., & Hammer, J. H. (2004). *A woman's guide to living with H.I.V. infection.* Baltimore: John Hopkins University Press.

Clarren, R. (2005, Summer). The green motel. *Ms.,* pp. 40–45.

Clay, R. A. (2003, April). An empty nest can promote freedom, improved relationships. *Monitor on Psychology,* pp. 40–41.

Clayton, A. H. (2002). Sexual dysfunction. In S. G. Kornstein & A. H. Clayton (Eds.), *Women's mental health: A comprehensive textbook* (pp. 263–273). New York: Guilford.

Cleary-Goldman, J. et al. (2005). Impact of maternal age on obstetric outcome. *Obstetrics & Gynecology, 105,* 983–990.

Clemetson, L. (2002, October 7). A neighborhood clinic helps fill the gap for Latinos without health care. *New York Times,* p. A12.

Cleveland, J. N., Stockdale, M., & Murphy, K. R. (2000). *Women and men in organizations: Sex and gender issues at work.* Mahwah, NJ: Erlbaum.

Cleveland, J. N., Vescio, T. K., & Barnes-Farrell, J. L. (2005). Gender discrimination in organizations. In R. L. Dipboye & A. Colella (Eds.), *Discrimination at work: The psychological and organizational bases* (pp. 149–176). Mahwah, NJ: Erlbaum.

Clewell, B. C., & Campbell, P. B. (2002). Taking stock: Where we've been, where we are, where we're going. *Journal of Women and Minorities in Science and Engineering, 8,* 255–284.

Cochran, C. C., Frazier, P. A., & Olson, A. M. (1997). Predictors of responses to unwanted sexual attention. *Psychology of Women Quarterly, 21,* 207–226.

Cochran, S. D. (2001). Emerging issues in research on lesbians' and gay men's mental health: Does sexual orientation really matter? *American Psychologist, 56,* 931–947.

Cockburn, A. (2003, September). 21st century slaves. *National Geographic,* pp. 2–25.

Cohen, D. L., & Petrie, T. A. (2005). An examination of psychosocial correlates of disordered eating among undergraduate women. *Sex Roles, 52,* 29–42.

Cohen, J. (2003, September 19). A home of their own. *New York Times,* pp. D1, D6.

Cohen, J. (2004). HIV/AIDS: India's many epidemics. *Science, 304,* p. 504.

Cohen, J. A., & Mannarino, A. P. (1998). Factors that mediate treatment outcome of sexually abused preschool children: Six- and 12-month follow-up. *Journal of the American Academy of Child & Adolescent Psychiatry, 37,* 44–51.

Cohen, P., et al. (2003). Variations in patterns of developmental transitions in the emerging adulthood period. *Developmental Psychology, 39,* 657–669.

Cohen, P. N., & Huffman, M. L. (2003). Occupational segregation and the devaluation of women's work across U.S. labor markets. *Social Forces, 81,* 881–908.

Cohen, R. (2004, November 28). In South Africa, denial is a form of protection. *New York Times,* p. WK3.

Cohen, S. A. (2005, February). Ominous convergence: Sex trafficking, prostitution and international family planning. *The Guttmacher Report on Public Policy,* pp. 12–14.

Cohler, B. J., & Nakamura, J. E. (1996). Self and experience across the second half of life. In J. Sadavoy, L. W. Lawrence, L. F. Jarvik, & G. T. Grossberg (Eds.), *Comprehensive review of geriative psychiatry—II,* 2d ed. (pp. 153–194). Washington, DC: American Psychiatry Publishing.

Coid, J., Petruckevitch, A., & Chung, W. (2003). Abusive experiences and psychiatric morbidity in women primary care attenders. *British Journal of Psychiatry, 183,* 332–339.

Coie, J. D., & Dodge, K. A. (1998). Aggression and antisocial behavior. In W. Damon (Series Ed.) & N. Eisenberg (Vol. Ed.), *Handbook of child psychology: Vol. 3, Social, emotional and personality development,* 5th ed. (pp. 779–862). New York: Wiley.

Col, N., & Komaroff, A. L. (2004, May 10). How to think about HT. *Newsweek,* p. 80.

Col, N. F., et al. (2004). Short-term menopausal hormone therapy for symptom relief. *Archives of Internal Medicine, 164,* 1634–1640.

Colbert, J. A., et al. (2004). The age at which women begin mammographic screening. *Cancer, 101,* 1850–1859.

Colcombe, S., & Kramer, A. F. (2003). Fitness effects on the cognitive function of older adults: A meta-analytic study. *Psychological Science, 14,* 125–130.

Cole, E. R., Zucker, A. N., & Duncan, L. E. (2001). Changing society, changing women (and men). In R. K. Unger (Ed.), *Handbook of the psychology of women and gender* (pp. 410–423). New York: Wiley.

Cole, J. B., & Guy-Sheftall, B. (2003). *Gender talk: The struggle for women's equality in African American communities.* New York: Random House.

Coley, R. L., & Chase-Lansdale, P. L. (1998). Adolescent pregnancy and parenthood: Recent evidence and future directions. *American Psychologist, 53,* 152–166.

Coll, C. T. G., Meyer, E. C., & Brillon, L. (1995). Ethnic and minority parenting. In M. H. Bornstein (Ed.), *Handbook of parenting.* Vol. 2, *Biology and ecology of parenting* (pp. 189–209). Mahwah, NJ: Erlbaum.

Collins, A. (1997). A psychological approach to the management of menopause. In B. G. Wren (Ed.), *Progress in the management of the menopause* (pp. 94–98). Pearl River, NY: Parthenon.

Collins, K. A., Bennett, A. T., & Hanzlick, R. (2000). Elder abuse and neglect. *Archives of Internal Medicine, 160,* 1567–1568.

Collins, K. S., & Simon, L. J. (1996). Women's health and managed care: Promises and challenges. *Women's Health Issues, 6* (1), 39–44.

Collins, N. L., & Feeney, B. C. (2004). An attachment theory perspective on closeness and intimacy. In A. Aron & D. J. Mashek, (Eds.), *Handbook of closeness and intimacy* (pp. 163–187). Mahwah, NJ: Erlbaum.

Collins, W. A. (2003). More than myth: The developmental significance of romantic relationships during adolescence. *Journal of Research on Adolescence, 13,* 1–24.

Coltrane, S. (1997, Spring). Families and gender equity. *National Forum, 77,* 31–34.

Coltrane, S. (2000). Research on household labor: Modeling and measuring the social embeddedness of routine family work. *Journal of Marriage and the Family, 62,* 1208–1233.

Coltrane, S., & Messineo, M. (2000). The perpetuation of subtle prejudice: Race and gender imagery in 1990s television advertising. *Sex Roles, 42,* 363–389.

Commonwealth Fund. (1993a). *The Commonwealth Fund survey of women's health.* New York: Author.

Commonwealth Fund. (1993b). *The untapped resource: The final report of the Americans Over 55 at Work program.* New York: Author.

Commonwealth Fund. (1997). *In their own words: Adolescent girls discuss health and health care issues.* New York: Author.

Commonwealth Fund. (1998). *The Commonwealth Fund 1998 survey of women's health.* New York: Author.

Compas, B. E., & Luecken, L. (2002). Psychological adjustment to breast cancer. *Current Directions in Psychological Science, 11,* 111–114.

Compian, L., & Hayward, C. (2003). Gender differences in opposite sex relationships: Interactions with puberty. In C. Hayward (Ed.), *Gender differences at puberty* (pp. 77–92). Cambridge: University Press.

Compton, W. M., et al. (2004). Prevalence of marijuana use disorders in the United States. *Journal of the American Medical Association, 291,* 2114–2121.

Comstock, G. (1991). *Television and the American child.* Orlando, FL: Academic Press.

Conkright, L., Flannagan, D., & Dykes, J. (2000). Effects of pronoun type and gender role consistency on children's recall and interpretation of stories. *Sex Roles, 43,* 481–497.

Conrad, C. (2005, July 22). The womanly art of negotiating. *Chronicle of Higher Education,* C2–3.

Consedine, N. S., et al. (2004). Fear, anxiety, worry, and breast cancer screening behavior: A critical review. *Cancer Epidemiology, Biomarkers & Prevention, 13,* 501–510.

Consolacion, T. B., Russell, S. T., & Sue, S. (2004). Sex, race/ethnicity, and romantic attractions: Multiple minority status adolescents and mental health. *Cultural Diversity and Ethnic Minority Psychology, 10,* 200–214.

Conti, N. E., & Kimmel, E. B. (1993). *Gender and cultural diversity bias in developmental textbooks.* Paper presented at the annual meeting of the Southeastern Psychological Association, Atlanta.

Cook, E., Heppner, M. J., & O'Brien, K. M. (2002). Career development of women of color and white women: Assumptions, conceptualization, and interventions from an ecological perspective. (Special Section). *Career Development Quarterly, 50,* 291–305.

Coombes, R. C., et al. (2004). A randomized trial of exemestane after two to three years of tamoxifen therapy in postmenopausal women with primary breast cancer. *New England Journal of Medicine, 350,* 1081–1092.

Cooper-Patrick, L., et al. (1999). Race, gender, and partnership in the patient-physician relationship. *Journal of the American Medical Association, 232,* 583–589.

Coovadia, H. (2004). Antiretroviral agents—How best to protect infants from HIV and save their mothers from AIDS. *New England Journal of Medicine, 351,* 289–291.

Corcoran, K., & Ellin, A. (2003, August 3). Shattering ceilings. *New York Times,* p. BU12.

Correa-de-Araujo, R. (2005). It's your health: Use your medications safely. *Journal of Women's Health, 14,* 16–18.

Correa-de-Araujo, R., Miller, E., Banthin, J. S., & Trinh, Y. (2005). Gender differences in drug use and expenditures in a privately insured population of older adults. *Journal of Women's Health, 14,* 73–80.

Cortina, L. M. (2004). Hispanic perspectives on sexual harassment and social support. *Personality and Social Psychology Bulletin, 30,* 570–584.

Cortina, L. M., & Magley, V. J. (2003). Raising voice, risking retaliation: Events following interpersonal mistreatment in the workplace. *Journal of Occupational Health Psychology, 8,* 247–265.

Cortina, L. M., Swan, S., Fitzgerald, L. F., & Waldo, C. (1998). Sexual harassment and assault: Chilling the climate for women in academia. *Psychology of Women Quarterly, 22,* 419–441.

Cosgrove, L., & Riddle, B. (2003). Constructions of femininity and experiences of menstrual distress. *Women & Health, 38,* 37–58.

Costello, C. B., & Stone, A. J. (Eds.). (2001). *The American woman 2001–2002.* New York: W. W. Norton.

Costello, C. B., & Wight, V. R. (2003). Taking it from here: Policies for the twenty-first century. In C. B. Costello, V. R. Wight, & A. J. Stone (Eds.), *The American woman 2003–2004: Daughters of a revolution—young women today* (pp. 127–142). New York: Palgrave Macmillan.

Costello, E. J., et al. (2003). Prevalence and development of psychiatric disorders in childhood and adolescence. *Archives of General Psychiatry, 60,* 837–844.

Costos, D., Ackerman, R., & Paradis, L. (2002). Recollections of menarche: Communication between mothers and daughters regarding menstruation. *Sex Roles, 46,* 49–59.

Cotter, D. A., Hermsen, J. M., Ovadia, S., & Vanneman, R. (2001). The glass ceiling effect. *Social Forces, 80,* 655–681.

Coulter, I., Jacobson, P., & Parker, L. E. (2000). Sharing the mantle of primary female care: Physicians, nurse practitioners, and physician assistants. *Journal of the American Medical Women's Association, 55,* 100–103.

Cowan, G. (2000). Beliefs about the causes of four types of rape. *Sex Roles, 42,* 807–823.

Cowley, G., & Murr, A. (2004, December 6). The new face of AIDS. *Newsweek,* pp. 76–79.

Cox, W. M., & Alm, R. (2005, February 28). Scientists are made, not born. *New York Times,* p. A19.

Cozzarelli, C., Wilkinson, A. V., & Tagler, M. J. (2001). Attitudes toward the poor and attributions for poverty. *Journal of Social Issues, 57,* 207–228.

Craig, R. S. (1992). The effect of television part on gender portrayals in television commercials: A content analysis, *Sex Roles, 26,* 197–211.

Crawford, M. (2001). Gender and language. In R. K. Unger (Ed.), *Handbook of the psychology of women and gender* (pp. 228–244). New York: Wiley.

Crawford, M., & MacLeod, M. (1990). Gender in the college classroom: An assessment of the "chilly climate" for women. *Sex Roles, 23,* 101–122.

Crawford, N. (2003, May). Parenting with a disability: The last frontier. *Monitor on Psychology,* pp. 68–70.

Creinin, M. D., et al. (2004). A randomized comparison of misoprostol 6 to 8 hours versus 24 hours after mifepristone for abortion. *Obstetrics & Gynecology, 103,* 851–859.

Crenshaw, A. B. (2002, June 2). Her next stop? Growing numbers of American women face retirement financially poor. *Washington Post,* pp. H1, H3.

Crimmins, E. M., Kim, J. K., & Hagedorn, A. (2002). Life with and without disease. *Journal of Women & Aging, 14,* 47–59.

Crockett, L. J. (1991). Sex roles and sex-typing in adolescence. In R. M. Lerner, A. C. Petersen, & J. Brooks-Gunn (Eds.), *Encyclopedia of adolescence,* Vol. 2 (pp. 1007–1017). New York: Garland.

Crombie, G., et al. (2005). Predictors of young adolescents' math grades and course enrollment intentions: Gender similarities and difference. *Sex Roles, 52,* 351–367.

Crosby, F. J. (1991). *Juggling: The unexpected advantages of balancing career and home for women and their families.* New York: Free Press.

Crosby, F. J., Iyer, A., Clayton, S., & Downing, R. A. (2003). Affirmative action: Psychological data and the policy debates. *American Psychologist, 58,* 93–115.

Crosby, R. A., et al. (2003). Value of consistent condom use: A study of sexually transmitted disease prevention among African American adolescent females. *American Journal of Public Health, 93,* 901–902.

Crouter, A. C., Manke, B. A., & McHale, S. M. (1995). The family context of gender intensification in early adolescence. *Child Development, 66,* 317–329.

Crowley, J. D. (2003). The anger of hope and the anger of despair: How anger relates to women's depression. In J. M. Stoppard & L. M. McMullen (Eds.), *Situating sadness. Women and depression in social context* (pp. 62–87). New York and London: New York University Press.

Crowley, K., Callanan, M. A., Tenenbaum, H. R., & Allen, E. (2001). Parents explain more often to boys than to girls during shared scientific thinking. *Psychological Science, 12,* 258–261.

Cuddy, A. J. C., & Fiske, S. T. (2002). Doddering but dear: Process, content, and function in stereotyping of older persons. In T. D. Nelson (Ed.), *Ageism: Stereotyping and prejudice against older persons* (pp. 3–26). Cambridge, MA: MIT Press.

Culp, L. N., & Beach, S. R. H. (1998). Marriage and depressive symptoms: The role and bases of self-esteem differ by gender. *Psychology of Women Quarterly, 22,* 647–663.

Cummings, A. L., & Leschied, A. W. (Eds.). (2002). Research and treatment for aggression with adolescent girls. *Mellen Studies in Social Work,* Vol. 5. Lewiston, NY: Edwin Mellen Press.

Cummings, S. R., (1999). The effect of raloxifene on risk of breast cancer in postmenopausal women. *Journal of the American Medical Association, 281,* 2189–2197.

Cunningham, M. (2001). The influence of parental attitudes and behaviors on children's attitudes toward gender and household labor in early adulthood. *Journal of Marriage and Family, 63,* 111–122.

Currin, L., Schmidt, U., Treasure, J., & Jick, H. (2005). Time trends in eating disorder incidence. *British Journal of Psychiatry, 186,* 132–135.

Curtis, G., & Schuler, J. (2004). *Your pregnancy week by week*, 5th ed. Cambridge, MA: DaCapo Press.

Curtis, L. H., et al. (2004). Inappropriate prescribing for elderly Americans in a large outpatient population. *Archives of Internal Medicine, 164,* 1621–1625.

Cushman, M., et al. (2004). Estrogen plus progestin and risk of venous thrombosis. *Journal of the American Medical Association, 292,* 1573–1580.

Cutter, J. A. (1999, June 13). Coming to terms with grief after a longtime partner dies. *New York Times*, p. WH10.

Dailard, C. (2002). Abstinence promotion and teen family planning: The misguided move for equal funding. *The Guttmacher Report on Public Policy, 5,* 1–3.

Dailard, C. (2003a). Marriage is no immunity from problems with planning pregnancies. *The Guttmacher Report on Public Policy,* pp. 10–13.

Dailard, C. (2003b). Understanding "abstinence": Implications for individuals, programs and policies. *The Guttmacher Report on Public Policy,* pp. 4–6.

Daly, E. (2005, February 8). Specialists trying to unravel the mystery of miscarriage. *New York Times,* pp. D5, D8.

Daly, K. (2004). Exploring process and control in families working nonstandard schedules. In A. C. Crouter & A. Booth (Eds.), *Work-family challenges for low-income parents and their children* (pp. 117–125). Mahwah, NJ: Erlbaum.

D'Amico, M., Baron, L. J., & Sissons, M. E. (1995). Gender differences in attributions about microcomputer learning in elementary school. *Sex Roles, 33,* 353–385.

Dan, A. J., & Rosser, S. V. (2003, Spring/Summer). Editorial. *Women's Studies Quarterly, 31,* pp. 6–24.

Dancer, L. S., & Gilbert, L. A. (1993). Spouses' family work participation and its relation to wives' occupational level. *Sex Roles, 28,* 127–145.

Daniluk, J. C. (1998). *Women's sexuality across the life span: Challenging myths, creating meanings.* New York: Guilford.

Daniluk, J. C. (1999). "When biology isn't destiny: Implications for the sexuality of women without children." *Canadian Journal of Counseling, 33,* 79–94.

Daniluk, J. C., & Towill, K. (2001). Sexuality education: What is it, who gets it, and does it work? In R. K. Unger (Ed.), *Handbook of the psychology of women and gender* (pp. 1023–1031). New York: Wiley.

Danner, F., Noland, F., McFadden, M., Dewalt, K., & Kotchen, J. M. (1991). Description of the physical activity of young children using movement sensor and observation methods. *Pediatric Exercise Science, 3,* 11–20.

D'Arcy, J. (1998, August 24). Marriage and family vs. career. *Hartford Courant,* pp. F1, F3.

Darling, C. A., Davidson, J. K., Sr., & Jennings, D. A. (1991). The female sexual response revisited: Understanding the multiorgasmic experience in women. *Archives of Sexual Behavior, 20,* 527–540.

Darroch, J. E., Frost, J. J., Singh, S., & the Study Team. (2001). *Teenage sexual and reproductive behavior in developed countries: Can more progress be made?* Occasional Report No. 3. New York: Alan Guttmacher Institute.

Das, M. (2000). Men and women in Indian magazine advertisements: A preliminary report. *Sex Roles, 43,* 699–716.

Daubman, K. A., Heatherington, L., & Ahn, A. (1992). Gender and the self-presentation of academic achievement. *Sex Roles, 27,* 187–204.

Daubman, K. A., & Sigall, H. (1997). Gender differences in perceptions of how others are affected by self-disclosure of achievement. *Sex Roles, 37,* 73–89.

D'Augelli, A. R. (2002). Mental health problems among lesbian, gay and bisexual youths ages 14 to 21. *Clinical Child Psychology and Psychiatry, 7,* 433–456.

Davey, E. H. (1998). Young women's expected and preferred patterns of employment and child care. *Sex Roles, 38,* 95–102.

David, H. P., & Lee, E. (2001). Abortion and its health effects. In J. Worell (Ed.), *Encyclopedia of women and gender* (pp. 1–14). San Diego: Academic Press.

David, S., & Knight, B. (2002, August). *Stress and coping among lesbian, gay, bisexual, and transgender older adults.* Paper presented at the meeting of the American Psychological Association, Chicago.

Davies, P. G., Spencer, S. J., & Steele, C. M. (2005). Clearing the air: Identity safety moderates the effects of stereotype threat on women's leadership aspirations. *Journal of Personality and Social Psychology, 88,* 276–287.

Daviglus, M. L., et al. (2004). Favorable cardiovascular risk profile in young women and long-term risk of cardiovascular and all-cause mortality. *Journal of the American Medical Association, 292,* 1588–1592.

Davies, P. T., Forman, E. M., Rasi, J. A., & Stevens, K. I. (2002). Assessing children's emotional security in the interparental relationship: The security in the interparental subsystem scales. *Child Development, 73,* 546–562.

Davis, M. K., & Gidycz, C. A. (2000). Child sexual abuse prevention programs: A meta-analysis. *Journal of Clinical Child Psychology, 29,* 257–265.

Davis, P. J. (1999). Gender differences in autobiographical memory for childhood emotional experiences. *Journal of Personality and Social Psychology, 76,* 498–510.

Davis, S. D., Crawford, M., & Sebrechts, J. (Eds.). (1999). *Coming into her own: Educational success in girls and women.* San Francisco: Jossey-Bass.

Davison, H. K., & Burke, M. J. (2000). Sex discrimination in simulated employment contexts: A meta-analytic investigation. *Journal of Vocational Behavior, 56,* 225–248.

Davison, K. K., & Birch, L. L. (2002). Processes linking weight status and self-concept among girls from ages 5 to 7 years. *Developmental Psychology, 38,* 735–748.

Davison, K. K., Susman, E. J., & Birch, L. L. (2003). Percent body fat at age 5 predicts earlier pubertal development among girls at age 9. *Pediatrics, 111,* 815–821.

Daw, J. (2001, October). Eating disorders on the rise. *Monitor on Psychology,* p. 21.

Daw, J. (2002, October). Is PMDD real? *Monitor on Psychology,* pp. 58–60.

Day, J. C., & Newburger, E. C. (2002). *The big payoff: Educational attainment and synthetic estimates of work-life earnings.* Current Population Reports P23–210. Washington, DC: U.S. Census Bureau.

Deal, J. J., & Stevenson, M. A. (1998). Perceptions of female and male managers in the 1990s: plu ca change . . . . *Sex Roles, 38,* 287–300.

DeAngelis, T. (2001, December). Are men emotional mummies? *Monitor on Psychology,* pp. 40, 41.

Deaux, K. (1999). An overview of research on gender: Four themes from 3 decades. In W. B. Swann, J. H. Langlois, & L. A. Gilbert (Eds.), *Sexism and stereotypes in modern society* (pp. 11–35). Washington, DC: American Psychological Association.

Deaux, K., & Stewart, A. J. (2001). Framing gendered identities. In R. K. Unger (Ed.), *Handbook of the psychology of women and gender* (pp. 84–97). New York: Wiley.

DeBell, M., & Chapman, C. (2004). *Computer and Internet use by children and adolescents in 2001.* U.S. Department of Education, National Center for Education Statistics. NCES 2004-014. Washington, DC: U.S. Department of Education.

DeGroot, J., & Fine, J. (2003). Integrating work and life: Young women forge new solutions. In C. B. Costello, V. R. Wight, & A. J. Stone (Eds.), *The American woman 2003–2004: Daughters of a revolution—young women today* (pp. 127–142). New York: Palgrave Macmillan.

de Guzman, M. R. T., Gustavo, C., Ontai, L. L., Koller, S. H., & Knight, G. P. (2004, August). Gender and age differences in Brazilian children's friendship nominations and peer sociometric ratings. *Sex Roles, 51,* 217–225.

DeJong Gierveld, J. (2004). Remarriage, unmarried cohabitation, living apart together: Partner relationships following bereavement or divorce. *Journal of Marriage and Family, 66,* 236–243.

Delaney, J., Lupton, M. J., & Toth, E. (1988). *The curse: A cultural history of menstruation.* Rev. ed. Urbana: University of Illinois.

de las Fuentes, C., & Vasquez, M. J. T. (1999). Immigrant adolescent girls of color: Facing American challenges. In N. G. Johnson, M. C. Roberts, & J. Worell (Eds.), *Beyond appearance: A new look at adolescent girls* (pp. 131–150). Washington, DC: American Psychological Association.

De Leon, B. (1995). Sex role identity among college students: A cross-cultural analysis. In A. M. Padilla (Ed.), *Hispanic psychology: Critical issues in theory and research.* Thousand Oaks, CA: Sage.

De Lisi, R., & Soundranayagam, L. (1990). The conceptual structure of sex role stereotypes in college students. *Sex Roles, 23,* 593–611.

DeLoach, C. P. (1989). Gender, career choice and occupational outcomes among college alumni with disabilities. *Journal of Applied Rehabilitation Counseling, 20,* 8–12.

Delsol, C., & Margolin, G. (2004). The role of family-of-origin violence in men's marital violence perpetration. *Clinical Psychology Review, 24,* 99–122.

DeNavas-Walt, C., Proctor, B. D., & Mills, R. J. (2004). Current Population Reports, P60–226. *Income, poverty, and health insurance coverage in the United States: 2003.* Washington, DC: U.S. Census Bureau.

Denizet-Lewis, B. (2004, May 30). Friends, friends with benefits and the benefits of the local mall. *New York Times Magazine,* pp. 30–35, 54–58.

Denmark, F. L. (1994). Engendering psychology. *American Psychologist, 49,* 329–334.

Denmark, F. L. (1999). Enhancing the development of adolescent girls. In N. G. Johnson, M. C. Roberts, & J. Worell (Eds.), *Beyond appearance: A new look at adolescent girls* (pp. 337–404). Washington, DC: American Psychological Association.

Denmark, F. L., Novick, K., & Pinto, A. (1996). Women, work, and family: Mental health issues. In J. E. Sechzer, S. M. Pfafflin, F. L. Denmark, A. Griffin, &

S. J. Blumental (Eds.), *Women and mental health* (pp. 101–117). New York: Academy of Sciences.

Denmark, F., Rabinowitz, V., & Sechzer, J. (2000). *Engendering psychology.* Needham Heights, MA: Allyn & Bacon.

DeParle, J. (1999, November 28). Early sex abuse common among welfare's women. *New York Times,* pp. Y1, Y20.

Depression across the lifespan. (2003, August). *National Women's Health Report, 25,* 6.

Depression & women. (2003, August). *National Women's Health Report, 25,* 1–4.

D'Erasmo, S. (2004, January 11). Lesbians on television: It's not easy being seen. *New York Times,* p. 1.

Derry, P. S. (2002). What do we mean by "The biology of menopause?" *Sex Roles, 46,* 13–23.

DeSouza, E. R. (2003, August). Antecedents and consequences of peer sexual harassment in Brazil. In E. R. DeSouza (Chair), *Sexual harassment of school-age students: A cross-cultural perspective.* Symposium presented at the meeting of the American Psychological Association, Toronto.

DeUgarte, C. M. et al. (2004). Female sexual dysfunction—from diagnosis to treatment. *Sexuality, Reproduction & Menopause, 2,* 139–145.

Deutsch, F. M., & Saxon, S. E. (1998). Traditional ideologies, nontraditional lives. *Sex Roles, 38,* 331–362.

DeVaus, D. (2002, Winter). Marriage and mental health. *Australian Institute of Family Studies, 62,* 26–32.

de Waal, F. B. M. (2002). Evolutionary psychology: The wheat and the chaff. *Current Directions in Psychological Science, 11,* 187–191.

DeZolt, D. M., & Henning-Stout, M. (1999). Adolescent girls' experiences in school and community settings. In N. G. Johnson, M. C. Roberts, & J. Worell (Eds.), *Beyond appearance: A new look at adolescent girls* (pp. 253–275). Washington, DC: American Psychological Association.

DeZolt, D. M., & Hull, S. H. (2001). Classroom and social climate. In J. Worell (Ed.), *Encyclopedia of women and gender* (pp. 257–264). San Diego: Academic Press.

Diagnoses of HIV/AIDS—32 states, 2002–2003. (2004). *Morbidity and Mortality Weekly Report, 53,* 1106–1110.

Diamond, L. M. (2000). Sexual identity, attractions, and behavior among young sexual-minority women over a 2-year period. *Developmental Psychology, 36,* 241–250.

Diamond, L. M. (2003a). Was it a phase? Young women's relinquishment of lesbian/bisexual identities over a 5-year period. *Journal of Personality and Social Psychology, 84,* 352–364.

Diamond, L. M. (2003b). What does sexual orientation orient? A biobehavioral model distinguishing romantic love and sexual desire. *Psychological Review, 110,* 173–192.

Diamond, L. M. (2004). Emerging perspectives on distinctions between romantic love and sexual desire. *Current Directions in Psychological Science, 13,* 116–119.

Diamond, M. (1997). Sexual identity and sexual orientation in children with traumatized or ambiguous genitalia. *Journal of Sex Research, 34,* 199–211.

Dickhäuser, O., & Stiensmeier-Pelster, J. (2002). Gender differences in computer work: Evidence for the model of achievement-related choices. *Contemporary Educational Psychology, 27,* 486–496.

DiClemente, R. J. et al. (2004). Efficacy of an HIV prevention intervention for African American adolescent girls: A randomized controlled trial. *Journal of the American Medical Association, 292,* 171–179.

Diekman, A. B., & Eagly, A. H. (1997, May). *Past, present, and future: Perceptions of change in women and men.* Paper presented at the meeting of the Midwestern Psychological Association, Chicago.

Diekman, A. B., Goodfriend, W., & Goodwin, S. (2004). Dynamic stereotypes of power: Perceptions of change and stability in gender hierarchies. *Sex Roles, 50,* pp. 201–215.

Diener, E., Gohm, C. L., Suh, M., & Oishi, S. (2000). Similarity of the relation between marital status and subjective well-being across cultures. *Journal of Cross-Cultural Psychology, 31,* 419–436.

Diener, E., & Seligman, M. E. P. (2004). Beyond money: Toward an economy of well-being. *Psychological Science in the Public Interest, 5,* 1–31.

Dierbeck, L. (2003). Choosing childlessness. In L. Slater, J. H. Daniel, & A. E. Banks (Eds.), *The complete guide to mental health for women* (pp. 40–47). Boston: Beacon Press.

Dietz, T. L. (1998). An examination of violence and gender role portrayals in video games: Implications for gender socialization and aggressive behavior. *Sex Roles, 38,* 425–442.

Dill, K. E., et al. (2001, August). *Violence, sex, race and age in popular video games: A content analysis.* Paper presented at the meeting of the American Psychological Association, San Francisco.

Dillon, S. (2002, June 15). Women tell of priests' abusing them as girls. *New York Times*, p. A11.

DiMatteo, M. R. (2004). Social support and patient adherence to medical treatment: A meta-analysis. *Health Psychology, 23*, 207–218.

DiMatteo, M. R., & Kahn, K. L. (1997). Psychosocial aspects of childbirth. In S. J. Gallant, G. Puryear Keita, & R. Royak-Schaler (Eds.), *Health care for women: Psychological, social, and behavioral influences* (pp. 175–186). Washington, DC: American Psychological Association.

DiNatale, M., & Boraas S. (2003). Young women, education, and employment. In C. B. Costello, V. R. Wight, & A. J. Stone (Eds.), *The American woman 2003-2004: Daughters of a revolution—young women today* (pp. 69–92). New York: Palgrave Macmillan.

Dingfelder, S. F. (2004, April). Gender bender. *Monitor on Psychology,* 48–49.

Dion, K. K., & Dion, K. L. (2001). Gender and relationships. In R. K. Unger (Ed.), *Handbook of the psychology of women and gender* (pp. 256–271). New York: Wiley.

Dion, K. L., & Cota, A. A. (1991). The Ms. stereotype: Its domain and the role of explicitness in title preference. *Psychology of Women Quarterly, 15*, 403–410.

Dion, K. L., & Schuller, R. A. (1990). Ms. and the manager: A tale of two stereotypes. *Sex Roles, 22*, 569–577.

Disparities in premature deaths from heart disease—50 states and the District of Columbia, 2001. (2004, February 20). *Morbidity and Mortality Weekly Report, 53*, pp. 121–125.

Dittmann, M. (2003, March). Coping with cancer through social connection. *Monitor on Psychology,* pp. 24–26.

Dixon, L., & Browne, K. (2003). The heterogeneity of spouse abuse: A review. *Aggression and Violent Behavior, 8*, 107–130.

Dodson, L., & Dickert, J. (2004). Girls' family labor in low-income households: A decade of qualitative research. *Journal of Marriage and Family, 66*, 318–332.

Dogar, R. (1999, Spring/Summer). STDs: Better safe than sorry. *Newsweek*, pp. 54–55.

Dominus, S. (2002, September 29). Shabana is late for school. *New York Times Magazine*, pp. 42–47, 56, 62–63, 118–120.

Dominus, S. (2004, October 24). Growing up with mom and mom. *New York Times Magazine*, pp. 68–75, 84, 143–144.

Donatelle, R. J., & Davis, L. G. (1998). *Access to health*. 5th ed. Boston: Allyn & Bacon.

Donnellan, M. B. et al. (2005). Low self-esteem is related to aggression, antisocial behavior, and delinquency. *Psychological Science, 16* 328–335.

Donohoe, M. (2005). Increase in obstacles to abortion: The American perspective in 2004. *Journal of the American Medical Women's Association, 60,* 16–25.

Donor-egg pregnancies called safe after age 50. (2002, November 12). *New York Times*, p. A27.

Doress-Worters, P. B., & Siegal, D. L. (1994). *The new ourselves growing older*. New York: Simon & Schuster.

Dorfman, L. T. (1995). Health, financial status, and social participation of retired rural men and women: Implications for educational intervention. *Educational Gerontology, 21,* 653–669.

Dorfman, L. T., & Rubenstein, L. M. (1993). Paid and unpaid activities and retirement satisfaction among rural seniors. *Physical & Occupational Therapy in Geriatrics, 12,* 45–63.

Döring, N. (2000). Feminist views of cybersex: Victimization, liberation, and empowerment. *Cyberpsychology & Behavior, 3,* 863–884.

Dotson, L. A., Stinson, J., & Christian, L. (2003). "People tell me I can't have sex": Women with disabilities share their personal perspectives on health care, sexuality, and reproductive rights. *Women & Therapy, 26,* 195–209.

Douglas, S. J., & Michaels, M. (2004). *The mommy myth: The idealization of motherhood and how it has undermined women*. New York: Free Press.

Dowden, R. (2002, January 27). Death by stoning. *New York Times Magazine*, pp. 28–31.

Dowling, W. (2001). Volunteerism among older women. In J. M. Coyle (Ed.), *Handbook on women and aging* (pp. 242–252). Westport, CT: Greenwood.

Downs, B. (2003). *Fertility of American women: June 2002*. Current Population Reports, P20–548. Washington, DC: U.S. Census Bureau.

Driscoll, M., & Groskop, V. (2003, January 5). Being a women isn't an illness. *Sun Times (London)*, p. 14.

Dube, K. (2004, June 18). What feminism means to today's undergraduates. *Chronicle of Higher Education*, p. B5.

Duenwald, M. (2002, July 16). Hormone therapy: One size clearly no longer fits all. *New York Times*, p. 16.

Duenwald, M. (2004, September 28). How young is too young to have a nose job and breast implants? *New York Times*, p. F5.

Duenwald, M., & Stamler, B. (2004, April 13). On their own, in the same boat. *New York Times,* pp. E1, E13.

Duff, J. L. (1996). *The best of friends: Exploring the moral domain of adolescent friendship.* Unpublished doctoral dissertation, Stanford University.

Duffy, J., Wareham, S., & Walsh, M. (2004). Psychological consequences for high school students of having been sexually harassed. *Sex Roles, 50,* 811–821.

Dugger, C. W. (2001, May 6). Modern Asia's anomaly: The girls who don't get born. *New York Times,* p. WK4.

Dugger, K. (1988). Social location and gender-role attitudes: A comparison of black and white women. *Gender & Society, 2,* 425–448.

Duncan, L. E., Peterson, B. E., & Ax, E. E. (2003). Authoritarianism as an agent of status quo maintenance: Implications for women's careers and family lives. *Sex Roles, 49,* 619–630.

Duncan, L. E., Wentworth, P. A., Owen-Smith, A., & LaFavor, T. (2002). Midlife educational, career, and family outcomes of women educated at two single-sex colleges. *Sex Roles, 47,* 237–247.

Dunham, K. J. (2003, August 26). Stay-at-home dads fight stigma. *New York Times,* pp. B1, B6.

Dunkle, K. L. (2004, May 1). Gender-based violence, relationship power, and risk of HIV infection in women attending antenatal clinics in South Africa. *The Lancet, 363,* 1415–1421.

Dunson, D. B., Baird, D. D., & Colombo, B. (2004). Increased infertility with age in men and women. *Obstetrics & Gynecology, 103,* 51–56.

Dush, C. M. K., Cohan, C., & Amato, P. (2003). Living together before marriage: Now common but still risky. *Journal of Marriage and the Family, 65,* 539–549.

Duxbury, L., & Higgins, C. (1994). Interference between work and family: A status report on dual-career and dual-earner mothers and fathers. *Employee Assistance Quarterly, 9,* 55–80.

Eagly, A. H. (1998). Gender and altruism. In D. L. Anselmi & A. L. Law (Eds.), *Questions of gender: Perspectives and paradoxes* (pp. 405–417). Boston: McGraw-Hill.

Eagly, A. H., & Carli, L. L. (1981). Sex of researchers and sex-typed communications as determinants of sex differences in influenceability: A meta-analysis of social influence studies. *Psychological Bulletin, 90,* 1–20.

Eagly, A. H., Diekman, A. B., Johannesen-Schmidt, M. C., & Koenig, A. M. (2004). Gender gaps in sociopolitical attitudes: A social psychological analysis. *Journal of Personality and Social Psychology, 87,* 796–816.

Eagly, A. H., & Johannesen-Schmidt, M. C. (2001). The leadership styles of women and men. *Journal of Social Issues, 57,* 781–797.

Eagly, A. H., Johannesen-Schmidt, M. C., & van Engen, M. L. (2003). Transformational, transactional, and laissez-faire leadership styles: A meta-analysis comparing women and men. *Psychological Bulletin, 129,* 569–591.

Eagly, A. H., & Johnson, B. T. (1990). Gender and leadership style: A meta-analysis. *Psychological Bulletin, 108,* 233–256.

Eagly, A. H., & Karau, S. J. (2002). Role congruity theory of prejudice toward female leaders. *Psychological Review, 109,* 573–598.

Eagly, A. H., Karau, S. J., & Makhijani, M. G. (1995). Gender and the effectiveness of leaders: A meta-analysis. *Psychological Bulletin, 117,* 125–145.

Eagly, A. H., Makhijani, M. G., & Klonsky, B. G. (1992). Gender and the evaluation of leaders: A meta-analysis. *Psychological Bulletin, 111,* 3–22.

Eagly, A. H., Wood, W., & Diekman, A. B. (2000). Social role theory of sex differences and similarities: A current appraisal. In T. Eckes & H. M. Trautner (Eds.), *The developmental social psychology of gender* (pp. 123–174). Mahwah, NJ: Erlbaum.

Eagly, A. H., Wood, W., & Johannesen-Schmidt, M. (2004). Social role theory of sex differences and similarities: Implications for the partner preferences of women and men. In A. H. Eagly, A. E. Beall, & R. J. Sternberg (Eds.), *The psychology of gender* (pp. 269–295). New York: Guilford.

Eaker, E. D., et al. (2004). Anger and hostility predict the development of atrial fibrillation in men in the Framingham offspring study. *Circulation, 109,* 1267–1271.

Eakin, E. (2002, March 30). Listening for the voices of women. *New York Times,* pp. A17, A19.

East, P. L., & Jacobson, L. J. (2001). The younger siblings of teenage mothers: A follow-up of their pregnancy risk. *Developmental Psychology, 37,* 254–264.

Eastman, V. J., & Utley, M. E. (2004, July). *Effect of pregnancy on judgments of a job applicant's qualifications.* Paper presented at the meeting of the American Psychological Association, Honolulu.

Eberhardt, J. L., & Fiske, S. T. (1998). Affirmative action in theory and practice: Issues of power, ambiguity, and gender versus race. In D. L. Anselmi & A. L. Law (Eds.), *Questions of gender: Perspectives and paradoxes* (pp. 629–641). Boston: McGraw-Hill.

Eccles, J. S. (2001). Achievement. In J. Worell (Ed.), *Encyclopedia of women and gender* (pp. 43–53). San Diego: Academic Press.

Eccles, J. S., Barber, B., & Jozefowicz, D. (1999). Linking gender to educational, occupational, and recreational choices: Applying the Eccles et al. model of achievement-related choices. In W. B. Swann, Jr., J. H. Langlois, & L. A. Gilbert (Eds.), *Sexism and stereotypes in modern society: The gender science of Janet Taylor Spence* (pp. 153–192). Washington, DC: American Psychological Association.

Eccles, J. S., Barber, B., Jozefowicz, D., Malanchuk, O., & Vida, M. (2002). Self-evaluations of competenece, task values and self-esteem. In J. Worell (Ed.), *Girls and adolescence.* Washington, DC: American Psychiatric Association.

Eccles, J. S., Freedman-Doan, C., Frome, P., Jacobs, J., & Yoon, K. S. (2000). Gender-role socialization in the family: A longitudinal approach. In T. Eckes & H. M. Trautner (Eds.), *The developmental social psychology of gender* (pp. 333–360). Mahwah, NJ: Erlbaum.

Eccles, J. S., & Roeser, R. W. (1999). School and community influences on human development. In M. H. Bornstein & M. E. Lamb (Eds.), *Developmental psychology: An advanced textbook,* 4th ed. (pp. 503–554). Mahwah, NJ: Erlbaum.

Eccles, J. S., Wigfield, A., & Schiefele, U. (1998). Motivation to succeed. In W. Damon (Series Ed.) & N. Eisenberg (Vol. Ed.), *Handbook of child psychology.* Vol. 3, *Social, emotional and personality development,* 5th ed. (pp. 1017–1095). New York: Wiley.

Eckert, P., & McConnell-Ginet, S. (2003). *Language and gender.* Cambridge: Cambridge University Press.

Eddleman, J., Essien, L., & Pollak, L. (2003, Spring/Summer). Success strategies. *AAUW Outlook,* p. 25.

Edwards, C. P., Knoche, L., & Kumru, A. (2001). Play patterns and gender. In J. Worell (Ed.), *Encyclopedia of women and gender* (pp. 809–815). San Diego: Academic Press.

Eggs shared, given, and sold. (2003). *The Lancet, 362,* 413.

Ehrenreich, B., & Hochschild, A. R. (2002). *Global woman: Nannies, maids, and sex workers in the new economy.* New York: Henry Holt.

Ehrmann, D. A. (2005). Polycystic ovary syndrome. *New England Journal of Medicine, 352,* 1223–1236.

Eisenberg, M. E., Neumark-Sztainer, D., & Story, M. (2003). Associations of weight-based teasing and emotional well-being among adolescents. *Archives of Pediatrics and Adolescent Medicine, 157,* 733–738.

Eisenberg, N. (2002). Prosocial development in early adulthood. *Journal of Personality and Social Psychology, 82,* 993–1006.

Eisenberg, N., & Fabes, R. A. (1998). Prosocial development. In W. Damon (Series Ed.) & N. Eisenberg (Vol. Ed.), *Handbook of child psychology.* Vol. 3, *Social, emotional and personality development,* 5th ed. (pp. 701–778). New York: Wiley.

Eisenberg, N., Martin, C. L., & Fabes, R. A. (1996). Gender development and gender effects. In D. C. Berliner & R. C. Calfee (Eds.), *The handbook of educational psychology* (pp. 358–396). New York: Simon & Schuster.

Eisenberg, N., & Morris, A. S. (2004). Moral cognitions and prosocial responding in adolescence. In R. M. Lerner & L. Steinberg (Eds.), *Handbook of adolescent psychology,* 2d ed. (pp. 155–188). Hoboken, NJ: Wiley.

Elder, J. (1997, June 22). Poll finds women are the health-savvier sex, and the warier. *New York Times,* p. WH8.

Elder, S. (2003, September). Europe's baby bust. *National Geographic,* p.1.

Ellin, A. (2002, April 21). Suddenly, 67 looks a lot closer. *New York Times,* p. BU9.

Ellin, A. (2004a, October 17). Helping grandparents help the grandkids. *New York Times,* p. BU9.

Ellin, A. (2004b, February 29). When it comes to salary, many women don't push. *New York Times,* p. BU7.

Elliott, G. C., Avery, R., Fishman, E., & Hoshiko, B. (2002). The encounter with family violence and risky sexual activity among young adolescent females. *Violence and Victims, 17,* 569–592.

Elliott, M. (2001). Gender differences in causes of depression. *Women & Mental Health, 33,* 163–177.

Elliott, N. (2004). Breast care should be better. *Women's Health in Primary Care, 7,* 464–465.

Ellis, B. J. (2004). Timing of pubertal maturation in girls: An integrated life history approach. *Psychological Bulletin, 130,* 920–958.

Ellis, B. J., & Garber, J. (2000). Psychosocial antecedents of variation in girls' pubertal timing: Maternal depression, stepfather presence, and marital and family status. *Child Development, 71,* 485–501.

Ellis, S. J. (2002). Student support for lesbian and gay human rights: Findings from a large-scale questionnaire study. In A. Coyle & C. Kitzinger (Eds.), *Lesbian and gay psychology: New perspectives* (pp. 239–254). Oxford, UK: BPS Blackwell.

Elmore, J. G., Armstrong, K., Lehman, C. D., & Fletcher, S. W. (2005). Screening for breast cancer. *Journal of the American Medical Association, 293,* 1245–1256.

Elrich, D. (1997, July 3). New video games: Despite promises, violence rules. *New York Times,* p. B1.

Elson, J. (2004). *Am I still a woman?* Philadelphia: Temple University Press.

Ens, C. Z., & Sinacore, A. (2001). Feminist theories. In J. Worell (Ed.), *Encyclopedia of women and gender* (pp. 469–480). San Diego: Academic Press.

Ensel, W. M., & Lin, N. (2004). Physical fitness and the stress process. *Journal of Community Psychology, 32,* 81–101.

Epstein, C. F., & Gambs, D. (2001). Sex segregation in education. In J. Worell (Ed.), *Encyclopedia of women and gender* (pp. 983–990). San Diego: Academic Press.

Epstein, R. H. (2001, November 27). Facing up to depression after a bypass. *New York Times,* p. D8.

Erel, O., Oberman, Y., & Yirmiya, N. (2000). Maternal versus nonmaternal care and seven domains of children's development. *Psychological Bulletin, 126,* 727–747.

Erikson, E. H. (1968). *Identity: Youth and crisis.* New York: Norton.

Erikson, E. H. (1980). *Identity and the life cycle.* New York: Norton.

Erkut, S., Marx, F., Fields, J. P., & Sing, R. (1999). Raising confident and competent girls: One size does not fit all. In L. A. Peplau, S. C. DeBro, R. C. Veniegas, & P. L. Taylor (Eds.), *Gender, culture, and ethnicity: Current research about women and men* (pp. 83–101). Mountain View, CA: Mayfield.

Espiritu, Y. L. (1997). *Asian American women and men: Labor, laws, and love.* Thousand Oaks, CA: Sage.

Estrogen therapy woes. (2004, March 3). *New York Times,* p. A15.

Etaugh, C. (1993). Maternal employment: Effects on children. In J. Frankel (Ed.), *The employed mother and the family context* (pp. 68–88). New York: Springer.

Etaugh, C., & Bridges, J. S. (2005). Midlife transitions. In J. Worell & C. Goodheart (Eds.), *Handbook of girls' and women's psychological health* (pp. 359–367). New York: Oxford University Press.

Etaugh, C., Bridges, J. S., Cummings-Hill, M., & Cohen, J. (1999). "Names can never hurt me?" The effects of surname use on perceptions of married women. *Psychology of Women Quarterly, 23,* 819–823.

Etaugh, C., & Conrad, M. (2004, July). *Perceptions of parents choosing traditional or nontraditional roles and surnames.* Poster presented at the meeting of the American Psychological Association, Honolulu, HI.

Etaugh, C., & Duits, T. (1990). Development of gender discrimination: Role of stereotypic and counterstereotypic gender cues. *Sex Roles, 23,* 215–222.

Etaugh, C., & Folger, D. (1998). Perceptions of parents whose work and parenting behaviors deviate from role expectations. *Sex Roles, 39,* 215–223.

Etaugh, C., & Fulton, A. (1995, June). *Perceptions of unmarried adults: Gender and sexual orientation (not social attractiveness) matter.* Paper presented at the meeting of the American Psychological Association, New York.

Etaugh, C., Grinnell, K., & Etaugh, A. (1989). Development of gender labeling: Effect of age of pictured children. *Sex Roles, 21,* 769–773.

Etaugh, C., Jones, N. A., & Patterson, K. (1995, August). *Gender comparisons and stereotypes: Changing views in introductory psychology textbooks.* Paper presented at the meeting of the American Psychological Association, New York City.

Etaugh, C., Levine, D., & Mennella, A. (1984). Development of sex biases in children: Forty years later. *Sex Roles, 10,* 913–924.

Etaugh, C., & Liss, M. B. (1992). Home, school, and playroom: Training grounds for adult gender roles. *Sex Roles, 26,* 129–146.

Etaugh, C., & Moss, C. (2001). Attitudes of employed women toward parents who choose full-time or part-time employment following their child's birth. *Sex Roles, 44,* 611–619.

Etaugh, C., & Nekolny, K. (1990). Effects of employment status and marital status on perceptions of mothers. *Sex Roles, 23,* 273–280.

Etaugh, C., & O'Brien, E. (2003, April). *Perceptions of parents' gender roles by preschoolers in traditional and egalitarian families.* Paper presented at the meeting of the Society for Research in Child Development, Tampa, FL.

Etaugh, C., & Poertner, P. (1991). Effects of occupational prestige, employment status, and mental status on perceptions of mothers. *Sex Roles, 24,* 345–353.

Etaugh, C., & Poertner, P. (1992). Perceptions of women: Influence of performance, marital, and parental variables. *Sex Roles, 26,* 311–321.

Etaugh, C., & Rathus, S. (1995). *The world of children.* Fort Worth, TX: Harcourt Brace.

Etaugh, C., & Roe, L. (2002, June). *"What's in a name?" Surname choice affects perceptions of women and men.* Poster presented at the meeting of the American Psychological Society, New Orleans.

Etaugh, C., Roe, L., & Zurek, R. (2003, July). *From "frogs and snails" to "Mr. Mom": Stereotypes of boys and men in children's books.* Poster presented at the European Congress of Psychology, Vienna.

Etaugh, C., & Spiller, B. (1989). Attitudes toward women: Comparison of traditional-aged and older college students. *Journal of College Student Development, 30,* 41–46.

Evans, E. M., Schweingruber, H., & Stevenson, H. W. (2002). Gender differences in interest and knowledge acquisition: The United States, Taiwan, and Japan. *Sex Roles, 47,* 153–168.

Evans, M. A., et al. (2003, April). *Gender constancy and sex-typed preferences: A meta-analytic integration.* Paper presented at the meeting of the Society for Research in Child Development, Tampa, FL.

Ewart, C. K., & Suchday, S. (2002). Discovering how urban poverty and violence affect health: Development and validation of a neighborhood stress index. *Health Psychology, 21,* 254–262.

Fabes, R. A., & Martin, C. L. (2003). *Exploring child development.* 2d ed. Boston: Allyn & Bacon.

Fabes, R. A., Martin, C. L., & Hanish, L. D. (2003). Young children's play qualities in same-, other-, and mixed-sex peer groups. *Child Development, 74,* 921–932.

Facio, E. (2001). Chicanas and aging: Toward definitions of womanhood. In J. M. Coyle (Ed.), *Handbook on women and aging* (pp. 335–350). Westport, CT: Praeger.

Fagot, B. I., & Leinbach, M. D. (1993). Gender-role development in young children: From discrimination to labeling. *Developmental Review, 13,* 205–224.

Fagot, B. I., Leinbach, M. D., & O'Boyle, C. (1992). Gender labeling, gender stereotyping, and parenting behaviors. *Developmental Psychology, 28,* 225–230.

Fagot, B. I., Rodgers, C. S., & Leinbach, M. D. (2000). Theories of gender role socialization. In T. Eckes & H. M. Trautner (Eds.), *The developmental social psychology of gender* (pp. 65–89). Mahwah, NJ: Erlbaum.

Fairweather, D., & Rose, N. R. (2004). Women and autoimmune diseases. *Emerging Infectious Diseases, 10,* 2005–2011.

Faludi, S. (1991). *Backlash: The undeclared war against women.* New York: Crown.

Families and Work Institute. (1995, May). *Women: The new providers.* Whirlpool Foundation Study, Part 1. New York: Author.

Family Caregiver Alliance. (2003). *Women and caregiving: Facts and figures.* Fact Sheet. San Francisco: Author.

Faria, G., & Belohlavek. (1995). Treating female adult survivors of childhood incest. In F. J. Turner (Ed.), *Differential diagnosis and treatment in social work,* 4th ed. (pp. 744–753). New York: Free Press.

Farmer, A., & Tiefenthaler, J. (2004). *Domestic violence and its impact on women's economic status, employers, and the workplace.* San Francisco: Blue Shield of California Foundation.

Farmer, H. S. (1997). Women's motivation related to mastery, career salience, and career aspiration: A multivariate model focusing on the effects of sex role socialization. *Journal of Career Assessment, 5,* 355–381.

Fassinger, R. E. (1994). Development and testing of the attitudes toward feminism and the women's movement (FWM) Scale. *Psychology of Women Quarterly, 18,* 389–402.

Fassinger, R. E. (1995). From invisibility to integration: Lesbian identity in the workplace. *The Career Development Quarterly, 44,* 148–167.

Fassinger, R. E. (2001). Women in nontraditional work fields. In J. Worell (Ed.), *Encyclopedia of women and gender* (pp. 1169–1180). San Diego: Academic Press.

Fausto-Sterling, A. (1992). *Myths of gender: Biological theories about women and men.* 2d ed. New York: Basic Books.

Fausto-Sterling, A. (2000, July/August). The five sexes, revisited. *The Sciences,* 18–23.

February is black history month. (2004, February). *Women's Psych-E, 3*(2).

Fechner, P. Y. (2003). The biology of puberty: New developments in sex differences. In C. Hayward (Ed.), *Gender differences at puberty* (pp. 17–28). Cambridge: University Press.

Federal Bureau of Investigation. (2002). *Hate crime statistics, 2001.* Washington, DC: Author.

Federal Glass Ceiling Commission. (1995a, March). *Good for business: Making full use of the nation's human capital*. Washington, DC: Author.

Federal Glass Ceiling Commission. (1995b, November). *A solid investment: Making full use of the nation's human capital*. Washington, DC: Author.

Feigelson, H. S., et al. (2004). Weight gain, body mass index, hormone replacement therapy, and postmenopausal breast cancer in a large prospective study. *Cancer Epidemiology Biomarkers & Prevention, 13*, 220–224.

Feingold, A. (1988). Cognitive gender differences are disappearing. *American Psychologist, 43*, 95–103.

Feingold, A. (1993). Cognitive gender differences: A developmental perspective. *Sex Roles, 29*, 91–112.

Feingold, A., & Mazzella, R. (1998). Gender differences in body image are increasing. *Psychological Science, 9*, 32–37.

Feiring, C., Taska, L., & Lewis, M. (2002). Adjustment following sexual abuse discovery: The role of shame and attributional style. *Developmental Psychology, 38*, 79–92.

Feist-Price, S., & Wright, L. B. (2003). African American women living with HIV/AIDS: Mental health issues. *Women & Therapy, 26*, 27–44.

Feldman, R. S. (1998). *Social psychology*. 2d ed. Upper Saddle River, NJ: Prentice Hall.

Feldman, R. S. (2000). *Development across the life span*. 2d ed. Upper Saddle River, NJ: Prentice Hall.

Feldman, S. (2003). How often should we screen for cervical cancer? *New England Journal of Medicine, 349*, 1495–1496.

Feldman, S., Byles, J. E., & Beaumont, R. (2000). "Is anybody listening?" The experiences of widowhood for older Australian women. *Journal of Women & Aging, 12*, 155–176.

Feldstein, K. (1998, April 13). Social Security's gender gap. *New York Times*, p. A27.

Feminization of AIDS. (2004, December 13). *New York Times*, p. 28.

Fergusson, D. M., & Woodward, L. J. (2000). Educational, psychosocial, and sexual outcomes of girls with conduct problems in early adolescence. *Journal of Child Psychology and Psychiatry, 41*, 779–792.

Ferris, L. E. (2004). Intimate partner violence. *British Medical Journal, 328*, 595–596.

Fiatarone, M. A., et al. (1994). Exercise training and nutritional supplementation for physical frailty in very elderly people. *New England Journal of Medicine, 33*, 1769–1775.

Field, A. E., et al. (2001). Peer, parent, and media influences on the development of weight concerns and frequent dieting among preadolescent and adolescent girls and boys. *Pediatrics, 107*, 54–60.

Field, A. E., et al. (2003). Relation between dieting and weight change among preadolescents and adolescents. *Pediatrics, 112*, 900–906.

Field, D., & Weishaus, S. (1992). Marriage over half a century: A longitudinal study. In M. Bloom (Ed.), *Changing lives* (pp. 269–273). Columbia: University of South Carolina Press.

Fielden, S. L., & Cooper, C. L. (2002). Managerial stress: Are women more at risk? In D. L. Nelson & R. J. Burke (Eds.), *Gender, work stress, and health* (pp. 19–34). Washington, DC: American Psychological Association.

Fielding, S. L., Edmunds, E., & Schaff, E. A. (2002). Having an abortion using mifepristone and home misoprostol: A qualitative analysis of women's experiences. *Perspectives on Sexual and Reproductive Health, 34*, 34–40.

Fields, J. (2003, June). *Children's living arrangements and characteristics: March 2002*. Washington, DC: U.S. Census Bureau.

Fields, J. (2004). *America's families and living arrangements: 2003*. Current Population Reports, P20–553. Washington, DC: U.S. Census Bureau.

Fields, J., & Casper, L. M. (2001). *America's families and living arrangements: March 2000*. Current Population Reports, P20–537, Washington, DC: U.S. Census Bureau.

Fine, M., & Carney, S. (2001). Women, gender, and the law: Toward a feminist rethinking of responsibility. In R. K. Unger (Ed.), *Handbook of the psychology of women and gender* (pp. 388–409). New York: Wiley.

Finer, L. B., & Henshaw, S. K. (2003). Abortion incidence and services in the United States in 2000. *Perspectives on Sexual and Reproductive Health, 35*, 6–15.

Fingeret, M. C., & Gleaves, D. H. (2004). Sociocultural, feminist, and psychological influences on women's body satisfaction: A structural modeling analysis. *Psychology of Women Quarterly, 28*, 370–380.

Fingerman, K. L. (2001). *Aging mothers and their adult daughters: A study in mixed emotions*. New York: Springer.

Fink, J. S., & Kensicki, L. J. (2002). An imperceptible difference: Visual and textual constructions of femininity in Sports Illustrated and Sports Illustrated for Women. *Mass Communication & Society, 5*, 317–339.

Finkelhor, D. (1990). Early and long-term effects of child sexual abuse: An update. *Professional Psychology: Research and Practice, 21,* 325–330.

Fish, J., & Wilkinson, S. (2003). Understanding lesbians' healthcare behaviour: The case of breast self-examination. *Social Science & Medicine, 56,* 235–245.

Fisher, S. Y., & Shelly, S. (2002). *The complete idiot's guide to personal finance in your 40s and 50s.* Indianapolis, IN: Alpha Books.

Fisher, T. D. (2004). Family foundations of sexuality. In J. H. Harvey, A. Welzel, & S. Sprecher (Eds.), *The handbook of sexuality in close relationships* (pp. 385–409). Mahwah, NJ: Erlbaum.

Fisher-Thompson, D. (1991, August). *Toys children request and receive: Sex and gender schema effects.* Paper presented at the meeting of the American Psychological Association, San Francisco.

Fisher-Thompson, D., Sausa, A. D., & Wright, T. F. (1995). Toy selection for children: Personality and toy request influences. *Sex Roles, 33,* 239–255.

Fiske, S. T. (2002, August). What we know now about bias and intergroup conflict, the problem of the century. *Current Directions in Psychological Science, 4,* 123–128.

Fiske, S. T., Bersoff, D. N., Borgida, E., Deaux, K., & Heilman, M. E. (1991). Social science research on trial: Use of sex stereotyping research in Price Waterhouse vs. Hopkins. *American Psychologist, 46,* 1049–1060.

Fiske, S. T., & Glick, P. (1995). Ambivalence and stereotypes cause sexual harassment: A theory with implications for organizational change. *Journal of Social Issues, 51,* 97–115.

Fiske, S. T., & Stevens, L. A. (1993). What's so special about sex? Gender stereotyping and discrimination. In S. Oskamp & M. Costanzo (Eds.), *Gender issues in contemporary society* (pp. 173–196). Newbury Park, CA: Sage.

Fitzgerald, L., Collinsworth, L. L., & Harned, M. S. (2001). Sexual harassment. In J. Worell (Ed.), *Encyclopedia of women and gender* (pp. 991–1004). San Diego: Academic Press.

Fitzgerald, L. F. (1996). Sexual harassment: The definition and measurement of a construct. In M. A. Paludi (Ed.), *Sexual harassment on college campuses: Abusing the ivory power* (pp. 25–47). Albany, NY: SUNY.

Fitzgerald, L. F. (2003). Sexual harassment and social justice: Reflections on the distance yet to go. *American Psychologist, 58,* 915–924.

Fitzgerald, M. H. (1990). The interplay of culture and symptoms: Menstrual symptoms among Samoans. *Medical Anthropology, 12,* 145–167.

Fitzpatrick, M. K., et al. (2004). Associations of gender and gender-role ideology with behavioral and attitudinal features of intimate partner aggression. *Psychology of Men & Masculinity, 5,* 91–102.

Fitzpatrick, T. R., & Vinick, B. (2005). The impact of husbands' retirement on wives' marital quality. *Journal of Family Social Work, 7,* 83–90.

Fivush, R., Brotman, M. A., Buckner, J. P., & Goodman, S. H. (2000). Gender differences in parent-child emotion narratives. *Sex Roles, 42,* 233–253.

Flanagan, C. (1993). Gender and social class: Intersecting issues in women's achievement. *Educational Psychologist, 28,* 357–378.

Flannagan, D., Baker-Ward, L., & Graham, L. (1995). Talk about preschool: Patterns of topic discussion and elaboration related to gender and ethnicity. *Sex Roles, 32,* 1–15.

Fleming, A. T. (2002, March 17). Maternal madness. *New York Times,* p. WK3.

Fleming, L. M., & Tobin, D. J. (2005). Popular child-rearing books: Where is Daddy? *Psychology of Men & Masculinity, 6,* 18–24.

Fletcher, G. J. O., et al. (2004). Warm and homely or cold and beautiful? Sex differences in trading off traits in mate selection. *Personality and Social Psychology Bulletin, 30,* 659–672.

Fletcher, V. (2005, January 14). Drunk girls under 14 ending up in hospital. *Daily Express (London),* p. 8.

Fogg, P. (2003, April 18). The gap that won't go away. Women continue to lag behind men in pay; the reasons may have little to do with gender bias. *Chronicle of Higher Education,* pp. A12–A15.

Follette, V. M., Alexander, P. C., & Higgs, D. C. (1991). Individual predictors of outcome in group treatment for incest survivors. *Journal of Consulting and Clinical Psychology, 59,* 150–155.

Forbes, G. B., Adams-Curtis, L. E., & White, K. B. (2004). First- and second-generation measures of sexism, rape myths and related beliefs, and hostility toward women: Their interrelationships and association with college students' experiences with dating aggression and sexual coercion. *Violence Against Women, 10,* 236–261.

Forbes, G. B., Adams-Curtis, L. E., White, K. B., & Holmgren, K. M. (2003). The role of hostile and benevolent sexism in women's and men's perceptions of the menstruating woman. *Psychology of Women Quarterly, 27,* 58–63.

Forbes, G. B., Doroszewicz, K., Card, K., & Adams-Curtis, L. (2004). Association of the thin body ideal, ambivalent sexism, and self-esteem with body acceptance and the preferred body size of college women in Poland and the United States. *Sex Roles, 50,* 331–345.

Ford, T. E., Ferguson, M. A., Brooks, J. L., & Hagadone, K. M. (2004). Coping sense of humor reduces effects of stereotype threat on women's math performance. *Personality and Social Psychology Bulletin, 30,* 643–653.

Foshee, V. A., et al. (2004). Assessing the long-term effects of the safe dates program and a booster in preventing and reducing adolescent dating violence victimization and perpetration. *American Journal of Public Health, 94,* 619–624.

Foster, M. D. (1999). Acting out against gender discrimination: The effects of different social identities. *Sex Roles, 40,* 167–186.

Fouts, G., & Burggraf, K. (1999). Television situation comedies: Female body images and verbal reinforcements. *Sex Roles, 40,* 473–481.

Fouts, G., & Burggraf, K. (2000). Television situation comedies: Female weight, male negative comments, and audience reactions. *Sex Roles, 42,* 925–932.

Fowers, B. J., Applegate, B., Tredinnick, M., & Slusher, J. (1996). His and her individualisms? Sex bias and individualism in psychologists' responses to case vignettes. *Journal of Psychology, 130,* 159–174.

Fowler, J. P. (2003). Aging with HIV: One woman's story. *Journal of Acquired Immune Deficiency Syndromes, 33,* S166–S168.

Frank talk about abortion. (2003, November 30). *New York Times,* p. WK8.

Frank, A. (1995). *The diary of a young girl: The definitive edition.* New York: Bantam Books.

Frank, S. J., Towell, P. A., & Huyk, M. (1985). The effects of sex-role traits on three aspects of psychological well-being in a sample of middle-aged women. *Sex Roles, 12,* 1073–1087.

Frankel, L. P. (2004). *Nice girls don't get the corner office 101. Unconscious mistakes women make that sabotage their careers.* New York: Warner.

Franklin, K. (1998, August). *Psychosocial motivations of hate crime perpetrators: Implications for educational interventions.* Paper presented at the meeting of the American Psychological Association, San Francisco.

Frankowski, B. L., & the Committee on Adolescence. (2004). Sexual orientation and adolescents. *Pediatrics, 113,* 1827–1832.

Frantz, D. (2000, November 3). Turkish women who see death as a way out. *New York Times,* p. A3.

Franzblau, S. H. (2002). Deconstructing attachment theory: Naturalizing the politics of motherhood. In L. H. Collins, M. R. Dunlap, & J. C. Chrisler (Eds.), *Charting a new course for feminist psychology* (pp. 93–110). Westport, CT: Praeger.

Franzoi, S. L., & Chang, Z. (2002). The body esteem of Hmong and Caucasian young adults. *Psychology of Women Quarterly, 26,* 89–91.

Frayne, S. M., et al. (2004). Effect of patient gender on late-life depression management. *Journal of Women's Health, 13,* 919–925.

Fraser, A. S., & Tinker, I. (2004). *Developing power: How women transformed international development.* New York: Feminist Press.

Fraser, M. B. (2002). *Solitaire: The intimate lives of single women.* New York: MacFarlane, Walter & Ross.

Frazier, P., et al. (2004). Correlates of levels and patterns of positive life changes following sexual assault. *Journal of Consulting and Clinical Psychology, 72,* 19–30.

Frazier, P., Arikian, N., Benson, S., Losoff, A., & Maurer, S. (1996). Desire for marriage and life satisfaction among unmarried heterosexual adults. *Journal of Social and Personal Relationships, 13,* 225–239.

Frazier, P. A. (2003). Perceived control and distress following sexual assault: A longitudinal test of a new model. *Journal of Personality and Social Psychology, 84,* 1257–1269.

Frasure-Smith, N., & Lespérance, F. (2005). Depression and coronary heart disease: Complex synergism of mind, body, and environment. *Current Directions in Psychological Science, 14,* 39–43.

Fredricks, J. A., & Eccles, J. S. (2002). Children's competence and value beliefs from childhood through adolescence: Growth trajectories in two male-sex-typed domains. *Developmental Psychology, 38,* 519–533.

Freeman, E. W., et al. (2004). Hormones and menopausal status as predictors of depression in women in transition to menopause. *Archives of General Psychiatry, 61,* 62–70.

French, D. C., Jansen, E. A., & Pidada, S. (2002). United States and Indonesian children's and adolescents' reports of relational aggression by disliked peers. *Child Development, 73,* 1143–1150.

Freud, S. (1925/1989). Some psychological consequences of the anatomical distinction between the sexes. In P. Gay (Ed.), *The Freud Reader* (pp. 670–678). New York: Norton.

Freud, S. (1938). The transformation of puberty. In A. A. Brill (Ed. and Trans.), *The basic writings of Sigmund Freud* (pp. 604–629). New York: Random House.

Fried, L. P., et al. (2004, March). A social model for health promotion for an aging population: Initial evidence on the Experience Corps model. *Journal of Urban Health, 81,* 64–78.

Friedan, B. (1963). *The feminine mystique.* New York: Norton.

Friedan, B. (1993). *The fountain of age.* New York: Simon & Schuster.

Friedman, D. E. (2001). Employee supports for parents with young children. *The Future of Children, 11(1),* 63–71.

Frieze, I. H. (2005). *Hurting the one you love. Violence in relationships.* Belmont, CA: Thomson Wadsworth.

Frieze, I. H., et al. (2003). Gender-role attitudes in university students in the United States, Slovenia, and Croatia. *Psychology of Women Quarterly, 27,* 256–261.

Frisch, R. E. (2002). *Female fertility and the body fat connection.* Chicago: University of Chicago Press.

Frone, M. R. (2003). Work-family balance. In J. C. Quick & L. E. Tetrick (Eds.), *Handbook of occupational health psychology* (pp. 143–162). Washington DC: American Psychological Association.

Frost, J., & McKelvie, S. (2004). Self-esteem and body satisfaction in male and female elementary school, high school, and university students. *Sex Roles, 51,* 45–54.

Frye, J. C. (1996). Affirmative action: Understanding the past and present. In C. Costello & B. K. Krimgold (Eds.), *The American woman 1996–1997* (pp. 33–43). New York: Norton.

Fulcher, M., Sutfin, E. L., & Patterson, C. J. (2003, April). *Parental sexual orientation, parental division of labor, and children's sex-typed occupational aspirations.* Paper presented at the meeting of the Society for Research in Child Development, Tampa, FL.

Fulkerson, J. A., & French, S. A. (2003). Cigarette smoking for weight loss or control among adolescents: Gender and racial/ethnic differences. *Journal of Adolescent Health, 32,* 306–313.

Fuller, B., et al. (2002). Does maternal employment influence poor children's social development? *Early Childhood Research Quarterly, 17,* 470–497.

Fuller-Thomson, E., & Minkler, M. (2003). Housing issues and realities facing grandparent caregivers who are renters. *The Gerontologist, 43,* 92–98.

Fulton, S. A., & Sabornie, E. J. (1994). Evidence of employment inequality among females with disabilities. *Journal of Special Education, 28,* 149–165.

Fultz, N. H., & Herzog, A. (2000). Urinary incontinence. In M. B. Goldman & M. E. Hatch (Eds.), *Women & health* (pp. 1202–1212). San Diego: Academic Press.

Furman, W. (2002). The emerging field of adolescent romantic relationships. *Current Directions in Psychological Science, 11,* 177–180.

Furnham, A., Reeves, E., & Budhani, S. (2002). Parents think their sons are brighter than their daughters: Sex differences in parental self-estimations and estimations of their children's multiple intelligences. *Journal of Genetic Psychology, 163,* 24–39.

Gaines, P. (2003). Daughters of the oft-forgotten continent. *AAUW Outlook,* pp. 22–24, 27.

Galambos, N. L. (2004). Gender and gender role development in adolescence. In R. M. Lerner & L. Steinberg (Eds.), *Handbook of adolescent psychology,* 2d ed. (pp. 233–262). Hoboken, NJ: Wiley.

Galambos, N. L., Leadbeater, B. J., & Barker, E. T. (2004). Gender differences in and risk factors for depression in adolescence: A 4-year longitudinal study. *International Journal of Behavioral Development, 28,* 16–25.

Galinsky, E. (2001, April). *Children's perspectives of employed mothers and fathers: Closing the gap between public debates and research findings.* Paper presented at the meeting of the Society for Research in Child Development, Minneapolis, MN.

Galinsky, E., & Bond, J. T. (1996). Work and family: The experiences of mothers and fathers in the U.S. labor force. In C. Costello & B. K. Krimgold (Eds.), *The American woman 1996–1997* (pp. 79–103). New York: Norton.

Gall, C. (2002, September 22). Long in dark, Afghan women say to read is finally to see. *New York Times,* pp. 1, 26.

Gallagher, C., & Busch-Rossnagal, N. A. (1991, March). *Self-disclosure and social support in the relationships of black and white female adolescents.* Poster presented at the Society for Research in Child Development, Seattle, WA.

Gallagher, W. (2001, November 13). Young love: The good, the bad, and the educational. *New York Times,* p. D6.

Gallant, S. J., & Derry, P. S. (1995). Menarche, menstruation, and menopause: Psychological research and future directions. In A. L. Stanton & S. J. Gallant (Eds.), *The psychology of women's health: Progress and challenges in research and application* (pp. 199–259). Washington, DC: American Psychological Association.

Galliano, G. (2003). *Gender: Crossing boundaries.* Belmont, CA: Wadsworth.

Galliher, R. V., Rostosky, S. S., Welsh, D. P., & Kawaguchi, M. C. (1999). Power and psychological well-being in late adolescent romantic relationships. *Sex Roles, 40,* 689–710.

Gallo, L. C., Matthews, K. A., Troxel, W. M., & Kuller, L. H. (2003). Marital status and quality in middle-aged women: Associations with levels and trajectories of cardiovascular risk factors. *Health Psychology, 22,* 453–463.

Gallor, S. (2003, January). An exploration of social support in the lives of ethnic minority lesbians and gay men. In R. E. Fassinger (Chair), *Results of the National Gay and Lesbian Experiences Study.* Symposium presented at the meeting of the American Psychological Association Multicultural Summit, Los Angeles.

Ganahl, D. J., Prinsen, T. J., & Netzley, S. B. (2003). A content analysis of prime time commercials: A contextual framework of gender representation. *Sex Roles, 49,* 545–551.

Gangestad, S. W., et al. (2004). Women's preferences for male behavioral displays change across the menstrual cycle. *Psychological Science, 15,* 203–207.

Gannon, L., & Ekstrom, B. (1993). Attitudes toward menopause: The influence of sociocultural paradigms. *Psychology of Women Quarterly, 17,* 275–288.

Gannon, L., Luchetta, T., Rhodes, K., Pardie, L., & Segrist, D. (1992). Sex bias in psychological research: Progress or complacency? *American Psychologist, 47,* 389–396.

Ganong, L. H., Coleman, M., Thompson, A., & Goodwin-Watkins, C. (1996). African American and European American college students' expectations for self and future partners. *Journal of Family Issues, 17,* 758–775.

Ganske, K. H., & Hebl, M. R. (2001). Once upon a time there was a math contest: Gender stereotyping and memory. *Teaching of Psychology, 28,* 266–268.

Garbers, S., et al. (2003). Barriers to breast cancer screening for low-income Mexican and Dominican women in New York City. *Journal of Urban Health, 80,* 81–91.

Gardner, R. M., Stark, K., Friedman, B. N., & Jackson, N. A. (2000). Predictors of eating disorder scores in children ages 6 through 14: A longitudinal study. *Journal of Psychosomatic Research, 49,* 1–7.

Garfinkel, P. (2002, February 24). As doctors on TV, women still battle the old clichés. *New York Times,* pp. AR17, 50.

Garnets, L. D., & Kimmel, D. C. (Eds.). (2003). *Psychological perspectives on lesbian and gay male experiences* (pp. 68–184). New York: Columbia University Press.

Garrow, D. J. (2004, May 9). Toward a more perfect union. *New York Times Magazine,* pp. 52–57.

Gartrell, N., et al. (2000). The national lesbian family study: 3. Interviews with mothers of five-year-olds. *American Journal of Orthopsychiatry, 70,* 542–548.

Gavey, N., & McPhillips, K. (1999). Subject to romance: Heterosexual passivity as an obstacle to women initiating condom use. *Psychology of Women Quarterly, 23,* 349–367.

Gaylord, S. (2001). Women and aging: A psychological perspective. In J. D. Garner & S. O. Mercer (Eds.), *Women as they age,* 2d ed. (pp. 49–68). New York: Haworth.

Gays win increasing protections in the workplace. (2003, Fall/Winter). *AAUW Outlook,* p. 6.

Geary, D. C. (2002). Sexual selection and human life history. In R. V. Kail (Ed.), *Advances in child development and behavior,* Vol. 30 (pp. 41–101). San Diego: Academic Press.

Geckler, J., & Fox, L. (2005, May). *Midwestern regional college students attitudes toward homosexuality.* Poster presented at the meeting of the Midwestern Psychological Association, Chicago.

Gelman, S. A., Taylor, M. G., & Nguyen, S. P. (2004). *Mother-child conversations about gender.* Boston: Blackwell Publishing.

Gender equality and the millennium development goals. (2003). Washington, DC: Gender and Development Group, World Bank.

Genetic testing for breast and ovarian cancer susceptibility: Evaluating direct-to-consumer marketing—Atlanta, Denver, Raleigh-Durham, and Seattle, 2003. (2003). *Morbidity and Mortality Weekly Report, 53*(27), 603–606.

Gennetian, L. A., & Miller, C. (2002). Children and welfare reform: A view from an experimental program in Minnesota. *Child Development, 73,* 601–620.

Genzlinger, N. (2004, January 20). An actress of a certain age eyes the beauty cult. *New York Times,* pp. B1, 5.

George, D., Carroll, P., Kersnick, R., & Calderon, K. (1998). Gender-related patterns of helping among friends. *Psychology of Women Quarterly, 22,* 685–704.

George, W. H., & Martinez, L. J. (2002). Victim blaming in rape: Effects of victim and perpetrator race, type of rape, and participant racism. *Psychology of Women Quarterly, 26,* 110–119.

Gerson, K. (1999). *Children of the gender revolution: Some theoretical questions and preliminary notes from the field.* Boston: Boston College Center for Work & Family.

Gibbons, C., & Jones, T. C. (2003). Kinship care: Health profile of grandparents raising their grandchildren. *Journal of Family Social Work, 7(1),* 1–14.

Gibbons, J. L. (2000). Gender development in cross-cultural perspective. In T. Eckes & H. M. Trautner (Eds.), *The developmental social psychology of gender* (pp. 389–415). Mahwah, NJ: Erlbaum.

Gibbs, N. (2002, April 15). Making time for a baby. *Time,* pp. 49–54.

Gibson, H. B. (1996). Sexual functioning in later life. In R. T. Woods (Ed.), *Handbook of the clinical psychology of aging* (pp. 183–193). New York: Wiley.

Giesbrecht, N. (1998). Gender patterns of psychosocial development. *Sex Roles, 39,* 463–478.

Gilbert, L. A. (1994). Reclaiming and returning gender to context: Examples from studies of heterosexual dual-earner families. *Psychology of Women Quarterly, 18,* 539–558.

Gilbert, L. A., & Rader, J. (2001). Counseling and psychotherapy: Gender, race/ethnicity, and sexuality. In J. Worell (Ed.), *Encyclopedia of women and gender* (pp. 265–277). San Diego: Academic Press.

Gilbert, L. A., & Scher, M. (1999). *Gender and sex in counseling and psychotherapy.* Boston: Allyn & Bacon.

Gilbert, S. (1998, May 19). Benefits of assistant for childbirth go far beyond the birthing room. *New York Times,* p. B17.

Gilbert, S. (1999, August 3). For some children, it's an after-school pressure cooker. *New York Times,* p. D7.

Gilbert, S. (2004, March 16). New clues to women veiled in black. *New York Times,* pp. D1, 7.

Giles, L. C., Glonek, G. F. V., Luczcz, M. A., & Andrews, G. R. (2005). Effects of social networks on 10-year survival in very old Australians: The Australian longitudinal study of aging. *Journal of Epidemiological Community Health, 59,* 574–579.

Giles, J. W., & Heyman, G. D. (2005). Young children's beliefs about the relationship between gender and aggressive behavior. *Child Development, 76,* 107–121.

Gil-Kashiwabara, E. F. (2002). Body image disturbance and disordered eating in African-American and Latina women. In L. H. Collins, M. R. Dunlap, and J. C. Chrisler (Eds.), *Charting a new course for feminist psychology* (pp. 282–306). Westport, CT: Praeger.

Gill, D. L. (2001). Sport and athletics. In J. Worell (Ed.), *Encyclopedia of women and gender* (pp. 1091–1100). San Diego: Academic Press.

Gill, T. M., et al. (2002). A program to prevent functional decline in physically frail, elderly persons who live at home. *New England Journal of Medicine, 347,* 1068–1074.

Gillespie, R. (2003, February). Childfree and feminine. Understanding the gender identity of voluntarily childless women. *Gender & Society, 17,* 122–136.

Gilligan, C. (1982). *In a different voice.* Cambridge, MA: Harvard University Press.

Gilligan, C. (1993). Joining the resistance: Psychology, politics, girls and women. In L. Weis & M. Fine (Eds.), *Beyond silenced voices* (pp. 143–168). Albany, NY: SUNY Press.

Gilligan, C. (2002). *Beyond pleasure.* New York: Knopf.

Giltay, E. J., et al. (2004). Dispositional optimism and all-cause and cardiovascular mortality in a prospective cohort of elderly Dutch men and women. *Archives of General Psychiatry, 61,* 1126–1135.

Gingrich, P. M. (2004). Management and follow-up of abnormal Papanicolaou tests. *Journal of the American Medical Women's Association, 59,* 54–60.

Ginorio, A. B., Gutiérrez, L., Cauce, A. M., & Acosta, M. (1995). Psychological issues for Latinas. In H. Landrine (Ed.), *Bringing cultural diversity to feminist psychology: Theory, research and practice* (pp. 241–263). Washington, DC: American Psychological Association.

Ginsburg, H. J., et al. (2002, June). *Sex differences in children's risk-taking revisited: Natural observations at the San Antonio Zoo.* Poster presented at the meeting of the American Psychological Society, New Orleans.

Ginty, M. M. (2000, August/September). What to ask your gynecologist. *Ms.,* pp. 64–68.

Giuliano, T. A., Popp, K. E., & Knight, J. L. (2000). Footballs versus Barbies: Childhood play activities as predictors of sport participation by women. *Sex Roles, 42,* 159–181.

Glass, T. A., de Leon, C. M., Marottoli, R. A., & Berkman, L. F. (1999). Population based study of social and productive activities as predictors of survival among elderly Americans. *British Medical Journal, 319,* 478–483.

Gleason, J. B., & Ely, R. (2002). Gender differences in language development. In A. McGillicuddy-DeLisi & R. DeLisi (Eds.), *Biology, society, and behavior: The development of sex differences in cognition. Advances in applied developmental psychology,* Vol. 21 (pp. 127–154). Westport, CT: Ablex.

Glenn, D. (2004, April 30). A dangerous surplus of sons? *Chronicle of Higher Education*, pp. 14–18.

Glick, P., & Fiske, S. T. (2001). An ambivalent alliance: Hostile and benevolent sexism as complementary justifications for gender inequality. *American Psychologist, 56*, 109–118.

Glick, P., et al. (2000). Beyond prejudice as simple antipathy: Hostile and benevolent sexism across cultures. *Journal of Personality and Social Psychology, 79*, 763–775.

Glied, S. (1998). The diagnosis and treatment of mental health problems among older women. *Journal of the American Medical Women's Association, 53*, 187–191.

Glomb, T. M., Munson, L. J., Hulin, C. L., Bergman, M. E., & Drasgow, F. (1999). Structural equation models of sexual harassment: Longitudinal explorations and cross-sectional generalizations. *Journal of Applied Psychology, 84*, 14–28.

Glud, E., et al. (2004). Hormone therapy and the impact of estrogen intake on the risk of ovarian cancer. *Archives Internal Medicine, 164*, 2253–2259.

Godbey, J. K., & Hutchinson, S. A. (1996). Healing from incest: Resurrecting the buried self. *Archives of Psychiatric Nursing, 10*, 304–310.

Godfrey, J. R. (2005). Toward optimal health: The experts discuss cardiovascular disease. *Journal of Women's Health, 14*, 4–10.

Goff, B. A., et al. (2004). Frequency of symptoms of ovarian cancer in women presenting to primary care clinics. *Journal of the American Medical Association, 291*, 2705–2712.

Gold, M. A., Wolford, J. E., Smith, K. A., & Parker, A. M. (2004). The effects of advance provision of emergency contraception on adolescent women's sexual and contraceptive behaviors. *Journal of Pediatric and Adolescent Gynecology, 17*, 87–96.

Goldberg, C. (1999, May 16). Wellesley grads find delicate balance. *Hartford Courant*, p. G3.

Goldberg, C. (2003, September 30). Unexpectedly expecting: Pregnant after 40. *Boston Globe*. Retrieved from http://www.boston.com/news/globe/health_science/articles/2003/09/30/

Goldfried, M. R. (2001). Integrating gay, lesbian and bisexual issues into mainstream psychology. *American Psychologist, 56*, 977–988.

Goldman, M. B., & Hatch, M. C. (2000). An overview of women and health. In M. B. Goldman & M. C. Hatch (Eds.), *Women & health* (pp. 5–14). San Diego: Academic Press.

Goldshmidt, O. T., & Weller, L. (2000). "Talking emotions": Gender differences in a variety of conversational contexts. *Symbolic Interaction, 23*, 117–134.

Goldstein, A. (2000, February 29). Breadwinning wives are on the rise. *Hartford Courant*, pp. A1, A7.

Goleman, D. (1995, September 6). Elderly depression tied to stroke. *New York Times*, p. B6.

Golombok, S., et al. (2003). Children with lesbian parents: A community study. *Developmental Psychology, 39*, 20–33.

Golombok, S., et al. (2004). Families created through surrogacy arrangements: Parent-child relationships in the first year of life. *Developmental Psychology, 40*, 400–411.

Golub, S. (1992). *Periods: From menarche to menopause*. Newbury Park, CA: Sage.

Gomez, M. J., et al. (2001). Voces abriendo caminos (Voices forging paths): A qualitative study of the career development of notable Latinas. *Journal of Counseling Psychology, 48*, 286–300.

Gondolf, E. W. (2004). Evaluating batterer counseling programs: A difficult task showing some effects and implications. *Aggression and Violent Behavior, 9*, 605–631.

Gonzalez, F. J., & Espin, O. M. (1996). Latino men, Latina women, and homosexuality. In R. P. Cabaj & T. S. Stein (Eds.), *Textbook of homosexuality and mental health* (pp. 583–593). Washington, DC: American Psychiatric Press.

Gonzalez, M. H., & Meyers, S. A. (1993). "Your mother would like me.": Self-presentation in the personal ads of heterosexual and homosexual men and women. *Personality and Social Psychology Bulletin, 19*, 131–142.

Good, C., Aronson, J., & Inzlicht, M. (2003). Improving adolescents' standardized test performance: An intervention to reduce the effects of stereotype threat. *Personality and Social Psychology Bulletin, 24*, 645–662.

Goodchilds, J. D. (2000, Summer). Afterword. *Journal of Social Issues*. Retrieved from http://www.findarticles.com/cf_dls/m0341/2_56/66419872/print.jhtml

Goode, E. (1999, May 20). Study finds TV trims Fiji girls' body image and eating habits. *New York Times*, p. A13.

Goode, E. (2000, May 19). Scientists find a particularly female response to stress. *New York Times*, p. A20.

Goode, E. (2003a, October 28). And still, echoes of a death long past. *New York Times*, pp. D1, D6.

Goode, E. (2003b, June 22). How to talk to teenage girls about weight? Very carefully. *New York Times*, p. WH8.

Gooden, A. M., & Gooden, M. A. (2001). Gender representation in notable children's picture books: 1995–1999. *Sex Roles, 45,* 89–101.

Goodman, M., et al. (2005, August). *Minority stress and psychological distress of lesbian and gay persons.* Poster presented at the meeting of the American Psychological Association, Washington, DC.

Goodwin, P. J., et al. (2001). The effect of group psychosocial support on survival in metastatic breast cancer. *New England Journal of Medicine, 345,* 1719–1726.

Goodwin, S. A., & Fiske, S. T. (2001). Power and gender: The double-edged sword of ambivalence. In R. K. Unger (Ed.), *Handbook of the psychology women and gender* (pp. 358–366). New York: Wiley.

Googins, B. K. (1991). *Work/family conflicts.* New York: Auburn House.

Gordon, R. A., Chase-Lansdale, P. L., & Brooks-Gunn, J. (2004). Extended households and the life course of young mothers: Understanding the associations using a sample of mothers with premature, low birth weight babies. *Child Development, 75,* 1013–1038.

Gorman, C., & Cole, W. (2004, March 1). Between the sexes. *Time,* pp. 54–56.

Gorman, J. (2004, April 27). Plastic surgery gets a new look. *New York Times,* pp. D1, D6.

Gose, B. (1995, February 10). Second thoughts at women's colleges. *Chronicle of Higher Education,* pp. A22–24.

Gottlieb, N. (1989). Families, work and the lives of older women. In J. D. Garner & S. O. Mercer (Eds.), *Women as they age: Challenge, opportunity, and triumph* (pp. 217–244). Binghamton, NY: Haworth.

Gould, L. (1990). X: A fabulous child's story. In A. G. Halberstadt & S. L. Ellyson (Eds.), *Social psychology readings: A century of research* (pp. 251–257). Boston: McGraw-Hill.

Gould, S. J. (1981). *The mismeasure of man.* New York: Norton.

Gourlay, M. L., & Brown, S. A. (2004). Clinical considerations in premenopausal osteoporosis. *Archives of Internal Medicine, 164,* 603–614.

Gowaty, P. A. (2001). Women, psychology and evolution. In R. K. Unger (Ed.), *Handbook of the psychology of women and gender* (pp. 53–65). New York: Wiley.

Gowers, S., & Bryant-Waugh, R. (2004). Management of child and adolescent eating disorders: The current evidence base and future directions. *Journal of Child Psychology and Psychiatry, 45,* 63–83.

Graber, J. A. (2004). Internalizing problems during adolescence. In R. M. Lerner & L. Steinberg (Eds.), *Handbook of adolescent psychology,* 2d ed. (pp. 587–626). Hoboken, NJ: Wiley.

Graber, J. A., & Brooks-Gunn, J. (1998). Puberty. In E. A. Blechman & K. D. Brownell (Eds.), *Behavioral medicine and women: A comprehensive handbook* (pp. 51–58). New York: Guilford.

Graber, J. A., & Brooks-Gunn, J. (2002). Adolescent girls' sexual development. In G. M. Wingood & R. J. DiClemente (Eds.), *Handbook of women's sexual and reproductive health* (pp. 21–42). New York: Kluwer Academic/Plenum.

Grady, D. (2002a, September 3). Hot flashes: Exploring the mystery of women's thermal chaos. *New York Times,* p. D5.

Grady, D. (2002b, March 5). Tests for breast cancer gene raise hard choices. *New York Times,* p. D6.

Grady, D. (2003, October 24). Women with genetic mutation at high risk for breast cancer, study confirms. *New York Times,* p. A15.

Grady, D. (2004a, April 14). Lung cancer affects sexes differently. *New York Times,* p. A18.

Grady, D. (2004b, March 18). Osteoporosis drug found safe to take for 10 years. *New York Times,* p. A19.

Grady, D. (2004c, September 24). Report of first birth for cancer survivor in a tissue implant. *New York Times,* pp. A1, A24.

Grady, D. (2004d, November 2). Vaccine works to prevent cervical cancer. *New York Times,* p. D7.

Grady, D. (2005, May 13). Therapies cut death risk, breast cancer study finds. *New York Times,* p. A10.

Grady-Weliky, T. A. (2003). Premenstrual dysphoric disorder. *New England Journal of Medicine, 348,* 433–438.

Graham, J. (2005, January 2). State sets standards on surrogate births. *Chicago Tribune,* pp. L1, L10.

Graham, S. (1997). "Most of the subjects were white and middle class": Trends in published research on African Americans in selected APA journals, 1970–1989. In L. A. Peplau & S. E. Taylor (Eds.), *Sociocultural perspectives in social psychology: Current readings* (pp. 52–71). Upper Saddle River, NJ: Prentice Hall.

Grall, T. S. (2004). *The condition of education 2004.* NCES 2004-007. U.S. Department of Education, National Center for Education Statistics. Washington, DC: U.S. Government Printing Office.

Grandparents raising grandchildren. (2002, June). *AARP Bulletin,* p. 27.

Granrose, C. S., & Kaplan, E. E. (1996). *Work-family role choices for women in their 20s and 30s: From college plans to life experiences*. Westport, CT: Praeger.

Gravois, J. (2005, January 7). Number of doctorates edges up slightly. *Chronicle of Higher Education*, pp. A24–A25.

Gray, J. (1992). *Men are from Mars, women are from Venus*. New York: HarperCollins.

Gray-Little, B., & Hafdahl, A. R. (2000). Factors influencing racial comparisons of self-esteem: A quantitative review. *Psychological Bulletin, 126,* 26–54.

Green, B. L., & Russo, N. F. (1993). Work and family roles: Selected issues. In F. L. Denmark & M. A. Paludi (Eds.), *Psychology of women: A handbook of issues and theories* (pp. 685–719). Westport, CT: Greenwood.

Green, R. J. (2004). Risk and resilience in lesbian and gay couples: Comment on Solomon, Rothblum, and Balsam (2004). *Journal of Family Psychology, 18,* 290–292.

Green, V. A., Bigler, R., & Catherwood, D. (2004). The variability and flexibility of gender-typed toy play: A close look at children's behavioral responses to counterstereotypic models. *Sex Roles, 51,* 371–386.

Greenberg, B. S., et al. (2003). Portrayals of overweight and obese individuals on commercial television. *American Journal of Public Health, 93,* 1342–1348.

Greenberg, S. H., & Springen, K. (2001, July 2). The baby blues and beyond. *Newsweek*, pp. 26–29.

Greene, B. (2003). Women of color and relationships. In L. Slater, J. H. Daniel, & A. E. Banks (Eds.), *The complete guide to mental health for women* (pp. 100–103). Boston: Beacon Press.

Greene, B. A., DeBacker, T., Ravindran, B., & Krows, A. J. (1999). Goals, values, and beliefs as predictors of achievement and effort in high school mathematics classes. *Sex Roles, 40,* 421–458.

Greene, C. K., & Stitt-Gohdes, W. L. (1997). Factors that influence women's choices to work in the trades. *Journal of Career Development, 23,* 265–278.

Greenfield, S. F. (2002). Women and alcohol use disorders. *Harvard Review of Psychology, 10,* 76–85.

Greenglass, E. R. (2002). Work stress, coping, and social support: Implications for women's occupational well-being. In D. L. Nelson & R. J. Burke (Eds.), *Gender, work stress and health* (pp. 85–96). Washington, DC: American Psychological Association.

Greenhaus, J. H., & Parasuraman, S. (2002). The allocation of time to work and family roles. In D. L. Nelson & R. J. Burke (Eds.), *Gender, work stress, and health* (pp. 115–128). Washington, DC: American Psychological Association.

Greenhouse, S. (2004, November 17). Abercrombie & Fitch bias case is settled. *New York Times*, p. A16.

Grimberg, A., Kutikov, J. K., & Cucchiara, A. J. (2005). Sex differences in patients referred for evaluation of poor growth. *Journal of Pediatrics, 146,* 212–216.

Grimmell, D., & Stern, G. S. (1992). The relationship between gender role ideals and psychological well-being. *Sex Roles, 27,* 487–497.

Grodstein, F., Clarkson, D. V. M., & Manson, J. E. (2003). Understanding the divergent data on postmenopausal hormone therapy. *New England Journal of Medicine, 348,* 645–650.

Grodstein, F., Lifford, K., Resnick, N. M., & Curhan, G. C. (2004). Postmenopausal hormone therapy and risk of developing urinary incontinence. *Obstetrics & Gynecology, 103,* 254–260.

Groesz, L. M., Levine, M. P., & Murnen, S. K. (2002). The effect of experimental presentation of thin media images on body satisfaction: A meta-analytic review. *International Journal of Eating Disorders, 31,* 1–16.

Gross, J. (2004a, April 23). Last hurdle for trailblazing women: The gold watch. Like men before them, professionals facing retirement ask what's next. *New York Times*, p. A19.

Gross, J. (2004b, May 31). Splitting up boys and girls, just for the tough years. School mixes single-sex classes in coed setting. *New York Times*, p. A16.

Gross, J. J., et al. (1997). Emotion and aging: Experience expression, and control. *Psychology and Aging, 12,* 590–599.

Gross, S. M., Ireys, H. T., & Kinsman, S. L. (2000). Young women with physical disabilities: Risk factors for symptoms of eating disorders. *Developmental and Behavioral Pediatrics, 21,* 87–96.

Grossman, A. H., D'Augelli, A. R., & Hershberger, S. L. (2000). Social support networks of lesbian, gay, and bisexual adults 60 years of age and older. *Journal of Gerontology: Psychological Sciences, 55B,* 171–179.

Grossman, A. H., D'Augelli, A. R., & O'Connel, T. S. (2001). Being lesbian, gay, bisexual, and 60 or older in North America. *Journal of Gay & Lesbian Social Services, 13,* 23–40.

Grossman, A. L., & Tucker, J. S. (1997). Gender differences and sexism in the knowledge and use of slang. *Sex Roles, 37,* 101–110.

Grossman, S. E., & Lundy, M. (2003). Use of domestic violence services across race and ethnicity by women aged 55 and older. *Violence Against Women, 9,* 1442–1452.

Grunbaum, J. A. (2004). Youth risk behavior surveillance—United States, 2003. *Morbidity and Mortality Weekly Report, 53.* No. SS-2.

Guastello, D. D., & Guastello, S. J. (2003). Androgyny, gender role behavior, and emotional intelligence among college students and their parents. *Sex Roles, 49,* 663–673.

Guidelines for psychotherapy with lesbian, gay, and bisexual clients. (2000). *American Psychologist, 55,* 1440–1451.

Gutek, B. A. (2001). Working environments. In J. Worell (Ed.), *Encyclopedia of women and gender* (pp. 1191–1204). San Diego: Academic Press.

Gutek, B. A., & Done, R. S. (2001). Sexual harassment. In R. K. Unger (Ed.), *Handbook of the psychology women and gender* (pp. 367–387). New York: Wiley.

Guterman, L. (2003, July 25). Not everyone's birthday is celebrated with a medical conference. *Chronicle of Higher Education,* p. A12.

Guzman, K. (2002, May 3). As wedding season looms, surname debate resumes. *Chicago Tribune,* pp. C1, C5.

Haag, P. (1999). *Voices of a generation: Teenage girls on sex, schools, and self.* Washington, DC: American Association of University Women.

Hackett, G., Betz, N. E., Casas, J. M., & Rocha-Singh, I. A. (1992). Gender, ethnicity, and social cognitive factors predicting the academic achievement of students in engineering. *Journal of Counseling Psychology, 39,* 527–538.

Hafemeister, T. L., & Jackson, S. (2000, February). Grandparent visitation: Who should decide? *APA Monitor,* p. 81.

Hafner, K., (1998, September 10). Girl games: Plenty and pink. *New York Times,* p. D8.

Hafner, K. (2003, August 21). 3 women and 3 paths, 10 years later. *New York Times,* pp. E1, E7.

Hafner, K. (2004, October 14). What do women game designers want? *New York Times,* pp. E1, E4.

Haj-Yahia, M. M. (2002). Beliefs of Jordanian women about wife-beating. *Psychology of Women Quarterly, 26,* 282–291.

Hall, E. J., & Rodriguez, M. S. (2003). The myth of postfeminism. *Gender & Society, 17,* 878–902.

Hall, J. A. (1996). Touch, status, and gender at professional meetings. *Journal of Nonverbal Behavior, 20,* 23–44.

Hall, J. A., Carter, J. D., & Horgan, T. G. (2000). Gender differences in nonverbal communication of emotion. In A. H. Fischer (Ed.), *Gender and emotion: Social psychological perspectives* (pp. 97–117). Paris: Cambridge University Press.

Hall, J. A., LeBeau, L. S., Reinoso, J. G., & Thayer, F. (2001). Status, gender, and nonverbal behavior in candid and posed photographs: A study of conversations between university employees. *Sex Roles, 44,* 677–692.

Hall, J. A., & Veccia, E. M. (1992). Touch asymmetry between the sexes. In C. L. Ridgeway (Ed.), *Gender, interaction, and inequality* (pp. 81–96). New York: Springer.

Hall, R. E. (2003, June). Eurocentric bias in women's psychology journals: Resistance to issues significant to people of color. *European Psychologist, 8,* pp. 117–122.

Hall, R. L., & Greene, B. (2002). Not any one thing: The complex legacy of social class on African American lesbian relationships. *Journal of Lesbian Studies, 6(1),* 85–109.

Hall, R. M., & Sandler, B. R. (1982). *The classroom climate: A chilly one for women?* Project on the Status and Education of Women. Washington, DC: Association of American Colleges.

Halliwell, E., & Dittmar, H. (2003). A qualitative investigation of women's and men's body image concerns and their attitudes toward aging. *Sex Roles, 49,* 675–684.

Hall Smith, P., White, J. W., & Holland, L. J. (2003). A longitudinal perspective on dating violence among adolescent and college-age women. *American Journal of Public Health, 93,* 1104–1109.

Halpern, D. F. (2000). *Sex differences in cognitive abilities.* 3d ed. Mahwah, NJ: Erlbaum.

Halpern, D. F. (2001). Sex difference research: Cognitive abilities. In J. Worell (Ed.), *Encyclopedia of women and gender* (pp. 963–971). San Diego: Academic Press.

Halpern, D. F. (2004a). A cognitive-process taxonomy for sex differences in cognitive abilities. *Current Directions in Psychological Science, 13,* 135–139.

Halpern, D. (2004b). Making it work: Recommendations for policies on working families. *Monitor on Psychology,* p. 5.

Halpern, D. (2004c). Transitions, reflections, resolutions. *Monitor on Psychology*, p. 5.

Halpern, D. (2005). Psychology at the intersection of work and family: Recommendations for employers, working families, and policymakers. *American Psychologist, 60*, 397–409.

Halpert, J. (2002, April 28). The nanny is late. You have a speech. What now? *New York Times*, p. BU8.

Hamby, S. L., & Koss, M. P. (2003). Shades of gray: A qualitative study of terms used in the measurement of sexual victimization. *Psychology of Women Quarterly, 27*, 243–255.

Hamida, S. B., Mineka, S., & Bailey, J. M. (1998). Sex differences in perceived controllability of mate value: An evolutionary perspective. *Journal of Personality and Social Psychology, 75*, 953–966.

Hamilton, B. E., Martin, J. A., & Sutton, P. D. (2004). *Births: Preliminary data for 2003*. National Vital Statistics Reports, 53, No. 9. Hyattsville, MD: National Center for Health Statistics.

Hamilton, M. C. (1991). Masculine bias in the attribution of personhood: People = male, male = people. *Psychology of Women Quarterly, 15*, 393–402.

Hamilton, M. C. (2001). Sex-related difference research: Personality. In J. Worell (Ed.), *Encyclopedia of women and gender* (pp. 973–981). San Diego: Academic Press.

Hampson, E., & Moffat, S. D. (2004). The psychobiology of gender: Cognitive effects of reproductive hormones in the adult nervous system. In A. H. Eagly, A. E. Beall, & R. J. Sternberg (Eds.), *The psychology of gender* (pp. 38–64). New York: Guilford.

Haninger, K., & Thompson, K. M. (2004). Content and ratings of teen-rated video games. *Journal of the American Medical Association, 291*, 856–865.

Hankin, B. L., & Abramson, L. Y. (2001). Development of gender differences in depression. *Psychological Bulletin, 127*, 773–796.

Hankin, S. (2004, Summer). Viagra or an Rx for sex? *Ms.*, p. 63.

Hanna, W. J., & Rogovsky, B. (1991). Women with disabilities: two handicaps plus. *Disability, Handicap & Society, 6*, 49–63.

Hanna, W. J., & Rogovsky, E. (1992). On the situation of African-American women with physical disabilities. *Journal of Applied Rehabilitation Counseling, 23*, 39–45.

Hanson, K., & Wapner, S. (1994). Transition to retirement: Gender differences. *International Journal of Aging and Human Development, 39*, 189–208.

Hanson, R. F., et al. (2001). Impact of childhood rape and aggravated assault on adult mental health. *American Journal of Orthopsychiatry, 71*, 108–119.

Hare-Mustin, R. T., & Marecek, J. (1990). On making a difference. In R. T. Hare-Mustin & J. Marecek (Eds.), *Making a difference: Psychology and the construction of gender* (pp. 1–21). New Haven, CT: Yale University Press.

Harm, N. J. (2001). Grandmothers raising grandchildren: Parenting the second time around. In J. D. Garner & S. O. Mercer (Eds.), *Women as they age,* 2d ed. (pp. 131–146). New York: Haworth.

Harmon, A. (2003, June 29). Online dating sheds its stigma as losers.com. *New York Times*, pp. YT1, 21.

Harmon, A. (2004, August 26). Internet gives teenage bullies weapons to wound from afar. *New York Times*, pp. A1, A21.

Harper, G. W., Jernewall, N., & Zea, M. C. (2004). Giving voice to emerging science and theory for lesbian, gay, and bisexual people of color. *Cultural Diversity and Ethnic Minority Psychology, 10*, 187–199.

Harper, M., & Schoeman, W. J. (2003). Influences of gender as a basic-level category in person perception on the gender belief system. *Sex Roles, 49*, 517–526.

Harris, A. C. (1994). Ethnicity as a determinant of sex role identity: A replication study of item selection for the Bem Sex Role Inventory. *Sex Roles, 31*, 241–273.

Harris, K. L., Melaas, K., & Rodacker, E. (1999). The impact of women's studies courses on college students of the 1990s. *Sex Roles, 40*, 969–977.

Harris, M. B. (1994). Growing old gracefully: Age concealment and gender. *Journal of Gerontology: Psychological Sciences, 49*, 149–158.

Harris, M. B., & Knight-Bohnhoff, K. (1996). Gender and aggression II: Personal aggressiveness. *Sex Roles, 35*, 27–42.

Harris, M. B., Page, P., & Begay, C. (1988). Attitudes toward aging in a southwestern sample: Effects of ethnicity, age, and sex. *Psychological Reports, 62*, 735–746.

Harris, R. J., & Firestone, J. M. (1998). Changes in predictors of gender role ideologies among women: A multivariate analysis. *Sex Roles, 38*, 239–252.

Harris, S. M. (1993). The influence of personal and family factors on achievement needs and concerns of African-American and Euro-American college women. *Sex Roles, 29*, 671–689.

Harrison, K. (2003). Television viewers' ideal body proportions: The case of the curvaceously thin woman. *Sex Roles, 48*, 255–264.

Harrison, L. J., & Ungerer, J. A. (2002). Maternal employment and infant-mother attachment security at 12 months postpartum. *Developmental Psychology, 38,* 758–773.

Harter, S. (1990). Adolescent self and identity development. In S. S. Feldman & G. R. Elliot (Eds.), *At the threshold: The developing adolescent* (pp. 352–387). Cambridge, MA: Harvard University Press.

Harter, S. (1998). The development of self-representations. In W. Damon (Series Ed.) & N. Eisenberg (Vol. Ed.), *Handbook of child psychology.* Vol. 3, *Social, emotional and personality development,* 5th ed. (pp. 553–617). New York: Wiley.

Harter, S. (1999). *The construction of the self: A developmental perspective.* New York: Guilford.

Hartley, H., & Tiefer, L. (2003, Spring/Summer). Taking a biological turn: The push for a "female Viagra" and the push for medicalization of women's sexual problems. *Women's Studies Quarterly, 31,* pp. 42–54.

Hartmann, K. E. et al. (2004). Quality of life and sexual function after hysterectomy in women with preoperative pain and depression. *Obstetrics & Gynecology, 104,* 701–709.

Hartup, W. W. (1993). Adolescents and their friends. In B. Laursen (Ed.), *New directions in child development.* No. 60, *Close friendships in adolescence* (pp. 3–22). San Francisco: Jossey-Bass.

Harville, M. L., & Rienzi, B. M. (2000). Equal worth and gracious submission: Judeo-Christian attitudes toward employed women. *Psychology of Women Quarterly, 24,* 145–147.

Harway, M. (2001). Mentoring and feminist mentoring. In J. Worell (Ed.), *Encyclopedia of women and gender* (pp. 743–748). San Diego: Academic Press.

Hasebe, Y., Nucci, L., & Nucci, M. S. (2004). Parental control of the personal domain and adolescent symptoms of psychopathology: A cross-national study in the United States and Japan. *Child Development, 75,* 815–828.

Haskell, K. (2003, November 30). When grandparents step into the child care gap, money can be scarce. *New York Times,* p. YT 29.

Haskell, M. (1998, February 8). Where the old boy always get the girl. *New York Times,* p. AR11.

Haskell, M., & Harmetz, A. (1998, March-April). Star power. *Modern Maturity, 41,* 32–40.

Hass, N. (2002, June 16). Hey dads, thanks for the love and support (and the credit card). *New York Times,* pp. ST1, SP2.

Hassan, M. A. M., & Killick, S. R. (2004). Negative lifestyle is associated with a significant reduction in fecundity. *Fertility and Sterility, 81,* pp. 384–392.

Hatala, M. N., & Prehodka, J. (1996). Content analysis of gay male and lesbian personal advertisements. *Psychological Reports, 78,* 371–374.

Hatch, L. R., & Thompson, A. (1992). Family responsibilities and women's retirement. In M. Szinovacz, D. J. Ekerdt, & B. H. Vinick (Eds.), *Families and retirement* (pp. 99–113). Newbury Park, CA: Sage.

Hattery, A. (2001). *Women, work, and family: Balancing and weaving.* Thousand Oaks, CA: Sage.

Hawkins, D. N., & Whiteman, S. D. (2004). Balancing work and family: Problems and solutions for low-income families. In A. C. Crouter and A. Booth (Eds.), *Work-family challenges for low-income parents and their children* (pp. 273–286). Mahwah, NJ: Erlbaum.

Hawkins, J. W., & Aber, C. S. (1993). Women in advertisements in medical journals. *Sex Roles, 28,* 233–244.

Hay, D. F., Payne, A., & Chadwick, A. (2004). Peer relations in childhood. *Journal of Child Psychology and Psychiatry, 45,* 84–108.

Hayden, T., & Kernaghan, C. (2002, July 6). Pennies an hour, and no way up. *New York Times,* p. A27.

Hayes, S. N., Weisman, C. S., & Clark, A. (2003). The Jacobs Institute of Women's Health report on the prevention of heart disease in women: Findings and recommendations from the "Women and heart disease: Putting prevention into primary care" conference. *Women's Health Issues, 13,* 115–121.

Haynie, D. L. (2003). Contexts of risk? Explaining the link between girls' pubertal development and their delinquency involvement. *Social Forces, 82,* 355–397.

Hayt, E. (2002, May 12). Admitting to mixed feelings about motherhood. *New York Times,* pp. ST1, ST2.

He, X. Z., & Baker, D. W. (2004). Body mass index, physical activity, and the risk of decline in overall health and physical functioning in late middle age. *American Journal of Public Health, 94,* 1567–1573.

Headlam, B. (2000, January 20). Barbie PC: Fashion over logic. *New York Times,* p. E4.

Health and wellness for women with disabilities. (2004, Winter). *Health Matters for Women Newsletter.*

Heart attacks' high toll on women. (2002, January 8). *New York Times,* p. D8.

Heatherington, L., et al. (1993). Two investigations of "female modesty" in achievement situations. *Sex Roles, 29,* 739–754.

Heckert, T. M. (2002). Gender differences in anticipated salary: Role of salary estimates for others, job characteristics, career paths, and job inputs. *Sex Roles, 47,* 139–151.

Hedley, M. (1994). The presentation of gendered conflict in popular movies: Affective stereotypes, cultural sentiments, and men's motivation. *Sex Roles, 31,* 721–740.

Hefferman, K. (1999). Lesbians and the internalization of societal standards of weight and appearance. *Journal of Lesbian Studies, 3(4),* 121–127.

Heffner, L. J. (2004). Advanced maternal age—How old is too old? *New England Journal of Medicine, 351,* 1927–1929.

Heilman, M. E. (2001). Description and prescription: How gender stereotypes prevent women's ascent up the organizational ladder. *Journal of Social Issues, 57,* 657–674.

Heilman, M. E., Wallen, A. S., Fuchs, D., & Tamkins, M. M. (2004). Penalties for success: Reactions to women who succeed at male gender-typed tasks. *Journal of Applied Psychology, 89,* 416–427.

Helgeson, V. S. (1994). Relation of agency and communion to well-being: Evidence and potential explanations. *Psychological Bulletin, 116,* 412–428.

Helgeson, V. S. (2002). *The psychology of gender.* Upper Saddle River, NJ: Prentice Hall.

HELP Network (2003). *Guns and domestic violence: A deadly combination.* Chicago: Author.

Helping the patient by helping the caretaker. (2000). *Health after 50: The John Hopkins Medical Letter, 12,* 3.

Helson, R. (1992). Women's difficult times and the rewriting of the life story. *Psychology of Women Quarterly, 16,* 331–347.

Helton, M. R. (2000). Prenatal care. In M. A. Smith & L. A. Shimp (Eds.), *20 common problems in women's health care* (pp. 65–89). New York: McGraw-Hill.

Helwig, A. A. (1998). Gender-role stereotyping: Testing theory with a longitudinal sample. *Sex Roles, 38,* 403–423.

Henderson, T. L. (2005). Grandparent visitation rights: Successful acquisition of court-ordered visitation. *Journal of Family Issues, 26,* 107–137.

Henderson-King, D., & Zhermer, N. (2003). Feminist consciousness among Russians and Americans. *Sex Roles, 48,* 143–155.

Hendrick, S. S. (2001). Intimacy and love. In J. Worell (Ed.), *Encyclopedia of women and gender* (pp. 633–643). San Diego, CA: Academic Press.

Hendy, H. M., et al. (2003). Comparison of six models for violent romantic relationships in college men and women. *Journal of Interpersonal Violence, 18,* 645–665.

Henig, R. M. (2004a, June 6). Sex without estrogen: Remedies for the midlife mind and body. *New York Times,* p. WH12.

Henig, R. M. (2004b, November 30). Sorry. Your eating disorder doesn't meet our criteria. *New York Times,* pp. D1, D9.

Henley, N. M. (1995). Body politics revisited: What do we know today? In P. J. Kalbfleisch & M. J. Cody (Eds.), *Gender, power, and communication in human relationships* (pp. 27–61). Hillsdale, NJ: Erlbaum.

Henley, N. M., Meng, K., O'Brien, D., McCarthy, W. J., & Sockloskie, R. J. (1998). Developing a scale to measure the diversity of feminist attitudes. *Psychology of Women Quarterly, 22,* 317–348.

Henningfield, J. E., Santera, P. B., & Stillman, F. A. (2005). Exploitation by design—could tobacco industry documents guide more effective smoking prevention and cessation in women? *Addiction, 100,* 735–736.

Henningsen, D. D. (2004). Flirting with meaning: An examination of miscommunication in flirting interactions. *Sex Roles, 50,* 481–489.

Henry, A. (2004). *Not my mother's sister. Generational conflict and third-wave feminism.* Bloomington, IN: Indiana University Press.

Henry, J. G. A. (2000). Depression and anxiety. In M. A. Smith & L. A. Shimp (Eds.), *20 common problems in women's health care* (pp. 263–301). New York: McGraw-Hill.

Herbert, S. E., & Bachanas, P. (2002). HIV/AIDS. In S. G. Kornstein, & A. H. Clayton (Eds.), *Women's mental health: A comprehensive textbook* (pp. 453–466). New York: Guilford.

Herdt, G. H., & Davidson, J. (1988). The Sambia "turnim-man": Sociocultural and clinical aspects of gender formation in male pseudohermaphrodites with 5-alpha-reductase deficiency in Papua New Guinea. *Archives of Sexual Behavior, 17,* 33–56.

Herek, G. M. (2000, Summer). Sexual prejudice and gender: Do heterosexuals' attitudes toward lesbians and gay men differ? *Journal of Social Issues, 56,* p. 251.

Herek, G. M., Cogan, S. C., & Gillis, J. R. (2002). Victim experiences in hate crimes based on sexual orientation. *Journal of Social Issues, 58,* 319–339.

Herek, G. M., et al. (1998). Correlates of internalized homophobia in a community sample of lesbians and gay men. *Journal of the Gay and Lesbian Medical Association, 2,* 17–25.

Herman, K., & West, S. A. (2003, Fall/Winter). Ensnared children in modern slavery. *AAUW Outlook*, pp. 16–19, 32.

Herman-Giddens, M. E., et al. (1997). Secondary sexual characteristics and menses in young girls seen in office practice: A study from the pediatric research in office settings network. *Pediatrics, 99*, 505–512.

Herman-Giddens, M. E., Kaplowitz, P. B., & Wasserman, R. (2004). Navigating the recent articles on girls' puberty in pediatrics: What do we know and where do we go from here? *Pediatrics, 113*, pp. 911–917.

Hertz, R., & Ferguson, F. I. (1998). Only one pair of hands: Ways that single mothers stretch work and family resources. *Community, Work, & Family, 1*, 13–37.

Heterosexual transmission of HIV—29 states, 1999–2002. (2004). *Morbidity and Mortality Weekly Report, 53*, 125–129.

Hetherington, E. M. (2004, July). *Lessons learned and unlearned in thirty five years of studying families*. Paper presented at the meeting of the American Psychological Association, Honolulu.

Hetherington, E. M., & Kelly, J. (2002). *For better or for worse: Divorce reconsidered*. New York: Norton.

Hewlett, S. (2002). *Creating a life: Professional women and the quest for children*. New York: Talk Miramax Books.

Heyl, A. R. (2004). The transition from career to retirement: Focus on well-being and financial considerations. *Journal of the American Medical Women's Association, 59*, 235–237.

Heyl, A. R. (2005). Climbing the ladder: Making the most of mentoring. *Journal of the American Medical Women's Association, 60*, 11–14.

Heywood, L. (1999, January 8). Despite the positive rhetoric about women's sports, female athletes face a culture of sexual harassment. *Chronicle of Higher Education*, pp. B4–B5.

Hickman, L. J., Jaycox, L. H., & Aronoff, J. (2004). Dating violence among adolescents. Prevalence, gender distribution, and prevention program effectiveness. *Trauma, Violence, & Abuse, 5*, 123–142.

Higginbotham, E., & Weber, L. (1996). Moving up with kin and community: Upward social mobility for Black and White women. In E. N. Chow, D. Wilkinson, & M. B. Zinn (Eds.), *Race, class, & gender: Common bonds, different voices* (pp. 125–148). Thousand Oaks, CA: Sage.

High percentage of inmates say they were abused as children. (1999, April 12). *New York Times*, p. A19.

Hill, E. J., Märtinson, V., & Ferris, M. (2004). New-concept part-time employment as a work-family adaptive strategy for women professionals with small children. *Family Relations, 53*, 282–292.

Hill, S. Y. (2000). Addictive disorders. In M. B. Goldman & M. C. Hatch (Eds.), *Women & health* (pp. 1042–1053). San Diego: Academic Press.

Hillis, S. D., et al. (2004). The association between adverse childhood experiences and adolescent pregnancy, long-term psychosocial consequences, and fetal death. *Pediatrics, 113*, 320–327.

Hillman, J. L., & Stricker, G. (1994). A linkage of knowledge and attitudes toward elderly sexuality: Not necessarily a uniform relationship. *Gerontologist, 34*, 256–260.

Hilton, N. Z., & Harris, G. T. (2005). Predicting wife assault. A critical review and implications for policy and practice. *Trauma, Violence, & Abuse, 6*, 3–23.

Hinden, S. (2001, September). Raw deal for women? *AARP*, pp. 18–20.

Hines, D. A., & Saudino, K. J. (2002). Intergenerational transmission of intimate partner violence. A behavioral genetic perspective. *Trauma, Violence, & Abuse, 3*, 210–225.

Hines, M. (2004a). Androgen, estrogen, and gender: Contributions of the early hormone environment to gender-related behavior. In A. H. Eagly, A. E. Beall, & R. J. Sternberg (Eds.), *The psychology of gender* (pp. 9–37). New York: Guilford.

Hines, M. (2004b). *Brain gender*. New York: Oxford University Press.

Hines, M., et al. (2002). Testosterone during pregnancy and gender role behavior of preschool children: A longitudinal population study. *Child Development, 73*, 1678–1687.

Hing, L. S. S., Bobocel, D. R., & Zanna, M. P. (2002). Meritocracy and opposition to affirmative action: Making concessions in the face of discrimination. *Journal of Personality and Social Psychology, 83*, 493–509.

Hirshbein, L. D. (2003). Biology and mental illness: A historical perspective. *Journal of the American Medical Women's Association, 58*, 89–94.

Ho, C. K. (1990). An analysis of domestic violence in Asian-American communities: A multicultural approach to counseling. In L. S. Brown & M. P. P. Root (Eds.), *Diversity and complexity in feminist therapy* (pp. 129–150). New York: Haworth Press.

Hoban, P. (2002, October 12). Single girls: Sex but still no respect. *New York Times*, pp. A19, A21.

Hochman, A. (2004, June). Don't panic. *Health*, pp. 99–103.

Hofferth, S. L., & Reid, L. (2002). Early childbearing and children's achievement and behavior over time. *Perspectives on Sexual and Reproductive Health, 34*, 41–49.

Hofferth, S. L., & Sandberg, J. F. (2001). How American children spend their time. *Journal of Marriage and Family, 63*, 295–308.

Hoffman, E. (2002, June). When couples clam up. *AARP Bulletin*, pp. 24–25.

Hoffman, L. W., & Youngblade, L. M. (2001, April). *Mothers' employment: Effects on families and children.* Paper presented at the meeting of the Society for Research in Child Development, Minneapolis, MN.

Hoffmann, M. L., Powlishta, K. K., & White, K. J. (2004). An examination of gender differences in adolescent adjustment: The effect of competence on gender role differences in symptoms of psychopathology. *Sex Roles, 50*, 795–810.

Hoffnung, M. (2004). Wanting it all: Career, marriage, and motherhood during college-educated women's 20s. *Sex Roles, 50*, 711–723.

Hogan, J. D., & Sexton, V. S. (1991). Women and the American Psychological Association. *Psychology of Women Quarterly, 15*, 623–634.

Hoge, W. (2002, December 7). Britain announces proposal for same-sex partnerships. *New York Times*, p. A8.

Hoggard, L. (2005, January 9). Why we're all beautiful now. *Observer (London)*, p. 4.

Hoglund, W. L., & Leadbeater, B. J. (2004). The effects of family, school, and classroom ecologies on changes in children's social competence and emotional and behavioral problems in first grade. *Developmental Psychology, 40*, 533–544.

Hogue, M., & Yoder, J. D. (2003). The role of status in producing depressed entitlement in women's and men's pay allocations. *Psychology of Women Quarterly, 27*, 330–337.

Holahan, C. K., & Sears, R. R. (1995). *The gifted group in later maturity.* Stanford, CA: Stanford University Press.

Holcomb, B. (1998). *Not guilty: The good news about working mothers.* New York: Scribner.

Holcomb, L. P., & Giesen, C. B. (1995). Coping with challenges: College experiences of older women and women with disabilities. In J. C. Chrisler & A. H. Hemstreet (Eds.), *Variations on a theme: Diversity and the psychology of women*. Albany, NY: SUNY.

Holland, A., & Andre, T. (1992). College students' attitudes toward women: A three-dimensional approach. *College Student Journal, 26*, 253–259.

Hollenshead, C. S., Wenzel, S. A., Lazarus, B. B., & Nair, I. (1996). The graduate experience in the sciences and engineering: Rethinking a gendered institution. In D. S. Davis, A. B. Ginorio, C. S. Hollenshead, B. B. Lazarus, & P. M. Raymond (Eds.), *The equity equation* (pp. 122–162). San Francisco: Jossey-Bass.

Hollingsworth, M. A., Tomlinson, M. J., & Fassinger, R. E. (1997, August). *Working it out: Career development among prominent lesbian women.* Paper presented at the meeting of the American Psychological Association, Chicago.

Holmes, M. D., & Kroenke, C. H. (2004, February). Beyond treatment: Lifestyle choices after breast cancer to enhance quality of life and survival. *Women's Health Issues, 14*, 11–13.

Holmes, S. E., & Cahill, S. (2004). School experiences of gay, lesbian, bisexual and transgender youth. *Journal of Gay & Lesbian Issues in Education, 1*, 53–66.

Holmes-Lonergan, H. A. (2003). Preschool children's collaborative problem-solving interactions: The role of gender, pair type, and task. *Sex Roles, 48*, 505–517.

Holroyd, S. (2002). Aging and elderly women. In S. G. Kornstein & A. H. Clayton (Eds.), *Women's mental health: A comprehensive textbook* (pp. 584–593). New York: Guilford.

Holroyd-Leduc, J. M., & Straus, S. E. (2004). Management of urinary incontinence in women. *Journal of the American Medical Association, 291*, 986–999.

Hong, S., Friedman, J., & Alt, S. (2003). Modifiable risk factors for the primary prevention of heart disease in women. *Journal of the American Medical Women's Association, 58*, 278–284.

Honig, M. (1996). Retirement expectations: Differences by race, ethnicity, and gender. *Gerontologist, 36*, 373–382.

Hook, J. L. (2004). Reconsidering the division of household labor: Incorporating volunteer work and informal support. *Journal of Marriage and Family, 66*, 101–117.

hooks, b. (1990). Feminism: A transformational politic. In D. L. Rhode (Ed.), *Theoretical perspectives in sexual difference* (pp. 185–193). New Haven, CT: Yale University Press.

Hopkins, A. B. (1996). *So ordered: Making partner the hard way.* Amherst: University of Massachusetts Press.

Horgan, T. G., Schmid Mast, M., Hall, J. A., & Carter, J. D. (2004). Gender differences in memory for the appearance of others. *Journal of Personality and Social Psychology Bulletin, 30,* 185–196.

Hornbacher, M. (1998). *Wasted: A memoir of anorexia and bulimia.* New York: Harper Perennial.

Hornblow, D. (2002, August 9). Cavalcade of white guys. *Hartford Courant,* pp. D1, D4.

Horner, M. S. (1972). Toward an understanding of achievement-related conflicts in women. *Journal of Social Issues, 28,* 157–176.

Horney, K. (1926/1974). The flight from womanhood: The masculinity-complex in women as viewed by men and women. In J. Strouse (Ed.), *Women and analysis: Dialogues on psychoanalytic views of femininity* (pp. 171–186). New York: Viking.

Horn-Ross, P. L., et al. (2004). Patterns of alcohol consumption and breast cancer risk in the California teachers study cohort. *Cancer Epidemiology Biomarkers & Prevention, 13,* 405–411.

Hourani, L. L., Yuan, H., & Bray, R. M. (2004). Psychosocial and lifestyle correlates of premenstrual symptoms among military women. *Journal of Women's Health, 13,* 812–821.

Howard, J. A., & Hollander, J. (1997). *Gendered situations, gendered selves: A gender lens on social psychology.* Thousand Oaks, CA: Sage.

Howes, C., & Aikins, J. W. (2002). Peer relations in the transition to adolescence. In R. V. Kail & H. W. Reese (Eds.), *Advances in child development and behavior,* Vol. 29 (pp. 195–230). San Diego: Academic Press.

How healthy are American women? (2003). *Women's Health in Primary Care, 6,* 452.

Hoyert, D. L., Kung, H-C., & Smith, B. L. (2005). *Deaths: Preliminary data for 2003.* National Vital Statitistics Reports, 53, No. 15.

Hsu, L. K. G. (2004). Eating disorders: Practical interventions. *Journal of the American Medical Women's Association, 59,* 113–124.

Hu, F. B., et al. (2004). Adiposity as compared with physical activity in predicting mortality among women. *New England Journal of Medicine, 351,* 2694–2703.

Hu, F. B., et al. (2002). Fish and omega-3 fatty acid intake and risk of coronary heart disease in women. *Journal of the American Medical Association, 287,* 1815–1821.

Hubbs-Tait, L. (1989). Coping patterns of aging women: A developmental perspective. In J. D. Garner & S. O. Mercer (Eds.), *Women as they age: Challenge, opportunity, and triumph,* (pp. 95–117). Binghamton, NY: Haworth.

Hudson, V. M., & denBoer, A. M. (2004). *Bare branches: Security implications of Asia's surplus male population.* Cambridge, MA: MIT Press.

Huffman, T., Chang, K., Rausch, P., & Schaffer, N. (1994). Gender differences and factors related to the disposition toward cohabitation. *Family Therapy, 21,* 171–184.

Hughes, I. A. (2004). Female development—All by default? *New England Journal of Medicine, 351,* 748–750.

Hughes, S. L., et al. (2004). Impact of the fit and strong intervention on older adults with osteoarthritis. *Gerontologist, 44,* 217–228.

Hull, N. E. H., & Hoffer, P. C. (2001, November 2). Teaching above the fray: A multidisciplinary approach to "Roe v. Wade." *Chronicle of High Education,* pp. B13–15.

Hulley, S. B., & Grady, D. (2004). The WHI estrogen-alone trial—Do things look any better? *Journal of the American Medical Association, 291,* 1769–1771.

Hulme, P. A., & Agrawal, S. (2004). Patterns of childhood sexual abuse characteristics and their relationships to other childhood abuse and adult health. *Journal of Interpersonal Violence, 19,* 389–405.

Hungerford, T. L. (2001). The economic consequences of widowhood on elderly women in the United States and Germany. *Gerontologist, 41,* 103–110.

Hurd, L. C. (2000). Older women's body image and embodied experience: An exploration. *Journal of Women & Aging, 12,* 77–97.

Hurley, D. (2005, April 19). Divorce rate: It's not as high as you think. *New York Times,* p. D7.

Hurme, S. B. (2002). *Perspectives on elder abuse.* Washington, DC: AARP.

Husseini, R. (2003, Fall). Murder as misdemeanor. *Ms.,* pp. 36–37.

Huston, A. C., & Wright, J. C. (1998). Mass media and children's development. In W. Damon (Series Ed.), I. E. Sigel, & K. A. Renninger (Vol. Eds.), *Handbook of child psychology,* Vol. 4, *Child psychology in practice,* 5th ed. (pp. 999–1058). New York: Wiley.

Hutchinson, M. K., et al. (2003, August). The role of mother-daughter sexual risk communication in reducing sexual risk behaviors among urban adolescent females: A prospective study. *Journal of Adolescent Health, 33,* 98–107.

Hutson-Comeaux, S. L., Westerhaus, E. K., & Snyder, R. (2002, June). *Personality, characteristics of women in male- and female-dominated occupations.* Poster presented at the meeting of the American Psychological Society, New Orleans.

Huyck, M. H. (1995). Marriage and close relationships of the marital kind. In R. Blieszner & V. H. Bedford (Eds.), *Handbook of aging and the family* (pp. 181–200). Westport, CT: Greenwood.

Hwang, K. (1997). Living with a disability: A woman's perspective. In M. L. Sipski & C. J. Alexander (Eds.), *Sexual function in people with disability and chronic illness: A health practitioner's guide* (pp. 119–130). Gaithersburg, MD: Aspen Publishers.

Hyde, J. S. (2003). Issues for women in middle age. In L. Slater, J. H. Daniel, & A. E. Banks (Eds.), *The complete guide to mental health for women* (pp. 48–50). Boston: Beacon Press.

Hyde, J. S., DeLamater, J. D., & Durik, A. M. (2001). Sexuality and the dual-earner couple. Part II: Beyond the baby years. *The Journal of Sex Research, 38,* 10–23.

Hyde, J. S., & Durik, A. M. (2000). Gender differences in erotic plasticity—Evolutionary or sociocultural forces? Comment on Baumeister (2000). *Psychological Bulletin, 126,* 375–379.

Hyde, J. S., Fennema, E., & Lamon, S. J. (1990). Gender differences in mathematics performance: A meta-analysis. *Psychological Bulletin, 107,* 139–155.

Hyde, J. S., & Jaffee, S. R. (2000, Summer). Becoming a heterosexual adult: The experiences of young women. *Journal of Social Issues, 56,* 283.

Hyde, J. S., Klein, M. H., Essex, M. J., & Clark, R. (1995). Maternity leave and women's mental health. *Psychology of Women Quarterly, 19,* 257–285.

Hyde, J. S., & Kling, K. C. (2001). Women, motivation, and achievement. *Psychology of Women Quarterly, 25,* 364–378.

Hyde, J. S., & Linn, M. C. (1988). Gender differences in verbal ability: A meta-analysis. *Psychological Bulletin, 104,* 53–69.

Hyde, J. S., & Mezulis, A. H. (2001). Gender difference research: Issues and outcome. In J. Worell (Ed.), *Encyclopedia of women and gender* (pp. 551–559). San Diego: Academic Press.

Hymowitz, K. S. (2002, Summer). The end of her story. *City Journal, 12(3),* 52–63.

Ibrahim, H. (Fall 2004/Winter 2005). Human rights, education, and women in northern Nigeria. *On Campus with Women, 34,* 7–9.

Iervolino, A. C., Hines, M., Golombok, S. E., Rust, J., & Plomin, R. (2005). Genetic and environmental influences on sex-typed behavior during the preschool years. *Child Development, 76,* 826–840.

Iglehart, J. K. (2002). Medicare's declining payments to physicians. *New England Journal of Medicine, 346,* 1924–1930.

Iglehart, J. K. (2003). The dilemma of Medicaid. *New England Journal of Medicine, 348,* 2140–2148.

Illinois Department on Aging. (2000). *Elder abuse and neglect program.* Springfield, IL: Author.

Indvik, J. (2004). Women and leadership. In P. G. Northouse (Ed.), *Leadership: Theory and practice* (pp. 265–299). Thousand Oaks, CA: Sage Publications.

Infertility: A guy thing. (2002, March 25). *Newsweek,* pp. 60–61.

Institute for Women's Policy Research. (2005, March). *Who are Social Security beneficiaries?* Washington, DC: Author.

International Labour Organization (2004). *Helping hands or shackled lives? Understanding child domestic labour and responses to it.* Geneva: Author.

Inter-Parlimentary Union. (2005). *Women in national parliaments.* Retrieved from http://www.ipu.org/wmn-eclassif.htm.

Ireland, M. L., & Nattiv, A. (Eds.) (2003). *The female athlete.* Philadelphia: W. B. Saunders.

Irvine, M. (2005, May 31). Anorexics seeking "skinny solidarity." *Peoria Journal Star,* pp. A1, A7.

Israel, B. (2002). *Bachelor girl: The secret history of single women in the twentieth century.* New York: William Morrow.

Iwamasa, G. Y., Sorocco, K. H., & Koonce, D. A. (2002). Ethnicity and clinical psychology. A content analysis of the literature. *Clinical Psychology Review, 22,* 931–944.

Jack, D. C. (2003). The anger of hope and the anger of despair: How anger relates to women's depression. In J. M. Stoppard & L. M. McMullen (Eds.), *Situating sadness: Women and depression in social context* (pp. 62–87). New York: New York University Press.

Jackson, L. A., & Ervin, K. S. (1991). The frequency and portrayal of Black females in fashion advertisements. *Journal of Black Psychology, 18,* 67–70.

Jackson, L. A., Ervin, K. S., Gardner, P. D., & Schmitt, N. (2001). Gender and the Internet: Women communicating and men searching. *Sex Roles, 44,* 363–379.

Jackson, L. A., Fleury, R. E., & Lewandowski, D. A. (1996). Feminism: Definitions, support, and correlates of support among female and male college students. *Sex Roles, 34,* 687–693.

Jackson, L. A., Gardner, P. D., Sullivan, L. A. (1992). Explaining gender differences in self-pay expectations: Social comparison standards and perceptions of fair pay. *Journal of Applied Psychology, 77,* 651–661.

Jackson, L. C., & Greene, B. (Eds.). (2000). *Psychotherapy with African American women: Innovations in psychodynamic perspectives and practice.* New York: Gullford.

Jackson, M. (2002, July 2). Companies adding benefits for care of the elderly. *New York Times,* p. BU8.

Jackson, R. A., et al. (2004). Perinatal outcomes in singletons following in vitro fertilization: A meta-analysis. *Obstetrics & Gynecology, 103,* 551–563.

Jackson, Y., & Warren, J. S. (2000). Appraisal, social support, and life events: Predicting outcome behavior in school-age children. *Child Development, 71,* 1441–1457.

Jacobi, C., et al. (2004). Coming to terms with risk factors for eating disorders: Application of risk terminology and suggestions for a general taxonomy. *Psychological Bulletin, 130,* 19–65.

Jacobs, J. A., & Gerson, K. (2001). Overworked individuals or overworked families?: Explaining trends in work, leisure, and family time. *Work and Occupations, 28,* 40.

Jacobs, J. E., Lanza, S., Osgood, D. W., Eccles, J. S., & Wigfield, A. (2002). Changes in children's self-competence and values: Gender and domain differences across grades one through twelve. *Child Development, 73,* 509–527.

Jacobs, R. H. (1997). *Be an outrageous older woman.* New York: HarperCollins.

Jacobsson, B., Ladfors, L., & Milsom, I. (2004). Advanced maternal age and adverse perinatal outcome. *Obstetrics & Gynecology, 104,* 727–733.

Jacobson, J. (2001, June 8). Female coaches lag in pay and opportunities to oversee men's teams. *Chronicle of Higher Education,* p. A38.

Jacoby, S. (2002, May). Are Medicare docs taking off? *AARP Bulletin Online.*

Jadva, V., et al. (2003). Surrogacy: the experiences of surrogate mothers. *Human Reproduction, 18,* 2196–2204.

Jaffe, E. (2004, January). Steele and Markus on "stereotype threat and black college students." *APS Observer,* pp. 22, 29.

Jaffe, M. L. (1998). *Adolescence.* New York: Wiley.

Jaffee, S., & Hyde, J. S. (2000). Gender differences in moral orientation: A meta-analysis. *Psychological Bulletin, 126,* 703–726.

Janofsky, M., & Schemo, D. J. (2003, March 16). The cadet life for many women: Sexual ordeals and internal rage. *New York Times,* pp. YT1, YT9.

Janssen, I., Craig, W. M., Boyce, W. F., & Pickett, W. (2004). Association between overweight and obesity with bullying behaviors in school-aged children. *Pediatrics, 113,* 1187–1194.

Jarrell, A. (2000, April 3). The face of teenage sex grows younger. *New York Times,* pp. B1, B8.

Jarviluoma, H., Moisala, P., & Vilkko, A. (2003). *Gender and qualitative methods.* Thousand Oaks, CA: Sage.

Jemal, A., et al. (2004). Annual report to the nation on the status of cancer, 1975–2001 with a special feature regarding survival. *Cancer, 101,* 3–27.

Jenkins, C. L. (2003). Widows and divorcees in later life. *Journal of Women & Aging, 15,* 1–6.

Jenkins, S. R. (2000). Introduction to the special issue: Defining gender, relationships, and power. *Sex Roles, 42,* 467–493.

Jernigan, D. H., Ostroff, J., Ross, C., & O'Hara, J. A. (2004). Sex differences in adolescent exposure to alcohol advertising in magazines. *Archives of Pediatrics & Adolescent Medicine, 158,* 629–634.

Jersild, D. (2002, May 31). Alcohol in the vulnerable lives of college women. *Chronicle of Higher Education,* pp. B10, B11.

Jessell, J. C., & Beymer, L. (1992). The effects of job title vs. job description on occupational sex typing. *Sex Roles, 27,* 73–83.

Jeter, R. F. (2000). Intimate relationships. In M. Biaggio & M. Hersen (Eds.), *Issues in the psychology of women* (pp. 173–198). New York: Kluwer.

Jha, A. K., et al. (2003). Differences in medical care and disease outcomes among Black and White women with heart disease. *Circulation, 110,* 1089–1094.

Joffe, C. (2003). Roe v. Wade at 30: What are the prospects for abortion prevention? *Perspectives on Sexual and Reproductive Health, 35,* 29–33.

John, R., Blanchard, P. H., & Hennessy, C. H. (2001). In J. M. Coyle (Ed.), *Handbook on women and aging* (pp. 290–325). Westport, CT: Praeger.

Johns, M., Schmader, T., & Martens, A. (2005). Knowing is half the battle: Teaching stereotype threat as a means of improving women's math performance. *Psychological Science, 16,* 175–179.

Johnson, A. G. (1997). *The gender knot: Unraveling our patriarchal legacy.* Philadelphia: Temple University Press.

Johnson, B. E., Kuck, D. L., & Schander, P. R. (1997). Rape myth acceptance and sociodemographic characteristics: A multidimensional analysis. *Sex Roles, 36,* 693–707.

Johnson, C. L. (1994). Differential expectations and realities: Race, socioeconomic status, and health of the oldest old. *International Journal of Aging and Human Development, 38,* 13–27.

Johnson, D. (2002, March 25). Until dust do us part. *Newsweek,* p. 41.

Johnson, D., et al. (2003). Studying the effects of early child care experiences on the development of children of color in the United States: Toward a more inclusive research agenda. *Child Development, 74,* 1227–1244.

Johnson, D., & Piore, A. (2004, October 18). At home in two worlds. *Newsweek,* pp. 53–54.

Johnson, D., & Rust, C. (2005, January 17). Who's babysitting the kids? A strange turn in the Andrea Yates saga. *Newsweek,* p. 37.

Johnson, D., & Scelfo, J. (2003, December 15). Sex, love and nursing homes. *Newsweek,* pp 54–55.

Johnson, D. R., & Scheuble, L. K. (1995). Women's marital naming in two generations: A national study. *Journal of Marriage and the Family, 57,* 724–732.

Johnson, L. A. (2004, October 14). Study links growth, breast cancer risk. *New York Times,* p. A3.

Johnson, L. A. (2005, April 25). Girls using steroids to get "toned" look. *Peoria Journal Star,* pp. A1, A7.

Johnson, M. A. (2004). Nutrition and aging—Practical advice for healthy eating. *Journal of the American Medical Women's Association, 59,* 262–269.

Johnson, S. M., & O'Connor, E. (2002). *The gay baby boom: The psychology of gay parenthood.* New York: New York University Press.

Johnson, W., McGue, M., Krueger, R. F., & Bouchard Jr., T. J. (2004). Marriage and personality: A genetic analysis. *Journal of Personality and Social Psychology, 86,* 285–294.

Johnston, D. & Swanson, D. (2003a). Invisible mothers: A content analysis of motherhood ideologies and myths in magazines. *Sex Roles, 49,* 21–33.

Johnston, D., & Swanson, D. (2003b). Undermining mothers: A content analysis of the representations of mothers in magazines. *Mass Communication and Society, 6,* 243–265.

Johnston, L. D., O'Malley, P. M., Bachman, J. G., & Schulenberg, J. E. (2005). *Monitoring the future national results on adolescent drug use: Overview of key findings, 2004.* (NIH Publication No. 05-5726.) Bethesda, MD: National Institute on Drug Abuse.

Jones, B. E. (2001). Is having the luck of growing old in the gay, lesbian, bisexual, transgender community good or bad luck? *Journal of Gay & Lesbian Social Services, 13,* 13–14.

Jones, C., & Shorter-Gooden, K. (2003). *Shifting: The double lives of Black women in America.* New York: Harper Collins

Jones, C. J., & Meredith, W. (2000). Developmental paths of psychological health from early adolescence to later adulthood. *Psychology and Aging, 15,* 351–360.

Jones, D. C. (2004). Body image among adolescent girls and boys: A longitudinal study. *Developmental Psychology, 40,* 823–835.

Jones, D. J., O'Connel, C., Gound, M., Heller, L., & Forehand, R. (2004). Predictors of self-reported physical symptoms in low income, inner-city African American women: The role of optimism, depressive symptoms, and chronic illness. *Psychology of Women Quarterly, 28,* 112–121.

Jones, M. (2003, March 16). The weaker sex. *New York Times Magazine,* p. 56.

Jones, S. M., & Dindia, K. (2004). A meta-analytic perspective on sex equity in the classroom. *Review of Educational Research, 74,* 443–471.

Jordan, J. V. (Ed.). (1997). *Women's growth in diversity: More writings from the Stone Center.* New York: Guilford.

Jordan, J. V., Banks, A. E., & Walker, M. (2003). Growth in connection: A relational-cultural model of growth. In L. Slater, J. H. Daniel, & A. E. Banks (Eds.), *The complete guide to mental health for women* (pp. 92–99). Boston: Beacon Press.

Josselson, R. (1994). Identity and relatedness in the life cycle. In H. A. Bosma, T. L. G. Graafsma, H. D. Groterant, & D. J. de Levita (Eds.), *Identity and development: An interdisciplinary approach* (pp. 81–102). Thousand Oaks, CA: Sage.

Josselson, R. (1996). *Revising herself: The story of women's identity from college to midlife.* New York: Oxford University Press.

Jovanovic, J., & Dreves, C. (1997, April). *Sex differences in students competency perceptions in science: Do classroom interactions play a role?* Paper presented at the meeting of the Society for Research in Child Development, Washington, DC.

Kahn, A. S. (2004). 2003 Carolyn Sherif Award address: What college women do and do not experience as rape. *Psychology of Women Quarterly, 28,* 9–15.

Kahn, A. S., et al. (2003). Calling it rape: Differences in experiences of women who do or do not label their sexual assault as rape. *Psychology of Women Quarterly, 27,* 233–242.

Kahn, J. (2004, May 30). The most populous nation faces a population crisis. *New York Times,* pp. WK1, WK5.

Kainen, A. (1995). Only your regrets. In B. Benatovich (Ed.), *What we know so far: Wisdom among women.* New York: St. Martin's Griffin.

Kaiser Family Foundation. (2001). *Inside-OUT: A report on the experiences of lesbians, gays, and bisexuals in America and the public's views on issues related to sexual orientation.* Menlo Park, CA: Author.

Kalb, C. (2004a, August 2). Fertility and the freezer. *Newsweek,* p. 52.

Kalb, C. (2004b, May 24). A shocking diagnosis. *Newsweek,* p. 57.

Kalb, C., & Springen, K. (2004, May 10). Putting it all together. *Newsweek,* pp. 55–56, 58, 61.

Kalev, H. D. (2004). Cultural rights or human rights: The case of female genital mutilation. *Sex Roles, 51,* 339–348.

Kalil, A., & Kunz, J. (2002). Teenage childbearing, marital status, and depressive symptoms in later life. *Child Development, 73,* 1748–1760.

Kalof, L., Eby, K. K., Matheson, J. L., & Kroska, R. J. (2001). The influence of race and gender on student self-reports of sexual harassment by college professors. *Gender & Society, 15,* 282–302.

Kamerman, S. B. (2000a). From maternity to parental leave policies: Women's health, employment, and child and family well-being. *Journal of the American Medical Women's Association, 55,* 96–99.

Kamerman, S. B. (2000b). Parental leave policies: An essential ingredient in early childhood education and care policies. *Social Policy Report, 14(2),* 1–15.

Kane, E. W. (2000). Racial and ethnic variations in gender-related attitudes. *Annual Review of Sociology, 26,* 419–439.

Kantrowitz, B. (2005, January 31). Sex and science. *Newsweek,* pp. 36–38.

Kaplan, G. A. (1992). Health and aging in the Alameda County study. In K. W. Schaie, D. Balzer, & J. S. House (Eds.), *Aging health behaviors and health outcomes* (pp. 69–88). Hillsdale, NJ: Erlbaum.

Karjane, H. K., Fisher, B. S., & Cullen, F. T. (2002). *Campus sexual assault: How American's institutions of higher education respond* Newton, MA: Education Development Center, Inc.

Karniol, R., Gabay, R., Ochion, Y., & Harari, Y. (1998). Is gender or gender-role orientation a better predictor of empathy in adolescence? *Sex Roles, 39,* 45–59.

Karraker, K. H., Vogel, D. A., & Lake, M. A. (1995). Parents' gender-stereotyped perceptions of newborns: The eye of the beholder revisited. *Sex Roles, 33,* 687–701.

Karrass, J., Braungart-Rieker, J. M., Mullins, J., & Lefever, J. B. (2002). Processes in language acquisition: The roles of gender, attention, and maternal encouragement of attention over time. *Journal of Child Language, 29,* 519–543.

Kasen, S., Cohen, P., Chen, H., & Castille, D. (2003). Depression in adult women: Age changes and cohort effects. *American Journal of Public Health, 93,* 2061–2066.

Kaslow, N. J., et al. (2004). Person factors associated with suicidal behavior among African American women and men. *Cultural Diversity and Ethnic Minority Psychology, 10,* 5–22.

Kates, E. (1996). Educational pathways out of poverty: Responding to the realities of women's lives. *American Journal of Orthopsychiatry, 66,* 548–556.

Katz, P. A. (1987). Variations in family constellation: Effects on gender schemata. In L. S. Liben & M. L. Signorella (Eds.), *Children's gender schemata: New directions for child development,* Vol. 38 (pp. 39–56). San Francisco: Jossey-Bass.

Katz, P. A. (1996). Raising feminists. *Psychology of Women Quarterly, 20,* 323–340.

Katz, P. A., & Walsh, V., (1991). Modification of children's gender-stereotyped behavior. *Child Development, 62,* 338–351.

Katz, S. J., Kabeto, M., & Langa, K. M. (2000). Gender disparities in the receipt of home care for elderly people with disability in the United States. *Journal of the American Medical Association, 284,* 3022–3027.

Katzenstein, L. (1999, June 13). Beyond the horror stories, good news about managed care. *New York Times,* p. WH6.

Kaufmann, J. A. (1996). Teenage parents and their offspring. Women and mental health. *Annals of the New York Academy of Sciences, 789,* 17–30.

Keel, P. K. (2005). *Eating disorders.* Upper Saddle River, NJ: Pearson Prentice Hall.

Keller, J. (2002). Blatant stereotype threat and women's math performance: Self-handicapping as a strategic means to cope with obtrusive negative performance expectations. *Sex Roles, 47,* 193–198.

Keller, J., & Dauenheimer, D. (2003). Stereotype threat in the classroom: Dejection mediates the disrupting threat effect on women's math performance. *Personality and Social Psychology Bulletin, 29,* 371–381.

Kelley, T. (2000, February 13). On campuses, warnings about violence in relationships. *New York Times,* p. L40.

Kelley-Moore, J. A., & Ferraro, K. F. (2004). The Black/White disability gap: Persistent inequality in later life? *Journals of Gerontology, 59,* S34–S43.

Kelly, A. M., et al. (2004). High body satisfaction in adolescent girls: Association with demographic, socio-environmental, personal, and behavioral factors. *Journal of Adolescent Health, 34,* 129.

Kendall, K. (1998). "When a woman loves a woman" in Lesotho: Love, sex, and the (Western) construction of homophobia. In S. O. Murray & W. Roscoe (Eds.), *Boy-wives and female-husbands: Studies of African homo-sexualities* (pp. 223–243). New York: St. Martin's.

Kendall-Tackett, K., Marshall, R., & Ness, K. (2003). Chronic pain syndromes and violence against women. *Women & Therapy, 26,* 45–56.

Kendler, K. S., Myers, J., & Prescott, C. A. (2005). Sex differences in the relationship between social support and risk for major depression: A longitudinal study of opposite-sex twin pairs. *American Journal of Psychiatry, 162,* 250–256.

Kennedy, D. (2002, June 2). An impatient sisterhood. *New York Times,* pp. AR9, AR22.

Kennedy, M. (2004, Spring). Cheaper than a cow. *Ms.,* pp. 50–53.

Kennedy, M. A., & Gorzalka, B. B. (2002). Asian and non-Asian attitudes toward rape, sexual harassment, and sexuality. *Sex Roles, 46,* 227–238.

Kennell, J. H., Klaus, M. H., McGrath, S., Robertson, S., & Hinkley, C. (1991). Continuous emotional support during labor in a U.S. hospital: A randomized clinical trial. *Journal of the American Medical Association, 265,* 2197–2201.

Kennell, J. H., & McGrath, S. (1993, March). *Perinatal effects of labor support.* Paper presented at the meeting of the Society for Research in Child Development, New Orleans.

Kerr, B. (1999, March 5). When dreams differ: Male-female relations on campus. *Chronicle of Higher Education,* pp. 87, 88.

Kersting, K. (2003a, May). Cognitive sex differences: A "political minefield." *Monitor on Psychology,* pp. 54–55.

Kersting, K. (2003b, October). Countering insidious stereotypes. *Monitor on Psychology,* pp. 34–35.

Keshavarz, H., et al. (2002). Hysterectomy surveillance—United States, 1994–1999. *Morbidity and Mortality Weekly Reports, Surveillance Summaries, 51 (SS 05),* 1–8.

Kessler, R. C., et al. (2004). Age and depression in the MIDUS survey. In O. G. Brim, C. D. Ryff, & R. C. Kessler (Eds.), *How healthy are we? A national study of well-being at midlife* (pp. 227–251). Chicago: University of Chicago Press.

Keyes, C. L. M., & Shapiro, A. D. (2004). Social well-being in the United States: A descriptive epidemiology. In O. G. Brim, C. D. Ryff, & R. C. Kessler (Eds.), *How healthy are we? A national study of well-being at midlife* (pp. 350–372). Chicago: University of Chicago Press.

Kiang, L., Moreno, A. J., & Robinson, J. L. (2004). Maternal preconceptions about parenting predict child temperament, maternal sensitivity, and children's empathy. *Developmental Psychology, 40,* 1081–1092.

Kiecolt-Glaser, J. K., & Newton, T. L. (2001). Marriage and health: His and hers. *Psychological Bulletin, 127,* 472–503.

Kiefer, A. K., & Shih, M. J. (2004, May). *Stereotype relevance and gender differences in performance attributions.* Poster presented at the meeting of American Psychological Society, Chicago.

Kilborn, P. T. (1999, May 31). Disabled spouses increasingly face a life alone and a loss of income. *New York Times,* p. A8.

Kilborn, P. T. (2004a, March 7). Alive, well and on the prowl, it's the geriatric mating game. *Scottsdale Journal,* p. YT12.

Kilborn, P. T. (2004b, May 2). An all-American town, a sky-high divorce rate. Economic woes strain Roanoke's marriages. *New York Times,* p. YT20.

Kilpatrick, D. G., et al. (2003). Violence and risk of PTSD, major depression, substance abuse/dependence, and comorbidity: Results from the National Survey of Adolescents. *Journal of Consulting and Clinical Psychology, 71,* 692–700.

Kim, J. E., & Moen, P. (2001a). Is retirement good or bad for subjective well-being? *Current Directions in Psychological Science, 10,* 83–86.

Kim, J. E., & Moen, P. (2001b). Moving into retirement: Preparation and transitions in late midlife. In M. Lachman (Ed.), *Handbook of midlife development* (pp. 487–527). New York: Wiley.

Kim, W. J., & Singh, T. (2004). Trends and dynamics of youth suicides in developing countries. *The Lancet, 363,* 1090.

Kimball, M. M. (1995). *Feminist visions of gender similarities and differences.* New York: Harrington Park.

Kimball, M. M. (1998). Gender and math: What makes a difference? In D. L. Anselmi & A. L. Law (Eds.), *Questions of gender: Perspectives and paradoxes* (pp. 446–460). Boston: McGraw-Hill.

Kimball, M. M. (2001). Gender similarities and differences as feminist contradictions. In R. K. Unger (Ed.), *Handbook of the psychology of women and gender* (pp. 66–83). New York: Wiley.

Kimm, S. Y. S., et al. (2002). Decline in physical activity in black girls and white girls during adolescence. *New England Journal of Medicine, 347,* 709–715.

Kimmel, D. G. (2002, August). *Ageism and implications for sexual orientation.* Paper presented at the American Psychological Association, Chicago.

Kimmel, E. B., & Crawford, M. (2001). Methods for studying gender. In J. Worell (Ed.), *Encyclopedia of women and gender* (pp. 749–758). San Diego: Academic Press.

Kimmel, M. (2001). Real men join the movement. In S. M. Shaw & J. Lee (Eds.), *Women's voices, feminist visions,* (pp. 536–540). Mountain View, CA: Mayfield.

King, A. C., et al. (2000). Personal and environmental factors associated with physical inactivity among different racial-ethnic groups of U.S. middle-aged and older women. *Health Psychology, 19,* 354–364.

King, A. C., Bernardy, N. C., & Hauner, K. (2003). Stressful events, personality, and mood disturbance: Gender differences in alcoholics and problem drinkers. *Addictive Behaviors, 28,* 171–187.

King, A. C., Rejeski, W. J., & Buchner, D. M. (1998). Physical activity interventions targeting older adults: A critical review and recommendations. *American Journal of Preventive Medicine, 15,* 316–333.

King, C., & Olsen, P. R. (2002, August 18). Follow the herd? Not her. *New York Times,* p. BU13.

King, K. M., et al. (2004). Sex differences in outcomes after cardiac catheterization: Effect modification by treatment strategy and time. *Journal of the American Medical Association, 291,* 1220–1225.

King, L. A., & King, D. W. (1990). Abbreviated measures of sex role egalitarian attitudes. *Sex Roles, 23,* 659–673.

King, M., et al. (2003). Mental health and quality of life of gay men and lesbians in England and Wales. *British Journal of Psychiatry, 183,* 552–558.

Kinsella, K., & Velkoff, V. A. (2001). *An aging world: 2001.* U.S. Census Bureau, Series P95/01-1. Washington, DC: U.S. Government Printing Office.

Kinsey, A. C., Pomeroy, W. B., Martin, C. E., & Gebhard, P. H. (1953). *Sexual behavior in the human female.* Philadelphia: Saunders.

Kinsler, K., & Zalk, S. R. (1996). Teaching is a political act: Contextualizing gender and ethnic voices. In K. F. Wyche, & F. J. Crosby (Eds.), *Women's ethnicities: Journeys through psychology* (pp. 27–48). Boulder, CO: Westview.

Kinzer, S. (2003, November 6). Dolls as role models, neither Barbie nor Britney. *New York Times,* pp. B1, B5.

Kirk, G., & Okazawa-Rey, M. (2001). *Women's lives: Multicultural perspectives.* 2d ed. Mountain View, CA: Mayfield.

Kitano, M. K. (1998). Gifted Latina women. *Journal for the Education of the Gifted, 21,* 131–159.

Kite, M. E. (2001). Changing times, changing gender roles: Who do we want women and men to be? In R. K. Unger (Ed.), *Handbook of the psychology of women and gender* (pp. 215–227). New York: Wiley.

Kite, M. E., et al. (2001). Women psychologists in academe: Mixed progress, unwarranted complacency. *American Psychologist, 56,* 1080–1098.

Kite, M. E., Stockdale, G., & Whitley, B. E. (2002, August). *Attitudes toward younger and older adults: A meta-analysis.* Paper presented at the meeting of the American Psychological Association, Chicago.

Kite, M. E., & Wagner, L. S. (2002). Attitudes toward older adults. In T. D. Nelson (Ed.), *Ageism: Stereotyping and prejudice against older persons* (pp. 129–161). Cambridge, MA: MIT Press.

Kitto, J. (1989). Gender reference terms: Separating the women from the girls. *British Journal of Social Psychology, 28,* 185–187.

Kitzinger, C. (1999). Researching subjectivity and diversity: Q-methodology in feminist psychology. *Psychology of Women Quarterly, 23,* 267–276.

Kitzinger, C., & Coyle, A. (2002). Introducing lesbian and gay psychology. In A. Coyle & C. Kitzinger (Eds.), *Lesbian and gay psychology: New perspectives* (pp. 1–29). Oxford, UK: BPS Blackwell.

Klaczynski, P. A., & Aneja, A. (2002). Development of quantitative reasoning and gender biases. *Developmental Psychology, 38,* 208–221.

Klein, A. A., & Larson, K. (2004, July). *Is "he" male? Interpretive and memory bias for pronouns.* Paper presented at the meeting of the American Psychological Association, Honolulu.

Klein, J. D., Graff, C. A., Green, A., & Kodjo, C. (2003). Adolescent pregnancy prevention: Impact of siblings who are teen parents. *Journal of Adolescent Health, 32,* 134–135.

Klein, K. P., & Rapp, S. R. (2004). Women's cognitive health: Postmenopausal dementia and the women's health initiative memory study. *Women's Health Issues, 14,* 71–74.

Klein, M. H., Hyde, J. S., Essex, M. J., & Clark, R. (1998). Maternity leave, role quality, work involvement, and mental health one year after delivery. *Psychology of Women Quarterly, 22,* 239–266.

Kleinfield, N. R. (2004, December 12). Bowed by age, battered by an addicted nephew and forced into begging and despair. *New York Times,* pp. 1, 56–57.

Kleyman, K. S., Stasson, M. F., Souza, J. G., Jr., & Gjerswold, K. L. (2004, May). *The effects of gender stereotypes on occupational judgments.* Poster presented at the meeting of American Psychological Society, Chicago.

Kline, G. H., et al. (2004). Timing is everything: Pre-engagement cohabitation and increased risk for poor marital outcomes. *Journal of Family Psychology, 18,* 311–318.

Kling, K. C., Hyde, J. S., Showers, C. J., & Buswell, B. N. (1999). Gender differences in self-esteem: A meta-analysis. *Psychological Bulletin, 125,* 470–500.

Klinger, R. L. (2002). Lesbian women. In S. G. Kornstein & A. H. Clayton (Eds.), *Women's mental health: A comprehensive textbook* (pp. 555–567). New York: Guilford.

Klohnen, E. C., & Luo, S. (2003). Interpersonal attraction and personality: What is attractive—self similarity, ideal similarity, complementarity, or attachment security? *Journal of Personality and Social Psychology, 85,* 709–722.

Klomsten, A. T., Skaalvik, E. M., & Espnes, G. A. (2004). Physical self-concept and sports: Do gender differences still exist? *Sex Roles, 50,* 119–127.

Klonoff, E. A., & Landrine, H. (1995). The schedule of sexist events: A measure of lifetime and recent sexist discrimination in women's lives. *Psychology of Women Quarterly, 19,* 439–472.

Kmiec, J., Crosby, J. F., & Worell, J. (1996). Walking the talk: On stage and behind the scenes. In K. F. Wyche & F. J. Crosby (Eds.), *Women's ethnicities: Journeys through psychology* (pp. 49–61). Boulder, CO: Westview.

Knickmeyer, N., Sexton, K., & Nishimura, N. (2002). The impact of same-sex friendships on the well-being of women: A review of the literature. *Women & Therapy, 25,* 37–59.

Knight, J. L., & Giuliano, T. A. (2001). He's a Laker; she's a "looker": The consequences of gender-stereotypical portrayals of male and female athletes by the print media. *Sex Roles, 45,* 217–229.

Knightley, P. (1999, September 20). Grandma led two lives. *New York Times,* p. A21.

Knodel, J., Watkins, S., & VanLandingham, M. (2003). AIDS and older persons: An international perspective. *Journal of Acquired Immune Deficiency Syndromes, 33,* S153–S165.

Knoops, K. T. B., et al. (2004). Mediterranean diet, lifestyle factors, and 10-year mortality in elderly European men and women. *Journal of the American Medical Association, 292,* 1433–1439.

Knox, S. S., & Czajkowski, S. (1997). The influence of behavioral and psychosocial factors on cardiovascular health in women. In S. J. Gallant, G. Puryear Keita, & R. Royak-Schaler (Eds.), *Health care for women: Psychological, social and behavioral influences* (pp. 257–272). Washington, DC: American Psychological Association.

Kobrynowicz, D., & Branscombe, N. R. (1997). Who considers themselves victims of discrimination? Individual difference predictors of perceived gender discrimination in women and men. *Psychology of Women Quarterly, 21,* 347–363.

Koch, R., Lewis, M. T., & Quinones, W. (1998). Homeless: Mothering at rock bottom. In C. G. Coll, J. L. Surrey, & K. Weingarten (Eds.), *Mothering against the odds: Diverse voices of contemporary mothers* (pp. 61–84). New York: Guilford.

Koenig, L. J., Doll, L. S., O'Leary, A., & Pequegnat, W. (Eds.) (2004). *From child sexual abuse to adult sexual risk: Trauma, revictimization, and intervention.* Washington, DC: American Psychological Association.

Kohlberg, L. (1966). A cognitive-developmental analysis of children's sex-role concepts and attitudes. In E. E. Maccoby (Ed.), *The development of sex differences* (pp. 82–173). Stanford, CA: Stanford University Press.

Kohlberg, L. (1985). *The psychology of moral development*. San Francisco: Harper & Row.

Kolata, G. (2002a, September 25). Abortion pill slow to win users among women and their doctors. *New York Times*, p. A1.

Kolata, G. (2002b, December 2). With no answers on risks, steroid users still say "yes." *New York Times*, pp. A1, A19.

Kolata, G. (2003, September 24). Death at 18 spurs debate over a pill for abortion. *New York Times*, p. A18.

Kolata, G. (2004a, May 11). The heart's desire. *New York Times*, pp. D1, D6.

Kolata, G. (2004b, March 9). Up in the air on hormones: Women under 50. *New York Times*, pp. D5, D8.

Kolata, G., & Moss, M. (2002, February 11). X-ray vision in hindsight: Science, politics and the mammogram. *New York Times*, p. A23.

Kolb, D., & Williams, J. (2003). *Everyday negotiation: Navigating the hidden agendas in bargaining*. San Francisco: Jossey-Bass.

Kolchakian, M. R., & Fassinger, R. E. (2003, January). Roles of identity in relationship functioning for diverse same-sex couples. In R. E. Fassinger (Chair), *Results of the National Gay and Lesbian Experiences Study*. Symposium presented at the meeting of the American Psychological Association Multicultural Summit, Los Angeles.

Konek, C. W., Kitch, S. L., & Shore, E. R. (1994). The future of women and careers: Issues and challenges. In C. W. Konek & S. L. Kitch (Eds.), *Women and careers: Issues and challenges* (pp. 234–248). Thousand Oaks, CA: Sage.

Konrad, A. M. (2003). Family demands and job attribute preferences: A 4-year longitudinal study of women and men. *Sex Roles, 49*, 35–46.

Konrad, A. M., Ritchie, J. E., Lieb, P., & Corrigall, E. (2000). Sex differences and similarities in job attribute preferences: A meta-analysis. *Psychological Bulletin, 126*, 593–641.

Kornstein, S. G., & Wojcik, B. A. (2002). Depression. In S. G. Kornstein & A. H. Clayton (Eds.), *Women's mental health. A comprehensive textbook* (pp. 147–165). New York: Guilford Press.

Koss, M. P., Baily, J. A., Yuan, N. P., Herrera, V. M., & Lichter, E. L. (2003). Depression and PTSD in survivors of male violence: Research and training initiatives to facilitate recovery. *Psychology of Women Quarterly, 27*, 130–142.

Koss, M. P., & Cleveland, H. H. (1997). Stepping on toes: Social roots of date rape lead to intractability and politicization. In M. D. Schwartz (Ed.), *Researching sexual violence against women: Methodological and personal perspectives* (pp. 4–21). Thousand Oaks, CA: Sage.

Koss, M. P., & Figueredo, A. J. (2004). Cognitive mediation of rape's mental health impact: Constructive replication of a cross-sectional model in longitudinal data. *Psychology of Women Quarterly, 28*, 273–286.

Koss, M. P., Goodman, L. A., Browne, A., Fitzgerald, L. F., Keita, G. P., & Russo, N. F. (1994). *No safe haven: Male violence against women at home, at work, and in the community*. Washington, DC: American Psychological Association.

Koss, M. P., & Hoffman, K. (2000). Survivors of violence by male partners: Gender and cultural considerations. In R. M. Eisler & M. Hersen (Eds.), *Handbook of gender, culture, and health* (pp. 471–490). Mahwah, NJ: Erlbaum.

Kossek, E. E., & Ozeki, C. (1998). Work-family conflict, policies, and the job-life satisfaction relationship: A review and directions for organizational behavior-human resources research. *Journal of Applied Psychology, 83*, 139–149.

Kowalski, R. M., & Chapple, T. (2000). The social stigma of menstruation: Fact or fiction? *Psychology of Women Quarterly, 24*, 74–80.

Krahé, B., Waizenhöfer, E., & Möller, I. (2003). Women's sexual agression against men: Prevalence and predictors. *Sex Roles, 49*, 219–232.

Krakauer, H. D., & Rose, S. M. (2000). The impact of group membership on lesbians' physical appearance. *Journal of Lesbian Studies, 6 (1)*, 31–43.

Kramarae, C. (2001). *The third shift: Women learning online*. Washington, DC: American Association of University Women.

Kramer, A., Lorenzon, D., & Mueller, G. (2004, January/February). Prevalence of intimate partner violence and health implications for women using emergency departments and primary care clinics. *Women's Health Issues, 14*, pp. 19–29.

Kramer, A. F., & Willis, S. L. (2002). Enhancing the cognitive vitality of older adults. *Current Directions in Psychological Science, 11*, 173–177.

Krantz, M. J., Leeman-Castillo, B. A., Watson, K. E., & Mehler, P. S. (2004). Coronary heart disease care in older women: Optimizing diagnostic and therapeutic decisions. *Journal of the American Medical Women's Association, 59*, 286–294.

Krause, N. (1993). Race differences in life satisfaction among aged men and women. *Journal of Gerontology: Social Sciences, 48,* S235–S244.

Kravetz, D., & Marecek, J. (2001). In J. Worell (Ed.), *Encyclopedia of women and gender* (pp. 457–468). San Diego: Academic Press.

Krebs, E. E., Ensrud, K. E., MacDonald, R., & Wilt, T. J. (2004). Phytoestrogens for treatment of menopausal symptoms: A systematic review. *Obstetrics & Gynecology, 104,* 824–836.

Kreider, R. M., & Simmons, T. (2003). *Marital status: 2000. Census 2000 brief.* Washington, DC: U.S. Census Bureau.

Kresevich, D. M. (1993, March). *Traditional and nontraditional career choices of elementary aged children.* Paper presented at the meeting of the Society for Research in Child Development, New Orleans.

Kristof, N. D. (2002, June 18). Women's rights: Why not? *New York Times,* p. A25.

Kristof, N. D. (2004a, February 14). Afghan women, still in chains. *New York Times,* p. A29.

Kristof, N. D. (2004b, October 6). Beaten Afghan brides. *New York Times,* p. A29.

Kristof, N. D. (2005, January 26). After the brothel. *New York Times,* p. A17.

Kroenke, C. H., et al. (2004). Functional impact of breast cancer by age at diagnosis. *Journal of Clinical Oncology, 22,* 1849–1856.

Kubany, E. S., et al. (2004). Cognitive trauma therapy for battered women with PTSD (CTT-BW). *Journal of Consulting and Clinical Psychology, 72,* 3–18.

Kuczynski, A. (2002a, February 7). F.D.A. plans to endorse a drug long endorsed by the vainer set. *New York Times,* pp. A1, A18.

Kuczynski, A. (2002b, June 23). Menopause forever. *New York Times,* p. ST12.

Kuhn, J. (2005, Winter). Feminism and childbirth (part 2 of 2). *The Feminist Psychologist,* p. 5.

Kuhn, M. (1991). *No stone unturned.* New York: Ballatine Books.

Kulig, K., Brener, N. D., & McManus, T. (2003). Sexual activity and substance use among adolescents by category of physical activity plus team sports participation. *Archives of Pediatrics and Adolescent Medicine, 157,* 905–912.

Kuppermann, M., et al. (2004). Effect of hysterectomy vs. medical treatment on health-related quality of life and sexual functioning. The medicine or surgery (Ms) randomized trial. *Journal of the American Medical Association, 291,* 1447–1455.

Kurdek, L. A. (1995). Lesbian and gay couples. In A. R. D'Augelli & C. J. Patterson (Eds.), *Lesbian, gay, and bisexual identities over the lifespan* (pp. 243–261). New York: Oxford University Press.

Kurman, J. (2004). Gender, self-enhancement, and self-regulation of learning behaviors in junior high school. *Sex Roles, 50,* 725–735.

Kurth, S. B., Spiller, S. S., & Travis, C. B. (2000). Consent, power, and sexual scripts: Deconstructing sexual harassment. In C. B. Travis & J. W. White (Eds.), *Sexuality, society, and feminism* (pp. 323–354). Washington DC: American Psychological Association.

Kurth, T., et al. (2003). Smoking and risk of hemorrhagic stroke in women. *Stroke, 34,* 2792–2795.

Kvigne, V. L., et al. (2004). Characteristics of children who have full or incomplete fetal alcohol syndrome. *Journal of Pediatrics, 145,* 635–640.

Kwong, M. J., Bartholomew, K., Henderson, A. J. Z., & Trinke, S. J. (2003). The intergenerational transmission of relationship violence. *Journal of Family Psychology, 17,* 288–301.

Labaton, V., & Martin, D. L. (2004). Introduction: Making what will become. In V. Labaton & D. L. Martin (Eds.), *The fire this time* (pp. xxi–xxxvii). New York: Anchor Books.

Laber, E. (2001, January 11). Men are from Quake, women are from Ultima. *New York Times,* pp. D1, D4.

Labre, M. P., & Walsh-Childers, K. (2003). Friendly advice? Beauty messages in Web sites of teen magazines. *Mass Communication & Society, 6,* 379–396.

Lacey, M. (2004, June 8). Genital cutting shows signs of losing favor in Africa. *New York Times,* pp. A3.

Laditka, J. N., & Laditka, S. B. (2003). Increased hospitalization risk for recently widowed older women and protective effects of social contacts. *Journal of Women & Aging, 15,* 7–28.

Lafferty, E. (2003, Fall). Queen Noor. The next chapter. *Ms.,* pp. 32–39.

Laflamme, D., Pomerleau, A., & Malcuit, G. (2002). A comparison of fathers' and mothers' involvement in childcare and stimulation behaviors during freeplay with their infants at 9 and 15 months. *Sex Roles, 47,* 507–518.

LaFrance, M. (2001a). Gender and social interaction. In R. K. Unger (Ed.), *Handbook of the psychology of women and gender* (pp. 245–255). New York: Wiley.

LaFrance, M. (2001b). Is rape natural? A review of "A natural history of rape: Biological bases of sexual coercion." *Contemporary Psychology, 46,* 377–379.

LaFrance, M., Hecht, M. A., & Paluck, E. L. (2003). The contingent smile: A meta-analysis of sex differences in smiling. *Psychological Bulletin, 129,* 305–334.

LaFraniere, S. (2005a, February 18). AIDS and custom leave African families nothing. *New York Times,* pp. A1, A6.

LaFraniere, S. (2005b). Entrenched epidemic: Wife-beating in Africa. *New York Times,* pp. A1, A8.

LaFromboise, T. D., Berman, J. S., & Sohi, B. K. (1994). American Indian women. In L. Comas-Díaz, & B. Greene (Eds.), *Women of color: Integrating ethnic and gender identities in psychotherapy* (pp. 30–71). New York: Guilford.

LaFromboise, T. D., Heyde, A. M., & Ozer, E. J. (1990). Changing and diverse roles of women in American Indian cultures. *Sex Roles, 22,* 455–476.

LaFromboise, T. D., Heyle, A. N., Ozer, E. M. (1999). Changing and diverse roles of women in American Indian cultures. In L. A. Peplau, S. C. DeBro, R. C. Veniegas, & P. L. Taylor (Eds.), *Gender, culture and ethnicity: Current research about women and men* (pp. 48–61). Mountain View, CA: Mayfield.

Lakkis, J., Ricciardelli, L. A., & Williams, R. J. (1999). Role of sexual orientation and gender-related traits in disordered eating. *Sex Roles, 41,* 1–16.

Lakoff, R. T. (1990). *Talking power: The politics of language.* New York: Basic Books.

Lalumiere, M. L., Blanchard, R., & Zucker, K. J. (2000). Sexual orientation and handedness in men and women: A meta-analysis. *Psychological Bulletin, 126,* 575–592.

Lambdin, J. R., et al. (2003). The animal = male hypothesis: Children's and adults' beliefs about the sex of non-sex specific stuffed animals. *Sex Roles, 48,* 471–482.

Lamberg, L. (2002). Younger children, more girls commit acts of violence. *Journal of the American Medical Association, 288,* 566–567.

Landesman, P. (2004, January 25). The girls next door. *New York Times Magazine,* pp. 30–39, 66–67, 72–75.

Lane, M., & Etaugh, C. (2001, July). *Is stereotyping of females declining in children's books? It depends on the measure you use.* Poster presented at the meeting of the Seventh European Congress of Psychology, London.

Laner, M. R., & Ventrone, N. A. (1998). Egalitarian daters/traditionalist dates. *Journal of Family Issues, 19,* 468–477.

Lannin, D. R., et al. (1998). Influence of socioeconomic and cultural factors on racial differences in late-stage presentation of breast cancer. *Journal of the American Medical Association, 279,* 1801–1807.

Lansky, A. J., et al. (2005). Gender differences in outcomes after primary angioplasty versus primary stenting with and without abciximals for acute myocardial infarction. *Circulation, 111,* 1611–1618.

L'Armand, K., et al. (2002, June). *Faculty-student romances: Effects of respondent gender and student status on judgments.* Poster presented at the meeting of the American Psychological Society, New Orleans.

LaRossa, R., Jaret, C., Gadgil, M., & Wynn, G. R. (2001). Gender disparities in Mother's Day and Father's Day comic strips: A 55-year history. *Sex Roles, 44,* 693–718.

Larson, R., & Wilson, S. (2004). Adolescence across place and time. Globalization and the changing pathways to adulthood. In R. M. Lerner & L. Steinberg (Eds.), *Handbook of adolescent psychology,* 2d ed. (pp. 299–330). Hoboken, NJ: Wiley.

Larson, R. W., & Verma, S. (1999). How children and adolescents spend time across the world: Work, play, and developmental opportunities. *Psychological Bulletin, 125,* 701–736.

Lasswell, M. (2002). Marriage and family. In S. G. Kornstein & A. H. Clayton (Eds.), *Women's mental health: A comprehensive textbook* (pp. 515–526). New York: Guilford.

Lauer, R. H., Lauer, J. C., & Kerr, S. T. (1995). The long-term marriage: Perceptions of stability and satisfactions. In. J. Hendricks (Ed.), *The ties of later life* (pp. 35–41). Amityville, NY: Baywood.

Laumann, E. O., et al. (2004). *The sexual organization of the city.* Chicago: University of Chicago Press.

Laumann, E. O., Gagnon, J. H., Michael, R. T., & Michaels, S. (1994). *The social organization of sexuality: Sexual practices in the United States.* Chicago: University of Chicago Press.

Laumann, E. O., & Mahay, J. (2002). The social organization of women's sexuality. In G. M. Wingood & R. J. DiClemente (Eds.), *Handbook of women's sexual and reproductive health* (pp. 43–70). New York: Kluwer Academic/Plenum.

Laumann, E. O., Paik, A., & Rosen, R. C. (1999). Sexual dysfunction in the United States: Prevalence and predictors. *Journal of the American Medical Association, 281,* 537–544.

Lauzen, M. M. (2003). *The celluloid ceiling: Behind-the-scenes and on-screen employment of women in the top 250 films of 2002.* MoviesByWomen.com

Lauzen, M. M., & Dozier, D. M. (2002). You look mahvelous: An examination of gender and appearance comments in the 1999–2000 prime-time season. *Sex Roles, 46,* 429–437.

Lavender, T., & Walkinshaw, S. A. (1998). Can midwives reduce postpartum psychological morbidity? A randomized trial. *Birth, 25,* 215–219.

Lawler, A. (2002). Engineers marginalized, MIT report concludes. *Science, 295,* 2192.

Lawler, A. (2004). Neuroscientist named MIT president. *Science, 305,* 1389.

Lawton, C. A., & Morrin, K. A. (1999). Gender differences in pointing accuracy in computer-simulated 3D mazes. *Sex Roles, 40,* 73–92.

Lawton, C. A., Blakemore, J. E. O., & Vartanian, L. R. (2003). The new meaning of Ms.: Single, but too old for miss. *Psychology of Women Quarterly, 27,* 215–220.

Leaper, C. (2000). The social construction and socialization of gender during development. In P. H. Miller & E. K. Scholnick (Eds.), *Toward a feminist developmental psychology* (pp. 127–152). Florence, KY: Taylor & Francis/Routledge.

Leaper, C. (2002). Parenting girls and boys. In M. H. Bornstein (Ed.), *Handbook of parenting,* 2d ed. (pp. 189–225). Mahwah, NJ: Erlbaum.

Leaper, C. (2004, July). *Gender-related variations in affiliative and assertive speech: Meta-analyses.* Paper presented at the American Psychological Association Convention, Honolulu.

Leaper, C., & Smith, T. E. (2004). A meta-analytic review of gender variations in children's language use: Talkativeness, affiliative speech, and assertive speech. *Developmental Psychology, 40,* 993–1027.

Leary, W. E. (1998, September 29). Older people enjoy sex, survey says. *New York Times,* p. B16.

Lee, F. R. (2004, July 3). Engineering more sons than daughters: Will it tip the scales toward war? *New York Times,* pp. A17, A19.

Lee, F. R. (2005, January 25). Driven by costs, fertility clients head overseas. *New York Times,* p. A1.

Lee, I. (2003). Physical activity in women. How much is good enough? *Journal of the American Medical Association, 290,* 1377–1379.

Lee, S. (2002). Health and sickness: The meaning of menstruation and premenstrual syndrome in women's lives. *Sex Roles, 46,* 25–35.

Lee, S. (2004). The new girls network: Women, technology, and feminism. In V. Labaton & D. L.

Martin (Eds.), *The fire this time* (pp. 84–104). New York: Anchor Books.

Lee, S., Colditz, G., Berkman, L., & Kawachi, I. (2003). Caregiving to children and grandchildren and risk of coronary heart disease in women. *American Journal of Public Health, 93,* 1939–1944.

Lee Badgett, M. V. (2003, September). *Variations on an equitable theme: Explaining international same-sex partner recognition laws.* Paper presented at the meeting "Same-sex couples, same-sex partnerships, and homosexual marriages," Stockholm University.

Leeb, R. T., & Rejskind, F. G. (2004). Here's looking at you, kid! A longitudinal study of perceived gender differences in mutual gaze behavior in young infants. *Sex Roles, 50,* 1–14.

Lefkowitz, E. S., & Fingerman, K. L. (2003). Positive and negative emotional feelings and behaviors in mother-daughter ties in late life. *Journal of Family Psychology, 17(4),* 607–617.

le Grange, D., et al. (2004). Bulimia nervosa in adolescents. A disorder in evolution? *Archives of Pediatrics and Adolescent Medicine, 158,* 478–482.

Lehr, S. (2001). The anomalous female and the ubiquitous male. In S. Lehr (Ed.), *Beauty, brains, and brawn: The construction of gender in children's literature* (pp. 193–207). Portsmouth, NH: Heinemann.

Leiblum, S. R. (Ed.). (1997). *Infertility: Psychological issues and counseling strategies.* New York: Wiley.

Leiblum, S., & Sachs, J. (2002). *Getting the sex you want: A woman's guide to becoming proud, passionate, and pleased in bed.* New York: Crown.

Leibson-Hawkins, B. (2004). *I'm too young to have breast cancer.* Washington, DC: Regnery Publishing.

Leinbach, M. D., & Fagot, B. I. (1993). Categorical habituation to male and female faces: Gender schematic processing in infancy. *Infant Behavior and Development, 16,* 317–322.

Leitner, M. J., & Leitner, S. F. (2004). *Leisure in later life,* 3d ed. Binghamton, NY: Haworth.

Leland, J. (2000a, March 20). Shades of gays. *Newsweek,* pp. 46–49.

Leland, J. (2000b, November 6). Silence ending about abuse in gay relationships. *New York Times,* p. A18.

Leland, J. (2003, October 19). I am woman. Now prepare to die. *New York Times,* pp. ST1, ST11.

Leland, J. (2004, March 23). He's retired, she's working, they're not happy. *New York Times,* pp. A1, A18.

Leland, J., & Miller M. (1998, August 17). Can gays convert? *Newsweek,* pp. 47–50.

Leman, P. J., Ahmed, S., & Ozarow, L. (2005). Gender, gender relations, and the social dynamics of children's conversations. *Developmental Psychology, 41,* 64–74.

Lengua, L. J., & Stormshok, E. A. (2000). Gender, gender roles, and personality: Gender differences in the prediction of coping and psychological symptoms. *Sex Roles, 42,* 787–819.

Lennon, M. C., Blome, J., & English, K. (2002). Depression among women on welfare: A review of the literature. *Journal of the Medical Women's Association, 57,* 27–32.

Leon, I. G. (2001). Perinatal loss. In N. L. Stotland and D. E. Stewart (Eds.), *Psychological aspects of women's health care,* 2d ed. (pp. 141–173). Washington, DC: American Psychiatric Press.

Leonard, D., & Jiang, J. (1999). Gender bias and the college predictions of the SATs: A cry of despair. *Research in Higher Education, 40,* 375.

LePage-Lees, P. (1997). Struggling with a nontraditional past: Academically successful women from disadvantaged backgrounds discuss their relationship with "disadvantage." *Psychology of Women Quarterly, 21,* 365–385.

Lerner, B. H. (2003, May 27). If biology is destiny, when shouldn't it be? *New York Times,* p. D7.

Lerner, J. S., Castellino, D. R., Lolli, E., & Wan, S. (2002). Children, families and work: Research findings and implications for policies and programs. In R. M. Lerner, F. Jacobs, & D. Wertlieb (Eds.), *Handbook of applied developmental science,* Vol. 1 (pp. 281–304). Thousand Oaks, CA: Sage.

Lerner, S. (2002, October 22). Good and bad marriage, boon and bane to health. *New York Times,* pp. D5, D8.

Lesbian community assesses health issues. (2004, June 20). *Associated Press.*

Lester, D., & Yang, B. (1998). *Suicide and homicide in the twentieth century: Changes over time.* Commack, AL: Nova Science.

Lethbridge-Cejku, M., Schiller, J. S., & Bernadel, L. (2004). *Summary health statistics for U.S. adults: National Health Interview Survey, 2002.* National Center for Health Statistics. *Vital Health Stat 10*(222).

Letherby, G., & Williams, C. (1999). "Non-motherhood: Ambivalent autobiographies." *Feminist Studies, 25,* 719–729.

Letourneau, E. J., Schoenwald, S. K., & Sheidow, A. J. (2004). Children and adolescents with sexual behavior problems. *Child Maltreatment, 9,* 49–61.

Leung, S. A., Ivey, D., Suzuki, L. (1994). Factors affecting the career aspirations of Asian Americans. *Journal of Counseling & Development, 72,* 404–410.

Levant, R. F. (1997, August). *Deconstructing Disney: Gender socialization through the lens of the cinema.* Paper presented at the meeting of the American Psychological Association, Chicago.

Leventhal, E. A. (1994). Gender and aging: Women and their aging. In V. J. Adesso, D. M. Reddy, & R. Flemming (Eds.), *Psychological perspectives on women's health* (pp. 11–35). Washington, DC: Taylor & Francis.

Leventhal, T., & Brooks-Gunn, J. (2004). A randomized study of neighborhood effects on low-income children's educational outcomes. *Developmental Psychology, 40,* pp. 488–505.

Levesque, K. (2003). Public high school graduates who participated in vocational/technical education: 1982–1998. *Education Statistics Quarterly, 5(3),* 33–39.

Levine, M. (2004, June 1). Tell the doctor all your problems, but keep it to less than a minute. *New York Times,* p. F6.

Levine, S. C., Huttenlocher, J., Taylor, A., & Langrock, A. (1999). Early sex differences in spatial skill. *Developmental Psychology, 35,* 940–949.

Levison, S. P., & Straumanis, J. (2002 September/October). FIPSE: Changing medical education forever. *Change,* pp. 19–26.

Levitt, H. M., & Hiestand, K. R. (2004). A quest for authenticity: Contemporary butch gender. *Sex Roles, 50,* 605–621.

Levy, G. D., Zimmerman, B., Barber, J., Martin, N., & Malone, C. (1998, May). *Preverbal awareness of gender roles in toddlers.* Poster presented at the meeting of the American Psychological Society, Washington, DC.

Levy, J. A., Ory, M. G., & Crystal, S. (2003, June 1). HIV/AIDS interventions for midlife and older adults: Current status and challenges. *Journal of Acquired Immune Deficiency Syndromes, 33,* S59–S67.

Lew, A. S., Allen, R., Papouchis, N., & Ritzler, B. (1998). Achievement orientation and fear of success in Asian American college students. *Journal of Clinical Psychology, 54,* 97–108.

Lewiecki, E. M. (2004, March). Bone density testing in the management of postmenopausal osteoporosis. *Women's Health in Primary Care, 7,* 84–95.

Lewin, T. (1997, September 30). Little talk on sexual diseases. *New York Times,* p. B15.

Lewin, T. (1999, October 3). Defining who can see the children. *New York Times,* p. WK3.

Lewin, T. (2001a, May 30). Program finds success in reducing teenage pregnancy. *New York Times,* p. A15.

Lewin, T. (2001b, September 10). Study finds little change in working mothers debate. *New York Times,* p. A26.

Lewin, T. (2002, May 30). U.S. defends anti-bias law on college sports. *New York Times,* p. A14.

Lewin, T. (2003, December 22). For more people in 20's and 30's, home is where the parents are. *New York Times,* p. A27.

Lewis Claar, R., & Blumenthal, J. A. (2003). The value of stress-management interventions in life-threatening medical conditions. *Current Directions in Psychological Science, 12(4),* 133–137.

Lewis, S. F., & Fremouw, W. (2001). Dating violence: A critical review of the literature. *Clinical Psychology Review, 21(1),* 105–127.

Lewittes, H. J. (1989). Just being friendly means a lot—women, friendship, and aging. In L. Grace & I. Susser (Eds.), *Women in the later years: Health, social, and cultural perspectives* (pp. 139–159). New York: Harrington Park Press.

Lex, B. W. (2000). Gender and cultural influences on substance abuse. In R. M. Eisler & M. Hersen (Eds.), *Handbook of gender, culture, and health* (pp. 255–297). Mahwah, NJ: Erlbaum.

Li, C. I., et al. (2003). Differences in breast cancer stage, treatment, and survival by race and ethnicity. *Archives of Internal Medicine, 163,* 49–56.

Li, Q. (1999). Teachers' beliefs and gender differences in mathematics: A review. *Educational Research, 41(1),* 63–76.

Liao, Y., et al. (2004). REACH 2010 Surveillance for health status in minority communities, 2001–2002. *Surveillance Summaries, 53* (No. SS-6).

Liben, L. S., & Bigler, R. S. (2002). The developmental course of gender differentiation. *Monographs of the Society for Research in Child Development.* Serial No. 269, Vol. 67, No. 2.

Liben, L. S., Bigler, R. S., & Krogh, H. R. (2001). Pink and blue collar jobs: Children's judgments of job status and job aspirations in relation to sex of worker. *Journal of Experimental Child Psychology, 79,* 346–363.

Liben, L. S., et al. (2002). The effects of sex steroids on spatial performance: A review and an experimental clinical investigation. *Developmental Psychology 38,* 236–253.

Lichter, E. L., & McCloskey, L. A. (2004). The effects of childhood exposure to marital violence on adolescent gender-role beliefs and dating violence. *Psychology of Women Quarterly, 28,* 344–357.

Ligos, M. (2001, January 14). How to scale back the hours but not the career. *New York Times,* p. BU10.

Liljestrand, J., & Gryboski, K. (2002). Women at risk of maternal mortality. In E. Murphy (Ed.), *Reproductive health and rights: Reaching the hardly reached* (pp. 121–128). Washington, DC: Program for Appropriate Technology in Health.

Lin, C. A. (1998). Uses of sex appeals in prime-time commercials. *Sex Roles, 38,* 461–475.

Lindner, K. (2004). Images of women in general interest and fashion magazine advertisements from 1955 to 2002. *Sex Roles, 51,* 409–421.

Lindsay, R., et al. (2002). Effect of lower doses of conjugated equine estrogens with and without medroxyprogesterone acetate on bone in early postmenopausal women. *Journal of the American Medical Association, 287,* 2668–2676.

Lindsey, E. W., & Mize, J. (2001). Contextual differences in parent-child play: Implications for children's gender role development. *Sex Roles, 44,* 155–176.

Linn, M. C., & Petersen, A. C. (1985). Emergence and characterization of sex differences in spatial ability: A meta-analysis. *Child Development, 56,* 1479–1498.

Lippa, R. A. (2005). *Gender, nature, and nurture.* 2d ed. Mahwah, NJ: Erlbaum.

Lippert, L. (1997). Women at midlife: Implications for theories of women's adult development. *Journal of Counseling & Development, 76,* 16–22.

Lips, H. M. (1997). *Sex and gender: An introduction.* 3d ed. Mountain View, CA: Mayfield.

Lips, H. M. (2003). The gender pay gap: Concrete indicator of women's progress toward equality. *Analyses of Social Issues and Public Policy, 3,* pp. 87–109.

Lips, H. M. (2004). The gender gap in possible selves: Divergence of academic self-views among high school and university students. *Sex Roles, 50,* 357–371.

Lipson, J. (2001, Fall). Pay equity: Fact or fiction? *Outlook,* pp. 14–18.

Lisi, D. (1993). Found voices: Women, disability, and cultural transformation. *Women & Therapy, 14,* 195–209.

Liss, M., Crawford, M., & Popp, D. (2004). Predictors and correlates of collective action. *Sex Roles, 50,* 771–779.

Liss, M., O'Connor, C., Morosky, E., & Crawford, M. (2001). What makes a feminist? Predictors and correlates of feminist social identity in college women. *Psychology of Women Quarterly, 25,* 124–133.

Little, M. V. (2005). Getting your financial priorities straight. *Journal of the American Medical Women's Association, 60,* pp. 9–10.

Littlefield, G. D., et al. (2000). Common themes in long-term lesbian relationships. *Family Therapy, 27,* 71–79.

Littleton, H. L., & Axsom, D. (2003). Rape and seduction scripts of university students: Implications for rape attributions and unacknowledged rape. *Sex Roles, 49,* 465–475.

Littleton, H. L., & Ollendick, T. (2003). Negative body image and disordered eating behavior in children and adolescents: What places youth at risk and how can these problems be prevented? *Clinical Child and Family Psychology Review, 6,* 51–66.

Littleton, K., Light, P., Barnes, P., Messer, D., & Joiner, R. (March, 1993). *Gender and software effects in computer based problem solving.* Paper presented at the meeting of the Society for Research in Child Development, New Orleans.

Liu, E., Kahan, M., & Wilson, L. (1999, August). *Physician attitudes and behavior towards male and female problem drinkers.* Paper presented at the meeting of the American Psychological Association, Boston.

Livson, F. B. (1983). Gender identity: A life span view of sex role development. In R. Weg (Ed.), *Aging: An international annual,* Vol. 1. *Sexuality in the later years: Roles and behavior* (pp. 105–114). Menlo Park, CA: Addison-Wesley.

Llabre, M. M., & Hadi, F. (1997). Social support and psychological distress in Kuwaiti boys and girls exposed to the Gulf crisis. *Journal of Clinical Child Psychology, 26,* 247–255.

Lloyd, T., Petit, M. A., Lin, H. M., & Beck, T. J. (2004). Lifestyle factors and the development of bone mass and bone strength in young women. *Journal of Pediatrics, 144,* 776–782.

Lloyd-Jones, D. M., et al. (2004). Parental cardiovascular disease as a risk factor for cardiovascular disease in middle-aged adults. *Journal of the American Medical Association, 291,* 2204–2211.

Loeb, S., Fuller, B., Kagan, S. L., & Carrol, B. (2004). Child care in poor communities: Early learning effects of type, quality, and stability. *Child Development, 75,* 47–65.

Longman, J. (2002, March 29). Debating the male coach's role. *New York Times,* pp. C13, C15.

Lott, B. (2002). Cognitive and behavioral distancing from the poor. *American Psychologist, 57,* 100–110.

Lott, B., & Bullock, H. E. (2001, Summer). Who are the poor? *Journal of Social Issues, 57,* 189–206.

Lott, B., & Maluso, D. (2001). Gender development: Social learning. In J. Worell (Ed.), *Encyclopedia of women and gender* (pp. 537–549). San Diego: Academic Press.

Lott, B., & Saxon, S. (2002). The influence of ethnicity, social class and context on judgments about American women. *Journal of Social Psychology, 142,* 481–499.

Lottes, I. L., & Kuriloff, P. J. (1992). The effects of gender, race, religion, and political orientation on the sex role attitudes of college freshmen. *Adolescence, 27,* 675–688.

Louie, B. (2001). Why gender stereotypes still persist in contemporary children's literature. In S. Lehr (Ed.), *Beauty, brains, and brawn* (pp. 142–151). Portsmouth, NH: Heinemann.

Lovejoy, M. (1998). "You can't go home again": The impact of women's studies on intellectual and personal development. *NWSA Journal, 10 (1),* 119.

Lowell, J. (2004, June 28). Have experience and wisdom, will travel. *Newsweek,* p. 14.

Lubinski, D., & Benbow, C. P. (1992). Gender differences in abilities and preferences among the gifted: Implications for the math-science pipeline. *Current Directions in Psychological Science, 1,* 61–66.

Lucas, R. E., Clark, A. E., Georgellis, Y., & Diener, E. (2003). Reexamining adaptation and the set point model of happiness: Reactions to changes in marital status. *Journal of Personality and Social Psychology, 84,* 527–539.

Lucas, V. A. (1992). An investigation of the health care preferences of the lesbian population. *Health Care for Women International, 13(2),* 221–228.

Luciano, L. (2003). The economics of young women today. In C. B. Costello, V. R. Wight, & A. J. Stone (Eds.), *The American woman 2003–2004: Daughters of a revolution—young women today* (pp. 143–163). New York: Palgrave Macmillan.

Lugaila, T., & Overturf, J. (2004, February). *Children and the households they live in: 2000.* Census 2000 Special Reports. Washington, DC: U.S. Census Bureau.

Lummis, M., & Stevenson, H. W. (1990). Gender differences in beliefs and achievement: A cross-cultural study. *Developmental Psychology, 26,* 254–563.

Luthar, S. S., & Sexton, C. C. (2004). The high price of affluence. In R. V. Kail (Ed.), *Advances in child development and behavior* (pp. 125–162). San Diego, CA: Elsevier.

Lutzker, J. R., Bigelow, K. M., Swenson, C. C., Doctor, R. M., Kessler, M. L. (1999). Problems related to child abuse and neglect. In S. D. Netherton, D. Holmes, & C. E. Walker (Eds.), *Child and adolescent psychological disorders: A comprehensive textbook* (pp. 520–548). New York: Oxford University Press.

Lyall, S. (2005, February 22). New course by Royal Navy: A campaign to recruit gays. *New York Times,* p. A1.

Lydon-Rochelle, M. T. (2004). Minimal intervention—nurse-midwives in the United States. *New England Journal of Medicine, 351,* 1929–1931.

Lynch, S. A. (1998). Who supports whom: How age and gender affect the perceived quality of support from family and friends. *Gerontologist, 38,* 231–238.

Lyness, J. M. (2004). Treatment of depressive conditions in later life. Real-world light for dark (or dim) tunnels. *Journal of the American Medical Association, 291,* 1626–1628.

Lyness, K. S., & Thompson, D. E. (1997). Above the glass ceiling? A comparison of matched samples of female and male executives. *Journal of Applied Psychology, 82,* 359–375.

Lyness, K. S., Thompson, C. A., Francesco, A. M., & Judiesch, M. K. (1999). Work and pregnancy: Individual and organizational factors influencing organizational commitment, timing of maternity leave, and return to work. *Sex Roles, 41,* 485–508.

Lyons, H. Z., Brenner, B. R., & Fassinger, R. E. (2003, January). Testing the role of experiences with heterosexism in the theory of work adjustment. In R. E. Fassinger (Chair), *Results of the National Gay and Lesbian Experiences Study.* Symposium presented at the American Psychological Association Multicultural Summit, Los Angeles.

Macalister, H. E. (2003). In defense of ambiguity: Understanding bisexuality's invisibility through cognitive psychology. *Journal of Bisexuality, 3,* 25–32.

MacCallum, F., & Golombok, S. (2002, July). *Families through surrogacy: Psychological implications.*

Paper presented at European Society of Human Reproduction and Embryology, Vienna.

Maccoby, E. E. (1998). *The two sexes: Growing up apart, coming together.* Cambridge, MA: Harvard University Press.

Maccoby, E. E. (2000). Perspectives on gender development. *International Journal of Behavioral Development, 24,* 398–406.

Maccoby, E. E. (2002). Gender and group process: A developmental perspective. *Current Directions in Psychological Science, 11,* 54–58.

Maccoby, E. E., & Jacklin, C. N. (1974). *The psychology of sex differences.* Stanford, CA: Stanford University Press.

MacGeorge, E. L., et al. (2004). The myth of gender cultures: Similarities outweigh differences in men's and women's provision of and responses to supportive communication. *Sex Roles, 50,* 143–175.

Mack, K.A., & Ory, M. G. (2003). AIDS and older Americans at the end of the twentieth century. *Journal of Acquired Immune Deficiency Syndromes, 33,* S68–S75.

Mack, K. A., et al. (2004). Health and sociodemographic factors associated with body weight and weight objectives for women: 2000 Behavioral Risk Factor Surveillance System. *Journal of Women's Health, 13,* 1019–1032.

MacMahon, K. M. A., & Lip, G. Y. H. (2002). Psychological factors in heart failure. *Archives of Internal Medicine, 162,* 509–516.

MacWilliams, B. (2003, October 3). Forced into prostitution. *Chronicle of Higher Education,* pp. A34–A36.

Madden, M. E., & Hyde, J. S. (1998). Integrating gender and ethnicity into psychology courses. *Psychology of Women Quarterly, 22,* 1–12.

Maestripieri, D. (2002, January). Developmental and evolutionary aspects of female attraction to babies. *Psychological Science Agenda, 18(1).* www.apa.org/science/psa

Magley, V. J. (2002). Coping with sexual harassment: Reconceptualizing women's resistance. *Journal of Personality and Social Psychology, 83,* 930–946.

Magley, V. J., Hulin, C. L., Fitzgerald, L. F., & DeNardo, M. (1999). Outcomes of self-labeling sexual harassment. *Journal of Applied Psychology, 84,* 390–402.

Mahaffy, K. A., & Ward, S. K. (2002). The gendering of adolescents' childbearing and educational plan: Reciprocal effects and the influence of social context. *Sex Roles, 46,* 403–417.

Mahalingam, R. (2003). Essentialism, culture, and beliefs about gender among the Aravanis of Tamil Nadu, India. *Sex Roles, 49,* 489–496.

Mahler, S. (2003). Anxiety disorders. In L. Slater, J. H. Daniel, & A. E. Banks (Eds.), *The complete guide to mental health for women* (pp. 197–203). Boston: Beacon Press.

Mahoney, S. (2003, November/December). Seeking love. *AARP Magazine,* 1–3.

Mail, P. D., Heurtin-Roberts, S., Martin, S. E., & Howard, J. (2002). *Alcohol use among America Indians and Alaska natives. Multiple perspectives on a complex problem.* NIH Publication No. 02-4231, pp. 3–369. Washington, DC: U.S. Department of Health and Human Services.

Maine, D., & Chavkin, W. (2002, Summer). Maternal mortality: Global similarities and differences. *Journal of the Medical Women's Association, 57,* 127–130.

Major, B. (1993). Gender, entitlement, and the distribution of family labor. *Journal of Social Issues, 49,* 141–159.

Major, B., Barr, L., Zubek, J., & Babey, S. H. (1999). Gender and self-esteem: A meta-analysis. In W. B. Swann, J. H. Langlois, & L. A. Gilbert (Eds.), *Sexism and stereotypes in modern society* (pp. 223–254). Washington, DC: American Psychological Association.

Major, B., Cozzarelli, C., Cooper, L., Zubek, J., Richards, C., Wilhite, M., & Gramzow, R. H. (2000). Psychological responses of women after first-trimester abortion. *Archives of General Psychiatry, 57,* 777–784.

Major, B., Richards, C., Cooper, M. L., Cozzarelli, C., & Zubek, J. (1998). Personal resilience, cognitive appraisals, and coping: An integrative model of adjustment to abortion. *Journal of Personality and Social Psychology, 74,* 735–752.

Major companies accused of sex discrimination. (2004, Fall/Winter). *AAUW Outlook,* p. 5.

Making the grade on women's health: A national and state report card, 2004. (2004, June). Washington, DC and Portland, OR: National Women's Law Center and Oregon Health & Science University.

Malamuth, N. M. (1996). The confluence model of sexual aggression: Feminist and evolutionary perspectives. In D. M. Buss & N. M. Malamuth (Eds.), *Sex, power, conflict: Evolutionary and feminist perspectives* (pp. 269–295). New York: Oxford University Press.

Malamuth, N. M., Sockloskie, R. J., Koss, M. P., & Tanaka, J. S. (1991). Characteristics of aggressors against women: Testing a model using a national sample of college students. *Journal of Consulting and Clinical Psychology, 59,* 670–681.

Maliti, T. (2004, October 9). Kenyan awarded Nobel Peace Prize. *Peoria Journal Star,* p. A3.

Malkin, A. R., Wornian, K., & Chrisler, J. C. (1999). Women and weight: Gendered messages on magazine covers. *Sex Roles, 40,* 647–655.

Malley-Morrison, K. (Ed.). (2004). *International perspectives on family violence and abuse.* Mahwah, NJ: Erlbaum.

Mankiller, W. (2004). Coda. In V. Labaton & D. L. Martin (Eds.), *The fire this time* (pp. 291–293). New York: Anchor Books.

Manlove, J., Ryan, S., & Franzetta, K. (2003). Patterns of contraceptive use within teenagers' first sexual relationships. *Perspectives on Sexual and Reproductive Health, 35,* 246–255.

Mannheim Research Institute for the Economics of Aging. (2005). *Health, ageing, and retirement in Europe.* Mannheim, Germany: Author.

Mansfield, P. K., et al. (1991). The job climate for women in traditionally male blue-collar occupations. *Sex Roles, 25,* 63–79.

Mansfield, P. K., Koch, P. B., & Voda, A. M. (1998). Qualities midlife women desire in their sexual relationships and their changing sexual response. *Psychology of Women Quarterly, 22,* 285–303.

Mansfield, P. K., Koch, P. B., & Voda, A. M. (2000). Midlife women's attributions for their sexual response changes. *Health Care for Women International, 21,* 543–559.

Marano, H. E. (1997, July 1). Puberty may start at 6 as hormones surge. *New York Times,* pp. B9, B12.

Marchbanks, P. A., et al. (2002). Oral contraceptives and the risk of breast cancer. *New England Journal of Medicine, 346,* 2025–2032.

Marcia, J. E. (1993). The relational roots of identity. In J. Krogers (Ed.), *Discussion on ego identity* (pp. 101–120). Hillsdale, NJ: Erlbaum.

Marecek, J. (2001). Disorderly constructs: Feminist frameworks for clinical psychology. In R. K. Unger (Ed.), *Handbook of the psychology of women and gender* (pp. 303–316). New York: Wiley.

Marecek, J., Crawford, M., & Popp, D. (2004). On the construction of gender, sex, and sexualities. In A. H. Eagly, A. E. Beall, and R. J. Sternberg (Eds.), *The psychology of gender,* 2d ed. (pp. 192–216). New York: Guilford.

Marecek, J., & Hare-Mustin, R. T. (1998). A short history of the future: Feminism and clinical psychology.

In D. L. Anselmi and A. L. Law (Eds.), *Questions of gender: Perspectives and paradoxes* (pp. 748–758). Boston: McGraw-Hill.

Mares, M-L., & Fitzpatrick, M. A. (2004). Communication in close relationships of older people. In J. F. Nussbaum & J. Coupland (Eds.), *Handbook of communication and aging research,* 2d ed. (pp. 231–250). Mahwah, NJ: Erlbaum.

Margolin, G., & Gordis, E. B. (2004). Children's exposure to violence in the family and community. *Current Directions in Psychological Science, 13,* 152–155.

Markey, C. N., Markey, P. M., & Birch, L. L. (2004). Understanding women's body satisfaction: The role of husbands. *Sex Roles, 51,* 209–216.

Markovits, H., Benenson, J., & Dolenszky, E. (2001). Evidence that children and adolescents have internal models of peer interactions that are gender differentiated. *Child Development, 72,* 879–886.

Markowe, L. A. (2002). Coming out as a lesbian. In A. Coyle & C. Kitzinger (Eds.), *Lesbian and gay psychology: New perspectives* (pp. 63–80). Oxford, UK: BPS Blackwell.

Markson, E. W. (2001). Sagacious, sinful or superfluous? The social construction of older women. In J. M. Coyle (Ed.), *Handbook on women and aging* (pp. 53–71). Westport, CT: Greenwood.

Markson, E. W., & Taylor, C. A. (1993). Real versus reel world: Older women and the Academy Awards. In N. D. Davis, E. Cole, & E. Rothblum (Eds.), *Faces of women and aging* (pp. 157–175). New York: Harrington Park Press.

Marler, J. H., & Moen, P. (2005). Alternative employment arrangements: A gender perspective. *Sex Roles, 52,* 337–349.

Marmot, M. (2003). Social resources and health. In F. Kessel, P. L. Rosenfield, & N. B. Anderson (Eds.), *Expanding the boundaries of health and social science* (pp. 259–285). New York: Oxford University Press.

Marquez, S. A. (1994). Distorting the image of hispanic women in sociology: Problematic strategies of presentation in the introductory text. *Teaching Sociology, 22,* 231–236.

Marrazzo, J. M. (2004). Barriers to infectious disease care among lesbians. *Emerging Infectious Diseases, 10,* 1974–1978.

Marrazzo, J. M., Coffey, P., & Bingham, A. (2005). Sexual practices, risk perception and knowledge of sexually transmitted disease risk among lesbian and bisexual women. *Perspectives on Sexual and Reproductive Health, 37,* 6–12.

Marriott, M. (2003, May 15). Fighting women enter the arena, no holds barred. *New York Times,* pp. E1, E7.

Marsh, H. W., Ellis, L. A., & Craven, R. G. (2002). How do preschool children feel about themselves? Unraveling measurement and multidimensional self-concept structure. *Developmental Psychology, 38,* 376–393.

Marshall, N. L. (1998). *Work and family today: Recent research at the Center for Research on Women,* pp. 102–105. Wellesley, MA: Wellesley College Center for Research on Women.

Marshall, N. L. (2004). The quality of early child care and children's development. *Current Directions in Psychological Science, 13,* 165–168.

Marshall, N. L., & Barnett, R. C. (1993). Work-family strains and gains among two-earner couples. *Journal of Community Psychology, 21,* 64–78.

Martin, C. L. (1995). Stereotypes about children with traditional and nontraditional gender roles. *Sex Roles, 33,* 727–751.

Martin, C. L. (1999). A developmental perspective on gender effects and gender concepts. In W. B. Swann, J. H. Langlois, & L. A. Gilbert (Eds.), *Sexism and stereotypes in modern society* (pp. 45–74). Washington, DC: American Psychological Association.

Martin, C. L. (2000). Cognitive theories of gender development. In T. Eckes & H. M. Trautner (Eds.), *The developmental social psychology of gender* (pp. 91–121). Mahwah, NJ: Erlbaum.

Martin, C. L., & Dinella, L. M. (2001). Gender development: Gender schema theory. In J. Worell (Ed.), *Encyclopedia of women and gender* (pp. 507–521). San Diego: Academic Press.

Martin, C. L., & Fabes, R. A. (2001). The stability and consequences of young children's same-sex peer interactions. *Developmental Psychology, 37,* 431–446.

Martin, C. L., & Little, J. K. (1990). The relation of gender understanding to children's sex-typed preferences and gender stereotypes. *Child Development, 61,* 1327–1439.

Martin, C. L., & Ruble, D. (2004). Children's search for gender cues. Cognitive perspectives on gender development. *Current Directions in Psychological Science, 13,* 67–70.

Martin, C. L., Ruble, D. N., & Szkrybalo, J. (2002). Cognitive theories of early gender development. *Psychological Bulletin, 128,* 903–933.

Martin, J. A., et al. (2003). *National Vital Statistics Reports, 52(10).* Hyattsville, MD: National Center for Health Statistics.

Martin, M. O., Mullis, I. V. S., Gonzalez, E. J., & Chrostowski, S. J. (2004). *TIMSS 2003 international science report.* Boston: Boston College.

Martin, S. L., et al. (2004, July). *Assault of women with disabilities: Research findings and clinical implications.* Paper presented at the meeting of the American Psychological Association, Honolulu.

Martire, L. M., & Parris Stephens, M. A. (2003). Juggling parent care and employment responsibilities: The dilemmas of adult daughter caregivers in the workforce. *Sex Roles, 48,* 167–173.

Marton, K. (2004, May 10). A worldwide gender gap. *Newsweek,* p. 94.

Marx, D. M., & Roman, J. S. (2002). Female role models: Protecting women's math test performance. *Personality and Social Psychology Bulletin, 28,* 1183–1193.

Mason, E. S. (1995). Gender differences in job satisfaction. *Journal of Social Psychology, 135,* 143–151.

Mason, G. (2002). *The spectacle of violence: Homophobia, gender, and knowledge.* London: Routledge.

Masser, B. M., & Abrams, D. (2004, November). Reinforcing the glass ceiling: The consequences of hostile sexism for female managerial candidates. *Sex Roles, 51,* 609–615.

Massoni, K. (2004). Modeling work: Occupational messages in Seventeen magazine. *Gender & Society, 18,* 47–65.

Masters, W. H., & Johnson, V. E. (1966). *Human sexual response.* Boston: Little, Brown.

Mastro, D. E., & Greenberg, B. S. (2000, Fall). The portrayal of racial minorities on prime time television. *Journal of Broadcasting & Electronic Media,* 690–703.

Mathers, C. D., et al. (2002). Global patterns of healthy life expectancy for older women. *Journal of Women & Aging, 14,* 99–117.

Matire, L. M., Stephens, M. A. P., & Townsend, A. L. (1998). Emotional support and well-being of midlife women: Role-specific mastery as a mediational mechanism. *Psychology and Aging, 13,* 396–404.

Matlin, M. W. (2001, May). *Wise and wonderful . . . or wrinkled and wretched: How psychologists and the rest of the world view older women.* Invited address presented at the Midwestern Psychological Association, Chicago.

Matlin, M. W. (2003). From menarche to menopause: Misconceptions about women's reproductive lives. *Psychology Science, 45,* 106–122.

Matthews, K. A., et al. (2004). Optimistic attitudes protect against progression of carotid atherosclerosis in healthy middle-aged women. *Psychosomatic Medicine, 66,* 640–644.

Mattingly, M. J., & Bianchi, S. M. (2003). Gender differences in the quantity and quality of free time: The U.S. experience. *Social Forces, 81,* 999–1030.

Mattis, J. S. (2002). Religion and spirituality in the meaning-making and coping experiences of African American women: A qualitative analysis. *Psychology of Women Quarterly, 26,* 309–321.

Mau, W. C. (2003). Factors that influence persistence in science and engineering career aspirations. *Career Development Quarterly, 51,* 234–243.

Mauthner, N. S. (2002). *The darkest days of my life: Stories of postpartum depression.* Cambridge, MA and London: Harvard University Press.

Mauthner, N. S. (2003). Imprisoned in my own prison. A relational understanding of Sonya's story of postpartum depression. In J. M. Stoppard & L. M. McMullen (Eds.), *Situating sadness. Women and depression in social context* (pp. 88–112). New York: New York University Press.

McCann, T. (2004, July). 2004 diversity survey: Women struggle to reach the top. *Chicago Lawyer,* 8–17, 76–77.

McClelland, M. M., Kessenich, M., & Morrison, F. J. (2003). Pathways to early literacy: The complex interplay of child, family, and sociocultural factors. In R. V. Kail (Ed.)., *Advances in child development and behavior, 31* (pp. 411–447). San Diego: Academic Press.

McCloud, A., et al. (2004). Relationship between alcohol use disorders and suicidality in a psychiatric population. *British Journal of Psychiatry, 184,* 439–445.

McClure, E. B. (2000). A meta-analytic review of sex differences in facial expression processing and their development in infants, children, and adolescents. *Psychological Bulletin, 126,* 424–453.

McConatha, J. T., et al. (2002, June). *Attitudes toward aging.* Poster presented at the meeting of the American Psychological Society, New Orleans.

McConnell, A. R., & Fazio, R. H. (1996). Women as men and people: Effects of gender-marked language. *Personality & Social Psychology Bulletin, 22,* 1004–1013.

McCowan, C. J., & Alston, R. J. (1998). Racial identity, African self-consciousness, and career decision making in African American college women. *Journal of Multicultural Counseling and Development, 26,* 28–38.

McCoy, W. D. (2002, June 11). Abundance of "cures" brings ills. *New York Times*, p. D6.

McCreary, D. R. (1994). The male role and avoiding femininity. *Sex Roles, 31*, 517–531.

McCree, D. H., et al. (2003, July). Religiosity and risky sexual behavior in African-American adolescent females. *Journal of Adolescent Health, 33*, 2–8.

McDonald, J. (2003). Eating disorders and disconnections. Telling the problem from the solution. In L. Slater, J. H. Daniel, & A. E. Banks (Eds.), *The complete guide to mental health for women* (pp. 228–237). Boston: Beacon Press.

McDonough, V. T. (2002, June 6). Between the lines. *Missoula Independent, 13*, pp. 1–2.

McFadden, D. (2002). Masculinization effects in the auditory system. *Archives of Sexual Behavior, 31*, 99–111.

McGarry, K., & Schoeni, R. F. (2003, December). *Widow poverty and out-of-pocket medical expenditures at the end of life*. PSC Research Report, Report No. 03-547. PSC Population Studies Center at the Institute for Social Research, University of Michigan.

McGeehan, P. (2004, August 22). What Merrill's women want. *New York Times*, pp. BU1, BU4.

McGill, H. C., & McMahan, C. A. (2003). Starting earlier to prevent heart disease. *Journal of the American Medical Association, 290*, 2320–2322.

McGinn, D. (2004, October 4). Mating behavior 101. *Newsweek*, pp. 44–45.

McGinn, D., & Skipp, C. (2002, June 3). Does Gran get it on? *Newsweek*, p. 10.

McGinnis, J. M., & Foege, W. H. (2004). The immediate vs the important. *Journal of the American Medical Association, 291*, 1263–1264.

McGirk, T., & Plain, S. (2002, February 18). Lifting the veil on sex slavery. *Time*, p. 8.

McGlynn, E. A., et al. (2003). The quality of health care delivered to adults in the United States. *New England Journal of Medicine, 348*, 2635–2645.

McGorty, E. K., Iyer, S. N., & Hunt, J. S. (2003, May). *The effect of patient sex on medical decision-making: A meta-analysis*. Paper presented at the meeting of the Midwestern Psychological Association, Chicago.

McHale, S. M., Corneal, D. A., Crouter, A. C., & Birch, L. L. (2001). Gender and weight concerns in early and middle adolescence: Links with well-being and family characteristics. *Journal of Clinical Child Psychology, 30*, 338–348.

McHale, S. M., Crouter, A. C., & Tucker, C. J. (1999). Family context and gender role socialization in middle childhood comparing girls to boys and sisters to brothers. *Child Development, 70*, 990–1004.

McHale, S. M., Crouter, A. C., & Tucker, C. J. (2001). Free-time activities in middle childhood: Links with adjustment in early adolescence. *Child Development, 72*, 1764–1778.

McHale, S. M., Kim, J. Y., Whiteman, S., & Crouter, A. C. (2004). Links between sex-typed time use in middle childhood and gender development in early adolescence. *Developmental Psychology, 40*, 868–881.

McHale, S. M., Shanahan, L., Updegraff, K. A., Crouter, A. C., & Booth, A. (2004). Developmental and individual differences in girls' sex-typed activities in middle childhood and adolescence. *Child Development, 75*, 1575–1593.

McHale, S. M., Updegraff, K. A., Helms-Erikson, H., & Crouter, A. C. (2001). Sibling influences on gender development in middle childhood and early adolescence: A longitudinal study. *Developmental Psychology, 37*, 115–125.

McKay, V. C., & Caverly, R. S. (2004). The nature of family relationships between and within generations: Relation between grandparent, grandchildren in later life. In J. F. Nussbaum & J. Coupland (Eds.), *Handbook of communication and aging research*, 2d ed. (pp. 251–272). Mahwah, NJ: Erlbaum.

McKelvey, M. W., & McKenry, P. C. (2000). The psychosocial well-being of black and white mothers following marital dissolution. *Psychology of Women Quarterly, 24*, 4–14.

McLean, R. (2005, April 22). Spanish parliament gives approval to bill to legalize same-sex marriages. *New York Times*, p. A12.

McLoyd, V. C. (1993). Employment among African-American mothers in dual-earner families: Antecedents and consequences for family life and child development. In J. Frankel (Ed.), *The employed mother and the family context* (pp. 180–226). New York: Springer.

McMillan, T. L., & Mark, S. (2004). Complementary and alternative medicine and physical activity for menopausal symptoms. *Journal of the American Medical Women's Association, 59*, 270–277.

McNamara, M. P. (2004, January 20). In fighting stereotypes, students lift test scores. *New York Times*, p. D7.

McNeely, C., et al. (2002). Mothers' influence on the timing of first sex among 14- and 15-year-olds. *Journal of Adolescent Medicine, 31*, 256–265.

McNeil, Jr., D. G. (2004, August 17). Facing middle age and AIDS. *New York Times*, pp. D1, D6.

McQuaide, S. (1998). Women at midlife. *Social Work, 43,* 21–31.

McSweeney, J. C., et al. (2003). Women's early warning symptoms of acute myocardial infarction. *Circulation,* pp. 2619–2623.

Meadows, S. (2002, June 3). Meet the gamma girls. *Newsweek,* pp. 44–50.

Medicine, B. (1988). Native American (Indian) women: A call for research. *Anthropology & Education Quarterly, 19,* 86–92.

Mednick, M. T., & Thomas, V. G. (1993). Women and the psychology of achievement: A view from the eighties. In F. L. Denmark & M. A. Paludi (Eds.), *Psychology of women: A handbook of issues and theories* (pp. 585–626). Westport, CT: Greenwood.

Menacker, F., Martin, J. A., MacDorman, M. F., Ventura, S. J. (2004). *Births to 10-14 year-old mothers, 1990–2002: Trends and health outcomes.* National Vital Statistics Reports, 53, No. 7. Hyattsville, MD: National Center for Health Statistics.

Ménard, K. S., et al. (2003). Gender differences in sexual harassment and coercion in college students: Developmental, individual, and situational determinants. *Journal of Interpersonal Violence, 18,* 1222–1239.

Menec, V. H. (2003). The relation between everyday activities and successful aging: A 6-year longitudinal study. *Journals of Gerontology, 58,* S74–S82.

Menendez, J. A., Vellon, L., Colomer, R., & Lupu, R. (2005, January 10). Oleic acid, the main monounsaturated fatty acid of olive oil, suppresses Her–2/*neu* (*erb* B–2) expression and synergistically enhances the growth inhibitory effects of trastuzumab (Herceptin™) in breast cancer cells with Her–2/*neu* oncogene amplification. *Annals of Oncology,* pp. 1–14.

Mercer, S. O., Garner, J. D., & Findley, J. (2001). Older women: A global view. In J. D. Garner & S. O. Mercer (Eds.), *Women as they age,* 2d ed. (pp. 13–32). New York: Haworth.

Merikangas, K. R., & Pollock, R. A. (2000). Anxiety disorders in women. In M. B. Goldman & M. C. Hatch (Eds.), *Women & health* (pp. 1010–1023). New York: Academic Press.

Merkin, D. (2004, May 2). Keeping the forces of decrepitude at bay. *New York Times Magazine,* pp. 64–67, 96–98.

Merline, A. C., et al. (2004). Substance use among adults 35 years of age: Prevalence, adulthood predictors, and impact of adolescent substance use. *American Journal of Public Health, 94,* 95–103.

Merrill, L. L., Newel, C. E., Milner, J. S., Hervig, L. K., & Gold, S. R. (1997). Prevalence of premilitary adult sexual victimization and aggression in a navy basic trainee sample. *U.S. Naval Health Research Center Report* (No. 97–4, pp. 1–14).

Merskin, D. (1999). Adolescence, advertising, and the ideology of menstruation. *Sex Roles, 40,* 941–957.

Messman-Moore, T. L., & Long, P. J. (2003). The role of childhood sexual abuse sequelae in the sexual revictimization of women. An empirical review and theoretical reformulation. *Clinical Psychology Review, 23,* 537–571.

Messner, M. A., Duncan, M. C., & Jensen, K. (1993). Separating the men from the girls: The gendered language of televised sports. *Gender & Society, 7,* 121–137.

Mestel, R. (2000, May 1). Sex in the shadow of illness and disability. *Los Angeles Times,* p. 1.

Metzl, J. M. (2003, Fall). Selling sanity through gender. *Ms.,* pp. 40–45.

Meyer, I. H. (2003). Prejudice, social stress, and mental health in lesbian, gay, and bisexual populations: Conceptual issues and research evidence. *Psychological Bulletin, 129,* 674–697.

Meyer, M. H., & Bellas, M. L. (1995). U.S. old-age policy and the family. In R. Bleiszner & V. H. Bedford (Eds.), *Handbook of aging and the family* (pp. 263–283). Westport, CT: Greenwood.

Mezulis, A. H., Abramson, L. Y., Hyde, J. S., & Hankin, B. L. (2004). Is there a universal positivity bias in attributions? A meta-analytic review of individual, developmental, and cultural differences in the self-serving attributional bias. *Psychological Bulletin, 130,* 711–747.

Michael, A., & Eccles, J. S. (2003). When coming of age means coming undone: Links between puberty and psychosocial adjustment among European American and African American girls. In C. Hayward (Ed.), *Gender differences at puberty* (pp. 277–303). Cambridge: University Press.

Michael, S. T., Crowther, M. R., Schmid, B., & Allen, R. S. (2003). Widowhood and spirituality: Coping responses. *Journal of Women & Aging, 15,* 145–166.

Michael, Y. L., Berkman, L. F., Colditz, G. A., & Kawachi, I. (2001). Living arrangements, social integration, and change in functional health status. *American Journal of Epidemiology, 153,* 123–131.

Michaud, S. L., & Warner, R. M. (1997). Gender differences in self-reported response to troubles talk. *Sex Roles, 37,* 527–540.

Michels, K. B., & Willett, W. C. (2004). Breast cancer—Early life matters. *New England Journal of Medicine, 351,* 1679–1681.

Michelson, W., & Tepperman, L. (2003). Focus on home: What time-use data can tell about caregiving to adults. *Journal of Social Issues, 59,* 591–610.

Milar, K. S. (2000). The first generation of women psychologists and the psychology of women. *American Psychologist, 55,* 616–620.

Milburn, S. S., Carney, D. R., & Ramirez, A. M. (2001). Even in modern media the picture is still the same: A content analysis of clipart images. *Sex Roles, 44,* 277–294.

Milkie, M. A., Bianchi, S. M., Mattingly, M. J., & Robinson, J. P. (2002). Gendered division of childrearing: Ideals, realities, and the relationship to parental well-being. *Sex Roles, 47,* 21–38.

Miller, B. A., & Downs, W. R. (2000). Violence against women. In M. B. Goldman & M. C. Hatch (Eds.), *Women & health* (pp. 529–540). San Diego: Academic Press.

Miller, B. C., Benson, B., & Galbraith, K. A. (2001). Family relationships and adolescent pregnancy risk: A research synthesis. *Developmental Review, 21,* 1–38.

Miller, B. C., & Moore, K. A. (1990). Adolescent sexual behavior, pregnancy, and parenting: Research through the 1980s. *Journal of Marriage and the Family, 52,* 1025–1044.

Miller, C., & Swift, K. (1991). *Words and women: Updated.* New York: HarperCollins.

Miller-Day, M. A. (2004). *Communication among grandmothers, mothers, and adult daughters.* Mahwah, NJ: Erlbaum.

Miller, J. B., & Stiver, I. P. (1997). *The healing connection.* Boston: Beacon Press.

Miller, K. K., et al. (2005). Medical findings in outpatients with anorexia nervosa. *Archives of Internal Medicine, 165,* 561–566.

Miller, K. S., Levin, M. L., Whittaker, D. J., & Xu, X. (1998). Patterns of condom use among adolescents: The impact of mother-adolescent communication. *American Journal of Public Health, 88,* 1542–1544.

Miller, P. (2004, Spring). Aborted rights. *Ms.,* pp. 14–15.

Miller, W. C., et al. (2004, May 12). Prevalence of chlamydial and gonococcal infections among young adults in the United States. *Journal of the American Medical Association, 291,* pp. 2229–2236.

Miner-Rubino, K., & Cortina, L. M. (2004). Working in a context of hostility toward women:

Implications for employees' well-being. *Journal of Occupational Health Psychology, 9,* 107–122.

Minto, C., Woodhouse, C., Ransley, P., & Creighton, S. (2003). The effect of clitoral surgery on sexual outcome in individuals who have intersex conditions with ambiguous genitalia: A cross-sectional study. *The Lancet, 361,* 1252–1257.

Mischel, W. (1966). A social-learning view of sex differences in behavior. In E. E. Maccoby (Ed.), *The development of sex differences* (pp. 56–81). Stanford, CA: Stanford University Press.

Misra, D. (2001). (Ed.). *Women's health data book: A profile of women's health in the United States,* 3d ed. Washington, DC: Jacobs Institute of Women's Health and The Henry J. Kaiser Family Foundation.

Misra, M., et al. (2004). Effects of anorexia nervosa on clinical, hematologic, biochemical, and bone density parameters in community-dwelling adolescent girls. *Pediatrics, 114,* 1574–1583.

Mitchell, B. S., & Stricker, G. (1998, August). *The quality of the grandparent-young adult relationship: How does it relate to attitudes toward older persons and personal anxiety towards aging?* Paper presented at the meeting of the American Psychological Association, San Francisco.

Mitka, M. (2004). Heart disease a global health threat. *Journal of the American Medical Association, 291,* 2533.

Mobily, K. E. (1992). Leisure, lifestyle, and lifespan. In M. L. Teague & R. D. MacNeil (Eds.), *Aging and leisure: Vitality in later life,* 2d ed. (pp. 179–206). Dubuque, IA: Brown & Benchmark.

Moen, P. (1996). Gender, age, and the life course. In R. H. Binstock & L. K. George (Eds.), *Handbook of aging and the social sciences,* 4th ed. (pp. 171–187). San Diego: Academic Press.

Moen, P., Kim, J. E., & Hofmeister, H. (2001). Couples' work/retirement transitions, gender, and mental quality. *Social Psychology Quarterly, 64,* 55–71.

Moffat, S. C., & Hampson, E. (1996). A curvilinear relationship between testosterone and spatial cognition in humans: Possible influence of hand preference. *Psychoneuroendocrinology, 21,* 323–337.

Mohler-Kuo, M., Dowdall, G. W., Koss, M. P., & Wechsler, H. (2004). Correlates of rape while intoxicated in a national sample of college women. *Journal of Studies on Alcohol, 65,* 37–45.

Mokdad, A. H., Marks, J. S., Stroup, D. F., & Gerberding, J. L. (2004). Actual causes of death in the United States, 2000. *Journal of the American Medical Association, 291,* 1238–1245.

Monastersky, R. (2005, March 4). Women and science: The debate goes. *Chronicle of Higher Education,* pp. 1, 12–16.

Mondschein, E. R., Adolph, K. E., & Tamis-LeMonda, C. S. (2000). Gender bias in mothers' expectations about infant crawling. *Journal of Experimental Child Psychology, 77,* 304–316.

Mongeau, P. A., Carey, C. M., & Williams, M. L. M. (1998). First date initiation and enactment: An expectancy violation approach. In D. J. Canary & K. Dindia (Eds.), *Sex differences and similarities in communication: Critical essays and empirical investigations of sex and gender in interaction* (pp. 413–426). Mahwah, NJ: Erlbaum.

Monsour, M. (2002). *Women and men as friends: Relationships across the life span in the 21st century.* Mahwah, NJ: Erlbaum.

Montepare, J. M., & Zebrowitz, L. A. (2002). A social-developmental view of ageism. In T. D. Nelson (Ed.), *Ageism: Stereotyping and prejudice against older persons* (pp. 77–125). Cambridge, MA: MIT Press.

Moos, R. (1985). *Perimenstrual symptoms: A manual and overview of research with the Menstrual Distress Questionnaire.* Stanford, CA: Stanford University.

Mor, N., & Winquist, J. (2002). Self-focused attention and negative affect: A meta-analysis. *Psychological Bulletin, 128,* 638–662.

Moracco, K. E., Runyan, C. W., & Butts, J. D. (2003). Female intimate partner homicide: A population-based study. *Journal of the American Medical Women's Association, 58,* 20–25.

Moradi, B., Fischer, A. R., Hill, M. S., Jome, L. M., & Blum, S. A. (2000). Does "feminist" plus "therapist" equal "feminist therapist"? *Psychology of Women Quarterly, 24,* 285–296.

Morahan-Martin J., & Schumacher, P. (1998, August). *Are Internet and computer experiences and attitudes related?: Gender differences.* Paper presented at the meeting of the American Psychological Association, San Francisco.

Morandi, P., et al. (2004). The role of aromatase inhibitors in the adjuvant treatment of breast carcinoma: The M.D. Anderson Cancer Center evidence-based approach. *Cancer, 101,* 1482–1489.

Mor-Barak, M. E., & Tynan, M. (1995). Older workers and the workplace. In F. J. Turner (Ed.), *Differential diagnosis and treatment in social work,* 4th ed. (pp. 59–73). New York: Free Press.

More women seemingly choosing c-sections. (2004, June 29). *Associated Press.*

Moreau, R., & Yousafzai, S. (2004, October 11). "Living dead" no more. *Newsweek,* p. 37.

Morell, C. (1993). "Intentionally childless women: Another view of women's development." *Affilia: Journal of Women & Social Work, 8,* 300–317.

Morgan, B. L. (1996). Putting the feminism into feminism scales: Introduction of a liberal feminist attitude and ideology scale (LFAIS). *Sex Roles, 34,* 359–390.

Morgan, L., & Kunkel, S. (2001). *Aging: The social context.* 2d ed. Thousand Oaks, CA: Pine Forge Press.

Morgan, R. (2002, November 29). Bisexual students face tension with gay groups. *Chronicle of Higher Education,* p. A31.

Mori, L., Bernat, J. A., Glenn, P. A., Selle, L. L., & Zarate, M. G. (1995). Attitudes toward rape: Gender and ethnic differences across Asian and caucasian college students. *Sex Roles, 32,* 457–467.

Morris, B. R. (2002, June 23). A disturbing growth industry: Web sites that espouse anorexia. *New York Times,* p. 8.

Morris, B. R. (2004a, June 6). Fighting dryness, with pills, gels and rings. *New York Times,* p. WH12.

Morris, B. R. (2004b, July 6). Older women, too, struggle with a dangerous secret. *New York Times,* pp. D5, D8.

Morris, J. F. (1998, August). *Use of therapy by lesbian and bisexual women of color.* Paper presented at the meeting of the American Psychological Association, San Francisco.

Morris, J. F., Balsam, K. F., & Rothblum, E. D. (2002). Lesbian and bisexual mothers and non-mothers: Demographics and the coming-out process. *Journal of Family Psychology, 16,* 144–156.

Morris, J. F., Waldo, C. R., & Rothblum, E. D. (2001). A model of predictors and outcomes of outness among lesbian and bisexual women. *American Journal of Orthopsychiatry, 71,* 61–71.

Morris, L. B. (2000, June 25). For the partum blues, a question of whether to medicate. *New York Times,* p. WH17.

Morrison, M. A., Morrison, T. G., & Sager, C. L. (2004, May). Does body satisfaction differ between gay men and lesbian women and heterosexual men and women? *Body Image, 1,* 127–138.

Morrongiello, B. A., & Dawber, T. (2000). Mothers' responses to sons and daughters engaging in injury-risk behaviors on a playground: Implications for sex differences in injury rates. *Journal of Experimental Child Psychology, 76,* 89–103.

Morrongiello, B. A., & Hogg, K. (2004). Mothers' reactions to children misbehaving in ways that can lead to injury: Implications for gender differences in children's risk taking and injuries. *Sex Roles, 50,* 103–118.

Morrow, M. (2002). Rational local therapy for breast cancer. *New England Journal of Medicine, 347,* 1270–1271.

Morrow, S. L., Gore, P. A., Jr., & Campbell, B. W. (1996). The application of a sociocognitive framework to the career development of lesbian women and gay men. *Journal of Vocational Behavior, 48,* 136–148.

Morrow-Howell, N., et al. (2003). Effects of volunteering on the well-being of older adults. *Journals of Gerontology, 58,* S137–S145.

Mortola, J. F. (2000). Premenstrual syndrome. In M. B. Goldman & M. C. Hatch (Eds.), *Women & health* (pp. 114–125). San Diego: Academic Press.

Mosca, L., et al. (2000). Awareness, perception, and knowledge of heart disease risk and prevention among women in the United States. *Archives of Family Medicine, 9,* 506–515.

Mosca, L., et al. (2004). Evidence-based guidelines for cardiovascular disease prevention in women. *Circulation, 109,* 672–693

Mosca, L., Ferris, A., Fabunmi, R., & Robertson, R. M. (2004). Tracking women's awareness of heart disease: An American Heart Association national study. *Circulation, 109,* 573–579.

Mosher, C. E., & Danoff-Burg, S. (2005). Agentic and communal personality traits: Relations to attitudes toward sex and sexual experiences. *Sex Roles, 52,* 121–129.

Mozaffarian, D., et al., (2005). Fish consumption and stroke risk in elderly individuals. *Archives of Internal Medicine, 165,* 200–206.

Mroczek, D. K. (2000). Age and emotion in adulthood. *Current Directions in Psychological Science, 10,* 87–90.

Muehlenhard, C. L., & Rodgers, C. S. (1998). Token resistance to sex: New perspectives on an old stereotype. *Psychology of Women Quarterly, 22,* 443–463.

Muehlenkamp, J. J., Swanson, J. D., & Brausch, A. M. (2005). Self-objectification, risk taking, and self-harm in college women. *Psychology of Women Quarterly, 29,* 24–32.

Mueller, K. A., & Yoder, J. D. (1997). Gendered norms for family size, employment, and occupation: Are there personal costs for violating them? *Sex Roles, 36,* 207–220.

Mulac, A., Bradac, J. J., & Gibbons, P. (2001). Empirical support for the gender-as-culture hypothesis. An intercultural analysis of male/female language differences. *Human Communication Research, 27,* 121–152.

Mulac, A. (1998). The gender-linked language effect: Do language differences really make a difference? In D. J. Canary & K. Dindia (Eds.), *Sex differences and similarities in communication: Critical essays and empirical investigations of sex and gender in interaction* (pp. 127–153). Mahwah, NJ: Erlbaum.

Mulac, A., et al. (1998). "Uh-huh. What's that all about?" Differing interpretations of conversational backchannels and questions as sources of miscommunication across gender boundaries. *Communication Research, 25,* 641–668.

Mulholland, A. M., & Mintz, L. B. (2001). Prevalence of eating disorders among African-American women. *Journal of Counseling Psychology, 48,* 111–116.

Mulick, P. S., & Wright, L. W. (2002). Examining the existence of biphobia in the heterosexual and homosexual populations. *Journal of Bisexuality, 2,* 47–64.

Mullis, I. V. S., Martin, M. O., Gonzalez, E. J., & Chrostowski, S. J. (2004). *TIMSS 2003 International Mathematics Report.* Boston: Boston College.

Munson, L. J., Miner, A. G., & Hulin, C. (2001). Labeling sexual harassment in the military: An extension and replication. *Journal of Applied Psychology, 86,* 293–303.

Murnen, S. K., & Smolak, L. (2000). The experience of sexual harassment among grade-school students: Early socialization of female subordination? *Sex Roles, 43,* 1–7.

Murnen, S. K., Wright, C., & Kaluzny, G. (2002). If "boys will be boys," then girls will be victims? A meta-analytic review of the research that relates masculine ideology to sexual aggression. *Sex Roles, 46,* 359–375.

Murnen, S. K., Smolak, L., Mills, J. A., & Good, L. (2003). Thin, sexy women and strong, muscular men: Grade-school children's responses to objectified images of women and men. *Sex Roles, 49,* 427–437.

Murphy, E. M. (2003). Being born female is dangerous for your health. *American Psychologist, 58,* 205–210.

Murray, B. (1998, October). Survey reveals concerns of today's girls. *APA Monitor, 29*, p. 12.

Murray, B. (1999, May). Friedan calls for more research on fathers and parenting. *APA Monitor, 30*, p. 10.

Murray, C. S., & Corson, J. R. (2004, May). *The role of peers in body dissatisfaction in men and women.* Poster presented at the meeting of American Psychological Society, Chicago.

Murray, L. R. (2003). Sick and tired of being sick and tired: Scientific evidence, methods, and research implications for racial and ethnic disparities in occupational health. *American Journal of Public Health, 93*, 221–226.

Murray, T., & Steil, J. (2000, August). *Construction of gender: Comparing children of traditional vs. egalitarian families.* Poster presented at the meeting of the American Psychological Association, Washington, DC.

Murrell, A. J. (1996). Sexual harassment and women of color: Issues, challenges, and future directions. In M. S. Stockdale (Ed.), *Sexual harassment in the workplace: Perspectives, frontiers, and response strategies* (pp. 51–66). Thousand Oaks, CA: Sage.

Murrell, A. J., Frieze, I. H., & Frost, J. L. (1991). Aspiring to careers in male- and female-dominated professions: A study of black and white college women. *Psychology of Women Quarterly, 15*, 103–126.

Murrell, A. J., & Jones, R. (1996). Assessing affirmative action: Past, present, and future. *Journal of Social Issues, 52*, 77–92.

Murthy, V. H., Krumholz, H. M., & Gross, C. P. (2004). Participation in cancer clinical trials. Race-, sex-, and age-based disparities. *Journal of the American Medical Association, 291*, 2720–2726.

Musick, M. A., & Wilson, J. (2003). Volunteering and depression: The role of psychological and social resources in different age groups. *Social Science & Medicine, 56*, 259–269.

Mustanski, B. S., et al. (2004). Genetic and environmental influences on pubertal development: Longitudinal data from Finnish twins at ages 11 and 14. *Developmental Psychology, 40*, 1188–1198.

Mutler, A. (2005, January 17). Children's author becomes oldest woman to give birth. *Independent (London)*, p. 20.

Muzio, C. (1996). Lesbians choosing children: Creating families, creating narratives. In J. Laird & R.-J. Green (Eds.), *Lesbians and gays in couples and families* (pp. 358–369). San Francisco: Jossey-Bass.

Myaskovsky, L., & Wittig, M. A. (1997). Predictors of feminist social identity among college women. *Sex Roles, 37*, 861–883.

Mydans, S. (2002, May 17). In Pakistan, rape victims are the "criminals." *New York Times*, p. A3.

Myers, D. J., & Dugan, K. B. (1996). Sexism in graduate school classrooms: Consequences for students and faculty. *Gender & Society, 10*, 330–350.

Nabel, E. G. (2000). Coronary heart disease—An ounce of prevention. *New England Journal of Medicine, 343*, 572–574.

Nagourney, E. (2004, September 28). Therapies; Mental, if not physical, benefits. *New York Times*, p. F6.

Nagourney, E. (2005, February 1). Mental health: Sweating depression away. *New York Times*, p. F6.

Nagurney, A. J., Reich, J. W., & Newsom, J. T. (2004). Gender moderates the effects of independence and dependence desires during the social support process. *Psychology and Aging, 19*, 215–218.

Naimi, T. S., et al. (2003). Binge drinking among U.S. adults. *Journal of the American Medical Association, 289*, 70–75.

Naples, N. A. (2003). *Feminism and method: Ethnography, discourse analysis and activist research.* New York: Routledge.

Nation: Faculty and staff. (2004, August 27). *Chronicle of Higher Education*, pp. 24–29.

Nation: Students. (2004, August 27). *Chronicle of Higher Education*, pp. 14–22.

National Alliance for Caregiving and AARP. (2004). *Caregiving in the U.S.* Bethesda, MD: Author.

National Campaign to Prevent Teen Pregnancy. (2003). *With one voice 2003: America's adults and teens sound off about teen pregnancy.* Washington, DC: Author.

National Center for Health Statistics. (2002). *Health, United States 2002.* Hyattsville, MD: Author.

National Center for Health Statistics. (2004). *Health, United States, 2004 with chartbook on trends in the health of Americans.* Hysttsville, MD: Author.

National Center for Injury Prevention and Control. (2003). *Costs of intimate partner violence against women in the United States.* Atlanta: Centers for Disease Control and Prevention.

National Center for Injury Prevention and Control. (2005). *Sexual violence: Fact sheet.* Washington, DC: Author.

National Center on Addiction and Substance Abuse (CASA) at Columbia University. (2002). *Teen tipplers: America's underage drinking epidemic.* New York: Author.

National Coalition for Women and Girls in Education. (2002). *Title IX at 30: Report card on gender equity.* Washington, DC: American Association of University Women.

National Council on Family Relations. (2003). *Family caregivers: Helping families meet the needs of older adults.* Minneapolis, MN: Author.

National Institute on Alcohol Abuse and Alcoholism. (2003, July). The genetics of alcoholism. *Alcohol Alert, 60.*

National Institutes of Health. (2003). *Alcohol: A women's health issue.* NIH Publication No. 03-4956, pp. 1–19. Washington, DC: U.S. Department of Health and Human Services.

National Institutes of Health. (2004). *Women's health in the U.S. Research on health issues affecting women.* NIH Publication No. 04-4697, pp. 1–29. Washington, DC: U.S. Department of Health and Human Services.

National Osteoporosis Foundation. (2002). *The physician's guide to prevention and treatment of osteoporosis.* Washington, DC: Author.

National Osteoporosis Foundation. (2004, Spring). Risk factors for osteoporosis. *Osteoporosis Clinical Updates, V(1),* 6.

National Partnership for Women & Families. (1998). *Balancing acts: Work/family issues on prime-time TV.* Washington, DC: Author.

National Science Foundation. (2003). *Gender differences in the careers of academic scientists and engineers: A literature review.* NSF 03-322. Arlington, VA: Author.

Navarro, M. (2001, February 13). Women in sports cultivating new playing fields. *New York Times,* pp. A1, C23.

Navarro, M. (2002, May 16). Trying to get beyond the role of the maid. *New York Times,* pp. B1, B4.

Navarro, M. (2004, September 19). When gender isn't a given. *New York Times,* p. 1.

Nayak, M. B., Byrne, C. A., Martin, M. K., & Abraham, A. G. (2003). Attitudes toward violence against women: A cross-nation study. *Sex Roles, 49,* 333–342.

Neff, K. D., & Terry-Schmitt, L. N. (2002). Youths' attributions for power-related gender attributes: Nature, nurture, or God? *Cognitive Development, 17,* 1185–1202.

Neff, L. A., & Karney, B. R. (2005). Gender differences in social support: A question of skill or responsiveness? *Journal of Personality & Social Psychology, 88,* 79–90.

Nelson, D. L., & Burke, R. J. (2002). A framework for examining gender, work stress, and health. In D. L. Nelson & R. J. Burke (Eds.), *Gender, work stress and health* (pp. 3–14). Washington, DC: American Psychological Association.

Nelson, D. L., Burke, R. J., & Michie, S. (2002). New directions for studying gender, work stress, and health. In D. L. Nelson & R. J. Burke (Eds.), *Gender, work stress, and health* (pp. 229–242). Washington, DC: American Psychological Association.

Nelson, H. D. (2004). Postmenopausal estrogen for treatment of hot flashes. Clinical applications. *Journal of the American Medical Association, 291,* 1621–1625.

Nelson, L. D., & LeBoeuf, R. A. (2002, February). *Why do men overperceive women's sexual intent? False consensus vs. evolutionary explanations.* Paper presented at the meeting of the Society for Personality and Social Psychology, Savannah, GA.

Nelson, L. J., Shanahan, S. B., & Olivetti, J. (1997). Power, empowerment, and equality: Evidence for the motives of feminists, nonfeminists, and antifeminists. *Sex Roles, 37,* 227–249.

Nelson, T. D. (Ed.). (2002). *Ageism: Stereotyping and prejudice against older persons.* Cambridge, MA: MIT Press.

Nesbitt, M. N., & Penn, N. E. (2000). Gender stereotypes after thirty years: A replication of Rosencrantz et al. (1968). *Psychological Reports, 87,* 493–511.

Netburn, D. (2002, May 26). Young, carefree, and hooked on sunlamps. *New York Times,* pp. ST1, ST7.

Netz, W. M., Becker, B. J., & Tenenbaum, G. (2005). Physical activity and psychological well-being in advanced age: A meta-analysis of intervention studies. *Psychology and Aging, 20,* 272–284.

Newby, J. H., et al. (2003). Spousal agression by U.S. Army female soldiers toward employed and unemployed civilian husbands. *American Journal of Orthopsychiatry, 73,* 288–293.

Newcombe, N. S. (2002, August). *Some unanswered questions about a sociobiological theory of sex differences in spatial ability.* Paper presented at the meeting of the American Psychological Association, Chicago.

Newman, J. (2000, April). How old is too old to have a baby? *Discover,* pp. 60–67.

Newman, L. S., Cooper, J. N., & Ruble, D. N. (1995). Gender and computers II. The interactive effects of knowledge and constancy on gender-stereotyped attitudes. *Sex Roles, 33,* 325–351.

New risks tied to hormone therapy. (2004, June 29). *New York Times,* p. A20.

Newton, K. M., Lacroix, A. Z., & Buist, D. S. M. (2000). Overview of risk factors for cardiovascular disease. In M. B. Goldman & M. C. Hatch (Eds.), *Women & health* (pp. 757–770). San Diego: Academic Press.

Newtson, R. L., & Keith, P. M. (2001). Single women in later life. In J. M. Coyle (Ed.), *Handbook on women and aging* (pp. 385–399). Westport, CT: Greenwood.

NICHD Early Child Care Research Network. (2002). Child-care structure→process→outcome: Direct and indirect effects of child-care quality on young children's development. *Psychological Science, 13,* 199–206.

NICHD Early Child Care Research Network. (2003). Does quality of child care affect child outcomes at age 4$^1/_2$? *Developmental Psychology, 39,* 451–469.

NICHD Early Child Care Research Network. (2004). Trajectories of physical aggression from toddlerhood to middle childhood. *Monographs of the Society for Research in Child Development, 69,* 1–146.

Nicolson, P. (2003). Postpartum depression: Women's accounts of loss and change. In J. M. Stoppard & L. M. McMullen (Eds.), *Situating sadness. Women and depression in social context* (pp. 113–138). New York: New York University Press.

Niemann, Y. F., Jennings, L., Rozelle, R. M., Baxter, J. C., & Sullivan, E. (1994). Use of free responses and cluster analysis to determine stereotypes of eight groups. *Personality and Social Psychology Bulletin, 20,* 379–390.

Niles, S. G. (2003, September). Career counselors confront a critical crossroad: A vision of the future. *Career Development Quarterly,* pp. 70–77.

Nishina, A., & Juvonen, J. (2005). Daily sports of witnessing and experiencing peer harassment in middle school. *Child Development, 76,* 435–450.

Nock, S. L. (1995). A comparison of marriages and cohabiting relationships. *Journal of Family Issues, 16,* 53–76.

Noland, V. J., et al. (2004). Is adolescent sibling violence a precursor to college dating violence? *American Journal of Health Behavior, 28,* S13–S23.

Nolen-Hoeksema, S. (2002). Gender differences in depression. In I. Gotlib, & C Hammen (Eds.), *Handbook of depression* (pp. 492–509). New York: Guilford.

Nolen-Hoeksema, S. (2003). *Women who think too much: How to break free of overthinking and reclaim your life.* New York: Henry Holt.

Nolen-Hoeksema, S., & Keita, G. P. (2003). Women and depression: Introduction. *Psychology of Women Quarterly, 27,* 89–90.

Nolen-Hoeksema, S., Larson, J., & Grayson, C. (1999). Explaining the gender difference in depressive symptoms. *Journal of Personality and Social Psychology, 77,* 1061–1072.

Noll, J. G., Trickett, P. K., & Putnam, F. W. (2003). A prospective investigation of the impact of childhood sexual abuse on the development of sexuality. *Journal of Consulting and Clinical Psychology, 71,* 575–586.

Nomaguchi, K. M., & Bianchi, S. M. (2004). Exercise time: Gender differences in the effects of marriage, parenthood, and employment. *Journal of Marriage and Family, 66,* 413–430.

Norris, P., & Inglehart, R. (2004, Spring). It's the *women,* stupid. *Ms.,* pp. 47–49.

North American Menopause Society. (2003). *Menopause guidebook.* Cleveland, OH: Author.

Nosek, B. A., Banaji, M. R., & Greenwald, A. G. (2002). Math = male, me = female, therefore math ≠ me. *Journal of Personality and Social Psychology, 83,* 44–59.

Not near the top. (2003, Fall/Winter). *AAUW Outlook,* p. 4.

Novack, L. L., & Novack, D. R. (1996). Being female in the eighties and nineties: Conflicts between new opportunities and traditional expectations among white, middle class, heterosexual college women. *Sex Roles, 35,* 57–77.

Nowell, A., & Hedges, L. V. (1998). Trends in gender differences in academic achievement from 1960 to 1994: An analysis of differences in mean, variance, and extreme scores. *Sex Roles, 39,* 21–43.

Nunes, K. L., de Bellefeuille-Percy, K., & Dowden, C. (2004, August). *Factors associated with attributions of blame, fault, responsibility, and causality to victims of sexual assault: A meta-analysis.* Poster presented at the meeting of the American Psychological Association, Honolulu.

Nussbaum, M. C. (2004). Women's education: A global challenge. *Signs: Journal of Women in Culture and Society, 29,* 325–355.

Nyad, D. (2004, August 15). The rise of the buff bunny. *New York Times,* p. ST7.

Oates, M. R., et al. (2004). Postnatal depression across countries and cultures: a qualitative study. *British Journal of Psychiatry, 184,* S10–S16.

Obeidallah, D. A., McHale, S. M., & Silbereisen, R. K. (1996). Gender role socialization and adolescents reports of depression: Why some girls and not others? *Journal of Youth and Adolescence, 25,* 776–786.

Oberman, Y., & Josselson, R. (1996). Matrix of tensions: A model of mothering. *Psychology of Women Quarterly, 20,* 341–359.

O'Brien, K., Friedman, S. C., Tipton, L. C., & Linn, S. G. (2000). Attachment, separation, and women's vocational development: A longitudinal analysis. *Journal of Counseling Psychology, 47,* 301–315.

O'Bryant, S. L., & Hansson, R. O. (1995). Widowhood. In R. Blieszner & V. H. Bedford (Eds.), *Handbook of aging and the family* (pp. 440–458). Westport, CT: Greenwood.

O'Connor, A. (2004, February 12). U.S. infant mortality rate rises slightly. Reversal points to advances that aid pregnancy but not survival. *New York Times,* p. A30.

Offman, A., & Matheson, K. (2004). The sexual self-perceptions of young women experiencing abuse in dating relationships. *Sex Roles, 51,* 551–560.

Ofstedal, M. B., Reidy, E., & Knodel, J. (2003, November). *Gender differences in economic support and well-being of older Asians.* Report No. 03-540. Population Studies Center at the Institute for Social Research, University of Michigan.

Oggins, J., Veroff, J., & Leber, D. (1993). Perceptions of marital interaction among Black and White newlyweds. *Journal of Personality and Social Psychology, 65,* 494–511.

O'Grady, K. (2003, Spring/Summer). New evidence about hormone replacement therapy: Turning the tide in the menopause wars. *Women's Studies Quarterly, 31,* pp. 137–144.

Ohye, B., Moore, C. W., & Braaten, E. (2003). Becoming a mother. A psychobiosocial transition in a woman's life. In L. Slater, J. H. Daniel, & A. E. Banks, (Eds.), *The complete guide to mental health for women* (pp. 18–30). Boston: Beacon Press.

Ojikutu, B. O., & Stone, V. E. (2005). Women, inequality, and the burden of HIV. *New England Journal of Medicine, 352,* 649–652.

Older Women's League. (1998). *Women, work, and pensions: Improving the odds for a secure retirement.* Washington, DC: Author.

Older Women's League. (2000). *Prescription for change: Why women need a Medicare drug benefit.* Washington, DC: Author.

Older Women's League. (2001). *State of older women in America.* Washington, DC: Author.

Older Women's League. (2002). *Social security privatization and women.* Washington, DC: Author.

Older Women's League. (2004). *A poor prognosis: Healthcare costs and aging.* Washington, DC: Author.

O'Leary, V. E., & Flanagan, E. H. (2001). Leadership. In J. Worell (Ed.), *Encyclopedia of women and gender* (pp. 645–656). San Diego: Academic Press.

Oliver, M. B., & Hyde, J. S. (1993). Gender differences in sexuality: A meta-analysis. *Psychological Bulletin, 114,* 29–51.

Oliver, M. B., & Sedikides, C. (1992). Effects of sexual permissiveness on desirability of partner as a function of love and high commitment to relationship. *Social Psychology Quarterly, 55,* 321–333.

Olkin, R. (2003). Women with physical disabilities who want to leave their partners: A feminist and disability-affirmative perspective. *Women & Therapy, 26,* 237–246.

Olkin, R., & Pledger, C. (2003). Can disability studies and psychology join hands? *American Psychologist, 58,* 296–304.

Olsen, D. (2002, June 7). Supreme court denies Tazewell grandparents visitation rights. *Peoria Journal Star,* pp. A1, A10.

Olson, J. P., & Warren, D. (2000). Hypertension and ischemic heart disease. In M. A. Smith, & L. A. Shimp (Eds.), *20 common problems in women's health care* (pp. 517–554). New York: McGraw-Hill.

Olson, S. L., & Ceballo, R. E. (1996). Emotional well-being and parenting behavior among low-income single mothers: Social support and ethnicity as contexts of adjustment. In K. F. Wyche & F. J. Crosby (Eds.), *Women's ethnicities: Journeys through psychology* (pp. 105–123). Boulder, CO: Westview.

Omar, H., & Griffith, J. R. (2004). Screening for dating violence: Should we screen or not? *Journal of Pediatric and Adolescent Gynecology, 17,* 53–55.

Omari, S. R., & Mitchell, J. (2003). The real deal: A qualitative analysis of body image attitudes of African American women in Mississippi. *The Researcher, 19(1),* 126–139.

Ompad, D. C., et al. (2005). Childhood sexual abuse and age at initiation of injection drug use. *American Journal of Public Health, 95,* 703–709.

Once behind the scenes, now in the fore. (1999, December). *APA Monitor,* p. 23.

O'Neil, J. (1999, February 2). Happy endings after difficult journeys. *New York Times,* p. D7.

O'Neil, J. (2003, September 23). Finding just the right cast, as fractures increase. *New York Times,* p. D6.

Onishi, N. (2002a, October 3). Globalization of beauty makes slimness trendy. *New York Times,* p. A4.

Onishi, N. (2002b, January 15). Medical schools show first sign of healing from Taliban abuse. *New York Times,* p. A10.

Orbuch, T. L., & Custer, L. (1995). The social context of married women's work and its impact on black husbands and white husbands. *Journal of Marriage and the Family, 57,* 333–345.

Orel, N. A. (2002, August). *The development of a gay, lesbian, and bisexual elders needs assessment scale.* Paper presented at the meeting of the American Psychological Association, Chicago.

Orenstein, C. (2004, June 9). Stepford is us. *New York Times,* p. A25.

Orenstein, C. (2005, Summer). The dialectic of fat. *Ms.,* pp. 46–49.

Orman, S. (2001). *The road to wealth: A comprehensive guide to your money—everything you need to know in good and bad times.* New York: Riverhead Books.

Ormerod, A. J., Vaile Wright, C., & Fitzgerald, L. F. (2003, August). Retaliation against military personnel following sexual harassment: Definition and correlates. In L. F. Fitzgerald (Chair), *Sexual harassment research in the military: Methodological and substantive advances.* Symposium presented at the meeting of the American Psychological Association, Toronto.

Orza, A. M., & Torrey, J. W. (1995). Teaching the psychology of women. In J. C. Chrisler & A. H. Hemstreet (Eds.), *Variations on a theme: Diversity and the psychology of women* (pp. 201–224). Albany, NY: SUNY Press.

Ossofsky, E. (2000, March 9). *A more secure retirement for workers: Proposals for ERISA reform.* Hearing before the Subcommittee on Employer-Employee Relations Committee on Education and the Workforce, U.S. House of Representatives.

O'Sullivan, L. F., Graber, J. A., & Brooks-Gunn, J. (2001). Adolescent gender development. In J. Worell (Ed.), *Encyclopedia of women and gender* (pp. 55–67). San Diego: Academic Press.

Oswald, D. L., & Harvey, R. D. (2003). A q-methodological study of women's subjective perspectives on mathematics. *Sex Roles, 49,* 133–142.

O'Toole, C., & Bregante, J. (1993). Disabled lesbians: Multicultural realities. In M. Nagler (Ed.), *Perspectives on disability: Text and readings on disability* (pp. 261–271). Palo Alto, CA: Health Markets Research.

Ozawa, M. N. (2004). Social welfare spending on family benefits in the United States and Sweden: A comparative study. *Family Relations, 53,* 301–309.

Ozer, E. J., Best, S. R., Lipsey, T. L., & Weiss, D. S. (2003). Predictors of posttraumatic stress disorder and symptoms in adults: A meta-analysis. *Psychological Bulletin, 129(1),* 52–73.

Ozer, E. M. (1995). The impact of childcare responsibility and self-efficacy on the psychological health of professional working mothers. *Psychology of Women Quarterly, 19,* 315–335.

Pacheco, S., & Hurtado, A. (2001). Media stereotypes. In J. Worell (Ed.), *Encyclopedia of women and gender* (pp. 703–708). San Diego: Academic Press.

Padavic, I., & Reskin, B. F. (2002). *Women and men at work.* 2d ed. Thousand Oaks, CA: Sage.

Padgett, D. (1999). Aging minority women. In L. A. Peplau, S. C. DeBro., R. C. Veniegas, & P. L. Taylor (Eds.), *Gender, culture and ethnicity: Current research about women and men* (pp. 173–181). Mountain View, CA: Mayfield.

Padgett, J., & Biro, F. M. (2003). Different shapes in different cultures: Body dissatisfaction, overweight, and obesity in African-American and Caucasian females. *Journal of Pediatric and Adolescent Gynecology, 16,* 349–354.

Palmore, E. B. (2001). Sexism and ageism. In J. M. Coyle (Ed.), *Handbook on women and aging* (pp. 3–13). Westport, CT: Praeger.

Paludi, M. A. (1996). Sexual harassment in college and university settings. In J. C. Chrisler, C. Golden, & P. D. Rozee (Eds.), *Lectures on the psychology of women* (pp. 325–337). New York: McGraw-Hill.

Pampel, F. C. (1998). National context, social change, and sex differences in suicide rates. *American Sociological Review, 63,* 744–758.

Panchaud, C., Singh, S., Feivelson, D., & Darroch, J. E. (2000). Sexually transmitted diseases among adolescents in developed countries. *Family Planning Perspectives, 32(1),* 24–32, 45.

Papalia, D. (2005). *A child's world: Infancy through adolescence.* 10th ed. New York: McGraw-Hill.

Pappert, A. (2000, June/July). What price pregnancy? *Ms.,* pp. 43–49.

Paradise, S. A. (1993). Older never married women: A cross cultural investigation. In N. D. Davis, E. Cole, & E. Rothblum (Eds.), *Faces of women and aging* (pp. 129–139). New York: Harrington Park Press.

Parent-Stevens, L., & Burns, E. A. (2000). Menstrual disorders. In M. A. Smith & L. A. Shimp (Eds.), *20 common problems in women's health care* (pp. 381–413). New York: McGraw Hill.

Parera, N., & Surís, J. C. (2004). Having a good relationship with their mother: A protective factor against sexual risk behavior among adolescent females? *Journal of Pediatric and Adolescent Gynecology, 17,* 267–271.

Parks, C. A., Hughes, T. L., & Matthews, A. K. (2004). Race/ethnicity and sexual orientation: Intersecting identities. *Cultural Diversity and Ethnic Minority Psychology, 10,* 241–254.

Parks, J. B., & Robertson, M. A. (2004). Attitudes toward women mediate the gender effect on attitudes toward sexist language. *Psychology of Women Quarterly, 28,* 233–239.

Parra, E. B., Arkowitz, H., Hannah, M. T., & Vasquez, A. M. (1995). Coping strategies and emotional reactions to separation and divorce in Anglo, Chicana, and Mexicana women. *Journal of Divorce & Remarriage, 23,* 117–129.

Parsons, E. M., & Betz, N. E. (2001). The relationship of participation in sports and physical activity to body objectification, instrumentality, and focus of control among young women. *Psychology of Women Quarterly, 25,* 209–222.

Partnership rights for gays. (2004, January 13). *New York Times,* p. A24.

Pasterski, V. L., et al. (2005). Prenatal hormones and postnatal socialization by parents as determinants of male-typical toy play in girls with congenital adrenal hyperplasia. *Child Development, 76,* 264–278.

Pastore, D., Fisher, M., & Friedman, S. (1996). Abnormalities in weight status, eating attitudes, and eating behaviors among urban high school students: Correlations with self-esteem and anxiety. *Journal of Adolescent Health, 18,* 312–319.

Pasupathi, M., & Löckenhoff, C. E. (2002). Ageist behavior. In T. D. Nelson (Ed.), *Ageism: Stereotyping and prejudice against older persons* (pp. 201–246). Cambridge, MA: MIT Press.

Patai, D., & Koertge, N. (2003, June 22). Tired brand of feminism still growing. *Arizona Republic,* p. V2.

Pate, R. R., Trost, S. G., Levin, S., & Dowda, M. (2000). Sports participation and health-related behaviors among U.S. youth. *Archives of Pediatric and Adolescent Medicine, 154,* 904–911.

Patel, J. D., Bach, P. B., & Kris, M. G. (2004). Lung cancer in U.S. women. *Journal of the American Medical Association, 291,* 1763–1768.

Patlak, M. (2003, December). Ovarian cancer: A tough fight may get easier. *Health, 35*–40.

Patrick, J. H., Cottrell, L. E., & Barnes, K. A. (2001). Gender, emotional support, and well-being among the rural elderly. *Sex Roles, 45,* 15–29.

Patterson, C. J. (2000). Family relationships of lesbians and gay men. *Journal of Marriage and the Family, 62,* 1052–1069.

Patterson, C. J., & Friel, L. V. (2000). Sexual orientation and fertility. In G. Bentley & N. Mascie-Taylor (Eds.), *Infertility in the modern world: Biosocial perspectives* (pp. 238–260). Cambridge: Cambridge University Press.

Patterson, C. J., Sutfin, E. L., & Fulcher, M. (2004). Division of labor among lesbian and heterosexual parenting couples: Correlates of specialized versus shared patterns. *Journal of Adult Development, 11,* 179–189.

Paul, E. L., & Hayes, K. A. (2002). The casualties of "casual" sex: A qualitative exploration of the phenomenology of college students' hookups. *Journal of Social and Personal Relationships, 19,* 639–661.

Paynter, N., et al. (2004, January 16). Declining prevalence of no known major risk factors for heart disease and stroke among adults—United States, 1991–2001. *Morbidity and Mortality Weekly Report, 53,* pp. 4–7.

Peacock, P. (1998). Marital rape. In R. K. Bergen (Ed.), *Issues in intimate violence* (pp. 225–235). Thousand Oaks, CA: Sage.

Pearson, S. M., & Bieschke, K. J. (2001). Succeeding against the odds: An examination of familial influences on the career development of professional African American women. *Journal of Counseling Psychology, 48,* 301–309.

Pedersen, S., & Seidman, E. (2004), Team sports achievement and self-esteem development among urban adolescent girls. *Psychology of Women Quarterly, 28,* 412–422.

Peirce, K. (1993). Socialization of teenage girls through teen-magazine fiction: The making of a new woman or an old lady? *Sex Roles, 29,* 59–68.

Peirce, K. (1997). Women's magazine fiction: A content analysis of the roles, attributes, and occupations of main characters. *Sex Roles, 37,* 581–593.

Pellegrini, A. D. (2001). A longitudinal study of heterosexual relationships, aggression, and sexual harassment during the transition from primary school through middle school. *Applied Developmental Psychology, 22,* 119–133.

Pellegrini, A. D., Kato, K., Blatchford, P., & Baines, E. (2002). A short-term longitudinal study of children's playground games across the first year of school: Implications for social competence and adjustment to school. *American Educational Research Journal, 39,* 991–1015.

Penn, N. E., et al. (2000). Health practices and health-care systems among cultural groups. In R. M. Eisler & M. Hersen (Eds.), *Handbook of gender, culture, and health* (pp. 105–137). Mahwah, NJ: Erlbaum.

Pennebaker, J. W., Mehl, M. R., & Niederhoffer, K. G. (2003). Psychological aspects of natural language use: Our words, our selves. *Annual Review of Psychology, 54*, 547–577.

Penner, A. M. (2003). International gender x item difficulty interactions in mathematics and science achievement tests. *Journal of Educational Psychology, 95*, 650–655.

Pennington, B. (2004, June 29). Title IX trickles down to girls of generation z. *New York Times*, pp. C19, C22.

Penninx, B. W. J. H., et al. (2002). Exercise and depressive symptoms. A comparison of aerobic and resistance exercise effects on emotional and physical function in older persons with high and low depressive symptomatology. *Journals of Gerontology Series B: Psychological Sciences and Social Sciences, 57*, pp. P124–P132.

Peplau, L. A. (1998). Lesbian and gay relationships. In D. L. Anselmi & A. L. Law (Eds.), *Questions of gender: Perspectives & paradoxes* (pp. 505–519). Boston: McGraw-Hill.

Peplau, L. A. (2002, August). *Venus and Mars in the laboratory: Current research on gender and sexuality.* Paper presented at the meeting of the American Psychological Association, Chicago.

Peplau, L. A., & Beals, C. P. (2001). Lesbians, gay men, and bisexuals in relationships. In J. Worell (Ed.), *Encyclopedia of women and gender* (pp. 657–666). San Diego: Academic Press.

Peplau, L. A., & Garnets, L. D. (2000). A new paradigm for understanding women's sexuality and sexual orientation. *Journal of Social Issues, 56*, 329–350.

Pepler, D. J., Madsen, K. C., Webster, C. D., & Levene, K. S. (Eds.). (2004). *The development and treatment of girlhood aggression.* Mahwah, NJ: Erlbaum.

Pérez-Peña, R. (2004, March 15). Use of midwives, a childbirth phenomenon, fades in city. *New York Times*, p. A21.

Perkins, D. F., Luster, T., Villarruel, F. A., & Small, S. (1998). An ecological risk-factor examination of adolescents' sexual activity in three ethnic groups. *Journal of Marriage and the Family, 60*, 660–673.

Perkins, K. P. (1992). Psychosocial implications of women and retirement. *Social Work, 37*, 526–532.

Perkins, K. P. (1995). Social (in)security: Retirement planning for women. *Journal of Women & Aging, 7*, 37–53.

Perkins, K. R. (1996). The influence of television images on black females' self-perceptions of physical attractiveness. *Journal of Black Psychology, 22*, 453–469.

Perlez, J. (2003, July 14). For these transvestites, still more role changes. *New York Times*, p. A4.

Perlez, J. (2004, June 22). Asian maids often find abuse, not riches, abroad. *New York Times*, p. A3.

Perlmutter, C., Hanlon, T., & Sangiorgio, M. (1994, August). Triumph over menopause. *Prevention*, pp. 78–87, 142.

Perls, T. T., & Fretts, R. C. (1998, June). Why women live longer than men. *Scientific American*, pp. 100–103.

Perry, S. (2002, July/August). Not-so-cosmic gender differences. *APS Observer, 15*, 24.

Perry-Jenkins, M., Seery, B., & Crouter, A. C. (1992). Linkages between women's provider-role attitudes, psychological well-being, and family relationships. *Psychology of Women Quarterly, 16*, 311–329.

Pesquera, B. M. (1993). In the beginning he wouldn't even lift a spoon: The division of household labor. In A. de la Torre & M. B. Pesquera (Eds.), *Building with our hands: New directions in Chicana studies* (pp. 181–195). Berkeley: University of California Press.

Peter, K., & Horn, L. (2005). *Gender differences in participation and completion of undergraduate education and how they have changed over time.* NCES 2005-169. U.S. Department of Education, National Center for Education Statistics. Washington, DC: U.S. Government Printing Office.

Peterson, C. (2000). The future of optimism. *American Psychologist, 55*, 44–55.

Peterson, H. B., et al. (2004). Hormone therapy: Making decisions in the face of uncertainty. *Archives of Internal Medicine, 164*, 2308–2312.

Peterson, R. D., & Bailey, W. C. (1992). Rape and dimensions of gender socioeconomic inequality in U.S. metropolitan areas. *Journal of Research in Crime and Delinquency, 29*, 162–177.

Peterson, Z. D., & Muehlenhard, C. L. (2004). Was it rape? The function of women's rape myth acceptance and definitions of sex in labeling their own experiences. *Sex Roles, 51*, 129–144.

Petitti, D. B. (2003). Combination estrogen-progestin oral contraceptives. *New England Journal of Medicine, 349*, 1443–1450.

Pettifor, A. E., Measham, D. M., Rees, H. V., & Padian, N. S. (2004, November). *Sexual power and HIV risk, South Africa.* Emerging Infectious Diseases [serial on the Internet]. Available from http://www.cdc.gov/ncidod/EID/vol10no11/04–0252.htm

Pew Research Center (2003). *Religious beliefs underpin opposition to homosexuality.* Washington, DC: Author.

Pfaff, L. A. and Associates. (1999). *Five-year study shows gender differences in leadership skills.* Kalamazoo, MI: Authors.

Phares, T. M., et al. (2004, July). Surveillance for disparities in maternal health-related behaviors—Selected states, pregnancy risk assessment monitoring system (PRAMS), 2000–2001. *Surveillance Summaries. Morbidity and Mortality Weekly Report, 53* (No. SS-4), 1–13.

Phillips, D., & Adams, G. (2001). Child care and our youngest children. *The Future of Children, 11(1),* 35–51.

Phillips, L. (2000). *Flirting with danger: Sexuality and violence in young women's hetero-relations.* New York: New York University Press.

Phillips, S. D., & Imhoff, A. R. (1997). Women and career development: A decade of research. *Annual Review of Psychology, 48,* 31–59.

Phipps, B. J. (1995). Career dreams of preadolescent students. *Journal of Career Development, 22,* 19–32.

Phipps, M. G., et al. (2002). Young maternal age associated with increased risk of neonatal death. *Obstetrics & Gynecology, 100,* 481–486.

Piccart-Gebhart, M. J. (2004). New stars in the sky of treatment for early breast cancer. *New England Journal of Medicine, 350,* 1140–1142.

Pierce, W. D., Sydie, R.A., Stratkotter, R., & Krull, C. (2003). Social concepts and judgments: A semantic differential analysis of the concepts feminist, man, and woman. *Psychology of Women Quarterly, 27,* 338–346.

Pietsch, J., Walker, R., & Chapman, E. (2003). The relationship among self-concept, self-efficacy, and performance in mathematics during secondary school. *Journal of Educational Psychology, 95,* 589–603.

Pigott, T. A. (2002). Anxiety disorders. In S. G. Kornstein & A. H. Clayton (Eds.), *Women's mental health: A comprehensive textbook* (pp. 195–221). New York: Guilford.

Pike, K. M., et al. (2001). A comparison of black and white women with binge eating disorder. *American Journal of Psychiatry, 158,* 1455–1460.

Piller, C. (1998, September). Women avoiding computer field as gender gap goes high tech. *Hartford Courant,* pp. A12–13.

Pimlott-Kubiak, S., & Cortina, L. M. (2003). Gender, victimization, and outcomes: Reconceptualizing risk. *Journal of Consulting and Clinical Psychology, 71,* 528–539.

Pinholster, G. (2005, February 18). New research casts doubt on surgery for infants born with male and female traits. *AAAS News Archives.* Available from http://www.aaas.org/news/releases/2005/0218gender.shtml.

Pinn, V. W. (2003). Sex and gender factors in medical studies: Implications for health and clinical practice. *Journal of the American Medical Association, 289,* 397–400.

Pinquart, M. (2003). Loneliness in married, widowed, divorced, and never-married older adults. *Journal of Social and Personal Relationships, 20,* 31–53.

Piran, N. (2001). Eating disorders and disordered eating. In J. Worell (Ed.), *Encyclopedia of women and gender* (pp. 369–378). San Diego: Academic Press.

Pittman, J. F., & Blanchard, D. (1996). The effects of work history and timing of marriage on the division of household labor: A life-course perspective. *Journal of Marriage and the Family, 58,* 78–90.

Plant, E. A., Hyde, J. S., Keltner, D., & Devine, P. G. (2000). The gender stereotyping of emotions. *Psychology of Women Quarterly, 24,* 81–92.

Plant, E. A., Kling, K. C., & Smith, G. L. (2004). The influence of gender and social role on the interpretation of facial expressions. *Sex Roles, 51,* 187–196.

Plichta, S. B. (1996). Violence and abuse: Implications for women's health. In M. M. Falik & K. S. Collins (Eds.), *Women's health: The commonwealth fund survey* (pp. 237–270). Baltimore, MD: Johns Hopkins University Press.

Plous, S., & Neptune, D. (1997). Racial and gender biases in magazine advertising: A content-analytic study. *Psychology of Women Quarterly, 21,* 627–644.

Plucker, J. A. (1996). Secondary science and mathematics teachers and gender equity: Attitudes and attempted interventions. *Journal of Research in Science Teaching, 33(7),* 737–751.

Polce-Lynch, M., Myers, B. J., Kilmartin, C. T., Forssmann-Falck, R., & Kliewer, W. (1998). Gender and age patterns in emotional expression, body image, and self-esteem: A qualitative analysis. *Sex Roles, 38,* 1025–1048.

Polivy, J., & Herman, C. P. (2002). Causes of eating disorders. In S. T. Fiske, D. L. Schacter, & C. Zahn-Waxler (Eds.), *Annual review of psychology, 53* (pp. 187–213). Palo Alto, CA: Annual Reviews.

Pollack, D. (2003). Pro-eating disorder Websites: What should be the feminist response? *Feminism & Psychology, 13,* 246–251.

Pomerantz, E. M., Ng, F. F., & Wang, Q. (2004). Gender socialization: A parent x child model. In A. H. Eagly, A. E. Beall, & R. J. Sternberg (Eds.),

The psychology of gender (pp. 120–144). New York: Guilford.

Pomerantz, E. M., & Ruble, D. N. (1998). The role of maternal control in the development of sex differences in child self-evaluative factors. *Child Development, 69,* 458–478.

Pomerleau, A., Bolduc, D., Malcuit, G., & Cossette, L. (1990). Pink or blue: Environmental gender stereotypes in the first two years of life. *Sex Roles, 22,* 359–367.

Poo, A. J., & Tang, E. (2004). Domestic workers organize in the global city. In V. Labaton & D. L. Martin (Eds.), *The fire this time* (pp. 150–165). New York: Anchor Books.

Popenoe, D., & Whitehead, B. D. (1999). *The state of our unions: The social health of marriage in America.* New Brunswick, NJ: National Marriage Project at Rutgers University.

Popp, D., et al. (2003). Gender, race, and speech style stereotypes. *Sex Roles, 48,* 317–325.

Population Action International. (1998). *Educating girls: Gender gaps and gains.* Washington, DC: Author.

Poran, M. A. (2002). Denying diversity: Perceptions of beauty and social comparison processes among Latina, black, and white women. *Sex Roles, 47,* 65–81.

Porter, K. H., Larin, K., & Primus, W. (1999). *Social security and poverty: A national and state perspective.* Washington, DC: Center on Budget and Policy Priorities.

Porzelius, L. K. (2000). Physical health issues for women. In M. Biaggio, & M. Hersen (Eds.), *Issues in the psychology of women* (pp. 229–249). New York: Kluwer.

Potoczniak, M. J., et al. (2003). Legal and psychological perspectives on same-sex domestic violence: A multisystemic approach. *Journal of Family Psychology, 17(2),* 252–259.

Poulin-Dubois, D., Serbin, L. A., & Derbyshire, A. (1998). Toddlers' intermodal and verbal knowledge about gender. *Merrill-Palmer Quarterly, 44,* 338–354.

Poulin-Dubois, D., Serbin, L., & Eischedt, J. (1997, April). *The construction of gender concepts between 12 and 24 months.* Paper presented at the meeting of the Society for Research in Child Development, Washington, DC.

Powell, S. R., & Yanico, B. J. (1991). A multimethod attitude study about women's roles and issues. *Psychology of Women Quarterly, 15,* 97–101.

Powers, P. S. (2002). Eating disorders. In S. G. Kornstein & A. H. Clayton (Eds.), *Women's mental health: A comprehensive textbook* (pp. 244–262). New York: Guilford.

Powlishta, K. K. (1997, May). *Social categorization and gender-role development.* Paper presented at the meeting of the Midwestern Psychological Association, Chicago.

Powlishta, K. K. (2001, April). *Own-sex favoritism and gender-role development.* Poster presented at the meeting of the Society for Research in Child Development, Minneapolis, MN.

Powlishta, K. K., Sen, M. G., Serbin, L. A., Poulin-Dubois, D., & Eichstedt, J. A. (2001). From infancy through middle childhood: The role of cognitive and social factors in becoming gendered. In R. K. Unger (Ed.), *Handbook of the psychology of women and gender* (pp. 116–132). New York: Wiley.

Pozner, J. L. (2004, Fall). The unreal world. *Ms.,* pp. 50–53.

Pradhan, A., & Bachmann, G. (2003). Today's therapeutic options for hot flashes. *Women's Health in Primary Care, 6,* 527–534.

Pratto, F., & Walker, A. (2004). The bases of gendered power. In A. H. Eagly, A. E. Beall, & R. J. Sternberg (Eds.), *The psychology of gender* (pp. 242–268). New York, NY: Guilford.

Prendergast, K. A., & Dalkin, A. C. (2004). Therapeutic options in the management of osteoporotic patients. *Women's Health in Primary Care, 7,* 185–193.

Prendergast, M. A. (2004). Do women possess a unique susceptibility to the neurotoxic effects of alcohol? *Journal of the American Medical Women's Association, 59,* 225–227.

Prentice, D. A., & Carranza, E. (2002). What women and men should be, shouldn't be, are allowed to be, and don't have to be: The contents of prescriptive gender stereotypes. *Psychology of Women Quarterly, 26,* 269–281.

Presser, H. B. (2004). Employment in a 24/7 economy: Challenges for the family. In A. C. Crouter and A. Booth (Eds.), *Work-family challenges for low-income parents and their children* (pp. 83–105). Mahwah, NJ: Erlbaum.

Price, J. L., Hilsenroth, M. J., Petretic-Jackson, P. A., & Bonge, D. (2001). A review of individual psychotherapy outcomes for adult survivors of childhood sexual abuse. *Clinical Psychology Review, 21,* 1095–1121.

Prinstein, M. J., & La Greca, A. M. (2004). Childhood peer rejection and aggression as predictors of adolescent girls' externalizing and health risk behaviors: A 6-year longitudinal study. *Journal of Consulting and Clinical Psychology, 72,* 103–112.

Proctor, B. D., & Dalaker, J. (2002). *Poverty in the United States: 2001.* Current Population Reports P60–219. Washington, DC: U.S. Census Bureau.

Proctor, B. D., & Dalaker, J. (2003). *Poverty in the United States: 2002.* U.S. Census Bureau, Current Population Reports, P60-222. Washington, DC: U. S. Government Printing Office.

Programme for International Student Assessment. (2004). *First results from PISA 2003.* London: Organization for Economic Cooperation and Development.

Propp, K. (2003). Pregnancy as a life passage. In L. Slater, J. H. Daniel, & A. E. Banks (Eds.), *The complete guide to mental health for women* (pp. 6–9). Boston: Beacon Press.

Pruchno, R. A. (1999). Raising grandchildren: The experiences of Black and White grandmothers. *The Gerontologist, 39,* 209–221.

Pryor, J. B., & Whalen, N. J. (1997). A typology of sexual harassment: Characteristics of harassers and the social circumstances under which sexual harassment occurs. In W. O'Donohue (Ed.), *Sexual harassment: Theory, research, and treatment* (pp. 129–151). Boston: Allyn & Bacon.

Pryzgoda, J., & Chrisler, J. C. (2000). Definitions of gender and sex: The subtleties of meaning. *Sex Roles, 43,* 553–569.

Purcell, P., & Stewart, L. (1990). Dick and Jane in 1989. *Sex Roles, 22,* 177–185.

Purdy, L. M. (1992). Another look at contract pregnancy. In H. B. Holmes (Ed.), *Issues in reproductive technology* (pp. 303–320). New York: Garland.

Putting the sex trade on notice. (2004, January 9). *New York Times,* p. A18.

Quatman, T., & Swanson, C. (2002). Academic self-disclosure in adolescence. *Genetic, Social, and General Psychology Monographs, 128,* 47–75.

Quatman, T., & Watson, C. M. (2001). Gender differences in adolescent self-esteem: An exploration of domains. *Journal of Genetic Psychology, 162,* 93–117.

Quinn, D. M., & Spencer, S. J. (2001, Spring). The interference of stereotype threat with women's generation of mathematical problem-solving strategies. *Journal of Social Issues,* pp. 55–72.

Quinn, J. B. (2001, February 17). Investing women aren't emotionally impaired. *Peoria Journal Star,* p. C2.

Quinn, P. C. (2002). Beyond prototypes: Asymmetries in infant categorization and what they teach us about the mechanisms guiding early knowledge acquisition. In R. V. Kail & H. W. Reese (Eds.), *Advances in child development and behavior,* Vol. 29 (pp. 161–193). San Diego: Academic Press.

Raag, T., & Rackliff, C. L. (1998). Preschoolers' awareness of social expectations of gender: Relationships to toy choices. *Sex Roles, 38,* 685–700.

Rabasca, L. (2000, October). The Internet and computer games reinforce the gender gap. *Monitor on Psychology,* pp. 32–33.

Rabinowitz, V. C., & Martin, D. (2001). Choices and consequences: Methodological issues in the study of gender. In R. K. Unger (Ed.), *Handbook of the psychology of women and gender* (pp. 29–52). New York: Wiley.

Radner, G. (1990). *It's always something.* New York: Avon.

Raffaelli, M., & Ontai, L. L. (2004). Gender socialization in Latino/a families: Results from two retrospective studies. *Sex Roles, 50,* 287–299.

Ragins, B. R. (1998, August). *The effect of legislation on workplace discrimination against gay employees.* Paper presented at the meeting of the American Psychological Association, San Francisco.

Ragins, B. R., & Cornwell, J. M. (2001). Pink triangles: Antecedents and consequences of perceived workplace discrimination against gay and lesbian employees. *Journal of Applied Psychology, 86,* 1244–1261.

Ragins, B. R., & Scandura, T. A. (1995). Antecedents and work-related correlates of reported sexual harassment: An empirical investigation of competing hypotheses. *Sex Roles, 32,* 429–455.

Rahman, Q., Kumari, V., & Wilson, G. D. (2003). Sexual orientation-related differences in prepulse inhibition of the human startle response. *Behavioral Neuroscience, 117,* 1096–1102.

Raisz, L. G. (2004). Homocysteine and osteoporotic fractures—Culprit or bystander? *New England Journal of Medicine, 350,* pp. 2089–2090.

Raley, R. K., & Wildsmith, E. (2004). Cohabitation and children's family instability. *Journal of Marriage and Family, 66,* 210–219.

Ralston, P. A. (2001). Midlife and older Black women. In J. M. Coyle (Ed.), *Handbook on women and aging* (pp. 273–289). Westport, CT: Praeger.

Ramchandani, P., & Jones, D. P. H. (2003). Treating psychological symptoms in sexually abused children. From research findings to service provision. *British Journal of Psychiatry, 183,* 484–490.

Ramey, F. H. (1995). Obstacles faced by African American women administrators in higher education: How they cope. *Western Journal of Black Studies, 19,* 113–119.

Ramirez, J. M. (2003). Hormones and aggression in childhood and adolescence. *Aggression and Violent Behavior, 8,* 621–644.

Ramsey, N. (2004, January 3). In Africa, girls fight a painful tradition. *New York Times,* p. A29.

Randolph, S. M. (1995). African American children in single-mother families. In B. J. Dickerson (Ed.), *African American single mothers: Understanding their lives and families* (pp. 117–145). Thousand Oaks, CA: Sage.

Rani, M., & Lule, E. (2004). Exploring the socioeconomic dimension of adolescent reproductive health: A multicountry analysis. *International Family Planning Perspectives, 30,* 110–117.

Rankin, S. R. (2003). *Campus climate for gay, lesbian, and transgender people: A national perspective.* New York: The Policy Institute of the National Gay and Lesbian Task Force.

Rapp, E. (2003, September 28). A pep talk for women to end all pep talks. *New York Times,* p. BU11.

Raschick, M., & Ingersoll-Dayton, B. (2004). The costs and rewards of caregiving among aging spouses and adult children. *Family Relations, 53,* 317–325.

Rathus, S., Nevid, J., & Fichner-Rathus, L. (2005). *Human sexuality in a world of diversity.* 5th ed. Boston: Allyn & Bacon.

Ratner, E. (1999). *The feisty woman's breast cancer book.* New York: Hunter House.

Räty, H., Vänskä, J., Kasanen, K., & Kärkkäinen, R. (2002). Parents' explanations of their children's performance in mathematics and reading: A replication and extension of Yee and Eccles. *Sex Roles, 46,* 121–128.

Rawlins, W. K. (2004). Friendships in later life. In J. F. Nussbaum & J. Coupland (Eds.), *Handbook of communication and aging research,* 2d ed. (pp. 273–304). Mahwah, NJ: Erlbaum.

Ray, E. B., & Miller, K. I. (1994). Social support, home/work stress, and burnout: Who can help? *Journal of Applied Behavioral Science 30,* 357–373.

Ray, K. L., & Hodnett E. D. (2003). Caregiver support for postpartum depression (Cochrane Review). *Cochrane Library,* Issue 4. Chichester, UK: Wiley.

Ray, O. (2004). How the mind hurts and heals the body. *American Psychologist, 59,* 29–40.

Rayman, P., Allshouse, K., & Allen, J. (1993). Resiliency amidst inequity: Older women workers in an aging United States. In J. Allen & A. Pifer (Eds.), *Women on the frontlines: Meeting the challenge of an aging America* (pp. 133–166). Washington, DC: Urban Institute Press.

Raymond, J., & Cowley, G. (2005, May 8). Targeting tumors. *Newsweek,* p. 13.

Read, J. (2004). Sexual problems associated with infertility, pregnancy, and ageing. *British Medical Journal, 329,* 559–561.

Ream, G. L., & Savin-Williams, R. C. (2002, August). *Development of religion-based homophobia among sexual-minority and heterosexual adolescents and young children.* Paper presented at the meeting of the American Psychological Association, Chicago.

Reame, N. K. (2001). Menstruation. In J. Worell (Ed.), *Encyclopedia of women and gender* (pp. 739–742). San Diego: Academic Press.

Rebar, R. W., & DeCherney, A. H. (2004). Assisted reproductive technology in the United States. *New England Journal of Medicine, 350,* 1603–1604.

Reed, M. E., Collinsworth, L. L., & Fitzgerald, L. F. (2005). There's no place like home: Sexual harassment of low income women in housing. *Psychology, Public Policy, and the Law, 11.*

Reeder, H. M. (2003). The effect of gender role orientation on same-and cross-sex friendship formation. *Sex Roles, 49,* 143–152.

Reeves, J. B., & Darville, R. L. (1994). Social contact patterns and satisfaction with retirement of women in dual-career/earner families. *International Journal of Aging and Human Development, 39,* 163–175.

Rehm, J., Gmel, G., Sempos, C. T., & Trevisan, M. (2002). Alcohol-related morbidity and mortality. *Alcohol Research & Health, 27,* 39–50.

Reichert, T., & Lambiase, J. (2003). *Sex in advertising: Perspectives on the erotic appeal.* Mahwah, NJ: Erlbaum.

Reichman, N. E., & McLanahan, S. S. (2001). Self-sufficiency programs and parenting interventions: Lessons from new chance and the teenage parent demonstration. *Social Policy Report, 15,* No. 2.

Reid, A., & Purcell, N. (2004). Pathways to feminist identification. *Sex Roles, 50,* 759–769.

Reid, P. T. (1999). Poor women in psychological research: Shut up and shut out. In L. A. Peplau, S. C. DeBro, R. C. Veniegas, & P. L. Taylor (Eds.), *Gender, culture and ethnicity: Current research about women and men* (pp. 336–352). Mountain View, CA: Mayfield.

Reid, P. T., & Kelly, E. (1994). Research on women of color: From ignorance to awareness. *Psychology of Women Quarterly, 18,* 477–486.

Reid, P. T., & Zalk, S. R. (2001). Academic environments: Gender and ethnicity in higher education. In J. Worell (Ed.), *Encyclopedia of women and gender* (pp. 29–42). San Diego: Academic Press.

Reijonen, J. H., Pratt, H. D., Patel, D. R., & Greydanus, D. E. (2003). Eating disorders in the adolescent population: An overview. *Journal of Adolescent Research, 18,* 209–222.

Reiner, W. G., & Gearhart, J. P. (2004). Discordant sexual identity in some genetic males with cloacal exstrophy assigned to female sex at birth. *New England Journal of Medicine, 350,* 333–341.

Reinhardt, R. (2002). Bisexual women in heterosexual relationships. *Journal of Bisexuality, 2,* 161–169.

Reisberg, L. (2000, November 10). A crossroads for women's colleges. *Chronicle of Higher Education,* pp. A50–A52.

Remer, P., & Oakley, D. (2005, Winter). Counselor self-disclosure. *The Feminist Psychologist,* pp. 8–10.

Remez, L. (2003). Few U.S. school-based health centers offer contraceptives on-site. *Perspectives on Sexual and Reproductive Health, 35,* 239–240.

Renk, K., et al. (2002). Prevention of child sexual abuse. Are we doing enough? *Trauma, Violence, & Abuse, 3,* 68–84.

Renk, K., et al. (2003). Mothers, fathers, gender role, and time parents spend with their children. *Sex Roles, 48,* 305–315.

Repetti, R. L., Taylor, S. E., & Seeman, T. E. (2002). Risky families: Family social environments and the mental and physical health of offspring. *Psychological Bulletin, 128,* 330–366.

Revenson, T. A. (2001). Chronic illness adjustment. In J. Worell (Ed.), *Encyclopedia of women and gender* (pp. 245–255). San Diego: Academic Press.

Reynolds, A. J., Temple, J. A., Robertson, D. L., & Mann, E. A. (2001). Long-term effects of an early childhood intervention on educational achievement and juvenile arrest. *Journal of the American Medical Association, 285,* 2339–2346.

Reynolds, J., & Wetherell, M. (2003). The discursive climate of singleness: The consequences of women's negotation of a single identity. *Feminism & Psychology, 13,* 489–510.

Rhoden, W. C. (2002, June 22). Destroying barriers women still face. *New York Times,* p. D2.

Ricciardelli, L. A., & McCabe, M. P. (2001). Children's body image concerns and eating disturbance: A review of the literature. *Clinical Psychology Review, 21,* 325–344.

Ricciuti, H. (2004a). On Mother's Day, a hopeful finding for single mothers and their children from a Cornell researcher. *The Journal of Educational Research, 97,* 5.

Ricciuti, H. (2004b). Single parenthood, achievement, and problem behavior in white, black, and hispanic children. *The Journal of Educational Research, 97,* 196–206.

Rice, J. K. (2001). Family roles and patterns, contemporary trends. In J. Worell (Ed.), *Encyclopedia of women and gender* (pp. 411–423). San Diego: Academic Press.

Rice, S. (2001). Sexuality and intimacy for aging women: A changing perspective. In J. D. Garner & S. O. Mercer (Eds.), *Women as they age,* 2d ed. (pp. 147–164). New York: Haworth.

Richards, H. M., Reid, M. E., Watt, G. C. M. (2002). Why do men and women respond differently to chest pain? A qualitative study. *Journal of the American Medical Women's Association, 57,* 79–81.

Richardson, P., & Lazur, A. (1995). Sexuality in the nursing home patient. *American Family Physician, 51,* 121–124.

Richardson, V. E. (2001). Mental health of elderly women. In J. D. Garner & S. O. Mercer (Eds.), *Women as they age,* 2d ed. (pp. 85–96). New York: Haworth.

Riche, M. F. (2003). Young women: Where they stand. In C. B. Costello, V. R. Wight, & A. J. Stone (Eds.). *The American woman 2003–2004: Daughters of a revolution—Young women today.* New York: Palgrave MacMillan.

Richie, B. S., et al. (1997). Persistence, connection, and passion: A qualitative study of the career development of highly achieving African American-Black and White women. *Journal of Counseling Psychology, 44,* 133–148.

Richman, E. L., & Shaffer, D. R. (2000). "If you let me play sports": How might sport participation influence the self-esteem of adolescent females? *Psychology of Women Quarterly, 24,* 189–199.

Rickert, V. I., Wiemann, C. M., & Berenson, A. B. (2000). Ethnic differences in depressive symptomatology in young women vary according to ethnicity and include physical or sexual assault, recent substance abuse, unemployment, age, and limited education. *Obstetrics & Gynecology, 95,* 55–60.

Rickert, V. I., Wiemann, C. M., Vaughan, R. D., & White, J. W. (2004). Rates and risk factors for sexual violence among an ethnically diverse sample of adolescents. *Archives of Pediatrics & Adolescent Medicine, 158,* 1132–1139.

Riddick, C. C. (1993). Older women's leisure activity and quality of life. In J. R. Kelly (Ed.), *Activity and aging: Staying involved in later life* (pp. 86–98). Newbury Park, CA: Sage.

Ridgeway, C. L. (2001). Gender, status, and leadership. *Journal of Social Issues, 57,* 637–655.

Riegle-Crumb, C. (2000). *International gender inequality in math and science education.* Unpublished doctoral dissertation, University of Chicago.

Rife, J. C. (2001). Middle-aged and older women in the work force. In J. M. Coyle (Ed.), *Handbook on women and aging* (pp. 93–111). Westport, CT: Greenwood.

Riger, S. (2000). *Transforming psychology: Gender in theory and practice.* Oxford: Oxford University Press.

Riger, S., & Staggs, S. L. (2004). Welfare reform, domestic violence and employment: What do we know, and what do we need to know? *Violence Against Women, 10,* 1–30.

Riggio, H. R., & Desrochers, S. (2005). The influence of maternal employment on the work and family attitudes of young adults. In D. F. Halpern & S. E. Murphy (Eds.), *From work-family balance to work-family interaction: Changing the metaphor* (pp. 177–196). Mahwah, NJ: Erlbaum

Riggs, J. M. (1997). Mandates for mothers and fathers: Perceptions of breadwinners and care givers. *Sex Roles, 37,* 565–580.

Riley, G. F., et al. (1999). Stage at diagnosis and treatment patterns among older women and breast cancer: An HMO and fee-for-service comparison. *Journal of the American Medical Association, 281,* 720–726.

Rimer, S. (1999, September 5). Gaps seen in treatment of depression in elderly. *New York Times,* pp. Y1, Y16.

Rimer, S. (2005, April 15). For women in sciences, slow progress in academia. *New York Times,* pp. Al, A15.

Rimm, E. B., & Stampfer, M. J. (2004). Diet, lifestyle, and longevity—The next steps? *Journal of the American Medical Association, 292,* 1490–1492.

Rintala, D. H., et al. (1997). Dating issues for women with physical disabilities. *Sexuality and Disability, 15,* 219–242.

Risman, B., & Schwartz, P. (2002, Spring). After the sexual revolution: Gender politics in teen dating. *Contexts,* pp. 16–24.

Rivers, I. (2002). Developmental issues for lesbian and gay youth. In A. Coyle & C. Kitzinger (Eds.), *Lesbian and gay psychology: New perspectives* (pp. 30–44). Oxford, UK: BPS Blackwell.

Rix, Sara E. (1990). Who pays for what? Ensuring financial security in retirement. In C. L. Hayes & J. M. Deren (Eds.), *Preretirement planning for women: Program design and research* (pp. 5–26). New York: Springer.

Roberto, K. A. (2001). Older women's relationships: Weaving lives together. In J. D. Garner & S. O. Mercer (Eds.), *Women as they age,* 2d ed. (pp. 115–129). New York: Haworth.

Roberts, B. W., Helson, R., & Klohnen, E. C. (2002). Personality development and growth in women across 30 years: Three perspectives. *Journal of Personality, 70,* 79–102.

Roberts, T. A. (2004). Female trouble: The menstrual self-evaluation scale and women's self-objectification. *Psychology of Women Quarterly, 28,* 22–26.

Roberts, T., Goldenberg, J., Power, C., & Pyszczynski, T. (2002). "Feminine protection": The effects of menstruation on attitudes toward women. *Psychology of Women Quarterly, 26,* 131–139.

Robertson, J., & Fitzgerald, L. F. (1990). The (mis)treatment of men: Effects of client gender role and life-style on diagnosis and attribution of pathology. *Journal of Counseling Psychology, 37,* 3–9.

Robertson, R. M. (2001). Women and cardiovascular disease: The risks of misperception and the need for action. *Circulation, 103,* 2318–2320.

Robin, L., et al. (2004, January). Behavioral interventions to reduce incidence of HIV, STD, and pregnancy among adolescents: A decade in review. *Journal of Adolescent Health, 34,* 3–26.

Robinson, C., & Miller, M. V. (2004). Emergent legal definitions of parentage in assisted reproductive technology. *Journal of Family Social Work, 8(2),* 21–51.

Robinson, D. T., Gibson-Beverly, G., & Schwartz, J. P. (2004). Sorority and fraternity membership and religious behaviors: Relation to gender attitudes. *Sex Roles, 50,* 871–877.

Robinson, J. D., Skill, T., & Turner, J. W. (2004). Media usage patterns and portrayals of seniors. In J. F. Nussbaum & J. Coupland (Eds.), *Handbook of communication and aging research,* 2d ed. (pp. 423–450). Mahwah, NJ: Erlbaum.

Robinson, T., et al. (1996). Ethnicity and body dissatisfaction: Are Hispanic and Asian girls at increased risk for eating disorders? *Journal of Adolescent Health, 19*, 384–393.

Roche, K. M., et al. (2005). Parenting influences on early sex initiation among adolescents. *Journal of Family Issues, 26*, 32–54.

Rogers, S. J., & DeBoer, D. D. (2001). Changes in wives' income: Effects in marital happiness, psychological well-being, and the risk of divorce. *Journal of Marriage and Family, 63*, 458–472.

Rohde, D. (2002, October 31). Attacks on schools for girls hint at lingering split in Afghanistan. *New York Times*, p. A1.

Rohde, D. (2003, October 26). India steps up effort to halt abortions of female fetuse. *New York Times*, p. YT3.

Roisman, G. I., Masten, A. S., Coatsworth, J. D., & Tellegen, A. (2004). Salient and emerging development tasks in the transition to adulthood. *Child Development, 75*, 123–133.

Romaine, S. (1999). *Communicating gender*. Mahwah, NJ: Erlbaum.

Romieu, I., et al. (2004). Carbohydrates and the risk of breast cancer among Mexican women. *Cancer Epidemiology Biomarkers & Prevention, 13*, 1283–1289.

Roovers, J. P. W. R., et al. (2003). Hysterectomy and sexual wellbeing: Prospective observational study of vaginal hysterectomy, subtotal abdominal hysterectomy, and total abdominal hysterectomy. *British Medical Journal, 327*, 774–778.

Roscoe, L. A., Malphurs, J. E., Dragovic, L. J., & Cohen, D. (2003). Antecedents of euthanasia and suicide among older women. *Journal of the American Medical Women's Association, 58*, 44–48.

Roscoe, W. (1998). *Changing ones: Third and fourth genders in North America*. New York: St. Martin's Press.

Rose, A. J. (2002). Co-rumination in the friendships of girls and boys. *Child Development, 73*, 1830–1843.

Rose, A. J., & Asher, S. R. (2004). Children's strategies and goals in response to help-giving and help-seeking tasks within a friendship. *Child Development, 75*, 749–763.

Rose, A. J., Swenson, L. P., & Waller, E. M. (2004). Overt and relational aggression and perceived popularity: Developmental differences in concurrent and prospective relations. *Developmental Psychology, 40*, 378–387.

Rose, S. (2000, Summer). Heterosexism and the study of women's romantic and friend relationships. *Journal of Social Issues, 56*, 315–328.

Rose, S., & Frieze, I. H. (1993). Young singles contemporary dating scripts. *Sex Roles, 28*, 499–509.

Rose, S. M. (2002). Introduction: Lesbian love and relationships. In S. M. Rose (Ed.), *Lesbian love and relationships* (pp. 1–3). Binghamton, NY: Harrington Park Press.

Rose, S. M., & Zand, D. (2002). Lesbian dating and courtship from young adulthood to midlife. In S. M. Rose (Ed.), *Lesbian love and relationships* (pp. 85–109). Binghamton, NY: Harrington Park Press.

Rosen, R. (2001). Epilogue: Beyond backlash. In S. M. Shaw & J. Lee (Eds.), *Women's voices, feminist visions* (pp. 552–559). Mountain View, CA: Mayfield.

Rosenberg, T. (2004, July 5). Mutilating Africa's daughters: Laws unenforced, practices unchanged. *New York Times*, p. A18.

Rosenblum C. (1991, October 31). Yipes! An eery metamorphosis is turning girls into turtles. *New York Times*, p. B1.

Rosenthal, E. (2003, July 20). Bias for boys leads to sale of baby girls in China. *New York Times*, p. YT6.

Ross, L. E., & Davis, A. C. (1996). Black-White college students' attitudes and expectations in paying for dates. *Sex Roles, 35*, 43–56.

Rossi, A. S. (2004). The menopausal transition and aging processes. In O. G. Brim, C. D. Ryff, & R. C. Kessler (Eds.), *How healthy are we? A national study of well-being at midlife* (pp. 153–201). Chicago: University of Chicago Press.

Rostosky, S. S., et al. (2004). Same-sex couple perceptions of family support: A consensual qualitative study. *Family Process, 43*, 43–57.

Rostosky, S. S., Wilcox, B. L., Wright, M. L. C., & Randall, B. A. (2004). The impact of religiosity on adolescent sexual behavior: A review of the evidence. *Journal of Adolescent Research, 19*, 677–697.

Roter, D. L., Hall, J. A., & Aoki, Y. (2002). Physician gender effects in medical communication. *Journal of the American Medical Association, 288*, 756–764.

Roth, R. (2003). Sexual and reproductive life of women: Gender equality in women's reproductive health in Western Europe and the U.S. *Psychology Science, 45*, 123–143.

Rothblum, E. D. (2002). Gay and lesbian body images. In T. F. Cash & T. Pruzinsky (Eds.), *Body images: A handbook of theory, research, and clinical practice* (pp. 257–265). New York: Guilford Publications.

Rothblum, E. D., & Brehony, K. A. (1991). The Boston marriage today: Romantic but asexual relationships among lesbians. In C. Silverstein (Ed.),

Gays, lesbians, and their therapists: Studies in psychotherapy (pp. 210–226). New York: W. Norton.

Rothblum, E. D., & Factor, R. (2001). Lesbians and their sisters as a control group: Demographic and mental health factors. *Psychological Science, 12*, 63–69.

Rothman, E. F., Hemenway, D., Miller, M., & Azrael, D. (2005). Batterers' use of guns to threaten intimate partners. *Journal of the American Medical Women's Association, 60*, 62–68.

Rotundo, M., Nguyen, D., & Sackett, P. R. (2001). A meta-analytic review of gender differences in perceptions of sexual harassment. *Journal of Applied Psychology, 86*, 914–922.

Rowley, L. M. C. (1999, August). *Women in dual-earner marriages: The impact of religious commitment on household task and management performance.* Paper presented at the meeting of the American Psychological Association, Boston.

Royak-Schaler, R., et al. (2003). Does access to screening through health maintenance organization membership translate into improved breast cancer outcomes for African American patients? *Journal of the American Medical Women's Association, 58*, 154–156.

Royak-Schaler, R., Lemkau, J. P., & Ahmed, S. M. (2002). Discussing breast cancer risk in primary care. *Journal of the American Medical Women's Association, 57*, 115–116.

Rozee, P. D., & Koss, M. P. (2001). Rape: A century of resistance. *Psychology of Women Quarterly, 25*, 295–311.

Rozin, P., Bauer, R., & Catanese, D. (2003). Food and life, pleasure and worry, among American college students: Gender differences and regional similarities. *Journal of Personality and Social Psychology, 85*, 132–141.

Rubin, J. Z., Provenzano, R., & Luria, Z. (1974). The eye of the beholder: Parents views on sex of newborns. *American Journal of Orthopsychiatry, 44*, 512–519.

Rubin, K. H., Bukowski, W., & Parker, J. G. (1998). Peer interactions, relationships, and groups. In W. Damon (Series Ed.) & N. Eisenberg (Vol. Ed.), *Handbook of child psychology*, Vol. 3. *Social, emotional and personality development*, 5th ed. (pp. 619–700). New York: Wiley.

Rubin, L. R., Nemeroff, C. J., & Russo, N. F. (2004). Exploring feminist women's body consciousness. *Psychology of Women Quarterly, 28*, 27–37.

Rubinstein, R. L. (1994). Adaptation to retirement among the never married, childless, divorced, gay and lesbian, and widowed. In A. Monk (Ed.), *The Columbia retirement handbook* (pp. 448–461). New York: Columbia University Press.

Rubinstein, S., & Caballero, B. (2000). Is Miss America an undernourished role model? *Journal of the American Medical Association, 283*, 1569.

Ruble, D. N., & Martin, C. L. (1998). Gender development. In W. Damon (Series Ed.) & N. Eisenberg (Vol. Ed.), *Handbook of child psychology*, Vol. 3. *Social, emotional and personality development*, 5th ed. (pp. 933–1016). New York: Wiley.

Rudman, L. A., & Fairchild, K. (2004). Reactions to counterstereotypic behavior: The role of backlash in cultural stereotype maintenance. *Journal of Personality and Social Psychology, 87*, 157–176.

Rudolph, K. D., & Hammen, C. (1999). Age and gender as determinants of stress exposure, generation, and reactions in youngsters: A transactional perspective. *Child Development, 70*, 660–677.

Rudolph, M. L., & Burt, V. K. (2003). Suicide in elderly women: Addressing this growing concern. *Women's Health in Primary Care, 6*, 281–289.

Ruiz, D. S., Zhu, C. W., & Crowther, M. R. (2003). *Not* on their own again: Psychological, social, and health characteristics of custodial African American grandmothers. *Journal of Women & Aging, 15*, 167–184.

Russell, D. E. H. (2001). Femicide: An international speakout. In D. E. H. Russell & R. A. Harmes (Eds.), *Femicide in global perspective* (pp. 128–137). New York: Teachers College Press.

Russell, M., & Carr, P. L. (2003). How to address eating disorders. An overview of screening and treatment in primary care. *Women's Health in Primary Care, 6*, 75–81.

Russell, M. M., Griffin, L. & Rajendran, A. (2003, August). *Effects of a psychoeducational group preventive intervention on dating violence.* Paper presented at the meeting of the American Psychological Association Conference, Toronto.

Russell, S. T., & Seif, H. (2002). Bisexual female adolescents: A critical analysis of past research, and results from a national survey. *Journal of Bisexuality, 2*, 73–94.

Russo, N. F. (1979). Overview: Roles, fertility and the motherhood mandate. *Psychology of Women Quarterly, 4*, 7–15.

Russo, N. F., & Vaz, K. (2001). Addressing diversity in the decade of behavior: Focus on women of color. *Psychology of Women Quarterly, 25*, 280–294.

Rust, J., et al. (2000). The role of brothers and sisters in the development of preschool children. *Journal of Experimental Child Psychology, 77,* 292–303.

Rust, P. C. (2000). Bisexuality: A contemporary paradox for women. *Journal of Social Issues, 56,* 205–221.

Rust, P. C. (Ed.) (2001a). *Bisexuality in the United States: A social science reader.* New York: Columbia University Press.

Rust, P. C. (2001b). Too many and not enough: The meanings of bisexual identities. *Journal of Bisexuality, 1,* 33–68.

Rutenberg, J. (2002, June 3). News anchors and the cathode-ray ceiling. *New York Times,* pp. C1, C8.

Rutter, M. (2003). Commentary: Causal processes leading to antisocial behavior. *Developmental Psychology, 39(2),* 372–378.

Rutter, M., et al. (2004). Sex differences in developmental reading disability. *Journal of the American Medical Association, 291,* 2007–2012.

Ryan, M. K., David, B., & Reynolds, K. J. (2004). Who cares? The effect of gender and context on the self and moral reasoning. *Psychology of Women Quarterly, 28,* 246–255.

Ryerson, A. B., Benard, V. B., & Major, A. C. (2005). *The national breast and cervical cancer early detection program 1991–2002 national report.* Atlanta: Centers for Disease Control and Prevention.

Sachs, S. (2001, August 15). Indians abroad get pitch on gender choice. *New York Times,* pp. A1, A24.

Sachs-Ericsson, N., Blazer, D., Plant, E. A., & Arnow, B. (2005). Childhood sexual and physical abuse and the 1-year prevalence of medical problems in the national comorbidity survey. *Health Psychology, 24,* pp. 32–40.

Sachs-Ericsson, N., & Ciarlo, J. A. (2000). Gender, social roles, and mental health: An epidemiological perspective. *Sex Roles, 43,* 605–628.

Sadker, M., & Sadker, D. (1994). *Failing at fairness: How America's schools cheat girls.* New York: Scribner.

Sadler, A. G., Booth, B. M., & Doebbeling, B. N. (2005). Gang and multiple rapes during military service: Health consequences and health care. *Journal of the American Medical Women's Association, 60,* 33–41.

Sadler, A. G., Booth, B. M., Mengeling, M. A., & Doebbeling, B. N. (2004). Life span and repeated violence against women during military service: Effects on health status and outpatient utilization. *Journal of Women's Health, 13,* 799–811.

Saewyc, E. M., Pettingell, S. L., & Skay, C. L. (2004). Hazards of stigma: The sexual and physical abuse of gay, lesbian, and bisexual adolescents in the U.S. and Canada. *Journal of Adolescent Health, 34,* 115–116.

Safir, M. P., et al. (2005). When gender differences surpass cultural differences in personal satisfaction with body shape in Israeli college students. *Sex Roles, 52,* 369–378.

Saftlas, A. F., et al. (2000). Racial disparity in pregnancy-related mortality associated with live birth: Can established risk factors explain it? *American Journal of Epidemiology, 152,* 413–419.

Sahyoun, N. R., Pratt, L. A., Lentzner, H., Dey, A., & Robinson, K. N. (2001). *The changing profile of nursing home residents: 1985–1997: Aging trends, No. 4.* Hyattsville, MD: National Center for Health Statistics.

St. John, W. (2002, May 20). The talk of the book world still can't sell. *New York Times,* pp. A1, A16.

Salganicoff, A., Wentworth, B., & Greene, L. (2003). Baby boom to generation X: Progress in young women's health. In C. B. Costello, V. R. Wight, & A. J. Stone (Eds.), *The American woman 2003–2004: Daughters of a revolution—young women today* (pp. 93–126). New York: Palgrave Macmillan.

Samuels, A. (2004, July 5). Smooth operations. *Newsweek,* pp. 48–49.

Sanchez-Hucles, J., & Hudgins, P. (2001). Trauma across diverse settings. In J. Worell (Ed.), *Encyclopedia of women and gender* (pp. 1151–1168). San Diego: Academic Press.

Sanchez-Hucles, J. V. (2003). Intimate relationships. In L. Slater, J. H. Daniel, & A. E. Banks (Eds.), *The complete guide to mental health for women* (pp. 104–120). Boston: Beacon Press.

Sanderson, C. A. (2004). *Health psychology.* New York: Wiley.

Sanderson, S., & Thompson, V. L. S. (2002). Factors associated with perceived paternal involvement in childrearing. *Sex Roles, 46,* 99–111.

Sandnabba, N. K., & Ahlberg, C. (1999). Parents' attitudes and expectations about children's cross-gender behavior. *Sex Roles, 40,* 249–263.

Sands, R. G. (1998). Gender and the perception of diversity and intimidation among university students. *Sex Roles, 39,* 801–815.

Sanger, C. (2000, January 5). The needs of the children. *New York Times,* p. A25.

Sanmartin, C., et al. (2004). *Joint Canada/United States survey of health, 2002–03.* Centers for Disease

Control and Prevention and *Statistics Canada*. Catalogue 82M0022-XIE.

Santelli, J. S., et al. (2003). Reproductive health in school-based health centers: Findings from the 1998–99 census of school-based health centers. *Journal of Adolescent Health, 32,* 443–451.

Santelli, J. S., et al. (2004). Initiation of sexual intercourse among middle school adolescents: The influence of psychosocial factors. *Journal of Adolescent Health, 34,* 200–208.

Santelli, J. S., Morrow, B., & Carter, M. (2004). Trends in contraceptive use among U.S. high school students in the 1990s. *Journal of Adolescent Health, 34,* 140.

Santora, M. (2005, January 30). U.S. is close to eliminating AIDS in infants, officials say. *New York Times,* pp. YT1, YT22.

Sanz de Acedo Lizarraga, M. L., & García Ganuza, J. M. (2003). Improvement of mental rotation in girls and boys. *Sex Roles, 49,* 277–286.

Saris, R. N., & Johnston-Robledo, I. (2000). Poor women are still shut out of mainstream psychology. *Psychology of Women Quarterly, 24,* 233–235.

Sarkisian, N., & Gerstel, N. (2004). Explaining the gender gap in help to parents: The importance of employment. *Journal of Marriage and Family, 66,* 431–451.

Sarto, G. E. (2004). The gender gap: New challenges in women's health. *Sexuality, Reproduction & Menopause, 2,* 9–14.

Sarwer, D. B., et al. (2005). Female college students and cosmetic surgery: An investigation of experiences, attitudes, and body image. *Plastic and Reconstructive Surgery, 115,* 931–938.

Sassler, S. (2004). The process of entering into cohabiting unions. *Journal of Marriage and Family, 66,* 491–505.

Saunders, K., & Kashubeck, S. (2002, August). *The relations among feminism, gender-role orientation, and psychological well-being in women.* Paper presented at the meeting of the American Psychological Association, Chicago.

Savin-Williams, R. C., & Diamond, L. M. (2004). Sex. In R. M. Lerner & L. Steinberg (Eds.), *Handbook of adolescent psychology,* 2d ed. (pp. 189–231). Hoboken, NJ: Wiley.

Savin-Williams, R. C., & Ream, G. L. (2003). Sex variations in the disclosure to parents of same-sex attractions. *Journal of Family Psychology, 17,* 429–438.

Sawaya, G. F., et al. (2003). Risk of cervical cancer associated with extending the interval between cervical-cancer screenings. *New England Journal of Medicine, 349,* 1501–1509.

Sayer, L. C., & Bianchi, S. M. (2000). Women's economic independence and the probability of divorce: A review and reexamination. *Journal of Family Issues, 21,* 906–943.

Saywitz, K. J., Mannarino, A. P., Berliner, L., & Cohen, J. A. (2000). Treatment for sexually abused children and adolescents. *American Psychologist, 55,* 1040–1049.

Scarborough, E. (2005, Winter). Constructing a women's history of psychology. *The Feminist Psychologist,* p. 6.

Schafer, J., Caetano, R., & Cunradi, C. B. (2004). A path model of risk factors for intimate partner violence among couples in the United States. *Journal of Interpersonal Violence, 19,* 127–142.

Schaidle, C. (2003, December 4). Manufacturers are playing makeup in creating more toys that appeal to both girls and boys. *Peoria Journal Star,* pp. C9–C10.

Scharf, M., Shulman, S., & Avigad-Spitz, L. (2005). Sibling relationships in emerging adulthood and in adolescence. *Journal of Adolescent Research, 20,* 64–90.

Schein, V. E. (2001). A global look at psychological barriers to women's progress in management. *Journal of Social Issues, 57,* 675–688.

Schemo, D. J. (2000a, December 28). Sex education with just one lesson: No sex. *New York Times,* pp. A1, A18.

Schemo, D. J. (2000b, October 4). Survey finds parents favor more detailed sex education. *New York Times,* pp. A1, A23.

Scherzer, L. (2002, Fall). Older & bolder. *Barnard Alumnae Magazine,* pp. 20–22.

Schewe, P. A. (Ed.). (2002). *Preventing violence in relationships: Interventions across the life span.* Washington, DC: American Psychological Association.

Schlenker, J. A., Caron, S. L., & Halteman, W. A. (1998). A feminist analysis of *Seventeen* magazine: Content analysis from 1945 to 1995. *Sex Roles, 38,* 135–150.

Schmader, T., Johns, M., & Barquissau, M. (2004). The costs of accepting gender differences: The role of stereotype endorsement in women's experience in the math domain. *Sex Roles, 50,* 835–850.

Schmaling, K. B. (2000). Poorly understood conditions. In M. B. Goldman & M. C. Hatch (Eds.), *Women & Health* (pp. 1055–1057). San Diego: Academic Press.

Schmitt, E. (2004, February 26). Rapes reported by servicewomen in the Persian Gulf and elsewhere. *New York Times,* pp. A1, A16.

Schmitt, M. T., Branscombe, N. R., Kobrynowicz, D., & Owen, S. (2002). Perceiving discrimination against one's gender group has different implications for well-being in women and men. *Personality and Social Psychology Bulletin, 28,* 197–210.

Schneider, L. S. (2004). Estrogen and dementia. Insights from the women's health initiative memory study. *Journal of the American Medical Association, 291,* 3005–3007.

Schneider, M. L., Moore, C. F., & Kraemer, G. W. (2004). Moderate level alcohol during pregnancy, prenatal stress, or both and limbic-hypothalamic-pituitary-adrenocortical axis response to stress in rhesus monkeys. *Child Development, 75,* 96–109.

Schneiderman, N. (2004). Psychosocial, behavioral, and biological aspects of chronic diseases. *Current Directions in Psychological Science, 13,* 247–251.

Schnieder, S. L. (2001). In search of realistic optimism: Meaning, knowledge, and warm fuzziness. *American Psychologist, 56,* 250–263.

Schoen, R., et al. (2002). Women's employment, marital happiness, and divorce. *Social Forces, 81,* 643–662.

Schoenberg, N. E., Peters, J. C., & Drew, E. M. (2003). Unraveling the mysteries of timing: Women's perceptions about time to treatment for cardiac symptoms. *Social Science & Medicine, 56,* 271–284.

Schoenborn, C. A., & Barnes, P. M. (2002). *Leisure-time physical activity among adults: United States, 1997–1998* (no. 325). Hyattsville, MD: National Center for Health Statistics.

Schooler, D., Ward, L. M., Merriwether, A., & Caruthers, A. (2004). Who's that girl: Television's role in the body image development of young White and Black women. *Psychology of Women Quarterly, 28,* 38–47.

Schroeder, K. A., Blood, L. L., & Maluso, D. (1992). An intergenerational analysis of expectations for women's career and family roles. *Sex Roles, 26,* 273–291.

Schulman, A. (2003). Female sexuality. In L. Slater, J. H. Daniel, & A. E. Banks (Eds.), *The complete guide to mental health for women* (pp. 82–91). Boston: Beacon Press.

Schulz, R., et al. (2003). End-of-life care and the effects of bereavement on family caregivers of persons with dementia. *New England Journal of Medicine, 349,* 1936–42.

Schulz, R., Martire, L. M., Beach, S. R., & Scheier, M. F. (2000). Depression and mentality in the elderly. *Current Directions in Psychological Science, 9,* 204–208.

Schumacher, J. A., & Leonard, K. E. (2005). Husbands' and wives' adjustment, verbal aggression, and physical aggression as longitudinal predictors of physical aggression in early marriage. *Journal of Consulting Psychology, 73,* 28–37.

Schwartz, L. M., Woloshin, S., Fowler, Jr., F. J., & Welch, H. G. (2004). Enthusiasm for cancer screening in the United States. *Journal of the American Medical Association, 291,* 71–78.

Schwartz, M. S., & Abell, S. C. (1999, August). *Body shape satisfaction and self-esteem: Exploring racial differences.* Paper presented at the meeting of the American Psychological Association, Boston.

Schwartz, P., & Rutter, V. (1998). *The gender of sexuality.* Thousand Oaks, CA: Pine Forge Press.

Sciolino, E. (2003, October 10). A prize, laureate says, "good for democracy." *New York Times,* p. A6.

Scott-Jones, D. (2001). Reproductive technologies. In J. Worell (Ed.), *Encyclopedia of women and gender* (pp. 919–932). San Diego: Academic Press.

Scott, K. D., Berkowitz, B., & Klaus, M. H. (1999). A comparison of intermittent and continuous support during labor: A meta-analysis. *American Journal of Obstetrics and Gynecology, 180,* 1054–1059.

Sears, D. O. (1997). College sophomores in the laboratory: Influences of a narrow data base on psychology's view of human nature. In L. A. Peplau & S. E. Taylor (Eds.), *Sociocultural perspectives in social psychology: Current readings* (pp. 20–51). Upper Saddle River, NJ: Prentice Hall.

Seem, S. R., & Clark, M. D. (2004, July). *Why Broverman et al again?* Poster presented at the meeting of the American Psychological Association, Honolulu.

Seibring, A. (2003). Living with infertility. In L. Slater, J. H. Daniel, & A. E. Banks (Eds.), *The complete guide to mental health for women* (pp. 10–17). Boston: Beacon Press.

Seitz, V. (1996). Adolescent pregnancy and parenting. In E. F. Ziegler, L. Kagen, & N. W. Hall (Eds.), *Children, families and government* (pp. 268–287). New York: Cambridge University Press.

Selingo, J. (1998, February 20). Science-oriented campuses strive to attract more women. *Chronicle of Higher Education,* A53–A54.

Sellers, N., Satcher, J., & Comas, R. (1999). Children's occupational aspirations: Comparisons by gender, gender role identity, and socioeconomic status. *Professional School Counseling, 2,* 314–317.

Sengupta, S. (2003, September 26). Facing death for adultery, Nigerian woman is acquitted. *New York Times*, p. A3.

Serbin, L. A., Moller, L. C., & Gulko, J. (1993). The development of sex-typing in middle childhood. *Monographs of the Society for Research in Child Development, 58* (Serial No. 232).

Serbin, L., et al. (2001). Gender stereotyping in infancy: Visual preferences for knowledge of gender-stereotyped toys in the second year. *International Journal of Behavioral Development, 25*, 7–15.

Serbin, L. A., et al. (2004). When aggressive girls become mothers: Problems in parenting, health, and development across two generations. In M. Putallaz & K. L. Bierman (Eds.), *Aggression, antisocial behavior, and violence among girls: A developmental perspective* (pp. 262–288). New York: Guilford.

Serbin, L. A., Moller, L. C., & Gulko, J. (1993). The development of sex-typing in middle childhood. *Monographs of the Society for Research in Child Development, 58*. Serial No. 232.

Serran, G., & Firestone, P. (2004). Intimate partner homicide: A review of the male proprietariness and the self-defense theories. *Aggression and Violent Behavior, 9*, 1–15.

Settersten, R. A., Jr., Furstenberg, F. F., & Rumbaut, R. G. (2005). On the frontier of adulthood: Theory, research, and public policy. Chicago: University of Chicago Press.

Sexual Assault Awareness Month—April 2005. *Morbidity and Mortality Weekly Report, 54*, 311.

Shakin, M., Shakin, D., & Sternglanz, S. H. (1985). Infant clothing: Sex labeling for strangers. *Sex Roles, 12*, 955–964.

Shapiro, J. P. (2001, May 21). Growing old in a good home. *U.S. News & World Report*, pp. 57–66.

Share, T. L., & Mintz, L. B. (2002). Differences between lesbians and heterosexual women in disordered eating and related attitudes. *Journal of Homosexuality, 42*, 89–106.

Sharps, M. J., Welton, A. L., & Price, J. L. (1993). Gender and task in the determination of spatial cognitive performance. *Psychology of Women Quarterly, 17*, 71–83.

Shaw, B. A., et al. (2004). Emotional support from parents early in life, aging, and health. *Psychology and Aging, 19(1)*, 4–12.

Shaw-Taylor, Y., Benokraitis, N. V. (1995). The presentation of minorities in marriage and family textbooks. *Teaching Sociology, 23*, 122–135.

Sheehy, G. (1991). *The silent passage*. New York: Random House.

Sheehy, G. (2002, May 12). It's about pure love. *Parade Magazine*, pp. 6–8.

Sheeran, P., Abraham, C., & Orbell, S. (1999). Psychosocial correlates of heterosexual condom use: A meta-analysis. *Psychological Bulletin, 125*, 90–132.

Sheets, V. L., & Lugar, R. (2005). Friendship and gender in Russia and the United States. *Sex Roles, 52*, 131–140.

Sheldon, J. P. (2004). Gender stereotypes in educational software for young children. *Sex Roles, 51*, 433–444.

Shellenbarger, S. (2004). *The breaking point: How female midlife crisis is transforming today's women*. New York: Holt.

Shelton, J. N., & Stewart, R. E. (2004). Confronting perpetrators of prejudice: The inhibitory effects of social costs. *Psychology of Women Quarterly, 28*, 215–223.

Shepela, S. T., & Levesque, L. L. (1998). Poisoned waters: Sexual harassment and the college climate. *Sex Roles, 38*, 589–611.

Sherman, M. (2002, June 23). Doubts on mammograms do not affect their use. *New York Times*, p. WH2.

Sherman, P. J., & Spence, J. T. (1997). A comparison of two cohorts of college students in responses to the male-female relations questionnaire. *Psychology of Women Quarterly, 21*, 265–278.

Sherman, S. R. (2001). Images of middle-aged and older women: Historical, cultural, and personal. In J. M. Coyle (Ed.), *Handbook on women and aging* (pp. 14–28). Westport, CT: Greenwood.

Sherry, B., et al. (2004). Attitudes, practices, and concerns about child feeding and child weight status among socioeconomically diverse White, Hispanic, and African-American mothers. *Journal of the American Dietetic Association, 104*, 215–221.

Sherwin, B. B. (2001). Menopause: Myths and realities. In N. L. Stotland & D. E. Stewart (Eds.), *Psychological aspects of women's health care* (pp. 241–259). Washington, DC: American Psychiatric Press.

Shields, S. A., & Eyssell, K. M. (2001). History of the study of gender psychology. In J. Worell (Ed.), *Encyclopedia of women and gender* (pp. 593–600). San Diego: Academic Press.

Shih, S., et al. (2004). Chlamydia screening among sexually active young female enrollees of health plans—United States, 1999–2001. *Morbidity and Mortality Weekly Report, 53*, 983–985.

Shorter-Gooden, K., & Washington, N. C. (1996). Young, black and female: The challenge of weaving an identity. *Journal of Adolescence, 19,* 465–475.

Shulman, J. L., & Horne, S. G. (2003). The use of self-pleasure: masturbation and body image among African American and European American women. *Psychology of Women Quarterly, 27,* 262–269.

Shupe, E. I., Cortina, L. M., Ramas, A., Fitzgerald, L. F., Salisbury, J. (2002). The incidence and outcomes of sexual harassment among Hispanic and non-Hispanic White women: A comparison across levels of cultural affiliation. *Psychology of Women Quarterly, 26,* 298–308.

Sices, L., et al. (2004). How do primary care physicians manage children with possible developmental delays? A national survey with an experimental design. *Pediatrics, 113,* 274–282.

Sidener, J. (2004, September 27). Digital dating. A growing number of seniors are looking for love online. *Peoria Journal Star,* pp. C5, C6.

Siegel, J. M. (2002, January). Body image change and adolescent depressive symptoms. *Journal of Adolescent Research, 17,* 27–41.

Sigal, J., et al. (2005). Cross-cultural reactions to academic sexual harassment: Effects of individualist vs. collectivist culture and gender of participants. *Sex Roles, 52,* 201–215.

Signorella, M. L., Bigler, R. S., & Liben, L. S. (1993). Developmental differences in children's gender schema about others: A meta-analytic review. *Developmental Review, 13,* 147–183.

Signorella, M. L., & Frieze, I. H. (1989). Gender schemes in college students. *Psychology: A Journal of Human Behavior, 26,* 16–23.

Signorielli, N. (1997, April). *A content analysis: Reflections of girls in the media.* Menlo Park, CA: Children Now and the Henry J. Kaiser Family Foundation.

Signorielli, N., & Bacue, A. (1999). Recognition and respect: A content analysis of prime-time television characters across the decades. *Sex Roles, 40,* 527–544.

Sikkema, K. J., Wagner, L. I., & Bogart, L. M. (2000). Gender and cultural factors in the prevention of HIV infection among women. In R. M. Eisler & M. Hersen (Eds.), *Handbook of gender, culture, and health* (pp. 299–320). Mahwah, NJ: Erlbaum.

Silverman, J. G., Raj, A., & Clements, K. (2004). Dating violence and associated sexual risk and pregnancy among adolescent girls in the United States. *Pediatrics, 114,* e220–e225.

Silverman, J. G., Raj, A., Mucci, L. A., & Hathaway, J. E. (2001). Dating violence against adolescent girls and associated substance use, unhealthy weight control, sexual risk behavior, pregnancy, and suicidality. *Journal of the American Medical Association, 286,* 572–579.

Silverstein, L. B. (1996). Fathering is a feminist issue. *Psychology of Women Quarterly, 20,* 3–37.

Silverstein, L. B., & Phares, V. (1996). Expanding the mother-child paradigm: An examination of dissertation research 1986–1994. *Psychology of Women Quarterly, 20,* 39–53.

Simmons, R. G., & Blyth, D. A. (1987). *Moving into adolescence: The impact of pubertal change and school context.* Hawthorne, NY: Aldine de Gruyter.

Simmons, T., & Dye, J. L. (2003*). Grandparents living with grandchildren: 2000.* Census 2000 Brief. Washington, DC: U.S. Census Bureau.

Simmons, T., & O'Connell, M. (2003). *Married-couple and unmarried-partner households: 2000.* Census 2000 Special Reports. Washington, DC: U.S. Census Bureau.

Simon, H. B. (2004, June). Longevity: The ultimate gender gap. *Science,* pp. 18–23.

Simon, R. J. (1998, October 2). What are the most pressing issues today in relations between men and women? Race and class drive most conflict now. *Chronicle of Higher Education,* p. B6.

Simon, R. W. (1995). Gender, multiple roles, role meaning, and mental health. *Journal of Health and Social Behavior, 36,* 182–194.

Simon, V. R., et al. (2005). *National Institutes of Health: Intramural and extramural support for research on sex differences, 2000–2003.* Washington, DC: Society for Women's Health Research.

Simons, R. L. (1996). The effect of divorce on adult and child adjustment. In R. L. Simons & Associates, *Understanding differences between divorced and intact families: Stress, interaction, and child outcome* (pp. 3–20). Thousand Oaks, CA: Sage.

Simpson, G. (1996). Factors influencing the choice of law as a career by Black women. *Journal of Career Development, 22,* 197–209.

Sims, M., Hutchins, T., & Taylor, M. (1998). Gender segregation in young children's conflict behavior in child care settings. *Child Study Journal, 28(1),* 1–16.

Singh, K., Robinson, A., & Williams-Green, J. (1995). Differences in perceptions of African American women and men faculty and administrators. *Journal of Negro Education, 64,* 401–408.

Singh, S., Darroch, J. E., Vlassoff, M., & Nadeau, J. (2003). *Adding it up: The benefits of investing in sexual and reproductive health care.* New York & Washington, DC: Alan Guttmacher Institute.

Sippola, L. K., Bukowski, W. M., & Noll, R. B. (1997). Dimensions of liking and disliking underlying the same-sex preference in childhood and early adolescence. *Merrill-Palmer Quarterly, 43,* 591–609.

Sit, D. (2004). Women and bipolar disorder across the life span. *Journal of the American Medical Women's Association, 59,* pp. 91–100.

Skaalvik, S. (2004). Gender differences in math and verbal self-concept, performance expectations, and motivation. *Sex Roles, 50,* 241–252.

Sklar, J. B. (2000). Elder and dependent adult fraud: A sampler of actual cases to profile the offenders and the crimes they perpetrate. *Journal of Elder Abuse & Neglect, 12,* 19–32.

Skoe, E. E. A., Cumberland, A., Eisenberg, N., Hansen, K., & Perry, J. (2002). The influences of sex and gender-idle identity on moral cognition and prosocial personality traits. *Sex Roles, 46,* 295–309.

Slater, A., & Tiggeman, M. (2002). A test of objectification theory in adolescent girls. *Sex Roles, 46,* 343–349.

Slaugher-Defoe, D. T., Addae, W. A., & Bell, C. (2002). Toward the future schooling of girls: Global status, issues, and prospects. *Human Development, 45,* 34–53.

Slentz, C. A., et al. (2004). Effects of the amount of exercise on body weight, body composition, and measures of central obesity. *Archives of Internal Medicine, 164,* 31–39.

Small, F. L., & Schultz, R. W. (1990). Quantifying gender differences in physical performance: A developmental perspective. *Developmental Psychology, 26,* 360–369.

Smallwood, S. (2002, April 5). Women still feel marginalized at MIT, study finds. *Chronicle of Higher Education,* p. A9.

Smetana, J. G., & Daddis, C. (2002). Domain-specific antecedents of parental psychological control and monitoring: The role of parenting beliefs and practices. *Child Development, 73,* 563–580.

Smetana, J. G., Metzger, A., & Campione-Barr, N. (2004). African American late adolescents' relationships with parents: Developmental transitions and longitudinal patterns. *Child Development, 75,* 932–947.

Smith, C., et al. (2004). A randomized controlled trial of ginger to treat nausea and vomiting in pregnancy. *Obstetrics & Gynecology, 103,* 639–645.

Smith, C. A., & Stillman, S. (2002a). Butch/femme in the personal advertisements of lesbians. *Journal of Lesbian Studies, 6(1),* 45–51.

Smith, C. A., & Stillman, S. (2002b). What do women want? The effects of gender and sexual orientation on the desirability of physical attributes in the personal ads of women. *Sex Roles, 46,* 337–342.

Smith, D. (2001, September). Harassment. *Monitor on Psychology,* pp. 38–40.

Smith, D. (2002, May). Studies garner groundbreaking data. *Monitor on Psychology,* pp. 44–45.

Smith, D. (2003, March). Angry thoughts, at-risk hearts. *Monitor on Psychology,* pp. 46–48.

Smith, D. (2005, January 16). Brown: Let women lead Africa out of poverty. *Sunday Times (London),* p. 8.

Smith, J., & Baltes, P. B. (1999). Life-span perspectives on development. In M. H. Bornstein, & M. E. Lamb (Eds.), *Development psychology: An advanced textbook,* 4th ed. (pp. 47–72). Mahwah, NJ: Erlbaum.

Smith, J., et al. (2003). Cervical cancer and use of hormonal contraceptives: A systematic review. *Lancet, 361,* 1159–1167.

Smith, K. (2002). *Who's minding the kids? Child care arrangements: Spring 1997.* Current Population Reports P70–86. Washington, DC: U.S. Census Bureau.

Smith, M. (1980). Sex bias in counseling and psychotherapy. *Psychological Bulletin, 87,* 392–407.

Smith, M. A., Boyd, L., Osuch, J. R., & Schwartz, K. (2000). Breast disorders. In M. A. Smith & L. A. Shimp (Eds.), *20 common problems in women's health care* (pp. 473–477). New York: McGraw-Hill.

Smith, R. A., & Saslow, D. (2002). Breast cancer. In G. M. Wingood & R. J. DiClemente (Eds.), *Handbook of women's sexual and reproductive health* (pp. 345–365). New York: Kluwer Academic/Plenum.

Smith, S., Pfeifer, S. M., & Collins, J. A. (2003). Diagnosis and management of female infertility. *Journal of American Medical Association, 290,* 1767–1770.

Smith, T. W. (1994). Attitudes toward sexual permissiveness: Trends, correlates, and behavioral connections. In A. S. Rossi (Ed.), *Sexuality across the life course* (pp. 63–97). Chicago: University of Chicago Press.

Smith, T. W. (1999). *The emerging 21st century American family.* Chicago: University of Chicago, National Opinion Research Center.

Smith, T. W. (2003). *American sexual behavior: Trends, socio-demographic differences, and risk behavior.* Chicago: National Opinion Research Center, University of Chicago.

Smith, T. Y. (2001). *The retention and graduation rates of 1993–99 entering science, mathematics, engineering and technology majors in 175 colleges and universities.*

Norman, OK: Center for Institutional Data Exchange and Analysis, University of Oklahoma.

Smock, P. J., & Manning, W. D. (2004). *Living together unmarried in the United States: Demographic perspectives and implications for family policy.* PSC Research Report No. 04–555, Institute for Social Research, University of Michigan.

Smolak, L., & Munstertieger, B. F. (2002). The relationship of gender and voice to depression and eating disorders. *Psychology of Women Quarterly, 26,* 234–241.

Smolak, L., Murnen S. K., & Ruble, A. E. (2000). Female athletes and eating problems: A meta-analysis. *Eating Disorders, 27,* 371–380.

Smolak, L., & Striegel-Moore, R. (2001). Body image concerns. In J. Worell (Ed.), *Encyclopedia of women and gender* (pp. 201–210). San Diego: Academic Press.

Snell, M. B. (2002, November/December). Good going. *Sierra,* pp. 26–27.

Snyder, N. M. (1994). Career women and motherhood: Child care dilemmas and choices. In C. W. Konek & S. L. Kitch (Eds.), *Women and careers: Issues and challenges* (pp. 155–172). Thousand Oaks, CA: Sage.

Söchting, I., Fairbrother, N., & Koch, W. J. (2004). Sexual assault of women. *Violence Against Women, 10,* 73–92.

Social Security Administration. (2002). *Social security: What every woman should know.* SSA Publication No. 05–10127. Washington, DC: Author.

Society for Adolescent Medicine. (2003). Eating disorders in adolescents: Position paper of the Society for Adolescent Medicine. *Journal of Adolescent Health, 33,* 496–503.

Society for Women's Health Research. (2005). *Women's fear of heart disease has almost doubled, but breast cancer remains the single most feared disease.* Washington, DC: Author.

Solarz, A. L. (Ed.). (1999). *Lesbian health: Current assessment and directions for the future.* Washington, DC: National Academy Press.

Solomon, C. G., & Dluhy, R. G. (2003). Rethinking postmenopausal hormone therapy. *New England Journal of Medicine, 348,* 579–580.

Solomon, S. E., Rothblum, E. D., & Balsam, K. F. (2004). Pioneers in partnership: Lesbian and gay male couples in civil unions compared with those not in civil unions, and married heterosexual siblings. *Journal of Family Psychology, 18,* 275–286.

Sommer, B. (2001). Menopause. In J. Worell (Ed.), *Encyclopedia of women and gender* (pp. 729–738). San Diego: Academic Press.

Sommer, B., et al. (1999). Attitudes toward menopause and aging across ethnic/racial groups. *Psychosomatic Medicine, 61,* 868–875.

Sommers-Flanagan, R., Sommers-Flanagan, J., & Davis, B. (1993). What's happening on music television? A gender role content analysis. *Sex Roles, 28,* 745–753.

Sonnert, G., & Holton, G. (1996). Career patterns of women and men in the sciences. *American Scientist, 84,* 63–71.

Sontag, D. (2002, November 17). Fierce entanglements. *New York Times Magazine,* 52–57, 62–63.

Sontag, S. (1979). The double standard of aging. In J. H. Williams (Ed.), *Psychology of women: Selected readings* (pp. 462–478). New York: Norton.

Sorenson, S. B. (1996). Violence against women: Examining ethnic differences and commonalities. *Evaluation Review, 20,* 123–145.

Sousa, C., Tieszen, L. A., & Yassen, J. (2003). Domestic violence. In L. Slater, J. H. Daniel, & A. E. Banks (Eds.), *The complete guide to mental health for women* (pp. 144–153). Boston: Beacon Press.

Sowers, M. R. (2000). Menopause: Its epidemiology. In M. B. Goldman & M. C. Hatch (Eds.), *Women & health* (pp. 1155–1168). New York: Academic Press.

Spanier, B. B. (1997). Sexism and scientific research. *National Forum, 77(2),* 26–30.

Sparks, E. E. (1998). Overcoming stereotypes of mothers in the African American context. In D. L. Anselmi & A. L. Law (Eds.), *Questions of gender: Perspectives & paradoxes* (pp. 220–232). Boston: McGraw-Hill.

Sparks, E. E., & Park, A. H. (2000). The integration of feminism and multiculturalism: Ethical dilemmas at the border. In M. M. Brabeck (Ed.) *Practicing feminist ethics in psychology* (pp. 203–224). Washington, DC: American Psychological Association.

Spataro, J., et al. (2004). Impact of child sexual abuse on mental health. *British Journal of Psychiatry, 184,* 416–421.

Speiser, P. W., & White, P. C. (2003). Congenital adrenal hyperplasia. *New England Journal of Medicine, 349,* 776–788.

Spence, J. T., & Buckner, C. E. (2000). Instrumental and expressive traits, trait stereotypes, and sexist attitudes: What do they signify? *Psychology of Women Quarterly, 24,* 44–62.

Spence, J. T., & Hahn, E. D. (1997). The Attitudes toward Women Scale and attitude change in college students. *Psychology of Women Quarterly, 21*, 17–34.

Spence, J. T., & Helmreich, R. L. (1978). *Masculinity & femininity: Their psychological dimensions, correlates, & antecedents.* Austin: University of Texas Press.

Spence, J. T., Helmreich, R. L., & Stapp, J. (1974). The Personal Attributes Questionnaire: A measure of sex-role stereotypes and masculinity-femininity. *JSAS Catalog of Selected Documents in Psychology, 4.* Ms. No. 617.

Spencer, J. M., et al. (2002). Self-esteem as a predictor of initiation of coitus in early adolescents. *Pediatrics, 109*, 581–584.

Spencer, S. J., Steele, C. M., & Quinn, D. M. (1999). Stereotype threat and women's math performance. *Journal of Experimental Social Psychology, 35*, 4–28.

Spicher, C. H., & Hudak, M. A. (1997, August). *Gender role portrayal on Saturday morning cartoons: An update.* Paper presented at the meeting of the American Psychological Association, Chicago.

Spiegel, D. (1998). Getting there is half the fun: Relating happiness to health. *Psychological Inquiry, 9*, 66–68.

Spiegel, D., Bloom, J. R., Kraemer, H. C., & Gottheil, E. (1989). Effect of psychosocial treatment on survival of patients with metastatic breast cancer. *Lancet, 2*, 888–891.

Spitzer, B. L., Henderson, K. A., & Zivian, M. T. (1999). Gender differences in population versus media body sizes: A comparison over four decades. *Sex Roles, 40*, 545–565.

Spitzer, R. L., et al. (Eds.). (1994). *DSM-IV casebook.* Washington, DC: American Psychiatric Association.

Spraggins, R. E. (2003). *Women and men in the United States: March 2002.* Current Population Reports, P20–544. Washington, DC: U.S. Census Bureau.

Spragins, E. (2003, August 3). Out of the classroom, back in the house. *New York Times*, p. BU9.

Sprecher, S., & Felmlee, D. (1997). The balance of power in romantic heterosexual couples over time from "his" and "her" perspectives. *Sex Roles, 37*, 361–379.

Springen, K. (2000, December 4). The right to choose. *Newsweek*, pp. 73–74.

Springen, K. (2004, November 1). Kids under the knife. *Newsweek*, pp. 59–60.

Springen, K. (2005, February 7). The miscarriage maze. *Newsweek*, pp. 63–64.

Springen, K., & Fragala, K. (2002, October 14). New hope in the war against breast cancer. *Newsweek*, p. 10.

Springen, K., & Kantrowitz, B. (2004, May 10). Alcohol's deadly triple threat. *Newsweek*, pp. 90–92.

Springen, K., & Seibert, S. (2005, January 17). Artful aging. *Newsweek*, pp. 57–65.

Srivastava, S., John, O. P., Gosling, S. D., & Potter, J. (2003). Development of personality in early and middle adulthood: Set like plaster or persistent change? *Journal of Personality and Social Psychology, 84*, 1041–1053.

Sroufe, L. A., Bennett, C., Englund, M., Urban, J., & Shulman, S. (1993). The significance of gender boundaries in preadolescence: Contemporary correlates and antecedents of boundary violation and maintenance. *Child Development, 64*, 455–466.

Stabiner, K. (2003, January 12). Where the girls aren't. They're not in computer science. Is it nature or conditioning? *New York Times Education Life*, p. 35.

Stacey, J., & Biblarz, T. J. (2001). (How) does the sexual orientation of parents matter? *American Sociological Review, 66*, 159–183.

Stack, S., & Eshleman, J. R. (1998). Marital status and happiness: A 17-nation study. *Journal of Marriage and the Family, 60*, 527–536.

Stake, J. E. (1997). Integrating expressiveness and instrumentality in real-life settings: A new perspective on the benefits of androgyny. *Sex Roles, 37*, 541–564.

Stake, J. E., & Malkin, C. (2003). Students' quality of experience and perceptions of intolerance and bias in the women's and gender studies classroom. *Psychology of Women Quarterly, 27*, 174–185.

Stake, J. E., Roades, L., Rose, S., Ellis, L., & West, C. (1994). The women's studies experience: Impetus for feminist activism. *Sex Roles. 18*, 17–24.

Stake, J. E., & Rose, S. (1994). The long-term impact of women's studies on students' personal lives and political activism. *Psychology of Women Quarterly, 18*, 403–412.

Stanley, A. (2002, January 13). For women, to soar is rare, to fall is human. *New York Times*, pp. BU1, 10.

Stanley, A. (2004, January 16). Women having sex, hoping men tune in. *New York Times*, pp. B1, 28.

Stanley, D., & Freysinger, V. J.(1995). The impact of age, health, and sex on the frequency of older adult's leisure activity participation: A longitudinal study. *Activities, Adaptation & Aging, 19*, 31–42.

Stanley, J. L. (2002). Young sexual minority women's perceptions of cross-generational friendships with older lesbians. In S. M. Rose (Ed.),

Lesbian love and relationships (pp. 139–148). Binghamton, NY: Harrington Park Press.

Stanton, A. L. (1995). Psychology of women's health: Barriers and pathways to knowledge. In A. L. Stanton & S. J. Gallant (Eds.), *The psychology of women's health: Progress and challenges in research and application* (pp. 3–21). Washington, DC: American Psychological Association.

Stark-Wroblewski, K., Yanico, B. J., & Lupe, S. (2005). Acculturation, internalization of Western appearance norms, and eating pathology among Japanese and Chinese international student women. *Psychology of Women Quarterly, 29,* 38–46.

Stearns, V., Beebe, K. L., Iyengar, M., & Dube, E. (2003). Paroxetine controlled release in the treatment of menopausal hot flashes. A randomized controlled trial. *Journal of the American Medical Association, 289,* 2827–2834.

Steele, C. M., Spencer, S. J., & Aronson, J. (2002). Contending with group image: The psychology of stereotype and social identity threat. In M. P. Zanna (Ed.), *Advances in experimental social psychology, 34,* 379–440.

Steele, J., James, J. B., & Barnett, R. C. (2002). Learning in a man's world: Examining the perceptions of undergraduate women in male-dominated academic areas. *Psychology of Women Quarterly, 26,* 46–50.

Steffens, D. C., et al. (2000). Prevalence of depression and its treatment in an elderly population: The Cache County study. *Archives of General Psychiatry, 57,* 601–607.

Steil, J. M. (2001). Family forms and member well-being: A research agenda for the decade of behavior. *Psychology of Women Quarterly, 25,* 344–363.

Steil, J. M., & Weltman, K. (1991). Marital inequality: The importance of resources, personal attributes, and social norms on career valuing and the allocation of domestic responsibilities. *Sex Roles, 24,* 161–179.

Steiner, M., & Born, L. (2002). Psychiatric aspects of the mentrual cycle. In S. G. Kornstein & A. H. Clayton (Eds.), *Women's mental health: A comprehensive textbook* (pp. 48–69). New York: Guilford.

Steiner, M., Dunn, E., & Born, L. (2003). Hormones and mood: From menarche to menopause and beyond. *Journal of Affective Disorders, 74,* 67–83.

Steinhauer, J. (1999, March 1). For women in medicine, a road to compromise, not perks. *New York Times,* pp. A1, A21.

Steinkamp, M. W., Harnisch, D. L., Walberg, H. J., & Tsai, S. (1985). Cross-national gender differences in mathematics attitude and achievement among 13-year-olds. *The Journal of Mathematical Behavior, 4,* 259–277.

Steinman, K. J., & Zimmerman, M. A. (2004). Religious activity and risk behavior among African American adolescents: Concurrent and developmental effects. *American Journal of Community Psychology, 33,* 155–161.

Steinpreis, R. E., Anders, K. A., & Ritzke, D. (1999). The impact of gender on the review of the curricula vitae of job applicants and tenure candidates: A national empirical study. *Sex Roles, 41,* 509–528.

Stephenson, J. (2002). AIDS knowledge gap. *Journal of the American Medical Association, 288,* 155.

Stern, M., & Karraker, K. H. (1989). Sex stereotyping of infants: A review of gender labeling studies. *Sex Roles, 20,* 501–521.

Sternberg, S. (2004, February 25). USA's youth at high risk for venereal diseases. *USA Today,* p. 6D.

Stewart, A. J., & Ostrove, J. M. (1998). Women's personality in middle age: Gender history, and midcourse corrections. *American Psychologist, 53,* 1185–1194.

Stewart, A. J., & Vandewater, E. A. (1999). "If I had it to do over again . . .": Midlife review, midcourse corrections, and women's well-being in midlife. *Journal of Personality and Social Psychology, 76,* 270–283.

Stewart, S. L., et al. (2004, June 4). Cancer mortality surveillance—United States, 1990–2000. *Surveillance Summaries, Morbidity and Mortality Weekly Report 2004, 53* (No. SS-3), 1–108.

Stice, E. (2002). Risk and maintenance factors for eating pathology: A meta-analytic review. *Psychological Bulletin, 128,* 825–848.

Stice, E., Burton, E. M., & Shaw, H. (2004). Prospective relations between bulimic pathology, depression, and substance abuse: Unpacking comorbidity in adolescent girls. *Journal of Consulting and Clinical Psychology, 72,* 62–71.

Stier, J. J. (2000, November). The easy lives of working moms. *Working Mother,* pp. 21–27.

Stith, S. M., et al. (2004, November/December). Intimate partner physical abuse perpetration and victimization risk factors: A meta-analytic review. *Aggression and Violent Behavior, 10,* pp. 65–98.

Stoffelmayr, B., Wadland, W. C., & Guthrie, S. K. (2000). Substance abuse. In M. A. Smith & L. A.

Shimp (Eds.), *20 common problems in women's health care* (pp. 225–262). New York: McGraw-Hill.

Stohs, J. H. (2000). Multicultural women's experience of household labor, conflicts, and equity. *Sex Roles, 42,* 339–361.

Stokes, J., Riger, S., & Sullivan, M. (1995). Measuring perceptions of the working environment for women in corporate settings. *Psychology of Women, 19,* 533–549.

Stolberg, S. G. (1998). Quandary on donor eggs: What to tell the children. *New York Times,* pp. Y1, Y14.

Stolberg, S. G. (2002, March 21). Minorities get inferior care, even if insured, study finds. *New York Times,* pp. A1, A30.

Stoney, C. M. (2003). Gender and cardiovascular disease: A psychobiological and integrative approach. *Current Directions in Psychological Science, 12,* 129–133.

Stoppard, J. M., & McMullen, L. M. (Eds.). (2003). *Situating sadness: Women's depression in social context.* New York: New York University Press.

Stotland, N. L. (2001). Induced abortion in the United States. In N. L. Stotland & D. E. Stewart (Eds.), *Psychological aspects of women's health care* (pp. 219–239). Washington, DC: American Psychiatric Press, Inc.

Straus, M. A., & Smith, C. (1990). Violence in Hispanic families in the United States: Incidence rates and structural interpretations. In M. A. Straus & R. J. Gelles (Eds.), *Physical violence in American families: Risk factors and adaptations to violence in 8,145 families* (pp. 341–367). New Brunswick, NJ: Transaction.

Strauser, D. R., et al. (2002, Jan.–March). Analyzing the differences in career thoughts based on disability status. (Differences in Career Thoughts). *Journal of Rehabilitation, 68,* 27–32.

Strauss, L. T., et al. (2004). Abortion surveillance—United States, 2001. *Morbidity and Mortality Weekly Report, 53* (SS09), 1–32.

Strauss, R. S. (2000). Childhood obesity and self-esteem. *Pediatrics, 105 (1),* e15.

Strawbridge, W. J., Camacho, T. C., Cohen, R. D., & Kaplan, G. A. (1993). Gender differences in factors associated with change in physical functioning in old age: A 6-year longitudinal study. *Gerontologist, 33,* 603–609.

Street, A. E., Stafford, J., & Bruce, T. A. (2003, Winter). Sexual harassment. *PTSD Research Quarterly, 14,* pp. 1–7.

Street, S., Kimmel, E. B., & Kromrey, J. D. (1995). Revisiting university student gender role perceptions. *Sex Roles, 33,* 183–201.

Street, S., Kromrey, J. D., & Kimmel, E. (1995). University faculty gender roles perceptions. *Sex Roles, 32,* 407–422.

Streppel, M. T., et al. (2005). Dietary fiber and blood pressure. *Archives of Internal Medicine, 165,* 150–156.

Strewler, G. J. (2004). Decimal point—Osteoporosis therapy at the 10-year mark. *New England Journal of Medicine, 350,* 1172–1174.

Strickland, B. R. (2000). Misassumptions, misadventures, and the misuse of psychology. *American Psychologist, 55,* 331–338.

Striegel-Moore, R. H., et al. (2003). Eating disorders in white and black women. *The American Journal of Psychiatry, 160,* 1326–1331.

Stroebe, M. S., & Stroebe, W. (1993). The mortality of bereavement: A review. In M. S. Stroebe, W. Stroebe, & R. D. Hanson (Eds.), *Handbook of bereavement* (pp. 208–226). London: Cambridge University Press.

Strong, T. H. (2000). *Expecting trouble: The myth of prenatal care in America.* New York: New York University Press.

Students and sexual harassment. (1999, May 25). *New York Times,* p. A30.

Stumpf, H., & Stanley, J. C. (1998). Stability and change in gender-related differences on the college board advanced placement and achievement tests. *Current Directions in Psychological Science, 7,* 192–196.

Subrahmanyam, K., Kraut, R., Greenfield, P. M., & Gross, E. (2001). New forms of electronic media. In D. G. Singer & J. L. Singer (Eds.), *Handbook of children and the media* (pp. 73–99). Thousand Oaks, CA: Sage.

Sue, D. (2000). Health risk factors in diverse cultural groups. In R. M. Eisler & M. Hersen (Eds.), *Handbook of gender, culture, and health* (pp. 85–103). Mahwah, NJ: Erlbaum.

Sue, D. W., Bingham, R. P., Porché-Burke, L., & Vasquez, M. (1999). The diversification of psychology: A multicultural revolution. *American Psychologist, 54,* 1061–1069

Suggs, W. (2003). A federal commission wrestles with gender equity in sports. *Chronicle of Higher Education,* pp. A41–A43.

Suggs, W. (2004, June 18). Small colleges lag on sports opportunities for women. *Chronicle of Higher Education,* pp. A1, A32–A36.

Suggs, W. (2005, April 8). Faces in a mostly white, male crowd. *Chronicle of Higher Education,* pp. A34–36.

Sugisawa, H., et al. (2002). The impact of social ties on depressive symptoms in U.S. and Japanese elderly. *Journal of Social Issues, 58(4),* 785–804.

Suicide and attempted suicide—China, 1990–2002. (2004). *Morbidity and Mortality Weekly Report, 53,* 481–483.

Summers-Effler, E. (2004). Little girls in women's bodies: Social interaction and the strategizing of early breast development. *Sex Roles, 51,* 29–44.

Sumner, K. E., & Brown, T. J. (1996). Men, women, and money: Exploring the role of gender, gender-linkage of college major and career-information sources in salary expectations. *Sex Roles, 34,* 823–839.

Surgeon General's Advisory on Alcohol Use in Pregnancy. (2005, March 11). *Morbidity and Mortality Weekly Report, 84,* 229.

Susman, E. J., Dorn, L. D., & Schiefelbein, V. L. (2003). Puberty, sexuality, and health. In I. Weiner (Ed.), *Handbook of psychology.* Vol. 6, *Developmental psychology* (pp. 295–324). (Vol. eds.: R. M. Lerner, M. A. Easterbrooks, & J. Mistry). Hoboken, NJ: Wiley.

Susman, E. J., & Rogol, A. (2004). Puberty and psychological development. In R. M. Lerner & L. Steinberg (Eds.), *Handbook of adolescent psychology,* 2d ed. (pp. 15–44). Hoboken, NJ: Wiley.

Susskind, J. E. (2003). Children's perception of gender-based illusory correlations: Enhancing pre-existing relationships between gender and behavior. *Sex Roles, 48,* 483–494.

Sved, M. S. (2001). Psychological aspects of lesbian health care. In N. L. Stotland & D. E. Stewart (Eds.), *Psychological aspects of women's health care* (pp. 549–570). Washington, DC: American Psychiatric Press, Inc.

Swearingen-Hilker, N., & Yoder, J. D. (2002). Understanding the context of unbalanced domestic contributions: The influence of perceiver's attitudes, target's gender, and presentational format. *Sex Roles, 46,* 91–98.

Swim, J. K., Aikin, K. J., Hall, W. S., & Hunter, B. A. (1995). Sexism and racism: Old-fashioned and modern prejudices. *Journal of Personality and Social Psychology, 68,* 199–214.

Swim, J. K., Borgida, E., Maruyama, G., & Myers, D. G. (1989). Joan McKay versus John McKay: Do gender stereotypes bias evaluations? *Psychological Bulletin, 105,* 409–429.

Swim, J. K., & Campbell, B. (2000). Sexism: Attitudes, beliefs, and behaviors. In R. Brown & S. Gaertner (Eds.), *Handbook of social psychology:* *Intergroup relations,* Vol. 4 (pp. 218–237). Cambridge, MA: Blackwell.

Swim, J. K., Mallett, R., & Stangor, C. (2004). Understanding subtle sexism: Detection and use of sexist language. *Sex Roles, 51,* 117–128.

Swim, J. K., Scott, E., Sechrist, G. B., Campbell, B., & Stangor, C. (2003). The role of intent and harm in judgments of prejudice. *Journal of Personality and Social Psychology, 84,* 944–959.

Switzer, J. Y. (1990). The impact of generic word choices: An empirical investigation of age- and sex-related differences. *Sex Roles, 22,* 69–82.

Sybert, V. P., & McCauley, E. (2004). Turner's syndrome. *New England Journal of Medicine, 351,* 1227–1238.

Sylvester, K. (2001). Caring for our youngest: Public attitudes in the United States. *The Future of Children, 11(1),* 53–61.

Szinovacz, M. (1991). Women and retirement. In B. B. Hess & E. W. Markson (Eds.), *Growing old in America,* 4th ed. (pp. 293–303). New Brunswick, NJ: Transaction.

Szinovacz, M., & Washo, C. (1992). Gender differences in exposure to life events and adaptation to retirement. *Journal of Gerontology: Social Science, 47,* S191–S196.

Szymanski, D. M. (2003). The feminist supervision scale: A rational/theoretical approach. *Psychology of Women Quarterly, 27,* 221–232.

Szymanski, D. M. (2005). Heterosexism and sexism as correlates of psychological distress in lesbians. *Journal of Counseling and Development, 83.*

Szymanski, D. M., Chung, Y. B., & Balsam, K. (2001). Psychosocial correlates of internalized homophobia in lesbians. *Measurement and Evaluation in Counseling and Development, 34,* 27–38.

Tai, Y. (2004, March 15). Shortage of females in China grows grave. *Washington Times,* p. 24.

Talaga, J. A., & Beehr, T. A. (1995). Are there gender differences in predicting retirement decisions? *Journal of Applied Psychology, 80,* 16–28.

Talbot, M. (2002, February 24). Girls just want to be mean. *New York Times Magazine,* pp. 24–29, 40, 58, 64–65.

Tamis-LeMonda, C. S., Shannon, J. D., Cabrera, N. J., & Lamb, M. E. (2004). Fathers and mothers at play with their 2- and 3-year olds: Contributions to language and cognitive development. *Child Development, 75,* 1806–1819.

Tang, M. (2003, September). Career counseling in the future: Constructing, collaborating, advocating. Career Counseling in the Next Decade. *Career Development Quarterly,* pp. 61–69.

Tanofsky-Kraff, M., et al. (2004). Eating-disordered behaviors, body fat, and psychopathology in overweight and normal-weight children. *Journal of Consulting and Clinical Psychology, 72,* 53–61.

Tariq, S. H., & Morley, J. E. (2003). Maintaining sexual function in older women: Physical impediments and psychosocial issues. *Women's Health in Primary Care, 6,* 157–162.

Tarkan, L. (2002, February 26). In many delivery rooms, a routine becomes less routine. *New York Times,* pp. D6, D8.

Tarkan, L. (2004, August 24). As a hormone substitute, soy is ever more popular, but is it safe? *New York Times,* pp. D5, D8.

Tarris, C. (2002, July 5). Are girls really as mean as books say they are? *Chronicle of Higher Education,* pp. B7–B9.

Tasker, F. (2002). Lesbian and gay parenting. In A. Coyle & C. Kitzinger (Eds.), *Lesbian and gay psychology: New perspectives* (pp. 81–97). Oxford, UK: BPS Blackwell.

Tasker, F., & Golombok, S. (1997). *Growing up in a lesbian family.* New York: Guilford.

Tavernise, S. (2004, October 14). Shielding women by teaching them they aren't chattel. *New York Times,* p. A14.

Taylor, C. R., Lee, J. Y., & Stern, B. B. (1995). Portrayals of African, Hispanic, and Asian Americans in magazine advertising. *American Behavioral Scientist, 38,* 608–621.

Taylor, K. (2001). How far can you flex? *Association Management, 53(3),* 58–64.

Taylor, K. L., et al. (2003). Psychological adjustment among African American breast cancer patients: One-year follow-up results of a randomized psychoeducational group intervention. *Health Psychology, 22,* 316–323.

Taylor, M., & Taylor L. (2003). *What are children for?* London: Short Books.

Taylor, P. L., Tucker, M. B., & Mitchell-Kernan, C. (1999). Ethnic variations in perceptions of men's provider role. *Psychology of Women Quarterly, 23,* 741–761.

Taylor, S. (2004, Summer). Being raised by my grandparents will help make me successful in life. *AARP, The GIC Voice,* p. 11.

Taylor, S. E. (2003). *The tending instinct.* New York: Henry Holt.

Taylor, S. E., et al. (2000). Biobehavioral responses to stress in females: Tend-and-befriend, not fight-or-flight. *Psychological Review, 107,* 411–429.

Taylor, S. E., et al. (2002). Sex differences in biobehavioral responses to threat: Reply to Geary and Flinn. *Psychological Review, 109,* 751–753.

Tedeschi, R., Park, C., & Calhoun, L. (Eds.). (1998). *Posttraumatic growth: Positive changes in the aftermath of crisis.* Mahwah, NJ: Erlbaum.

Tenenbaum, H. R., & Leaper, C. (2002). Are parents' gender schemas related to their children's gender-related cognitions? A meta-analysis. *Developmental Psychology, 38,* 615–630.

Tenenbaum, H. R., & Leaper, C. (2003). Parent-child conversations about science: The socialization of gender inequities. *Developmental Psychology, 39,* 34–47.

Thabes, V. (1997). A survey analysis of women's long-term, postdivorce adjustment. *Journal of Divorce & Remarriage, 27,* 163–175.

Theriault, S. W., & Holmberg, D. (1998). The new old-fashioned girl: Effects of gender and social desirability on reported gender-role ideology. *Sex Roles, 39,* 97–112.

This year's freshmen at 4-year colleges: A statistical profile. (2002, February 1). *Chronicle of Higher Education,* pp. A36–37.

This year's freshmen at 4-year colleges: A statistical profile. (2005, February 4). *Chronicle of Higher Education,* p. A33.

Thomas, A., & White, R. (1996). A study of gender differences among school psychologists. *Psychology in the Schools, 33,* 351–359.

Thomas, E. (2003, July 7). The war over gay marriage. *Newsweek,* pp. 38–45.

Thomas, J. J., & Daubman, K. A. (2001). The relationship between friendship quality and self-esteem in adolescent girls and boys. *Sex Roles, 45,* 53–65.

Thomas, J. L., Sperry, L., & Yarbrough, M. S. (2000). Grandparents as parents: Research findings and policy recommendations. *Child Psychiatry and Human Development, 31,* 3–22.

Thomas, J. R., & French, K. E. (1985). Gender differences across age in motor performance: A meta-analysis. *Psychological Bulletin, 98,* 260–282.

Thomas, T. (2005, January 16). So when is a woman too old to give birth? *Sunday Express (London),* pp. 55–57.

Thompson, G. (1999, March 30). New clinics seek patients among lesbians, who often shun health care. *New York Times*, p. 25.

Thompson, S. J., & Johnston, L. (2004). Risk factors of gay, lesbian, and bisexual adolescents: Review of empirical literature and practice implications. *Journal of Human Behavior in the Social Environment, 8,* 111–128.

Thomsen, S. R., Weber, M. M., & Brown, L. B. (2002). The relationship between reading beauty and fashion magazines and the use of pathogenic dieting methods among adolescent females. *Adolescence, 37,* 1–18.

Thorne, B. (1993). *Gender play: Girls and boys in school.* New Brunswick, NJ: Rutgers University Press.

Thornhill, R., & Palmer, C. T. (2000). *A natural history of rape: Biological bases of sexual coercion.* Cambridge, MA: MIT Press.

Tidball, M. E., Smith, D. G., Tidball, C. S., & Wolf-Wendel, L. E. (1999). *Taking women seriously: Lessons and legacies for educating the majority.* Phoenix, AZ: American Council on Education.

Tiedemann, J. (2000). Parents' gender stereotypes and teachers' beliefs as predictors of children's concept of their mathematical ability in elementary school. *Journal of Educational Psychology, 92,* 144–151.

Tiefer, L. (2001). A new view of women's sexual problems: Why new? Why now? *Journal of Sex Research, 38,* 89–96.

Tiggemann, M. (2001). The impact of adolescent girls' life concerns and leisure activities on body dissatisfaction, disordered eating, and self-esteem. *Journal of Genetic Psychology, 62,* 133–142.

Tilberis, L. (1998). *No time to die.* London: Little, Brown.

Timmerman, G. (2003). Sexual harassment of adolescents perpetrated by teachers and by peers: An exploration of the dynamics of power, culture, and gender in secondary schools. *Sex Roles, 48,* 231–244.

Tischler, L. (2004, February). Where are the women? *Fast Company,* 52–60.

Tjaden, P., & Thoennes, N. (2000). *Extent, nature, and consequences of intimate partner violence: Findings from the national violence against women survey.* Washington, DC: National Institute of Justice.

Tobach, E. (2001). Development of sex and gender: Biochemistry, physiology, and experience. In J. Worell (Ed.), *Encyclopedia of women and gender* (pp. 315–332). San Diego: Academic Press.

Toller, P. W., Suter, E. A., & Trautman, T. C. (2004). Gender role identity and attitudes toward feminism. *Sex Roles, 51,* 85–90.

Tolman, D. L. (2002). *Dilemmas of desire: Teenage girls talk about sexuality.* Cambridge, MA: Harvard University Press.

Tolman, D. L., & Brown, L. M. (2001). Adolescent girls' voices: Resonating resistance in body and soul. In R. K. Unger (Ed.), *Handbook of the psychology of women and gender* (pp. 133–155). New York: Wiley.

Tolman, D. L., Striepe, M. I., & O'Sullivan, L. F. (2003). How do we define sexual health for women? In L. Slater, J. H. Daniel, & A. E. Banks (Eds.), *The complete guide to mental health for women.* Boston: Beacon Press.

Tolou-Shams, M., et al. (2002, August). *Sexual orientation and ethnicity: Predictors of domestic violence in women.* Paper presented at the meeting of the American Psychological Association, Chicago.

Tomich, P. L., & Schuster, P. M. (1996). Gender differences in the perception of sexuality: Methodological considerations. *Sex Roles, 34,* 865–874.

Torpy, J. M. (2002). Birth labor. *Journal of the American Medical Association, 288,* 1432.

Torpy, J. M. (2004). Hysterectomy. *Journal of the American Medical Association, 291,* 1526.

Torpy, J. M. (2005). Suicide. *Journal of the American Medical Association, 293,* 2558.

Torres, B., et al. (2004, November). *Effective communication to prevent infectious disease in women.* Emerging Infectious Diseases. Serial on the Internet. http://www.cdc.gov/ncidod/EID/vol10no11/04–06 23_13.htm

Torres, S. (1987). Hispanic-American battered women: Why consider cultural differences? *Response to the Victimization of Women and Children, 10,* 20–21.

Torres, S. (1991). A comparison of wife abuse between two cultures: Perception, attitudes, nature, and extent. *Issues in mental health nursing: Psychiatric nursing for the 90's: New concepts, new therapies, 12,* 113–131.

Torrez, D. J. (2001). The health of older women: A diverse experience. In J. M. Coyle (Ed.), *Handbook on women and aging* (pp. 131–148). Westport, CT: Greenwood.

Tougas, F., Brown, R., Beaton, A. M., & Joly, S. (1995). Neosexism: Plus ça change, plus c'est pareil. *Personality and Social Psychology Bulletin, 21,* 842–849.

Toussaint, D. (2003, September/October). Outward bound. *Bride's,* p. 346.

Townsend, T. G. (2002). The impact of self-components on attitudes toward sex among African-American preadolescent girls: The moderating role of menarche. *Sex Roles, 47,* 11–20.

Travis, C. B. (2005). 2004 Carolyn Sherif award address: Heart disease and gender inequity. *Psychology of Women Quarterly, 29,* 15.

Travis, C. B., & Compton, J. D. (2001). Feminism and health in the decade of behavior. *Psychology of Women Quarterly, 25,* 312–323.

Treas, J., & Spence, M. (1994). Family life in retirement. In A. Monk (Ed.), *The Columbia retirement handbook* (pp. 419–432). New York: Columbia University Press.

Treas, J., & Widmer, E. D. (2000). Married women's employment over the life course: Attitudes in cross-national perspective. *Social Forces, 78,* 1409–1436.

Trebay, G. (2003, September 2). The skin wars start earlier & earlier. *New York Times,* p. C12.

Trice, A. D., Hughes, M. A., Odom, C., Woods, K., & McClellan, N. C. (1995). The origins of children's career aspirations: IV. Testing hypotheses from four theories. *Career Development Quarterly, 43,* 307–322.

Trickett, P. K., & Gordis, E. B. (2004). Aggression and antisocial behavior in sexually abused females. In M. Putallaz & K. L. Bierman (Eds.), *Aggression, antisocial behavior, and violence among girls: A developmental perspective* (pp. 162–185). New York: Guilford.

Trippet, S. E., & Bain, J. (1992). Reasons American lesbians fail to seek traditional health care. *Health Care for Women International, 13(2),* 145–153.

Trivits, L. C., & Repucci, N. D. (2002). Application of Megan's Law to juveniles. *American Psychologist, 57,* 690–704.

Troisi, R., & Hartge, P. (2000). Ovarian cancer. In M. B. Goldman & M. C. Hatch (Eds.), *Women & health* (pp. 907–915). New York: Academic Press.

Troxel, W. M., Matthews, K. A., Gallo, L. C., & Kuller, L. H. (2005). Marital quality and occurrence of the metabolic syndrome in women. *Archives of Internal Medicine, 165,* 1022–1027.

Tsui, L. (1998). The effects of gender, education, and personal skills self-confidence on income in business management. *Sex Roles, 38,* 363–373.

Tucker, C. M., & Herman, K. C. (2002). Using culturally sensitive theories and research to meet the academic needs of low-income African-American children. *American Psychologist, 57,* 762–773.

Tucker, M. B., & Mitchell-Kernan, C. (1995). *The decline in marriage among African Americans: Causes, consequences, and policy implications.* New York: Russell Sage.

Tuggle, C. A., Huffman, S., & Rosengard, D. S. (2002). A descriptive analysis of NBC's coverage of the 2000 Summer Olympics. *Mass Communication & Society, 5,* 361–375.

Turkle, S. (2002, March 7). Lord of the hackers. *New York Times,* p. A27.

Turner, B. F., & Turner, C. B. (1991). Through a glass, darkly: Gender stereotypes for men and women varying in age and race. In B. B. Hess & E. W. Markson (Eds.), *Growing old in America,* 4th ed. (pp. 137–150). New Brunswick, NJ: Transaction.

Turner, J. S., & Helms, D. B. (1989). *Contemporary adulthood.* 4th ed. Fort Worth, TX: Holt, Rinehart & Winston.

Twenge, J. M. (1997a). Attitudes toward women, 1970–1995: A meta-analysis. *Psychology of Women Quarterly, 21,* 35–51.

Twenge, J. M. (1997b). Changes in masculine and feminine traits over time: A meta-analysis. *Sex Roles, 36,* 305–325.

Twenge, J. M. (2001). Changes in women's assertiveness in response to status and roles: A cross-temporal meta-analysis, 1931–1993. *Journal of Personality and Social Psychology, 81,* 133–145.

Twenge, J. M., & Crocker, J. (2002). Race and self-esteem: Meta-analyses comparing Whites, Blacks, Hispanics, Asians and American Indians and comment on Gray-Little and Hafdahl (2000). *Psychological Bulletin, 128,* 371–408.

Tyler, K. A. (2002). Social and emotional outcomes of childhood sexual abuse: A review of recent research. *Agression and Violent Behavior, 7,* 567–589.

Tyre, P. (2002, June 10). "R" is for retirement. *Newsweek,* p. 48.

Tyre, P., & Pierce, E. (2003, September 14). Ma, I'll be at the spa. *Newsweek,* p. 10.

Uchitelle, L. (2001, June 26). Women forced to delay retirement. *New York Times,* p. A1.

UCLA study looks at women in treatment. (2000, March). *Research Findings: National Institute on Drug Abuse, 14,* 58.

Ullman, S. E. (2002). Rape avoidance: Self-protection strategies for women. In P. A. Schewe (Ed.), *Preventing violence in relationships: Interventions across the life span.* (pp. 137–162). Washington, DC, US: American Psychological Association.

Ullman, S. E. (2003). A critical review of field studies on the link of alcohol and adult sexual assault in women. *Aggression and Violent Behavior, 8,* 471–486.

Ullman, S. E. (2004). Sexual assault victimization and suicidal behavior in women: A review of the literature. *Aggression and Violent Behavior, 9,* 331–351.

Ullman, S. E., & Brecklin, L. R. (2003). Sexual assault history and health-related outcomes in a national sample of women. *Psychology of Women Quarterly, 27,* 46–57.

Umbach, P. D., et al. (2004). *Women students at coeducational and women's colleges: How do their experiences compare?* Bloomington, IN: Indiana University Center for Postsecondary Research.

U.N. offers action plan for a world aging rapidly. (2002, April 14). *New York Times,* p. YNE5.

UNAIDS. (2003). *AIDS epidemic update: December 2003.* Geneva: Author.

UNAIDS. (2004). *2004 report on the global AIDS epidemic.* Geneva: Author.

UNAIDS. (2005). *AIDS in Africa. Three scenarios to 2025.* Geneva: Author.

Underwood, A. (2004, May 10). Fresh weapons for an old battle. *Newsweek,* pp. 64, 66, 69.

Unger, J. B., & Seeman, T. E. (2000). Successful aging. In M. B. Goldman & M. C. Hatch (Eds.), *Women & health* (pp. 1238–1251). New York: Academic Press.

Unger, R. K. (2001). Women as subjects, actors, and agents in the history of psychology. In R. K. Unger (Ed.), *Handbook of the psychology of women and gender* (pp. 3–16). New York: Wiley.

UNICEF. (2000). Domestic violence against women and girls. *Innocenti Digest,* No. 6.

UNICEF. (2004). *Afghanistan—Progress of provinces.* Multiple indicator cluster survey 2003. Afghanistan: Author.

UNIFEM. (2003). *Not a minute more: Ending violence against women.* New York: Author.

United Nations Population Fund. (2004). *UNFPA state of world population 2004. The Cairo consensus at ten: Population, reproductive health and the global effort to end poverty.* New York: Author.

Upchurch, D. M., et al. (2004). Social and behavioral determinants of self-reported STD among adolescents. *Perspectives on Sexual and Reproductive Health, 36,* 276–287.

Upchurch, D. M., & Kusunoki, Y. (2004, May/June). Associations between forced sex, sexual and protective practices, and sexually transmitted diseases among a national sample of adolescent girls. *Women's Health Issues, 14,* pp. 75–84.

Updegraff, K. A., McHale, S. M., & Crouter, A. C. (2000). Adolescents' sex-typed friendships: Does having a sister versus a brother matter? *Child Development, 21,* 1597–1610.

UPI. (2004, March 29). *Aspirin may help fight ovarian cancer.* Retrieved April 25, 2004, from http://www.nlm.nih.gov/medlineplus/news/fullstory_16836.html

Urquiza, A. J., & Goodlin-Jones, B. L. (1994). Child sexual abuse and adult revictimization with women of color. *Violence and Victims, 9,* 223–232.

U.S. Bureau of Labor Statistics. (2005). *Women in the labor force: A data book.* Washington, DC: Author.

U.S. Census Bureau, International Database. (1997, 1995). http://www.census.gov/International/Aging Statistics.htm

U.S. Census Bureau. (2003a). *Custodial mothers and fathers and their child support: 2001.* Current Population Reports, pp. 60–225. Washington, DC: Author.

U.S. Census Bureau. (2003b). *Educational attainment in the United States: March 2001 and March 2002.* Current Population Reports. Washington, DC: Author.

U.S. Census Bureau. (2003c). *Statistical profile of the United States.* 123d ed. Washington, DC: U.S. Government Printing Office.

U.S. Census Bureau. (2004a). *Educational attainment in the United States: 2003.* Current Population Reports. Washington, DC: Author.

U.S. Census Bureau. (2004b, July 29). *Grandparents day 2004: Sept. 12.* CB04-FF.15.

U.S. Census Bureau. (2005a). *Educational attainment in the United States: 2004.* Current Population Reports. Washington, DC: Author.

U.S. Census Bureau. (2005b, January 31). *Women's History Month (March). Facts for Features.* CB05-FF.04

Usdansky, M. L. (2000, March 8). Numbers show families growing closer as they pull apart. *New York Times,* p.10.

U.S. Department of Education. (2004). *The condition of education 2004 in brief.* Washington, DC: Author.

U.S. Department of Health and Human Services (USDHHS). (1999). *1998 national household survey on drug abuse.* Washington, DC: U.S. Government Printing Office.

U.S. Department of Health and Human Services. (2004a). *2002 National survey of family growth (NSFG).* Washington, DC: Author.

U.S. Department of Health and Human Services. (2004b). *Bone health and osteoporosis: A report of the Surgeon General.* Rockville, MD: Author.

U.S. Department of Labor. (n.d.). *Affirmative action at OFCCP: A sound policy and a good investment.* Employment Standards Administration, Office of Federal Contract Compliance Programs. Washington, DC: Author.

Utter, J., Neumark-Sztainer, D., Wall, M., & Story, M. (2003). Reading magazine articles about dieting and associated weight control behaviors among adolescents. *Journal of Adolescent Health, 32,* 78–82.

Utz, R. L., et al. (2004). The daily consequences of widowhood. The role of gender and intergenerational transfers on subsequent housework performance. *Journal of Family Issues, 25,* 683–712.

Vaccarino, V., et al. (2005). Sex and racial differences in the management of acute myocardial infarction, 1994 through 2002. *New England Journal of Medicine, 353,* 671–681.

Vandello, J. A., & Cohen, D. (2004). When believing is seeing: Sustaining norms of violence in cultures of honor. In M. Schaller & C. Crandall (Eds.), *The psychological foundations of culture* (p. 281–304). New York: Erlbaum.

Vandewater, E. A., Ostrove, J. M., & Stewart, A. J. (1997). Predicting women's well-being in midlife: The importance of personality development and social role involvements. *Journal of Personality and Social Psychology, 72,* 1147–1160.

Vandewater, E. A., & Stewart, A. J. (1997). Women's career commitment patterns and personality development. In M. E. Lachman & J. B. James (Eds.), *Multiple paths of midlife development* (pp. 375–410). Chicago: University of Chicago Press.

Van Evra, J. (2004). *Television and child development.* 3d ed. Mahwah, NJ: Erlbaum.

Vanfraussen, K., Ponjaert-Kristoffersen, I., & Brewaeys, A. (2003). Family functioning in lesbian families created by donor insemination. *American Journal of Orthopsychiatry, 73,* 78–90.

Vangelisi, A. L., & Daly, J. A. (1997). Gender differences in standards for romantic relationships: Different cultures or different experiences? *Personal Relationships, 4,* 203–219.

VanLeuvan, P. (2004). Young women's science/ mathematics career goals from seventh grade to high school graduation. *Journal of Educational Research, 97,* 248–267.

Van Steenhouse, A. (2002). *Empty nest . . . full heart. The journey from home to college.* Denver, Co: Simpler Life Press.

Van Willigen, M., & Drentea, P. (2001). Benefits of equitable relationships: The impact of sense of fairness, household division of labor, and decision making power on perceived social support. *Sex Roles, 44,* 571–597.

Vasquez, M. J. T., & de las Fuentes, C. (1999). American-born Asian, African, Latina, and American Indian adolescent girls: Challenges and strengths. In N. G. Johnson, M. C. Roberts, & J. Worell (Eds.), *Beyond appearance: A new look at adolescent girls* (pp. 151–173). Washington, DC: American Psychological Association.

Vasta, R., Knott, J. A., & Gaze, C. E. (1996). Can spatial training erase the gender differences on the water-level task? *Psychology of Women Quarterly, 20,* 549–567.

Vastag, B. (2001). CDC says rates are up for gonorrhea, down for syphilis. *Journal of the American Medical Association, 285,* p. 155.

Vastag, B. (2002). Hormone replacement therapy falls out of favor with expert committee. *Journal of the American Medical Association, 287,* 1923–1924.

Vastag, B. (2003). Breast cancer racial gap examined. No easy answers to explain disparities in survival. *Journal of the American Medical Association, 290,* 1838–1842.

Vaughan, K. K., & Fouts, G. T. (2003). Changes in television and magazine exposure and eating disorder symptomatology. *Sex Roles, 49,* 313–320.

Velkoff, V. A., & Lawson, V. A. (1998). *Gender and aging: Caregiving.* 1B/98-3. Washington, DC: U.S. Bureau of the Census.

Veniegas, R. C., & Conley, T. D. (2000). Biological research on women's sexual orientations: Evaluating the scientific evidence. *Journal of Social Issues, 56,* 267–282.

Ventura, S. J., Abma, J. C., Mosher, W. D., & Henshaw, S. (2003). *Revised pregnancy rates, 1990–97, and new rates for 1998–99: United States.* National Vital Statistics Reports, Vol. 52 No. 7. Hyattsville, MD: National Center for Health Statistics.

Vermeer, H. J., Boekaerts, M., & Seegers, G. (2000). Motivational and gender differences: Sixth grade students' mathematical problem-solving behavior. *Journal of Educational Psychology, 92,* 308–315.

Vermeulen, M. E., & Minor, C. W. (1998). Context of career decisions: Women reared in a rural community. *Career Development Quarterly, 46,* 230–245.

Vescio, T. K., et al. (2005). Power and the creation of patronizing environments. The stereotype-based behaviors of the powerful and their effects on female performance in masculine domains. *Journal of Personality and Social Psychology, 88,* 658–672.

Vesely, S. K., et al. (2004). The potential protective effects of youth assets from adolescent sexual risk behaviors. *Journal of Adolescent Health, 34,* 356–365.

Victory, R., et al. (2004, October). *Reduced risks in oral contraceptive users: Results from the women's health initiative.* Paper presented at the meeting of the American Society for Reproductive Medicine, Philadelphia, PA.

Vigil, J. M., Geary, D. C., & Byrd-Craven, J. (2005). A life history assessment of early childhood sexual abuse in women. *Developmental Psychology, 41,* 553–561.

Viki, G. T., Abrams, D., & Hutchison, P. (2003). The "true" romantic: Benevolent sexism and paternalistic chivalry. *Sex Roles, 49,* 533–537.

Vilhjalmsson, R., & Kristjansdottir, G. (2003). Gender differences in physical activity in older children and adolescents: The central role of organized sport. *Social Science & Medicine, 56,* 363–374.

Villarosa, L. (2002a, June 4). At elders' home, each day is Valentine's Day. *New York Times,* pp. D6, D10.

Villarosa, L. (2002b, June 25). Making an appointment with the stork. *New York Times,* p. 9.

Villarosa, L. (2002c, December 3). To prevent sexual abuse, abusers step forward. *New York Times,* pp. D5, D8.

Villarosa, L. (2003, December 23). More teenagers say no to sex, but experts aren't sure why. *New York Times,* pp. D6, D8.

Villarosa, L. (2004, April 5). AIDS fears grow for Black women. *New York Times,* pp. A1, A13.

Viswanathan, A. K., et al. (2005). Smoking and the risk of endometrial cancer: Results from the Nurses' Health Study. *International Journal of Cancer, 114,* 996–1001.

Vitaliano, P. P., Young, H. M., & Zhang, J. (2004). Is caregiving a risk factor for illness? *Psychological Science, 13,* 13–16.

Vitaliano, P. P., Zhang, J., & Scanlan, J. M. (2003). Is caregiving hazardous to one's physical health? A meta-analysis. *Psychological Bulletin, 129(6),* 946–972.

Voelker, R. (2002). Elder abuse and neglect a new research topic. *Journal of the American Medical Association, 288,* 2254–2256.

Vogt, A. (1997, August 24). Even in virtual reality, it is still a man's world. *Chicago Tribune,* Sec. 13, pp. 1, 6.

Voracek, M., & Fisher, M. L. (2002). Shapely centre-folds? Temporal changes in body measures: Trend analysis. *British Medical Journal, 325,* 1447–1448.

Votruba-Drzal, E., Coley, R. L., & Chase-Lansdale, P. L. (2004). Child care and low-income children's development: Direct and moderated effects. *Child Development, 75,* 296–312.

Voyer, D., Nolan, C., & Voyer, S. (2000). The relation between experience and spatial performance in men and women. *Sex Roles, 43,* 891–915.

Voyer, D., Voyer, S., & Bryden, M. P. (1995). Magnitude of sex differences in spatial abilities: A meta-analysis and consideration of critical variables. *Psychological Bulletin, 117,* 250–270.

Vyrostek, S. B., Annest, J. L., & Ryan, G. W. (2004). Surveillance for fatal and nonfatal injuries—United States, 2001. *Morbidity and Mortality Weekly Report.* Surveillance Summaries 53, (No. SS-7).

W/F balance becomes the major job concern; telework a potential solution. (1999, March 23). *National Report on Work & Family, 12,* p. 45.

Wadyka, S. (2004, September 21). For women worried about fertility, egg bank is a new option. *New York Times,* pp. D5, D8.

Wagner, M. (1992, April). *Being female—A secondary disability? Gender differences in the transition experiences of young people with disabilities.* Paper presented at the meeting of the American Educational Research Association, San Francisco.

Wahab, S., & Olson, L. (2004). Intimate partner violence and sexual assault in Native American communities. *Trauma, Violence, & Abuse, 5,* pp. 353–366.

Wainer, H., & Steinberg, L. S. (1992). Sex differences in performance in the mathematics section of the scholastic aptitude test: A bidirectional validity test. *Harvard Educational Review, 62,* 323–336.

Wainright, J. L., Russell, S. T., & Patterson, C. J. (2004). Psychosocial adjustment, school outcomes, and romantic relationships of adolescents with same-sex parents. *Child Development, 75,* 1886–1898.

Waisberg, J., & Page, S.(1988). Gender role nonconformity and perceptions of mental illness. *Women & Health, 14,* 3–16.

Waitkevicz, H. J. (2004). Lesbian health in primary care. *Women's Health in Primary Care, 7,* 134–139.

Waldfogel, J. (2001). International policies toward parental leave and child care. *The Future of Children, 11(1),* 99–111.

Waldman, A. (2002, January 9). Young women back in school, race to catch up. *New York Times,* p. A10.

Waldrop, D. P. (2004). Caregiving issues for grandmothers raising their grandchildren. *Journal of Human Behavior in the Social Environment, 7,* 201–223.

Walker, L. E. A. (2001). Battering in adult relations. In J. Worell (Ed.), *Encyclopedia of women and gender* (pp. 169–188). San Diego: Academic Press.

Walker, L. J. (1991). Sex differences in moral reasoning. In W. M. Kurtines & J. L. Gewirtz (Eds.), *Handbook of moral behavior and development.* Vol. 2, *Research* (pp. 333–367). Hillsdale, NJ: Erlbaum.

Walker, T. (2005, February 28). Parents. Again. Some grandparents who raised their grandchildren are now raising their great-grandchildren. *Peoria Journal Star,* p. C6.

Wallis, C. (2004, March 22). The case for staying home. *Time,* 51–59.

Walsh, P. N., & LeRoy, B. (2004). *Women with disabilities aging well: A global view.* Baltimore, MD: Brookes.

Walsh, P. V., Katz, P. A., & Downey, E. P. (1991, April). *A longitudinal perspective on race and socialization in infants and toddlers.* Paper presented at the meeting of the Society for Research in Child Development, Kansas City, KS.

Walsh-Bowers, R. (1999). Fundamentalism in psychological science: The publication manual as bible. *Psychology of Women Quarterly, 23,* 375–392.

Walsh, T. (2004). The future of research on eating disorders. *Appetite, 42,* 5–10.

Walter, C. A. (2000). The psychosocial meaning of menopause: Women's experiences. *Journal of Women & Aging, 12,* 117–131.

Walter, C. A. (2003). *The loss of a life partner: Narratives of the bereaved.* New York: Columbia University Press.

Walther-Lee, D., & Stricker, G. (1998, August). *The basis of closeness between grandchildren and grandparents.* Paper presented at the meeting of the American Psychological Association, San Francisco.

Wang, L., et al. (2004). Stress and dysmenorrhoea: A population based perspective study. *Occupational and Environmental Medicine, 61,* 1021–1026.

Wangby, M., Bergman, L. R., & Magnusson, D. (1999). Development of adjustment problems in girls: What syndromes emerge? *Child Development, 70,* 678–699.

Ward, C. A. (2000). Models and measurements of psychological androgyny: A cross-cultural extension and theory and research. *Sex Roles, 43,* 529–552.

Ward, L. M. (2002). Does television exposure affect emerging adults' attitudes and assumptions about sexual relationships? Correlational and experimental confirmation. *Journal of Youth and Adolescence, 31,* 1–15.

Ward, L. M., & Caruthers, A. (2001). Media influences. In J. Worell (Ed.), *Encyclopedia of women and gender* (pp. 687–701). San Diego: Academic Press.

Ward, L. M., Hansbrough, E., & Walker, E. (2005). Contributions of music video exposure to black adolescents' gender and sexual schemas. *Journal of Adolescent Research, 20,* 143–166.

Wardle, J., et al. (2004). Socioeconomic variation in attitudes to eating and weight in female adolescents. *Health Psychology, 23,* 275–282.

Wark, P. (2005, January 14). Going solo: Why fathers are out of the picture. *Times (London),* pp. 4–5.

Warner, J. (2005). *Perfect madness: Motherhood in the age of anxiety.* New York: Riverhead books.

Warner, J., et al. (2004). Rates and predictors of mental illness in gay men, lesbians and bisexual men and women. *British Journal of Psychiatry, 185,* pp. 479–485.

Warshaw, C. (2001). Women and violence. In N. L. Stotland & D. E. Stewart (Eds.), *Psychological aspects of women's health care* (pp. 477–548). Washington, DC: American Psychiatric Press, Inc.

Warshaw, R. (1988). *I never called it rape: The Ms. report on recognizing, fighting, and surviving date and acquaintance rape.* New York: Harper & Row.

Wartella, E., Caplovitz, A. G., & Lee, J. H. (2004). From Baby Einstein to Leapfrog, from Doom to The Sims, from instant messaging to Internet chat rooms: Public interest in the role of interactive media in children's lives. *Social Policy Report, 18(4),* 3, 5–11, 13–14, 16–19.

Wartik, N. (2001, June 24). Paying a price for drinking men under the table. *New York Times,* p. WH4.

Wartik, N. (2002, June 23). Hurting more, helped less? *New York Times,* pp. WH1, WH6, WH7.

Wasco, S. M. (2003). Conceptualizing the harm done by rape. Applications of trauma theory to experiences of sexual assault. *Trauma, Violence, & Abuse, 4,* 309–322.

Washington, D. L., & Bird, C. E. (2002). Sex differences in disease presentation in the emergency department. *Annuals of Emergency Medicine, 40,* 461–463.

Wasti, S. A., & Cortina, L. M. (2002). Coping in context: Sociocultural determinants of responses to sexual harassment. *Journal of Personality and Social Psychology, 83,* 394–405.

Wathen, C. N., & MacMillan, H. L. (2003). Interventions for violence against women. *Journal of the American Medical Association, 289,* 589–600.

Watkins, P. L., & Whaley, D. (2000). Gender role stressors and women's health. In R. M. Eisler & M. Hersen (Eds.), *Handbook of gender, culture, and health* (pp. 43–62). Mahwah, NJ: Erlbaum.

Watson, C. M., Quatman, T., & Edler, E. (2002). Career aspirations of adolescent girls: Effects of achievement level, grade, and single-sex school environment. *Sex Roles, 46,* 323–335.

Watson, E. (1995). Comfort. In B. Benatovich (Ed.). *What we know so far: Wisdom among women.* New York: St. Martin's Griffin.

Watt, H. M. G. (2004). Development of adolescents' self-perceptions, values, and task perceptions according to gender and domain in 7th-through 11th-grade Australian students. *Child Development, 75,* 1556–1574.

Waxman, S. (2005, February 21). "Simpsons" animates gay nuptials, and a debate. *New York Times,* p. A17.

Way, N. (1995). "Can't you see the courage, the strength that I have?" Listening to urban adolescent girls speak about their relationships. *Psychology of Women Quarterly, 19,* 107–128.

Wayne, J. H., & Cordeiro, B. L. (2003). Who is a good organizational citizen? Social perception of male and female employees who use family leave. *Sex Roles, 49,* 233–246.

Wearing, B. (1998). *Leisure and feminist theory.* Thousand Oaks, CA: Sage.

Weatherall, A. (1999). Exploring a teaching/research nexus as a possible site for feminist methodological innovation in psychology. *Psychology of Women Quarterly, 23,* 199–214.

Weatherall, A. (2002). *Gender, language, and discourse.* London: Routledge.

Weber, L., & Higginbotham, E. (1997). Black and white professional-managerial women's perceptions of racism and sexism in the workplace. In E. Higginbotham & M. Romero (Eds.), *Women and work: Exploring race, ethnicity, and class* (pp. 153–175). Thousand Oaks, CA: Sage.

Wechsler, H., Lee, J. E., Kuo, M., Seibring, M., Nelson, T. F., & Lee, H. (2002). Trends in college binge drinking during a period of increased prevention efforts. *Journal of American College Health, 50,* 203–217.

Weeks, W. A., & Nantel, J. (1995). The effects of gender and career stage on job satisfaction and performance behavior: A case study. *Journal of Social Behavior and Personality, 10,* 273–288.

Wei, G. S., & Herbers, J. E., Jr. (2004). Reporting elder abuse: A medical, legal, and ethical overview. *Journal of the American Medical Women's Association, 59,* 248–254.

Weichold, K., Silbereisen, R. K., & Schmitt-Rodermund, E. (2003). Short-term and long-term consequences of early versus late physical maturation in adolescents. In C. Hayward (Ed.), *Gender differences at puberty* (pp. 241–276). Cambridge: University Press.

Weinberg, D. H. (2004). *Evidence from census 2000 about earnings by detailed occupation for men and women.* Washington, DC: U. S. Census Bureau.

Weinberg, M. S., Williams, C. J., & Pryor, D. W. (1994). *Dual attraction: Understanding bisexuality.* New York: Oxford University Press.

Weingarten, K., Surrey, J. L., Coll, C. G., & Watkins, M. (1998). Introduction in C. G. Coll, J. L. Surrey, & K. Weingarten (Eds.), *Mothering against the odds: Diverse voices of contemporary mothers* (pp. 1–14). New York: Guilford.

Weinraub, B., & Rutenberg, J. (2003, July 29). Gay-themed TV gains a wider audience. *New York Times,* pp. A1, C5.

Weinraub, M., et al. (1984). The development of sex role stereotypes in the third year: Relationships to gender labeling, gender identity, sex-typed toy preferences, and family characteristics. *Child Development, 55,* 1493–1503.

Weinstock, H., Berman, S., & Cates, W. (2004). Sexually transmitted diseases among American youth: Incidence and prevalence estimates, 2000. *Perspectives on Sexual and Reproductive Health, 36,* 6–10.

Weisgram, E. S., & Bigler, R. S. (2004, May). *Belief in the altruistic value of math and science affects girls' interest.* Poster presented at the meeting of American Psychological Society, Chicago.

Weitz, R., & Gordon, L. (1993). Images of black women among Anglo college students. *Sex Roles, 28,* 19–34.

Wellington, S., & Giscombe, K. (2001). Women and leadership in corporate America. In C. B. Costello & A. J. Stone (Eds.), *The American woman 2001–2002: Getting to the top* (pp. 87–106). New York: Norton.

Welty, F. K. (2001). Cardiovascular disease and dyslipidemia in women. *Archives of Internal Medicine, 161,* 514–522.

Wentz, E., Gillberg, C., Gillberg, I. C., & Rastam, M. (2001). Ten-year follow-up of adolescent-onset anorexia nervosa: Psychiatric disorders and overall functioning scales. *Journal of Child Psychology and Psychiatry, 42,* 613–622.

Wenzel, A., Jackson, L. C., & Brendle, J. R. (2004). Psychopathology, sexuality, and the partner relationship. In J. H. Harvey, A. Wenzel, & S. Sprecher (Eds.), *The handbook of sexuality in close relationships* (pp. 545–571). Mahwah, NJ: Erlbaum.

Werner, E. E. (2004). What can we learn about resilience from large-scale longitudinal studies? In S. Goldstein & R. Brooks (Eds.), *Handbook of resilience in children,* Chapter 7. New York: Kluwer.

Werner, E. E., & Smith, R. S. (2001). *Journeys from childhood to midlife: Risk, resilience and recovery.* Ithaca, NY: Cornell University Press.

Werner-Wilson, R. J. (1998). Gender differences in adolescent sexual attitudes: The influence of individual and family factors. *Adolescence, 33,* 519–531.

West, C. M. (2002). Black battered women: New directions for research and black feminist theory. In L. H. Collins, M. R. Dunlap, & J. C. Chrisler (Eds.), *Charting a new course for feminist psychology* (pp. 216–237). Westport, CT: Praeger.

West, C. M. (2002). Lesbian intimate partner violence: Prevalence and dynamics. In S. M. Rose (Ed.), *Lesbian love and relationships* (pp. 121–127). Binghamton, NY: Harrington Park Press.

Weuve, J., et al. (2004). Physical activity, including walking, and cognitive function in older women. *Journal of the American Medical Association, 292,* 1454–1461.

Whaley, R. B. (2001). The paradoxical relationship between gender inequality and rape: Toward a refined theory. *Gender & Society, 15,* 529–553.

Whelehan, P. (2001). Cross-cultural sexual practices. In J. Worell (Ed.), *Encyclopedia of women and gender* (pp. 291–302). San Diego: Academic Press.

Whiffen, V. E. (2001). Depression. In J. Worell (Ed.), *Encyclopedia of women and gender* (pp. 303–314). San Diego: Academic Press.

Whiffen, V. E., & MacIntosh, H. B. (2005). Mediators of the link between childhood sexual abuse and emotional distress. *Trauma, Violence, & Abuse, 6,* pp. 24–39.

Whiston, S. C., & Keller, B. K. (2004). The influences of the family of origin on career development: A review and analysis. *The Counseling Psychologist, 32,* 493–568.

White, B. H., & Kurpius, S. E. R. (2002). Effects of victim sex and sexual orientation on perceptions of rape. *Sex Roles, 46,* 191–200.

White, J. W. (2001). Aggression and gender. In J. Worell (Ed.), *Encyclopedia of women and gender* (pp. 81–93). San Diego: Academic Press.

White, J. W., Donat, P. L. N., & Bondurant, B. (2001). A developmental examination of violence against girls and women. In R. K. Unger (Ed.), *Handbook of the psychology women and gender* (pp. 343–357). New York: Wiley.

White, J. W., & Kowalski, R. M. (1994). Deconstructing the myth of the nonaggressive woman: A feminist analysis. *Psychology of Women Quarterly, 18,* 487–508.

White, J. W., Russo, N. F., & Travis, C. B. (2001). Feminism and the decade of behavior. *Psychology of Women Quarterly, 25,* 267–279.

Whitley, B. E. (2001a, May). *Gender-role beliefs and attitudes toward homosexuality.* Paper presented at the meeting of the Midwestern Psychological Association, Chicago.

Whitley, B. E. (2001b, August). *Racial/ethnic differences in attitudes toward homosexuality: A meta-analysis.* Paper presented at the meeting of the American Psychological Association, San Francisco.

Whitley, B. E. (2002, August). *Authoritarianism and social dominance orientation as predictors of heterosexist and racial attitudes.* Paper presented at the meeting of the American Psychological Association, Chicago.

Whitley, B. E., Jr., McHugh, M. C., & Frieze, I. H. (1986). Assessing the theoretical models for sex differences in causal attributions of success and failure. In J. S. Hyde & M. C. Linn (Eds.), *The psychology of gender: Advances through meta-analysis* (pp. 102–135). Baltimore, MD: Johns Hopkins.

Whittaker, T. (1996). Violence, gender and elder abuse. In B. Fawcett, B. Featherstone, J. Hearn, & C. Toft (Eds.), *Violence and gender relations: Theories and interventions* (pp. 147–160). Thousand Oaks, CA: Sage.

Wichstrom, L., & Hegna, K. (2003). Sexual orientation and suicide attempt: A longitudinal study of the general Norwegian adolescent population. *Journal of Abnormal Psychology, 112,* 144–151.

Wigfield, A., & Eccles, J. S. (2002). The development of competence beliefs, expectancies for success, and achievement values from childhood through adolescence. In A. Wigfield & J. S. Eccles (Eds.), *Development of achievement motivation* (pp. 91–120). San Diego: Academic Press.

Wilcox, S., et al. (2003). Psychosocial and perceived environmental correlates of physical activity in rural and older African American and white women. *The Journals of Gerontology, 58,* P329–P337.

Wilcox, S., et al. (2003). The effects of widowhood on physical and mental health, health behaviors, and health outcomes: The women's health initiative. *Health Psychology, 22,* 513–522.

Wiley, D., & Bortz, W. M., II. (1996). Sexuality and aging—Usual and successful. *Journal of Gerontology: Medical Science, 51A (3),* M142–M146.

Wilkinson, J. A., & Ferraro, K. F. (2002). Thirty years of ageism research. In T. D. Nelson (Ed.), *Ageism: Stereotyping and prejudice against older persons* (pp. 339–358). Cambridge, MA: MIT Press.

Wilkinson, S. (2002). Lesbian health. In A. Coyle & C. Kitzinger (Eds.), *Lesbian and gay psychology: New perspectives* (pp. 117–134). Oxford, UK: BPS Blackwell.

Willemsen, T. M. (2002). Gender typing of the successful woman—A stereotype reconsidered. *Sex Roles, 46,* 385–391.

Willetts-Bloom, M. C., & Nock, S. L. (1994). The influence of maternal employment on gender role attitudes of men and women. *Sex Roles, 30,* 371–389.

Williams, A. (2004). E-dating bubble springs a leak. *New York Times,* pp. ST1, ST6.

Williams, A. (2005, April 3). Casual relationships, yes—Casual sex, not really. *New York Times,* pp. 1, 12.

Williams, J. (2002, June 17). How academe treats mothers. *Chronicle of Higher Education.* http://career network.com

Williams, J. E., & Best, D. L. (1990). *Measuring sex stereotypes: A multination study.* Newbury Park, CA: Sage.

Williams, M. K., McCandies, T., & Dunlap, M. R. (2002). Women of color and feminist psychology: Moving from criticism and critique to integration and application. In L. H. Collins, M. R. Dunlap, & J. C. Chrisler (Eds.), *Charting a new course for feminist psychology* (pp. 65–89). Westport, CT: Praeger.

Williams, N., & Leiblum, S. L. (2002). Sexual dysfunction. In G. M. Wingood & R. J. DiClemente (Eds.), *Handbook of women's sexual and reproductive health* (pp. 303–328). New York: Kluwer Academic/ Plenum.

Williams, R., & Wittig, M. A. (1997). "I'm not a feminist, but . . ." Factors contributing to the discrepancy between pro-feminist orientation and feminist social identity. *Sex Roles, 37,* 885–904.

Williams, R. B., Barefoot, J. C., & Schneiderman, N. (2003). Psychosocial risk factors for cardiovascular disease. More than one culprit at work. *Journal of American Medical Association, 290,* 2190–2192.

Williams, T. J., et al. (2000). Finger-length ratios and sexual orientation. *Nature, 404,* 455–456.

Williams-Nickelson, C. (2005, January). Women mentoring women. *gradPSYCH, 3,* p. 11.

Williamson, J., Softas-Nall, B., & Miller, J. (2001, August). *Grandmothers raising grandchildren: Challenges and rewards.* Paper presented at the meeting of the American Psychological Association, San Francisco.

Willis, F. N., & Carlson, R. A. (1993). Singles ads: Gender, social class, and time. *Sex Roles, 29,* 387–404.

Willson, A. E., & Hardy, M. A. (2002). Racial disparities in income security for a cohort of aging American women. *Social Forces, 80,* 1283–1306.

Wilson, J. F. (1997). Changes in female students' attitudes toward women's lifestyles and career choices during a psychology of women course. *Teaching of Psychology, 24,* 50–52.

Wilson, M. C. (2004, Summer). Closing the leadership gap. *Ms.,* pp. 14–15.

Wilson, R. (2004a, January 23). Louts in the lab. *Chronicle of Higher Education,* A7–A9.

Wilson, R. (2004b, December 3). Where the elite teach, it's still a man's world. *Chronicle of Higher Education,* pp. A8–A14.

Windle, M., & Windle, R. C. (2002). Alcohol use and women's sexual and reproductive health. In G. M. Wingood & R. J. DiClemente (Eds.), *Handbook of women's sexual and reproductive health* (pp. 153–171). New York: Kluwer Academic/Plenum.

Wingood, G. M., & DiClemente, R. J. (2002). HIV/AIDS. In G. M. Wingood & R. J. DiClemente (Eds.), *Handbook of women's sexual and reproductive health* (pp. 281–301). New York: Kluwer Academic/ Plenum.

Winstead, B. A., & Griffin, J. L. (2001). Friendship styles. In J. Worell (Ed.), *Encyclopedia of women and gender* (pp. 481–492). San Diego: Academic Press.

Winston, C. A. (2003). African American grandmothers parenting AIDS orphans: Concomitant grief and loss. *American Journal of Orthopsychiatry, 73,* 91–100.

Winterich, J. A. (2003). Sex, menopause, and culture. Sexual orientation and the meaning of menopause for women's sex lives. *Gender & Society, 17,* 627–642.

WISER. (2002). *Widowhood: Why women need to talk about this issue.* Washington, DC: Women's Institute for a Secure Retirement.

Wisocki, P. A. (1998). The experience of bereavement by older adults. In M. Hersen & V. Van Hasselt (Eds.), *Handbook of clinical geropsychology* (pp. 431–448). New York: Plenum.

Wisocki, P. A., & Skowron, J. (2000). The effects of gender and culture on adjustment to widowhood. In R. M. Eisler & M. Hersen (Eds.), *Handbook of gender, culture, and health* (pp. 429–448). Mahwah, NJ: Erlbaum.

Wloszczyna, S. (2003, June 2). It's in to be out in pop culture. *USA Today,* pp. 9B, 10B.

Wolchik, S. A., et al. (2002). Six-year follow-up of preventive interventions for children of divorce. *Journal of the American Medical Association, 288,* 1874–1881.

Wolf, R. S. (2001). Support groups for older victims of domestic violence. *Journal of Women & Aging, 13,* 71–83.

Wolfe, D. A., et al. (2003). Dating violence prevention with at-risk youth: A controlled outcome evaluation. *Journal of Consulting and Clinical Psychology, 71,* 279–291.

Wolfe, D. A., et al. (2004). Predicting abuse in adolescent dating relationships over 1 year: The role of child maltreatment and trauma. *Journal of Abnormal Psychology, 113,* 406–415.

Wolfe, V. (2002, August). *Similarities and differences between heterosexual and same-sex domestic violence.* Paper presented at the meeting of the American Psychological Association, Chicago.

Wolk, A., et al. (1998). A prospective study of association of monounsaturated fat and other types of fat with risk of breast cancer. *Archives of Internal Medicine, 158,* 41–45.

Women and disability. (2004, July). *Women's Psych-E, 3* (5).

Women and heart health: From prevention to intervention. (2005, February). *National Women's Health Report, 27*(1), 1–4.

Women heed warnings about stroke better than men do. (1998, March). *APA Monitor,* p. 9.

Wood, E., Desmarais, S., & Gugula, S. (2002). The impact of parenting experience on gender stereotyped toy play of children. *Sex Roles, 47,* 39–49.

Wood, J. T. (1994). *Gendered lives: Communication, gender, and culture.* Belmont, CA: Wadsworth.

Wood, W., & Eagly, A. H. (2002). A cross-cultural analysis of the behavior of women and men: Implications for the origins of sex differences. *Psychological Bulletin, 128,* 699–727.

Woodhill, B. M., & Samuels, C. A. (2003). Positive and negative androgyny and their relationship with psychological health and well-being. *Sex Roles, 48,* 555–565.

Wooster, R., & Weber, B. L. (2003). Breast and ovarian cancer. *New England Journal of Medicine, 348,* 2339–2347.

Worell, J. (1996). Opening doors to feminist research. *Psychology of Women Quarterly, 20,* 469–485.

Worell, J. (2001). Feminist interventions: Accountability beyond symptom reduction. *Psychology of Women Quarterly, 25,* 335–343.

Worell, J., & Etaugh, C. (1994). Transforming theory and research with women: Themes and variations. *Psychology of Women Quarterly, 18,* 443–450.

Worell J., & Johnson, D. M. (2001). Feminist approaches to psychotherapy. In J. Worell (Ed.), *Encyclopedia of women and gender* (pp. 425–437). San Diego: Academic Press.

Worell, J., & Remer, P. (2003). *Feminist perspectives in therapy: Empowering diverse women.* Hoboken, NJ: Wiley.

Worell, J., Stilwell, D., Oakley, D., & Robinson, D. (1999). Educating about women and gender: Cognitive, personal, and professional outcomes. *Psychology of Women Quarterly, 23,* 797–811.

World Health Day—April 7, 2005. (2005). *Morbidity and Mortality Weekly Report, 54,* 309.

World Health Organization. (2004). *World report on knowledge for better health.* Geneva: Author.

World Health Organization. (2002). *World report on violence and health.* Geneva: Author.

Wortman, C. M., Wolff, K., & Bonanno, G. A. (2004). Loss of an intimate partner through death. In D. J. Mashek & A. Aron (Eds.), *Handbook of closeness and intimacy* (pp. 305–320). Mahwah, NJ: Erlbaum.

Wright, V. C., et al. (2004, April 30). Assisted reproductive technology surveillance United States, 2001. *Morbidity and Mortality Weekly Report, 53,* pp. 1–20.

Wrosch, C., Schulz, R., & Heckhausen, J. (2004). Health stresses and depressive symptomatology in the elderly: A control-process approach. *Current Directions in Psychological Science, 13,* 17–20.

Wu, C-H., et al. (2002). Epidemiological evidence of increased bone mineral density in habitual tea drinkers. *Journal of the American Medical Association, 162,* 1001–1006.

Wyatt, G. E., et al. (2002). Sexual abuse. In G. M. Wingood & R. J. DiClemente (Eds.), *Handbook of women's sexual and reproductive health* (pp. 195–216). New York: Kluwer Academic/Plenum.

Wyche, K. F. (2001). Sociocultural issues in counseling for women of color. In R. K. Unger (Ed.), *Handbook of the psychology of women and gender* (pp. 330–340). New York: Wiley.

Wyche, K. F., & Crosby, F. J. (Eds.). (1996). *Women's ethnicities: Journeys through psychology.* Boulder, CO: Westview.

Wylie, K. (2004). Gender related disorders. *British Medical Journal, 329,* 615–617.

Xu, X., et al. (2005). Prevalence of and risk factors for intimate partner violence in China. *American Journal of Public Health, 95,* 78–85.

Yaffe, K. (2003). Hormone therapy and the brain: Déjà vu all over again? *Journal of the American Medical Association, 289,* 2717–2719.

Yaffe, K., et al. (2001). A prospective study of physical activity and cognitive decline in elderly women. *Archives of Internal Medicine, 161,* 1703–1708.

Yardley, J. (2004, December 21). Rural exodus for work fractures Chinese family. *New York Times,* pp. A1–A8.

Yardley, J. (2005, January 31). Fearing future, China starts to give girls their due. *New York Times,* p. A3.

Yates, A., Edman, J., & Aruguete, M. (2004). Ethnic differences in BMI and body/self-dissatisfaction among whites, Asian subgroups, Pacific Islanders, and African-Americans. *Journal of Adolescent Health, 34,* 300–307.

Yeung, D. Y. L., Tang, C. S., & Lee, A. (2005). Psychosocial and cultural factors influencing expectations of menarche: A study on Chinese premenarcheal teenage girls. *Journal of Adolescent Research, 20,* 118–135.

Yoder, J. D. (2000). Women and work. In M. Biaggio & M. Hersen (Eds.), *Issues in the psychology of women* (pp. 71–91). New York: Kluwer.

Yoder, J. D., & Aniakudo, P. (1999). "Outsider within" the firehouse: Subordination and difference in the social interactions of African American women firefighters. In L. A. Peplau, S. C. DeBro., R. C. Veniegas, & P. L. Taylor (Eds.), *Gender, culture and ethnicity: Current research about women and men* (pp. 135–152). Mountain View, CA: Mayfield.

Yoder, J. D., & Kahn, A. S. (1992). Toward a feminist understanding of women and power. *Psychology of Women Quarterly, 16,* 381–388.

Yoder, J. D., & Kahn, A. S. (2003). Making gender comparisons more meaningful: A call for more attention to social context. *Psychology of Women Quarterly, 27,* 281–290.

Yoon, D. P., & Lee, E. O. (2004). Religiousness/spirituality and subjective well-being among rural elderly Whites, African Americans, and Native Americans. *Journal of Human Behavior in the Social Environment, 10,* 191–211.

Young, J. R. (2003, September 12). Sexual assault of female Air Force Academy cadets is much more common than reported, survey finds. *Chronicle of Higher Education, 50,* p. A31.

Younger, B. A., & Fearing, D. D. (1999). Parsing items into separate categories: Developmental change in infant categorization. *Child Development, 70,* 291–303.

Yunger, J. L., Carver, P. R., & Perry, D. G. (2004). Does gender identity influence children's psychological well-being? *Developmental Psychology, 40,* 572–582.

Zabin, L. S., & Cardona, K. M. (2002). Adolescent pregnancy. In G. M. Wingood & R. J. DiClemente (Eds.), *Handbook of women's sexual and reproductive health* (pp. 231–253). New York: Kluwer Academic/Plenum.

Zablotsky, D., & Kennedy, M. (2003, June 1). Risk factors and HIV transmission to midlife and older women: Knowledge, options, and the initiation of safer sexual practices. *Journal of Acquired Immune Deficiency Syndromes, 33,* S122–S130.

Zager, K., & Rubenstein, A. (2002). *The inside story on teen girls.* Washington, DC: American Psychological Association.

Zahn-Waxler, C., & Polanichka, N. (2004). All things interpersonal: Socialization and female aggression. In M. Putallaz & K. L. Bierman (Eds.), *Aggression, antisocial behavior, and violence among girls: A developmental perspective* (pp. 48–68). New York: Guilford.

Zalk, S. R. (1991, Fall). Task force report response of mainstream journals to feminist submissions. *Psychology of Women: Newsletter,* pp. 10–12.

Zebrowitz, L. A., & Montepare, J. M. (2000). Too young, too old: Stigmatizing adolescents and elders. In T. F. Heatherton, R. E. Kleck, M. R. Hebl, & J. G. Hull (Eds.), *The social psychology of stigma* (pp. 334–373). New York: Guilford.

Zernike, K. (2001, April 8). The reluctant feminist. *New York Times,* pp. ED 34–35.

Zernike, K. (2003a, November 30). Just saying no to the dating industry. *New York Times,* pp. ST1, ST12.

Zernike, K. (2003b, December 16). Teenagers want more advice from parents on sex, study says. *New York Times,* p. A32.

Zettel, L. A., & Rook, K. S. (2004). Substitution and compensation in the social networks of older widowed women. *Psychology and Aging, 19,* 433–443.

Zhou, Q., et al. (2002). The relations of parental warmth and positive expressiveness to children's empathy-related responding and social functioning: A longitudinal study. *Child Development, 73,* 893–915.

Zill, D. G., Toussaint, L. A., & Pittman, D. R. (2004, May). *Portrayal of female and minority athletes in Sports Illustrated: 1988–2002.* Poster presented at the meeting of American Psychological Society, Chicago.

Zink, T., Jacobson, C. J., Regan, S., & Pabst, S. (2004). Hidden victims: The healthcare needs and experiences of older women in abusive relationships. *Journal of Women's Health, 13,* 898–908.

Zink, T., & Sill, M. (2004). Intimate partner violence and job instability. *Journal of the American Medical Women's Association, 59,* 32–35.

Zubenko, G. S., et al. (2002). Genome survey susceptibility loci for recurrent, early-onset major depression: Results at 10 cM resolution. *American Journal of Medical Genetics, 114,* 413–422.

Zucker, A. N. (2004). Disavowing social identities: What it means when women say, "I'm not a feminist, but . . ." *Psychology of Women Quarterly, 28,* 423–435.

Zucker, A. N., Ostrove, J. M., & Stewart, A. (2002). College-educated women's personality development in adulthood: Perceptions and age differences. *Psychology and Aging, 17,* 236–244.

Zucker, K. J. (2001). Biological influences on psychosocial differentiation. In R. K. Unger (Ed.), *Handbook of the psychology of women and gender* (pp. 101–115). New York: Wiley.

Zucker, K. J., Bradley, S. J., Oliver, G., & Blake, J. (1996). Psychosexual development of women with congenital adrenal hyperplasia. *Hormones and Behavior, 30,* 300–318.

Zuger, A. (1998, January 6). Do breast self-exams save lives? Science still doesn't have answer. *New York Times,* pp. B9, B15.

NAME INDEX

SUBJECT INDEX

Photo Credits

p. 1: Steve Mason/Getty Images—Photodisc; p. 7: Courtesy of Wellesley College Archives/Notman; p. 12: Mary Jane Murawka; p. 16: Michael Newman/PhotoEdit; p. 27: Bill Aron/PhotoEdit; p. 45: Picture Desk, Inc./Kobal Collection; p. 47: Sharie Kennedy/CORBIS—NY; p. 47b: Tony Freeman/PhotoEdit; p. 49: Jaap Buitendijk/©Warner Bros./Photofest; p. 54: Courtesy of Unilever; p. 59: Courtesy of the Knoxville NewsSentinal Company; p. 64: Robert Brenner/PhotoEdit; p. 70: Johns Hopkins University Press; p. 77: Laura Dwight/PhotoEdit; p. 90: Branson Reynolds/Index Stock Imagery, Inc.; p. 98: Shirley Zeiberg/Pearson Education/PH College; p. 104: Richard Hutchings/Photo Researchers, Inc.; p. 105: AP Wide World Photos; p. 107a: Tony Freeman/PhotoEdit; p. 107b: David Young-Wolff/PhotoEdit; p. 111: Courtesy of Claire Etaugh; p. 113: Robert Harbison; p. 121: Robert Harbison; p. 127: Oscar Burriel/Latin Stock/Science Photo Library/Custom Medical Stock Photo, Inc.; p. 133: Jeff Greenberg/PhotoEdit; p. 136: David Young-Wolff/PhotoEdit; p. 137: Myrleen Ferguson Cate/PhotoEdit; p. 152: Will Hart; p. 156: David Young-Wolff/PhotoEdit; p. 160: Adam Smith/Getty Images, Inc.—Taxi; p. 171: Bill Bachmann/Photo Researchers, Inc.; p. 174: Martin Meyer/CORBIS—NY; p. 178: Stockbyte; p. 185: Cleo Photography/PhotoEdit; p. 189: Roger Tully/Getty Images Inc.—Stone Allstock; p. 194: Tom Stewart/Corbis/Bettmann; p. 202: Panos Pictures; p. 208: David Young-Wolff/PhotoEdit; p. 215: AP Wide World Photos; p. 221: Sean Sprague/The Image Works; p. 226: Cleve Bryant/PhotoEdit; p. 230: Adam Smith/SuperStock, Inc.; p. 232: Tony Freeman/PhotoEdit; p. 242: Dana White/PhotoEdit; p. 258: AP Wide World Photos; p. 264: Yann Layma/Getty Images Inc.—Stone Allstock; p. 271: Michael Newman/PhotoEdit; p. 276: Robert Harbison; p. 277: Courtesy of Claire Etaugh; p. 286: Ed Bock/CORBIS—NY; p. 297: EyeWire Collection/Getty Images—Photodisc; p. 304: AP Wide World Photos; p. 315: Lou Dematteis/The Image Works; p. 319: Gordon, Larry Dale/Getty Images Inc.—Image Bank; p. 328: Bruce Ayres/Getty Images Inc.—Stone Allstock; p. 331: Macduff Everton/The Image Works; p. 340: Michael Krasowitz/Getty Images, Inc.—Taxi; p. 347: Bill Aron/PhotoEdit; p. 358: Bob Mahoney/The Image Works; p. 361: Jose Luis Pelaez/CORBIS—NY; p. 371: Jim Cummins/Getty Images, Inc.—Taxi; p. 376: Jonathan Nourok/PhotoEdit; p. 384: Stuart Cohen/The Image Works; p. 388: Yoav Levy/Phototake NYC; p. 393: A. Ramey/PhotoEdit; p. 400: Charles Gupton/Stock Boston; p. 414: Photolibrary.Com; p. 417: David Young-Wolff/PhotoEdit; p. 420: AP Wide World Photos; p. 433: Corbis/Bettmann; p. 439: Getty Images—Photodisc; p. 443: Michael Newman/PhotoEdit; p. 451: Bruce Ayres/Getty Images Inc.—Stone Allstock; p. 460: Shehzad Noorani /Panos Pictures; p. 467: Mark Peterson/CORBIS—NY; p. 468: Lorena Ros/Panos Pictures; p. 482: Ames Tribune/AP Wide World Photos; p. 489: Ron Rovtar; p. 492: Corbis/Bettmann; p. 499: AP Wide World Photos.